THINK
SOCIOLOGY

JOHN D. CARL
Rose State College

Prentice Hall
Upper Saddle River   London   Singapore
Toronto   Tokyo   Sydney   Hong Kong   Mexico City

Editorial Director: Leah Jewell
Editor-in-Chief: Dickson Musslewhite
Editorial Project Managers: Vanessa Gennarelli
    and Maggie Barbieri
Editorial Assistant: Nart Varoqua
Director of Marketing: Brandy Dawson
Senior Marketing Manager: Kelly May
Marketing Assistant: Elaine Almquist
Director of Market Development: Maureen Prado Roberts
Full-Service Project Management: Natalie Wright,
    Patricia Gordon, Bernadette Enneg, Adam Noll,
    and Jennifer Plum Auvil/Words & Numbers
Production Liaison: Cheryl Keenan
Senior Operations Supervisor: Sherry Lewis
Operations Specialist: Christina Amato
Line Art Illustrations: Words & Numbers
AV Project Manager: Mirella Signoretto

Manager of Design Development: John Christiana
Art Director, Text and Cover Design: Kasia Mrozek
Manager, Visual Research: Beth Brenzel
Photo Researcher: Kathy Ringrose
Manager, Rights and Permissions: Zina Arabia
Image Permission Coordinator: Ang'John Ferreri
Manager, Cover Visual Research & Permissions: Karen Sanatar
Front Cover Art: Jupiter Images/Comstock/Alamy
Back Cover Art: Alloy Photography/Veer
Media Director: Karen Scott
Lead Media Project Management: Melanie McFarlane
Lead Media Project Manager: Diane Lombardo
Supplements Editor: Mayda Bosco
Composition: Words & Numbers
Printer/Binder: Courier/Kendallville
Cover Printer: Lehigh Lithographers
This book was set in 8.5/12 Helvetica Neue Light.

To the important women in my life,
Keven, Sara, and Caroline. **I love you all.**

Credits and acknowledgments borrowed from other sources and reproduced with permission in this textbook appear on appropriate page within text or on page 324.

Library of Congress Cataloging-in-Publication Data
Carl, John D.
Think sociology / John D. Carl.
    p. cm.
Includes bibliographical references and index.
ISBN-13: 978-0-13-175459-1 (alk. paper)
ISBN-10: 0-13-175459-9 (alk. paper)
ISBN-13: 978-0-205-63209-1 (alk. paper)
ISBN-10: 0-205-63209-2 (alk. paper)
1. Sociology. 2. Sociology–Research. 3. Sociology–Methodology. I. Title.
HM585.C365 2010
301—dc 22   2008047352

10 9 8 7 6 5 4 3 2

Prentice Hall
is an imprint of

www.pearsonhighered.com

Student ISBN-13:   978-0-13-175459-1
Student ISBN-10:   0-13-175459-9
Exam Copy ISBN-13:   978-0-205-63209-1
Exam Copy ISBN-10:   0-205-63209-2

BRIEF CONTENTS

01
SOCIOLOGY
An Introduction
to the Foundations of Sociology 2

02
SOCIOLOGICAL RESEARCH
How Do We Learn About Society? 28

03
CULTURE
A Framework for the Individual 46

04
SOCIAL STRUCTURE
AND INTERACTION
Micro and Macro Orientations 64

05
SOCIALIZATION
The Process of Fitting into Society 82

06
GROUPS AND SOCIETIES
Understanding Our Environment 100

07
SOCIAL CLASS IN THE UNITED STATES
Stratification in a Modern Society 118

08
GLOBAL STRATIFICATION
Wealth and Poverty in the World 136

09
POPULATION
AND ENVIRONMENTAL IMPACT
How Do Societies Deal
with Growing Numbers? 154

10
RACE AND ETHNIC
STRATIFICATION
Is It a Question of Color? 172

11
GENDER STRATIFICATION
The Social Side of Sex 190

12
AGING AND HEALTH
The Graying of Society 208

13
CRIME AND THE LEGAL SYSTEM
How Do Societies Respond
to Crime and Deviance? 226

14
MARRIAGE AND FAMILY
How Do Societies
Perpetuate Themselves? 244

15
EDUCATION AND RELIGION
How Do Societies Pass
on Information? 262

16
ECONOMY AND POLITICS
How Do Societies Support
and Govern Themselves? 280

17
SOCIAL MOVEMENTS, COLLECTIVE
BEHAVIOR, AND SOCIAL CHANGE
How Do Societies Change? 298

CONTENTS

01

SOCIOLOGY
An Introduction to the Foundations of Sociology 2

Get the Topic: What Is Sociology? 5
Sociology Defined 5
Developing a Sociological Imagination 5
Emile Durkheim's Theory on Suicide 7
  Individual Choice and Social Forces 8

Think Sociologically: What Are the Characteristics of the Three Major Sociological Paradigms? 9
The Functionalist's Worldview 10
  Herbert Spencer 11 • Emile Durkheim 12
Functionalism in the United States 12
  Talcott Parsons 12 • Robert Merton 12 • Criticisms of Functionalism 13
The Conflict Theorist's Worldview 14
  Karl Marx 14 • Harriet Martineau 15 • W. E. B. Du Bois 16
  Jane Addams 16 • John Bellamy Foster 17 • Criticisms of Conflict Theory 18
The Symbolic Interactionist's Worldview 18
  George Herbert Mead 19 • Herbert Blumer 20 • Erving Goffman 20 • Howard Becker 20 • Criticisms of Symbolic Interactionism 22
The Three Paradigms: How Are They Interrelated? 22
  Applying Sociological Theories 23

Discover Sociology in Action: Why Is Community Learning Important to a Society? 25
Getting Involved in Sociology—Community Learning 25

02

SOCIOLOGICAL RESEARCH
How Do We Learn About Society? 28

Get the Topic: What Are Research Methods? 30
Objectivity 31
Variables 31
Cause and Correlation 32
Scientific Method: What Are the Six Steps of Social Research? 32
  Field Research 36 • Measures of Central Tendency 38
  Evaluating Data 38 • How to Read a Table 38 • Ethical Concerns 40 • The Ethics of Humphreys 40

Think Sociologically: How Do Sociologists Use Research Methods? 41
Quantitative and Qualitative Methods 41
Triangulation 42
Research Methods and the Three Paradigms 42

Discover Sociology in Action: How Is Research Involved in Social Policy and Community Learning? 43
Social Policy and Statistics 43
Community Learning—Needs Assessments 43

03

CULTURE
A Framework for the Individual 46

Get the Topic: What Is Culture? 48
Material Culture 49
Nonmaterial Culture 49
  Symbols 49 • Language 49 • Gesture 51 • Values 51
Additional Values 54
Norms and Sanctions 54
  Folkways 54 • Mores 54
The Study of Culture 54
  Ethnocentrism and Cultural Relativism 55 • Cultural Lag and Culture Shock 55 • Ideal Versus Real Culture 56
  Subcultures and Countercultures 56 • Multiculturalism and Assimilation 56

Think Sociologically: What Differentiates One Culture From Another? 58
Symbolic Interactionism—A Crisis of Values 58
  Traditional Values vs. Secular Values 58 • The Three Hypotheses 58 • Baker's Conclusion 58
Functionalism—Communitarianism 59
Conflict Theory—The McDonaldization of the United States 59
  Negative Effects of McDonaldization 59

Discover Sociology in Action: How Does Culture Influence Sociological Theory and Study? 61
Social Policy: Multiculturalism and Assimilation 61

04

SOCIAL STRUCTURE AND INTERACTION
Micro and Macro Orientations 64

Get the Topic: What Elements Create a Social Structure? 66
Macrosociology and Microsociology 66
  Social Structure 67
  Stages of Societal Change 70 • Social Institutions 71
  Holding Society Together 72
Micro Orientations: Social Interactions 74
  Personal Space 74 • Dramaturgy 75

Think Sociologically: How Do the Three Paradigms View Social Structures? 76
An Example of Symbolic Interactionism: The Thomas Theorem and the Social Creation of Reality 76
An Example of Functionalism: Studying Essential Features of Functional Social Structures 76
An Example of Conflict Theory: Deliberate Efforts to Weaken the Structure and Culture of Native Americans 77

Discover Sociology in Action: How Can Social Policies Improve Society? 79
Social Policy—The Perry Preschool Project 79

05

SOCIALIZATION
The Process of Fitting into Society 82

Get the Topic: What Is Socialization? 84

The Nature vs. Nurture Debate—What Makes Us
    Who We Are? 85
    Feral and Isolated Children 86
Theorists on Socialization 87
    Cooley's Looking-Glass Self 87 • George Herbert Mead—
    The Three Stages of the "I-Me" Self 87
Agents of Socialization 92
    The Family: Parenting Styles and Reciprocal Socialization 92
    Social Class: Opportunities for Socialization 93
    Neighborhood 93

Can We Be "Resocialized"? Experiencing the Total
    Institution 93

Think Sociologically: How Do the Three Theoretical
Paradigms View Socialization? 94

Symbolic Interactionism and Resocialization 94
Functionalism 94
    Religion 94 • Education 94
Conflict Theory—What Forces Socialize Us? 95

Discover Sociology in Action: How Does Understanding
Socialization Help Us Improve the Community? 97
Applying Sociological Thinking in the World, Social Policy,
    and Title IX 97

06

GROUPS AND SOCIETIES
Understanding Our Environment 100

Get the Topic: What Are the Characteristics of Social
Groups? 102
    Primary and Secondary Groups 103 • In-Groups and
    Out-Groups 104 • Reference Groups 105
    Group Size, Structure, and Interaction 106 • Leadership
    Styles 106 • Conformity 107
    Social Capital and Social Networks 109
Formal Organizations 110
    Voluntary Associations 110 • Organizations and
    Bureaucracies 110 • Characteristics of Bureaucracy 111

Think Sociologically: How Do Sociologists View Social
Groups? 112

Functionalism and Leadership 112
    Leadership 101: What Every Leader Needs to Know 112
Conflict Theory—Marx, Bureaucracy, and Democratic
    Organizations 113
Symbolic Interactionism—Creating a Just and Democratic
    Workplace 113

Discover Sociology in Action: How Does a Parent's
Civic Engagement Affect a Child's Future Political
Involvement? 115

Adult Civic Engagement and Childhood Activities 115
Leading Groups 115

07

SOCIAL CLASS IN THE UNITED STATES
Stratification in a Modern Society 118

Get the Topic: What Is Social Stratification? 121
    Income Distribution 121 • Wealth Distribution 122
How Does the United States Define Poverty? 122
    Power 123 • Prestige 123
    Class Structure in the United States 124
    Neighborhoods and Social Class 127 • Education and
    Social Class 127
Social Mobility 128

Think Sociologically: What Are the Theories Behind Social
Stratification? 129

Functionalism 129
Conflict Theory 130
Symbolic Interactionism 130

Discover Sociology in Action: What Social Policies Have
Been Created to Ease Poverty? 132

Social Policy: Welfare for the Poor 132
Social Policy: Minimum Wage 133

08

GLOBAL STRATIFICATION
Wealth and Poverty in the World 136

Get the Topic: What Is Global Stratification? 138
Global Stratification 138
    Population and Geographic Area 139 • Income 139
    Measures of Stratification in Underdeveloped Nations 140
    Measures of Stratification in Developed Nations 141
    Quality of Life 141
Social Systems 142
    Slavery 142 • Caste Systems 143 • Class Systems 143

Think Sociologically: What Are the Theories Behind Global
Stratification? 146

Global Stratification: No Longer a Third World 146
    Immanuel Wallerstein's World Systems Theory 146
    Neocolonialism 147 • Globalization 147
Functionalism 148
Conflict Theory 148
Symbolic Interactionism 149

Discover Sociology in Action: What Is Being Done to Assist
Underdeveloped Countries? 151

Social Policy: Foreign Aid 151

09

POPULATION
AND ENVIRONMENTAL IMPACT
How Do Societies Deal with Growing Numbers? 154

Get the Topic: What Is Demography? 157
Population by the Numbers 157
    Tools for Studying Population 157
Malthusian Theory 162

Demographic Transition Theory 163
Issues Associated with Population Growth 163
    Food Shortage and Hunger 163 • Economic Implications 163

Think Sociologically: What Is Environmental Sociology? 164
Human Exemptionism 164
Environmental Sociology 164
    Environmental Justice 165

Discover Sociology in Action: How Can Governments Control Populations? 168
Population Control Programs 168

10

RACE AND ETHNIC STRATIFICATION
Is It a Question of Color? 172

Get the Topic: What Is the Difference Between Race and Ethnicity? 175
Census Definitions 175
    Majority and Minority Groups 176 • Racism 176
    Patterns of Interaction 178
    Prejudice vs. Discrimination 181 • Institutional Discrimination in the United States 181
    Causes for Prejudice and Discrimination 182
    Segregation 182
Racial Stratification in the United States 183
    Income 183 • Education 184

Think Sociologically: What Causes Racist Attitudes, and How Do These Attitudes Affect People? 184
Symbolic Interactionism: Color-Blind Racism 184

Discover Sociology in Action: How Does Affirmative Action Help Minority Groups in the United States? 187
Affirmative Action 187

11

GENDER STRATIFICATION
The Social Side of Sex 190

Get the Topic: What Is the Difference Between Gender and Sex? 193
Gender vs. Sex 193
    Gender Construction 193
Patriarchy and Sexism 194
Gender Roles 194
    Gender Roles and the Media 195 • The Fluidity of Gender Roles: Indonesia's Bugis People 195
Gender and Inequality 196
    Gender and Education 197 • Gender and the Workplace 198 Gender and Politics 199
Feminism 200
    First-Wave Feminism 200 • Second-Wave Feminism 200 Third-Wave Feminism 200

Think Sociologically: What Are the Perspectives on Gender and Gender Inequality? 201
Feminist Theory 201
    Liberal vs. Radical Feminism 202
Functionalism 202
Conflict Theory 202
Symbolic Interactionism 202

Discover Sociology in Action: What Policies Are in Place to Prevent Sexual Harassment and Domestic Violence? 205
Social Policy: Stopping Sexual Harassment and Gender Violence 205

12

AGING AND HEALTH
The Graying of Society 208

Get the Topic: How Do Health and Aging Affect Social Stratification? 211
Health Defined 211
    Social Epidemiology 211
Health in the United States: Living off the Fat of the Land 213
    Childhood Obesity 213 • Stigmatization of the Obese 214 Obesity and Race 214
Health Care 215
    The Uninsured 215 • Costs of Services 215 • Health Care: An International Comparison 215 • Health Care and the Elderly—Medicare 216
Aging: The Graying of the United States 216
    Aging and Demographic Change in the United States 216
    The "Sandwiched" Generation 217
    Concerns About Aging 219

Think Sociologically: What Theories Exist About the Aging Process? 220
Functionalism—Disengaging from Society 220
Symbolic Interactionism—Living an Active Lifestyle 220
Conflict Theory—Aging and Inequality 221

Discover Sociology in Action: What Are the Advantages and Disadvantages of the Health Care System in the United States for the Elderly? 223
Social Security and Medicare 223

13

CRIME AND THE LEGAL SYSTEM
How Do Societies Respond to Crime and Deviance? 226

Get the Topic: What Is Crime? 228
Deviance vs. Crime 228
    What is Deviance? 229
    Crime Statistics 229 • Crime Trends 230
    Societal Responses to Crime and Deviance 232
    Prison and the Characteristics of Prison Inmates 233

Think Sociologically: Why Does Crime Exist? 235
Historical Roots of Deviance and Crime Theories 235
    The Positivist School 235 • Biological Perspectives on Crime and Deviance 235 • The Classical School 235 • Psychological Perspectives on Crime and Deviance 236
Functional Explanations of Crime and Deviance 236
    Theory of Anomie 236
Social Interaction Theories 237
    Differential Association Theory 237 • Social Control Theories 237
Symbolic Interactionist Theory 238
    Labeling Theory 238
Social Conflict Theory 238
General Theories of Crime Causation 238

Discover Sociology in Action: How Do We Deal With Crime? 240

Crime Control: The Criminal Justice System 240
  Police 240 • Courts 240 • Death Penalty 240

14

MARRIAGE AND FAMILY
How Do Societies Perpetuate Themselves? 244

Get the Topic: What Is a Family? 246

Marriage and Family 246
  Forms of Marriage and Family 247 • Trends of the
  American Family 248
  Phases of the Family 251

Think Sociologically: Is the Family in Decline? 256

Symbolic Interactionism 256
Conflict Theory 257
Functionalism 257
  Popenoe's Erosion of the Family 257

Discover Sociology in Action: What Do Future Families
Look Like? 259

Gay Marriage vs. Civil Unions vs. Nothing 259

15

EDUCATION AND RELIGION
How Do Societies Pass on Information? 262

Get the Topic: How Do Societies Pass on Information? 265

Education in Society 265
  Hidden Curriculum 266 • Roots of Modern Education
  Systems 266 • Education Throughout the World 266
  Educational Discrepancies in Race and Gender 267
  Teacher Expectancy and Attainment 268 • Academic
  Achievement 268 • Education and Religion 270
Religion 270
  Types of Religion 270 • Organization in Religion 272
  • Religion in Society 272 • Religion and the Economy 273
  • Changes in Religion 273

Think Sociologically: How Does Religion Affect Society? 274

Symbolic Interactionism 274
Functionalism 275
Conflict Theory 275

Discover Sociology in Action: What Social Policies Help
Children Get a Better Education? 277

Improving Education with School Vouchers 277

16

ECONOMY AND POLITICS
How Do Societies Support
and Govern Themselves? 280

Get the Topic: What Are the Systems of Economics and
Politics? 283

Economic Systems 283
  Capitalism 283 • Socialism 284 • Democratic

  Socialism 285 • Convergence of Capitalism
  and Socialism 285 • The U.S. Economy: A System
  in Crisis 286
Global Economy 287
  Corporations: Spreading Across the Globe 287
  Trade Agreements: Embargoes and NAFTA 287
Political Systems 287
  Traditional 287 • Charismatic 287 • Rational-Legal
  Authority 287
Types of Government 288
  Monarchy 288 • Authoritarianism 288 • Democracy 288
Politics in the United States 289
  Political Parties 289
  Political Funding 290
The Nature of Power 290
  Military and the Use of Force 290

Think Sociologically: How Do Sociologists View
Economic and Political Systems? 293

  Functionalism 293
  Conflict Theory 293
  Symbolic Interactionism 293

Discover Sociology in Action: How Does the System Work
for Veterans? 295

Lack of Assistance for Veterans 295
  Substandard Conditions at Walter Reed 295

17

SOCIAL MOVEMENTS, COLLECTIVE BEHAVIOR, AND SOCIAL CHANGE
How Do Societies Change? 298

Get the Topic: What Drives Social Change? 301

Shifts in Society 301
  Technology 302
Resistance to Change 302
  Collective Behavior 304
  Nature of Social Movements 306
  Types of Social Movements 308 • Revolutionary Social
  Movements 309

Think Sociologically: What Are the Theories Behind Social
Movements? 309

Conflict Theory 309
Functionalism 310
Symbolic Interactionism 310
  Framing Processes 310

Discover Sociology in Action: How Do Social Movements
Influence Sociological Theory and Study? 313

Social Policy: Corporate Average Fuel Economy 313

Acknowledgements viii
About the Author ix
Glossary 316
Endnotes 324
Photo Credits 340
Index 342

ACKNOWLEDGMENTS

In so many ways, this text started long before I was trained in sociology. I owe a debt of gratitude to my parents, Helen and John, who taught me the value of hard work, and finishing what you start. I also thank my sisters, Mary, Kathy, and Laurie for teaching me not to take myself too seriously and supporting the changes I've made in my life. As a student, I had many fine professors who inspired me, challenged me, and encouraged me to look at the world in a critical way. They too, are in this text. I understand that any author requires support and encouragement. I am especially indebted to my wife, who has always supported my goals and dreams and never complained. Keven, you are an amazing person and I am eternally grateful you are my wife. My daughters, Sara and Caroline, also sacrificed hours of my time to allow me to write while offering their support through this process.

While my name is under the title of this book, it should be obvious to everyone that no single person could create a piece of work like this on his own. I would like to thank the many people involved for their support and assistance.

In 2004, my book representative, Amanda Crotts suggested I consider writing a book. She gave my name to Jeanne Bronson and the sociology editor, Chris DeJohn, and the seeds of this book took root. Since that time, many different hands have touched parts of this manuscript. The team of professionals who bring you this text are an amazing group of people who are almost too numerous to mention. However, special thanks go to Dickson Musslewhite, Maggie Barbieri, Nancy Roberts, Cheryl Keenan, Vanessa Gennarelli, Susanna Lesan, and Leah Jewell. Kasia Mrozek created the beautiful design of this book. I have also had the pleasure of working with the following staff at *Words & Numbers*: Natalie Wright, Adam Noll, Patricia Gordon, Bernadette Enneg, and Jennifer Plum Auvil and thank them for their commitment in implementing the editorial and production processes. Each of you helped shape this text and I am grateful for that assistance.

Each chapter of this book went through an extensive review process. I am grateful to the members of my editorial review board for their work to make sure that the information in this book is both accurate and up to date. Special thanks go to:

Robbie Akhere, *Central Piedmont Community College*
Angie Andrus, *Fullerton College*
Margaret Choka, *Pellissippi State Technical Community College*
Carlos Garcia, *San Jose State University*
Kevin Keating, *Broward College*
Kathleen Lowney, *Valdosta State University*
Marcie Sheumaker, *Southern Illinois University at Carbondale*

Over the years spent writing this text many of my colleagues offered ideas, support, and constructive comments along the way, for which I am exceedingly grateful. Special thanks go to Kathy Carey, Baillie Dunlap, James Hochtritt, Michael Lovegrove, Keith Thrasher, Arnold Waggoner, Bret Wood, John Wood, and Michelle Yelle. I am also very grateful to work at a college where the administration supports faculty goals and encourages scholarship. I am indebted to the college leadership for their support during this project.

I also wish to thank some of my friends and peers at the University of Oklahoma and beyond. Specifically, I wish to thank my friend and mentor, Craig St. John for teaching me the love of sociology. My thanks also to Loretta Bass, Anne Beutel, Carlos Garcia, Tom Burns, and Bob Franzese for their advice and direction.

Finally, I wish to thank the students who over the years helped me learn to communicate complex issues in ways that they can understand. The design of this book is for you. The language, art, layout, and topics covered were all selected with you in mind. Faculty may select books, but students read them. Over the years, I listened to my students and hope I have created a textbook that teaches them the wonders of the science of sociology.

Sincerely,
JOHN D. CARL

JOHN CARL'S interest in sociology grew from his interests and job experiences after college, which included working in hospitals, schools, churches and prisons. John reflects, "In these many diverse encounters, I continued to notice how often the structures of society frequently did not support the change so desperately sought after by the individual. I began to reflect on my sociology courses from my undergraduate work and decided to return to graduate school to study sociology."

At the University of Oklahoma, he became passionate about the study of Criminology and Stratification, completing his Ph.D. while teaching full time at Rose State College. John says, "I found that every part of my life, to this point, fit perfectly with the study of sociology. It is a diverse and exciting field that helps each of us understand our world."

Today, teaching remains his primary focus. John Carl has excelled in the classroom, winning awards for his teaching and working to build and improve the sociology program at Rose State College. "I teach the introductory class every semester because I believe it is the most important course in any department. It is where students get the foundation they need for their continued study of sociology. In these classes, my goal is simple: to teach students to think sociologically so that they can consider any new event in the light of that thought."

When asked why he wrote *THINK Sociology,* the answer was simple: "This book is truly a labor of love for me. I wanted to write a book that is filled with examples used in the classroom and written in a language that students can understand without compromising the core concepts of sociology."

John lives in Oklahoma with his family: wife Keven, and daughters, Sara and Caroline. In his free time, John plays golf, gardens, throws pottery, and plays his guitar. He continues to move from the classroom to community by being active in non-profit leadership in his home community and providing training to non-profit boards so they may better achieve their goals. John suggests, "It is all part of sociology, not only to understand the world in which we live, but to take that understanding from the classroom and use it to improve the community."

JOHN CARL welcomes your comments and suggestions about this **THINK Sociology** text at: **jcthinksociology@gmail.com**

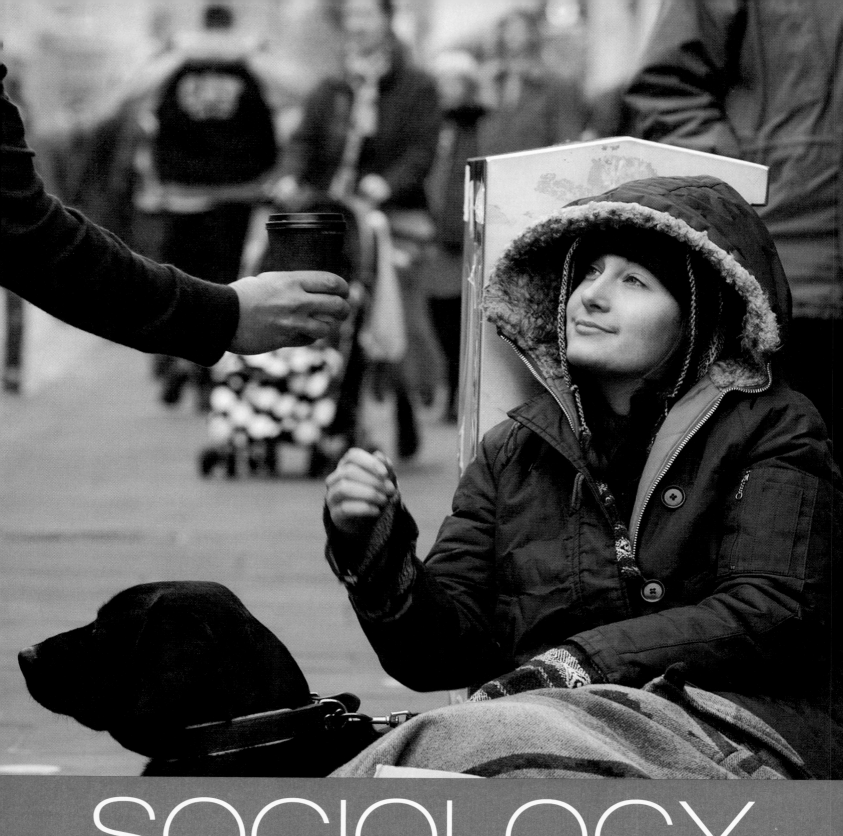

SOCIOLOGY

"Like you,

I know people who drink, people who do drugs, and bosses who have tantrums and treat their subordinates like dirt. They all have good jobs. Were they to become homeless, some of them would surely also become "alcoholics," "addicts," or "mentally ill." Similarly, if some of the homeless women who are now so labeled were to be magically transported to a more usual and acceptable setting, some of them—not all, of course—would shed their labels and take their places with the rest of us somewhere on the spectrum of normality.

"There are many homeless people in America and that is a shame. Shame on you, shame on me, shame on America. Shame because it is the result of choices we have made, shame because it does not have to be. . . . Homeless people are homeless because they do not have a place to live.

"The connection between homelessness and poverty points to major system failures at the lower and sometimes middle level of our wage-labor hierarchy. The major failure is the inability of the system, even in the best of times, to provide jobs for all who are able and willing to work. Every day, millions of would-be workers are told that our society has nothing for them to do, that they are not needed, that they and their dependents are surplus.

"Another major system failure, equally destructive, is the fact that a growing number of men and women—individuals and heads of families—are workers but remain poor. . . . These workers file papers, mop floors, clean the tables, or guard whatever needs guarding. At the end of the day, they say "OK, I've done what you asked me to do. What am I worth?" And our society answers, through the employer, "Not much. Not even enough to live on."[1]

An Introduction *to the* Foundations of Sociology

CHAPTER 01

In **Tell Them Who I Am: The Lives of Homeless Women,** professor and sociologist Elliot Liebow gives a voice to the homeless women he encounters. The homeless are no longer anonymous people on the street corner; they now have names and faces.

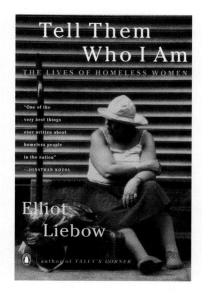

The homeless are often viewed as nameless, faceless, voiceless people loitering on street corners and huddled under bridges. It's easy for us to turn a blind eye to the problem if we don't feel a personal connection to the man panhandling on the sidewalk or the woman seeking warmth beneath a flimsy cardboard box.

Nobody chooses to be homeless, Liebow writes, but sometimes circumstances turn against him or her. Homelessness can happen anywhere, even on a college campus, as I found out one semester: I learned that one of my students often stayed in the library until closing time. She didn't have a place to live, so she read in the library until closing and then walked to a local store to sleep in the clothing aisles. She was pregnant, and her parents had kicked her out of the house. Of course, none of this was planned; it simply happened. And I was left, like Liebow, to wonder why a country as developed as the United States has allowed homelessness to become a "normal" part of its culture.

Liebow's book is a blueprint of what sociology is all about. He gathers information, explains his findings, and then thinks about the bigger picture. He questions social policies and draws his own conclusions. A sociologist like Liebow does not try to pinpoint one specific cause of homelessness in the United States. Instead, he tackles the issue from all angles.

SOCIOLOGY

is defined as — a science guided by the basic understanding that "the social matters: our lives are affected, not only by our individual characteristics, but by our place in the social world"

and should be studied using a — **Sociological Imagination—** the ability to look beyond the individual as the cause for success and failure and see how one's society influences the outcome

and examines the relationship between

Functionalists
- Auguste Comte
- Herbert Spencer
- Emile Durkheim
- Albion Small
- Talcott Parsons
- Robert Merton

Conflict Theorists
- Karl Marx
- Harriet Martineau
- W.E.B. Du Bois
- Jane Addams
- John Bellamy Foster

Symbolic Interactionist
- George Herbert Mead
- Herbert Blumer
- Erving Goffman
- Howard Becker

and was founded by sociologists such as

Symbolic Interactionism
- focuses on how people interact in their everyday lives with their society's symbols
- is a micro orientation on the individual and how he or she interacts with the social environment

get the topic: WHAT IS SOCIOLOGY?

Sociology Defined

How do you define sociology? You might say that it's the study of society, the study of how people live, or the study of people's interactions with one another. This is all true, but these answers only scratch the surface. According to the American Sociological Association, **sociology** is a science guided by the basic understanding that "the social matters: our lives are affected, not only by our individual characteristics but by our place in

> **SOCIOLOGY** is a science guided by the basic understanding that "the social matters: our lives are affected, not only by our individual characteristics but by our place in the social world."

the social world."[2] Like any science, sociologists seek to understand the facts of a situation while keeping an open mind about what they are studying. In addition to this, we strive to keep our personal opinions at bay.

MAKE CONNECTIONS

Using Video Games to Study Sociology

Have you ever wanted to control someone else's actions? Leave it to video games to allow you to act out such a fantasy. One of the most popular is *The Sims*, a strategic computer game that simulates real life. You decide when your character sleeps, eats, and even bathes. More recently, the game *Façade* has sprung forth a similar idea. While *The*

Sims and *Façade* play up the entertainment factor, they also provide a lesson in sociology.

Players of *The Sims* and *Façade* manipulate characters in a virtual world to see the effect certain behaviors have on the characters' lives. Your characters become depressed when they have little interaction with others, just like in real life.

The Sims and *Façade* allow you to study the effect people's actions have on themselves and others. The best part is that in the simulated world, the consequences are not real, so

you don't have to be afraid to test how extreme behaviors affect your characters.

>>> **ACTIVITY** Think about a real-world theory you'd like to use *The Sims* or *Façade* to test. How would you use the game to test the theory? What do you think the outcome of your study will be? Write a few paragraphs describing your proposed sociological study. If you have access to either of these video games, go ahead and test your theory!

Developing a Sociological Imagination

One of my students recently lost her job at a nearby automotive factory. She attended classes during the day and worked at a convenience store at night. Being a single mother of two, she had no one to watch her kids while she was at work. Without supervision, her children were falling

behind in school, hanging out on street corners, and getting into trouble. Like many single parents, she had no other options and no idea what else to do.

When we think of kids in trouble, many of us probably blame the parent. But, in this situation, does the blame rest solely on her shoulders? Famous American sociologist C. Wright Mills (1916–1962) would say no. Mills asserted that people must understand how outside forces contribute

Individual Choice vs. Social Forces
- **Solidarity**—the level of connectedness a person feels to others in the environment
- **Social Control**—the social mechanisms that regulate a person's actions

and is studied using one of three theoretical paradigms

Functionalism
- views society as a system of interrelated parts
- is a macro orientation because it studies how social structures affect how a society works

and

Conflict Theory
- studies issues such as race, gender, social class, criminal justice, and international relations
- is a macro orientation because it studies how the struggle for resources holds society together

and

to someone's situation. In other words, Mills wanted us to develop a **sociological imagination**—the ability to look beyond the individual as the cause for success and failure and see how one's society influences the outcome.[3]

Developing a sociological imagination helps you understand your place in a complex world. We must grasp both the history and the biography of a situation to generate this imagination. Mills argued that most of us see social issues through biography; that is, our personal point of view.[4] This **micro**, or small-scale, reference focuses our attention on the individual. We must also understand how history and social structure affect the individual. By including this **macro**, or large-scale, point of view in our imagining of the social world, we can understand it more clearly. These factors influence both our individual choices and our interpretation of events. So, using the sociological imagination gives us more than an individualistic interpretation of the world.[5]

Let's consider my student's situation this time using our sociological imaginations. Is outsourcing labor to blame for her situation? When U.S. companies close because of cheaper overseas labor, workers in the United States suffer. Ultimately, the goal of most businesses is to make the biggest profit possible, so owners can't resist the lure of hiring cheap labor. With gas and food prices skyrocketing,

> **When working-class parents struggle to put food on the table, some might blame their predicament on a lack of education or motivation.** People using a sociological imagination, however, might attribute other forces, such as rising gas prices, to the parents' predicament.

many businesses must adjust their budgets accordingly and find less expensive ways of doing things. Some people win and others lose, as in my student's case. If my student had not lost her job, would her children still be in trouble? Probably not. She reported that when working her old job, she was home every day when they got home from school. Now, she rarely sees them. What's clear is that when thinking sociologically about an issue, simple answers rarely explain the complexities of human situations.

Emile Durkheim's Theory on Suicide

There are often several biographical, social, and historical causes for every event—from homelessness to unemployment to suicide. Using a sociological imagination means that we consider the impact on the individual from these points of view. Ever wonder why someone would commit suicide? Suicide is perhaps the most personal type of death, and yet in the 1897 book *Suicide*, sociologist Emile Durkheim (1858–1917) proposed that two social forces, solidarity and social control, influence the chance of a person taking his or her own life.[6] **Solidarity** refers to the level of connectedness a person feels to others in the environment, and **social control** refers to the social mechanisms that regulate a person's actions.[7] These two social forces are independent factors that help predict the type of suicide someone might commit.

When people lack solidarity, **egoistic suicides** occur. People who commit these suicides have few social connections, feel isolated and alone, and are more likely to fall into despair. Of course, this doesn't mean that all "loners" are suicidal. It only shows that having low levels of solidarity increases the odds for egoistic suicides.

Solidarity levels also influence the likelihood of **altruistic suicides**. These suicides result when the level of solidarity is exceptionally high. Because the individual is deeply connected to a group, he or she views the best interests of the group as superior to all other interests. This particular analysis might explain the rationale behind *kamikaze* pilots and suicide bombers.

SOCIOLOGICAL IMAGINATION is the ability to look beyond the individual as the cause for success and failure and see how one's society influences the outcome.

MICRO means small-scale.

MACRO means large-scale.

SOLIDARITY refers to the level of connectedness and integration a person feels to others in the environment.

SOCIAL CONTROL refers to the social mechanisms that regulate a person's actions.

EGOISTIC SUICIDES are suicides that result from a lack of solidarity, occurring among those who have few social connections, feel isolated and alone, and are more likely to fall into despair.

ALTRUISTIC SUICIDES are suicides that occur when the level of solidarity is exceptionally high and when the individual views the group's interest as superior to all other interests.

∨
∨
∨ **Durkheim identified four different types of suicide—egoistic, altruistic, fatalistic, and anomic**—illustrated in the graphic below.[8]

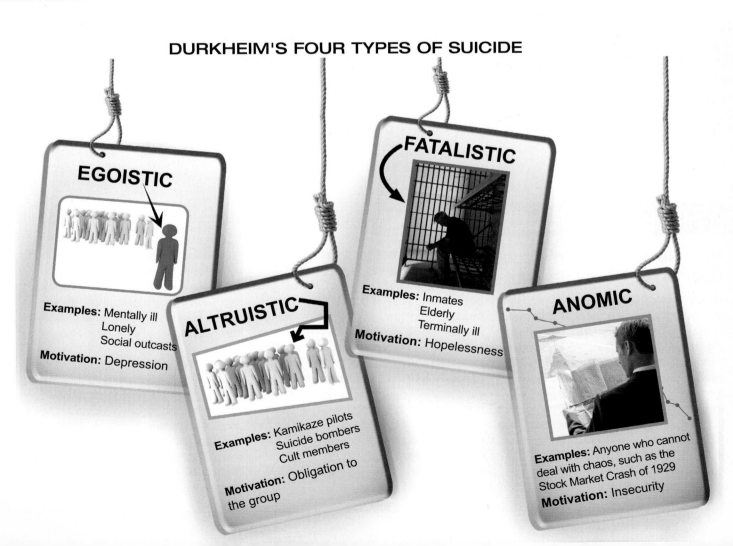

DURKHEIM'S FOUR TYPES OF SUICIDE

EGOISTIC

Examples: Mentally ill
Lonely
Social outcasts

Motivation: Depression

ALTRUISTIC

Examples: Kamikaze pilots
Suicide bombers
Cult members

Motivation: Obligation to the group

FATALISTIC

Examples: Inmates
Elderly
Terminally ill

Motivation: Hopelessness

ANOMIC

Examples: Anyone who cannot deal with chaos, such as the Stock Market Crash of 1929

Motivation: Insecurity

FATALISTIC SUICIDES are suicides that result from a lack of social control.

ANOMIC SUICIDES are suicides that occur as a result of social unrest.

PARADIGM refers to a theoretical framework through which scientists study the world.

FUNCTIONALISM is a theoretical framework that defines society as a system of interrelated parts.

CONFLICT THEORY is a theoretical framework that views society as an unequal system that brings about conflict and change.

SYMBOLIC INTERACTIONISM is a theoretical framework that focuses on how people interact with others in their everyday lives.

Unlike altruistic suicides, **fatalistic suicides** are related to the level of one's social control. This type of suicide happens when a person feels that his or her future is bleak and there is no way for the situation to improve. Individuals who live in hopeless environments—such as prisons and long-term health-care facilities—are more likely to commit fatalistic suicide.

During times of social unrest, **anomic suicides** increase. Anomie refers to social instability caused by a wearing away of social standards. Durkheim predicted that modernization and industrialization would bring an increase in anomic suicides because society's rules for appropriate behavior were changing. As a result, many of the social institutions that had once regulated society, such as religion, lose their power.[9] In times of civic unrest, certain individuals will decide that living through the chaos is more than they can handle, so they will take their own lives.

Although Durkheim's theory is more than a century old, it's still an important way to consider the tension between social forces and individual choice.

Suicide might be seen as an individual decision, but there are many social factors that seem to influence suicide rates. We cannot use these factors to specifically predict who will and will not kill themselves, but we can understand that one's environment influences the rate of suicide in a society. Other factors such as one's family makeup, and the relative size of a group of people born during the same time period also play a role.[10]

INDIVIDUAL CHOICE AND SOCIAL FORCES

You've probably guessed by now that social factors often influence our personal choices. They provide a context in which we make decisions. Again, consider the act of suicide. Most of my students suggest that this is totally an individual choice, and in fact it is. However, certain trends arise in the data on suicides that indicate people who are at higher risk of taking their own lives.

Time of year, profession, and age all predict the likelihood of suicide. According to the Centers for Disease Control and Prevention:

- Suicide rates in the United States are lowest in winter and highest in spring. During the winter holidays, most people are surrounded by friends and family. However, in the spring this socialization may end. The lack of integration might increase the odds of an egoistic suicide.

- Police officers have a high risk of suicide. Perhaps this is because they work long hours and are exposed to violent and graphic scenes. Add to this fact that they have easy access to guns, and you can see some structural characteristics that may lead them to fatalistic thinking and suicide.

- Generally, the rate of suicide increases with age. Furthermore, men are more likely to commit suicide than women. Men over the age of 65 have the highest rates of suicide in the United States. This may also be due to fatalism, because when people age, they may have more illnesses and/or physical limitations that increase the risk of suicide.[11]

It is important for you to note that these factors do not cause individuals to commit suicide per se, however they do indicate groups who are at risk of killing themselves. When sociologists examine an issue, such as suicide, homelessness, or any other social event, they use their sociological imagination to help consider how social factors influence an individual's choice. How do sociologists use the sociological imagination to study the larger world? Let's examine three important theoretical perspectives and the sociologists who helped develop them.

THINK SOCIOLOGICALLY

Homelessness—Individual Choice vs. Social Factors

Have you ever heard someone argue that people choose to be homeless? You might have even made the argument yourself. In *Tell Them Who I Am: The Lives of Homeless Women,* Liebow says, "it is, perhaps, all too easy to fall into homelessness, but being there is not easy at all."[12] When many people are living paycheck to paycheck, it's not hard to imagine someone waking up one day and finding that they don't have enough money to pay a mortgage or buy groceries.

Liebow finds that most homeless women are actually working-class women who have fallen on hard times. Once these women "fall into homelessness," they find it tough to climb out of that dark hole. Finding work is especially difficult because employers shy away from hiring people who have no home. Even if a homeless woman actually finds a job, many times her wages will not be enough to pay for a house, especially when she must spend a good part of her salary on transportation to get to work. The rest of her money is likely to be spent on food for her family and other necessities. As a result, her children grow up in an environment with little privacy and few role models for success.

Although Liebow does not suggest that homelessness is impossible to overcome, he does argue that society is doing little to help. With the cards seemingly stacked against homeless people, what choice do they *really* have?

>>> **ACTIVITY** Visit a homeless shelter in your community. Talk to the people there and find out how social factors contributed to their situation. How did they arrive at the shelter? What was their life like before? Write a paragraph describing one of the people you met and analyzing the factors that led to that person's homelessness.

think sociologically: WHAT ARE THE CHARACTERISTICS OF THE THREE MAJOR SOCIOLOGICAL PARADIGMS?

Before I ever knew anything about sociology, I had a worldview. Being born in the United States to a religious, working-class family, my parents' teachings shaped my point of view. Had I been born in China, Chad, or Chile, I would likely think differently about the world. How do you view the world? What personal beliefs or ideas do you value most? It might be difficult to respond to these questions, but I bet you have some pretty definitive answers. When sociologists take in the world, they do it through a **paradigm**—a theoretical framework through which scientists study the world.

In the United States, most sociologists view the world through three major paradigms—functionalism, conflict theory, and symbolic interactionism. **Functionalism** is a theoretical framework that defines society as a system of interrelated parts. This paradigm is a macro approach to sociological study because it focuses on larger social structures rather than individuals. When you think about functionalism, it may be helpful to think about the human body. The body has built-in mechanisms that help it maintain a normal body temperature. If you are stranded outside in freezing temperatures, you will start shivering in an attempt to regulate your body temperature. Society is similar in many ways. When something happens to throw a social system off-kilter, certain forces step in to help balance things out again.

Conflict theory is a theoretical framework that views society as being in a constant struggle over scarce resources. This constant struggle inevitably results in an unequal system. Similar to functionalism, conflict theory is also a macro approach, as this theory is concerned with various interested groups battling for power. Inequality of wealth and power in society is often the focus of modern conflict theory. For example, conflict theorists might examine how the chasm between the rich and the poor affects people's opportunities in our society. It's no surprise that children who come from privileged backgrounds can afford to receive the best educations, participate in organized sports, and take music lessons. However, children from poorer families may not get these same opportunities, and this lack of opportunity puts them at a disadvantage.

Symbolic interactionism is a theoretical framework that focuses on how individual interactions between people influences them and how these interactions can impact society. Symbolic interactionism is primarily a micro approach to sociology because it is concerned with the individual's role in creating society. The use of "symbols," such as words, gestures, body language, and facial expressions, influence how people communicate. Our actions communicate meaning. For example, if you're having a "bad day," what does that mean? One student once told me he had a "bad day" every time it rained. If that is the case, could such a definition of reality influence how you behave toward others on your job or in the classroom? How might his "bad day" influence the "days" of others? Interactionists constantly seek to understand how small interactions influence the larger society.

>>> In April 2008, more than 200 women and children were removed from a polygamist ranch in El Dorado, Texas, because of an alleged report of child abuse on the ranch. **How might being raised on a polygamist ranch influence one's worldview?**

that a society's structures create homelessness (functionalism), and people with wealth and power control those structures and are generally abusive to the poorest of the poor (conflict theory). Those who experience homelessness often create in themselves self-fulfilling prophecies that help them remain mired in their plight (symbolic interactionism). Liebow uses each of these ideas to create a complete view of why homelessness exists in our society.

Now that you have a general understanding of each paradigm and know what kinds of questions they ask, let's take a closer look at each one. We'll begin with the oldest of the sociological paradigms—functionalism.

As you can see, sociologists often approach their study of society from either a macro or micro perspective. In sociology, the macro approach is most commonly used, as it examines larger social groups and institutions and their effects on society. This is part of what separates sociology from psychology, as psychology operates on a micro level by studying the workings of the human mind. Although some sociological studies focus on the individual, the primary concern is the effect that these individuals have on the rest of society and the influence that society has on the individual. Each sociological paradigm can combine aspects of macro and micro approaches, and yet they all seek to understand the process by which people influence society and society affects them.

Sociologists from each paradigm often analyze similar issues, such as why homelessness exists or how children learn about the social world. However, the questions they ask as they analyze these issues differ. The chart below illustrates how functionalists, conflict theorists, and symbolic interactionists approach learning about society.

Sociologists use these questions to help them build theories about the world. So, is one school of thought better than the others? Not necessarily. In fact, most sociologists' worldview is rather eclectic or diverse. They may use each paradigm to illuminate different issues or use all three to look comprehensively at a single issue. If you consider Elliot Liebow's work, for example, you'll see that he uses bits and pieces of each paradigm to understand homelessness. Liebow finds

The Functionalist's Worldview

Although philosophers have always tackled the issues surrounding how people and society fit together, it was not until French philosopher Auguste Comte (1798–1857) coined the term *sociology* that the discipline got its name.[13] The functionalist paradigm owes much to Comte, who is considered the father of sociology.

Comte felt that sociology should strive to discover **social laws**—statements of fact that are unchanging under given conditions and can be used as ground rules for any study of society. In order to discover these laws, Comte proposed that we study **social statics**, or the existing structural elements of society, and **social dynamics**, or the change in those elements. He believed that by discovering the interplay between structures and dynamics we could develop social laws that would help improve society. To date, we have no social laws, but some sociologists are still trying to develop them. Although few people follow Comte's theories today, his basic ideas are the groundwork on which functionalism is based.

As we've discussed, functionalism is a theoretical framework that defines society as a system of interrelated parts. These parts work in concert with one another to satisfy the needs of society as a whole. According to functionalists, society is relatively stable, which means that things occur in society for a specific function and those functions help maintain stability.

Social institutions such as the family, economy, educational system, and political system are critical for society to function properly.

COMPARING THE THEORETICAL PARADIGMS

	Functionalism	Conflict Theory	Symbolic Interactionism
Level of Analysis	Macro	Macro	Micro
Core Questions	• What keeps society functioning smoothly? • What are the parts of society and how do they relate? • What are the intended and unintended outcomes of an event?	• How are wealth and power distributed in society? • How do people with wealth and power keep them? • Are there groups that get ahead in this society and why? • How are society's resources and opportunities divided?	• How do people co-create the society? • How does social interaction influence, create, and sustain human relationships? • Do people change behavior from one setting to another, and if so, why?

∧
∧ It's hard to spot the light-colored moth in this photograph, isn't it? The
∧ moth's coloring is probably a result of natural selection. **Moths with colors
that stand out in their environment often die out, leaving behind the "best fit"
members of the species.**

Understanding how these and other social institutions work in a society is of great interest to functionalists. Since these parts are interrelated, each has an impact on the others. Remember my student who lost her job? The economic system influenced the family system, which may, if her children continue to get into trouble, interact with the criminal justice system. By this example, you can see that performing functional analysis can be quite complex.

Functionalism suggests that a society's values and norms provide the foundation for the rules and laws that it creates. These norms regulate the relationships between social institutions. Therefore, general agreement on these norms must occur for a society to achieve balance.

All of the social structures, from the minor day-to-day interactions with friends to the complex cultural traditions and customs, work together to keep society running. Functionalists, however, have differing views about how these structures cooperate with one another. Some compare society to living, breathing organisms, others analyze the expected and unexpected outcomes of a social event, while still others wonder what exactly it is that holds a society together. Although it's the oldest theoretical approach, functionalism remains an important way to consider society. On the next few pages, we'll investigate some early functionalists and you can see who these ideas come from. Early theorists like Herbert Spencer and Emile Durkheim contributed to the growth and development of the functionalist perspective.

HERBERT SPENCER

Herbert Spencer (1820–1903) was a British intellectual whose ideas furthered the development of functionalism. Spencer's study of sociology was informed by Charles Darwin's theory of natural selection. Darwin argued that natural selection—a process resulting in the evolution of organisms best adapted to the environment—makes evolution occur. Spencer viewed society as a biological organism, and as such, it can evolve, thrive, or die. For him, some societies are "more fit" than others because they adapt better to changes in the environment. From Spencer, you can see a type of thinking often called **"social Darwinism"**—a notion that suggests strong societies survive and weak ones become extinct.[14]

Spencer's idea informs a social theory that, in essence, evaluates the superiority or inferiority of a society based on its ability to be strong and survive. For example, in a recent class discussion about homelessness, one of my students stated, "Homeless people can't follow the rules that everyone else does; their homelessness is their own fault." Do you see Spencer's ideas in her comments? How do her words reflect the idea of social Darwinism? On the macro level, do you think some societies are superior to others? Would you suggest that the United States reached its success due to its own merit? If so, you think a bit like a social Darwinist.

EMILE DURKHEIM

Like Spencer, French intellectual Emile Durkheim (1858–1917) also viewed society as an organism. You should recognize Durkheim's name from our discussion of suicide earlier in the chapter. Durkheim was one of the first true sociologists, in that he used data to test theories. His work provides the basis for much of functionalist thought.

Durkheim's work suggested that solidarity is a vital component that holds society together. Solidarity integrates, or holds society together, because people see themselves as unified. He points out that the type of society influences the type of solidarity. Durkheim divided solidarity into two different types, mechanical and organic. **Mechanical solidarity** refers to the state of community bonding in traditional societies in which people share beliefs and values and perform common activities. It's this bond that works to keep society running smoothly.[15]

As societies become more complex, their type of solidarity changes from mechanical to organic. **Organic solidarity** occurs when people live in a society with a diverse division of labor. Division of labor refers to the many different jobs we have today. This forces people to depend on one another for survival. Ask yourself, when was the last time you ate something you either grew or killed yourself? For most of us, the answer is never. Food is essential for survival, and yet most of us require a complex division of labor to feed ourselves. Truckers, grocers, and farmers all must do their part so we can eat.[16] This organic connection ensures that we get the things we need and holds society together. Beliefs remain important in a modern society, but what binds people together is their organic solidarity.[17]

Durkheim's ideas about solidarity are just the tip of the iceberg, though. A number of American thinkers drew inspiration from Durkheim and expanded his ideas into what is known as functionalist thought.

Functionalism in the United States

After Albion Small created the first department of sociology in 1892 at the University of Chicago, a new academic discipline began to emerge across the United States.[18] This budding science provided social thinkers a place to study the workings of society. One of these thinkers was Talcott Parsons.

TALCOTT PARSONS

Functionalist Talcott Parsons (1902–1979) was a giant in the field of sociology in the United States. Parsons was interested in creating grand theories that attempted to explain every aspect of the human experience and how social systems interconnect. For Parsons, society was much like a bicycle wheel, made up of independent yet interdependent parts. When properly balanced, each independent spoke connected to the hub keeps the wheel spinning. But if just one spoke breaks on your wheel, the entire wheel will eventually fall out of balance. Similarly, society is an interrelated system, and if one part fails to work, the whole system suffers.[19]

Parsons also commented on the inertia of social systems, meaning that they tend to remain at rest, if they are at rest, or stay in motion, if already in motion. For example, when you go bowling, you must take a bowling ball and use your own force to make it roll down the alley. Once the ball starts rolling, it tends to keep rolling until the pins and the end of the alley stop it. Although the friction from the floor may slow it down, some other force must stop it. Parsons pointed out that the social world acts the same way. Thus, in order to change a society, some great force must impact the system or it will remain unchanged. This is because societies naturally will find a balance. Thus change is unlikely and often disruptive. Of course, once the process of change starts, the system will continue on that path until some counterreaction occurs due to social inertia.[20]

ROBERT MERTON

Functionalist Robert K. Merton (1910–2003), a contemporary of Parsons, sought to create a middle-range theory that could bridge the gap

<<< **Amish farm communities** in Pennsylvania **have mechanical solidarity because everyone lives in much the same way, does the same things, and shares the same values.**

between grand theories and the study of individual parts of society. He did this by breaking society into parts and studying them individually to better understand the whole.[21] This idea is widely accepted in sociology today, as most sociologists have an area of expertise, be it race, gender, crime, inequality, population, or a host of other issues. It is possible to spend a career pursuing knowledge in one of these areas, seeking to create theories of the middle range that describe these issues and how they influence society. Merton's work also shows how sociologists are rarely "pure" theorists in any area.

One of Merton's greatest theoretical contributions to functionalism was his understanding that social realities have both intended and unintended **functions**—social factors that affect people in a society. Merton identified two types: **manifest functions**, or factors that lead to an expected consequence or outcome, and **latent functions**, or factors that lead to an unforeseen or unexpected consequence. Merton suggested that when looking at any social event, sociologists should ask the question, "For whom is this functional?" By doing this, we'll do a complete analysis because we'll consider both manifest and latent functions. For example,

MECHANICAL SOLIDARITY refers to the state of community bonding in traditional societies in which people share beliefs and values and perform common activities.

ORGANIC SOLIDARITY occurs when people live in a society with a diverse division of labor.

FUNCTIONS are social factors that affect people in a society.

MANIFEST FUNCTIONS are functions that lead to an expected consequence or outcome.

LATENT FUNCTIONS are functions that lead to unforeseen or unexpected consequences.

one could argue that the manifest function of outsourcing jobs is to improve a company's profits while providing cheaper goods to consumers. However, the latent function of such a system creates tension for families whose jobs are lost, like my student. For Merton, one cannot complete a functional analysis without considering both manifest and latent functions.[22]

THE FUNCTIONALISTS—AT A GLANCE

CRITICISMS OF FUNCTIONALISM

In the mid-20th century, functionalism was the dominant theoretical approach. However, its dominance has waned in more recent years. Critics of functionalism sometimes claim that this paradigm does not take into account the influences of wealth and power on the formation of society. From a purely functionalist point of view, all social structures exist because they meet some need. For example, years ago in the town in which I live, downtown area stores had hitching posts in front of them. Now they're gone because no one rides a horse for transportation anymore. If and when cars become obsolete, society will find some other way to deal with transportation issues. However, in the meantime, cars serve an essential function for society.

Functionalists are accused of supporting the status quo, even when it may be harmful to do so. Consider the invention of the automobile. Certainly it has made society more mobile and provides freedom of movement for millions. And yet, if we fail to consider the latent consequences of this invention, we do not fully understand it. Thus, supporting the car means supporting the air pollution, acres of parking lots, and potential accidents that come with it.

Functionalists suggest that societies will naturally find a balance point on their own. If change occurs, it will do so slowly, and this is actually in the best interest of society. However, if you think about certain social problems such as homelessness, is this something that should be addressed slowly or quickly? Although it is easy to point out that certain individual traits may lead some to live in shelters, is it really good for anyone to have people sleeping on the streets? The lack of affordable housing in society remains a problem. Although Liebow argues that the United States does not have enough cheap housing or high-paying work for all of its citizens, he points out that a lack of a decent wage drives much of the poverty that results in homelessness. In this way, he criticizes the functional argument that the balance point is fair. Thus, is the United States really a "land of opportunity" for everyone?

As you consider homelessness or other societal issues, ask yourself for whom is the system functional? Or whom does the system benefit? Functionalists might argue that society works for the greatest number of people. Change will arise when problems become "big enough." However, critics would argue that this belief results in many minorities being ignored. Who speaks for the homeless? What choice did my student have about globalization and the loss of her job? The functionalist perspective often fails to recognize how inequalities in social class, race, and gender cause an imbalance in our society.

The conflict theory paradigm arose as a response to some of functionalism's weaknesses. Conflict theorists want to analyze how these social inequalities affect society as a whole.

The Conflict Theorist's Worldview

Remember, conflict theory is a theoretical framework that views society in a struggle for scarce resources. So, what is scarce? Two main concerns for conflict theorists are economic wealth and power. Such theorists acknowledge that we live in an unequal society. Why? It could be because there is not enough "stuff" to go around, or it could be because those with the "stuff" don't want to let go of it. In either case, conflict theory suggests that we're all struggling for more "stuff," whether that "stuff" is power in a marriage or wealth in the world.

Conflict theorists, like functional ones, tend to focus on macro issues, viewing how society's structures contribute to the conflict. Modern conflict theorists often look at the inequality of a capitalist economic system. Such a system breeds inequality, as it rewards some at the expense of others. Once you have power, you want to keep it. For this reason, the wealthy elites are more likely to create advantages for themselves, even if their actions put others at a disadvantage.

In general, the essence of conflict theory suggests that a pyramid structure of power and wealth exists in society. The elite at the top of the pyramid determine the rules for those below them. Under such a system, laws, institutions, and traditions support their authority. When Liebow discusses the lack of adequate wages and the shame we all deserve because we permit homelessness to exist, he is in essence suggesting that those of us who are not homeless are, in part, responsible for those who are because we allow the system to ignore these people.

Many theorists who use the conflict paradigm might examine macro conflicts between different groups of society, different countries, or different social classes. The study of inequality in sociology always involves a consideration of conflict theory. Thus, you can see the paradigm applied to social class, race, gender, marriage, religion, population, environment, and a host of other social phenomena. If you believe that discrimination, ageism, sexism, racism, and classism occur in society because some people have the power to inflict their desires over others, then you think like a conflict theorist.

Modern feminist theory, or the study of how gender affects the experiences and opportunities of men and women, often takes a conflict-oriented point of view. Women throughout the world are still placed in positions subordinate to men. In some countries, this might mean women cannot choose their husbands, while in this country it may be more linked to opportunities afforded to women. You'd be very hard-pressed to find women CEOs in the biggest companies. Of the top 500 companies in the United States, women lead fewer than 20.[23] Feminists often suggest this occurs because men want to maintain their positions of power in society and strive to keep women out. Do you see the conflict perspective here?

A student once pointed out that women often find themselves at the short end of the "financial stick" and powerful people take advantage of the poor. She was adamant about her views and refused to change her opinion. When I labeled her views as Marxist, she immediately took offense and denied my claim. However, it was evident to me that her views originated from the thoughts of Karl Marx, a founder of conflict theory.

KARL MARX

Karl Marx (1818–1883) was a German theorist, social activist, and writer who analyzed the effects of capitalism—an economic system in which private individuals own businesses and control the economy. Believing that capitalism corrupted human nature, Marx hoped for a utopia in which equality reigned. At his core, Marx was not that different from Comte because he wished to understand society to improve it for all.

Marx suggested that in a capitalist system, the **bourgeoisie,** or members of the capitalist class, own most of the wealth because they control the businesses. Since increasing profit is their first goal, owners pay workers as little as possible. Liebow, too, notices this when he encounters homeless women who actually have some form of employment, but don't make enough money to afford housing. Employers generally pay these women as little as possible, and the women have no way to fight the system.

Marx called the workers in a capitalist system the **proletariat,** or members of the poor working class. They do all the work and the owners reap all the benefits. The proletariat live in an unending cycle in which they work for low pay and then use those wages to survive. According to Marx, workers will never get ahead if they do not share in the wealth they create.

Why don't workers do something to change their fate? Marx suggested that it was because people had a **false consciousness,** or a lack of understanding of their position in society. The workers felt that they were alone in their plight. Marx proposed that the workers must develop **class consciousness**, or an understanding of one's position in the system. Marx suggested that most workers do not truly understand how capitalism enslaves them. They think if they work hard, they'll get by and perhaps thrive. Marx argued that these ideas were fantasy.

Marx believed that once workers recognized their positions, they would unite to end their tyranny. He proposed an overthrow of the private ownership of capitalism, and instead suggested socialism. In such a system, the government controls the economic system, ensuring that all people share in the profits generated by their own labor.

However, Marx didn't suggest that long-term government repression was necessary to enforce communism on people. He knew that the government would initially have to force the bourgeoisie to give up their wealth because it takes force to make powerful people give up their power.

In 2008, Wachovia Bank's CEO Ken Thompson was forced to step down from his post after receiving pressure from the bank's board. For several months, the board criticized Thompson's work,

blaming a loss of more than $700 million on him. During these months, Thompson did damage control to help regain the confidence of investors and the board, but his efforts failed. Thompson did not step down willingly; those on top do whatever it takes to stay there.[24]

Marx believed the same would be true in society. However, he believed that members of the capitalist class would willingly share their wealth once they saw the benefits of communal living. Our true human nature is to live in harmony, sharing everything equally.[25]

Sociologists' opinions on Marxist theory vary. While some may hope for a type of class con-

sciousness to arise and replace our current system, others think he oversimplified class struggle. His simple system of social class is difficult to apply to a complex postindustrial capitalist society, and even if you try, where would you draw the line between owners and workers? My student actually owned stock in the company that let her go, so was she a worker or an owner? Seems like both.

Marxist theory clearly remains active in today's discussions of sociology. Marx felt that economic power should be in the hands of the people because wealth corrupts human nature.

These ideas continue to inspire sociologists. Let's next look at the work of four conflict theorists, Martineau, Du Bois, Addams, and Foster, to study how gender, race, and class affect a society.

HARRIET MARTINEAU

Harriet Martineau (1802–1876), like Karl Marx, came from a bourgeois family and received the benefits and status that came with such a class distinction. However, she hoped that capitalism and industrialization would bring greater justice and opportunity. Martineau, one of the first female sociologists, did not just examine the inequalities in the economic system, she also focused on the inequality between the sexes.

In the book *Society in America*, Martineau analyzed the impact of slavery, the position of women in society, and the social customs within U.S. political and economic systems.[26] She points out out how these systems favor men who hold the power in society.

Martineau's studies noted hypocrisy and favoritism in the United States. For example, only white men could vote in the United States, despite the nation's democratic ideals. Enslaved people and women did not have equal opportunities for political, economic, and educational involvement. Martineau pointed out that some people did not have the same opportunities as others. She not only paved the way for other female sociologists, but also expanded people's thinking about the world, enlightening what would become the conflict paradigm.[27]

CYCLE OF WEALTH IN A CAPITALIST SYSTEM

The Bourgeoisie

spends their wages in businesses owned by

owns the wealth and exploits

The Proletariat

W.E.B. DU BOIS

W. E. B. Du Bois (1868—1963) was an African American conflict theorist who agreed with a great deal of Marx's thinking. After attending Fisk University, Du Bois moved on to Harvard, where he would eventually complete both his undergraduate and graduate work. His writings are vast, but he is often credited for initiating the study of race in America. He was particularly interested in issues of racial inequality in the United States.[28]

In his book *The Philadelphia Negro*, Du Bois showed that poverty among African Americans in the United States was primarily the result of prejudice and discrimination.[29] In the book, he reviewed the history of African Americans in Philadelphia and connected that history to the problems his contemporaries were facing. Implying that slavery and capitalism led to African Americans' problems, Du Bois pointed out that history was influential over the present. He also noted that African Americans of his time had to live in two worlds, a white one and a black one. In one world, they were second-class citizens, while in the other they were equals. This idea, which Du Bois termed "double consciousness," created tension and conflict for African Americans. He felt that with greater assimilation into the mainstream culture, African Americans would eventually lead better-quality lives.[30]

In many respects, Du Bois was the first and perhaps most influential sociologist to study race in the United States. He was a social activist, and he became more interested in working to improve life on the African continent and less interested in life in the United States. Du Bois eventually came to believe that African Americans would never be equal to whites because the white population would not allow this. For this reason, he left the United States and spent his remaining years in Africa.

When Du Bois saw extreme poverty, oppressive governments, and many wars in Africa, he realized that colonizing Europeans caused many of these problems. **Colonialism was a primary way for European powers to generate wealth for capitalists while doing little to improve the lives of the African poor.** Du Bois increasingly believed that the greed of the United States and western Europe was the cause of war and poverty throughout the world. **To counter this, promoting economic justice and equality helps the world be at peace.**[31]

V
V
V Martineau's studies revealed inequality in the U.S. democratic system. What about today? **Is the U.S. system fair for each person in the photograph below?**

JANE ADDAMS

Laura Jane Addams (1860—1935) was born in Cedarville, Illinois. Addams's father, a businessman and politician who worked to elect Lincoln and strongly opposed slavery, raised her. Jane earned a bachelor of arts degree from Rockford Women's Seminary in 1882, then traveled to Europe, where she saw things that changed her life.

In Toynbee Hall, Addams witnessed the settlement house movement.[32] The settlement house movement supported the

THE CONFLICT THEORISTS — AT A GLANCE

KARL MARX

Equal Wealth = Peace

JANE ADDAMS

Ignorance + Structural Barriers = Poverty

W.E.B. DU BOIS

Greed − War + Poverty

HARRIET MARTINEAU

Democratic Power for All!

JOHN BELLAMY FOSTER

Capitalism = Destruction of Earth

idea that poverty results from ignorance and structural barriers, not from failings in the morality of the person. The settlement house workers actually lived and worked in the slums. Jane and a friend, Ellen Gates Starr, decided to create a settlement house in Chicago. In 1889, they opened Hull-House with these three principles:

1. Workers would live in the slums to better understand the problems there.
2. Every person has dignity and worth regardless of race/ethnicity, gender, or social class.
3. Dedication, education, and service can overcome ignorance, disease, and other problems often associated with poverty.

Offering services from medical to educational, Addams also used her position at Hull-House to write articles and books on a variety of topics like the rights of women and the poor. In many ways, Hull-House became a laboratory for the application of sociological principles. In 1931, Jane Addams won the Nobel Peace Prize for her lifetime of service and dedication to peace.[33]

Through her teaching, writing, and action, Jane Addams embodied the best of sociology principles. Along with Albion Small, she helped found the American Sociological Association and often guest lectured in sociology classes at the University of Chicago. In order to understand the poor, Addams felt that she must live among them. Once she comprehended this situation, she wrote about it to inform others. These theories impacted her work at Hull-House. These are the steps you will take in learning to think like a sociologist.

JOHN BELLAMY FOSTER

John Bellamy Foster, a contemporary professor of sociology, often writes using a conflict paradigm. His work is primarily concerned with the negative effects of capitalism on society and the planet as whole. In his article, "The End of Rational Capitalism," he points out that purely capitalist economies, or economies in which markets are totally free, are disappearing throughout the world.

In free-market capitalism, businesses seek short-term rewards by working to expand markets. They do not care about long-term consequences. As a result, Foster argues that businesses' pursuit of wealth has created environmental and global problems, including the existence of extreme global poverty and inequality.

Foster argues that markets cannot "solve problems" because there are no profits to be had from such an endeavor. Often, people suggest that the United States is the wealthiest country in the world because we have worked harder and used the capitalist system to give opportunity and incentive to people. Foster reminds us that such a perspective ignores important parts of history, namely the period after World War II when most of the "industrialized world" was destroyed (except the United States), and the expansion of the U.S. economy was largely related to building up these devastated countries. This had very little to do with the superiority of the American capitalist system. Issues such as the fall of the USSR and the privatization of the Chinese economy seem to indicate that capitalism has won and is "superior" to socialism. However, totally

<<< This is a collage of flags from many of the world's most populous and powerful nations. **Do any of these flags have meaning to you?**

The Symbolic Interactionist's Worldview

Symbolic interactionism focuses on how communication influences the way people's interactions with each other create the social world in which we live. Symbolic interactionists believe that the root of society comes from its symbols. They suggest that the symbols we use are arbitrary, meaning that they vary from culture to culture.

Do you write with a pen or la pluma? Neither is wrong; one is a label in English, the other in Spanish. **As long as you are with other people who speak the same language, you can interact.**

free-market capitalism will result in the destruction of the environment and the exploitation of workers throughout the world.[34] The long and short of it is that capitalism cannot continue to expand because we are reaching a stagnant point according to Foster.

CRITICISMS OF CONFLICT THEORY

Critics of conflict theory often accuse it of being too radical. This paradigm often becomes synonymous with the idea that powerful people oppress the weak. However, most people seem to agree that the roles and rules of society "make sense." For example, even after we discussed globalization and the depletion of factory jobs in the United States, my student who lost her job still felt that the U.S. system was "fair." She said, "it still makes sense to me, even though I'm being hurt by it." This illustrates the reality that most people in society tend to agree with the status quo. Certainly, some are victimized by racism, sexism, and other prejudices, but most members of society seem to agree that things are generally fine.

A simple reading of conflict theory can also seem to make the notion of conflict seem like a "bad" thing. However, doesn't competition breed excellence? When I played baseball, I never worked harder than when my team got a new member, a young man who also played second base. I worked even harder to maintain my spot on the roster. Starting positions are rare, and the "conflict" actually improved my play.

After examining the works of functionalists and conflict theorists you're probably thinking in a macro manner. Whether you're using functionalism or conflict theory, you are thinking like many sociologists. Yet one more paradigm remains. If you believe that the way to change the world is through the individual, you might find symbolic interactionism appealing.

A long time ago, I enrolled in a language school in Mexico. I lived with a family who spoke no English, and my teachers only spoke to us in Spanish. At first, I was totally lost. I clung to the members of the family with whom I lived as if I were a little child. However, I soon began to learn the language. It is amazing how our need to communicate with others helps us learn. Although the words or accents sound different, communication is central to all human interactions.

Of course, words are not the only symbols. Consider the photograph of flags from countries around the world. The flag that probably has meaning for you is the U.S. flag. However, people from China, Brazil, Belgium, or the United Kingdom probably feel the same way about their flags as you do about yours. These symbols represent entire nations, and yet you cannot identify many of them and they probably don't hold much interest to you. This is because the importance of a symbol is rooted in the culture from which it comes. Just as language varies between people, so, too, do their symbol systems.

As you can see then, for interactionists, society is fluid thing. It is always in a process of change because how we use symbols and what they mean to us is constantly changing. For example, when I was in school, teachers might tell ethnic jokes, such as "Polack" jokes. Of course, now most of you have not ever heard these jokes. Why? Because people began to define such humor as unacceptable.

You can see then, that our definition of what has value depends on our understanding of it. Context and setting affects our understanding of a social event. You certainly behave differently in church than you do in a bar or on a golf course. Social order results when the members of society share common definitions of what is appropriate.

Disputes arise when we do not share the same definitions. Think about an argument you've had with someone recently. Did the fight stem from a different interpretation of meaning? For example, if your roommate eats your food without asking your permission, you might interpret that behavior as disrespectful and rude. However, he might feel that his behavior shows that the two of you are friends and share everything with one another.

Symbolic interactionism is the most micro of sociological approaches, as it often studies the activities of individuals and then draws connections to larger society from these. Studies of relationships, race, deviance, and even social movements can all use a symbolic interactionist approach.

Interactionists argue that individuals have the power to co-create the world, to make it what they want it to be. People develop standards and norms through a process of interacting with others. This way, we learn what is "normal" and acceptable behavior. Widespread social acceptance of a behavior is the main criterion in declaring it to be "normal," and we quickly learn that different situations allow for different behaviors. For example, if you're dating someone, kissing good night is a perfectly acceptable behavior. However, trying to kiss a co-worker good-bye could result in your being charged with sexual harassment.

Symbolic interactionism is a distinctly American way of looking at the world. In many ways it blends sociology and psychology. Let's take a look at the work of its founder, George Herbert Mead.

GEORGE HERBERT MEAD

Symbolic interactionism was the brainchild of George Herbert Mead (1863–1931), an American sociologist from the University of Chicago. After his death in 1931, Mead's former students were so committed to him that they combined his articles, notes, and lectures into the book *Mind, Self, and Society*. This book introduced a new theory called symbolic interactionism.[35]

In his book *Mind, Self, and Society*, Mead suggests that the root of society is the symbols that teach us to understand the world. We then use these symbols to develop a sense of self, or identity. It is this identity that we then take into the world and interact with other identities to create society. Thus, the building blocks of society start with our minds, the place we interpret symbols.

How do you learn to interpret symbols? Mead suggests that we do this through the micro interactions we have every day. When I was born, my parents named me John. When I got older, if someone

called, "John," I turned my head. Eventually, I learned nuances of the symbol John. For example, if my mother yelled my name, I knew I was in trouble. Mead argues that all these various symbols enter our minds, where their meaning is interpreted and we are told how to react. Mead suggests that this process is never-ending; therefore, we have a fluid sense of who we are. Our selves can change, and they do change based on how we interpret the symbols thrown our way.

In this way, your self develops. **Self** is your identity. It's what makes you who you are and separates you from others. According to Mead, you couldn't have a self without symbols or without someone to pass those symbols to you. In other words, you learn who you are through others.

In middle school, did you ever feel embarrassed by your parents? Do you feel the same level of embarrassment today? The answer to both questions is probably yes *and* no. When I ask this in class, most of my students report that they don't find their parents nearly as embarrassing as they used to. Why does this occur? It is because when you're young, you don't have a well-developed sense of self. You are anxious, taking your cue from others as to what is "cool" or acceptable. You worry that your parents' actions might reflect upon you. As you grow older, you've experienced thousands of interactions that have taught you who you are. This is why, the older you get, the less embarrassing your parents seem. You know yourself much better now than you did in middle school.

Mead proposed that symbols build society. Symbols have meaning, and meaning directs our lives. The symbols a society uses help us understand the people in that society. In the United States, we have accepted that we need the word "homeless" to discuss people who cannot afford housing. Symbols help us define a situation and determine what we should do about it. For example, Liebow finds that people often assign labels, such as "addict," "alcoholic," or "mentally ill," to the homeless, but not as often to people who have jobs. Some even use addiction as an excuse not to help the homeless—*Oh, he or she is just an addict*. If potential employers believe in these labels, then they will be less likely to hire homeless people, perpetuating a system that keeps them homeless.

▶▶▶ GO GL🌐BAL

Homeless Labels Around the World

Assigning negative labels to the homeless occurs not only in the United States, but also in countries all over the world. In Finland during the 1980s, homelessness became associated with alcoholism. People related the two ideas so closely that the government in Finland had to step in to prevent such negative stereotyping. In China and India, people connect homelessness with a lack of governmental registration, which means that the homeless aren't seen as true citizens. In Peru, children living on the street are called *piranitas*, or little piranhas, which implies that they are dangerous and likely to resort to criminal behavior. People in Bangladesh equate homelessness with having a lack of morals.[36]

Criminal, alcoholic, immoral—these are only a handful of labels that exist for the homeless around the world. As Liebow noted, negative labels make it even more difficult for homeless individuals to rise above their situation. If people who are homeless are given an opportunity and adequate support, they can be just as successful and stable as any other members of society.

HERBERT BLUMER

Symbolic interactionist Herbert Blumer (1900–1987), a disciple of George Herbert Mead and former chair of the University of California, Berkeley sociology department, established three basic premises that define the symbolic interactionist perspective:

1. Human beings behave toward things on the basis of the meanings they ascribe to those things.
2. The meaning of such things is derived from, or arises out of, the social interaction that one has with others and society.
3. These meanings are handled in and modified through an interpretive process used by the person in dealing with the things he or she encounters.[37]

What does he mean? First, we all react to situations and people based on how we perceive them. Have you ever noticed that you can "dis" your mom, but if someone else does, you get defensive? This is because you ascribe meaning to the act of dissing that it's OK for someone in the family, but when outsiders join in, you circle the wagons and defend the group.

How did your feelings emerge? They probably occurred from the many years in which your mother cared for you. While she may drive you crazy sometimes, she certainly fed you, tucked you in at night, and nurtured you when you were sick. In other words, the social interactions you had with her support the meaning you ascribe to who can and cannot dis her.

Blumer proposed that the primary focus of the interactionist approach involves studying individual interactions with symbols. This micro focus places great importance on the idea that symbols have great power to affect society as a whole. The way we talk about something creates the way we deal with it. Consider this example: In the 1950s, many whites spoke using racial slurs. Today, such language is socially unacceptable. Has this change eliminated racism? Certainly not, but the level of racism in the United States has certainly declined. Are these two factors connected? Blumer would suggest that they are. Words convey meaning and meaning creates reality. Eliminating racist language moves society closer to eliminating racism.

Normally, people interpret the words and actions of those around them and determine their behavior based on this interpretation. This results in rational behavior, meaning that we tailor our responses to the setting after we've interpreted the reactions. However, in a group setting our behaviors are somewhat different. Generally, Blumer suggests that in a group setting we react without the same degree of thought we use in an individual decision. At some point, people stop thinking rationally and act in ways that they might not consider acceptable in a different setting. Last football season, our college team was losing an important game. A man in the stands became extremely distraught; four-letter words came from his mouth like steam out of Old Faithful. The stands were filled not with sailors, but with men, women, and children, and I'm sure this man would never have behaved this way at a PTA meeting. So why did this happen? Blumer would suggest that it was the result of collective excitement, an intense emotional behavior that makes it hard for us to think and act rationally. This is what Blumer calls **contagion**, a rapid, irrational mode in which people do not think rationally or clearly. In such a setting, they "lose their heads" and react emotionally, not rationally. In this way, you can see that individual interactions can create social realities. I was thankful that at that game I had not taken my youngest child, but a man in the crowd eventually told the man to watch his mouth because there were children around. Initially, the foul-mouthed man seemed angry to be scolded in public, but he quickly "cooled down" as he noticed that a number of people around him were watching his behavior closely. How do we react when others are watching? Sociologist Erving Goffman developed a theory about this.

> **Goffman's primary insight is that we are constantly trying to manage the impressions that others have of us. Impression management is the action we use to control what others think of us.** When the angry man at the football game "calmed down," it was probably because he was a season ticket-holder and he knew that we'd all see him again next week. He didn't want to come off as the "jerk who cusses."

ERVING GOFFMAN

Canadian sociologist Erving Goffman (1922-1982) developed a theory he called **dramaturgy**, a theory of interaction in which all life is like acting. Goffman uses this theory to compare daily social interactions to the gestures of actors on a stage. People are constantly "acting" in order to convince people of the character that they wish to portray to the outside world. Not to say that people are always "faking it," but rather that people are concerned about what the rest of the world will think of them, and they adjust their social interactions accordingly.

Frequently, we alter our behavior without much deliberate thought. For example, if you are on a first date, do you behave differently than the way you do with an old friend? Usually, on a first date you dress differently, talk differently, and eat carefully. You may be nervous, but you will also, without thinking about it, change your behavior. Why? Because you are taking extra care to make a good first impression, even if it means not being completely yourself. Goffman points out that managing impressions involves a complex series of actions and reactions. As a person gets older and has more "practice" in socializing, he or she may be better equipped to gauge the reactions that their actions will receive.[38] Chapter 4 provides more detail on dramaturgy.

HOWARD BECKER

Howard Becker, a sociologist from Chicago, suggests that human action is related to the labels attached to it. In his book, *Outsiders: Studies in the Sociology of Deviance*, Becker suggests that a label is attached to a certain behavior when a group with powerful social status labels it deviant. He suggests that deviance is rooted in the reactions and responses of others to an individual's acts.

The label of deviant, or conformist for that matter, is applied when people see our behavior and react to it. This sets up a self-fulfilling prophecy for behavior as people seek an identity that will match up to the expectations that others hold of them. Becker applied these ideas to the study of deviant behavior, but the idea of labeling theory applies to all identity issues, including gender, sexual orientation, and personal identity.

CONTAGION is a rapid, irrational mode in which people do not think rationally or clearly.

DRAMATURGY is a theory of interaction in which all life is like acting.

Consider the example of a five-year-old girl who has been labeled a "good girl." The theory would suggest that somewhere along the line, she did what others expected of her and that these people had power over her. Her parents asked her to take a bath and she did. She received a positive reward, "she's a good girl," and through repeated events throughout her life, she developed that sense of self whereby she never does anything remotely "dangerous" or out of line and always takes a bath. However, if this "good girl" becomes a "terrible teen" and her parents label her as a delinquent, she might stop bathing and start smoking. Becker would suggest that the label we ascribe to people has a major influence on their behavior.

THE SYMBOLIC INTERACTIONISTS — AT A GLANCE

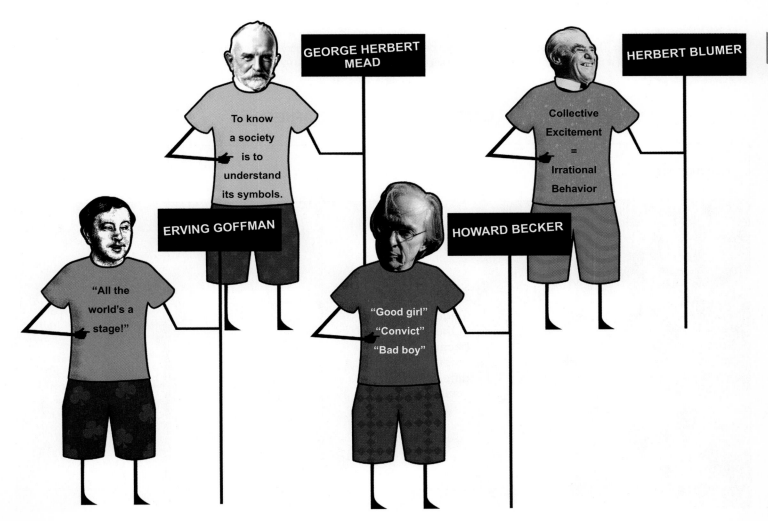

GEORGE HERBERT MEAD

To know a society is to understand its symbols.

HERBERT BLUMER

Collective Excitement = Irrational Behavior

ERVING GOFFMAN

"All the world's a stage!"

HOWARD BECKER

"Good girl" "Convict" "Bad boy"

CRITICISMS OF SYMBOLIC INTERACTIONISM

Critics of symbolic interactionism suggest that this perspective ignores the coercive effects of social structure, focusing too much on the power of the individual to co-create his or her world. If, for example, you're a slave, it doesn't matter whether or not you reject the ownership symbol or not. If you try to leave, you'll be punished.

Of course, we are all born into a culture and social setting. We don't create them as we go along. As a result, your parents, neighborhood, and nation of birth all influence how you see things. Had you been born in a different time or in a different culture, you might have believed totally different things.

The Three Paradigms— How Are They Interrelated?

In the sports arena, we tend to associate phenomenal players with the teams on which they play. The player's name and the team name become synonymous. Michael Jordan and the Chicago Bulls. Tom Brady and the New England Patriots. Derek Jeter and the New York Yankees. You get the idea. The same is true of sociologists—we associate the theorist with the paradigm that he or she favored or had a hand in developing. For example, Marx is a symbol of conflict theory, whereas Comte and functionalism go hand in hand. However, sometimes it can be tricky to confine sociologists to such a tight box because they might use parts of each paradigm in their analyses. In fact, I know of no colleague of mine who is a "purist" in anything. That's because no single paradigm perfectly fits every situation. To get a complete picture, many sociologists use all three paradigms. In this way, the three paradigms are interrelated and work together to help us figure out why society is the way it is.

Think about sociologist Robert Merton and his concept of latent and manifest consequences. He takes a functionalist stance, but adds to it the notion that intended and unintended results can arise. Thus, we should ask, for whom is this functional? Can you see a bit of conflict theory here? Like Merton, symbolic interactionist Howard Becker also blurs the lines between the paradigms.

Becker's labeling theory can be linked to conflict theory because the labeling tradition suggests that those with power determine what is and is not labeled as deviant or criminal. In other words, the power of the label influences the outcome of the individual, but people with the ability to get what they want done put the label on us. Like a conflict theorist, Becker acknowledges that a system of inequality exists within our society. Consider this question: Why are cigarettes legal, while marijuana is illegal? Labeling theorists would argue that this is because people with power smoke cigarettes, but not pot. If powerful people ever started smoking pot, the practice would become legal.

We've seen how conflict theory overlaps with both functionalism and symbolic interactionism, but does functionalism ever overlap with symbolic interactionism? When Emile Durkheim suggests that values unify people, he sounds a bit like George Herbert Mead. The solidarity of a society for Durkheim is related to what it values, and he acknowledges that values change as societies become more modern.

The point for you as a student of sociology is to beware that just because a sociologist is classified as a functionalist, conflict theorist, or symbolic interactionist, that doesn't mean that he or she won't use other points of view in making an analysis of the world. In fact, at times, a theorist's point of view can be so eclectic that he can't be pinned down into a single category. This sentiment is especially true of sociologist Max Weber (1864–1920).

OVERLAPPING THEORIES

Functionalism		Conflict Theory		Symbolic Interactionism
Everything in the social world exists because it has both an intended outcome and an unintended outcome.	Power differentials (conflict theory) often indicate for whom things are functional and for whom they are not (functionalism).	Inequality exists in the social world because of differences between different groups' wealth and power.	People in power create labels and assign them to others (conflict theory), and these labels influence the outcomes of the individual (symbolic interactionism).	Labels are attached to certain individuals; this practice sets up a self-fulfilling prophecy as people try to match their behavior to their labels.

Max Weber — Theorist Who Transcends Categorization

To me, Max Weber (1864–1920) is the German counterpart of Emile Durkheim because he wrote about a great variety of topics, used data in his analysis, and laid the foundations for high-quality sociological research. In his work, students often see a variety of ideas that seem to blend different schools of thought. Yet, he wrote at a time before many of these "schools" were clearly defined or established.

Because Weber wrote partly as a response to some of Karl Marx's ideas, many consider him a conflict theorist. Weber accepted that social classes influence our outcomes; however, he felt Marx's social class system was too simple. He proposed that all people have economic, political, and cultural conflicts that are related to their relative social position. As a result, being an owner does not necessarily make you important in society. Wealth is important, but political power and social standing are also important.

In other ways, Weber appeared to take a more functional approach, particularly when he discussed how bureaucracies function in society. Bureaucracies, which will be discussed in depth in Chapter 6, are formal organizations that are organized into a hierarchy of smaller departments. You might think of a large corporation or a government agency as a bureaucracy. Weber proposed that rational and ideal bureaucracies naturally occur because we need them. They provide clear lines of authority, divide tasks so that workers can specialize, and clearly define rules and expectations. Under such a type of leadership, societies and large organizations function smoothly and improve the function of society. Although Weber was well aware that few perfect bureaucracies existed, he argued that responsible leadership will tend toward the ideal because Western society is increasingly focused on achieving goals, and a rational bureaucracy is an efficient way to achieve those goals.[39]

Other colleagues of mine have suggested that Weber's ideas seem to lay the foundation for the symbolic interactionist school of thought.

>>> Is Max Weber (pronounced *VAY-bur*) a conflict theorist? A functionalist? A symbolic interactionist? Or is he all three? **Sociologists everywhere disagree on how to classify Weber. That's because his views are so varied that he almost defies categorization.**

Why? Because he pointed out how values influence our goals and affect our behaviors. In his book, *The Protestant Ethic and the Spirit of Capitalism,* Weber clearly linked a person's religious value to the societal creation of a capitalist economy. For him, capitalism arose in the Western world primarily because a religious value system that he called "the Protestant Ethic" emphasizes the accumulation of wealth as a marker of God's favor on a person.

Furthermore, Weber also discussed how values are important to the study of sociology. For example, he understood that sociologists are at risk of approaching their profession with personal values that might influence the outcome of their study. Weber stressed that sociology should be value-free. In other words, sociologists should study society as it is, not as they would like it to be. They should put their biases aside when analyzing a topic. He implied that personal values may impact social research, and therefore sociologists must strive to put such values aside when they make their analyses.

So, where does your professor put Weber? The more you read about social theorists, the more you will find that most of them blend ideas from all schools of thought.

APPLYING SOCIOLOGICAL THEORIES
Now it's time to think like a sociologist. Thinking like a sociologist means that you understand the topic, and you examine it from one or more of the three sociological theories covered in this section. Consider the problem of homelessness in a society. How might a functionalist view homelessness? How might a conflict theorist view it? A symbolic interactionist?

WRAP YOUR MIND AROUND THE THEORY

Functionalists look for the function of any issue. **Food banks, functionalists argue, make a dysfunctional system like homelessness function in a society.**

FUNCTIONALISM

Functionalists suggest society works as an interrelated system. Communitarians understand that if society is to run smoothly, the government, the local community, and the business sector must all work together for the well-being of all. The root of society is the local community; it anchors this societal tree. The government carries the will of the people to the economic system, thereby functioning as the trunk of this tree. The leaves of a tree make the sugar that allows the entire plant to live. Of course, leaves without roots blow over, and roots without leaves die.

CONFLICT THEORY

Conflict theorists would view homelessness as a sign of inequality in society. Conflict theorists focus on social classes and their drastic differences in wealth, power, and prestige. They believe that the upper class controls society's wealth and resources and exploits the lower class. If the upper class shared its wealth, conflict theorists argue, then homelessness would be cut down dramatically.

WHAT CAUSES HOMELESSNESS IN A SOCIETY?

SYMBOLIC INTERACTIONISM

Because symbolic interactionists view things on a smaller scale, they would explore how homelessness affects the way individuals act toward one another. These theorists would ask: How do individuals behave toward one another? What labels do individuals assign to homelessness? How do non-homeless people interact with homeless people?

The **inequality of wealth** in a society **is a leading cause of homelessness.**

Look at each picture. **How do you think each pair of people is acting toward each other? Do you think there are differences between pairs?**

discover sociology in action: WHY IS COMMUNITY LEARNING IMPORTANT TO A SOCIETY?

Getting Involved in Sociology—Community Learning

In *Tell Them Who I Am: The Lives of Homeless Women*, Elliot Liebow discusses how he often "loaned" money to many homeless women who had absolutely none. He was always careful to consider the money a "loan" because he knew that simply giving it to them would show that he thought of them as nothing more than panhandlers. Liebow figured he wouldn't get the money back, but he didn't mind.[40] His goal was to treat the women with dignity and earn their trust. Liebow was practicing community learning. **Community learning** occurs when individuals and groups work to identify and address issues of public concern.

It's easy for people to believe that social problems are so widespread that there is nothing we can do about them. Often, we feel so out of touch with the world around us that we do not vote, we do not know our neighbors, and we cannot name our town council members. Community learning, however, can help you see things with fresh eyes. Working in the community expands your understanding of sociology and your world.

ACTIVITIES

1. What community learning opportunities are available in your area? Surf the Web to find local shelters, food banks, or other organizations in your community. Choose an organization and volunteer there. Write about your experience.
2. Research your local and state governments. Who are the important government officials? What roles do they play in the government? What policies and issues do they support?
3. Homelessness is just one of many issues that plague today's society. What other social issues do you think are important to address and why? How would you try to solve these problems?

Liebow's study of the homeless showed him that homelessness is a widespread problem, and there is plenty of blame to go around. There are too many people who don't understand the problem, just ignore it, or both. When I worked at a local day shelter during my undergraduate days, I realized I had a lot to learn. One day, while serving lunch, I noticed that one of the patrons became quite irritated. "Hot dogs again!" he screamed. In shock, I thought that he had no right to complain when he could be eating nothing for lunch. An older and more experienced volunteer must have noticed my face because she said to me, "Sometimes, so many people look past them, that they just have to yell so you'll know they're there." That sobering comment brought me back to my senses. When you actually take a minute to view the world from someone else's perspective, you'll find it hard to just sit around and do nothing.

From Classroom to Community | Helping the Homeless

"Homeless people are just a bunch of drug addicts, aren't they?"

I wasn't surprised when Theo, one of my first-year sociology students, made this comment during a lecture. However, I was disappointed because I knew that many people around the world share this view. After a lively debate on the subject, I realized I hadn't changed Theo's mind, so I challenged him to volunteer at a local homeless shelter.

Day after day, Theo worked with the families at the shelter—feeding, clothing, and talking with them. While at the shelter, he met a homeless mother who had been the victim of domestic violence.

"When I looked into that mother's face and the face of her children, I realized how narrow my viewpoint had been," Theo remarked to me later. "How did I ever think you could label an entire group of people?"

At the end of Theo's volunteer period, he wrote a paper for class revealing how much he had learned about the homeless. He even decided to continue working at the shelter. Volunteering made him feel like he was making a difference in the lives of the people he encountered, and he knew they were making a difference in his. Theo's experiences helped him realize that the people at the shelter were just like him. The only difference was that they had fallen on some bad luck.

Theo's story shows how moving out of the classroom and into the community helps people gain a new perspective. They can get out of their individual boxes and view the world as a sociologist would.

WHAT IS SOCIOLOGY? 5

a science guided by the basic understanding that the social matters: our lives are affected not only by our individual characteristics, but by our place in the social world

WHAT ARE THE CHARACTERISTICS OF THE THREE MAJOR SOCIOLOGICAL PARADIGMS? 9

functionalism: defines society as a system of interrelated parts; primarily a macro orientation because it focuses on larger social structures rather than individuals

conflict theory: views society as an unequal system that brings about conflict and change; focuses on macro issues and supports the idea that the struggle for scarce resources holds a society together; concerned with inequality as it relates to wealth and power

symbolic interactionism: focuses on how individual people interact with other people in their everyday lives; studies how the use of "symbols" influence how people communicate; follows a micro approach because it is concerned with the individual's role in creating society

WHY IS COMMUNITY LEARNING IMPORTANT TO A SOCIETY? 25

provides you with a fresh perspective and expands your understanding of sociology and your world

get the topic: WHAT IS SOCIOLOGY?

Sociology Defined 5
Developing a Sociological Imagination 5
Emile Durkheim's Theory on Suicide 7
The Functionalist's Worldview 10

Functionalism in the United States 12
The Conflict Theorist's Worldview 14
The Symbolic Interactionist's Worldview 18

The Three Paradigms—How Are They Related? 22
Getting Involved in Sociology—Community Learning 25

Theory

FUNCTIONALISM 10

- society is a system of connected parts working together to keep society intact
- it is important to consider the function of any issue
- society is fairly stable, which means that things occur in society for a specific function
- suggests society will find a balance point of its own

CONFLICT THEORY 14

- focuses on social classes and their drastic differences in wealth, power, and prestige
- upper class controls society's wealth and resources and exploits the lower class
- once a group has power, they want to keep it, so they are likely to create advantages for themselves

SYMBOLIC INTERACTIONISM 18

- believes the root of society comes from its symbols
- society is fluid, meaning it is always in the process of change because the symbols we use and their interpretations change
- disputes arise when people do not share the same definitions of symbols

Key Terms

sociology is a science guided by the basic understanding that "the social matters: our lives are affected, not only by our individual characteristics but by our place in the social world." 5

sociological imagination is the ability to look beyond the individual as the cause for success and failure and see how one's society influences the outcome. 6

micro means small-scale. 6

macro means large-scale. 6

solidarity refers to the level of connectedness and integration a person feels to others in the environment. 7

social control refers to the social mechanisms that regulate a person's actions. 7

egoistic suicides are suicides that result from a lack of solidarity, occurring among those who have few social connections, feel isolated and alone, and are more likely to fall into despair. 7

altruistic suicides are suicides that occur when the level of solidarity is exceptionally high and when the individual views the group's interest as superior to all other interests. 7

fatalistic suicides are suicides that result from a lack of social control. 8

anomic suicides are suicides that occur as a result of social unrest. 8

paradigm refers to a theoretical framework through which scientists study the world. 9

functionalism is a theoretical framework that defines society as a system of interrelated parts. *9*

conflict theory is a theoretical framework that views society as an unequal system that brings about conflict and change. *9*

symbolic interactionism is a theoretical framework that focuses on how people interact with others in their everyday lives. *9*

social laws are statements of fact that are unchanging under given conditions and can be used as ground rules for any kind of society. *10*

social statics are the existing structural elements of society. *10*

social dynamics are the change in existing structural elements of society. *10*

social Darwinism is a notion that suggests strong societies survive and weak ones become extinct. *11*

mechanical solidarity refers to the state of community bonding in traditional societies in which people share beliefs and values and perform common activities. *12*

organic solidarity occurs when people live in a society with a diverse division of labor. *12*

functions are social factors that affect people in a society. *13*

manifest functions are functions that lead to an expected consequence or outcome. *13*

latent functions are functions that lead to unforeseen or unexpected consequences. *13*

bourgeoisie refers to members of the capitalist class. *14*

proletariat refers to members of the poor working class. *15*

false consciousnes is a person's lack of understanding of his or her position in society. *15*

class consciousness is an understanding of one's position in the class system. *15*

self refers to a person's identity and what makes that person different from others. *19*

contagion is a rapid, irrational mode in which people do not think rationally or clearly. *20*

dramaturgy is a theory of interaction in which all life is like acting. *20*

community learning occurs when individuals and groups work to identify and address issues of public concern. *25*

Sample Test Questions

These multiple-choice questions are similar to those found in the test bank that accompanies this textbook.

1. Which of the following is a criticism of conflict theory?
   a. It overlooks that fact that many willingly accept society's rules.
   b. It does not recognize the differences between social classes.
   c. It fails to acknowledge social inequality.
   d. It is unsympathetic to homelessness.

2. Which of the following questions might a symbolic interactionist ask about the social world?
   a. Why does inequality exist in society?
   b. Why do income disparities occur between the races?
   c. How do social institutions keep society running smoothly?
   d. How does a particular social setting affect a person's behavior?

3. Erving Goffman's theory of dramaturgy suggests that
   a. people behave similarly in a variety of situations.
   b. people change their behavior to fit the setting they are in.
   c. people's behavior has little to do with others' perceptions of them.
   d. people's behavior is not affected by the behavior of others around them.

4. Which could be considered a latent function of slavery in the United States?
   a. The ease in which crops were harvested
   b. The increase in the growth of crops
   c. The mistreatment of African slaves
   d. The wealth farmers generated

5. All of the following are macro orientations *except*
   a. functionalism.
   b. conflict theory.
   c. social Darwinism.
   d. symbolic interactionism.

ESSAY

1. The three sociological paradigms often overlap with one another. Choose a sociologist discussed in the chapter. Discuss how his or her ideas connect to all three sociological paradigms.

2. Why is it important for a sociologist to use a sociological imagination? What consequences might arise if he or she failed to use this way of thinking?

3. What sort of attitudes concerning homelessness might a symbolic interactionist discourage?

4. Why is suicide a compelling sociological issue?

5. Describe possible manifest and latent functions of a law that would legalize drugs.

WHERE TO START YOUR RESEARCH PAPER

To learn more about sociology as a scientific discipline, go to
http://www.asanet.org

To find useful information about the famous figures of sociology, go to
http://www2.pfeiffer.edu/~lridener/DSS/INDEX.HTML

To find an in-depth sociology dictionary, go to
http://www.webref.org/sociology/sociology.htm

For more information about sociology departments in the United States, go to http://www.sociolog.com/us_links/

To find a guide for sociological Internet sources, go to
http://www.socioweb.com/

For more information about the study of symbolic interactionism, go to
http://www.soci.niu.edu/~sssi/

To find an online journal of sociology, go to
http://www.ou.edu/special/freeinq/

To find a Web site dedicated to finding out the truth about urban myths, go to http://www.truthorfiction.com/

To find an excellent source for different information on sociology, go to
http://www.trinity.edu/~mkearl/theory.html

ANSWERS: 1. a; 2. d; 3. b; 4. c; 5. d

Remember to check www.thethinkspot.com **for additional information, downloadable flashcards, and other helpful resources.**

SOCIOLOGICAL
RESEARCH

"Observation

of the tearoom encounters. . . is made doubly difficult when the observer is an object of suspicion. Any man who remains in a public washroom for more than five minutes is apt to be either a member of the vice squad or someone on the make.

"I assumed the role of the voyeur—a role superbly suited for sociologists and the only lookout role that is not overtly sexual. . . By serving as a voyeur-lookout, I was able to move around the room at will. . . and to observe all that went on without alarming my respondents or otherwise disturbing the action.

"Identification of the sample was made by using the automobile license registers of the states in which my respondents lived. . . friendly policemen gave me access to the license registers without asking to see the numbers or becoming too inquisitive about the type of "market research" in which I was engaged.

"Realizing that the majority of my participant sample were married—and nearly all of them quite secretive about their deviant activity—I was faced with the problem of how to interview. . . Clearly, I could not knock on the door of a suburban residence and say, 'Excuse me, I saw you engaging in a homosexual act in a tearoom last year, and I wonder if I might ask you a few questions.' Having already been jailed, locked in a restroom, and attacked. . . I had no desire to conclude my research with a series of beatings.

"My research in tearooms required such a disguise. Does it then constitute a violation of professional ethics?…

Are there, perhaps, some areas of human behavior that are not fit for social scientific study at all? Should sex, religion, suicide, or other socially sensitive concerns be omitted from the catalogue of possible fields of sociological research?…[S]everal have suggested to me that I should have avoided this research subject altogether. Their contention has been that in an area of such sensitivity it would be best to 'let sleeping dogs lie.' I doubt that there are any 'sleeping dogs' in the realm of human interaction. . . Even if there are, sexual behavior in public places is not among them.

"The wonder to me is not that some sociologist might endanger his ethical integrity and that of his profession by standing around in public lavatories making mental notes on the art of fellatio. . . Concern about 'professional integrity,' it seems to me, is symptomatic of a dying discipline. Let the clergy worry about keeping their cassocks clean; the scientist has too great a responsibility for such compulsions!

"I believe that preventing harm to his respondents should be the primary interest of the scientist. We are not, however, protecting a harassed population of deviants by refusing to look at them. . . Our concern about possible research consequences for our fellow 'professionals' should take a secondary place to the concern for those who may benefit from our research."[1]

How Do We Learn About Society?

CHAPTER 02

In *Tearoom Trade: Impersonal Sex in Public Places,* **Laud Humphreys concludes that men use tearooms because** they're bisexual or gay, and **the social stigma of being openly gay is too great to endure.**

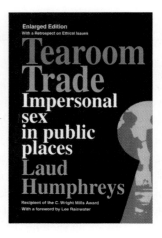

Politics and scandal seem to go hand in hand. In 2007, the world learned of U.S. Senator Larry Craig's visits to "tearooms"— public places, a men's room in this case, that serve as locations for sex acts between men. After his arrest, Senator Craig pled guilty to disorderly conduct in an airport restroom.[2] Sociologists immediately pointed to research by Laud Humphreys, detailed in his book, *Tearoom Trade.*[3] His findings were somewhat surprising. Fifty-four percent of the men participating in tearooms were married and living with their wives and children, while only fourteen percent were openly gay men.

Although Humphreys' research calls into question many ethical concerns, his studies prove that it's only through the use of sound scientific research that sociologists can learn. In our ongoing quest to think like a sociologist, this chapter will arm you with a precise understanding of research method weapons.

get the topic: WHAT ARE RESEARCH METHODS?

RESEARCH METHODS are the scientific procedures that sociologists use to conduct research and develop knowledge about a particular topic.

Hearing jargon like "sociological research" and "statistical analysis" may trigger horrid visions of crunching numbers, learning terms, and memorizing formulas for hours on end. However, learning the actual nitty-gritty of research methods is very different from that. While it's true that research requires dealing with data and measurements, it also allows you to delve into the behaviors of your society. **Research methods** are the scientific procedures that sociologists use to conduct research and develop knowledge about a particular topic. So, to fully understand what sociology *is*, you have to be aware of what a sociologist *does*. And that means learning to think and act like a sociologist.

As we discussed in Chapter 1, the first step in thinking like a sociologist is to comprehend the topic, and part of this involves understanding certain terms and research methods.

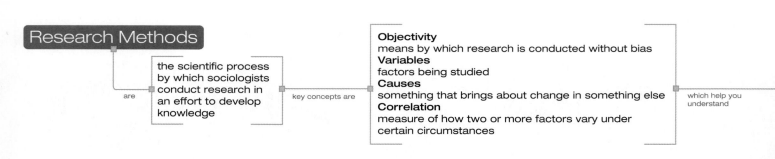

Research Methods

are · the scientific process by which sociologists conduct research in an effort to develop knowledge

key concepts are ·

Objectivity
means by which research is conducted without bias
Variables
factors being studied
Causes
something that brings about change in something else
Correlation
measure of how two or more factors vary under certain circumstances

which help you understand

Step 6
Share and Publish Results

now you can complete

Qualitative
words, pictures, or photos
Quantitative
numeric form

which can be

Objectivity

The first concept in a sociologist's repertoire should be objectivity, the foundation for all sociological research. For sociologists, **objectivity** is the ability to conduct research without allowing personal biases or prejudices to influence them. They must put their own opinions and preconceived notions aside to study human behavior objectively. Being objective may seem simple, but it can be very difficult in practice. We all have our own opinions and prejudices, which can skew an objective point of view. For example, if you're studying the implication of ethics violations among NBA referees, your research might be swayed if you feel a particular referee has treated your favorite team unfairly. In that case, it's probably unwise to start this study after a bad call just cost your team a playoff game.

Whether you're studying NBA referees or researching tearoom encounters in your area, it's important to be objective. Sociologist Max Weber (1864–1920) applied the term *verstehen*—understanding the meaning of action from the actor's point of view—to his research.[4] Weber argued that only when a researcher completely detaches himself or herself from a subject could accurate conclusions be drawn. When conducting a sociological study, you must enter your subject's world and check your personal prejudices at the door.

Variables

It may be impossible to erase your own biases, but you can become aware of them and train yourself to see beyond them. Once you've accounted for your prejudices, you can then focus on the variables you will observe. Two types of variables exist in all kinds of research: independent and dependent. **Independent variables** are variables that are deliberately manipulated to test the response in an experiment, and **dependent variables** are the response to the manipulated variable. In other words, the dependent variable *depends* on the independent variable. Let's say you want to know if there's a connection between playing a musical instrument and doing well in school. In this case: playing an instrument = the independent variable, and your GPA = the dependent variable. When testing these two variables, a person's academic success, or lack thereof, is dependent upon whether or not he or she plays a musical instrument.

To determine the effect of playing an instrument on GPA accurately, though, you'll need to control these variables. **Control variables** are variables that are kept constant to accurately test the impact of an independent variable. These variables must be controlled because they might influence the results, which would lead the researcher to a false conclusion. If you compare the GPAs of students who play instruments to the GPAs of students who don't play instruments, you have to make sure that all other factors are equal. If all the students who don't play instruments also have learning disabilities, then you'll get skewed results. You'd have no way of determining whether the students' disability caused the poor GPA or if it was the absence of a musical gift. Control variables ensure that you are testing *only* the independent variable.

∧ Max Weber's idea of *verstehen* suggested that **sociologists step out of their own shoes and into their subject's shoes when conducting a study.**

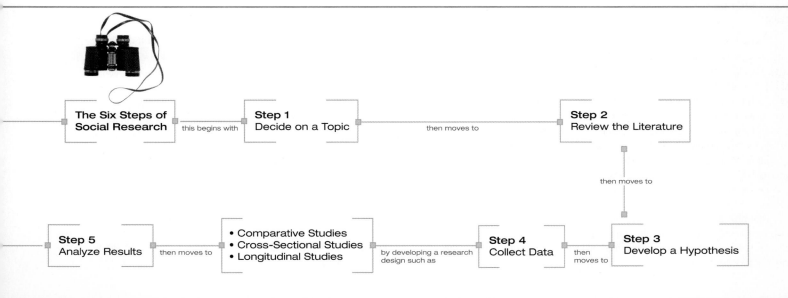

The Six Steps of Social Research — this begins with — Step 1 Decide on a Topic — then moves to — Step 2 Review the Literature

then moves to

Step 3 Develop a Hypothesis

Step 4 Collect Data — then moves to

by developing a research design such as — • Comparative Studies • Cross-Sectional Studies • Longitudinal Studies

Step 5 Analyze Results — then moves to

CAUSAL RELATIONSHIP is a relationship in which one condition leads to a certain consequence.

CAUSATION is the relationship between cause and effect.

CORRELATION is an indication that one factor might be the cause for another factor.

POSITIVE CORRELATION includes two variables that move in a parallel direction.

NEGATIVE CORRELATION occurs when variables move in opposite directions.

SPURIOUS CORRELATION occurs when two variables appear to be related, but actually have a different cause.

SOCIAL RESEARCH is investigation conducted by social scientists.

LITERATURE REVIEW is a study of relevant academic articles and information.

THEORY is a comprehensive and systematic explanation of events that lead to testable predictions.

HYPOTHESIS involves a suggestion about how variables relate.

CONCEPTS are abstract ideas that are impossible to measure.

OPERATIONALIZING is turning abstract ideas into something measurable.

Cause and Correlation

A **causal relationship** is one in which a condition or variable leads to a certain consequence. To understand causal relationships, you need to recognize the difference between causation and correlation. **Causation** is the relationship between cause and effect. Suppose I let go of a pencil. Gravity *causes* the pencil to fall to the floor. According to the law of gravity, the same cause results in the same effect every time. Correlations, unlike causes, are not laws because they do not guarantee a certain effect. Instead, a **correlation** is an indication that one factor *might* be a cause for another factor. Consider this correlation using the variable we discussed: Students who play musical instruments generally have higher GPAs than students who don't play an instrument. There is a correlation between the study of music and one's GPA. However, that doesn't mean that playing an instrument will always result in a higher GPA. There are other factors that come into play, such as how much you study and whether you apply what you learn. Unlike gravity, the correlation between instrumental music and grades is not a *law*.

Causes always create the same effects; correlations don't. Although it's likely that there is a relationship between getting good grades and playing an instrument, it's not a sure thing.

There are three types of correlations—positive, negative, and spurious. A **positive correlation** involves two variables moving in a parallel direction. In other words, you can find a positive correlation when variables increase or decrease together. Take the relationship between one's level of education and income. It has been observed that people with higher levels of education earn higher incomes.[5] This is a positive correlation because both variables trend in the same direction. A second type of relationship between variables is called a **negative correlation**, which occurs when the variables move in opposite directions. So, if you notice your grades slip as your Internet surfing or TV watching increases, that is a negative correlation. The third type is a spurious correlation. Spurious means not genuine or authentic, so a **spurious correlation** occurs when two variables appear to be related, but actually have a different cause. So, if you're looking at statistical data and notice that ice cream sales and the drowning rate are both increasing, that doesn't mean that someone eating a hot fudge sundae is destined to drown in a swimming pool. Another

factor is probably affecting these statistics. In this case, these increases are likely occurring in the hot summer months, when more people happen to be buying ice cream and going swimming. This proves that researchers should always be wary of spurious correlations.

Scientific Method: What Are the Six Steps of Social Research?

Doing sociological research follows many of the same procedures as any type of scientific research. After all, sociology is the scientific study of society. By requiring a logical and organized series of steps, sociologists ensure accurate results. In the next section of this chapter, we will review the six steps of **social research**, or investigation conducted by social scientists. As with any type of research, you first need to decide what topic you want to find out more about.

1 **Decide on a Topic** The first stage of the research model involves determining what you want to study. In order to take this step, researchers bring to light a question they want answered. Sociologists select topics on the basis of importance, personal interest, or the availability of research.

2 **Review the Literature** After you select a topic, you'll need to perform a **literature review**, which is a study of relevant academic articles and information. This is essentially an organized effort to research your topic. Literature reviews let you know what other researchers think about a particular topic and what they have discovered through their research. For example, if you were still examining how playing instruments affects one's GPA, you might review scholarly articles written by sociologists who've examined the same idea. Viewing their methodology will help you improve upon their work and avoid making any of the same mistakes they made.

3 **Develop a Hypothesis** After you have completed the initial research of your topic, it is time to formulate a hypothesis. It is important not to confuse a hypothesis with a theory. A **theory** is a comprehensive and systematic explanation of events that lead to testable predictions. These testable predictions are the basis for what we call a hypothesis.[6] A **hypothesis** involves a suggestion about how variables relate. For example, my hypothesis that students who play a musical instrument will have high GPAs is dependent on the theory that students who earn good grades are more likely to play an instrument than students who earn bad grades, and that music is part of the reason they do better. My hypothesis is a way for me to test that theory by manipulating variables. In this case, the two variables are playing an instrument and the student's grades.

Concepts and Operationalizing Variables

So how are we supposed to measure these variables anyway? You might notice that the two variables above are not very specific. What does it mean to *play* an instrument? Will playing once a week be enough? Do you have to be an exceptional musician, or can your music be mediocre? Also, what does a *good* GPA entail exactly? Is 3.1 a good GPA? In order to create a testable hypothesis, we'll need to be a bit more specific. Right now, "playing a musical instrument" and getting a "good grade" are just **concepts**, or abstract ideas that are impossible to measure. Turning these abstract ideas into something measurable is called **operationalizing** the variables. If you operationalize "playing an instrument" into "hours spent playing the instrument," you now have a variable that's measurable in minutes. Likewise, we can change the relative idea of "a better grade" into a more measurable "grade of A." Now that we have a hypothesis, we can move on to designing a research strategy.

4 **Collect Data** You have a hypothesis, so now what? Now you'll have to test that hypothesis to see whether data support or refute your idea. Collecting data means using a research design to help you. A **research design** refers to the process used to find information. Designs need to be both logical and orderly so that the research is reliable and valid. A logical, orderly design isn't the only thing that'll guarantee your research is up to snuff. For research to be **reliable**, or able to be trusted, you must measure things the same way, every time. If you alter your measuring technique in any way, your results could easily change. **Validity** assures that you're actually measuring the thing you set out to measure in the first place. In our example, you wouldn't want your professor to use your musical taste to determine what kind of grade you get in class. To collect data that are both reliable and valid, sociologists use a variety of strategies, which include conducting studies.

RESEARCH DESIGN refers to the process used to find information.

RELIABLE means able to be trusted.

VALIDITY assures that you're actually measuring the thing you set out to measure in the first place.

COMPARATIVE STUDIES use data from different sources in order to evaluate them against each other.

CROSS-SECTIONAL STUDIES look at one event at a single point in time.

LONGITUDINAL STUDIES include data from observations over time using a cohort.

COHORT is a specific group of people used in a study.

Comparative, Cross-Sectional, and Longitudinal Studies

Comparative studies use data from different sources in order to evaluate them against each other. International comparisons often use data from different countries and put them side by side. You should be aware, though, that comparative data across cultures might have methodological problems. For example, the definition of a drug offense differs greatly between the Netherlands and the United States. What passes as taboo in one country might be perfectly permissible in another.

The majority of available data in sociology are the result of cross-sectional studies. Like a camera capturing a singular moment, **cross-sectional studies** look at an event at a single point in time. Researchers may use a variety of cross-sectional studies to try to track trends in society. However, these may not always include data gathered from the same people. To learn how specific people change over time with the changes in society, researchers conduct longitudinal studies.

Longitudinal studies include data from observations over time using a specific group of people called a **cohort**. These types of studies allow the researcher to provide measures of the same group over a period of time. The period of time can be extensive, and researchers frequently take multiple measures over a period of years. Although this longitudinal information can be expensive and time-consuming to gather, it is useful in illustrating trends and showing how segments of society change.

MAKE CONNECTIONS

Country Music and Suicide

Back in 1992, researchers wanted to study the relationship between country music and its listeners. Researchers Steven Stack and Jim Gundlach found positive correlations between country music airplay and white male suicide rates in metropolitan areas.[7] According to their research, common themes in country music created a subculture that essentially led men to suicide. These themes include problems with personal relationships, including divorce and infidelity, alcohol consumption, and general hardships like work problems or death. Sara Evans's *Cheatin'*, Toby Keith's *Get Drunk and Be Somebody,* and Johnny Paycheck's *Take This Job and Shove It* are all songs that fit these themes.

The researchers took data from 49 different metropolitan areas in the United States. To prevent a spurious conclusion, they used poverty, divorce, gun availability, and region of the country as control variables. For example, because divorce has a strong influence on the suicide rate, the researchers had to make sure that this variable didn't affect their results. In their analysis, they showed that the white male suicide rates were positively correlated with the amount of radio airtime of country music.

The conclusion was that country music contributed to an ideology that supported suicide. Because people tend to listen to songs many times, the power of their thematic message is stronger than other media. These themes help create a subculture in which individuals perceive a world full of sadness, drinking, and exploitation.

Following this research, a statistical and methodological debate raged. Sociologists Maguire and Snipes tried to retest the data, but failed to duplicate Stack and Gundlach's 1992 results.[8] Maguire and Snipes claimed the original authors were mistaken because they did not take into account how other factors in their subjects' lives might have contributed to their actions. Stack and Gundlach stuck by their research. In a series of articles, each designed to respond to the other, these two camps argued over which side's research was valid.

Can you see problems with the research, particularly as associated with spuriousness and correlation? Is it possible that there is another relationship being depicted? For example, since white men are more likely to listen to country music than other ethnic groups, perhaps more country music is aired in metropolitan areas with higher concentrations of white men.[9]

>>> **ACTIVITY** Pick three songs within a particular genre, (i.e., hip-hop, rock, pop) and examine their lyrics. Do these songs express anything about the culture in which we live? If so, how do you think this affects people who listen to this type of music? Is there a spurious correlation?

Could country music have **led** this man **to the edge?**

Serious Drug Problems: The United States versus the Netherlands

Just based on the statistics below, it would seem that the United States has a serious drug problem compared to the Netherlands. But is that really the case? Well, that depends on how you define a drug offense. The United States and the Netherlands have very different drug policies that have been characterized as "overly punitive policies vs. overly permissive."[10]

The Dutch believe the best course of action with drugs is to implement a harm reduction approach, which minimizes risks typically associated with drug use, instead of total drug suppression.[11] In the Netherlands, a harm reduction approach includes increased drug treatment and needle exchange programs. Drug use is a public health problem, not a criminal one. Since Dutch authorities believe "soft" drugs, like cannabis, are ultimately harmless and simply associated with youthful indiscretion, marijuana is legalized in small amounts. Moreover, the predominant thinking regarding these soft drug users is that they are less likely to get mixed up with hard drugs, like cocaine or heroin. Therefore, the focus is less on incarceration and more on treatment and prevention.[12]

The United States, on the other hand, has arrested hundreds of thousands of people for possession and use of marijuana. In 2006, there were over 1.8 million state and local arrests for drug violations. Of these, 39.1 percent or 738,915 arrests were for marijuana possession, and only 4.8 percent were for marijuana sale and manufacturing.[13] These possession arrests may not have been made in the Netherlands, which reflects a methodological problem. The numbers for drug offenses generally reflect the ideologies each country has about drug policy enforcement and prevention.

Source: Based on The Eighth United Nations Survey on Crime Trends and the Operations of Criminal Justice Systems, 2002, *United Nations Office on Drugs and Crime, Centre for International Crime Prevention*.

Survey

A **survey** is an investigation of the opinions or experience of a group of people by asking them questions. In sociological research, surveys are necessary to gauge valuable information. Institutions ranging from government agencies to marketing teams rely on survey responses to determine how the general public feels about their policies or their products. Surveys include interviews and questionnaires. Seeing as how it would be nearly impossible to survey every single individual within a specific population, researchers need to be more focused.

How to Conduct a Survey

Sociologists generally use the following seven steps to conduct a survey:

1. Clarify Your Purpose – What do I want to find out?

2. Define Your Population – Who do I want to study?

3. Choose a Sample – I can't study everyone so I have to choose a few people to represent the entire population.

4. Prepare Questions.

5. Decide How to Collect Data – Do I want to conduct face-to-face interviews or hand out surveys?

6. Collect the Data.

7. Record, Analyze, and Interpret the Data.

Populations

For starters, researchers need to determine the specific **populations**, or target groups, from which they wish to gain information. Perhaps you're interested in discovering what commuter students think about the parking situation on campus. Ideally you'd ask every student with a car on campus, but that would take a lot of time and money. Because researchers also have limits on their resources, they have to practice **parsimony**, or extreme unwillingness to use resources, so that they get the most for their effort.

Samples

To get the most bang for their buck, sociologists only give surveys to a **sample**, or subset of the population, selected for research. In order to produce a reliable result, samples should represent an accurate picture of the population.

When sociologists study a part of the population, the percentages in the sample should reflect the percentages of women, racial minorities, and other groups that exist in the population. In short, the sample needs to look like the population so we can generalize the findings. **Generalization** is the extent that what is learned from a sample can be applied to the population from which the sample is taken. Would it be fair to take the results of Humphreys' research and apply it to every male who enters a bathroom in the United States? Certainly not. Why? Humphreys' research was conducted in the St. Louis area, meaning that his findings may or may not reflect bathroom behavior in California, Texas, or New York. Humphreys did not claim that one could take the results of his study and apply them to the entire country. To do that would require a special type of sampling.

A **random sample** is a group of subjects arbitrarily chosen from a defined population. This type of sample increases the chances that the sample represents the population. Randomness means that everyone in the population has an equal chance of selection for the sample. However, few true random samples exist, especially if the entire country is the target population. But, random samples are the true research method that allows a social scientist to know his or her sample looks like the population.

Many national surveys, therefore, rely on random samples and can, with as few as 1,000 people, make predictions about what Americans think about specific issues. Although sample size can affect the power of the predictions, after a certain point the advantage of a bigger sample becomes almost irrelevant. Thus, samples are usually as small as possible. However, if you want to use the survey for a variety of purposes, it might be a smart practice to make the sample bigger. This is called **oversampling**. You need to oversample if the group you wish to study makes up a small percentage of the whole population. Let's say exit pollers conducting a random survey of people who voted in the 2008 Democratic primary wanted to know how many Latino voters supported Senator Barack Obama. Since Latinos make up approximately 13 percent of the U.S. population, a random sample of 1,000 people would correlate to roughly 130 Latinos. This sample size is too small to be meaningful; therefore, a larger one is required to increase the odds that it accurately represents the Latino population.

Selection Effects and Samples of Convenience

Even though random samples are preferred, other types of samples are often used. Researchers may use a **sample of convenience**, which is a non-random sample available to the researcher. These are simply people we can find to study. These samples often suffer from **selection effects;** that is, the likelihood that a nonrepresentative sample may lead to inaccurate results.

Think back to Laud Humphreys' study of tearooms. His results showed that 54 percent of men involved in tearooms were married. Does that mean over half of all men participating in tearooms were married? No, it only signals that 54 percent of men taking part in his study were married. However, his findings do imply that the majority of men participating in all tearooms might be married. Why? Because Humphreys used a sample of convenience. Of course, nonrandom samples can be quite valuable because they help illustrate a problem, illuminate issues, and test theories, but one cannot generalize the findings from them to the larger population. Therefore, all men who frequent tearooms probably don't look like the men in Humphreys' study.

Experiments

Like any good scientist, a sociologist uses experiments to test ideas. In an experiment, researchers hope to control variables in order to test causes and effects. Sociological experiments do the same thing, but some may test people's interactions or other social causes of human behavior. Read the *Think Sociologically* feature to learn about a series of experiments Stanley Milgram conducted in the 1960s.

Milgram Obedience Study

Social psychologist Stanley Milgram created a series of experiments to test a subject's ability to reject the orders of a perceived superior. In the experiment, two subjects enter a room where a man in a lab coat meets them. This individual, called "the experimenter," takes on the role of the authority figure. The subjects are told they are going to be a part of a study to test the effects of punishment on learning. One of the subjects roleplays as the "teacher," while the other—who is secretly one of Milgam's assistants—is the "learner."

The subjects are then led into a room where the "learner" is strapped into a chair with electrodes attached to him. The experimenter assures both subjects that while pain will result, no permanent damage will occur.

The teacher is placed in front of an electroshock machine and separated from the learner. If the learner failed to recall a series of paired words, the teacher was supposed to administer an electric shock. With each error, the teacher was instructed to increase the voltage. In reality, the learner was only acting and never received a shock, unbeknownst to the teacher.

Throughout the experiment, some subjects would pause when they heard learners cry "ouch"

or "I want to quit." The scripted responses also included groans, screams, and even silence. When teachers questioned whether they should continue to inflict pain on the learner, they were told, "Please go on" and/or "You must go on."

Milgram found that 65 percent of the teachers administered up to 450 volts, even when there was no reply and despite the fact that the dial on the machine for this voltage read "danger."

Milgram points out that subjects would shock others to unconsciousness and even death on the command of a stranger who represented authority. Thus, Milgram suggests that when faced with an authority figure, most people follow orders even if those orders go against their better judgment.[14]

> If you were the teacher in Milgram's research, **what action would you have taken based on the learner's response?**

Hawthorne Effect

The seminal Milgram experiment documented what happens when a subject is unaware that he is being experimented on. But what about people who are cognizant of the experiment? In the 1930s an electric company hired researchers to test worker productivity in its Hawthorne Works factory outside Chicago. After pretesting worker performance, researchers made the lighting brighter. They quickly noticed that brighter lights seemed to make people work harder. However, when they later turned down the lights, productivity increased once again. In fact, every step the researchers took helped boost the workers' productivity.

Why did every change, even ones that seemed like it might hinder productivity, have the same effect? Researchers believed it was because the subjects knew they were being studied. Thus, the **Hawthorne effect** was coined for occurrences in which people

behave differently because they know they are part of an experiment.[15] Unlike the experiment at the Hawthorne factory, Milgram's experiment used subjects who did not know they were being studied. When conducting experiments and studies, sociologists must make sure that the Hawthorne effect does not influence their findings.

FIELD RESEARCH

It would be difficult to study society without actually mingling with the people you're observing. Therefore, researchers need to venture out and conduct studies in a natural setting. This **field research** takes the sociologist out into the streets. There are three common methods of field research—participant observation, case studies, and ethnography.

Participant Observation

In *Tearoom Trade*, Laud Humphreys describes how he "assumed the role of the voyeur" by observing the men who engaged in public sex without actively participating himself. Humphreys practiced **participant observation**, a type of field research in which the researcher poses as a person who is normally in the environment. Participant observation decreases the chances of the Hawthorne effect because subjects do not know they're being studied.

As a voyeur, Humphreys learned signals to use to inform participants of police presence or accidental passersby. Eager to find out more information about the men, Humphreys needed to expand the sample further. This led him to secretly record some participants' personal information. About a year later, posing as a health survey researcher, Humphreys visited many of the men in their homes. By becoming a participant in the men's activities and misleading them to gain access to their personal lives, Humphreys gained the men's trust and was able to conduct his study more freely.

Case Studies

Unlike participant observations, **case studies** investigate one person or event in detail. Such a study is able to illuminate a complex issue through the lens of an individual case. Isabelle, a feral child who had spent most of her six years in a dark room with minimal human contact, is an example of a case study.[16] This case study includes not only a history of neglect both emotionally and physically, but also provides a compelling tale about experts who worked to develop her potential. When Isabelle was discovered, she could communicate using only grunts and invented gestures. Remarkably, Isabelle was able to improve her social skills and fully integrate into mainstream society. Some critics believe case studies are subjective because it's tricky to generalize the findings of an individual case to fit a larger group.[17] For example, the findings in Isabelle's case don't fit *all* feral children because some might not be able to fully develop.

Ethnography

An **ethnography** is a research method that aims to understand the social perspective and cultural values of a particular group by participating with or getting to know their activities in detail. In 1991, Ralph Weisheit articulated the complex nature of Illinois' illegal marijuana crop economy, showing that often there is more involved than simply a desire to support the illegal drug trade. Interviewing about 30 marijuana farmers in rural Illinois, Weisheit presented a context for this phenomenon by showing that growers often have different motives for their illegal deeds. Marijuana farmers fall into one of three groups—*hustlers, pragmatists,* and *communal cultivators.* Hustlers grow marijuana for the large profits and are clearly driven by a desire for the money. Pragmatists, the largest group of growers, generally don't use the drug. Instead, they farm marijuana because they are in financial trouble often caused by poor prices of legitimate cash crops or a desire to provide better support for their families. Communal growers cultivate marijuana because they wish to use the drug themselves, and this is a method to secure access to it. They sell their surplus, but their primary goal is personal use. In each case, the threat of incarceration is not a great enough deterrence to cause any of the growers to stop their illegal activity.[18]

Secondary Data Analysis

Sociologists don't always have to collect new data. Instead, sociologists sometimes need to access **secondary data**, or data that others have already collected and published. The process of using and analyzing data others have collected is known as **secondary data analysis.** A variety of data sources exist for sociologists to use. Not surprisingly, the World Wide Web contains many of these sources. Census data, crime statistics, journal entries, and transcripts of speeches are just a few of the examples of secondary data found on the Web.

HAWTHORNE EFFECT occurs when people behave differently because they know they are part of an experiment.

FIELD RESEARCH is research conducted in a natural setting.

PARTICIPANT OBSERVATION is a type of field research in which the researcher poses as a person who is normally in the environment.

CASE STUDIES are investigations of one person or event in detail.

ETHNOGRAPHY is a research method that aims to understand the social perspective and cultural values of a particular group by participating with or getting to know their activities in detail.

SECONDARY DATA are data that others have already collected and published.

SECONDARY DATA ANALYSIS is the process of using and analyzing data that others have collected.

Method	Example	Pros	Cons
Survey	Interview	• Sampling process lets researcher apply data from a few subjects to an entire population	• Time-consuming • Difficult to find participants
Experiments	Manipulation of variables to study human behavior	• Gives researcher specific quantitative data	• Ethical concerns put restrictions on the way human subjects can be used
Field Research	Case study	• Can study behavior in a natural environment • Can be inexpensive	• Time-consuming • Ethical concerns put restrictions on the way human subjects can be used
Secondary Data Analysis	Another sociologist's analysis of population data	• Inexpensive • Reduces time spent to collect data	• Data not collected for the purpose in which you are using it • Data could be biased by the collector

Research Methods: How Do They Measure Up?

5 **Analyze Results** The fifth step of the scientific method, analyzing results, involves the dreaded "S-word." No, not *that* word. The term I'm thinking of is *statistical* analysis. Because sociological research can delve into very complex statistics, it's important that you learn a few basics that will help you confidently confront any statistics you encounter now or in the future.

MEASURES OF CENTRAL TENDENCY

You know how news outlets report on the national price of a gallon of gasoline? Sometimes, the price you hear on the radio ends up being lower—or higher—than the one at the pump. This is because the reporters were only finding a measure of **central tendency**. To put it simpler, researchers look at an

> ### John's Test Scores
>
> Test 1: 90
> Test 2: 70
> Test 3: 80
> Test 4: 20
> Test 5: 80

array of numbers and find the ones that are in the middle. There are three measures of central tendency—mean, median, and mode. Imagine that a student received the test scores listed above. How would you calculate the mean, median, and mode?

Mean

A **mean** is an average. You add up all the scores and then divide by the number of scores. John's mean score is 68. Does this average accurately measure his performance? He failed one exam, but received a C or better on all other tests. It doesn't seem fair that one bad grade leaves John with a D average for the class. That's the problem with calculating mean scores. Extremely high or low scores can have dramatic impact on statistical means.

> 90 + 70 + 80 + 20 + 80 = 340
> 340 ÷ 5 = 68
> Mean = 68

Median

When you're cruising down the highway— after blowing your savings on that full tank of gas—you might notice the northbound lanes are separated from southbound ones by a median. In statistical analysis, the **median** refers to the midpoint in a distribution of numbers. If you line up the numbers from lowest to highest, the median is the one in the middle. The median does not vary

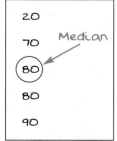

when you have extremely high or extremely low values in the distribution. John's median score is 80.

Mode

The **mode** refers to the most common value in a distribution of numbers. Extremely high or low scores do not impact this measure either. It's possible to have more than one mode in a distribution of numbers. In our simple example, 80 is the mode because it occurs twice. You will notice that the modal score in this example is the same as the median. Both give John a final grade of a B. Which measure of central tendency best shows John's performance?

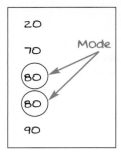

Most colleges have a policy of using averages to calculate grades. However, when I review grades at the end of the semester, I frequently take all three measures of central tendency into account. In most cases, the mean is close to the median and the mode. However, an extreme score can alter the mean score dramatically, as in John's case. If you have a low score on an exam, consider asking your professor to consider other measures of central tendency to calculate your performance. It might just raise your grade!

EVALUATING DATA

Evaluating and interpreting data are important parts of conducting research. What's the use of gathering data if you don't know what to do with them? It's vital to be able to make sense of the data you collect. The tables and graphs you will encounter during the research process may seem daunting at first. But it's really not as complicated as you might think, as long as you know what steps to take.

HOW TO READ A TABLE

The table to the right provides regional HIV and AIDS statistics reported in 2007. Laud Humphreys wrote *Tearoom Trade* in the 1970s, before the start of the HIV and AIDS outbreak during the 1980s. If Humphreys had conducted his study after this time, he might have examined how this disease affected his subjects, if at all. What do the data in the table tell you?

If you struggled to make sense of the table, don't worry. You're not alone. Fortunately, the four simple steps that follow will help make reading this and other tables second nature to you.

1. Carefully read the title of the table. Ask yourself: What do I expect the table to show me?

2. Notice the structure of the table. This one is made up of columns and rows. The columns represent a specific category, such as "Adults and Children Living with HIV," and the rows list data from each geographic region.

3. This table has an important subheading. In italics, you see the phrase, *"Figures shown in millions."* In a table with large number values, it is quite common to shorten the number by placing it in a category. This means that more than 22 million adults and children are living with HIV in sub-Saharan Africa."

4. Read any text and notes provided below the table.
   - The asterisk sign next to "Oceania" in the table indicates that the word will be defined below.

- The note provides information about the data in the table. In this table, the data for 2007 are not considered final. Final data for this year will be published in the 2008 issue.
- The source note indicates where the original data are located.

Now review the table again. Do the data make more sense now?

6 **Share and Publish Results** Doing research is important; however, if we don't share what we learn with others, our work is meaningless. Sharing allows others to read and use your findings in their own research, which ultimately expands the base of knowledge.

Publishing requires an appropriate writing style. Most sociology research follows the American Sociological Association style. In the ASA style guide, you'll find standards for using language and directions on how to cite sources appropriately. If you need a quick style guide, be sure to visit their Web site at http://www.asanet.org/.

Regional HIV and AIDS Statistics in 2007 (Figures shown in millions)			
Region	Adults and Children Living with HIV	Adults and Children Newly Infected with HIV	Adult and Child Deaths Due to AIDS
Sub-Saharan Africa	22.5	1.7	1.6
Middle East and North Africa	0.38	0.035	0.025
South and Southeast Asia	4.0	0.34	0.27
East Asia	0.80	0.092	0.032
Oceania*	0.075	0.014	0.0012
Latin America	1.6	0.1	0.058
Caribbean	0.23	0.017	0.011
Eastern Europe and Central Asia	1.6	0.15	0.055
Western and Central Europe	0.76	0.031	0.012
North America	1.3	0.046	0.021
TOTAL	33.2	2.5	2.1

* Oceania refers to the islands and archipelagos of the central and south Pacific, including Australia, Malay Archipelago, Melanesia, Micronesia, New Zealand, and Polynesia.

Notes: Updating estimates is an ongoing process. Final regional estimates for 2007 will be published in the 2008 report on the global AIDS epidemic.

Source: Data from "2007 AIDS Epidemic Update," *Joint United Nations Programme on HIV/AIDS and World Health Organization.*

ETHICAL CONCERNS

Have you ever had to do something that violated your personal beliefs or values? Of course you have. Sociologists struggle with this issue all the time. Sometimes, a sociologist's findings have the potential to hurt or embarrass the human subjects of a particular study. Deciding how to protect human subjects is a major concern for sociological researchers. In *Tearoom Trade*, Humphreys addressed some of the ethical questions that surrounded much of his research.

Ethics is a system of values or principles that guide one's behavior. For some, it means following the law, and for others, trusting one's gut. The American Sociology Association's code of ethics lays down standards for sociological research. Five general principles make up ethical practice in sociology.[20]

1 **Professional competence** refers to the obligation to limit our research, teaching, and other activities to our area of expertise. Sociologists ensure competence in their work through ongoing professional training. Competent researchers know their limits and consult with others who have greater expertise when necessary.

2 **Integrity** suggests that when researching, teaching, and providing service, sociologists act in an honest and fair manner. Misleading subjects or deliberately making false statements is unethical.

3 **Professional and scientific responsibility** is a researcher's obligation to treat others with professional courtesy. When reviewing other sociologists' work, we confront theoretical or statistical issues in a manner that is honest, not hostile.

4 **Respect for people's rights, dignity, and diversity** is a foundational sociological belief. Sociologists believe that discrimination based on differences between people is contrary to the core values of the discipline.

5 **Social responsibility** is a professional responsibility to serve the community. Understanding that sociology is more than an activity in a classroom or the research lab, we take what we know and apply it for the good of all people.

THE ETHICS OF HUMPHREYS

After reviewing the five pillars of ethical behavior, do you think Humphreys engaged in unethical practices? Humphreys used tearoom subjects without their knowledge. Risking their anonymity for his research by recording personal information, Humphrey suggests that this is justified in order to gain this knowledge. Others might suggest he failed to respect his subjects' dignity and worth.

In Humphreys' defense, the code of ethics was not in place when he conducted his research. This code, in fact, was the result of studies like Humphreys' investigation of the tearoom trade. Studies like Humphreys' also prompted the federal government to play a role in research ethics. The government established an institutional review board, which must review all grant applications from colleges and universities that want federal funding to conduct research using human subjects.

Nonetheless, researchers who study deviant behaviors suggest that deception is essential in collecting accurate information. The issue of how to use deception is a critical question in field research. If you fully disclose what you are doing, how can you be sure the Hawthorne effect is not affecting your results? If you deceive, how can you protect the subjects' dignity and worth? That's why a debate on ethics rages on within the sociological research community today.

So the question is how can you avoid ethical dilemmas? One way is to get the consent of your subject. Hand out an informed consent form before the study begins. Informed consent means that the research subject understands the general purpose of the study and its main features. If the researcher is using deception, subjects deserve to know when they will find out the truth. Subjects must know that they can cease their participation at any time without risk to themselves.

>>> Despite the differences in these people's ethnic backgrounds, **sociologists should strive to value each of them equally.**

think sociologically: HOW DO SOCIOLOGISTS USE RESEARCH METHODS?

No single research method applies only to functionalism, conflict theory, or symbolic interactionism. But these theoretical frameworks do lend themselves to using types of data in different ways. The basis for these differences is often quantitative and qualitative data.

Quantitative and Qualitative Methods

If you were asked to rank your motivation on a scale of 1–5, with 5 being highly motivated, your response would be an example of quantitative data. Simply put, the term **quantitative data** refers to data based on numbers. Another example includes researched numbers, such as the number of Asian American students that attend historically black colleges. Laud Humphreys used the information he received from his subjects to create quantitative data. After interviewing his subjects, Humphreys calculated their responses and found that a much lower number than he expected—only 14 percent—of his total subjects were openly gay men.

Qualitative data may include words, pictures, photos, or any other type of information that comes to the researcher in a non-numerical form. When Humphreys posed as a market researcher and interviewed his subjects in their homes, he was collecting qualitative data. One common type of qualitative data is a **content analysis**—a type of research in which the sociologist looks for common words or themes in newspapers, books, or structured interviews.

Both quantitative and qualitative data require evaluation. The way in which the evaluation is measured is different, but both allow sociologists to better understand an issue.

The choice to use either qualitative or quantitative data pertains to all three theoretical perspectives, but there are some general trends that appear. Functional and conflict theorists tend to address more structural issues, and so they often use quantitative measurements. Conversely, symbolic interactionists might prefer qualitative data because they deal with the words and meanings attached to events. Whichever way you slice it, there is no hard and fast rule that connects a particular theoretical paradigm to a singular research method. Both qualitative and quantitative data can be appropriate.

Think about the research methods we discussed earlier in the chapter. How would you classify those methods? Are they quantitative or qualitative?

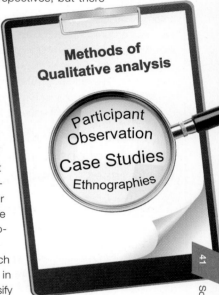

Methods of Qualitative analysis

Participant Observation
Case Studies
Ethnographies

METHODS OF QUANTITATIVE ANALYSIS

CROSS-SECTIONAL STUDIES

COMPARATIVE STUDIES

LONGITUDNAL STUDIES

SURVEYS

EXPERIMENTS

Triangulation

Triangulation is the process of using multiple approaches to study a phenomenon. Just as a centrist politician triangulates by co-opting issues from both sides of the political spectrum, sociologists often use triangulation to include aspects of both qualitative and quantitative analysis. For example, if you want to study the influence of hip-hop music on white, teenage, suburban culture, you might look at the quantitative data of hip-hop CD sales among white teens. Afterward, you'd conduct in-depth qualitative interviews with the consumers who buy hip-hop to gauge how the music influences their lives. When you follow this process, you're triangulating the issue, or studying it from multiple points of view. Triangulation allows you to better explain a social event because you use two or more methods to study it.[21]

If you relied on only one method, you might draw an inappropriate conclusion about a social issue because all the facts are not available.

Triangulation helps researchers use **the strengths of one approach** to **compensate for the weaknesses in another.**

Research Methods and the Three Paradigms

Although our theoretical paradigm does not dictate the research method we use, it does affect how we interpret data. Conflict theorists and functionalists can look at the same data and come to different conclusions. Imagine that a conflict theorist and a functionalist studied data showing the rise of income inequality in a community. In other words, the gap between the "haves" and the "have-nots" in the community is widening. How might the two sociologists interpret the data? Remember, both functionalists and conflict theorists have a macro-orientation, so they study how a certain issue affects the whole society and not individual people. However, functionalists examine how a certain issue functions in a society, whereas conflict theorists study how the unequal distribution of goods affects society.

Functionalists studying the data might suggest that income inequality serves the society well, as more rich people are able to start businesses and invest in long-term projects that will one day make society better for everyone. These businesses might one day be able to employ the poor members of the community and help them rise above their situation. Functionalists would not view the income inequality as a negative phenomenon. Conflict theorists, meanwhile, might suggest that the same numbers show that the rich exploit the poor and that this exploitation is only getting worse. You can see how two researchers look at the same data and come to different conclusions.

Because symbolic interactionists have a micro-orientation, they might focus more on how the income inequality affected people at an individual level. These researchers might study wealthy individuals' perceptions of the poor and low-income individuals' perceptions of the rich. They might examine how being poor affects an individual's lifestyle. For example, how does the lack of money affect the kind of clothes that a person wears or the place he or she lives. Here too, you can see, the same set of data can be interpreted differently depending on the theoretical lens through which the data are viewed.

Using Triangulation to Examine the Tearoom Trade

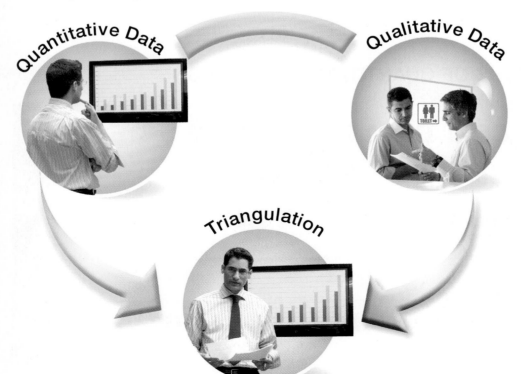

Quantitative Data

Qualitative Data

Triangulation

<<< Although Humphreys did not use the triangulation in his study of the tearoom trade, **here's how someone might use this method to study the issue.**

discover sociology in action:
HOW IS RESEARCH INVOLVED IN SOCIAL POLICY AND COMMUNITY LEARNING?

The American Sociological Association's code of ethics calls sociologists to take action in their communities. Working on social policies and participating in community-learning projects are just two of the ways sociologists can better the community.

Social Policy and Statistics

Social policies arise because people recognize a problem and take action to deal with it. Often the first step is to get more information about the problem, which involves analyzing statistics. When consuming statistical evidence, it's important that you:

• **Beware the Headline.** News organizations titillate the public with sensational headlines such as "Airline Accident Rate is Highest in 13 Years." The problem here is that the rate of airline accidents was really declining. In this instance, the writer misused the word "rate." Instead, the writer should have stated that the *gross number* of airline accidents had increased.[22]

• **Check Term Definitions.** Each researcher makes decisions about how to measure certain constructs. Beware of any study using value-laden terms such as "conservative" or "liberal" without properly defining them. What you consider "liberal" might not be interpreted the same way by your neighbor or a community in another state.

• **Find Out Who Funded the Study.** Groups who fund research often have an interest in the outcome. You should always consider the possibility that stakeholders want to use research to support their positions.

ACTIVITIES

1. Check out the online resources at your college library. Which search engines does your college suggest are best for sociological research? Make a list. Then write a paragraph evaluating each one.
2. Conduct a class survey. Talk with your professor and create a 10-question survey to give to your classmates about something that interests you.
3. Have a class discussion about Humphreys' claim that the end justifies the means. How can a researcher truly hope to find out about a subculture without deception?

Remember, objectivity is the foundation of sociological research. Be on the lookout for groups or individuals with ulterior motives.

• **Look for Spuriousness and Selection Effects.** When reading research, ask yourself: Could something else be causing this result? Has the researcher really looked at every possible angle?

• **Look for Agendas.** Agendas are often political in nature. Many times politicians quote statistics, but that doesn't mean they're true. Regardless of party affiliation, many politicians choose to manipulate statistics to make their claims appear stronger than they actually are.[23]

Community Learning—Needs Assessments

As you consider how to assist your local communities, one research method might be exceptionally valuable: a needs assessment. A **needs assessment** is an analysis that studies the needs of a specific group and presents the results in a written statement. There are three key questions to ask when you're doing a needs assessment:

1. What information is needed?
2. What is the background of this situation?
3. How will we collect this information?

Your methodological training can help you help others in your community. But don't forget, statistics are everywhere, and you need to understand them in order to evaluate research accurately.

From Classroom to Community Volunteering at the Rec Center

"I can't believe the building has changed so much within a year,"
Kathryn, one of my first-year sociology students, remarked at the grand reopening of a local recreation center that provided after school and weekend activities for troubled youth. As a volunteer at the center last year, Kathryn noticed that many of the center's rooms were empty and unused. She knew that if the rooms were put to use, the kids' attendance would skyrocket. Since she didn't know why the rooms were unused or even how the center should use them, Kathryn decided to conduct a needs assessment.

"I met with the directors of the center and learned that they didn't have the funds necessary to renovate the empty rooms," she said. "But the directors agreed that giving the kids more options at the center might beef up their interest."

After meeting with the board, Kathryn spoke to staff members to find out how they proposed to use the empty rooms. She met with potential investors and found several interested parties. A quick examination of the public records found that 40 percent of the city's population was within the recreation center's target age group. Armed with this information, Kathryn met with the board of directors again. This time she proposed her own ideas for how to renovate the space and how the center could fund the renovations. Kathryn worked alongside the board to create two computer rooms and a game room. Like many sociologists, Kathryn identified a need, analyzed data, and found a way to meet that need in the end.

02

WHAT **ARE RESEARCH METHODS?**   30

the scientific procedures that sociologists use to conduct research and develop knowledge about a particular topic

HOW **DO SOCIOLOGISTS USE RESEARCH METHODS?**   41

through analysis of quantitative data using cross-sectional studies, comparative studies, longitudinal studies, surveys, and experiments; through analysis of qualitative data using participant observation, case studies, and ethnographies

HOW **IS RESEARCH INVOLVED IN SOCIAL POLICY AND COMMUNITY LEARNING?**   43

through analysis of statistics and by conducting needs assessments

get the topic: WHAT ARE RESEARCH METHODS?

Objectivity   30
Variables   30
Cause and Correlation   32
Scientific Method: What Are the Six Steps of Social Research?   32

Quantitative and Qualitative Methods   41
Triangulation   42
Research Methods and the Three Paradigms   42

Social Policy and Statistics   43
Community Learning—Needs Assessments   43

Key Terms

research methods are the scientific procedures that sociologists use to conduct research and develop knowledge about a particular topic.   30

objectivity is the ability to conduct research without allowing personal biases or prejudices to influence you.   31

independent variables are variables that are deliberately manipulated in an experiment.   31

dependent variables are the response to the manipulated variable.   31

control variables are variables that are kept constant to accurately test the impact of an independent variable.   31

causal relationship is a relationship in which one condition leads to a certain consequence.   32

causation is the relationship between cause and effect.   32

correlation is an indication that one factor might be a cause for another factor.   32

positive correlation includes two variables that move in a parallel direction.   32

negative correlation occurs when variables move in opposite directions.   32

spurious correlation occurs when two variables appear to be related, but actually have a different cause.   32

social research is investigation conducted by social scientists.   32

literature review is a study of relevant academic articles and information.   32

theory is a comprehensive and systematic explanation of events that lead to testable predictions.   32

hypothesis involves a suggestion about how variables relate.   32

concepts are abstract ideas that are impossible to measure.   32

operationalizing is turning abstract ideas into something measurable.   32

research design refers to the process used to find information.   33

reliable means able to be trusted.   33

validity assures that you're actually measuring the thing you set out to measure in the first place.   33

comparative studies use data from different sources in order to evaluate them against each other.   33

cross-sectional studies look at one event at a single point in time.   33

longitudinal studies include data from observations over time using a cohort.   33

cohort is a specific group of people used in a study.   33

survey is an investigation of the opinions or experience of a group of people by asking them questions.   35

populations are target groups from which researchers want to get information.   35

parsimony is extreme unwillingness to use resources.   35

sample is a subset of a population.   35

generalization is the extent that what is learned from a sample can be applied to the population from which the sample is taken.   35

random sample is a group of subjects arbitrarily chosen from a defined population.   35

oversampling is the process of taking a bigger sample if the group you wish to study makes up a small percentage of the whole population.   35

sample of convenience is a nonrandom sample available to the researcher.   35

selection effects are the likelihood that a nonrepresentative sample of the population may lead to inaccurate results.   35

Hawthorne effect occurs when people behave differently because they know they are part of an experiment.   36

field research is research conducted in a natural setting.   36

participant observation is a type of field research in which the researcher poses as a person who is normally in the environment.   37

case studies are investigations of one person or event in detail.   37

ethnography is a research method that aims to understand the social perspective and cultural values of a particular group by participating with or getting to know their activities in detail.   37

secondary data are data that others have already collected and published.   37

secondary data analysis is the process of using and analyzing data that others have collected. *37*

central tendency is the numbers in the middle of an array of numbers. *38*

mean is an average. *38*

median refers to the midpoint in a distribution of numbers. *38*

mode refers to the most common value in a distribution of numbers. *38*

ethics is a system of values or principles that guide one's behavior. *40*

quantitative data refer to data based on numbers. *41*

qualitative data include words, pictures, photos, or any other type of information that comes to the researcher in a non-numeric form. *41*

content analysis is a type of research in which the sociologist looks for common words or themes in newspapers, books, or structured interviews. *41*

triangulation is the process of using multiple approaches to study a phenomenon. *42*

needs assessment is an analysis that studies the needs of a specific group and presents the results in a written statement. *42*

Sample Test Questions

These multiple-choice questions are similar to those found in the test bank that accompanies this textbook.

1. "Children who participate in organized sports are less likely to suffer from obesity later in life." This statement is an example of a

   a. causal relationship.
   b. positive correlation.
   c. negative correlation.
   d. spurious correlation.

2. Which of the following research steps requires developing a logical research design?

   a. Collecting data
   b. Analyzing results
   c. Deciding on a topic
   d. Developing a hypothesis

3. What kind of study tells you what other researchers think about a particular topic?

   a. Literature review
   b. Longitudinal study
   c. Comparative study
   d. Cross-sectional study

4. The ethical principle that refers to staying within one's area of expertise is

   a. integrity.
   b. social responsibility.
   c. professional competence.
   d. professional and scientific responsibility.

5. Which measure of central tendency is not affected by extreme high or low scores?

   a. Mean
   b. Mode
   c. Average
   d. Median

ESSAY

1. How could you argue that Humphreys' study of the tearoom trade violated ethical standards of sociological study?

2. What caveats should you keep in mind when reading statistical evidence?

3. Suppose you were conducting a study of how people of different racial and ethnic backgrounds felt about a particular political candidate. How might you collect quantitative data for this study? How might you collect qualitative data?

4. How could the Hawthorne effect influence the results of a study on office productivity?

5. Provide an example of a theory. Next, explain how you would use that theory to form a hypothesis.

WHERE TO START YOUR RESEARCH PAPER

For more information on all countries, including maps and profiles, go to http://www.cia.gov/cia/publications/factbook/index.html

To find United Nations data on children, go to http://www.unicef.org/statistics/index.html

To find more information on national and international population projections and reports as well as inequality and poverty numbers, go to http://www.census.gov

To learn more about the World Values Survey (which includes data from surveys of 66 countries), go to http://wvs.isr.umich.edu/

To find religious data on the Web, go to http://www.adherents.com/

For comparison data on education, go to http://nces.ed.gov/

For more information on the world population report, data, and trends, go to http://www.un.org/esa/population/unpop.htm

To find summary data on topics related to population growth, go to http://www.prb.org/

To find information on health indicators, international comparisons or health care systems, and health-related data, go to http://www3.who.int/whosis/menu.cfm

To find international data and analysis of poverty and wealth throughout the world, go to http://www.worldbank.org/

ANSWERS: 1. c; 2. a; 3. a; 4. c; 5. d

Remember to check www.thethinkspot.com **for additional information, downloadable flashcards, and other helpful resources.**

CULTURE

"At different

times in our history, different cities have been the focal point of a radiating American spirit. In the late eighteenth century, for example, Boston was the center of a political radicalism that ignited a shot heard round the world—a shot that could not have been fired any other place but the suburbs of Boston. At its report, all Americans, including Virginians, became Bostonians at heart. In the mid-nineteenth century, New York became the symbol of the idea of a melting-pot America—or at least a non-English one—as the wretched refuse from all over the world disembarked at Ellis Island and spread over the land their strange languages and even stranger ways. In the early twentieth century, Chicago, the city of big shoulders and heavy winds, came to symbolize the industrial energy and dynamism of America. If there is a statue of a hog butcher somewhere in Chicago, then it stands as a reminder of the time when America was railroads, cattle, steel mills and

entrepreneurial adventures. If there is no such statue, there ought to be, just as there is a statue of a Minute Man to recall the Age of Boston, as the Statue of Liberty recalls the Age of New York.

"Today, we must look to the city of Las Vegas, Nevada, as a metaphor for our national character and aspiration, its symbol a thirty-foot-high cardboard picture of a slot machine and a chorus girl. For Las Vegas is a city entirely devoted to the idea of entertainment, and as such proclaims the spirit of a culture in which all public discourse increasingly takes the form of entertainment. Our politics, religion, news, athletics, education, and commerce have been transformed into congenial adjuncts of show business, largely without protest or even much popular notice. The result is that we are a people on the verge of amusing ourselves to death."[1]

A Framework
for the Individual

CHAPTER 03

---In his book *Amusing Ourselves to Death* professor and social commentator Neil Postman sounds a sociological alarm, warning readers that a **culture based purely on technology and TV is not necessarily a culture worth enjoying.**

If we become caught up in a culture of mindless entertainment, he argues, we spend our time thinking about insignificant trivia and ignoring important issues. We are at risk of killing our culture because people are too busy focusing on the insignificant.

Is Postman's warning nothing more than hyperbole? Not necessarily. Recently, I watched a family sitting at a table eating frozen custard. The mother listened to her iPod as a Nintendo DS game hypnotized her son. The father talked on his cell phone, and the five-year-old daughter seemed totally bored because she had no electronic toy or anyone to talk to. This technophilic family was clearly caught up in our country's culture of instant, constant entertainment.

Entertainment is not all bad, as Postman points out, but pursuing entertainment at all costs affects our relationships and our nation. Of course, there's more to culture than movies, slot machines, and electronic gizmos. In fact, culture forms the foundation of society and frames our perception of life.

We are rapidly becoming a society that focuses on trivia. We all know who's dating who in Hollywood and which TV star recently got arrested, but can we name the vice president?

get the topic: WHAT IS CULTURE?

CULTURE is the language, beliefs, values, norms, behaviors, and material objects that are important enough to pass on to future generations of a society.

The languages we speak and the behavioral codes we follow may seem perfectly natural to us, but there's nothing "natural" about culture: It is a framework built by and for human societies. We adopt our **culture** from those who came before us.

If you want to think like a sociologist, you'll need to understand not only the definition of culture but also how culture affects our lives. Because we see the world through the lens of our culture, it's easy for us to take our cultural orientation for granted, accepting it without much thought. In fact, we're often not even aware of the ways in which culture guides (or misguides) our thoughts and actions. The fact that you may only speak English, for example, is indicative of the culture in which you grew up. Had the Spanish or French run the English out of the United States in the 1600s, you might greet your friends, "¡Hola!" or "Bonjour!" The tangible and intangible aspects of culture have a significant impact on your daily life.

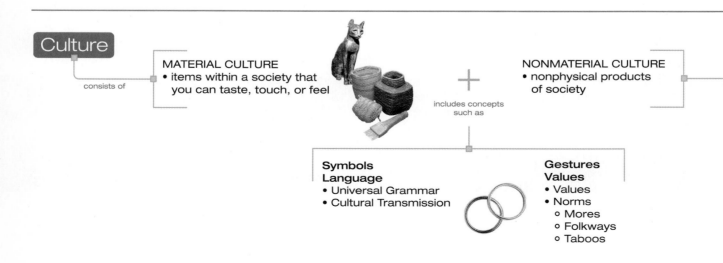

Material Culture

One category of culture is **material culture**: items within a society that you can taste, touch, or feel. The jewelry, art, music, clothing, architecture, and crafts a society creates are all examples of material culture. Of course, the natural resources available to a culture can influence that culture's creations. For example, while seven countries (the United States, Japan, Russia, Canada, Germany, France, and the United Kingdom) use more than 46 percent of the world's electricity and oil, these countries combined hold only about 12 percent of the world's population. What do these statistics tell you about material culture? On a tour of these countries, you'd be likely to stumble across plenty of cars, air conditioners, heaters, blow dryers, and a host of other modern conveniences. If you took a trip to Nigeria, though, you'd notice that a lack of access to energy also influences material culture. Nigeria is the ninth largest country in the world, yet it ranks 71st in the world's electricity use and 42nd in the world's use of oil. Few people own a car, and many live without regular access to electricity.[2]

Nonmaterial Culture

Not all elements of culture are items you can touch, see, or buy at your local mall. **Nonmaterial culture** consists of the nonphysical products of society, including our symbols, values, rules, and sanctions.

SYMBOLS

What do you think of when you see the U.S. flag? To most of us, it's more than just a piece of cloth—it's a symbol. **Symbols** represent, suggest, or stand for something else. They can be words, gestures, or even objects, and they often represent abstract or complex concepts. For example, wedding rings represent a legal bond of marriage and an emotional bond of love between two people. Each culture determines the meaning of its own symbols and uses these symbols to share thoughts and concepts with others. During the 2008 presidential campaign, a metal lapel pin in the shape of the U.S. flag took on a surprising amount of symbolism—or rather, its absence did.

> **MATERIAL CULTURE** consists of items within a culture that you can taste, touch, and feel.
>
> **NONMATERIAL CULTURE** consists of the nonphysical products of society, including our symbols, values, rules, and sanctions.
>
> **SYMBOLS** represent, suggest, or stand for something else.
>
> **LANGUAGE** is a system of speech and/or written symbols used to convey meaning and communicate.

Democratic presidential candidate Barack Obama at times chose not to wear a flag pin, and for some Americans, his empty lapel symbolized a lack of patriotism. The pin's occasional absence became a source of irritation for many people, and Obama was forced to publicly address the issue. Symbols are powerful things.

LANGUAGE

Language is a system of speech and/or written symbols used to convey meaning and communicate. Some languages exist only in the oral tradition, while other languages are expressed through both speech and writing systems, but all cultures use some form of language. The United Nations reports that currently, there are more than 6,000 different languages on the planet. Due to conquest, commerce, and failure to write down some languages, about half of these are in danger of extinction.[3]

Two main factors determine the number of speakers of a language: population size and colonial history. China and India are the world's largest countries by population, a fact that single-handedly explains the large percentage of people who speak Mandarin Chinese and Hindi. The English language is widely spoken throughout the world, but this has little to do with Great Britain's population size. If you've ever heard the phrase, "The sun never sets on the British Empire," you know that the British Empire once owned territory on every continent. As Great Britain colonized countries around the world from the 1700s to the 1900s, English was introduced to these places.

The Study of Culture

may be influenced by
- Ethnocentrism
- Xenophobia
- Xenocentrism
- Cultural Relativism

and should focus on
- **Ideal Culture**—the values to which a culture aspires
- **Real Culture**—the way people actually behave

and might discuss

+

- **Subcultures**—subsets of the dominant culture that have distinct values, beliefs, and norms
- **Countercultures**—subcultures whose values and/or beliefs are in opposition to the dominant group

- **Multiculturalism**—concept that supports the inherent value of different cultures in a society
- **Assimilation**—process by which minority groups adapt to the dominant culture

∨
∨ **Language influences how we perceive**
∨ **things,** which in turn influences our experience of the world. Our experiences help us develop language, **but our use of language also influences our experience.**[6]

Universal Grammar

The famous linguist Noam Chomsky suggests that human beings' ability to use language comes from common roots.[4] All languages contain what Chomsky calls a "universal grammar." This term refers not to particular language rules but to the way in which languages are constructed. Chomsky theorizes that, among other things, commonalities in sentence construction and word pronunciation connect languages throughout the world. Furthermore, he says, universal grammar begins in children at about the same age, regardless of culture. Chomsky's observations suggest that humans have an innate need for language.

Research by Coppola and Newport supports much of Chomsky's theory. In their study of deaf subjects who were isolated and knew no official sign language, Coppola and Newport found that these people's "home sign language" (i.e., language that they developed themselves) follows a predictable grammatical style.[5] For instance, the subject of a sentence generally appears at the beginning of the statement. Such findings point to an innate logic in the construction of language and support Chomsky's theory of universal grammar.

Cultural Transmission

Language is a useful tool, but is it culturally crucial? There's plenty of evidence to support the idea that a system of communication is, in fact, a critical aspect of culture. Culture often passes from one generation to the next through language. We call this phenomenon **cultural transmission**. Thanks to cultural transmission, you can use information others have learned to improve your own life. Cultural transmission also helps spread technology: Scientific studies of electricity and the development of microwave technology and the microchip made today's cell phones and computers possible.

Language not only advances our knowledge; it also brings us together by helping us create social consensus, or agreement. If you and I were to meet, we could use language to exchange ideas, debate, or decide on a course of action. Language is inherently social: It serves as a tool for sharing past memories, making plans, and building relationships.

>>> The lyrics of rap music often prize material culture. **Why do you think this is?**

The Sapir-Whorf Hypothesis

It's difficult to overstate the importance of language in our lives. Benjamin Whorf, a student of anthropologist Edward Sapir, suggested that language and thinking patterns are directly connected. Sapir and Whorf reached this conclusion, known as the **Sapir-Whorf hypothesis,** after studying many different languages and the people who spoke them.[7] The Sapir-Whorf hypothesis proposes two key points:

1. The differences in the structure of language parallel differences in the thinking of the people who speak languages.

2. The structure of a language strongly influences the speaker's worldview.

Have you ever considered how much language actually influences our thinking? Imagine that the English language had no words for right, left, front, or back. Would you still be able to understand these concepts? Probably not. An aboriginal group from Cape York Peninsula in Australia has no words for relative locations; instead, the group has words for absolute location, such as east, west, north, and south. Most members of the group do learn English, so they have an understanding of relative location. However, if they do not learn English at an early age, they struggle when asked to describe their location in relative terms.[8] Ongoing research into the Sapir-Whorf hypothesis suggests that because language influences thinking, it also influences culture.

GESTURE

Although language is a primary component of nonmaterial culture, it's not the only one. Another symbol system that differs by culture is gesture. **Gestures** are symbols we make using our bodies, such as facial expressions, hand movements, eye contact, and other types of body language. A gesture's symbolic meaning can vary widely between cultures: When I worked as a counselor to a Native American man, I interpreted my client's refusal to make eye contact with me as a sign of distrust until I learned that in his culture, looking someone in the eye is considered rude.

GESTURES are symbols we make using our bodies, such as facial expressions, hand movements, eye contact, and other types of body language.

VALUES are a part of a society's nonmaterial culture that represent cultural standards by which we determine what is good, bad, right, or wrong.

VALUE PAIRS help us define values, usually in terms of opposites.

VALUE CLUSTERS are two or more values that support each other.

VALUE CONFLICT occurs when two or more values are at odds.

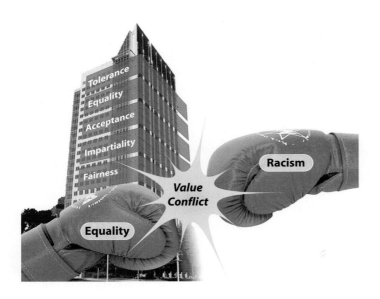

VALUES

Values, part of a society's nonmaterial culture, represent cultural standards by which we determine what is good, bad, right, or wrong. Sometimes, these values are expressed as proverbs or sayings that teach us how to live. Do you recognize the phrase, "Life is like a box of chocolates—you never know what you're going to get"? This modern-day saying is popular today among those who embrace life's unpredictability. Cultures are capable of growth and change, so it's possible for a culture's values to change over time.

Value pairs help us define values, usually in terms of opposites. For every positive value, we have a negative one. We may also hold values that support or contradict our other values. **Value clusters** are two or more values that support each other. Let's say you value both equality and tolerance. These values form a value cluster because they are similar concepts that strengthen each other. When two or more values are at odds, however, a **value conflict** occurs. For example, equality and racism are conflicting values.

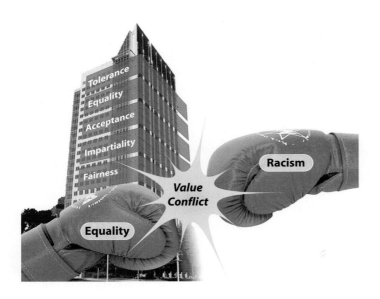

▶▶▶ GO GLⒼBAL

International Gestures Quiz

Think you know what it means to give a high five in Honduras or a thumbs-up in Thailand? Test your body language IQ to find out if you're culturally savvy.

1. How would you let a French person know he's boring you to tears?
    a. pat your mouth and let out a giant yawn
    b. mime playing an imaginary flute
    c. push your nose with your middle and index fingers

2. Your Puerto Rican friend wiggles her nose at you. What's she saying?
    a. "What's going on?"
    b. "I smell a rat—literally."
    c. "My nose itches!"

3. Which gesture is considered offensive in Egypt?
    a. using the right hand for eating
    b. showing someone the sole of your shoe
    c. walking hand in hand with someone

ANSWERS: 1. b; 2. a; 3. b

"The **differences in the structure of language parallel differences in the thinking of the speakers** of those languages."

Fifteen U.S. Values According to Sociologist ROBIN WILLIAMS

If someone asked you to list the values of people in today's society, what would you include? Famous sociologist Robin Williams (*not the comedian*) suggests there are fifteen dominant values in the United States.[9]

1 **Achievement and Success**. What do you want to accomplish with your life? Each of us has our cwn definition of success. For some it means having a high income, for others a college degree, still others simply want a better life than their parents had. Since success is an abstract concept, we often look at our achievements to determine whether or not we've been successful.

2 **Activity and Work**. It's what you might call the American dream: With enough hard work, anyone can pave a path to success. Thanks in part to this widely held belief, work has become a strong cultural value in the United States. We don't like when others call us "lazy" or "idle," and we fill free time with hobbies and activities. In fact, we spend more time on the job than most people in the industrialized world.[10]

3 **Moral Orientation**. U.S. citizens have a tendency toward absolute ethical judgments regarding what is good, bad, right, or wrong. For example, when President George W. Bush suggested in 2003 that North Korea, Iran, and Iraq formed an "axis of evil," he was using an absolute moral orientation.

4 **Humanitarianism.** In the United States, many people are generous and value philanthropy. In times of crisis, we are willing to help. After Hurricane Katrina in 2005, people all over the country assisted the residents of New Orleans and the Gulf Coast area. Organizations raised more than $3.27 billion, including about $1 billion in the first three weeks.[11]

5 **Efficiency and Practicality.** People in the United States seek the most benefit for the least effort. We believe that efficiency helps us achieve goals quickly and easily.

6 **Progress**. People who value progress believe in "moving forward" by making changes and proposing ideas designed to improve society. For example, you (and most of the people you know) probably believe that, to some extent at least, new technology improves life. This belief is one motivator behind the One Laptop Per Child program, which sends kid-friendly, wireless-enabled laptops to developing countries in an attempt to increase children's educational opportunities.[12]

7 **Material Comfort.** If you've ever felt like you have too much "stuff"—and yet you still want more—you're far from alone. The desire for material comfort drives many of us to buy bigger homes and fill them with things that make our lives easier, like wireless Internet. There are more Wi-Fi hotspots in the United States than in the United Kingdom, the Russian Federation, and Taiwan combined.

8 **Equality.** Since the Declaration of Independence was penned, people in the United States have embraced the notion that all people should be treated equally regardless of race, gender, social class, or religious background. However, we don't always put our egalitarian values into practice. For example, female CEOs ran only 12 Fortune 500 companies in 2007. This gender disparity reflects women's struggle to achieve equality in the workplace.

9 **Freedom.** Generally, U.S. citizens place high value on civil liberties and the rights of the individual. Civil liberties limit the power of the government in our daily lives. We value our freedom to speak our minds, hold independent beliefs, and follow the religious practices of our choice.

10 **External Conformity.** Don't underestimate the power of a group to influence your choices. If you value external conformity, you're probably eager to fit in with those around you. When you were in high school, for example, other students probably influenced your desire to have the latest and greatest clothes, shoes, or haircut.

<<< Judging from the quantity of belongings strewn across the lawn, it's safe to say that **this family places a high value on material comfort.**

It's customary for players and fans alike to remove their hat, place their right hand on their hearts, and sing the national anthem before sporting events. Why do so at an event that has nothing to do with politics, patriotism, or war?

11 **Science and Secular Rationality**. In the United States, scientific proof and rational thought aren't concepts to be sneezed at. The essence of the scientific method is to use logic, order, and rational thought to attain knowledge. Many of us believe that logic and science can solve any problem that arises, including complex issues such as a cure for cancer or a solution to global warming.

12 **Nationalism and Patriotism**. We use the term civil religion to describe national pride and patriotism when it takes on an almost religious context.[13] In our everyday lives, you and I might engage in ritualistic patriotism without much thought. For example:

• **What** does singing the national anthem before sporting events have to do with sports?

• **What** does starting the school day with the pledge of allegiance have to do with learning?

13 **Democracy**. As any politician running for elected office would be happy to tell you, voting is a valuable aspect of civic engagement in our democracy. For a significant number of U.S. citizens, inspiring democratic systems of government in other nations is valuable, too. In the past 18 years, the number of electoral democracies in the world has doubled. Although more than half of the countries in the world have democracies, not all of those countries give their residents the freedoms U.S. citizens take for granted. In 2005, Freedom House reported that only 89 of the 122 electoral democracies are "free" in the same sense as the United States is.[14]

14 **Individual Personality**. When Williams discusses "individual personality," he's talking about individualism, or the tendency to look at the world through the lens of the individual rather than the lens of family or community. If you have an individualist worldview, you believe that people are autonomous—in other words, people's choices and actions are not predetermined by their positions in society. Because individualists tend to place personal goals ahead of group goals, tension often develops in groups of individualists.[15]

15 **Racism and Related Group Superiority**. According to Williams, racism is a value in the United States, though not a positive one. Historical examples of racism toward non-Caucasian citizens abound, but racism is very much a contemporary issue. The town of Jena, Louisiana, made national headlines when, in 2006, nooses were hung from a tree and six African-American students were charged with attempted murder for beating up a white student. The case of the "Jena Six" makes it painfully clear that the United States continues to struggle with issues of race.[16]

▶▶▶ GO GL🌐BAL

Individualistic and Collectivistic Views

Individualism, while it may be a core U.S. value, is hardly universal across the globe; people in countries such as Japan are more apt to see things through the lens of collectivism.[17] In a collectivist culture, interdependence is valued over independence, group goals valued over individual wants and needs.[18]

How do our individualist or collectivist views affect us in practical terms? For starters, let's consider how we respond to questions. Research has shown that people from more collective societies, such as China and Japan, are less likely to answer with extremes on surveys. On a survey that allows participants to strongly agree, agree, disagree, and strongly disagree, U.S. citizens are more likely to choose "strongly agree" and "strongly disagree," whereas Chinese and Japanese participants tend to choose the less extreme responses.[19]

Important cultural differences like these can inform business situations. For example, research has found that a culture's orientation, whether individualistic or collectivist, does influence economic development, and vice versa. When individualist U.S. businesses enter collectivist countries without well-established legal codes, regulations, and court systems, these U.S. companies are likely to find that their business strategies don't succeed as well. Collectivist nations' business styles often differ from those of U.S. companies; In China, for example, businesspeople greatly value *guanxi*, or relationship development. While people working in the United States might not be used to building strong interpersonal relationships with potential business partners before even starting to work on a project, this type of in-depth relationship cultivation is critical in China. U.S. companies must be sensitive to cultural differences and adapt their business practices accordingly to be successful.[20]

Additional Values

Because Williams' list of U.S. values is more than 30 years old, I believe that today's society warrants the addition of two new values. Look at any magazine cover, and you will see images of youthful, physically fit bodies and people in sexy, intimate poses. That's because today's society values these traits.

1 **Physical Fitness and Youthfulness.** People in the United States value a youthful appearance and a physically fit body. This is perhaps strange in a country that has increasingly high rates of obesity.[21] Yet, if you describe beauty, it's likely to be in terms of being young and physically fit.

2 **Sexuality and Romance.** John D'Emilio and Estelle B. Freedman detail the history of sexuality in the United States.[22] Reviewing data about sex over time, they conclude that we are becoming an increasingly sexualized society. This claim shouldn't be surprising—music, television, and magazines all tend to glorify sexuality. Linked to feelings about sexuality is romantic love, which involves sexual attraction and feelings of affection. In our society, nothing speaks to our value of romance like Valentine's Day. Every February 14th, about half of adult consumers buy 13 billion dollars of roses and other gifts to show their love.[23]

Norms and Sanctions

How can people uphold and enforce their values in everyday life? First of all, they might develop rules for appropriate behavior based on those values. We call these rules norms. **Norms** are conditional; they can vary from place to place. In 2003 the Las Vegas Convention and Visitors Authority launched the advertising tagline "What Happens Here, Stays Here." The tourism board wanted visitors to frequent their city's casinos, bars, shows, and restaurants without feeling guilty about how participation at these places may contradict their cultural values. Las Vegas is now known as a place to escape from cultural norms in other cities; the norm in Vegas is for people to enjoy entertainment without regret.

Norms provide the justification for sanctions. A **sanction** is a prize or punishment you receive when you either abide by a norm or violate it. If you do what you are supposed to do, you get a positive sanction; if you break the rules, you earn a negative sanction.

Most sanctions are informal, like when your friend rolls her eyes at your terrible joke. However if we violate a law or some formal written rule, we receive a formal negative sanction. A speeding ticket is one example of a formal sanction. Sanctions, both positive and negative, can reinforce a culture's values by rewarding people who hold those values and punishing those who have opposing values.

FOLKWAYS

Folkways are informal types of norms. They provide a framework for our behavior and are based on social expectations. Because they are less serious types of norms, the sanctions applied are less severe than for other types of norms. For example, if you see a person struggling with packages, you will hold the door for him or her. If you let the door slam on the person, you might be considered rude, but you won't go to jail. Folkways are often social customs that, when violated, call for minor, informal negative sanctions.

MORES

Although folkways are informal norms, mores (pronounced MORE-ayes) are more serious. **Mores** are norms that represent a community's most important values. A **taboo** is an act that is socially unacceptable. For example, if you murder a person, you've violated one of society's mores.. People who violate mores are given a particularly serious type of formal negative sanction. Acts that lead us to feel revulsion, such as murder, are taboos.[24]

The Study of Culture

When you study culture, it's a good idea to consider whether a particular behavior or event is a cultural universal, or common to all cultures. For example, funeral rites are a cultural universal because all cultures have methods of disposing of the dead. Many specific cultural norms surround funerals and death, however, these norms vary widely from culture to culture. In what is now known as Micronesia, anthropologist Bronislaw Malinowski witnessed a funeral ritual in which native islanders ate part of the dead person to maintain a connection.[25] After eating, they would vomit in an attempt to create distance from the deceased. This Micronesian funeral norm probably differs greatly from your own culture's norm.

<<< In 2007 **Richard Gere** caused a stir when he **kissed actress Shilpa Shetty** on the cheek at a public event in India. **While this gesture is common** in the United States, it's considered a **vulgar act in India.**

ETHNOCENTRISM AND CULTURAL RELATIVISM

When studying culture from a sociological perspective, you must not allow your personal biases to complicate your understanding. **Ethnocentrism** occurs when a person uses his or her own culture to judge another culture. Nearly all people in the world are ethnocentric, but ethnocentrism is potentially dangerous to sociologists because it can lead to incorrect assumptions about different cultures.[26]

Xenophobia refers to fear and hostility toward people who are from other countries or cultures. The United States has a long history of xenophobia. When the United States entered World War II after Japan bombed Pearl Harbor in 1941, people in the United States began to fear Japanese Americans and locked many in internment camps.

∧
∧
∧ Propaganda posters popped up all over the nation after the Japanese bombed Pearl Harbor. **Terrifying images of Japanese soldiers terrorizing women and children in the United States led to widespread xenophobia.**

Perspectives of a Central American Hotel Room

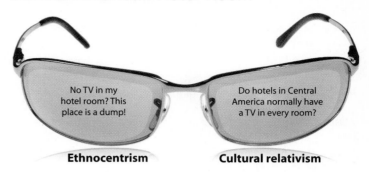

No TV in my hotel room? This place is a dump!

Do hotels in Central America normally have a TV in every room?

Ethnocentrism   **Cultural relativism**

When **traveling in Central America**, I noticed that even in very nice hotels there was **rarely a television in the room.** I viewed this observation through an **ethnocentric** lens based on my **cultural expectations**, but I was also able to view it through an **objective, prejudice-free lens of cultural relativism**.

Not all personal biases result in a negative view of foreign cultures. Sometimes, we engage in **xenocentrism** when we perceive other groups or societies as superior to our own. When living in Mexico, I noticed that my host family watched very little television. Instead, the family spent time discussing ideas. I remember wishing that people in my own culture would follow suit and interact with one another more.

Thinking like a sociologist means striving to practice cultural relativism when studying other cultures. **Cultural relativism** consists of a deliberate effort to appreciate a group's ways of life in its own context, without prejudice. Philosophers sometimes refer to this effort as **normative relativism** because it bases the evaluation of a society on that society's own norms. In some Islamic countries, for instance, women are not encouraged to seek education. Within the context of these countries, this practice could be interpreted as a normal function of that culture. However, if women in the United States were not allowed to get an education, the practice would seem unfair because it would violate U.S. cultural norms. When we engage in normative relativism, we evaluate acts within their cultural contexts.

Some people, however, argue that there are universal human values that are standards by which we should evaluate cultures.[27] According to this argument, women in every culture should be educated, and any culture that does not allow this is inferior and exploitive of women.

CULTURAL LAG AND CULTURE SHOCK

Cultural lag happens when social and cultural changes occur at a slower pace than technological changes. This is often the case when new technology enters and changes a culture. In the late 1970s, scientists were concerned with the deforestation of poorer regions of the world. People used most of the felled lumber to heat stoves for cooking. To combat this problem, solar stoves were developed. However, initial tests in Africa and Haiti showed that people were reluctant to use these stoves. After learning of the stoves' benefits, people's reluctance waned, and today more than 120 million solar stoves are used around the world.[28]

CULTURE SHOCK occurs when a person encounters a culture foreign to his or her own and has an emotional response to the differences between the cultures.

SUBCULTURE is a subset of the dominant culture that has distinct values, beliefs, and norms.

COUNTERCULTURES are groups with value systems that are in opposition to the dominant group's values.

MULTICULTURALISM is a concept that supports the inherent value of different cultures within society.

ASSIMILATION is the process by which minority groups adopt the patterns of the dominant culture.

GLOBAL VILLAGE refers to the "shrinking" of the world through immediate electronic communications.

Have you ever been to a foreign country and marveled at how the culture differed from your own? If so, you were probably experiencing culture shock. **Culture shock** occurs when a person encounters a culture foreign to his or her own and has an emotional response to the differences between the cultures. During my time in Mexico, I was stunned to discover that the electricity went out every afternoon. My host family planned their cooking schedule around the predictable power outages. It took some time, but I eventually accepted this cultural difference.

IDEAL VERSUS REAL CULTURE

Is there a difference between culture as we'd like it to be and culture as it really is? Often, the answer is yes. Ideal culture represents the values to which a culture aspires, and real culture represents a culture's actual behaviors. Democracy, for example, has always been part of the ideal culture of the United States, but voter turnouts for the 1996, 2000, and 2004 presidential elections indicate that many people don't show democratic values and turn out to vote.

SUBCULTURES AND COUNTERCULTURES

Groups with a common interest may form a subculture. A **subculture** is a subset of the dominant culture that has distinct values, beliefs, and norms.

In complex societies, subcultures allow people to connect with other people who have similar interests. Churches, civic organizations, clubs, and even online communities can become subcultures.

When you read the term counterculture, images of mafia organizations

When a subculture expresses values or beliefs that are in direct opposition to the dominant group's values, it becomes a counterculture.

and violent motorcycle gangs might come to mind. These groups are **countercultures** because their value systems are in opposition to the dominant group's values. Sometimes, countercultures can merge with and change the dominant culture. For example, in the Roman Empire, Christianity was once banned and practicing Christians were fed to the lions. However, Christianity later became the official religion of the empire.

MULTICULTURALISM AND ASSIMILATION

If you move to a new country, you'll bring along not only material belongings but also concealed cultural baggage. It can be tricky to "unpack" that baggage, but you'll need to find a way to adapt to your new culture. **Multiculturalism** is a concept that supports the inherent value of different cultures within society. Proponents of multiculturalism think that immigrants should maintain links to aspects of their original culture—such as language, cultural beliefs and traditions, and religion—while also integrating into their new culture. However, opponents of multiculturalism worry that this practice keeps groups from adapting to the dominant culture.

Assimilation is the process by which minority groups adopt the patterns of the dominant culture. If a minority group completely abandons its previous culture in favor of a new one, that group is likely to experience rapid assimilation. One method by which the U.S. government tried to force rapid assimilation involved taking Native American children from their parents and placing them in boarding schools to teach them "white ways." However, many Native American students left the boarding schools unprepared to live in either the dominant culture or their own culture.[29]

MAKE CONNECTIONS

The Subcultures of Facebook

Are you a member of a Facebook subculture? Considering that Facebook has more than 69 million active users worldwide, you probably are. Facebook, an online social networking site, helps connect people through mutual interests. When you use this site, your friends are always at your fingertips.

When you join Facebook, you create a profile that includes personal information, interests, beliefs, or hobbies. The more information you include, the larger your world can become, because Facebook connects you to others in the system who have similar characteristics. For example, you can connect to people who have the same class schedule or belong to the same fraternity and/or sorority. You're linked to people who have similar values, or your subculture of friends.

Like any culture or subculture, Facebook has norms and sanctions. Many Facebook users believe that the more friends you have, the more popular you are. One norm for interacting with friends on the site is to "poke" a person. The person you poke may poke you back or ignore your poke. An informal sanction might occur if your poke goes unanswered. A formal sanction can

occur if a friend deletes you from his or her friends list. Though nontraditional, Facebook creates a virtual community in which people interact with others who share norms and values.

>>> **ACTIVITY** Log on to a social networking site, like Facebook, and identify a culture.
- **MAKE** a list of the values of that culture.
- **HOW** are these values distinct from the values on pages 52–54?
- **HOW** are they similar?

Global Village

In the 1960s, Marshall McLuhan popularized the term "**global village**," which refers to the "shrinking" of the world through immediate electronic communications.[30] McLuhan's work suggests that time and space differences are rapidly becoming irrelevant as a result of technology. But is technology really bringing people closer together?

Before the advent of the Internet, Stanley Milgram conducted an experiment in an attempt to determine whether it really is a small world after all.[31] Milgram found people from different areas of the United States and sent them on a hunt for strangers. He asked them to mail a letter to a target person, whom they did not know, using only their social networks. He provided only the subject's name and town of residence but nothing else. After passing through the hands of between two and ten people, the letters eventually found their targets. Now that the Internet plays such a large role in our lives, could our separation be even shorter than it was in the 1960s? How many links would it take you to connect with a student in Japan?

Dodds et al. used the Internet to conduct a similar study.[32] Through e-mail, Dodds sent more than 60,000 people on a target hunt to find 18 people in 13 different countries. Their results were astonishingly similar to Milgram's results. Although these findings certainly support the notion of a small world, they do not suggest that the world is any smaller today than it was in Milgram's time.

^
^ **Twitter, a social-networking/micro-blogging**
^ **device, allows users to alert their friends (with "Tweets") to their current activities via instant message or RSS feed.** Twitter, in effect, encourages users to know all the actions of their friends in real time. **Do programs like Twitter make the world feel smaller? Why or why not?**

THINK SOCIOLOGICALLY

Technology and Cultural Change

In *Amusing Ourselves to Death: Public Discourse in the Age of Show Business*, Neil Postman discusses television's impact on U.S. culture. Television is the primary means of communication for news and information in the United States. Fewer people read newspapers and magazines. Do the media affect the message?

Marshall Fishwick would say that they do. According to him, many aspects of life that make us human are not computable.[33] Your laptop cannot feel, create beauty, or think. Your MP3 player talks to you; it does not listen. Like Fishwick, Postman argues that technology, such as television, provides a passive type of engagement for the user. Postman suggests that this creates a nation of people who cannot think. This inability increases the odds that we will accept overly simple solutions to extremely complex problems, which will destroy our culture in the long run.

Of course, not everyone believes that technology will destroy our culture. In *Culture and Technology*, Andrew Murphie and John Potts argue that technology has improved society. For example, Murphie and Potts argue that the technology of writing "transformed human consciousness" because it brought about new ways of thinking. Technological advancements, such as the Internet and television, inspire creativity and innovation, and open up a world of opportunity for a society. They claim that technology does not limit a society, as Fishwick and Postman suggest, but it gives people the tools to continue to improve their lives.[34] Is our culture becoming a technopoly? A technopoly is a society that values technological change for its own sake. In such a culture, having the latest upgrade is most important. Fishwick suggests that our culture is experiencing a tyranny of technology, while Murphie and Potts argue that culture and technology are so tightly linked that we can't really separate one from the other. What do you think? Has technology really improved society?

think sociologically: WHAT DIFFERENTIATES ONE CULTURE FROM ANOTHER?

Now we will turn to the major theoretical perspectives on culture. The theoretical perspectives affect how sociologists view language, gestures, and values in a culture.

Symbolic Interactionism— A Crisis of Values

Symbolic interactionists explore how language, gestures, or values affect a culture. If a symbolic interactionist were to study values in U.S. society, he or she might ask: How are values defined in the United States? Are U.S. values weakening? Is the United States experiencing a moral decline?

TRADITIONAL VALUES VS. SECULAR VALUES

In *America's Crisis of Values*, author Wayne Baker investigates whether a crisis of values really exists.[35] Baker surmises that proponents of a decline of values usually support one of three arguments: the trend hypothesis, the comparative hypothesis, or the distribution hypothesis. He compares traditional and secular values over time.

Traditional values include the importance of religion and God, absolute standards of good and evil, importance of the family, deference to authority, male dominance in economic and political life, and intolerance of certain moral issues such as abortion, homosexuality, divorce, and suicide. Secular values emphasize reason and logic. Ignoring religion and custom when determining government and social decisions, accepting low levels of religious beliefs and relative standards of good and evil, and questioning authority are all examples of secular values.

THE THREE HYPOTHESES

The comparative hypothesis suggests that the values in U.S. society are inferior to those found in other modern democracies. The argument proposes that our individualist and traditional values result in higher rates of murder, poverty, and out-of-wedlock births. When Baker compared value statements from a variety of countries, he found more similarities than differences, which lends no support to the comparative hypothesis.

The distribution hypothesis or, as Baker also refers to it, "the culture war thesis" suggests that the United States is involved in a culture war. According to this theory, two morally opposed groups (one liberal, one conservative) fight for control of the media, government, and society. Here again, Baker finds no evidence to support the idea that the United States is divided into two opposed groups fighting for moral high ground.

BAKER'S CONCLUSION

Using data gathered from the U.S. public over a 30-year span, Baker concludes that U.S. citizens are becoming more traditional and less secular. Baker's results may come as a surprise to pundits who love to chatter about culture wars. His findings suggest that U.S. citizens have more similar values today than they did 30 years ago. In fact, the country's traditional values have become stronger over time. Yet, many who espouse these values suggest that secular rational values are "winning," when in fact they are not. Baker suggests that the United States' purported "crisis of values" is nothing more than an illusion fueled by rhetoric.

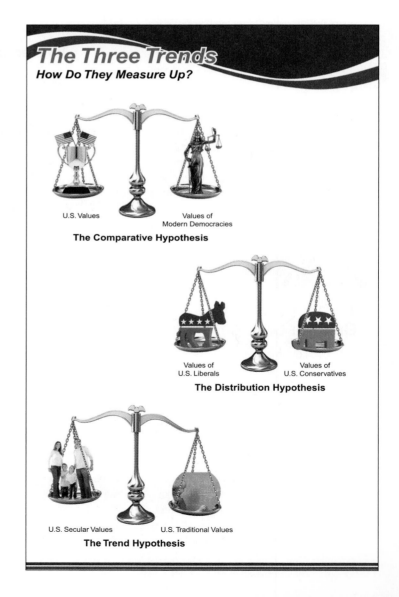

The Three Trends
How Do They Measure Up?

U.S. Values   Values of Modern Democracies
The Comparative Hypothesis

Values of U.S. Liberals   Values of U.S. Conservatives
The Distribution Hypothesis

U.S. Secular Values   U.S. Traditional Values
The Trend Hypothesis

>>> The trend hypothesis asserts that **traditional values are losing ground to secular ones.**

Functionalism— Communitarianism

When functionalists look at the importance of culture, they often consider how culture works to hold society together. Functionalists suggest that culture binds society through shared values and norms and the interaction of social structures. Noted sociologist Amitai Etzioni has explored these systems in U.S. society.

Amitai Etzioni is one of the foundational creators of communitarianism—a functional approach to the understanding of culture in the United States.[36] This theory suggests that for society to function properly, it must have a balanced relationship between the community, the market, and the government. Etzioni stresses that to build a society that works, its members must see themselves as individuals and as part of a community. Communitarians are not communists. Unlike communists, communitarians believe in free markets and private ownership of business. However, they stress that a sense of community must exist to check excesses of either the government or the market place.

Conflict Theory—The McDonaldization of the United States

Conflict theorists suggest that society is united in a struggle for scarce resources. Unequal distribution of wealth means that some people win and others lose. But how do you win? Are there predictable patterns of interaction that can bring about financial success? McDonald's restaurant is successful because it prizes efficiency, practicality, and affordability. Sociologist George Ritzer suggests that U.S. society models itself after a McDonald's restaurant through a process he calls "McDonaldization."[37]

Using a conflict theory rooted in the work of economist/sociologist/political scientist Max Weber, Ritzer notes that efficient bureaucracies succeed in business. In a capitalist system, those who follow the McDonaldization process are likely to be financially successful.

1 **Efficiency**. When a business practices efficiency, consumers benefit from the low prices that the business offers. The McDonaldization of efficiency means customers do the employees' work. If you go to McDonald's, you usually carry the food to the table yourself, and in some parts of the country, you might fill your own drink as well.

2 **Calculability**. McDonald's counts every item, from the pickles on the hamburger to the number of chicken tenders in a box. Quantity is valued, and quality is less relevant. McDonaldized societies measure success by the number of tasks completed on time. If the quality of the task is mediocre, we often accept it as long as it is finished on schedule.

3 **Predictability**. Finding a product that is predictable decreases the risk of business failure. In this way, our culture has taken a page from the fast-food industry. Food from Taco Bell tastes the same whether you purchase it in San Antonio or Boston. Predictability increases reward and decreases risk to both the business owner and the consumer.

4 **Technology**. Businesses gain more control over their products when they use technology to limit human error. This trend helps increase profits because business owners are able to hire fewer people.

NEGATIVE EFFECTS OF MCDONALDIZATION

Ritzer warns that the use of technology dehumanizes our culture. People use ATMs or self-checkout lines for convenience. However, using these forms of technology shows that society values speed through a checkout line over human interaction. In the long run, is this healthy for today's society?

McDonaldization trades convenience for high quality and ensures high profits for business owners. Innovation and creativity suffer, but short-term profits rise. By replacing workers with technology, wages drop and inequality increases, leading to conflict between business owners and workers.

Morgan Spurlock's 2004 documentary *Super Size Me* showed how eating McDonald's food every day for one month negatively affected his health. **Even though McDonald's is a perfect example of efficiency, calculability, and technology, does the restaurant chain really help our society win?**

WRAP YOUR MIND AROUND THE THEORY

The roots of mangroves grow in water, shown here in Papua New Guinea.

FUNCTIONALISM

Functionalists suggest society works as an interrelated system. Communitarians understand that if society is to run smoothly, the government, the local community, and the business sector must all work together for the well-being of all. The root of society is the local community; it anchors this societal tree. The government carries the will of the people to the economic system, thereby functioning as the trunk of this tree. The leaves of a tree make the sugar that allows the entire plant to live. Of course, leaves without roots blow over, and roots without leaves die.

CONFLICT THEORY

Conflict theorists point out that members of society struggle for what is scarce. In our society, that usually involves wealth and power because of the McDonaldization process. Short term rewards increase power and wealth of the few. The costs to society are irrelevant. Las Vegas casinos frequently make money off of people who are not wealthy. These consumers gamble for the entertainment value and because they believe gambling will make them wealthy. In reality, it's the casino owners who become wealthier.

IS YOUR COUNTRY LOSING TRADITIONAL VALUES TO SECULAR ONES?

SYMBOLIC INTERACTIONISM

Interactionists suggest that culture is rooted in the values expressed by the people who live within it. Politicians use symbols to articulate that which they believe is important. Successful candidates are able to attract votes from a wide variety of people; so, in general, they do not have extreme values. Many people in today's society get their information about politicians from television news. Neil Postman argues that news programs use sound bites from politicians to sum up their complex views in single phrases. Can people truly understand politicians' values from a single sentence?

New York senator Hillary Rodham Clinton and Illinois senator Barack Obama were in a close race throughout most of the 2008 Democratic Presidential Primaries because they **both appealed to a wide variety of people.**

Slot machines are a popular form of casino entertainment **because of the lights, sounds, and interactive nature of the game.**

discover sociology in action: HOW DOES CULTURE INFLUENCE SOCIOLOGICAL THEORY AND STUDY?

Social Policy — Multiculturalism and Assimilation

In recent years, more than 15 states in the United States have passed laws that require immigrants to understand English in order to use public services. Some "English-only" laws simply state that English is the official state language, while others prohibit giving state applications, forms, and driver's license exams in any language other than English.[38]

When discussing the social polices related to the English-only movement, sociologists often use the terms "multiculturalism" and "assimilation." Supporters of multiculturalism believe that people should be allowed to adapt to a new culture.. People who favor assimilation often criticize multiculturalism because they believe that immigrants should adapt to society. Society does not need to adapt to immigrants.

Is one theory better than the other is? Sociologist Ruben Rumbaut explores immigrant assimilation by reviewing a variety of studies.[39] Traditionally, experts believed that assimilation occurred in a linear process. Immigrants began to assimilate by learning the language and then incorporated other parts of the culture into their lives. Rumbaut finds that this linear idea is not valid. Assimilation varies based on the immigrant's time of entry into the country and country of origin. Many of today's immigrants come from countries with little understanding of industrialization and democracy, which limits the process by which they assimilate. Under these conditions, coerced rapid assimilation has a negative impact on successful immigrant adaptation. Recent research shows that immigrants improve their chances of successful adaptation if they remain tied to their own culture and remain bilingual.[40]

Those who support aggressive assimilation policies view the policies as a way to functionally support the country's unity and ease the fear that a bilingual society would negatively affect the country. Interestingly, as an individual's education level increases, the likelihood of supporting "English only" laws decreases. Therefore, college graduates are more likely to realize that successful immigrant adaptation occurs slowly and cannot be forced.[41]

ACTIVITIES

1. Research the laws in your state. In what languages other than English can a person take a driver's license test?
2. Imagine that you moved to another country and were banned from speaking English. How might you feel? What would you do to adapt?
3. Visit an English as a second language classroom in a school in your community. Ask the teacher about the importance of language in cultural transmission.

From Classroom to Community | Assisting Immigrants

"I didn't know what I was getting into."

Sonya, a 22-year-old, bilingual, United States-born Latino student uttered these words when reflecting on an experience she had while working on a civic engagement project. When Sonya began volunteering at a local Latino development organization that offered legal, medical, and psychological help to Spanish-speaking immigrants, she could not imagine the life lessons she would learn.

"After the first week, I was given a case of an immigrant woman who needed help **getting medical care for her children,**"

Sonya recalled. The woman spoke very little English, and her husband had left her and her children about a year earlier. As a legal citizen of the United States, the woman was entitled to public assistance. However, she did not know how to get it.

The process was long and arduous, but Sonya did not falter. She followed the woman through the system and appealed each rejection along the way. Eventually, Sonya was able to help the woman find daycare assistance and food stamps, and she helped the woman collect child support from her ex-husband. The experience taught Sonya how not speaking English cripples many immigrants in the United States.

"If you can't speak English very well, you

cannot really negotiate the system. Even legal immigrants suffer in such an environment.

Fortunately, the Latino society is closely knit and more collective. This helped her to survive.

Without her community's support she would have had no hope to make a new and better life for herself and her children."

03

WHAT **IS CULTURE?**   48

the language, beliefs, values, norms, behaviors, and material objects that are important enough to pass on to future generations of a society

WHAT **DIFFERENTIATES ONE CULTURE FROM ANOTHER?**   58

language, gestures, values, perception and categorization of experiences, actions, norms, interaction of social structures, and struggle for scarce resources

HOW **DOES CULTURE INFLUENCE SOCIOLOGICAL THEORY AND STUDY?**   61

culture: affects how we perceive things; guides our thoughts and actions; must be studied while keeping these differences in mind

get the topic: WHAT IS CULTURE?

Material Culture   49
Nonmaterial Culture   49
Additional Values   54
Norms and Sanctions   54

The Study of Culture   54
Symbolic Interaction—A Crisis of Values   58
Functionalism—Communitarianism   59
Conflict Theory—The McDonaldization of the
    United States   59

Social Policy: Multiculturalism and Assimilation   61

Theory

FUNCTIONALISM   58

- culture (shared values and norms) holds society together through shared values and norms
- interaction of social structures
- society must have a balanced relationship between the community, the market, and the government
- communitarians (free markets and private ownership of businesses)

CONFLICT THEORY   59

- society struggles for resources
- societies win resources by using McDonaldization process (efficiency, calculability, predictability, and technology)

- convenience over quality
- only the wealthy benefit: wages drop, inequality increases, short-term profits rise

SYMBOLIC INTERACTIONISM   59

- traditional vs. secular values
- three hypotheses: trend, comparison, and distribution
- individualist and traditional values result in higher rates if murder, poverty, and out-of-wedlock births
- U.S. citizens becoming more traditional, not secular

Key Terms

culture is the language, beliefs, values, norms, behaviors, and material objects that are passed on to future generations of society.   *48*

material culture consists of items within a culture that you can taste, touch, and feel.   *49*

nonmaterial culture consists of the nonphysical products of society, including our symbols, values, rules, and sanctions.   *49*

symbols represent, suggest, or stand for something else.   *49*

language is a system of speech and/or written symbols used to convey meaning and communicate.   *49*

cultural transmission is culture passing from one generation to the next through language.   *50*

Sapir-Whorf hypothesis is a hypothesis, first advanced by Edward Sapir in 1929 and subsequently developed by Benjamin Whorf, that the structure of a language determines a native speaker's perception and categorization of experience.   *50*

gestures are symbols we make using our bodies, such as facial expressions, hand movements, eye contact, and other types of body language.   *51*

values are a part of a society's nonmaterial culture that represent cultural standards by which we determine what is good, bad, right, or wrong.   *51*

value pairs help us define values, usually in terms of opposites.   *51*

value clusters are two or more values that support each other.   *54*

value conflict occurs when two or more values are at odds.   *51*

norms are rules developed for appropriate behavior based on specific values that are conditional.   *54*

sanction is a prize or punishment you receive when you either abide by a norm or violate it.   *54*

folkways are informal types of norms.   *54*

mores are norms that represent a community's most important values.   *54*

taboo is an act that is socially unacceptable.   *54*

ethnocentrism occurs when a person uses his or her own culture to judge another culture.   *55*

xenophobia refers to fear and hostility toward people who are from other countries or cultures.   *55*

xenocentrism is perceiving other groups or societies as superior to your own. *55*

cultural relativism means making a deliberate effort to appreciate a group's ways of life without prejudice. *55*

normative relativism is the evaluation of a society based on that society's norms. *55*

cultural lag happens when social and cultural changes occur at a slower pace than technological changes. *55*

culture shock occurs when a person encounters a foreign culture and has an emotional response to the differences between the cultures. *56*

subculture is a subset of the dominant culture that has distinct values, beliefs, and norms. *56*

countercultures are groups with value systems that are in opposition to the dominant group's values. *56*

multiculturalism is a concept supporting the inherent value of different cultures

within society. *56*

assimilation is the process by which minority groups adopt the patterns of the dominant culture. *56*

global village refers to the "shrinking" of the world through immediate electronic communications. *57*

Sample Test Questions

These multiple-choice questions are similar to those found in the test bank that accompanies this textbook.

1. Norms include all of the following *except*
   a. folkways.
   b. mores.
   c. rules for behavior.
   d. definitions of beauty.

2. Which of the following statements is *false*?
   a. Values may cluster, but they cannot contradict.
   b. Values remain the same over time.
   c. Values are often defined by their opposite.
   d. Values exist in all societies.

3. Gestures are part of
   a. assimilation.
   b. material culture.
   c. nonmaterial culture.
   d. multiculturalism.

4. How does a counterculture form?
   a. When a subculture's values differ from the dominant group's values
   b. When a group maintains likes to aspects of their original culture
   c. When the dominant culture does not accept part of the group
   d. When the subculture adopts the values of the dominant culture

5. In order for sociologists to practice cultural relativism when studying polygamists in the United States, they must consider
   a. U.S. laws.
   b. U.S. norms.
   c. polygamist norms.
   d. cultural universals.

ESSAY

1. What aspects of Las Vegas culture may lead to the city's culture death?
2. How does culture influence sociological theory and study?
3. How might individualism lead to conflict?
4. How can a business benefit from the McDonaldization process?
5. How did Wayne Baker determine whether a crisis of values really exists in the United States?

WHERE TO START YOUR RESEARCH PAPER

To learn more about the McDonaldization of America, go to http://www.mcdonaldization.com

To find more information about attending college while traveling the world, go to http://www.semesteratsea.com

To learn more about the Small World project (the online experiment to test the idea that any two people in the world can be connected through only six others), go to http://smallworld.columbia.edu

To learn more about the communitarian movement, go to http://www.gwu.edu/~ccps/index.html

To find urban legends and myths as well as their origins and why they are not true, see http://www.snopes.com

For more information on international study options, go to http://www.studyabroad.com, http://www.studyabroadlinks.com

To find vital information to consider before studying abroad, go to http://travel.state.gov/travel/living/studying/studying_1238.html

For more information on international volunteering, go to http://www.crossculturalsolutions.org

To learn more about the Peace Corp, go to http://www.peacecorps.gov

ANSWERS: 1. a; 2. b; 3. c; 4. a; 5. c

Remember to check www.thethinkspot.com **for additional information, downloadable flashcards, and other helpful resources.**

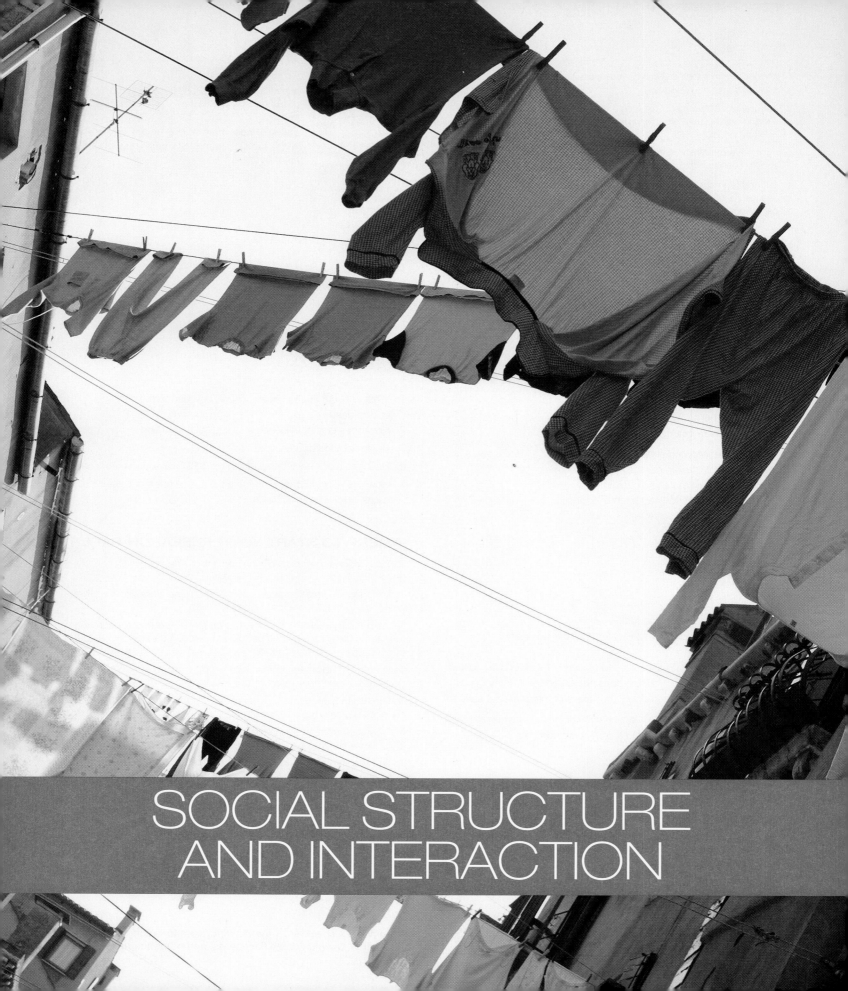

SOCIAL STRUCTURE
AND INTERACTION

"Being

poor is worse in the United States than it is in France. First, the French poor are less poor: the French welfare state is better equipped to redistribute income, and it has not experienced the rise in poverty seen in the United States in recent years. Second, poverty is mostly associated with long term unemployment in France, whereas in the United States the minimum wage is so low as to create a large segment of impoverished workers. Third, the French poor are less isolated than the American poor because the French public housing projects are more racially and ethnically diverse and bring together employed and unemployed people. By contrast, American public housing projects tend to contain a relatively homogenous population of unemployed urban blacks. French workers also have a less negative image of the poor than American counterparts, given the presence among the poor of many native-born whites, their lesser geographic concentration, and the weaker stigmatization of public project dwellers. Also, American mass media reinforce the association between poverty and blackness by underrepresenting whites in reporting on the poor."[1]

65

Micro *and* Macro Orientations

By studying workers in the United States and France, **Michèle Lamont illustrates that there is a clear link between the small-scale and large-scale components of a society.**

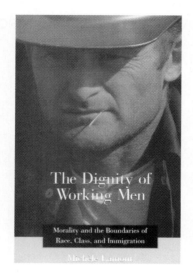

While working as a landscaper during my undergrad days, I witnessed firsthand the link Lamont describes in *The Dignity of Working Men: Morality and the Boundaries of Race, Class, and Immigration.* Most of the men with whom I worked had high school diplomas, but none had any hope of having a career that did not include manual labor. Although we were all poor, I noticed a distinct difference between the ways whites interpreted their life chances compared with members of minority groups. One day, a panhandler came by and asked for a dollar. A white co-worker immediately launched into a vicious rant about the man's lazy lifestyle before he stormed off. I continued to watch as a Mexican American worker reached into his pocket and gave the man a dollar. I remember wondering about this disparity. Now I see that it's related to Lamont's claim that individual decisions are related to large-scale issues; in this case it was race.

One's race, Lamont argues, colors his or her opinions of general social issues like poverty. Whites in the United States, for example, are more likely to ascribe economic success or failure to individual or moral causes, while African American workers view poverty as related to failures within the structures of the society. As you view any society, you'll find that the small interactions and the large components combine to create the social world.

get the topic: WHAT ELEMENTS CREATE A SOCIAL STRUCTURE?

Macrosociology and Microsociology

When Oceanic Flight 815 crashes in the middle of the ocean on the hit TV show *Lost,* the survivors find themselves washed up on the shores of a seemingly uncharted desert island. After recovering from the initial shock of the crash, some survivors search the island for signs of life or danger. Another group scours the wreckage for food and water. Still others battle mysterious clouds of black smoke and fend off polar bears; this *is* a fictional TV show after all, but you get the idea. Very quickly, fixed social positions are established. The survivors become hunters, warriors, builders, and cooks.

It soon becomes apparent that rescue is not imminent, so the survivors find ways to deal with death, crime, and outsiders. Rules are put into place and leaders are chosen. The survivors use their various medical, outdoors, and military experiences to help one another survive.

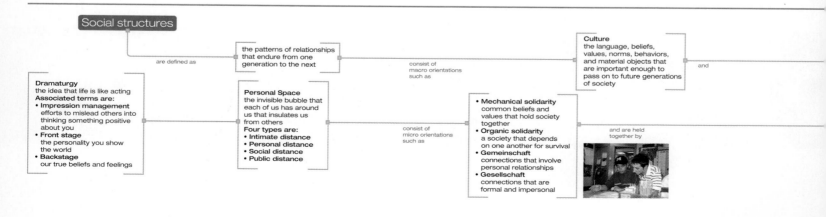

Social structures are defined as **the patterns of relationships that endure from one generation to the next** consist of macro orientations such as **Culture** the language, beliefs, values, norms, behaviors, and material objects that are important enough to pass on to future generations of society and

Dramaturgy
the idea that life is like acting
Associated terms are:
• **Impression management**
efforts to mislead others into thinking something positive about you
• **Front stage**
the personality you show the world
• **Backstage**
our true beliefs and feelings

Personal Space
the invisible bubble that each of us has around us that insulates us from others
Four types are:
• Intimate distance
• Personal distance
• Social distance
• Public distance

consist of micro orientations such as

• **Mechanical solidarity**
common beliefs and values that hold society together
• **Organic solidarity**
a society that depends on one another for survival
• **Gemeinschaft**
connections that involve personal relationships
• **Gesellschaft**
connections that are formal and impersonal

and are held together by

What does this example show us? It draws attention to two important components of society: the macro (large) elements and the micro (small) elements. On the island, the survivors developed both macro structures to accomplish needed tasks and micro orientations to ensure that their society would run smoothly. **Macrosociology** is the study of large-scale society, focusing on the social structures that exist within a society and examining how those structures create the social world. **Microsociology** deals primarily with the small interactions of daily life.

SOCIAL STRUCTURE

You've probably never had to think too hard about the way a society functions. That's because we often have an inherent understanding of how our society is structured. **Social structures** are patterns of relationships that endure from one generation to the next. They are the arrangement of systems—such as marriage, education, and work—by which people in a society interact and are able to live together.

Consider your position as a college student. When you first arrived on campus, you quickly learned that recruiters are not counselors and that talking with your professor about financial aid is probably not going to get you the correct information. The patterns of these relationships dictate their function. You learn academic information from faculty, and you get student loan advice from personnel in the financial aid office. The pattern of these relationships does not change much over time and becomes part of a university's culture.

Culture

Culture, discussed in depth in Chapter 3, is the language, beliefs, values, norms, behaviors, and material objects that are important enough to pass on to future generations of a society. The embedded structure of culture touches every aspect of our lives and is a large part of our society.

Groups

Groups are any number of people with similar norms, values, and behaviors who frequently interact with one another. Knitting clubs, government agencies, religious cults—all of these are groups. Residents living in the same apartment complex aren't necessarily a group because they may rarely hang out together.

Sociologist Charles H. Cooley suggests that we divide ourselves into two types of groups: primary and secondary.[2] **Primary groups** are small, intimate, and enduring. Your family and close friends are primary groups to which you belong. **Secondary groups** are formal, superficial, and temporary. Your relationship to your classmates is probably a secondary group. The line between these two types of groups is not always clear-cut, but we have far more secondary groups than primary ones. You'll learn more about groups and group interactions in Chapter 6.

MACROSOCIOLOGY is the study of large-scale society, focusing on the social structures that exist within a society and examining how those structures create the social world.

MICROSOCIOLOGY is the study of the small interactions of daily life.

SOCIAL STRUCTURES are patterns of relationships that endure from one generation to the next.

GROUPS are any number of people with similar norms, values, and behaviors who frequently interact with one another.

PRIMARY GROUPS are groups that are small, intimate, and enduring.

SECONDARY GROUPS are groups that are formal, superficial, and temporary.

SOCIAL CLASS is a group with similar access to power, wealth, and prestige.

Social Class

Social class, which will be discussed in more detail in Chapter 7, refers to a group with similar access to power, wealth, and prestige. The importance of social class varies depending upon the society. In the United States, for example, the working class makes up about 30 percent of the population.[3] The members of this social class are often the swing voters at election time. Although they are often treated as a unified group, Michèle Lamont's research finds that the working class frequently remains divided along racial lines.

Your social class can have a profound impact on your life, especially the length of it. Studies have shown that one's social class can affect his or her health, happiness, and life span. In England, researchers have found that the life expectancy of professional women is far longer than women who are unskilled laborers.

85.1 years
Life expectancy of a woman from a high social class, such as a doctor, lawyer, or accountant

78.1 years
Life expectancy of a woman from a low social class, such as an unskilled laborer, maid, or messenger

Source: Data from the "Wealthy, Healthy, and Aged 85: The Women Living Even Longer" by Jill Sheerman.

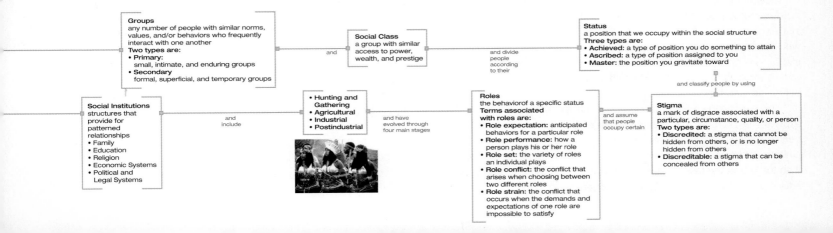

Groups
any number of people with similar norms, values, and/or behaviors who frequently interact with one another
Two types are:
• **Primary:**
  small, intimate, and enduring groups
• **Secondary**
  formal, superficial, and temporary groups

and

Social Class
a group with similar access to power, wealth, and prestige

and divide people according to their

Status
a position that we occupy within the social structure
Three types are:
• **Achieved:** a type of position you do something to attain
• **Ascribed:** a type of position assigned to you
• **Master:** the position you gravitate toward

and classify people by using

Social Institutions
structures that provide for patterned relationships
• Family
• Education
• Religion
• Economic Systems
• Political and Legal Systems

and include

• Hunting and Gathering
• Agricultural
• Industrial
• Postindustrial

and have evolved through four main stages

Roles
the behavior of a specific status
Terms associated with roles are:
• **Role expectation:** anticipated behaviors for a particular role
• **Role performance:** how a person plays his or her role
• **Role set:** the variety of roles an individual plays
• **Role conflict:** the conflict that arises when choosing between two different roles
• **Role strain:** the conflict that occurs when the demands and expectations of one role are impossible to satisfy

and assume that people occupy certain

Stigma
a mark of disgrace associated with a particular, circumstance, quality, or person
Two types are:
• **Discredited:** a stigma that cannot be hidden from others, or is no longer hidden from others
• **Discreditable:** a stigma that can be concealed from others

Social Class in China:

While some cultures don't have a rigid social class system, others have a well-established system. Take, for example, the Hukou system used in China immediately after the Communist Revolution. Under this system, once a person registered in a specific geographic area—rural or urban—he or she was not allowed to move far beyond the area. This fixed system gave city dwellers the advantages of better access to education and more opportunity for advancement than those living in rural areas.

Today, groups of workers in rural areas are predominantly male and make up emerging social classes. In the rural areas of modern China, being connected to the government is far less important than it is in urban areas where Communist party membership can be vital to a person's success. Therefore, in urban areas class systems are significantly different than they are in rural areas. For one thing, they're much more fluid and allow for more movement than rural divisions do.

In the rigid rural class system, people do not have much freedom to move up and down the hierarchy. The rural system from top to bottom includes cadres, capitalists, managers, household business owners, professionals, wage laborers, and peasants.

For the urban class, the system is more flexible. The urban social class system from top to bottom includes capitalist entrepreneurs, intellectuals and professionals, members of the middle and working class, and the poor.

Because of the increasing fluidity of China's social systems, people are able to change the social class in which they belong. Receiving an education and owning a business are two ways that people raise their social standing.[4]

Social Status

Visit a trendy Hollywood hotspot like Spago's, and you'll probably wait hours for a table, if you can even get in at all. Of course, if you're Brad Pitt or Angelina Jolie, you'll be whisked in through the front door with an army of paparazzi chronicling your every move. So what's the difference? Pitt and Jolie are movie stars, and you're not. And in our fame-obsessed society, celebrities have reached a certain social status. **Status** refers to the position that a person occupies within the social structure and is often closely linked to social class. The wealthier and more powerful you are, the higher your social status will be. Often, a person's value to society does not determine his or her social status. For example, doctors enjoy high social status, while garbage collectors are looked down upon. However, if we had no more garbage collectors, a social crisis would arise more quickly than if we had no more doctors.

Sociologists divide status into two different types: achieved and ascribed. **Achieved status** refers to a type of position that someone earns or does something to attain. When you finish your college degree, you'll have *achieved* the position of college graduate. **Ascribed status** describes a position in society that is given or assigned. For example, socialite Paris Hilton's fame is an ascribed status. Because she was born into a wealthy and famous family, she draws attention at red-carpet events and enjoys the privileges of a celebrity. Paris didn't choose to be wealthy, just like you didn't choose your gender, race, or ethnicity. Ascribed statuses are given to us at birth—we do not make a decision to choose them.

Most of us occupy a number of positions in our lives. For example, I am an author, college professor, husband, father, son, and brother, just to name a few. Since we all occupy more than one status in life, we will gravitate toward one that we call a **master status**. The master status may be what is most important to us, such as our status as a parent, or what is most important to others, such as one's race or economic standing.

People often perceive individuals who have high status to be experts in fields other than their professions. Oldmeadow et al. find that personal status impacts others' perceptions.[5] In a study of student athletes, Oldmeadow found that team captains have a higher status than the rest of the team.[6] Thus, team members are likely to follow the advice of their captains even in areas unrelated to their particular sport.[7] The status of being a captain carries with it power. Some statuses in our society, such as judge, doctor, and professor, carry instant authority. People in other positions may be discounted when giving their opinions. For example, although a student may have more knowledge in a particular area, he or she may defer to the professor's wisdom on the topic because the professor has achieved a certain status and is deemed wise.

Status is an important social construct because **the positions we occupy lead to the roles we play.**

Social Roles

When you enter a classroom, you sit in the chairs designated for students. You don't go to the front of the room and stand behind the podium. You understand that your status is that of a student and so you play the role of student, not teacher. A **role** is the behavior of a specific status, and your status affects the role you play. If the professor asked you to lecture without any advance notice, you'd probably think something was wrong. This is because the roles we play come with certain expectations about how to play those roles.

Role expectations are the anticipated behaviors for a particular role. When you go to the doctor, you do as the doctor says, even if you have never met him or her before. This is because the statuses of doctor and patient define the roles. However, if the doctor is rude or obviously uninterested in your care, you'll say he or she has a "bad bedside manner." We tend to view people as less capable when they do not fill their role expectations as socially gracefully as we would hope.

Role expectations dominate our lives. When you refer to a "bad date," it's usually because you expected one thing and got something else. We evaluate **role performance** on whether or not a person plays the role in a manner we expect. It's important to remember that role expectations can be reasonable or unreasonable. If you expect your professor to make this course a cakewalk, you're probably going to be disappointed because you have an unreasonable expectation. If you then trash your instructor on a rate-your-professor Web site, it's because you judged his or her performance negatively based on your role expectation.

Robert Merton clarifies other important components of roles.[8] We all play a variety of roles, which makes up our role set. As a college student, you might also play the role of child, employee, parent, or spouse, and when playing these multiple roles, you might find you have to choose between the competing demands of those roles—a phenomenon known as **role conflict**. This happens when you need to study for a final exam to satisfy your role as a student the same night you need to attend your dad's retirement party to satisfy your role as a child.

At other times, we may feel **role strain**. This occurs when the demands and expectations of one role are impossible for us to satisfy. You might feel role strain when deciding whether to go out to a party on Saturday night or cram for the midterm that Monday.

The ways in which status and roles influence our lives often goes unnoticed. We expect the cashier at the grocery store to take our money and send us on our way. If he or she talks too much, we might get annoyed. The setting influences our expectations.

For example, in Iran, the Supreme Leader of the nation is the ultimate religious authority who is also the highest ranking authority figure in the government. Meanwhile, the president of Iran has far less political power, especially in areas of governmental policy. These roles are just the opposite in the United States, where religious leaders may influence political decisions, but are not allowed to implement laws and policies directly. The variety of statuses and roles depends upon the type of society.

Stigmas

Any convict who's been released from prison will tell you that life on the "outside" is no picnic. That's because people who serve time for a crime and then rejoin society carry with them the label of "ex-con" for the rest of their lives. In other words, we attach a **stigma**, or a mark of disgrace associated with a particular status, quality, or person, to the ex-convict. Sometimes, one's age, religion, sexual orientation, economic status, or race can result in a stigma.

STATUS is the position that you occupy within the social structure, which is often closely linked to social class.

ACHIEVED STATUS is a type of position that you earn or do something to attain.

ASCRIBED STATUS is a position in society that is given or assigned.

MASTER STATUS is the status toward which we gravitate.

ROLE is the behavior of a specific status.

ROLE EXPECTATIONS are the anticipated behaviors for a particular role.

ROLE PERFORMANCE is the degree to which a person plays the role in a manner we expect.

ROLE CONFLICT is a phenomenon occurring when one is forced to choose between the competing demands of multiple roles.

ROLE STRAIN occurs when the demands and expectations of one role are impossible for us to satisfy.

STIGMA is a mark of disgrace associated with a particular status, quality, or person.

DISCREDITED STIGMA is a stigma that cannot be hidden from others or is no longer hidden from others.

DISCREDITABLE STIGMA is a stigma that can be concealed from others.

Sociologist Erving Goffman suggests that we all have a positive ideal identity that we hope others will accept.[9] Unfortunately, a stigma points out the differences between our ideal and real selves. There are two types of stigma—discredited stigma and discreditable stigma. A **discredited stigma** is a stigma that cannot be hidden from others, or is no longer hidden from others. A person with a physical handicap has a discredited stigma. A **discreditable stigma** is a stigma that can be concealed from others, such as sexual orientation, STDs, and criminal history.

For example, in *The Dignity of Working Men,* Lamont describes how white and African American workers stigmatized others. Many white workers were more likely to hold the poor in contempt and view African Americans as lazy, unmotivated individuals, whereas many African American workers viewed whites as domineering, controlling, and lacking warmth.

<<< Here, the roles seem to have reversed. We'd normally expect the adult to play the role of the doctor, while the child plays the role of the patient.

STAGES OF SOCIETAL CHANGE

As societies change over time, the complexity of social interaction also changes. With increasing population and technological advancement, societies have become more diverse, which leads to changes in the social structures. American sociologist Gerhard E. Lenski is one of the few theorists who maintain an evolutionary view of society. According to Lenski et al., the evolution of society consists of four main stages—hunting and gathering, agricultural, industrial, and postindustrial.[10]

Hunting and Gathering Societies

Have you ever wondered how you might survive if you were forced to become a hunter-gatherer? Recently, some friends and I took a camping trip to the Boundary Waters Canoe Area in northern Minnesota. In such a place, you have only what you bring with you. And if you want to eat, you'd better learn how to fish. I can't say we had much luck living off the land; the one fish I did manage to catch was hardly enough to feed us all. Luckily, the dehydrated food in our backpacks was enough to sustain us.

Of course, the first hunter-gatherers didn't rely on dehydrated food to survive, but they did live off the land and focused most of their efforts on finding food. Archeological evidence supports the idea that Homo sapiens lived as hunters and gatherers approximately 50,000 years ago. Beginning in the Neolithic period, hunters and gatherers existed in small groups of approximately 150 people for about 2,000 generations. Over this period, their culture and population changed slowly.[11]

In hunting and gathering societies, an individual's status and role were closely linked. Thus, the status of tribal leader was often given to the strongest person or the best hunter. Because there were few roles for people to play in these types of societies, Lenski suggested that the division of labor in hunting and gathering societies was very limited.[12] Everyone in the society had to be involved in the production of food for survival.

Successful hunters and gatherers adapted to their environment. Geography professor Jared Diamond shows that food supply and available natural resources dictate a great deal about the form of society.[13] People living in areas with abundant food were able to hunt and gather for longer periods than those living in cold climates. Geological differences fostered human innovation. For example, farming and raising animals occurred in areas that supported crop growth and had a suitable climate for animals. This transition ushered in the agricultural stage of society.

Agricultural Societies

Approximately 10,000 years ago, people began to move from hunting and gathering to agrarian-based societies.[14] With this change, society became more complex. Lenski et al. divided agricultural societies into two groups: (1) pastoral and horticultural societies and (2) agricultural groups.[15]

Pastoral and horticultural societies appeared when humans learned to domesticate plants and animals. Members of these societies learned to use simple hand tools to till the soil and plant seeds in order to grow grains for food. They figured out that certain grains could be planted in soft ground. Likewise, they developed ways to raise certain types of animals in captivity, such as cows, goats, and chickens, which increased their food supply and allowed them to become less nomadic.[16]

Around 5,000 to 7,000 years ago, some groups took yet another step in the evolution of society. With the invention of the plow, agricultural societies arose. The simple technology of the animal-drawn plow—a sharp, hard piece of stone, wood, or metal that tills the soil—helped people cultivate lands that were previously unusable. The dramatic increase in food production promoted the growth of cities.[17] These agrarian city-states were often quite large, with up to one million people. Humans lived for approximately 500 generations in agrarian cultures.[18]

The Stages of Societal Change

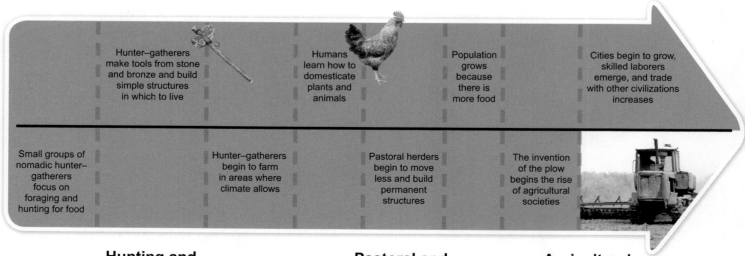

Hunter–gatherers make tools from stone and bronze and build simple structures in which to live

Humans learn how to domesticate plants and animals

Population grows because there is more food

Cities begin to grow, skilled laborers emerge, and trade with other civilizations increases

Small groups of nomadic hunter–gatherers focus on foraging and hunting for food

Hunter–gatherers begin to farm in areas where climate allows

Pastoral herders begin to move less and build permanent structures

The invention of the plow begins the rise of agricultural societies

Hunting and Gathering Societies

Pastoral and Horticultural Societies

Agricultural Societies

Industrial Societies

During the 17th and 18th centuries, the Western world experienced an industrial revolution. Complex machines, such as the steam engine, encouraged the growth of industry. Steam-powered machines made human labor more efficient because the machines could perform a simple task quickly and repeatedly without rest.[19] The steam engine revolutionized the clothing industry, for example, because fabric no longer had to be hand-woven. Machines mass-produced fabric, which reduced the cost of labor.

This basic idea, using technology to create goods, greatly expanded the surplus of industrial societies. Farming techniques improved through mechanization, and early tractors expanded the farmable land even more. Fewer people were required to produce sufficient food for the population, which allowed for even more specialization of labor. As a result, more new types of jobs were created that ultimately led to new statuses and roles.

Lenski et al. suggested that industrial societies actually have less social inequality than agrarian societies.[20] This is largely because the increasing technology and surplus improve the standard of living. Even the poorest people in industrial societies have access to goods and services that are unavailable in agrarian societies. Working-class men, like the group Lamont studies in *The Dignity of Working Men*, exist in industrial societies.

The industrial society lasted only nine generations in some parts of the world, although it continues in others. The change occurred in some areas as a new form of society began—the postindustrial society.[21]

Postindustrial Societies

The term *postindustrial society* refers to the societal change that occurs when people move from an economy based on manufacturing to one based on service and technology. Such societies still require basic food and manufactured goods, but seek them from other countries. Before this stage, it's possible for a society to live off its natural resources. Since postindustrial societies can no longer meet their own needs, energy, food, and goods must be imported. These societies have become societies vested in a technology that grew exponentially with the invention of the microchip.

Sociologist Daniel Bell suggested three key characteristics of a postindustrial society: (1) a shift from manufacturing to services, (2) the centrality of the new science-based industries, and (3) the rise of new technical elites. These characteristics bring about changes in status and power.[22] The creation of wealth is no longer rooted in controlling land or building factories. Power and wealth are associated with who controls and develops the latest technology. Thus, Bill Gates became the richest man in the world by developing computer software.

Postindustrial societies have great surpluses of wealth and goods. Their material culture is the most developed of all societal forms. Consider the fact that even the poorest person in your neighborhood probably owns a phone or a television. Although these societies do not provide dramatic changes in where people live or how they are governed, the advances of technology expand divisions of labor and increase international interdependence.

SOCIAL INSTITUTIONS

Although hunting and gathering, agricultural, industrial, and post-industrial societies are very different, they all share — social institutions. **Social institutions** are structures that provide for patterned relationships.

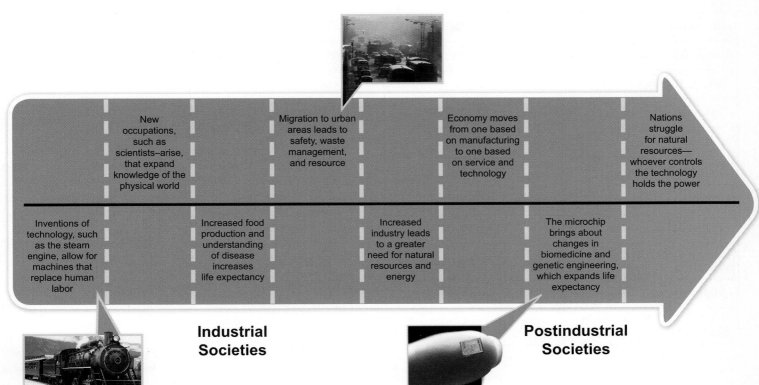

Industrial Societies

New occupations, such as scientists–arise, that expand knowledge of the physical world

Inventions of technology, such as the steam engine, allow for machines that replace human labor

Increased food production and understanding of disease increases life expectancy

Migration to urban areas leads to safety, waste management, and resource

Increased industry leads to a greater need for natural resources and energy

Economy moves from one based on manufacturing to one based on service and technology

The microchip brings about changes in biomedicine and genetic engineering, which expands life expectancy

Nations struggle for natural resources— whoever controls the technology holds the power

Postindustrial Societies

GEMEINSCHAFT refers to community connections involving personal relationships based on friendship and kinship ties, such as family.

GESELLSCHAFT refers to societal connections that are more formal and impersonal.

In other words, the roles and statuses are already established and the members of society merely need to step into them. It's important to note that the specifics of these institutions change with the type of society and the culture of the people being studied.

Family

Families, which are discussed in greater detail in Chapter 14, are a cultural universal. The form of the family may have changed a great deal throughout human history, but the institution of family has remained constant.[23] Families teach the value of sharing and mutual support. They provide safety and security needs for their members, pass on important values, and offer a safe haven for raising children and caring for the elderly.

Educational and Religious Systems

Two more cultural universals, education and religion (discussed in depth in Chapter 15), assist in socialization. Educational systems transfer the knowledge and information of the society to new members and can be both formal and informal.

Every region has some type of educational system, even though every child does not always participate in that system.

Secondary School Net Enrollment Rate in World Regions, 2006	
Developed Regions	**92%**
Developing Regions	**54%**
Sub-Saharan Africa	25%
Oceania	33%
Southern Asia	54%
Western Asia	58%
Northern Africa	60%
Southeastern Africa	63%
Latin America & the Caribbean	67%
Eastern Asia	68%
Transitional Countries in South and Eastern Europe	84%

Source: Data from the United Nations, *The Millennium Development Goals Report,* 2007

Religious practice varies a great deal depending upon a person's culture, but most religions unify people through an organized system of beliefs. By bringing people together, religion stabilizes society and provides a framework for people to live their lives.

Economic Systems

From the time of the earliest hunters and gatherers to today, societies have needed a system that helps people get what they need. Economic systems (discussed in Chapter 16) allow for the consumption, production, and orderly transition of goods from one person to another. If, for example, you want a new TV, you understand how to trade money to get it. Without an economic system, people either do without or steal. Either option would make for a dangerous and chaotic society.

Early economic systems involved bartering—the trading of goods from one person to another. As societies became more complex, the currency of coins and money became the default value source, allowing for quicker and easier transitions of goods and services. Although bartering is often thought of as an ancient system, there are modern-day examples of the barter system on Web sites such as Craigslist. Craigslist gives users a forum to post free classified ads for jobs, internships, housing, and personals.

To keep a society's economic system running smoothly and efficiently, rules must be established. That's why every society has political and legal systems to help establish rules for society at large.

Political and Legal Systems

Ever since the first chief in the first hunter-gatherer tribe was named, people have been involved in politics. Political systems, which are described in Chapter 16, distribute power in a society, and power is the key component of any political system, whether a dictatorship or democracy. As you consider the importance of political systems, it's crucial to understand how power is used.

Political power is used to create laws or rules that dictate right and wrong in society. So, the political and legal systems are integrally linked. When someone with power sees something that's wrong, he or she is likely to create a law to fix it. The legal system serves the vital function of enforcing those laws to maintain social order and promote unity.

Although the form may vary, family, education, religion, economics, politics, and legislation exist in every form of society. That makes these institutions social facts. As we have seen, societies become more complex as they develop; this complexity witnesses the replacement of many of the old ways of living and thinking.

HOLDING SOCIETY TOGETHER

On May 3, 1999, tornadoes ravaged the Midwest. In the immediate aftermath, I volunteered to help the survivors. As a sociologist, I was amazed to see the extent of people's generosity. All we had to do was tell the media we needed something, and as soon our request was on the air, the items would arrive. Why? Because in the Midwest, a tornado cleanup tends to unify people.

What exactly holds a society together? Solidarity. That's the "glue" that binds a society.

Mechanical and Organic Solidarity

Think back to Chapter 1, when you first learned about Emile Durkheim and solidarity, the shared values, needs, and beliefs of a society. He suggested that simple forms of society have mechanical solidarity, whereas organic solidarity holds more complex societies together. In societies with mechanical solidarity, people's common beliefs and practices help bind them together. On the other hand, the interdependence of the people is what holds societies with organic society together. Durkheim's idea led German sociologist Ferdinand Tonnies to investigate how the form of society affects the interactions that we might have.

Gemeinschaft and Gesellschaft

Society can be classified into two distinct groups: *Gemeinschaft* (or community) and *Gesellschaft* (or society).[24] **Gemeinschaft** connections involve personal relationships based on friendship and kinship ties, such as the family. A society's form can also influence the type of group. For example, small bands of hunters and gatherers live in communal societies because they have very little division of labor. This creates a group that exists with shared values, goals, and beliefs.

Often we also engage in groups considered as **Gesellschaft**. These relationships are more formal and impersonal. Urban life is filled with many impersonal interchanges, so groups living here are more likely to occur in industrial and postindustrial societies. In such a society, social status, role, and social class become very important. Are you interested in knowing the janitor who cleans the classroom? You're probably only

aware that the seats and floor are clean. Tonnies suggested that as societies grow more complex, many of our interactions invariably become more impersonal.

As you review these ideas, you can see that large cities tend toward *Gesellschaft* relationships, while smaller ones tend to be more *Gemeinschaft*. That means the size of your immediate area influences your daily life.[25] This idea leads sociologists to look for other common behavior patterns. To do this, we turn from large-scale observations and review the sociological study of small orientations.

∧
∧
∧ Since people have virtually the same job, **mechanical solidarity** creates a common moral order that **holds people together.**

THINK SOCIOLOGICALLY

Social Class and Character Traits

In *The Dignity of Working Men: Morality and the Boundaries of Race, Class, and Immigration*, Michèle Lamont describes how working-class men view members of the upper class. Many believe that a person's class connotes specific traits. For example, an "auto mechanic describes himself as mid-

dle class because he shares, '[T]his whole idea of being concerned a little more about other things rather than your immediate self. That for me starts to define middle class.'"[26] Working-class men pick up on this feeling from middle-class workers that they are somehow morally inferior. Working-class men believe middle-class workers purposefully distance themselves from people "who are not

their own kind."[27] They point out specific attributes they associate with middle-class behavior, such as insensitivity, snobbery, and narrow-mindedness.

Generally, when people hear the terms working, middle, and upper class, they think of occupation and salary, not necessarily character. But do these terms also connote specific personal characteristics?

PERSONAL SPACE is the invisible bubble that each of us has around us that insulates us from others.

INTIMATE DISTANCE is distance reserved for those with whom we are very close.

PERSONAL DISTANCE is distance that ranges from 18 inches to 4 feet; this distance is for normal conversations.

SOCIAL DISTANCE is distance that ranges from about 4 feet to 12 feet and is usually reserved for formal settings.

PUBLIC DISTANCE is the zone of interaction that is used in highly formal settings; this distance includes everything greater than 12 feet.

IMPRESSION MANAGEMENT is management of the impression that the performer makes on others.

FRONT STAGE is what the audience sees, or the part of ourselves that we present to others.

BACKSTAGE is the demeanor that incorporates our true feelings and beliefs.

Just as you adjust the personal distance between yourself and others depending on the situation, you probably also adjust your behavior so that it's appropriate for the setting you're in. **When you're in public, you often show off your best self to others and hide what you don't want them to see.**

Micro Orientations: Social Interactions

Generally, macro orientations take for granted that society exists. Additionally, less emphasis is placed on the ways in which societies are held together. Thus, symbolic interactionists tend to study the "how" of society, as opposed to the "what." Instead of observing what binds a society together, these sociologists seek to discover how that society is held together.

Communication is one component of the "how" of the social world. However, communication involves more than simply having conversations. From verbal interaction to physical distance, effective communication requires knowledge of the things that inform how we communicate with one another. One of those things, **personal space**, refers to the invisible bubble that each of us has around us that insulates us from others.

PERSONAL SPACE

How do you feel when someone stands very close to you during a conversation? It's a little uncomfortable, right? Even if the person is a friend, your natural impulse is to back away.

Our feelings about personal space often depend upon the setting and the person with whom we are interacting. For example, in order for a doctor to properly examine you, she needs to enter your personal space. In a different setting, you would never allow such behavior. Although socially appropriate amounts of personal space vary between cultures, Edward Hall suggests that people in the United States have four discrete zones of personal space.[28]

1 We reserve **intimate distance** for those with whom we are very close. This zone covers roughly from 0 to 18 inches. We generally reserve this distance for intimate encounters, but these conditions may vary depending on setting.

2 **Personal distance** ranges from 18 inches to 4 feet. Normal conversations occur at a personal distance. When you share secrets with a friend, you automatically lean in to an intimate distance. Once the whispering is over, though, you will automatically return to a personal distance.

Zones of Personal Space

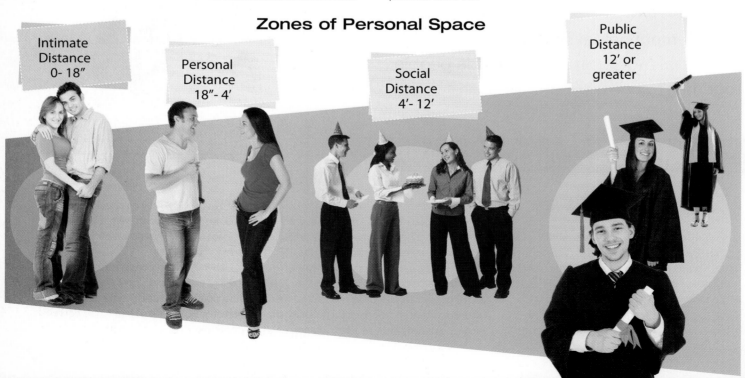

Intimate Distance 0- 18"

Personal Distance 18"- 4'

Social Distance 4'- 12'

Public Distance 12' or greater

3 **Social distance** ranges from about 4 feet to 12 feet and is usually reserved for formal settings. When you go on a job interview, for instance, you generally sit at what sociologist Edward Hall called "social distance."[29] Social encounters at this distance are not very personal. This distance allows the speaker to be heard, but does not presume any friendship.

4 **Public distance** refers to the zone of interaction that is used in highly formal settings. This distance includes everything greater than 12 feet. When you sit in the back of the classroom, you guarantee that you will maintain a public distance from your professor. Public distance also occurs during political speeches, at churches, and at formal events. Speakers are separate from the listener, and, generally, the audience shows respect and deference to the speaker.

DRAMATURGY

"All the world's a stage," Shakespeare wrote in *As You Like It*. Though he wasn't technically a sociologist, the Bard may have been more accurate than he realized. Erving Goffman developed a theory of interaction called dramaturgy, which suggests that life is like acting.[30] Social actors enter every situation with two possible selves. The first, the performer, attempts to manage the impressions that he or she makes on others. Goffman termed this effort **impression management**.

EMBARRASSMENT is a state that occurs when we realize our act has failed.

FACE-SAVING WORK is a reaction to embarrassment in the form of either humor, anger, or retreat.

For example, if you think someone having an iced mocha at the corner coffee shop is attractive, you might want to make contact with him or her. As you approach, hoping to look "cool," you are entering the **front stage**. This is what the audience sees. Most of us live our lives on the front stage.

Of course, we are more than our front stage acts. **Backstage** demeanor incorporates our true feelings and beliefs. Most people do not show their backstage personas very often. We usually save that version of ourselves for our very closest family and friends.

Returning to our coffee shop example, let's assume that as you approach this person, you trip and fall. Obviously, you'll be embarrassed. **Embarrassment** occurs when we realize our act has failed. It's hard to pull off looking "cool" and tripping at the same time. When this type of mismatch happens, we engage in **face-saving work**. People generally choose one of three different options when they engage in face-saving work: humor, anger, or retreat.

Using humor, you can turn an embarrassing situation into a self-deprecating joke. This gives you the chance to impress upon the person that you have your act together because you can laugh at yourself.

In an angry reaction to this embarrassing situation, you may start cussing. This reaction is an attempt to say to the audience, "I'm powerful, even though I'm on the floor."

Efforts to retreat when we become embarrassed involve simply an attempt to escape. After all, our act has failed, and we want to leave the stage as soon as possible. The premise of Southwest Airlines' series of "Want to Get Away" ads, which feature people in uncomfortable situations, is based on this particular face-saving concept.

Goffman suggests that we would be wise to distrust most of what we see in other people because almost every interaction is front stage behavior. A wise student of Goffman can use impression management to get ahead in the world. Look at the Make Connections box and review the research there by Wayne and Liden.[31]

In March 2008, Eliot Spitzer, governor of New York, came under fire after news leaked that he was involved in a prostitution scandal and money laundering. Politicians try to craft their front stage selves to appear family oriented and honest; however, their backstage selves may tell a different story. **What other types of occupations require a person to have a highly controlled front stage demeanor?**[32]

MAKE CONNECTIONS

Using Impression Management to Get Ahead in the Workplace

No matter where you start your career, you probably hope to climb the ladder of success while you're there. You can impress your boss and chart your course to the corner office of your dreams by following the simple steps below.

Wayne and Liden showed that successful impression management techniques positively affect an employee's performance rating.[33] They found three components that influence successful performance reviews:

demographic similarity, supervisor-focused impression management, and self-focused impression management. **Demographic similarity** means that you share characteristics such as race, gender, or age, with your boss, coworkers, or others you encounter. **Supervisor-focused impression management** techniques involve flattering your boss and agreeing with your boss's opinions (or at least avoiding disagreements whenever possible). **Self-focused impression management** techniques include acting modest about your accomplishments (even if that modesty is false), boasting occasionally about your successes, and showing your

friendliness and self-assuredness through smiles and eye contact.

Most of us like people who are like us, and bosses are no different. By using either self-focused or supervisor-focused impression management techniques, you can advance your career and look forward to the day when your employees use impression management techniques to impress *you*.

>>> **ACTIVITY** The next time you hang out with a friend, act as though your friend is your boss and use the impression management techniques listed above. Record how he or she responds and share it with your class.

think sociologically: HOW DO THE THREE PARADIGMS VIEW SOCIAL STRUCTURES?

Now let's turn our attention from the specific terms and concepts of the macro/micro world, and look at it through the lens of the three sociological paradigms.

An Example of Symbolic Interactionism: The Thomas Theorem and the Social Creation of Reality

From the interactionist point of view comes the Thomas Theorem: "If men define situations as real, they are real in their consequences."[34] This statement describes the social construction of reality.

Think back to the chapter opener about how race can help dictate your own personal reality. White workers are more apt to view success as a personal achievement and are less concerned with issues such as equal opportunities or affirmative action. Many African Americans also believe in the "American Dream," but they understand there are obstacles that must be overcome in order to get there. Both groups believe that success is possible, but they have different opinions on what it takes to be successful. The social creation of reality emphasizes personal power; however, it does not deny the importance of social structures and their effect on us. We attach the meaning of events to them.

An Example of Functionalism: Studying Essential Features of Functional Social Structures

When functionalists study a topic, they often ask how various elements fit together. Social institutions and structures serve essential functions in a society. As you study social structures in later chapters, you will see a general functional framework that applies in virtually all cases. Durkheim (1858–1917) called these essential features "functional requisites."[35] Consider the five primary tasks of society that create social structures: (1) adaptation and replacement, (2) orientation and socialization, (3) production and economy, (4) social order, and (5) unity and purpose.

Adaptation and Replacement Effective and functional societies must get their needs met to survive. Jared Diamond suggests that

societies collapse unless they can accomplish certain tasks, including adapting to changes in the environment.[36] Adaptations are also essential for accommodating the changing relationships that a society has with the world around it.

Besides adapting to environmental and political changes, societies must also replace people who either die or leave the group. Without continually replacing people, societies cannot carry on.

Socialization and Orientation Closely tied to replacement are socialization and orientation of new members. When children are born, they need to be socialized into the group. Socialization and orientation are vital to the continuation of a society because these processes allow new members to join and assign them roles. In "traditional societies," this assigning of roles might include gender-specific tasks such as men hunting or women caring for children. In a postindustrial society, socialization and orientation can be much more formal and include teaching related social norms.

DEMOGRAPHIC SIMILARITY refers to shared characteristics such as race, gender, or age.

SUPERVISOR-FOCUSED IMPRESSION MANAGEMENT refers to techniques that involve flattering your boss and agreeing with your boss's opinions (or at least avoiding disagreements whenever possible).

SELF-FOCUSED IMPRESSION MANAGEMENT refers to techniques that include acting modest about your accomplishments (even if that modesty is false), boasting occasionally about your successes, and showing your friendliness and self-assuredness through smiles and eye contact.

∧
∧ **According to Durkheim, there are "functional requisites" that hold society together.** Think of the five tasks listed as puzzle pieces; if you're missing one, the puzzle isn't complete.

Socialization is not possible without some means to communicate. Societies create a system of symbols that include language and gestures to orient new members and to pass on information to the next generation. Socialization takes place in schools and families as well as through media, religion, and other structures found in various forms of society.

Production and Economy Production The ability of a society to meet its needs through its environment is the most important idea associated with this task. Simple societies create a material culture based on the resources at hand, whereas more complex societies trade with other groups to get the goods and services they need.[37] People within complex societies require an economic system to simplify the trading of goods and services. Although the exact nature of the economic system differs between societies, people always need a way to make or acquire the goods and services they need.

Social Order Because every society has people who cannot follow the rules, social norms and sanctions must be created to deal with these lawbreakers. In simple societies, force and strength might rule the day, whereas in complex societies, people settle disputes through legal battles. Not all societies have written laws, but they all socialize their members to promote social order.

Unity and Purpose Unity is achieved through common thoughts, beliefs, and attitudes. The United States is built on common ideals, not common heritage. Those shared thoughts united people, leading them to create a new country. Unity is also achieved through a sense of purpose, which gives a society some goal to achieve. This purpose holds people together, causing them to work together in times of trial.[38]

An Example of Conflict Theory: Deliberate Efforts to Weaken the Structure and Culture of Native Americans

In order to understand the interaction of micro and macro components, consider the conflict perspective of the interaction of Native Americans with European settlers. Be aware that the connections Native Americans had with whites varied, which makes historical sociological generalizations very difficult.

Long before whites arrived in North America, a variety of different Native American cultures emerged. Although tribal societies did fight between themselves, Native Americans clashed violently with the influx of Europeans in the country. Eventually, the newcomers assumed that every inch of land was open for settlement, and conflict increased.

After the so-called Indian Wars, the remaining Native Americans endured a process known as Americanizing. Striving to change both micro and macro components of Native American life, the goal was to teach them "white ways." The acculturation of Native Americans involved deliberate efforts to make them a part of the "melting pot" of the United States.[39]

When whites dominated various Native American cultures, they generally did so out of a desire to control land and gain wealth. Policies such as the Dawes Act were purportedly enacted to help Native Americans. However, the Dawes Act allowed whites guardianship over Native American lands. These policies did little more than dismantle the reservations in an effort to turn Native Americans into farmers.

Perhaps the most abusive form of Americanization involved the use of boarding schools. These schools existed to "educate" Native Americans by trying to destroy their culture and teach them to be "white" instead. The schools took children from their parents early in life and barred them from speaking their native tongue. Frequently, these children were not allowed to visit their parents at all. The misguided motivation behind the Americanization effort was supported by the desire to change the next generation of Native Americans into good citizens of the United States. Without any power to control their own lives, these children fit into neither the white world nor their own.[40]

The structures of family and the entire Native American population were weakened because the children were removed, thus leaving parents with no role to fill and children without the support they needed. Consequently, a generation of people was unschooled in their own culture. Whites saw the efforts to Americanize natives as a social program designed to help them assimilate, but Native Americans saw it as an example of cultural genocide.[41]

WRAP YOUR MIND AROUND THE THEORY

How do you think **these two people** from *Crash* might **define their situations?**

SYMBOLIC INTERACTIONISM

Symbolic interactionists believe that a person's social creation of reality may take into account social issues such as job opportunities, welfare policies, and unemployment. Experiences with these issues can have an effect on people, causing them to alter their creation of reality. Recall how impression management can be used to help you get ahead on the job. Bosses may take demographic differences into account. For example, in the 2004 movie *Crash*, Farhad, a Persian shop owner, incorrectly assumes that his Hispanic locksmith looted his shop. Farhad's belief that Hispanic men cannot be trusted leads him to take matters dramatically into his own hands.

WHY IS THERE SUCH A DISTINCTION BETWEEN THE WORKING CLASS AND OTHER CLASSES IN THE UNITED STATES?

FUNCTIONALISM

Social institutions and structures are essential functions for society. Sociologists believe that there are five basic structures necessary for a society to function. However, just because society is getting its needs met, this does not mean individual members of society are also having their needs fulfilled. The United States has a stable social structure, but millions and millions of people are living at or below the poverty level. Functionalists might suggest that for both the rich and poor, the economic system rewards those with ability and drive, while the system allows those who are less motivated to fall behind of their own merits. In Lamont's book, white factory workers tend to be functionalist while minorities see things differently. Why do you think there is a difference? Should people rethink the causes of poverty?

CONFLICT THEORY

Conflict theorists study issues such as race, social class, and inequality. After Hurricane Katrina hit the Gulf Coast and flooded parts of Louisiana, Mississippi, and Alabama, the federal government's response to the citizens there was widely criticized. Many people alleged that aid was delayed because a majority of struggling citizens were poor African Americans. Did the citizens' social class really affect their treatment? In Michèle Lamont's *The Dignity of Working Men,* she points out the current isolation of the U.S. poor from the rest of society. Public housing projects in most of the United States consist of homogenous populations in urban environments. Compare this to another country, like France, where public housing areas are racially, ethnically, and economically more diverse. Conflict theorists would perceive a pattern of inequality for the U.S. poor that does not occur on an international level.

Even though we are living in a stable society, millions of Americans are living in poverty. **How should society adapt to help these individuals?**

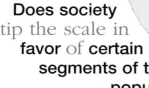

Does society tip the scale in **favor** of **certain segments of the population?**

discover sociology in action: HOW CAN SOCIAL POLICIES IMPROVE SOCIETY?

In our culture, social policies are applied in an effort to improve society. High-quality preschool is one such policy that provides an interaction between macro and micro components.

Social Policy— The Perry Preschool Project

Does early intervention assist children in negotiating the macro and micro components of American society? One study set out to find the answer by following students at Michigan's Perry Elementary School from 1960 to the present day.[42] Students enrolled in the preschool program there attended school for two and a half hours each morning, five days a week. Each child also received a weekly home visit from a teacher, during which the teacher worked with students on academic skills and guardians on parenting skills. All of the children were living in poverty at the time of the project.

The cost of this program was high when compared with standard preschool programs, mostly because teachers were extremely well qualified and were paid accordingly. The results support the notion that high-quality early childhood education improves students' lives in the long term, despite the students' socioeconomic backgrounds.

> **ACTIVITIES**
>
> 1. Visit a Head Start program in your area. Talk to the staff and the clients, and learn why early intervention is important. Consider spending some time helping them as a student volunteer.
> 2. What type of public funding does your state provide for preschool education? Does the state rank day care centers based on quality? If so, how?
> 3. Aside from preschool, what features act to strengthen U.S. society? What features weaken it?

In 2002, when the original Perry Preschool participants were about 40 years old, Lawrence Schweinhart examined their lives. The students who had participated in the revolutionary program reported better educational outcomes, higher salaries, and fewer arrests compared to those who did not participate. Furthermore, although the program was expensive to run, it actually saved money over the 42-year period. Most students in the program did not ultimately require special education, welfare, or incarceration, so fewer tax dollars were spent on these programs. Schweinhart's study shows that high-quality early childhood intervention can create significant positive changes in students' lives, the communities where they lived, and our society as a whole.[43]

Social policies, like preschool, help improve society. However, the quality of implementation drastically affects the outcome of the programs.

From Classroom to Community } Giving Kids a Head Start

Janet, a student in a sociology course, decided to volunteer at Head Start, a national educational program similar to the Perry Preschool Project that, largely due to a lack of funding, has never attained Perry's level of success.

She told our class, "The first thing I noticed was that the entire program was about socialization. The teachers taught the kids about rules and how to fit in. The children and parents both attend different classes designed to help them adapt to school and eventually be successful in it."

During her time as a volunteer, Janet helped set up classrooms, file necessary papers, and supervise the children during free time. "Playing with the kids was my favorite thing to do. I discovered that many of the things with which I was raised are rare for these children. For example, their clothes and toys were often used and torn. Some came to Head Start for lunch because their parents could not always afford food for them."

Janet saw her time at Head Start through the lenses of both functionalists and conflict theorists. "I couldn't help but think that this program was really there to help teach children how to fit into school and the larger society. In that way, it supports social control components of society and socializes children.

"However, the lack of staff and funding seemed to be the major issue facing my placement. I couldn't help but wonder why the program was so underfunded. It seems like people should be able to do more to help these kids learn."

WHAT ELEMENTS CREATE A SOCIAL STRUCTURE?   66

macrosociology and microsociology

HOW DO THE THREE PARADIGMS VIEW SOCIAL STRUCTURE?   76

functionalism: social institutions and structures serve essential functions in a society
conflict theory: the structure and culture of the underprivileged are deliberately weakened for the benefit of the dominant group
symbolic interactionism: social construction of reality: "If men define situations as real, they are real in their consequences"

HOW CAN SOCIAL POLICIES IMPROVE SOCIETY?   79

high-quality preschool programs: improve the lives of the participants; decrease the amount of funding needed for other social programs (special education, welfare)

get the topic: WHAT ELEMENTS CREATE A SOCIAL STRUCTURE?

Macrosociology and Microsociology   66
Micro Orientations: Social Interactions   74
An Example of Symbolic Interactionism: The Thomas Theorem and the Social Creation of Reality   76

An Example of Functionalism: Studying Essential Features of Functional Social Structures   76

An Example of Conflict Theory: Deliberate Efforts to Weaken the Structure and Culture of Native Americans   77
Social Policy—The Perry Preschool Project   79

Theory

FUNCTIONALISM   76

- social institutions and structures are essential functions for society
- five primary tasks of society that create social structures: (1) adaptation and replacement, (2) orientation and socialization, (3) production and economy, (4) social order, (5) unity and purpose
- just because society is having its needs met, this does not mean individual members of society are also having their needs fulfilled

CONFLICT THEORY   77

- study issues such as race, social class, and inequality

- conflict theorists perceive a pattern of inequality for the U.S. poor that does not occur on an international level, such as Hurricane Katrina relief

SYMBOLIC INTERACTIONISM   76

- a person's social creation of reality may take into account social issues such as job opportunities, welfare policies, unemployment, and access to a living wage
- experiences with these issues can have an effect on people, causing them to alter their creation of reality

Key Terms

macrosociology is the study of large-scale society, focusing on the social structures that exist within a society and examining how those structures create the social world.   67

microsociology is the study of the small interactions of daily life.   67

social structures are patterns of relationships that endure from one generation to he next.   67

groups are any number of people with similar norms, values, and behaviors who frequently interact with one another.   67

primary groups are groups that are small, intimate, and enduring.   67

secondary groups are groups that are formal, superficial, and temporary.   67

social class is a group with similar access to power, wealth, and prestige.   67

status is the position that you occupy within the social structure, which is often closely linked to social class.   68

achieved status is a type of position that you earn or do something to attain.   68

ascribed status is a position in society that is given or assigned.   68

master status is the status toward which we gravitate.   68

role is the behavior of a specific status.   68

role expectations are the anticipated behaviors for a particular role.   68

role performance is the degree to which a person plays the role in a manner we expect.   68

role conflict is a phenomenon occurring when one is forced to choose between the competing demands of multiple roles.   69

role strain occurs when the demands and expectations of one role are impossible for us to satisfy.   69

stigma is a mark of disgrace associated with a particular status, quality, or person.   69

discredited stigma is a stigma that cannot be hidden from others or is no longer hidden from others.   69

(continued)

discreditable stigma is a stigma that can be concealed from others. *69*

social institutions are structures that provide for patterned relationships. *71*

Gemeinschaft refers to community connections that involve personal relationships based on friendship and kinship ties, such as family. *73*

Gesellschaft refers to societal connections that are more formal and impersonal. *73*

personal space is the invisible bubble that each of us has around ourselves to insulate us from others. *74*

intimate distance is distance reserved for those with whom we are very close. *74*

personal distance is distance that ranges from 18 inches to 4 feet; this distance is for normal conversations. *74*

social distance is distance that ranges from about 4 feet to 12 feet and is usually reserved for formal settings. *75*

public distance is the zone of interaction that is used in highly formal settings; this distance includes everything greater than 12 feet. *75*

impression management is management of the impression that the performer makes on others. *75*

front stage is what the audience see, or the part of ourselves that we present to others. *75*

backstage is the demeanor that incorporates our true feelings and beliefs. *75*

embarrassment is a state that occurs when we realize our act has failed. *75*

face-saving work is a reaction to embarrassment in the form of either humor, anger, or retreat. *75*

demographic similarity refers to shared characteristics such as race, gender, or age. *76*

supervisor-focused impression management refers to techniques that involve flattering your boss and agreeing with your boss' opinions (or at least avoiding disagreements whenever possible). *76*

self-focused impression management refers to techniques that include acting modest about your accomplishments (even if that modesty is false), boasting occasionally about your successes, and showing your friendliness and self-assuredness through smiles and eye contact. *76*

Sample Test Questions

These multiple-choice questions are similar to those found in the test bank that accompanies this textbook.

1. In what kind of society is the economy based on service and technology?
   a. Industrial
   b. Agricultural
   c. Postindustrial
   d. Hunting and gathering

2. Craigslist is an example of a modern-day
   a. social institution.
   b. political system.
   c. barter system.
   d. religious group.

3. Which of the following systems distributes power in a society?
   a. Legal
   b. Political
   c. Economic
   d. Educational

4. Which of the following groups is the best example of a *Gemeinschaft* relationship?
   a. A large city
   b. A soccer team
   c. A government
   d. A large corporation

5. Which of the five tasks of society allows new members to join and assigns roles to the new members?
   a. Socialization and orientation
   b. Adaptation and replacement
   c. Production and economy
   d. Unity and purpose

ESSAY

1. What are the differences between an industrial society and a post-industrial society?
2. How do societies demonstrate adaptation and replacement for survival? Give examples.
3. Why is it important to observe the conventions of personal space?
4. Explain how a group might change from a *Gemeinschaft* to a *Gesellschaft*.
5. Which systems would a conflict theorist target when addressing the issue of poverty? Why?

WHERE TO START YOUR RESEARCH PAPER

For more information on sociological theories, especially the works of Durkheim and Marx, go to
http://www2.uwsuper.edu/HPS/MBALL/DEAD_SOC.HTM

To learn more about the agricultural revolution and its transition from hunting and gathering, go to
http://www.wsu.edu/gened/learn-modules/top_agrev/agrev-index.html

For a detailed view of hunting and gathering in New Guinea, go to
http://www.climatechange.umaine.edu/Research/projects/NewGuinea.html

To learn more about how elevated social status may help people live longer lives, go to http://www.newscientist.com/article/dn10972-social-status-helps-you-live-longer.html

For more information on impression management as an important factor in business success, go to
http://changingminds.org/index.htm
http://www.impressionmanagement.com/
http://www.salesvantage.com/article/view.php?w5857&Using_Impression_Management_to_Excel_in_Your_Career/

To learn more about Head Start, go to
http://www.acf.hhs.gov/programs/hsb/hsweb/index.jsp

ANSWERS: 1. c; 2. c; 3. b; 4. b; 5. a

Remember to check www.thethinkspot.com **for additional information, downloadable flashcards, and other helpful resources.**

SOCIALIZATION

WHAT IS SOCIALIZATION?
HOW DO THE THREE THEORETICAL PARADIGMS
   VIEW SOCIALIZATION?
HOW DOES UNDERSTANDING SOCIALIZATION
   HELP US IMPROVE THE COMMUNITY?

"People

don't come to Temple City to be discovered, they come to be left alone . . . Before the disruption of that quiet [street] in November of 1970, the residents of one small house behind the row of royal palms were known to their neighbors as the quietest family of all.

"The disruption was spectacular—enough so to earn a week's worth of stories in the Los Angeles Times . . . *"GIRL, 13, PRISONER SINCE INFANCY, DEPUTIES CHARGE; PARENTS JAILED,"* . . . *"MYSTERY SHROUDS HOME OF ALLEGED CHILD PRISONER."*

"The ensuing inquiries found the girl to be a teenager, though she weighed only fifty-nine pounds and was only fifty-four inches tall. She was in much worse physical shape than at first suspected: she was incontinent, could not chew solid food and could hardly swallow, could not focus her eyes beyond twelve feet, and, according to some accounts, could not cry . . . She could not hop, skip, climb, or do anything requiring the extension of her limbs . . . [and] she could not talk . . .

"The girl is referred to not by her real name but by her scientific alias, Genie—the name used in the symposium papers, the psychology magazines, and the textbooks contrived in order to protect the child's identity.

"The story of Genie, has come to seem to me . . . twin histories; that of a young woman trying desperately, heroically, and ultimately unsuccessfully, to transcend the confining horrors of her childhood, and that of researchers . . . In a mutual quest, the successes and failures of scientist and subject became linked.

"Genie had appeared to them out of a little room and they had thought . . . that here was someone of whom they might ask questions and whom might be able to respond . . . It turned out the scientists had not freed Genie from the little room; instead she had ushered them in."[1]

The Process of Fitting *into* Society

In *Genie: A Scientific Tragedy*, Russ Rymer chronicles how **Genie's father locked her in a small room, fearing his daughter was mentally retarded.**

In a dark, gloomy room, a 13-year-old girl sits tied to a toddler's potty chair. Left for days on end, she rarely sees the light of day or interacts with others. Guttural utterances and a few recognizable words are all that she can muster. Unfortunately, this girl isn't some fictional character from a movie; she's an actual girl whom scientists dubbed "Genie." Equipped with absolutely no social skills, Genie materialized from her room into a human society with which she had no experience.

When Genie was finally rescued in November of 1970, experts found that a lack of nurturing and care had left her ill prepared to interact with others.

Thinking about Genie, I'm reminded of my own children and how important it is to speak to them, read to them, and interact with them. Such interaction is vital for a child to know who he or she is. Rymer's work explores the questions: What happens to someone who lives in absolute isolation during his or her formative years? What can science do for such a person? And, does a lack of early socialization pose long-term problems for a person?

get the topic: WHAT IS SOCIALIZATION?

SOCIALIZATION is the process that teaches the norms, values, and other aspects of a culture to new group members.

How do you know what language to speak? What does a red light mean? From the minute you are born, you are being socialized into the world around you. At a football game I recently attended, a young man did not remove his hat during the national anthem. Offended, an older man reached over and snatched the hat off the young man's head. Each man's values, in terms of respect for his country, were miles apart. How did they learn these differing values? Through socialization, of course.

Socialization is the process that teaches the norms, values, and other aspects of a culture to new group members. As such, it is a lifelong process of creating and maintaining group membership. Countless sociologists and psychologists have studied how people become socialized, which has led to the development of several socialization theories.

Socialization theory claims that the person we become is the result of our environment. According to sociologist Talcott Parsons, introduced in Chapter 1, socialization requires people to learn and internalize society's values.[2] In other words, we accept and integrate the values of the group as our own. These social values constantly surround us, but they often go unexamined.

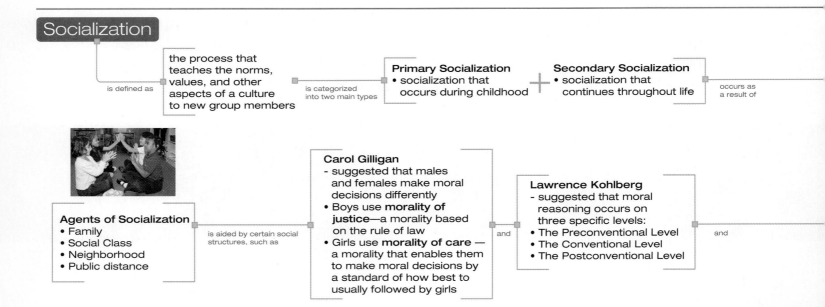

Socialization

is defined as → **the process that teaches the norms, values, and other aspects of a culture to new group members**

is categorized into two main types →

Primary Socialization
• socialization that occurs during childhood

Secondary Socialization
• socialization that continues throughout life

occurs as a result of

Agents of Socialization
• Family
• Social Class
• Neighborhood
• Public distance

is aided by certain social structures, such as

Carol Gilligan
- suggested that males and females make moral decisions differently
• Boys use **morality of justice**—a morality based on the rule of law
• Girls use **morality of care** — a morality that enables them to make moral decisions by a standard of how best to usually followed by girls

and

Lawrence Kohlberg
- suggested that moral reasoning occurs on three specific levels:
• The Preconventional Level
• The Conventional Level
• The Postconventional Level

and

At what point in our lives does socialization take place? Parsons and Bales argue that most socialization occurs during childhood.[3] Orville Brim refers to this early socialization as **primary socialization**.[4] Parents are their children's first teachers; they pass on values, rules, language, religious beliefs, and an unending list of social norms. However, socialization is also reciprocal because children also influence their parents. Before I had children, I thought I knew about parenting, but each child teaches me something new as I try to socialize them. Because socialization is an unending cycle, we are at times the "socializer" and at other times the "socialized."[5] This dynamic, whereby socialization continues throughout our lives is considered **secondary socialization**.[6] As you experience life-changing events—like going to college, beginning a career, or getting married—new socialization occurs. At each stage of life, we encounter new norms, values, and expectations. We learn to accept and integrate them as we adapt to our environment. In a sense, the socialization process makes us who we are. Why might Genie's lack of primary socialization have lasting effects on her life?

The Nature vs. Nurture Debate — What Makes Us Who We Are?

As one theorist said, "We, and all other animals, are machines created by our genes."[7] Pure "**nature**" theorists believe that the genes we get from our parents at conception are the primary causes of human behaviors—in short, our genetic makeup determines who we are. For example, a biologist studying Genie might argue that her genetics determined how she coped with and survived her predicament. Had her genetic makeup been different, she might have emerged from the room with little or no side effects.

In the 20th century, social scientists began to fight biologists' belief that nature is the sole determinant of who we are. Those who believe in "**nurture**," like philosopher John Locke, propose that our environment influences the way we think, feel, and behave.[8] Supporters of this idea assert that socialization molds us like pieces of clay, particularly during early childhood. Many nurture theorists believe that a social process teaches people who they are and how they fit into their world. For some-

PRIMARY SOCIALIZATION is socialization that occurs during childhood.

SECONDARY SOCIALIZATION is the dynamic whereby socialization continues throughout our lives.

NATURE THEORY states that the genes we get from our parents at conception are the primary causes of human behaviors.

NURTURE THEORY states that our environment influences the way we think, feel, and behave.

one like Genie, who lacked such nurturing, her ability to cope within society could be greatly affected.

Extreme proponents on both sides of the nature/nurture debate have difficulty sorting out this issue. Although it is true that our genes do not necessarily dictate our destiny, it's also true that our biological makeup is what interacts with the environment in the first place. Noted biologist and author Paul Ehrlich supports a blended point of view. In Ehrlich's book he notes, "We can't partition the responsibility for aggression, altruism, or charisma between DNA and upbringing. In many such cases, trying to separate the contributions of nature and nurture to an attribute is rather like trying to separate the contributions of length and width to the area of a rectangle, which at first glance also seems easy. When you think about it carefully, though, it proves impossible."[9]

∧
∧ **Does our genetic makeup really determine**
∧ **who we will become? Or do other factors come into play, such as the way our parents care for us?** Where do you stand on the nature vs. nurture debate?

Nature
• the belief that genetic and biological heredity are the primary causes of human behaviors

or

Nurture
• the belief that the way in which we think, feel, and behave are the results of our environment

has inspired many theorists to explain how people become socialized, such as

Charles H. Cooley
• proposed the theory of "looking-glass self," which states that the self develops through a process of reflection

and

George Herbert Mead
- proposed that the self consists of two parts the "I" and the "Me"
- suggested that the self develops in three stages:
• The Imitation Stage
• The Play Stage
• The Game Stage

and

Jean Piaget
- proposed that people go through a four-stage process of cognitive development:
• The Sensorimotor Stage
• The Preoperational Stage
• The Concrete Operational Stage
• The Formal Operational Stage

and

Erik Erikson
- proposed that people develop a personality in eight psychosocial stages
- at each stage we experience a crisis that upon resolving will have an effect on our ability to deal with the next one

The Eight Stages:
• Infancy
• Toddlerhood
• Preschooler
• Elementary School

• Adolescence
• Young Adulthood
• Middle Adulthood
• Late Adulthood

Rhesus Monkey Study

Which is more important to our survival—nature or nurture? To find out, researchers Harry and Margaret Harlow conducted numerous experiments with rhesus monkeys.[10] One of the most famous was designed to test which need is greater: the need for physical contact or the need for biological sustenance. The Harlows raised monkeys in isolation and eventually presented them with two artificial "mothers." The first "mother"—which was simply a hard wire frame with a wooden head—provided food. The other "mother" provided no food at all but was made of soft, cuddly material. The Harlows noticed that frightened baby monkeys sought comfort with the soft "mother" and not with the "mother" that fed them. They drew the conclusion that the key component of infant-mother bonding is not the providing of food, but the presence of comfort. The Harlows' findings, while not directly applicable to human development, support the idea that socialization, i.e., nurture, is a key building block in normal development.

The Harlows' conclusion supports Genie's story. The Genie team concluded that she was not retarded from birth, but due to her deprivation early in life, she would never be "normal." Her arrested development proves how sustenance is actually secondary to comfort as a necessary component for human development. Genie's growth as a person was stunted due to her lack of socialization.

FERAL AND ISOLATED CHILDREN

Tales of **feral**, or wild, children raised by animals are not limited to works of fiction like *Tarzan* or *The Jungle Book*. Newspapers and tabloids often feature sensational headlines about the discoveries of such children. Unfortunately, there are too many stories about children held captive at the hands of abusive and/or mentally unstable parents. Although these stories are staples on the nightly news, we rarely explore or even think about what happens to these children as a result of their isolation. How does human contact, or the lack thereof, affect the people we become?

In April 2008, the story of Josef Fritzl — an Austrian father who had imprisoned his daughter in a basement dungeon for 24 years—attracted worldwide coverage on all the cable news networks. During this time, Fritzl repeatedly abused and raped his imprisoned daughter Elisabeth, even impregnating her seven times. One child died, Fritzl and his wife were raising three children, and the remaining three were left in the dungeon with little human contact. Until the rescue, the three isolated children had never seen the light of day, and they communicated using only simple grunts and gestures.[11] The future of the Fritzl children and their mother remains to be seen. They've surely got intense therapy and a long struggle ahead of them. Will the children ever become socialized?

Some clues might be found when looking back at the story of Genie, who was discovered in California in 1970. When authorities removed the child from her home, they immediately began to care for her.[12] A group of experts, known as "the Genie team," observed that Genie could not walk normally and understood only a few words. Additionally, she had problems eating solid food and still needed diapers. However, after her rescue, Genie made rapid progress. She quickly learned to dress and go to the toilet herself. She also learned to walk more normally. Her language skills began to develop, and within a few months, her vocabulary of only five to ten words had expanded to more than 100 words.[13]

Unfortunately, despite the massive efforts to help Genie, she never caught up with her peers. "The Genie team" concluded that her delayed progress was the result of missing key points in her social development. Because this lack of socialization kept her brain from fully developing, Genie must now live in a home for mentally retarded adults.[14]

Not all feral children have such difficulty becoming socialized. Isabelle, a feral child whose

Average Vocabularies of Children by Age

12-18 months	2 years	3 years	4 years	5 years

Source: Based on *Stages of Language Development* by Louis De Maio.

<<< **Shortly after Genie's rescue, she developed a vocabulary of more than 100 words.** How does Genie's vocabulary compare to children raised in a more "typical" way?

grandfather locked her in a darkened room with her deaf-mute mother, was discovered at age six. She communicated only through gestures, which her mother taught her. Experts put Isabelle through a rigorous socialization process. Surprisingly, Isabelle learned quickly. After two months, she was able to speak in sentences, and after about 18 months she had a vocabulary of 1500–2000 words. Ultimately, Isabelle was able to go to school and function normally with children her own age.[15]

Humans need other humans in order to live and to develop normally. Our human nature is not necessarily instinctual. If it were, Genie would have been able to catch up developmentally to her peers.

Deprivation of human interaction is perhaps more detrimental to humans than being underfed or physically abused. If we are to achieve our full potential, we need others to socialize us. The nurturing we experience in our early lives ultimately affects who we are and who we will become.

Theorists on Socialization

Socialization is a process that theorists have been studying for decades. Many of these theorists, from sociologists to psychologists, have made significant contributions to our understanding of the development of self and the development of morality. Like a never-ending college course, we're enrolled in "socialization" until the day we die. In that sense, we're constantly learning about ourselves.

COOLEY'S LOOKING–GLASS SELF

Charles H. Cooley is one of the central theorists of the development of the self. His notion of the "**looking-glass self**" proposes that, like a mirror, the self develops through a process of reflection. That said, one's self is also established through interactions with others. According to Cooley, this process contains three steps:

1. We imagine how our behaviors will look to others.
2. We interpret others' reactions to our behaviors.
3. We develop a self-concept.[16]

Although Cooley's ideas were developed more than a century ago, modern scholars remain interested in them. King-To Yeung and John Levi Martin, contemporary sociologists who study the processes of the "looking-glass self," used Cooley's theory to test the internalization of self-understanding.[17] Their research found general support for the theory that our self-concept involves interpreting and internalizing others' perceptions about us. Yeung and Martin showed that the importance of our relationships is the key factor in determining how we internalize others' perceptions of us. This is why our parents influence us more than our local bank tellers do.[18]

GEORGE HERBERT MEAD — THE THREE STAGES OF THE "I-ME" SELF

Another theory about how humans develop the self was explored in symbolic interactionist George Herbert Mead's *Mind, Self, and Society*. For Mead, the self is that part of personal identity that has both self-aware-

---

FERAL means wild.

LOOKING-GLASS SELF is the theory that the self develops through a process of reflection, like a mirror.

"I" SELF is the subjective part of the self.

"ME" SELF is the objective part of the self.

IMITATION STAGE is Mead's first stage of development, which is the period from birth to about age 2, and is the stage at which children merely copy the behaviors of those around them.

PLAY STAGE is Mead's second stage of development, which occurs around the ages of 2-4 years, during which children play roles and begin to take on the characteristics of important people in their world.

GAME STAGE is Mead's third stage of development that never truly ends, and is the stage in which we begin to understand that others have expectations and demands placed upon them.

THE GENERALIZED OTHER is our sense of others.

---

ness and self-image.[19] Like Cooley, Mead agreed that the development of self involves interaction with others.

For Mead, though, the self consists of two parts: the "I" and the "Me." These two parts essentially create the self through their interaction. The "**I" Self** is the part of us that is an active subject, our subjective sense of who we are. It seeks self-fulfillment, asking, "What do *I* want?" In contrast, the "**Me" Self** is the objective part of the self; the part of our self-concept that questions how others might interpret our actions. The "Me" understands the symbols that others give us, and seeks to find favorable reactions to our behaviors from others.[20]

According to Mead, the self develops in three stages. The first is the **imitation stage**, which is the period from birth to about age 2. At this stage, children merely copy the behaviors of those around them. They don't attribute meaning to their actions, nor do they understand the implications of their behavior. For instance, when you see your baby sister clapping her hands, she's probably just imitating something she's seen and not actually giving you a round of applause.

Children enter the **play stage** around the ages of 2–4 years. Here, children play roles and begin to take on the characteristics of important people in their world. By playing roles, children see others as separate from themselves. They understand that their actions can affect other people, and vice versa. Mead claimed that, through play, children learn to find a sense of who they are and how to best interact with others in their society. At this stage, you're likely to see little boys tie blankets around their necks and pretend to be superheroes.

During our early school years, we enter what Mead called the **game stage**, a stage that never truly ends. It is in the game stage that we begin to understand that others have expectations and demands placed upon them. Mead termed this sense of others "**the generalized other.**"

Through understanding others we are able to adjust or evaluate our own behavior based on factors such as culture and society. Developing a concept of the generalized other helps us understand other people's roles, norms, and expectations. This concept is important if we are to fit into society and live intimately with others.[21] The idea of little league sports best represents this stage.

When children are involved in a team sport like baseball or basketball, they must understand each position's roles and responsibilities in order to play the game. Not everyone can hit or shoot; everyone has a job to do or we can't play the game.

Erik Erikson's Eight Stages of Development

Erik Erikson proposed that humans develop a personality in eight psychosocial, or psychological and social, stages. (See page 89 for a complete list of each stage.) During each stage, we experience a particular **psychosocial crisis** that will be resolved either positively or negatively, and each outcome will have an effect on our ability to deal with the next one.[22]

According to Erikson, the crisis at each stage of development must be resolved positively before you can successfully master subsequent stages. Think back to Genie. She was imprisoned from the infancy stage through the elementary school stage, so did she ever truly become socialized? The answer is no. Although Genie did make some initial progress, she regressed after her first foster parents severely punished her for vomiting. Genie refused to open her mouth for fear it might happen again and responded in the only way she knew how: silence.[23] Genie's case helps illustrate Erikson's theory that failing to master one stage can mean that a person will fail the subsequent stages.

Jean Piaget's Theory of Cognitive Development

While Erikson's research focused on personality development, the work of Jean Piaget focused on **cognitive development**, which relates to a person's ability to think and reason. Since the way we think helps shape our self-concept, cognition (thinking) plays a significant role in socialization. Simply put, Piaget found that children don't think like adults. His four-stage theory of cognitive development has become an important basis for much educational theory, particularly as it applies to teaching young children.

When my daughter was an infant, nearly everything she touched went directly into her mouth. It didn't matter if it was a stuffed panda, board book, or a long red millipede. If she could reach it, it was going in her mouth. According to Piaget, this is the way babies learn. At the **sensorimotor stage** (birth to age 2 years), infants learn to experience and think about the world through their senses and motor skills. During this period, children develop a sense of "object permanence," the understanding that objects outside themselves still exist even when they are not in view.[24] For example, play "peek-a-boo" with an infant and you'll notice that the baby expresses surprise when you cover your face, followed by great joy when you reveal it. Near the end of the sensorimotor stage, peek-a-boo loses its allure and object permanence exists.

At the **preoperational stage** (ages 2 through 7 years), the ability to speak grows rapidly. Although children have already learned some words and phrases, their ability to use and interpret symbols is limited. Children will generally identify objects by a single characteristic. If you show a child the letters *C-A-T*, for example, the child is likely to read each individual letter aloud. It is unlikely that she will link them together into the word *cat*. Linking multiple symbols together is difficult for a preoperational thinker. By the end of this stage, however, a child can say the word *ball*, draw a picture of a ball, point to a ball on the floor, and understand that all of these mean the same thing.[25]

During the **concrete operational stage** (ages 7 through 12 years), children can think about objects in the world in more than one way and start to understand causal connections in their surroundings. They can think logically about some objects and events. For example, they learn that even though a plain sheet of white paper is folded into a paper airplane, it is still that same piece of white paper. Children at this stage can also imagine what other people might be thinking or feeling. Piaget believed we can't understand the "position" of others until we have passed through some developmental state. Children gain this ability during the concrete operational stage.[26]

Only at the **formal operational stage** (ages 12 years and above) do people become able to comprehend abstract thought. Because they're testing their ability to reason and comprehend the complexities of their world, children at this stage often argue with those in authority. Unsure of themselves, they're testing their thinking. Understanding abstract mathematical principles, such as algebra, becomes possible at this stage, and we become able to understand more deeply the interactions of concrete reality with abstract ideals.[27]

Piaget argued that it could be frustrating and traumatizing to force children to learn ahead of their cognitive capacities. In other words, it serves no purpose to try to teach geometry to a first-grader. Expecting a child to act like an adult is both impossible and unfair.[28]

> Each of the theorists—Cooley, Mead, Erikson, and Piaget—provides a different view of the development of self. **All these theorists agree that a person's development continues throughout life. These theories present human development as a type of staircase process.** Children who miss one or more stages of socialization generally fail to reach successful completion of their development, as was the case for Genie.

Erikson's Eight Stages of Development

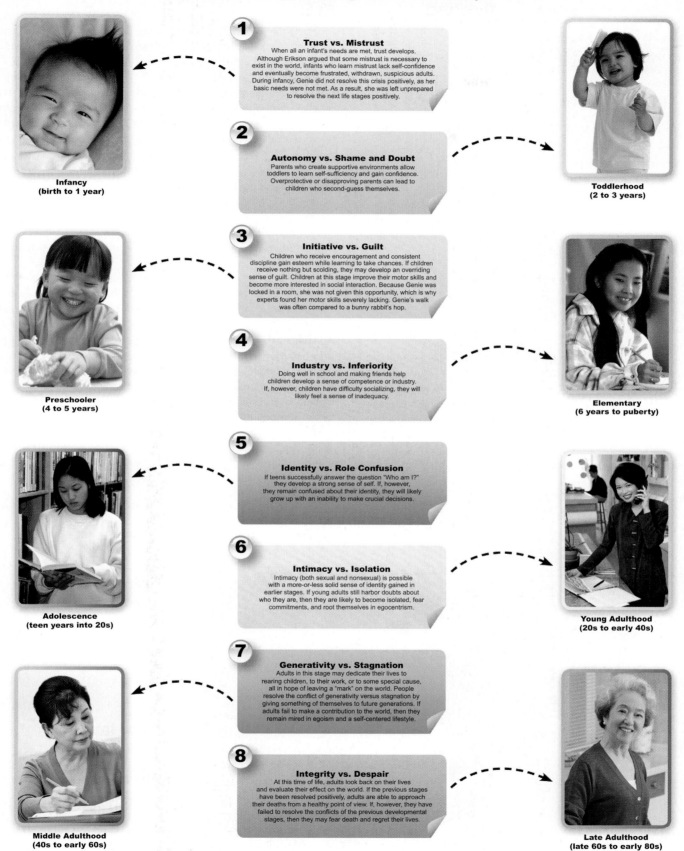

1

Trust vs. Mistrust
When all an infant's needs are met, trust develops. Although Erikson argued that some mistrust is necessary to exist in the world, infants who learn mistrust lack self-confidence and eventually become frustrated, withdrawn, suspicious adults. During infancy, Genie did not resolve this crisis positively, as her basic needs were not met. As a result, she was left unprepared to resolve the next life stages positively.

Infancy
(birth to 1 year)

Toddlerhood
(2 to 3 years)

2

Autonomy vs. Shame and Doubt
Parents who create supportive environments allow toddlers to learn self-sufficiency and gain confidence. Overprotective or disapproving parents can lead to children who second-guess themselves.

3

Initiative vs. Guilt
Children who receive encouragement and consistent discipline gain esteem while learning to take chances. If children receive nothing but scolding, they may develop an overriding sense of guilt. Children at this stage improve their motor skills and become more interested in social interaction. Because Genie was locked in a room, she was not given this opportunity, which is why experts found her motor skills severely lacking. Genie's walk was often compared to a bunny rabbit's hop.

Preschooler
(4 to 5 years)

Elementary
(6 years to puberty)

4

Industry vs. Inferiority
Doing well in school and making friends help children develop a sense of competence or industry. If, however, children have difficulty socializing, they will likely feel a sense of inadequacy.

5

Identity vs. Role Confusion
If teens successfully answer the question "Who am I?" they develop a strong sense of self. If, however, they remain confused about their identity, they will likely grow up with an inability to make crucial decisions.

Adolescence
(teen years into 20s)

Young Adulthood
(20s to early 40s)

6

Intimacy vs. Isolation
Intimacy (both sexual and nonsexual) is possible with a more-or-less solid sense of identity gained in earlier stages. If young adults still harbor doubts about who they are, then they are likely to become isolated, fear commitments, and root themselves in egocentrism.

7

Generativity vs. Stagnation
Adults in this stage may dedicate their lives to rearing children, to their work, or to some special cause, all in hope of leaving a "mark" on the world. People resolve the conflict of generativity versus stagnation by giving something of themselves to future generations. If adults fail to make a contribution to the world, then they remain mired in egoism and a self-centered lifestyle.

Middle Adulthood
(40s to early 60s)

Late Adulthood
(late 60s to early 80s)

8

Integrity vs. Despair
At this time of life, adults look back on their lives and evaluate their effect on the world. If the previous stages have been resolved positively, adults are able to approach their deaths from a healthy point of view. If, however, they have failed to resolve the conflicts of the previous developmental stages, then they may fear death and regret their lives.

Source: Based on *Childhood and Society* by Erik Erikson.

PRECONVENTIONAL LEVEL is the first stage of moral development that lasts through the elementary school years; at this level, children make their moral judgements within a framework of hedonistic principles.

HEDONISM is seeking pleasure over pain.

CONVENTIONAL LEVEL is the second stage of moral development that arises before puberty and uses the lens of norms and rules to determine what is right and wrong.

POSTCONVENTIONAL LEVEL is the third stage of moral development that refers to a morality based on abstract principles.

MORALITY OF JUSTICE is morality based on the rule of law.

MORALITY OF CARE is morality decided by a standard of how best to help those who are in need.

Theories of Moral Development

How do we know what's right and what's wrong? Do girls learn about morals differently from boys? These are just two of the questions that theories of moral development seek to answer.

Kohlberg's Theory of Moral Development

Building upon the work of Piaget, the prominent theorist Lawrence Kohlberg suggested that moral reasoning occurs on three specific levels: preconventional, conventional, and postconventional. Each level describes different ways in which we make moral decisions.[29]

During the **preconventional level,** which lasts through the elementary school years, children make their moral judgments within a framework of **hedonism**—seeking pleasure over pain.[30] In other words, children judge right from wrong on the basis of what feels good or right to them. If a little boy notices that drawing on the walls results in a visit to the "naughty stool," chances are he won't take the crayons to the walls again.

The **conventional level** arises before puberty and uses the lens of norms and rules to determine what is right and wrong.[31] Basically, what is "right" is obedience to the rules. Rather than question the logic behind why those rules were established, a child simply does what he or she is told. The child may not understand *why* kicking his sister is wrong; he just understands that he shouldn't do it because "Mommy says so." Following the expectations of the family or group is valuable in and of itself. Doing your duty and respecting authority are the hallmarks of this level of development.

Kohlberg's third stage of moral development, the **postconventional level**, refers to a morality based on abstract principles. These may be rooted in political beliefs, religious beliefs, or a combination of both. Kohlberg suggests that the "good" includes adherence to agreed-upon principles rather than rules.[32] Such principles guide all decisions and provide a seamless web of morality for us all. For example, during the civil rights movement of the 1950s and 1960s, countless African American college students held sit-ins at segregated lunch counters, museums, libraries, and many other public places. Although their behavior broke the Jim Crow laws of the time, these students believed their behavior was "right" because they were drawing attention to laws that were morally wrong.

Although Kohlberg's own research supported his theory, more recent scholars question some of his assumptions. For example, Charles Helwig and Urszula Jasiobedzka found that children's moral judgments about law and lawbreaking occur earlier in life than Kohlberg's theory proposed.[33] Preschoolers may abide by the rules because they believe rule-breaking is wrong. In addition, moral reasoning doesn't always correlate with moral behavior. Using Kohlberg's schema, Colby and Damon showed that people at the highest levels of moral development act the same as people at lower levels of moral development. Instead, the situation influences people's behavior.[34] Take speeding, for example. Although everyone knows it's against the law, many people speed when they believe they won't be caught. These and other questions about Kohlberg's theory of moral development led Carol Gilligan to propose another point of view in 1982.

<<< It's hard to imagine that the simple act of sitting at a lunch counter could be illegal. **The unfairness of laws** such as these **led many students of all races to hold peaceful sit-ins across the South in hopes of abolishing Jim Crow laws.**

Carol Gilligan and the "Morality of Care"

Carol Gilligan suggested that Kohlberg's theories were valid, though only when discussing the development of male morality. To Gilligan, his conclusions were biased against women because Kohlberg only studied men initially.[35] This, in turn, led him to erroneously assume men and women developed moral decisions similarly without actually studying women. Do men and women approach moral decisions differently?

I recently faced a moral decision while shopping at my local discount store. The cashier gave me $10 too much change. Being a bit of a miser, I immediately noticed her mistake. I'm human, so I considered keeping the money, but then I began to wonder what might happen if I took the money. Was it my fault that the cashier made a mistake? Would she get in trouble when she came up short at the end of her shift? All of these thoughts ran through my mind. Of course, I gave her the money back. Gilligan would argue that my gender influenced the way I approached my decision; women would follow a slightly different process.

After investigating women's experiences with morality, Gilligan concluded that moral decisions arise from two different principles: the morality of justice and the morality of care. She agreed that boys primarily follow what she called a **morality of justice**, a morality based on the rule of law. However, girls learn a **morality of care**, which enables them to make moral decisions by a standard of how best to help those who are in need.[36]

To study the differences between moral development in boys and girls, Gilligan proposed a real-life moral dilemma to young male and female subjects. Gilligan used the story of "Mr. Heinz and the Druggist," a tale that Kohlberg also used in his research. The general idea of the story is this: Mr. Heinz's wife is sick with a potentially fatal disease. Luckily, their small-town pharmacy is the only place around that carries the life-saving medication that his wife needs. The problem is the drug costs an astronomical $10,000, and the druggist refuses to sell it for any less. Should Mr. Heinz steal the drug?

Gilligan found that most male subjects used logic when answering the question. Many boys believed that Mr. Heinz should steal the medication, even though it's legally wrong. Boys reasoned that the judge would likely be lenient on Mr. Heinz because of the circumstances. In short, the boys answered the question like a math problem: $x + y = z$. The girl subjects, however, considered the personal relationships involved. Girls worried that Mr. Heinz might go to jail, which could make his wife sicker and leave no one around to care for her or provide her with medicine. They also tried to think of other ways for Mr. Heinz to get the drug so that he would not have to leave his wife. Girls were more concerned about how Mr. Heinz's actions would affect the dynamic between him and his wife.

Modern research provides mixed support for Gilligan's assertion of gender differences in moral reasoning. In short, it appears that girls and boys learn *both* morality of care and morality of justice. The two types of morality are not exclusive to one gender over the other.[37] Some find-

Kohlberg and Gilligan's Theories of Moral Development

"Both boys and girls go through the same three stages—preconventional, conventional, and postconventional—to develop their morality."
— Lawrence Kohlberg

"Boys and girls develop their morality differently. Boys generally develop a morality of justice, while girls develop a morality of care."
— Carol Gilligan

ings show that since girls advance through the stages of moral development faster than boys, they actually develop postconventional morality at earlier ages.[38] The most important aspect, perhaps, is the link between ego development and the moralities of care and justice. Because girls develop faster than boys, they present a morality of care more quickly than boys.[39]

Either way, Gilligan and Kohlberg both agree that moral reasoning follows a developmental process and that the surroundings affect that process. Although the precise gender differences may not be as clearly distinguished as Gilligan initially believed, and Kohlberg's age groups may be more flexible than he proposed, both theories show that we learn to make moral decisions in different ways.

Agents of Socialization

We learn socialization with outside help from different **agents of socialization**, which are the people and groups that shape our self-concept, beliefs, and behavior. So what social structures, or agents, help us become socialized?

THE FAMILY: PARENTING STYLES AND RECIPROCAL SOCIALIZATION

Few things in life shape us more than our parents. Because both my parents worked full time, I learned at an early age that one must work to live. I started working at 13 and am still working today, as evidenced by my writing this book on nights, weekends, and summer vacations. My parents also valued education. Although they never completed college, they encouraged us kids to go. Sometimes, I wonder what my life would have been like if I had had different parents. What if my parents were drug addicts? Or illiterate? Or members of the wealthiest elite in the country (my personal favorite)? My point is merely that children don't select their parents, and yet family is one of the most important agents of socialization.

When parents socialize their children, they do so in two different ways. First, they create safe environments by providing emotional support through love, affection, and nurturing. Second, parents provide social control by teaching their children appropriate behaviors. Parents do this by using force, coercion, threats, or rewards.[40] If parents are not successful at providing these things for their children, the results can be disastrous. Genie's father, for example, locked her in a dark room on a potty for days on end. She didn't receive the love and nurturing she needed as a child, which led to socialization problems after she was rescued.

Sociologist Diana Baumrind explored how parental discipline affects children. Although disciplining children is a cultural universal, the manner in which it occurs varies by culture and family style. Baumrind observed that parenting styles have a substantial effect on individual socialization outcomes.[41] Parents who practice an **authoritative style** listen to their children's input while consistently enforcing the preset rules. Children reared in such an environment integrate into the world with the most ease because they exhibit high levels of self-esteem and possess the capacities for independence and cooperation with others.

Whereas authoritative parents practice a balanced style of child-rearing, permissive and authoritarian parents represent opposite extremes, and neither produces positive outcomes. **Permissive style** parents provide high levels of support but an inconsistent enforcement of rules. This results in a child who does not understand boundaries and expectations. The teenagers on MTV's *My Super Sweet 16* who are showered with lavish gifts and extravagant parties by their affluent parents may be ill-equipped to deal with the disappointments and responsibilities that are sure to come later in life. Conversely, children reared by **authoritarian style** parents experience high levels of social control but low levels of emotional support. Such children understand the rules but have no relational reasons to obey them when their parents are not looking. Often, the most rebellious youths are by-products of very strict households. Baumrind suggests that these two styles of parenting produce children with lower self-esteem and less self-assurance.[42]

Three Parenting Styles

Source: Based on *Current Patterns of Parental Authority* by Diana Baumind.

▶▶ GO GLOBAL

Parenting in Asian Cultures

Do the parenting styles that Baumrind describes apply in all cultures? Ruth Chao studied how the parenting styles of Chinese families affected children.[43] In order to explore the perception of Chinese school-children as successful and well behaved, Chao observed how parents interacted with their children.[44] The mothers she observed provided high levels of control, but also high levels of sacrifice and personal closeness to their children. Parents in China expect their children to meet high standards of both individual achievement and social conformity. In general, Chinese children meet these standards. The parents in this culture are authoritative; children receive adequate emotional support and know that their hard work will gain the family's approval.

In another study, sociologist Min Zhou proposed that Confucian philosophy, with its emphasis on family loyalty, acts as a social control mechanism that supports Asian children's success.[45] Studies of Vietnamese immigrant children living in enclaves in the United States show similar findings to those of Chao. They show that second-generation immigrant children who remain linked to their families and culture have better outcomes with regard to educational attainment and the likelihood that they will stay in school.[46] Culture plays an important role in psychologists' and sociologists' interpretations about family socialization.

SOCIAL CLASS: OPPORTUNITIES FOR SOCIALIZATION

Family isn't the only agent of socialization; our social class also affects us. Numerous studies show connections between social class and socialization. Melvin Kohn's research found that working-class parents focus on their children's obedience to authority, whereas middle-class parents showed greater concern about the motivations for their children's behavior.[47] Because working-class parents are closely supervised at their jobs, they are more likely to demand this same conformity from their children. Therefore, the mother who is used to punching a clock at the assembly line is more likely to expect a home environment in which her children do their chores at set times.

Our social class affects us in many ways that we do not anticipate and may not even recognize. The availability of piano lessons, art classes, and little-league sports teams all socialize children; however, these experiences are typically available only to middle- and upper-income families. Children of less affluent families tend to miss these socialization opportunities. Social class affects not only the type of experiences we have, but also their quality and quantity.

NEIGHBORHOOD

Anyone who's ever visited a dormitory building before making a decision to live there believes that the "right" dorm matters. The same is true of choosing a neighborhood in which to live because your social class is often tied to the kind of neighborhood you live in. Noted sociologist William J. Wilson looked at how inner-city poverty brought with it the disadvantages of poor schools, weak social structures, high crime rates, and rampant drug use.[48] Wilson argued that poor people are truly disadvantaged because their community offers few role models for anything else. Children who grow up in these communities are likely to make poor decisions. Studies have shown that neighborhood has significant negative effects on IQ, teen pregnancy, and high school dropout rates.[49]

Neighborhoods also influence economically privileged children. Children who grow up in more affluent neighborhoods often do better in

school, have lower rates of teen pregnancy, and higher IQ scores.[50] Neighborhoods can also predict how far you may go in school, showing that the higher the socioeconomic status of the neighborhood, the higher the educational attainment.[51] Neighborhood effects also apply to voluntary associations for children. A predicting factor in the sport children will play is correlated to their neighborhoods.[52] For example, a sport like skiing that requires expensive equipment is more likely to played by children of well-to-do families because they can afford the upkeep and travel to the slopes.

Of course, just because parents are affluent does not mean that they will be great parents or that their children will be successfully socialized. The reverse is also true; a parent who has very limited financial means may be a very good parent.

Can We Be "Resocialized"? Experiencing the Total Institution

Resocialization is the process of learning new norms, values, attitudes, and behaviors and abandoning old ones. This process involves more than the kinds of secondary socialization that occur when we marry or take a new job. Yoda, the noted Jedi philosopher, says it best in the film *The Empire Strikes Back;* sometimes, "You must unlearn what you have learned."

The most effective forms of resocialization occur in **total institutions** that isolate people from outside influences so they can be reformed and controlled.[53] People may enter total institutions voluntarily, as in the case of non-draftees that enlist in military boot camps, or involuntarily, as in the case of inmates in mental institutions and prisons. Regardless, total institutions have certain characteristics:

1. There is one authority, and activities take place in specific locations.

2. Carefully structured activities control the participants.

3. Authorities carefully screen all information from outside the institution.

4. Rules and roles are clearly defined.

5. A strict hierarchy exists within the institution.

6. Total institutions restrict individual choice.

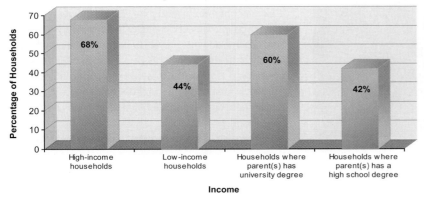

The Effect of Income and Education on Children's Participation in Organized Sports in Canada

Percentage of Households

- High-income households: 68%
- Low-income households: 44%
- Households where parent(s) has university degree: 60%
- Households where parent(s) has a high school degree: 42%

Income

Participation in Organized Sports

Source: Based on "Organized Sports Participation Among Children," 2005.

think sociologically: HOW DO THE THREE THEORETICAL PARADIGMS VIEW SOCIALIZATION?

Symbolic Interactionism and Resocialization

We've seen how symbolic interactionists interpret society's symbols as a means for people to create a sense of self. We've also learned how the self develops under ordinary conditions. But how might development inside a total institution affect a person's sense of self?

Sociologist Harold Garfinkel explored the similarities in the ways prison inmates and military enlistees are resocialized upon entering those total institutions.[54] Garfinkel points out that these institutions "welcome" new members through some form of degrading ceremony designed to humiliate the person. This humiliation is required to "break them down" so that resocialization is possible. Inmates and enlistees may both have their heads shaved and their "street clothes" taken away. After putting on uniforms, their individual style of dress is erased in order to look like everyone else. In boot camp and under the control of the institution, the new recruit has no choice in when he or she will eat, sleep, or bathe. Similarly, inmates receive numbers to replace their names, are given uniforms to wear, and are told where they will sleep, when they will eat, and how they will spend their allocated "free" time. In both cases, the goal is to strip away former identity and resocialize the person into someone who will be obedient to commands.

Through resocialization, the institution controls all aspects of a person's life.[55] The techniques that total institutions use change the inmate or soldier's internal thinking, which in turn changes his or her sense of self.

∧
∧
∧ **Prison inmates are stripped of their individual identities so that they can be transformed into people who willingly follow the orders** of those in authority.

Functionalism

While symbolic interactionists study the effect of institutions on individuals, functionalists examine how certain institutions, specifically religion and education, function in society. An institution's function, and the individual's relationship to that institution, helps determine what role it plays in the development of self.

RELIGION

In every U.S. election, Christian fundamentalists are a key voting bloc that politicians court by campaigning on "family values." Though the idea of such values is malleable depending on the issues, it's clear that the members of this group share a common set of beliefs that finds its foundation in religion.

From Muslim practitioners to Orthodox Jews and Buddhist monks, all world religions provide frames of reference for believers. These frameworks include beliefs, values, and behaviors in keeping with the teachings of that religion. Religions teach about life, death, and all of life's transitions in between. The religious socialization that results from this teaching process has measurable effects.

Sociologists Charles Tittle and Michael Welch studied the links between religiosity and juvenile delinquency and found that they were inversely related. The more religious the juvenile, the less likely he or she is to be delinquent.[56] Harold Grasmick and colleagues found weaker, but similar, results with respect to adults and behaviors such as tax cheating and littering.[57] This research shows that religion can play a role in forming our behavior.

EDUCATION

Out of a typical seven-hour school day, students in secondary schools in the United States spend only about three hours doing academic activities.[58] Instead, students are learning the **"hidden curriculum"**–lessons taught in school that are unrelated to academic learning. School teaches you to deal with peers who are sometimes cruel.[59] If students successfully negotiate the dangers of their neighborhoods and the various power struggles that go on in their schools, they feel a sense of satisfaction. Mock elections and saluting the flag help foster citizenship among students. Schools also socialize children by setting regulations that structure the school day. Students must show up on time, get along with others, follow teachers' expectations, wait in lines, and follow the rules.[60]

When families and schools cooperate to teach children to follow the rules, they help create a society that has fewer lawbreakers. When neighborhoods support these ideals, children grow up feeling part of something important. In the event that the family is dysfunctional, or the school does not work, or the neighborhood is infecting them with negative ideas about the society, this too socializes children. Negative outcomes usually result. Society functions best when social institutions cooperate.

Conflict Theory—What Forces Socialize Us?

Recall that conflict theory suggests that power relationships influence our perceptions. To guide our actions, societies use **gender socialization** to teach their members how to express their masculinity or femininity. **Gender**, which will be discussed in greater detail in Chapter 11, refers to the expectations of behavior and attitude that a society considers proper for males and females. If and when these expectations limit one gender in favor of the other, it usually occurs as a result of differences in power.

Conflict theorists often argue that **men use their power to dominate and limit women.**

MAKE CONNECTIONS

Fictional Tales and Gender

From *Aesop's Fables* to the Brothers Grimm, folktales symbolize the innocence of childhood. But a closer analysis shows how these folktales shape how children perceive gender. Most folktales follow a typical pattern in which a dependent woman relies exclusively on a strong man to save her from harm. Think about the story of Rapunzel—the girl with the long, golden hair who is trapped in a tower by a witch. In the story, Rapunzel is merely a piece of property, given away by her father in exchange for his life. While trapped in the tower, Rapunzel is dependent on the witch and unable to escape. Rapunzel, afraid of the witch's wrath, remains in the tower alone and refuses the prince's help to escape. The prince goes blind because he is unable to save the beauty. Young children, especially young girls, who read these tales internalize the idea that being submissive and reliant on men is a desired trait.

These stereotypes are not just a part of archaic folktales; they also appear in modern works of fiction. Television programs like *Grey's Anatomy* and *Desperate Housewives* feature female characters who reinforce generalizations about gender roles. That said, there are a number of stereotype-breaking charac-

ters like those featured on *Buffy the Vampire Slayer* and *Lost*. Even in the *Harry Potter* series, Hermione Granger, Harry's sidekick, is a secondary character and yet she is always saving the day. Real life does not work as it does in fiction. Not all men can be heroes, and passivity and dependency rarely bring women success in the modern world.

>>> **ACTIVITY** Think about a movie or TV show you've seen or a book you've read recently. What gender stereotypes, if any, are depicted on the screen or the page? Does the work defy any traditional gender stereotypes? Write a paragraph analyzing the work you chose.

GENDER BIAS IN THE MEDIA

When Senator Hillary Clinton ran for the Democratic nomination in the 2008 presidential race, one of the major issues involved how the pundits and politicos treated the first viable woman to run for the highest office in the land. Clinton's supporters pointed to the disproportionate amount of attention given to their candidate's appearance and noted a perceived gender bias in the coverage of her campaign.

Any print or electronic resource that is used to communicate to a wide audience is referred to as **mass media**.

Products of mass media—books, magazines, television, radio, movies, music, and newspapers—are everywhere, and their influence on culture is inescapable. **The media play a role in our socialization because they transmit stories, values, and attitudes.**

Consider the effect the media have in determining gendered stereotypes through sexual imagery. Kirstie Farrar and her colleagues reviewed the sexual images that aired during "prime-time" television hours. They found that images on shows like *The Bachelor* and *One Tree Hill* tended to reinforce the notion that women are primarily sexual objects.[61] These and other images supported the dominant male/submissive female paradigm. They also found that 64 percent of the television shows during the 2000–2001 season contained sexual messages, and that sexual intercourse occurred in 14 percent of the shows. For conflict theorists, these findings suggest that such imagery is an effort by those in power to maintain it. Men are the primary decision makers for large media corporations, so are they responsible for perpetuating these ideas about gender roles?

Because of the way gender roles are defined in society, it can take several years to see through the generalizations. I can remember realizing during my freshman year in college that my father and I had never hugged, primarily because of gender ideals about men touching each other. The next time I returned home, I gave him a big hug as soon as he answered the door. From that day forth, hugging was no longer taboo at our house. In this simple way, my father and I changed our gender socialization.

WRAP YOUR MIND AROUND THE THEORY

In order for a society to function, **functionalists argue that people adapt their behavior to the norms and values of the institutions in that society.**

FUNCTIONALISM

According to functionalists, socialization occurs when people internalize society and enact its norms, values, and roles. In high schools across the country, students struggle with the choice to conform and practice "normal" behavior or to think outside the box. Those who step outside the box are often stigmatized and labeled as "different." These individuals are not "functioning" because they don't conform to the rules set by the society's institutions. Institutions, such as religion and education, serve their function. To keep a society running smoothly, people adapt to the norms and values of their particular institutions. In short, people become socialized when they learn and accept what a society expects of them.

HOW DO PEOPLE BECOME SOCIALIZED?

?

CONFLICT THEORY

Conflict theorists believe that the "haves" and the "have-nots" are socialized differently. Children who come from middle- and upper-class backgrounds are more likely to participate in organized sports, take music or art lessons, and have Internet access in their homes. Taking part in activities such as these teaches children how to interact with others and learn what society expects of them. Impoverished children sometimes find themselves at a disadvantage because they are less likely to have these experiences. Of course, material wealth is not the only determinant of whether one becomes socialized. However, parents' material wealth does put some children at an advantage.

SYMBOLIC INTERACTIONISM

Symbolic interactionists believe that socialization is the major determinant of human nature. People develop their sense of self by incorporating how others interpret their behavior. The symbols we encounter, such as other people's interpretations of our behavior, help shape who and what we become. Genie, the feral child discovered in 1970, was not given the opportunity to interact with others during her formative years. As a result, she was unable to fully develop her own identity when she was thrust into the social world. As we saw in Mead's theory of the "I" and the "Me," people develop their sense of self though their interaction with others.

Children who participate in organized sports learn how to interact with others in the social world. **Having little or no opportunities to play sports can limit a child's socialization.**

If the students in class snicker and whisper while the child gives his report, how might the child interpret these symbols? How might he feel about himself?

discover sociology in action:
HOW DOES UNDERSTANDING SOCIALIZATION HELP US IMPROVE THE COMMUNITY?

Applying Sociological Thinking in the World, Social Policy, and Title IX

Auguste Comte, the founder of sociology, urged us to use our knowledge about society to improve society. Lawmakers have used that philosophy to enact various **social policies**, deliberate strategies designed to correct recognized social problems. The 1972 educational amendment, commonly known as **Title IX**, is one such attempt to implement sociological knowledge. Named the Patsy T. Mink Equal Opportunity in Education Act in honor of its principle author—a Hawaiian congresswoman who felt that gender discrimination in public schools must be stopped—the act prohibits the exclusion of any person from participation in an educational program on the basis of gender.[62]

Title IX became important when it was used to allocate funding for extracurricular activities like sports. Before 1972, very few girls were involved in sports partly because few sports existed for girls. In the three decades since Title IX, however, those numbers have skyrocketed:

- Female participation in high school sports has increased 800 percent.
- Female participation in intercollegiate athletics has increased 400 percent.
- Girls now make up 42 percent of high school athletes.

SOCIAL POLICIES are deliberate strategies designed to correct recognized social problems.

TITLE IX is a 1972 educational amendment that prohibits the exclusion of any person from participation in an education program on the basis of gender.

- Women now make up 42 percent of Division I varsity college athletes.
- Women receive 43 percent of Division I athletic scholarship dollars.
- Women's college sports receive about one dollar for every two spent on men's programs.[63]

You can see that a social policy designed to give equal opportunities to both genders has increased women's athletic participation. However, these numbers also indicate that the goal of actual equality has not yet been met. Today, girls may have many more athletic role models than they did 30 years ago, but they do not yet receive equal funding for sports programs in their schools. Although women outnumber men on college campuses, funding remains largely in the hands of male sports. A quick look at the difference in television budgets between the men's and women's NCAA Final Four basketball tournaments demonstrates the disparity. Sports play a big role in a child's socialization, and both genders should have the opportunity to participate equally.

ACTIVITIES

1. How does your college deal with Title IX? Are male and female scholarships equal? Are they in compliance?
2. What agents of socialization influenced you the most when you were growing up? What influences you the most now?
3. Read stories of feral children, such as Genie. What is the importance of early socialization on development? Have researchers made any strides in socializing feral children?
4. Visit a developmental disability hospital in your area and talk to the staff and parents. Can the best efforts at socialization overcome nature? Write about your findings.

From Classroom to Community › Children's Hospital

When David, one of my sociology students, decided to do his service learning project at a local children's hospital for the developmentally disabled, he was not prepared for the experiences he was about to have.

"Before I started my volunteerism," he said,

"I had a clear understanding of the socialization process. I'd studied Genie and knew how difficult it was to socialize children who had developmental delays."

David realized that many of the children, unlike Genie, came from loving families and had received all kinds of therapy from a very early age. But David found that despite all the assistance they received, something about their development was delayed.

"Some children had physical delays, while others had cognitive ones," he recalled. David was particularly interested in a 12-year-old boy who was born deaf, blind, and mentally retarded.

"He was a really difficult case because I couldn't figure out how to communicate with him. He interacted mostly through touch. Yet when you reached out to help him, he often hit you and wildly swung his arms around in the air."

Children with development delays that influence communication often experience problems with socialization.

"It seemed that about all my patient could do was hit people and eat.

I could not help but wonder how this boy would come to know who he was and where he fit in the world. Without communication, it seems almost impossible."

WHAT **IS SOCIALIZATION?**   84

the process that teaches the norms, values, and other aspects of a culture to new group members

HOW **DO THE THREE THEORETICAL PARADIGMS VIEW SOCIALIZATION?**   94

functionalism: institutions, like religion and education, are useful in socializing individuals

conflict theory: societies use gender socialization to teach members how to express their femininity and masculinity

symbolic interactionism: total institutions are successful in resocializing people by altering their sense of self

HOW **DOES UNDERSTANDING SOCIALIZATION HELP US IMPROVE THE COMMUNITY?**   97

through social policies that are designed to give equal opportunities to both genders

get the topic: WHAT IS SOCIALIZATION?

The Nature vs. Nurture Debate—
    What Makes Us Who We Are?   85
Theorists on Socialization   87
Agents of Socialization   92

Can We Be "Resocialized"? Experiencing the
    Total Institution   93
Symbolic Interactionism and Resocialization   94
Functionalism   94

Conflict Theory—What Forces Socialize Us? 95
Applying Sociological Thinking in the World,
    Social Policy, and Title IX   97

Theory

FUNCTIONALISM   94

- socialization occurs when people internalize society and enact its norms, values, and roles
- people who don't internalize norms are stigmatized and labeled as "different"
- people become socialized when they learn and accept what society expects of them

CONFLICT THEORY   95

- the "haves" and the "have-nots" are socialized differently

- taking part in activities teaches children how to interact with others and learn what society expects of them
- children who come from middle- and upper-class backgrounds are more likely to participate in organized activities than some impoverished children who are unable to participate

SYMBOLIC INTERACTIONISM   94

- socialization is the major determinant of human nature
- people develop their sense of self by incorporating how others interpret their behavior

Key Terms

socialization is the process that teaches the norms, values, and other aspects of a culture to new group members.   84

primary socialization is socialization that occurs during childhood.   85

secondary socialization is the dynamic whereby socialization continues throughout our lives.   85

nature theory states that the genes we get from our parents at conception are the primary causes of human behaviors.   85

nurture theory states that our environment influences the way we think, feel, and behave.   85

feral means wild.   86

looking-glass self is the theory that the self develops through a process of reflection, like a mirror.   87

"I" self is the subjective part of the self.   87

"me" self is the objective part of the self.   87

imitation stage is Mead's first stage of development, which is the period from birth to about age 2, and is the stage at which children merely copy the behaviors of those around them.   87

play stage is Mead's second stage of development, which occurs around the ages of 2–4 years, during which children play roles and begin to take on the characteristics of important people in their world.   87

game stage is Mead's third stage of development that never truly ends, and is the stage in which we begin to understand that others have expectations and demands placed upon them.   87

the generalized other is our sense of others.   87

psychosocial crisis is a crisis occurring during each of Erikson's stages that will be resolved

either positively or negatively, and each outcome will have an effect on our ability to deal with the next one.   88

cognitive development is a person's ability to think and reason.   88

sensorimotor stage is the stage (birth to age 2 years) at which infants learn to experience and think about the world through their senses and motor skills.   88

preoperational stage is the stage (ages 2 through 7 years) at which the ability to speak grows rapidly.   88

concrete operational stage is the stage (ages 7 through 12 years) at which children can think about objects in the world in more than one way and start to understand causal connections in their surroundings.   88

formal operational stage is the stage (ages 12 years and above) at which people become able to comprehend abstract thought. *88*

preconventional level is the first stage of moral development that lasts through elementary school years; at this level, children make their moral judgments within a framework of hedonistic principles. *90*

hedonism is seeking pleasure over pain. *90*

conventional level is the second stage of moral development that arises before puberty and uses the lens of norms and rules to determine what is right and wrong. *90*

postconventional level is the third stage of moral development that refers to a morality based on abstract principles. *90*

morality of justice is morality based on the rule of law. *91*

morality of care is morality decided by a standard of how best to help those who are in need. *91*

agents of socialization are the people and groups who shape our self-concept, beliefs, and behavior. *92*

authoritative style is a parenting style in which parents listen to their children's input while consistently enforcing the preset rules. *92*

permissive style is a parenting style in which parents provide high levels of support but an inconsistent enforcement of rules. *92*

authoritarian style is a parenting style with which children experience high levels of social control but low levels of emotional support. *92*

resocialization is the process of learning new norms, values, attitudes, and behaviors and abandoning old ones. *93*

total institutions are places in which the most effective forms of resocialization can occur because they isolate people from outside influences so they can be reformed and controlled. *93*

hidden curriculum refers to the lessons taught in school that are unrelated to academic learning. *94*

gender socialization teaches members of society how to express their masculinity or femininity. *95*

gender is the expectations of behavior and attitude that a society considers proper for males and females. *95*

mass media include any print or electronic resource that is used to communicate to a wide audience. *95*

social policies are deliberate strategies designed to correct recognized social problems. *95*

Title IX is a 1972 educational amendment that prohibits the exclusion of any person from participation in an educational program on the basis of gender. *97*

Sample Test Questions

These multiple-choice questions are similar to those found in the test bank that accompanies this textbook.

1. During which of Erikson's eight stages would a person develop a strong sense of self?
   a. Trust vs. mistrust
   b. Initiative vs. guilt
   c. Industry vs. inferiority
   d. Identity vs. role confusion

2. According to Piaget, at what stage of cognitive development does a child's ability to speak grow rapidly?
   a. Sensorimotor stage
   b. Preoperational stage
   c. Concrete operational stage
   d. Formal operational stage

3. The preconventional level, conventional level, and postconventional level are stages of
   a. moral development.
   b. social development.
   c. creative development.
   d. language development.

4. Which of the following is *not* an example of a total institution?
   a. A prison
   b. The military
   c. A university
   d. A rehabilitation clinic

5. Which researcher developed the morality of care and the morality of justice?
   a. Erik Erikson
   b. Carol Gilligan
   c. Lawrence Kohlberg
   d. George Herbert Mead

ESSAY

1. How did Piaget describe the stage at which a child learns to speak?
2. What is the difference between authoritative style and authoritarian style parenting?
3. Why is resocialization important in total institutions?
4. Conflict theorists often argue that men use their power to dominate and limit women. Provide an example of gender bias in the media and explain how it supports this theory.
5. In the terms of Erikson's theory, how was Genie's development stunted?

WHERE TO START YOUR RESEARCH PAPER

For more information on "Child of our Time: Socialization Information from British Broadcasting Service" (a BBC interactive discussion on socialization of children with links to online quizzes and expert opinions), go to
http://www.open2.net/childofourtime/tv_pages/art_socialization_1.htm

For in-depth articles on the field of evolutionary psychology, relating the development of the brain and how social settings influence a person's development, go to
http://www.psych.ucsb.edu/research/cep/

To find data on child socialization and marital adjustment, go to
http://www.parentsurf.com

For more information on education and health care for parents and children, go to http://www.kidsource.com/

To learn more about how media influences society (particularly the sociological perspective on media and society), go to
http://www.public.asu.edu/~zeyno217/365/notes1.html

To find more information on Mama Feeta and her work in caring for the children of war-torn Liberia, go to
http://www.shinefoundation.org/

For more information on centers that work with people who have developmental delays, go to
http://www.miusa.org/ncde/

ANSWERS: 1. d; 2. b; 3. a; 4. c; 5. b

Remember to check www.thethinkspot.com **for additional information, downloadable flashcards, and other helpful resources.**

GROUPS AND SOCIETIES

WHAT ARE THE CHARACTERISTICS
OF SOCIAL GROUPS?
HOW DO SOCIOLOGISTS VIEW GROUP
LEADERSHIP?
HOW DOES A PARENT'S CIVIC ENGAGEMENT
AFFECT A CHILD'S FUTURE POLITICAL
INVOLVEMENT?

"We will

consider an extraordinary subculture, the Oneida community, sharing an unusual set of religious beliefs and following an individual with unusual personal magnetism, John Humphrey Noyes. He exercised what is referred to as charismatic authority. This refers to the power made legitimate by a leader's exceptional personal or emotional appeal to his or her followers . . . Noyes was able to lead and inspire without relying on established rules or traditions.

"Noyes acquired a reputation for being a radical, and although he was granted his license to preach in 1833, he was not a success. At one point . . . he declared himself to be without sin . . . For the next few years [Noyes] traveled through New York and New England . . . spreading the doctrine of Perfectionism: people could live without sin . . . Given the proper environment, therefore man could lead a perfect or sinless life . . .

"In 1844 . . . the perfectionists adopted economic communalism as a way of life. They commenced to share their work, their food, their living quarters, and their resources . . . In 1846 the group began to share spouses. As might have been predicted, once the Perfectionists began the practice of spouse sharing, the word soon spread . . . Amidst rumors of mob violence—John Humphrey

Noyes was indicted . . . on the grounds of adultery. He was released pending trial . . . and on the advice of his lawyer . . . fled to New York . . . [O]ther Perfectionist centers were available to him. One such spot was a fairly large tract of land along Oneida creek in New York State . . .

"With several hundred people living under one roof, the Oneidans had an interesting problem in human relations . . . Practically everything the perfectionists did was designed to play down the "I" in favor of the "we." Members ate . . . worked . . . and played together. They shared their property, they shared their sexual partners. And they shared their children . . .

"The religious practices of the Oneidans also served to reinforce primary-group association . . . Perfectionists dispensed with most of the formal aspects of religion. They maintained no church, held no prayer services . . . Neither baptismal nor communion services were utilized . . . At the same time, religion was a central part of the Oneidan's daily lives . . . rather than special religious celebrations . . . Perfectionists believed that every day should involve religious awareness . . . And they believed that by listening to John Humphrey Noyes—and his followers' teachings—they were listening to the voice of God."[1]

101

Understanding Our
Environment

In *Extraordinary Groups: An Examination of Unconventional Lifestyles*, **Richard Schaefer and William Zellner chronicle the rise and fall of** social groups, including **the Oneida group—a utopian society led by John Humphrey Noyes.**

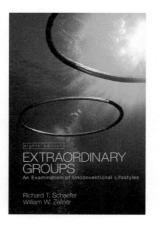

In a world without sin, where polygamy reigns and formal religion is shunned, one man, believed by his followers to be God, leads with an iron fist. This sounds like the deep voice of a movie trailer, but instead it's the real life story of John Humphrey Noyes.

Even if you aren't familiar with Noyes and his Oneida group, the remnants of this group have crept into your daily life. Any time you've eaten with Oneida silverware, you're using utensils that come from a community that believed it could live without sin and where monogamy was unnatural for both men and women. All that remains of the community, which dissolved in 1879, is the famous Oneida silverware corporation.

We only need examine Noyes's leadership, the members' interactions with one another, and their ultimate dissolution to understand what can make a group triumph or flop.

get the topic: WHAT ARE THE CHARACTERISTICS OF SOCIAL GROUPS?

SOCIAL GROUPS are groups that consist of two or more people who interact with one another and share a common identity.

At the 2008 Super Bowl in Arizona, approximately 73,000 people sat in the stands to watch the underdog Giants eke out a nail-biting victory over the undefeated Patriots.[2] That same year, there were more than 100,000 U.S. troops deployed in Iraq. It's probably safe to say that both the number of Super Bowl attendees and troops in Iraq were very high, but would you classify them both as social groups? The values and goals of an army are unified, while a football crowd—especially one that is evenly divided between fans of each team—is not. When 73,000 people gather to watch the Super Bowl, they're considered a crowd. But 100,000 troops fighting and working together on the frontlines of a battlefield? That's a **social group**.

<<< These people work in the same building, maybe even in the same office. But **are these people a social group?**

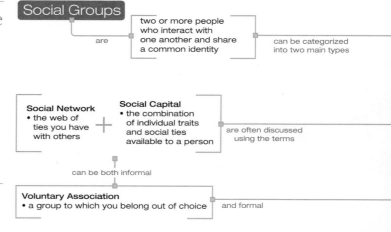

Social Groups

are → two or more people who interact with one another and share a common identity → can be categorized into two main types

Social Network
• the web of ties you have with others

+

Social Capital
• the combination of individual traits and social ties available to a person

→ are often discussed using the terms

can be both informal

Voluntary Association
• a group to which you belong out of choice   and formal

Whether we're aware of it or not, we all belong to a social group in some way or another—families, close friends, teammates, classmates, clubs, and organizations are all examples of groups to which we belong. Few of us could live totally self-reliant lives, so we find groups on which to depend. Of course, not all groups are the same. For all intents and purposes, your membership in your family is permanent, but you might not work with the same people for the rest of your life. Although no two groups are alike, they do have two commonalities; the members of the group share something in common, and they identify each other as members of that group.

PRIMARY AND SECONDARY GROUPS

We've already established that classmates qualify as a social group with shared goals and values. If you have this relationship with your classmates, why might you refrain from spilling your guts to your chemistry lab partner? Because we have different types of groups that dictate how we interact within them.

According to sociologist Charles H. Cooley, groups can be divided into two main categories—primary and secondary. *Primary groups* are small, intimate, and long-lasting.[3] Our most immediate relationships, such as relationships with family members and close friends, form primary groups. The Oneida community created a primary group by sharing everything, including spouses and children. Oneidans had a communal society in which all adults were married to each other and the community collectively raised the children.

More importantly, primary groups help us to determine who we are. Because our primary groups are usually made up of our relatives and closest friends, their presence and influence are constant reminders of how we see ourselves. It is through these relationships that we create our "looking-glass selves," which is discussed in detail in Chapter 5. By reflecting their perceptions back to us, primary relationships provide valuable feedback.

Secondary groups, on the other hand, are formal, superficial, and last for a short or fixed time.[4] These groups generally come together to meet some specific goal or purpose. If you join a civic organization in order to help put on a parade, you are joining a secondary group. Such groups provide **bounded relationships** that exist only under specific conditions. For example, you and your co-workers might "do lunch," but you probably wouldn't invite them to a family function. Co-workers form a group that is usually of secondary importance to you.

Formal types of social norms heavily influence the way we interact in secondary groups. These norms direct our actions and frame our communication. For example, you might ask your mailman about the weather, but you probably wouldn't get into a debate about climate change. Moreover, the types of norms we follow when interacting affects the way we feel about the group. If we are close and informal, we may fit in with the group, making it feel more like a primary one. If not, we can easily feel like outsiders.

PRIMARY VS. SECONDARY GROUPS

- Secondary relationships are transferable.
- Primary relationships play a variety of roles.
- Secondary relationships are impersonal and unemotional and involve limited communication.
- Primary relationships are filled with emotion and involve open communication.
- Secondary relationships have specialized roles.
- Primary relationships are not easily replaced.

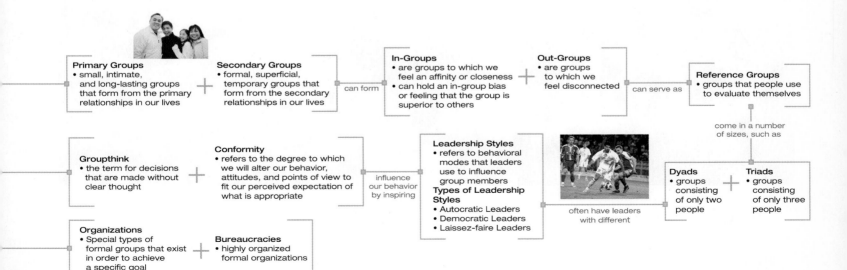

Primary Groups
- small, intimate, and long-lasting groups that form from the primary relationships in our lives

can form

Secondary Groups
- formal, superficial, temporary groups that form from the secondary relationships in our lives

In-Groups
- are groups to which we feel an affinity or closeness
- can hold an in-group bias or feeling that the group is superior to others

Out-Groups
- are groups to which we feel disconnected

can serve as

Reference Groups
- groups that people use to evaluate themselves

come in a number of sizes, such as

Groupthink
- the term for decisions that are made without clear thought

Conformity
- refers to the degree to which we will alter our behavior, attitudes, and points of view to fit our perceived expectation of what is appropriate

influence our behavior by inspiring

Leadership Styles
- refers to behavioral modes that leaders use to influence group members

Types of Leadership Styles
- Autocratic Leaders
- Democratic Leaders
- Laissez-faire Leaders

often have leaders with different

Dyads
- groups consisting of only two people

Triads
- groups consisting of only three people

Organizations
- Special types of formal groups that exist in order to achieve a specific goal

Bureaucracies
- highly organized formal organizations

IN-GROUPS AND OUT-GROUPS

In the words of supermodel-turned-reality-show-host Heidi Klum on *Project Runway,* "One day you're in, and the next day, you're out." Klum's catchphrase, which is used to discuss whether an aspiring designer's fashions are in or out of style, is not just true of clothes, but also of social groups. If you've ever had to wait for what seemed like hours on the sidelines—while all the popular kids are getting chosen for the team—you were hoping to be welcomed into the in-group of people who don't have to wait until last to be chosen.

An **in-group** is a group to which we feel an affinity or closeness. For this reason, we often have a strong sense of loyalty to an in-group. Most people hold an **in-group bias**, the feeling that their in-group is superior to others.[5] The ABC reality series *Wife Swap* perfectly illustrates how some families engage in in-group bias. The show, in which the mothers of two very different families exchange places for a period of time, usually features participants who believe theirs is the best way to raise a family. The mothers are then confronted by the strange interactions of another's family. Each mother considers the other family an out-group.

An **out-group** is a group from which we are disconnected. We often hold negative biases toward out-groups and may even feel very competitive toward them. We see this all the time in sports. Ask any member of Red Sox Nation about the Yankees, and you're likely to be met with unvarnished vitriol. The same will probably happen if you ask Yankees fans about the Red Sox. In both cases, each respective fan group holds an out-group bias toward the other fan group. This is especially true in partisan politics in which skirmishes between Democrats and Republicans can erupt over the most mundane issues. The members of the Oneida community came together to form a type of in-group. Members of the group were fiercely loyal to one another and shunned those who lived in the "outside" world.

Sociologist Robert Merton suggests that our biases come from our position in society.[6] We see the traits of our group as acceptable while we hold the views of out-groups as unreasonable. Generally, people hold a bias toward out-groups; however, there are a number of factors that impact whether these biases are positive or negative.[7] For example, social outcasts in high school can hold either a positive or negative bias toward the "popular" group. If the outcasts know that nothing can change their outsider status, then they're likely to hold the cool kids in contempt. If, on the other hand, an outcast hopes to one day penetrate the cool group, he or she holds a positive bias toward them. In a sense, outcasts place the in-group on a pedestal if they think they can join them, and they knock this group down if they feel joining the group is impossible.[8]

Judging from the expressions on the faces **of Heidi and crew** on the set of the fashion design competition *Project Runway,* **the designer frock** they're viewing is definitely a fashion "don't."

Sociologists Tajfel and Turner suggest that everyone seeks a positive social identity.[9] This pursuit is the root cause of in-group and out-group biases. We may point out the negative differences in others to elevate our own identity, even if the differences are insignificant. Go to an Internet message board where posters are discussing a hypothetical battle between Superman and the Incredible Hulk, and you might observe some heated wrath being spewed as each camp take sides. This seemingly innocuous conversation can quickly devolve into a flame-throwing contest between angry fanboys. By poking fun at the other, the groups make themselves feel superior.

Position and power are other factors that can impact our perception of in-groups and out-groups. The workplace is common ground for these biases. Courtney Von Hippel studied temporary employees' out-group biases.[10] Temps who actually wanted a full-time job desired their co-workers' acceptance.[11] Meanwhile, temps who didn't expect permanent employment resented full-time employees because they didn't need to feel accepted.[12] In other words, it was highly unlikely that full-timers were taking these temps out to lunch.

IN-GROUP is a group to which we feel an affinity or closeness.

IN-GROUP BIAS is the feeling that a person's in-group is superior to others.

OUT-GROUP is a group from which we are disconnected.

REFERENCE GROUP is the group that you use to evaluate yourself.

REFERENCE GROUPS

In nearly every situation, we compare ourselves to another person or group. For example, you might not have a need for a new cell phone, but if one of your best friends keeps going on and on about his new iPhone, you might find yourself visiting your local wireless phone dealer so you're not left out. Since we cannot make judgments about our own behavior in isolation, we often use others to assess our behavior.[13] Sociologists refer to the group you use to evaluate yourself as a **reference group**.

REFERENCE GROUPS, though, are not necessarily in-groups because we don't have to belong to them. **If, for example, you are studying to be a neurosurgeon,** you might talk to surgeons at your local hospital **about the duties and challenges of the career.** But simply thinking like a surgeon doesn't make you one. **They're just a reference group to help guide who you are and who you will become.**

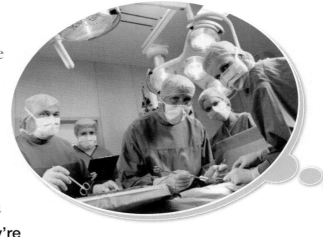

▶▶▶ GO GLOBAL

In and Out in Japan

Xenophobia, the fear of outsiders, is a powerful example of out-group bias. In Japan, only those with 100% Japanese lineage are considered Japanese.[14] Foreigners who move to Japan and live there for years might eventually be able to gain citizenship, but will never "become Japanese," nor will their children.[15] In this way, Japanese society alienates itself from other cultures. "True" Japanese people in Japan form an in-group, whereas all other non-native or different peoples form an out-group.

Throughout history, it's been customary for the Japanese to create out-groups, ostracize them, and then hold that group responsible for current social problems.[16] During the early 1900s, many Korean people were brought into Japan as migrant workers to meet the nation's industrialization needs.[17] Japanese society immediately began to look at the Korean population as outsiders. Association with the population was frowned upon, and cultural integration was impossible. In fact, in present-day Japan, Koreans cannot gain full citizenship. However, leaders are working to change laws in order to recognize Koreans as full-fledged Japanese citizens.

>>> **ACTIVITY** Research a country other than Japan. What in- and out-groups are part of that country's society? How are members of the out-groups treated? Discuss your findings with a classmate.

DYAD is a group consisting of only two people.

TRIAD is a group consisting of three people.

LEADERSHIP STYLE is a behavioral mode that leaders use to influence group members.

AUTOCRATIC LEADERS are leaders who determine the group policies and assign tasks.

DEMOCRATIC LEADERS are leaders who strive to set group policy by discussion and agreement.

LAISSEZ-FAIRE LEADERS are leaders who lead by absence and may in fact not want to be leaders at all.

CONFORMITY is the degree to which we will alter our behavior, attitudes, and points of view to fit into our perceived expectation of what is appropriate.

GROUPTHINK is the term for group decisions that are made without objective thought.

GROUP SIZE, STRUCTURE, AND INTERACTION

Groups come in all shapes and sizes. When the Oneida group began in 1849, there were 87 original members.[18] The group grew to a total of 306 members before dissolving in the late 1800s. Part of the reason the Oneida community broke up was due to its size—the large group size led to infighting among its members. As a group gets larger, maintaining in-group feelings becomes harder. Smaller groups tend to be more intimate and less official, making them easier to maintain.

The smallest and strongest form of a group is a **dyad**, a group consisting of only two people. The two members become very close, intimate, and connected. Think of a happy marriage as an example of a strong dyad. Such closeness is not possible in larger groups. Paradoxically, a dyad can also be unstable because either member can unilaterally decide to dissolve the group.[19] If someone has ever dumped you, you probably understand this principle.

When a third member enters a twosome, a **triad**, or group of three, forms. In a triad, mediation, alliances, and competition are likely. For example, if two members of the triad are at odds, the third member can act as a mediator to resolve the conflict. Triads can also allow for alliances between two of the members, potentially against the third, which weakens the group. If two friends ever teamed up against you, then you understand this principle. When alliances occur, the chance for competition among the members increases, which can lead to dissolution of the group. As a result, sociologist Georg Simmel referred to the triad as the weakest group size.[20]

As group size grows, there are greater opportunities for potential interactions, but also more formality and less intimacy. Family gatherings are great places to see this theory play out in real life. At a recent family gathering, I closely watched the interactions taking place as people slowly began to arrive. When the group size was small, people remained together, sitting in the same room and holding a single conversation. However, as the size grew to greater than ten, having one large conversation became impossible. I noticed people breaking off into subgroups. Some played games, others went outside, and still others stayed in the kitchen sampling the holiday goodies. Such divisions are normal even among close families. The group was simply too large to allow for one conversation.

If you attend a concert in a large arena, you'll probably talk only to those with whom you came, right? You and others are sandwiched into tight surroundings, and you may be actually physically touching someone you don't know, yet you probably won't talk to that person. Ironically, our sense of group often gets smaller when we're in large crowds. As a population increases in size and becomes denser, our perception of group size becomes smaller.[21] As crowds get larger, they become more stressful to us. In order to reduce the stress, we retreat into smaller, safer groups, thus limiting the interactions in the group and the stress of being in the crowd.

According to Hamburger et al., **the size of the group affects the group's ability to cooperate in a task.**[22] This phenomenon explains why reducing class size in public schools is a major issue in education policy. **Smaller groups accomplish more in less time than larger ones do.**

LEADERSHIP STYLES

In many groups, there are always those individuals who stand apart from the crowd and become leaders, either officially or unofficially. If you've watched any season of *Survivor,* you know that often tribe leaders emerge. Tribe leaders provide food for the group, instructions for building shelter, and unity among the tribe members. Since leadership makes others more conscious of the person, leaders on *Survivor* often have a huge target on the backs even though their contributions are usually crucial to the tribe's success.

According to Lewin et al., leadership can be summarized by three distinct styles.[23] **Leadership style** refers to a behavioral mode that leaders use to influence group members. Leadership style varies between autocratic, democratic, and laissez-faire styles. **Autocratic leaders** determine the group policies and assign tasks.[24] These strict authoritarians inform you, "It's my way or the highway." Conversely, **democratic leaders** strive to set group policy by discussion and agreement.[25] They hope for consensus and are likely to ask for your opinion on matters. Finally, **laissez-faire leaders** lead by absence and may in fact not want to be leaders at all.[26] They set few goals and do only what must be done.

Whichever style you've encountered, there are some important points to remember about leadership style as it applies to social groups:

1. There is no "right" type of leadership style.
2. Successful leaders adapt the style to the situation.
3. The process of leadership impacts both the group members and the leader.
4. Leadership styles are learnable.
5. Different styles can be effective in certain situations and/or with certain groups of people.[27]

CONFORMITY

Because it takes the rare individual to stand out and be a leader, most members of a group are followers in some way. **Conformity** refers to the degree to which we will alter our behavior, attitudes, and points of view to fit into our perceived expectation of what is appropriate. Everyone hopes to "fit in," but would you change your opinion of what you think is true in order to fit into a group?

Psychologist Solomon Asch wanted to test the impact of groups on people's perception in 1952.[28] Asch set up groups so that only one member was not aware that the rest were actors. Then, he showed the pseudo-group a series of cards like those shown below. He asked them to match the lines on card 2 to the line they saw on card 1. At first, the confidants chose correctly and the group could easily make unified decisions. However, over time the confidants began to make deliberate mistakes in order to test the desire to achieve group conformity. Amazingly, about a third of the participants went along with the group, even though it was in error. Such a phenomenon is more common than you might think. When people are in a group, they often want to conform to the majority and don't offer an opinion that goes against the grain.

>>> When you're with a crowd, **do you find that you change your behavior to match everyone? Or do you march to your own drummer?**

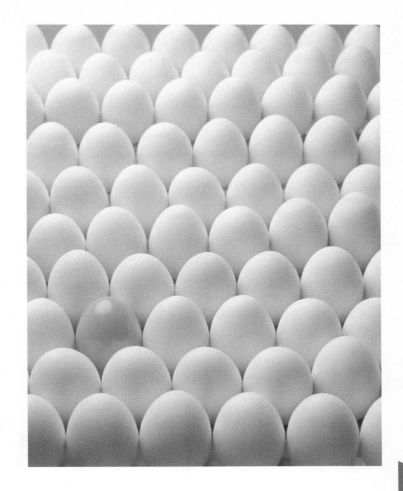

ASCH'S CARDS

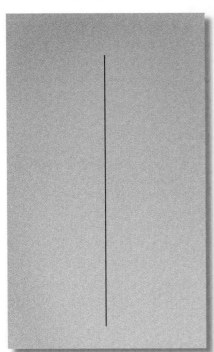

CARD 1

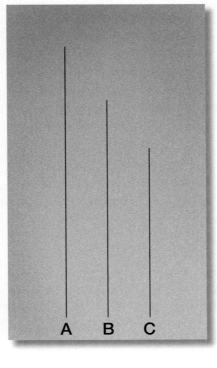

CARD 2

A   B   C

Groupthink

At times, group conformity becomes so strong that a group will not consider other ideas or influences. Extremely cohesive groups or ones with very strong leaders might make decisions using groupthink.[29] **Groupthink** is the term for group decisions that are made without objective thought. When a group is in this mode, people conform to what they believe is the consensus of the rest of the group. They often make decisions that they would not make as individuals. Extreme group conformity leads to groupthink. It frequently results in bad decisions that people later agree were a mistake. Groupthink is more likely when the following conditions are present:

- **Cohesiveness:** Groups that are highly connected are more likely to engage in groupthink. If, for example, you were to join a board of directors that the same people had led for 10 years, odds are groupthink is occurring. This group is likely to be very interconnected and to think they have ironed out all the possible solutions to the potential problems.
- **Threats:** When groups encounter an external threat, solidarity increases because common enemies unify groups.
- **A Strong Leader:** If the leader has a domineering style or is charismatic enough, groups will usually accept the leader's will. Although a strong leader is important to a group's progress, it can also increase the odds of groupthink because few will want to take on the leader.[30]

MAKE CONNECTIONS

A History of Groupthink

Sociologist Irving Janis pinned down eight shortcomings that are likely to result from groupthink decisions.[31] We can use these criteria as standards to evaluate any decision and determine if groupthink was involved. Groupthink in U.S. politics is hardly anything new. Janis points out that political leaders often run the risk of making poor decisions because of this phenomenon. The failed U.S. invasion of Cuba, known as the Bay of Pigs, fits the bill.[32] Think about past U.S. leaders' decisions to invade nations such as Iraq. Was groupthink behind these decisions?

1 **Illusion of invulnerability.** Groupthink creates excessive optimism that the desired outcome will occur. Some have suggested that the 2003 invasion of Iraq arose from an illusion of invulnerability. When the United States launched its "Shock and Awe" campaign in 2003, media coverage gave citizens the impression that the war would be easily won.[33] The military was supposed to dominate Iraq rapidly, quickly winning the war on terror and suffering few casualties in the process.

2 **Collective rationalization.** Members ignore warnings as irrelevant and will not reconsider the assumptions of the decision. Some have suggested that the 2003 invasion of Iraq arose from collective rationalization. Critics point to President Bush's "Bring 'em on" and Vice President Cheney's proclamation that "We'll be greeted as liberators" as examples of such thinking.[34]

3 **Belief in inherent morality.** People in the group believe their cause is just and right. In a 2001 speech, President George W. Bush claimed, "Either you are with us, or you are with the terrorists."[35] This led many citizens to reconsider their opposition to the war.

4 **Stereotyped views of out-groups.** Groupthink is likely when members view themselves as the "good guys" and their opponents as the "bad guys." When the United States invaded Iraq to overthrow the government of Saddam Hussein, many of my students held negative stereotypes of the Iraqi people, believing them to be "cold-blooded terrorists."

∧∧∧ **What conditions** do you think **are contributing to** this **groupthink?**

5 **Direct pressure on dissenters.** Members of the group who disagree are under pressure to keep quiet if they dissent. Frequently, the group will not allow any voicing of disagreement. In his 2004 book *Plan of Attack*, journalist Bob Woodward suggests that members of President George W. Bush's presidential cabinet effectively isolated dissenters of the war in Iraq.[36] Moreover, many critics of the administration were labeled "unpatriotic" and accused of "not supporting the troops" if they expressed contradictory opinions.

6 **Self-censorship.** Group members squelch their doubts and fail to express reservations they may have about the proposal. When group members see dissenters punished or isolated, they will self-censor in order to avoid punishment from a strong leader. In the time leading up to the war in Iraq, many media outlets, such as *The New York Times* and NBC News, tended to downplay anti-war stories due to pressure from the Bush administration.[37]

7 **Illusion of unanimity.** The group leadership in particular mistakes a pressured majority view for unanimity. For example, in an interview with ABC News, former Secretary of State Colin Powell admitted that his public support for the war in Iraq came from his loyalty to President Bush and not his personal convictions.[38] When Powell silenced his personal convictions, he gave the appearance of unanimity.

8 **Self-appointed mind guards.** Certain members play the role of protector of the leader, shielding him or her from information and ideas that might be contradictory to the group's decision. Many television media stations could be considered mind guards because they rarely, if ever, aired views that could be considered counterproductive to the war.

>>> **ACTIVITY** Think about your own life. How has groupthink played a role in a past decision you've made? Do you regret that decision now? Evaluate your choice using the eight shortcomings of groupthink. Did all eight factor into your decision?

SOCIAL CAPITAL AND SOCIAL NETWORKS

When you think of all the possible things that brought you to this point in your life, you're basically thinking about social capital. **Social capital** is a sociological concept that refers to the individual and collective resources available to a person. Social capital includes the institutions, relationships, attitudes, and values that influence interactions among people and contribute to economic and social development. Coleman suggests that social capital impacts all aspects of our lives and affects the choices and options available to us.[39]

Most of us use this kind of capital to find jobs, colleges, and other opportunities. For example, my first job was repairing bicycles in a local bike shop. I got the job because my mother knew the owner. Later on, a friend helped me find my second job at a fast-food chicken restaurant. Of course, I had to do the work and keep the job, but my friends and family were a part of my social capital that helped me gain employment.

Although Coleman suggests that social capital is functional for society and individuals, Bourdieu, a conflict theorist, views it as an economic resource.[40] Consider legacy admissions: a policy in which applicants to a highly touted private university are admitted based on their family's history with the school. Such a practice tends to benefit wealthier students because they are more likely to have family members who are alumni. In short, our social and familial contacts can help us get a foot in the door of a place to which we might have otherwise been denied access.

The social contacts that people make, when culled together, comprise a social network, which is one component of social capital. Basically, a **social network** is the web of ties you have with others. Networks usually include people with similar values, beliefs, and identities. They allow us to gain important information and may even open doors of opportunity. In the 21st century, social networking has taken on an even greater importance for Web-savvy individuals. Sites such as MySpace, Facebook, and LinkedIn serve as virtual alternatives to traditional networks. The power of the Internet allows people to expand their network exponentially.

SOCIAL CAPITAL is a sociological concept that refers to the individual and collective resources available to a person.

SOCIAL NETWORK is the web of ties you have with others.

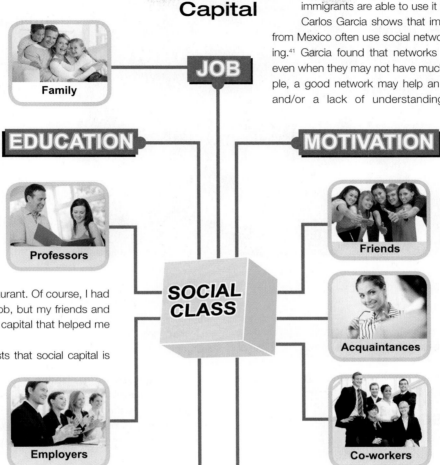

Social Capital

Family — JOB

EDUCATION — Professors

MOTIVATION — Friends

SOCIAL CLASS

Acquaintances

Employers

Co-workers

GENDER — RACE

Classmates

∧∧∧ Your **social capital** is a combination of **internal and external** resources.

To see the value of a social network, look at how recent immigrants are able to use it to their advantage. Sociologist Carlos Garcia shows that immigrants to the United States from Mexico often use social networks to get jobs and find housing.[41] Garcia found that networks allow immigrants to succeed even when they may not have much personal capital.[42] For example, a good network may help an immigrant overcome illiteracy and/or a lack of understanding of the English language. Immigrants use three different forms of networking:

1 **Traditional networks:** These include primary group relationships with family and close friends. Often Mexican immigrants obtain job leads from family and friends, which can impact decisions they make about where they will live.[43]

2 **Church networks:** These networks connect people based on their religious affiliation and offer many of the same benefits as a traditional one. Mexican immigrants often use church affiliations in order to expand the scope of their networks.[44]

3 **Contract networks:** These involve employers seeking workers. During Garcia's research, meatpacking plants sent agents to Mexico to contract with potential laborers, guaranteeing them work if they could get to the United States. Contract networks provide necessary economic resources, whereas traditional and church networks provide social and emotional support.[45]

Sometimes, you don't have to depend on a strong network to succeed. Weak ties can also be immensely valuable to us. For example, you may hear about a job opening from someone sitting next to you in class. Even though your classmate isn't necessarily in your primary group, this tip could prove much more valuable than information from your family or friends. Granovetter suggests that weak ties play a vital role in social capital because they expand our networks, thus expanding our possibilities.[46]

<<< Our view of an organization depends upon our involvement with it. For example, a prison can be a **utilitarian organization** for the prison guards, **a normative organization** for people who volunteer to lead Alcoholics Anonymous groups with the inmates, **and a coercive organization** to the inmates themselves.

Formal Organizations

When you hang out with friends or family, you let your guard down and forget about all the rules. That's because these social groups are informal. Other groups you're affiliated with, such as your local bowling league or country club, are probably formal organizations. **Formal organizations** are groups created for a certain purpose and built for maximum efficiency.

VOLUNTARY ASSOCIATIONS

Through joining a team, singing in a choir, or helping in a soup kitchen, you can make a **voluntary association**. In 1995, political scientist Robert Putnam showed that participation in these kinds of associations is declining.[47] Take bowling leagues, for example. The number of bowling leagues is decreasing, while the number of people bowling has not changed. People are joining organizations less frequently, creating a more individual and isolated society. The social capital of our entire society may be suffering from shrinking social networks, despite our using networks to increase our outcomes and improve our lives.

Voluntary associations have life-changing effects on communities. For example, in an area of Nepal where high fertility rates were an increasing problem, more individuals became involved in voluntary associations—like credit bank groups, women's groups, agricultural groups, and youth groups. As memberships increased, the likelihood of Nepalese people using contraception also increased.[48] People who lived in neighborhoods that had a number of possible voluntary associations were more likely to use contraceptives than people who lived in relatively isolated communities. Through fostering a better sense of community among individuals, voluntary associations helped control fertility rates.

ORGANIZATIONS AND BUREAUCRACIES

Organizations come in a variety of types and sizes. Some organizations are formed to help a cause, such as the Sierra Club. Others, like the popular furniture store IKEA, serve to make money. All organizations are alike in that they are formal groups that exist to achieve a desired goal. Sociologist Amitai Etzioni suggested that the type of organization ultimately determines our membership in it.[49] For example, when you get a job at a department store or office building, you're joining a **utilitarian organization**.[50] Members join utilitarian organizations because they receive wages in exchange for work. **Normative organizations**, though, exist in order to achieve a worthwhile goal.[51] If you volunteer at normative organization, such as a soup kitchen, you do so because you believe feeding the homeless serves an essential purpose in society.

While we willingly join utilitarian and normative organizations, we do not join **coercive organizations** by choice.[52] Members of coercive organizations, like prison inmates or rehab patients, don't join voluntarily; outside forces of authority bring them into the organization.

Whether utilitarian, normative, or coercive, organizations have some important qualities that keep them running smoothly.

- **Division of labor:** Tasks are clearly defined and divided, and members understand their roles and expectations.
- **Concentration of power:** Organizations concentrate power in the hands of a few, who can then use that power to control the institution.
- **Methods of succession:** Membership in the organization allows for the replacement of all roles, including leaders.[53]

Within all organizations, a structure exists, though some may be more formal than others. **Formal structure** refers to the explicit rules, goals, and guidelines of the organization. Organization charts, policy and procedure manuals, and established titles and roles are all part of the formal structure of an organization. You can see such formal structures develop in any student organization that elects presidents, vice presidents, and other officers. **Informal structures** consist of friendships, allegiances, and loyalties among members of the organization. All organizations have informal structures, and these often make the organization run smoothly.

CHARACTERISTICS OF BUREAUCRACY

If you've ever had to wait in line for hours to renew your driver's license, only to hear "I can't help you. You'll have to wait over there," then you know some of the frustrations that come with a large bureaucracy. **Bureaucracies** are formal organizations that are organized into a hierarchy of smaller departments. Bureaucracies often have an impersonal feel when one department doesn't have much contact with another. Since a better method of organization has not yet been found, it looks like they are here to stay.

Max Weber was one of the early sociologists to discuss the idea of bureaucracy.[54] Weber proposed that no matter what a formal organization's purpose might be, all ideal bureaucracies display certain characteristics.

Weber and the Iron Cage

For Weber, bureaucratization was a logical extension of formal rational thought.[55] **Formal rationality** refers to the reasonable actions organizations and bureaucracies take to achieve goals in the most effective way. If Weber's theory sounds familiar, it's because George Ritzer used the same theory in his discussion of the McDonaldization of the United States included in Chapter 3.[56]

According to Weber, any organization that grows large enough will inevitably strive toward formal rationality and bureaucracy. However, such a highly structured bureaucracy can cause the members to feel trapped in a dehumanizing "**iron cage**" that turns them into little more than robots accomplishing tasks. Weber proposed that this iron cage, while problematic from a personal level, is actually a good thing because it helps the organization thrive and places its needs above the needs of the individual.

The power of the bureaucracy often moves from the top down, meaning that leaders of the group make decisions, and those lower on the organizational chart complete these tasks. This setup forces leaders to be accountable for the actions of the bureaucracy and increases their control. However, this hierarchy strips workers of having a say in decision making.

With all the decision-making power at the top, inefficiencies can occur. If leaders don't understand what is happening at the lower levels of the organization, they can easily lead it astray. For example, while I was working as an intake social worker, the agency hired a new director. The director decided that instead of seeing a social worker first, all potentially new clients should first have nurses assess their medical condition. Both the nurses and I voiced our objections, but the director overruled us. As a result, many of

our new clients found out that after spending hours in the agency, they were not eligible for service. Many wasted hours resulted, and eventually the director went back to the old system.

The division of labor in a bureaucracy can also be a negative. Workers may become alienated from the organization's purpose and only focus on their specific tasks. For example, a factory worker who spends hours putting tires on cars might notice a broken windshield but not say anything because "it's not his job." Such a feeling arises from an impersonal organizational culture.

Although written rules and regulations let workers know what is expected of them, strict enforcement of these rules stifles creativity and imagination. Workers might not be inclined to speak up in order to implement a new idea or to perform tasks that do not fall under their job description.

Now that we have discussed the role of groups and group interaction in society, it's time to think sociologically about these groups.

FORMAL ORGANIZATIONS are groups created for a certain purpose and built for maximum efficiency.

VOLUNTARY ASSOCIATION is the act of joining an organization that offers no pay and that expands social networks through interaction.

ORGANIZATIONS are formal groups that exist to achieve a desired goal.

UTILITARIAN ORGANIZATION is an organization in which people receive wages in exchange for work.

NORMATIVE ORGANIZATIONS are organizations that exist to achieve a worthwhile goal.

COERCIVE ORGANIZATIONS are organizations that people are forced to join.

FORMAL STRUCTURES are the explicit rules, goals, and guidelines of an organization.

INFORMAL STRUCTURES are friendships, allegiances, and loyalties among members of an organization.

BUREAUCRACIES are formal organizations that are organized into a hierarchy of smaller departments.

FORMAL RATIONALITY is the reasonable actions that organizations and bureaucracies take to achieve goals in the most effective way.

IRON CAGE is a concept introduced by Max Weber that refers to the way in which bureaucracies make workers feel trapped and turn them into little more than robots accomplishing tasks.

Weber's Characteristics of Bureaucracy

Division of Labor
Workers are assigned specific, specialized tasks.

Hierarchy of Authority
Decision-making power moves from the top (supervisors) down to workers in lower positions.

Rules and Regulations
Rules and regulations guide a bureaucracy's actions to ensure that tasks are performed uniformly.

Impersonality
Workers perform "without hatred or passion," meaning that all clients are treated equally.

Technical Qualifications
Hiring and promotions are based on a worker's ability to perform a task.

think sociologically: HOW DO SOCIOLOGISTS VIEW GROUP LEADERSHIP?

Functionalism and Leadership

What makes someone a good leader? Influential functionalism theorist John C. Maxwell provides a model of leadership made up of five levels.[57] Think about leaders you know who exhibit these qualities.

LEADERSHIP 101: WHAT EVERY LEADER NEEDS TO KNOW

The true measure of leadership is influence on others. If you lack this ability, no one will follow you. The style of leadership—autocratic, democratic, or laissez-faire—you employ does not directly affect your level of leadership. An autocratic leader can be just as influential as a democratic leader. However, Maxwell suggests that all leaders begin at the most basic level.[58]

Level 1: *Positional leaders: People follow the leader because they must.*

This level serves as the most basic type of leadership. Simply put, other people give positional leaders the reins of leadership. They don't rely on vision or charisma to lead others; instead, people follow them because of their title. When you enter the workforce, the hierarchy of your company determines who your supervisor will be, and it is part of your job to follow that person's lead. In the overall scheme of things, though, the positional leader and the people he or she oversees are just cogs in a machine. This type of leader has the least amount of influence.

Level 2: *Permission leaders: People follow because they want to.*

> Successful leaders eventually understand that there is more to leadership that merely being the boss.

Although positional leaders often lack personal relationships with their followers, permission leaders take the opposite tack. These leaders generate followers willingly precisely because they develop personal relationships with them. A permission leader doesn't merely view workers as a means to an end; instead, they work together because they enjoy each other's company. Such a leader has considerably more influence because their followers are actually invested in the relationship, and, by extension, the task that is to be completed.

Level 3: *Production leaders: People follow because of what you have done.*

At this level of leadership, goals are met with minimum effort because the leader sets the example. Production leaders spur a sense of accomplishment in the people who follow them and clearly communicate a vision of what can be. They then go out and perform just as hard as everyone else. Production leaders are also willing to make difficult decisions and take the blame for failures. Kobe Bryant is known to be quiet and introspective off the basketball court. But on the court, he is unquestionably his team's leader because his effort and skills inspire the rest of his teammates to perform better.

Level 4: *People development: People follow because they are empowered.*

Rather than demonstrating their own skills to set an example, empowering leaders help people meet their potential by encouraging them to accomplish tasks they might have previously felt were impossible. By developing people, an empowering leader accomplishes tasks more easily because the team feels they are capable and competent. An example of this type of leadership is demonstrated in President John F. Kennedy's famous words, "Ask not what your country can do for you; ask what you can do for your country."

Level 5: *Personhood: People follow because of who you are.*

It can take many years for people to attain this highest level of influence. Such leaders must spend a lot of time cultivating relationships with people and developing communication skills. But once this level is reached, they will be able to inspire their followers to exceed their potential and willingly sacrifice for them.

Maxwell suggests that all leaders have the potential to climb this ladder of influence, but every new leader starts at the first level. Successful leaders eventually understand that there is more to leadership than merely being the boss.

THINK SOCIOLOGICALLY

Leadership in the Oneida Community

John Humphrey Noyes displayed each of Maxwell's levels of effective leadership in the way he oversaw the Oneida community. Since Noyes was the founder of the community, anyone who joined had to follow his lead.

Both Noyes and his early followers believed that he had "divine commission," or was sent by a higher power to lead the group. Noyes believed so strongly in his right to lead that he said, "I would never connect myself with any individual or association in religion unless I were acknowledged leader," and many did acknowledge him.[59] Similar to Maxwell's first level of leadership, Noyes' followers were influenced by his title as divine leader. As more members joined, Noyes formed personal relationships with each of them and cultivated a more loyal following.

Noyes was able to sustain his leadership by practicing the "sinless life" he often preached. This influenced his followers to believe in the collective cause of the community. There was no question that the Oneida community was governed as an absolute monarchy. In this society, authority came from the Noyes at the top and the members supported his decisions.

Noyes did not completely rule on his own, though. Like Maxwell suggested, leaders succeed because they empower others. Once Noyes discovered loyal individuals, he often employed them as his advisors. At the height of his power, Noyes had climbed to the top of the leadership ladder. His followers were willing to make whatever sacrifices were necessary to remain members of this community.

∧
∧
∧
Marx believed that **bureaucracy was actually a "hierarchy of knowledge."** The **leaders trust workers** to handle all the details, while the **workers trust the leaders** to handle the general outcome. Based on this idea, **Marx believed each side deceived the other,** which ultimately **benefited the bourgeoisie.**[60] Do you agree with Marx's interpretation of bureaucracy? Why or why not?

Conflict Theory—Marx, Bureaucracy, and Democratic Organizations

While Weber saw both the positive and negative aspects of bureaucracy, Karl Marx believed that "bureaucracy [was] a circle from which one [could not] escape." For Marx, bureaucracy provided no essential function for society. It was just another way for the bourgeoisie to exploit workers more efficiently and gain more wealth and control for themselves.

You'd probably expect workers to fight against bureaucratic systems. However, Marx's theory suggests that employees who oppose a bureaucracy's leadership are easily discovered, reprimanded, or fired. Is this the most beneficial for productivity? Studies show that a democratic, instead of an autocratic leadership style, actually increases worker productivity. Democratic leaders encourage workers to participate in production decisions, and this participation increases profits and productivity.[61] It seems that a more inclusive leadership style helps both the workers and the owners.

Greater labor participation in leadership roles does not mean that the company will succeed. In studies by Hammer et al., increased laborer participation on boards of directors does not translate to increased profits.[62] In fact, such involvement is counterproductive for future planning because workers and management tend to have differing points of view. Workers focus primarily on job protection, while managers are interested in appeasing stockholders.

Symbolic Interactionism— Creating a Just and Democratic Workplace

After graduating from college, you probably have high hopes of landing your dream job. The sad fact is that for four out of five people in the United States, their daily grind is a nightmare.[63] It appears that U.S. citizens hate their jobs more than ever before.

Negative feelings like these have symbolic interactionists wondering: How do workers' attitudes toward their jobs impact productivity and job satisfaction? This is a question that can keep a human resources administrator up at night. When people have a level of personal control over the outcomes of their jobs, they are more connected to their work.[64] For example, if a programmer has designed a software prototype that catches her supervisor's eye, she is more likely to feel a stronger connection to the company.

Joyce Rothschild suggests that traditional bureaucracies create ineffective work environments because workers are disconnected.[65] Studying Eastern European capitalist and communist countries in the late 1970s and early 1980s, Rothschild found similar feelings of disconnection in both environments.[66] Workers experienced little ability to innovate and change their work environment in the centrally organized government-owned businesses of Eastern Europe. This top-down management style is very similar to that of Western capitalist bureaucracies. Rothschild's conclusion was clear—restrictive work environments equal inefficient and unproductive workers.[67]

In contrast, team approaches in management encourage democracy in the workplace.[68] Teams in the workplace are likely to be more connected to their jobs because individuals can connect to other team members. From the perspective of an interactionist, such a change could be linked to a changing definition of business success. As workers become more educated, they expect to have more input in the work they do. After completing your degree, you'll probably seek a job that includes you in the process of deciding how to do your work. It's a good position to strive for. Jobs like these allow people to have a sense of satisfaction both at work and in their personal lives.

WRAP YOUR MIND AROUND THE THEORY

Today, Oprah Winfrey is one of the most influential women in the world, but she did not start off that way. After beginning her career in 1971 at a small TV station in Nashville, **she worked her way through the levels of leadership. Since then, she expanded her audience so much that people have described her influence to be greater than most political and religious leaders, aside from the Pope.**[69]

FUNCTIONALISM

When studying groups, functionalists might examine the group's values and behaviors, particularly those of the group's leader. Successful groups often have successful leaders, so studying a group's leadership and how it impacts other members is important. John Maxwell points out that while anyone can be a "boss," only specific people can become a leader. He created a model outlining the five levels of leadership and proposed that each level depicts an increase in influence and empowerment in workers. Even Oneida community founder John Humphrey Noyes went through these steps before he was able to become powerful. Eventually, he was able to influence hundreds of people to follow him and start his own community of loyal followers.

CONFLICT THEORY

Since conflict theorists focus on macro issues and their relationship to society, they would take note of the arguments surrounding bureaucracy. While Weber saw bureaucracy as an extension of formal rational thought, Marx viewed it as a tool of the rich to keep the working class down. Critics of Marx have pointed out that democratic environments actually improve productivity and profits. However, if a democratic environment is not implemented, then bureaucracy can be stifling for the worker and the organization. To keep control over the Oneida group, Noyes created 48 departments for community organizations and 21 committees to supervise these departments.[70] While Weber may have viewed this system as rational, Marx would claim it was a tool used to keep control.

HOW DO DIFFERENT PERSPECTIVES VIEW GROUP LEADERSHIP?

SYMBOLIC INTERACTIONISM

Symbolic interactionists realize that along with leadership, personal attitude has a big effect on job performance and satisfaction. People feel good about themselves and their jobs when they feel they have a certain level of control over their actions. Rothschild suggests that workers feel disconnected under traditional bureaucracies, which create unproductive environments. Symbolic interactionists view a democratic work environment as more satisfactory for workers because it helps them feel connected to their jobs. Noyes tried to create a sense of connection in the Oneida community through criticism sessions in which people could release their aggression. Although these sessions seemed to be therapeutic, they were actually useful in controlling the community through shame.[71] People gained a sense of power over the community when they could take part in disciplining its members.

What do you see when you look at this picture? **Is it an organized business, or is it a tool to maintain oppression?**

When people have a certain level of control over their jobs, **they are much more likely to feel connected and satisfied.** This, in turn, **makes them more productive in the** organization.

discover sociology in action: HOW DOES A PARENT'S CIVIC ENGAGEMENT AFFECT A CHILD'S FUTURE POLITICAL INVOLVEMENT?

I always vote. Why? Primarily because my parents did. During my childhood, they stressed the importance of being involved in my government and community. My mother always said, "If you don't care, why should anyone else?"

Adult Civic Engagement and Childhood Activities

Since the 1960s, civic organizations have witnessed a sharp decline in participation, which could certainly lead to a society that is less interconnected and has a lower level of social capital.[72] As a result, a number of social problems can arise, one of which is voter apathy.

Could participation in voting and politics be related to what you did when you were younger? Daniel McFarland and Reuben Thomas suggest your involvement as a child impacts your willingness to engage in political action in the future.[73] The authors tested children and controlled for a variety of factors, including the parents' socioeconomic status and education.[74] They found that involvement in activities that encouraged public speaking and/or community service increased the likelihood of political involvement in adult life.[75] Perhaps this is because participants become involved in communities and see the benefits of such involvement.

These findings have direct implications on social policies and civic engagement. Schools that encourage students to become involved in their communities build active citizens. Not only does service learning help you take what you learn in the classroom and use it in the community, but you are also more likely to remain civically engaged.

ACTIVITIES

1. Visit with a professor and discuss your ideas about leadership in the classroom and on your college campus. What does your professor do to inspire followers to his or her discipline?
2. Does your college offer courses or clubs to train you in leadership skills? If so, what are they? If not, where in your local community can you find such opportunities?
3. Do you vote? Do your classmates vote? Why or why not?
4. Read other stories from *Extraordinary Groups: An Examination of Unconventional Lifestyles*. What sociological components make groups last? What happens to the group to cause it to die out?

Leading Groups

As you take your learning from the classroom to the community, you may find yourself leading groups. Effective group work practice requires you to have an understanding of how groups work and a level of comfort with group leadership. How do you gain these things?

The first thing you should ask is, "What are the group's goals?" Depending on the group's goals, your work may be quite different. If you are supervising a call center for a political campaign, your goal may be as simple as monitoring the hours other volunteers work, or you may need to keep their motivation up. No matter what type of group you lead, you need to be able to provide direction if the group gets off-track.

From Classroom to Community | Registering Voters

Janice, a student in my class, was also studying political science. She earned extra credit by helping to register voters for an upcoming election. In a report for her poli-sci class, she detailed how people reacted when asked if they were registered to vote.

"Lots of people just walked by the table and tried to ignore me, Some people actually got mad if I asked them why they weren't registered to vote.

"I couldn't understand that. My parents always voted, and so the thought that college students wouldn't care shocked me. Of course, my sociology class helped shed light on the problem. The U.S. government is such a large bureaucracy that many people feel like they don't matter. I guess they're too busy with their primary groups to care much about secondary groups."

WHAT **ARE THE CHARACTERISTICS OF SOCIAL GROUPS?** 102

two commonalities: the members of the group share something in common, and they identify each other as members of that group

HOW **DO SOCIOLOGISTS VIEW GROUP LEADERSHIP?** 112

functionalism: leaders are measured by their influence on others
conflict theory: for Marx, bureaucracy was a way to exploit workers, so the bourgeoisie could gain wealth
symbolic interactionism: workers' attitudes toward their jobs impact productivity and job satisfaction

HOW **DOES A PARENT'S CIVIC ENGAGEMENT AFFECT A CHILD'S FUTURE POLITICAL INVOLVEMENT?** 115

increases the likelihood of political involvement in adult life

get the topic: WHAT ARE THE CHARACTERISTICS OF SOCIAL GROUPS?

Formal Organizations 110
Functionalism and Leadership 112
Conflict Theory—Marx, Bureaucracy, and Democratic Organizations 113

Symbolic Interactionism—Creating a Just and Democratic Workplace 113
Adult Civic Engagement and Childhood

Activities 115
Leading Groups 115

Theory

FUNCTIONALISM 112

- examines the group's values and behaviors, particularly the group's leader
- successful groups often have successful leaders
- Maxwell's five levels of leadership

CONFLICT THEORY 113

- democratic leadership styles increase worker productivity
- if a democratic environment is not implemented, then bureaucracy can be stifling for the worker and the organization

- greater participation in leadership roles does not mean the company will succeed

SYMBOLIC INTERACTIONISM 113

- along with leadership, personal attitude has a big effect on job performance and satisfaction
- people feel good about themselves and their jobs when they feel they have a certain level of control over their actions
- democratic work environments help people feel connected to their jobs

Key Terms

social groups are groups that consist of two or more people who interact with one another and share a common identity. *102*

bounded relationships are relationships that exist only under specific conditions. *103*

in-group is a group to which we feel an affinity or closeness. *104*

in-group bias is the feeling that a person's in-group is superior to others. *104*

out-group is a group from which we are disconnected. *104*

reference group is the group you use to evaluate yourself. *105*

dyad is a group consisting of two people. *106*

triad is a group consisting of three people. *106*

leadership style is a behavioral mode that leaders use to influence group members. *106*

autocratic leaders are leaders who determine the group policies and assign tasks. *106*

democratic leaders are leaders who strive to set group policy by discussion and agreement. *106*

laissez-faire leaders are leaders who lead by absence and may not want to be leaders at all. *106*

conformity is the degree to which we will alter our behavior, attitudes, and points of view to fit into our perceived expectation of what is appropriate. *107*

groupthink is the term for group decisions that are made without objective thought. *107*

social capital is a sociological concept that refers to the individual and collective resources available to a person. *109*

social network is the web of ties you have with others. *109*

formal organizations are groups created for a certain purpose and built for maximum efficiency. *110*

voluntary association is the act of joining an organization that offers no pay and that expands social networks through interaction. *110*

organizations are formal groups that exist to achieve a desired goal. *110*

utilitarian organization is an organization in which people receive wages in exchange for work. *110*

normative organizations are organizations that exist to achieve a worthwhile goal. *110*

coercive organizations are organizations that people are forced to join. *110*

formal structure is the explicit rules, goals, and guidelines of the organization. *110*

informal structures are friendships, allegiances, and loyalties among members of the organization. *110*

bureaucracies are formal organizations that are organized into a hierarchy of smaller departments. *111*

formal rationality is the reasonable actions organizations and bureaucracies take to achieve goals in the most effective way. *111*

iron cage is a concept introduced by Max Weber that refers to the way in which bureaucracies make workers feel trapped and turn them into little more than robots accomplishing tasks. *111*

Sample Test Questions

These multiple-choice questions are similar to those found in the test bank that accompanies this textbook.

1. What type of leader sets few goals and does only what must be done?

- **a.** Totalitarian leader
- **b.** Autocratic leader
- **c.** Democratic leader
- **d.** Laissez-faire leader

2. A soup kitchen is an example of a

- **a.** coercive organization.
- **b.** utilitarian organization.
- **c.** normative organization.
- **d.** democratic organization.

3. Which of the following is *not* a characteristic common to all properly functioning organizations?

- **a.** Division of labor
- **b.** Methods of succession
- **c.** Voluntary participation
- **d.** Concentration of power

4. Which organization did Weber call a logical extension of formal rational thought?

- **a.** Democracy
- **b.** Bureaucracy
- **c.** Coercive organization
- **d.** Informal organization

5. By a functionalist's standard, the greatest measure of a leader is

- **a.** influence.
- **b.** charisma.
- **c.** authority.
- **d.** intimidation.

ESSAY

1. How and why are social networks of great use to immigrants?

2. Why is groupthink a potentially dangerous method of decision making?

3. What are the potential pitfalls of the three leadership styles discussed in this chapter?

4. Which leadership style did John Humphrey Noyes employ as leader of the Oneida group? Explain.

5. Why is a dyad considered the strongest form of a group?

WHERE TO START YOUR RESEARCH PAPER

To find out how you can be a leader, go to http://www.holsteinfoundation.org/pdffile/EGL02.pdf

To learn more about the skills needed for leadership, go to http://www.livingskillslibrary.com/html/Leadership%201%20Models.html

To find Max Weber's notes and original texts, go to http://www.sociosite.net/topics/weber.php

For more information on the sociology of Georg Simmel, go to http://www.sociosite.net/topics/sociologists.php#simmel

For information on America Reads and how you can become a school volunteer, go to http://www.ed.gov/inits/americareads/index.html

Remember to check www.thethinkspot.com **for additional information, downloadable flashcards, and other helpful resources.**

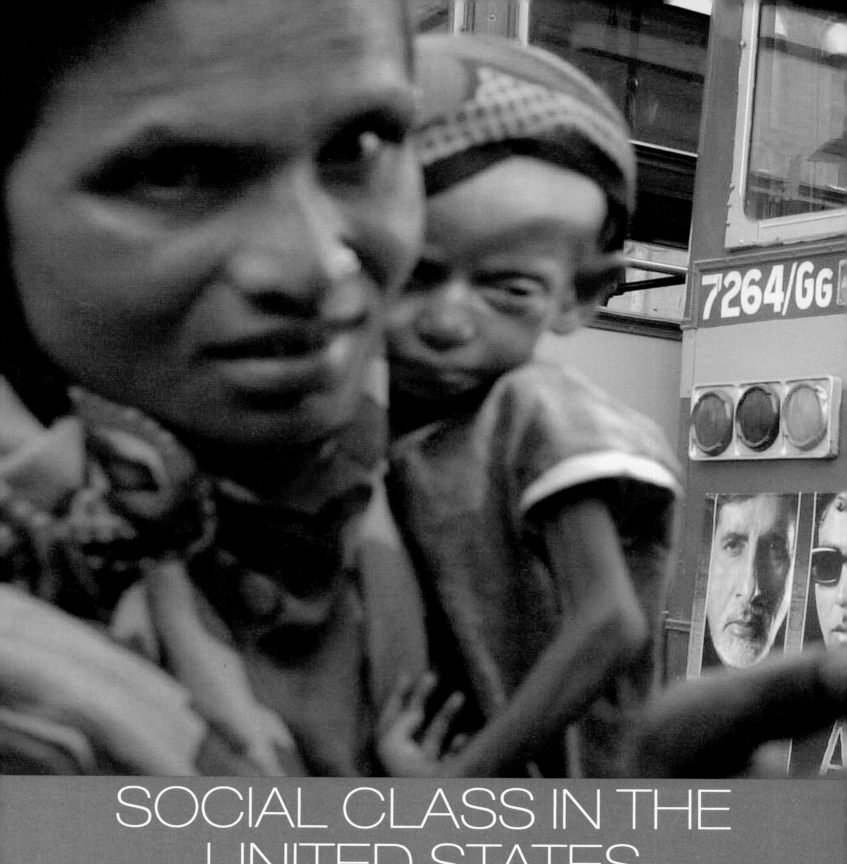

SOCIAL CLASS IN THE UNITED STATES

WHAT IS SOCIAL STRATIFICATION?
WHAT ARE THE THEORIES BEHIND SOCIAL STRATIFICATION?
WHAT SOCIAL POLICIES HAVE BEEN CREATED TO EASE POVERTY?

"It is no surprise that many Americans believe a whole host of social ills can be traced to the lapse in judgment that a poor, unmarried woman shows when she bears a child she can't afford. The solution to these problems seems obvious to most Americans: these young women should wait to have children until they are older and more economically stable, and they should get married first. It is indeed true that if more of these mothers married their children's fathers, fewer would be poor.

"What is striking about the body of social science evidence is how little of it is based on the perspectives and life experiences of the women who are its subjects. We provide new ideas about the forces that may be driving the trend by looking at the problems of family formation through the eyes of 162 low-income single mothers living in eight economically marginal neighborhoods. Their stories offer a unique point of view on the troubling questions of why low-income, poorly educated young women have children they can't afford and why they don't marry.

"To most middle-class observers, a poor woman with children but no husband, diploma, or job is either a victim of her circumstances or undeniable proof that American society is coming apart at the seams. But in the social world inhabited by poor women, a baby born into such conditions represents an opportunity to prove one's worth.

"For the poor and affluent alike, marriage is now much less about sex, co-residence, and raising children than it used to be. Whereas most couples used to view marriage as a starting point in their quest to achieve a series of life goals, today the poor insist on meeting these goals before marriage.

"If the poor shared both the middle class's marriage standards and their childbearing behaviors, few Americans would question their behavior. What troubles most middle-class citizens is why women don't wait until they are married to have children. The poor view childlessness as one of the greatest tragedies in life.

"The public often assumes that early childbearing is the main reason why so many girls from poor inner city areas fail to complete high school, go on to college, gain valuable work skills, or earn decent wages, but there is virtually no evidence to support this idea. Disadvantaged girls who bear children have about the same long-term earnings trajectories as similarly disadvantaged youth who wait until their mid or late twenties to have a child. In other words, early childbearing is highly selective of girls whose other characteristics—family background, cognitive ability, school performance, mental health status, and so on—have already diminished their life chances so much that an early birth does little to reduce them much further."[1]

Stratification *in a* Modern Society

CHAPTER 07

In *Promises I Can Keep: Why Poor Women Are Putting Motherhood Before Marriage*, Kathryn Edin and Maria Kefalas interviewed women from poor neighborhoods in Philadelphia to find out why unmarried women chose to have children.

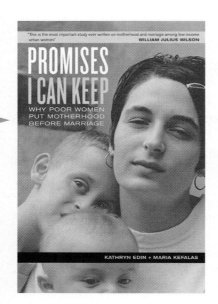

On the hit TV show *Ugly Betty,* Betty's thirty-something sister Hilda became pregnant as a teenager and has been raising her son as a single mother ever since. Sure, Hilda's fashion-loving, chic son Justin is a fictional character, but he represents an important demographic in the United States today: children who are born out of wedlock. In 2004, 32 percent of all children born in the United States were born to women who had never been married, divorced, or widowed.[2] Why are so many women having children out of wedlock?

Kathryn Edin and Maria Kefalas found that most of these women thought that being a mother would be their most important life accomplishment.

In a world where circumstances leave these women little hope for their futures, children make their lives meaningful. Marriage, however, does not hold the same promise. To these women, the cost of marrying a man who could be unreliable, unfaithful, and abusive far outweighs the financial benefits that marriage might bring.

Statistics show that single mothers are often impoverished and lack the resources they need to raise their children. Many have difficulty finding work, and the jobs they do get pay little. Lack of education also limits their ability to improve their circumstances. These women make up only one part of the poor in the United States. How does social position affect a person's life? As sociologists, we want to find out.

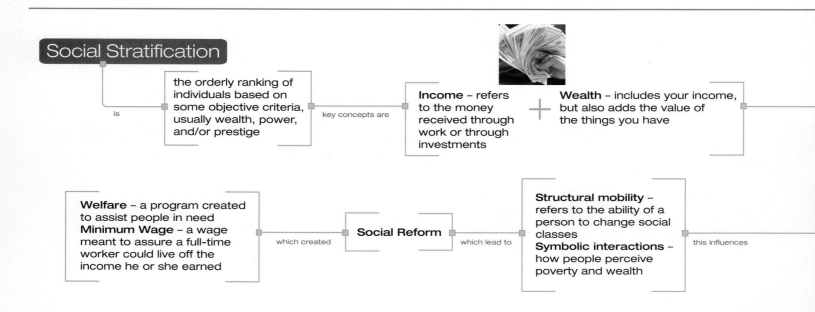

Social Stratification

is → the orderly ranking of individuals based on some objective criteria, usually wealth, power, and/or prestige

key concepts are → **Income** – refers to the money received through work or through investments

+ **Wealth** – includes your income, but also adds the value of the things you have

Welfare – a program created to assist people in need
Minimum Wage – a wage meant to assure a full-time worker could live off the income he or she earned

which created → **Social Reform**

which lead to → **Structural mobility** – refers to the ability of a person to change social classes
Symbolic interactions – how people perceive poverty and wealth

this influences

get the topic: WHAT IS SOCIAL STRATIFICATION?

It seems that it's in our nature to rank things. Pick up any magazine at the end of a given year, and you're sure to find "top ten" lists ranking the best (or worst) movies, albums, or books of the year. For example, David Letterman has made the Top Ten List his signature bit on the *Late Show with David Letterman*. Sociologists also like to rank individuals based on objective criteria, usually including wealth, power, or prestige. **Social stratification** relates to the ranking of people and the rewards they receive based on an objective criteria, often including wealth, power, and/or prestige.

All forms of society have ways to rank, or stratify, the members of their populations, but the level of stratification can vary a great deal between societies.[3] Some societies may use political power to separate people by giving party members special privileges unavailable to others.

For example, in the United States' "closed" presidential primary elections, party members are the only ones who are allowed to vote. Societies might use wealth to stratify people into social classes as well; the more money you have, the higher your status. Still others use birth status and family of origin as a means to divide people; certain families regarded as "nobility" hold privileged positions.

In the United States, we tend to divide groups by their access to wealth and/or income. **Income** refers to the money received for work or through investments. Whether it's the paycheck you get at the end of every month or the dividends you receive from your stock investments, the money you receive regularly is considered income. **Wealth**, on the

> **SOCIAL STRATIFICATION** is the ranking of people and the rewards they receive based on an objective criteria, often including wealth, power, and/or prestige.
>
> **INCOME** is the money received for work or through investments.
>
> **WEALTH** is all of your material possessions, including income.

other hand, refers to all your material possessions, including income. If you were to take everything you owned—your car, your computer, clothes, etc.—and sell it all at a fair market value, you could probably raise a considerable sum that would be more than your monthly income. It's important to know the difference between the two and to understand how each of these factors can affect your social standing.

INCOME DISTRIBUTION

When I was a college student, I could put everything I owned in the back of my Honda Civic. I worked for 25 cents above the minimum wage, and I had few expenses. I earn much more now than I did in college, but my expenses have also increased significantly as I married, bought a house, and started a family. In the United States, there is a diverse group of income earners. The entire income of the country can be divided into five groups, each with the same number of households. Among these groups, the poorest 20 percent of the country's earners received only 3.4 percent of the total income, whereas the top 20 percent received 50.5

<<< **Some societies use birth as a way to stratify their people. Although Japan is a democracy with a prime minister, nobility** such as Emperor Akihito and Empress Michiko **are among Japanese society's most elite and wealthy members.**

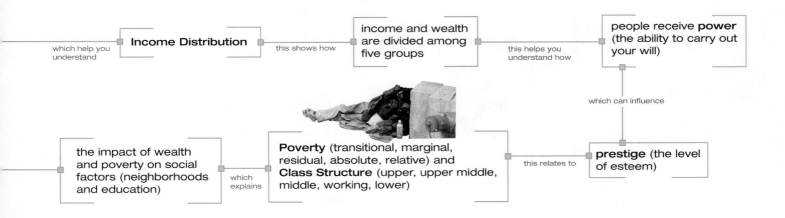

which help you understand → **Income Distribution** → this shows how → income and wealth are divided among five groups → this helps you understand how → people receive **power** (the ability to carry out your will)

which can influence

the impact of wealth and poverty on social factors (neighborhoods and education) → which explains → **Poverty** (transitional, marginal, residual, absolute, relative) and **Class Structure** (upper, upper middle, middle, working, lower) → this relates to → **prestige** (the level of esteem)

TRANSITIONAL POVERTY is a temporary state of poverty that occurs when someone loses a job for a short time.

MARGINAL POVERTY is a state of poverty that occurs when a person lacks stable employment.

RESIDUAL POVERTY is chronic and multigenerational poverty.

ABSOLUTE POVERTY is poverty so severe that one lacks resources to survive.

RELATIVE POVERTY is a state of poverty that occurs when we compare ourselves to those around us.

percent. The median, or midpoint, household income is $48,201. However, one of every five households in the United States has an income of $11,352 or lower. Meanwhile, five percent of all households earn more than $174,012.[4] If income trends continue, the rich are going to get richer. From 1970-2000, income for the bottom 90 percent of taxpayers actually dropped by 0.1 percent. Meanwhile, the top 10 percent of households saw income increases ranging from 89.5-558 percent.[5] Consider the pay of corporate executives. The ratio of a CEO's pay to a worker's pay was $24 to $1 in 1965, meaning that for every dollar a worker earned, the CEO made $24. By 2000, the ratio increased to $300 to $1.[6]

WEALTH DISTRIBUTION

This change in income only worsens the wealth disparity in the United States. When stocks, bonds, and many other items are included, it turns out that the top one percent of U.S. wealth holders controls more total wealth than the bottom 90 percent.[7] This means that a relatively small group of people control most of the country's money and assets.

The wealth distribution of the United States shows other trends as well. Generally, men have more wealth than women do. Stocks and personal residences make up the two largest categories of wealth. Top wealth holders in the United States are predominantly married (49 percent) or widowed (26 percent).[8] Wealth distribution also shows geographic trends. What does the map below tell you about wealth in the United States?

In 2000, Keister and Moller found that wealth inequality had worsened over a 34-year period

between 1962 and 1995.[9] They show that wealth has grown for the top wealth holders. At the same time, the percentage of the U.S. population with more debt than assets increased eight percent.

How Does the United States Define Poverty?

Sociologists have several different ways of defining poverty. **Transitional poverty** is a temporary state that occurs when someone loses a job for a short time. **Marginal poverty** occurs when a person lacks stable employment. For example, if your job is lifeguarding at a pool during the summer season, you might experience marginal poverty when the season ends. The next, more serious level, **residual poverty**, is chronic and multigenerational. People who live in a seemingly never-ending cycle of poverty that passes on to their children and grandchildren experience this type of poverty. A person who experiences **absolute poverty** is so poor that he or she doesn't have resources to survive. The people who are starving to death in the Darfur region of the Sudan are living in absolute poverty. **Relative poverty** is a state that occurs when we compare ourselves to those around us. You might experience relative poverty if you feel like your cell phone is old and insufficient compared with your friend's phone.

The U.S. government defines poverty much differently. The government establishes a poverty line in order to determine what services are needed and by whom. If a family's income is below that line, assistive services such as food, health care, and job placement programs are available.[10] If your income is above the line, you receive little or no government assistance. Using a national standard for poverty may be misleading. Consider the cost of living where you live—are the costs the same elsewhere in the country? A one-room apartment in Manhattan might go for as much or more than a much bigger house in Arkansas. Costs for many things vary depending upon the location in the country, and yet the poverty line is the same in 48 states.[11]

In addition to region, gender also comes into play; women are more likely to be poor than are men. The women Edin and Kefalas interviewed were affected by this gender bias known as the feminization of poverty. For example, median annual earnings for men are $41,386, whereas the median for women is $31,858. Women earn 77 cents for every dollar that men earn.[12] Poverty is particularly concentrated in female-headed households. Many women have low-paying jobs that barely support their family's needs. Women of color run into even greater barriers.[13]

Millionaires in the United States in 2006

More wealth is located on the coasts — Washington, California, New York, Pennsylvania, Florida, and New Jersey have the highest number of millionaires.

Texas
• One of the richest states with the 9th highest poverty rate. Why might this be?

NEW YORK
• 368,388 millionaires live in New York.
• Has the 15th highest poverty rate in United States, which could be related to Wilson's claim that urban areas are prone to higher poverty.

Number of millionaires in the United States, by State

| 0 – 49,999 | 50,000– 99,999 | 100,000 – 199,999 | 200,000 – 700,000 |

Source: *The Geography of American Poverty*, U.S. Census Bureau, www.Census.gov, February 7, 2008.

POWER

Another measure of stratification is **power**—the ability to carry out your will and impose it on others. In college classrooms, teachers possess great power. They select the textbooks, the topics the class will cover, and the order in which they will cover them. In short, all college instructors have a great deal of power over what is in their classes, and students' only power is to enroll or drop the course. Why are things this way? Because the power to educate in college is **delegated**, meaning given or assigned, to faculty by the college or university. Members of Congress have delegated power when they represent the people who elected them. They can use this power to authorize the deployment of troops into a military conflict or steward the economy into or out of a recession.[14]

Individuals have varying amounts of power, but no one has totally unlimited power. C. Wright Mills suggested that within the United States a small group called the **power elite** holds immense power.[15] The power elite come from three distinct but related groups: high-ranking political officials, corporate leaders, and military leaders. They decide what information and knowledge to share with the rest of us, and they use their social position and influence to direct the country's decisions. For example, there are five media giants: Time Warner, Disney, News Corporation, Bertelsmann of Germany, and Viacom.[16] As one of the five largest media corporations, the Disney Corporation listed $35.5 billion in revenue for the year 2007. The people in charge of this company, such as former Disney CEO Michael Eisner and current CEO Robert Iger, are counted as members of society's power elite.[17]

Most politicians must be voted into power, but who exercises their right to vote? People with high incomes and people who've achieved high levels of education are more likely to vote than their less wealthy, less-educated neighbors.[18] So what does this mean? Older, wealthier, educated people are making key decisions for the entire country. How does this affect the kinds of politicians we elect, the social measures we pass, and the economic packages we approve?

> **POWER** is the ability to carry out your will and impose it on others.
>
> **DELEGATED** means given or assigned.
>
> **POWER ELITE** is a small group of people who hold immense power.
>
> **PRESTIGE** is the level of esteem associated with one's status and social standing.

PRESTIGE

Prestige refers to the level of esteem associated with our status and social standing. Most of us want others to hold us in high regard, but various types of jobs hold differing levels of prestige. Generally, low-paying jobs have less prestige because of the stigma attached to such jobs. Not only do low-wage workers struggle to pay the bills, they also struggle to earn respect in a society that stigmatizes their work.

Prestigious jobs are generally ranked on a scale from 0 to 100, with 0 being the lowest. As you might suspect, physicians and lawyers top the list with ratings of 86 and 75; and street corner drug dealers bring up the rear with a 13.[19]

A prestigious job may carry its benefits into other areas of life. For example, you might take a stock tip from a successful start-up CEO, but I doubt you'd take the advice of a minimum-wage-earning grocery bagger. You don't expect someone who works as a bagger to be able to give you a great stock tip. Otherwise, why would he or she be working in such a low-status job? Occupational prestige varies a great deal between jobs and shows the general respect we have for certain work. Few people look at their newborn baby and hope she'll grow up to become a fry cook rather than a doctor.

Wealth, power, and prestige are the basis for the stratification system used to characterize the population, so these three components can also be used to analyze the class system of the United States.

►►► GO GLOBAL

From One Extreme to Another

The United States has the greatest percentage of children living in poverty compared with other industrial democracies.[20] In our country, 17.4 percent of children under the age of 18 live in poverty,[21] and 17 percent of these children live in households classified as "food insecure," which are households that change the quantity or quality of their food or frequently skip meals because of limited incomes.[22] In 2005, seven percent of the children living in the United States lived in extreme poverty.[23] These families have incomes below 50 percent of the poverty threshold.[24]

Ironically, the United States leads the world in the total number of millionaires as

well as the highest percentage of new millionaires.[25] Many of these millionaires run for positions in government or contribute large donations to political causes. In fact, of the 100 members in the 1995 Senate, 40 were millionaires.[26]

<<< Although there are government programs designed to help the poor, many **impoverished children may suffer from lack of nutritious food, dirty living conditions, and poor health.**

CLASS STRUCTURE IN THE UNITED STATES

If someone asked you what your social class is, what would you say? I often ask students to identify their social class. More often than not, they claim to be part of the "middle class." In fact, most people in the United States claim to belong to the middle class.[27] But are their claims accurate? If you had to divide the United States into classes, how would you make class distinctions?

Sociologists have varying opinions on how many classes there should be and what constitutes each class. For our discussion, however, let's look at five different social classes in the United States: upper class, upper middle class, middle class, working class, and lower class. Ask yourself how your membership to one class or the other might influence your perspective, opportunities, and long-term outcomes.

Upper/Elite Class

The **upper** or **elite class** is very small in number and holds significant wealth. We've already learned that only about 1 percent of the population belongs to this group.[28] Since there are about 300 million people in the country, approximately three million people are considered "upper class." The upper class possesses much of the country's "old money," which affords them great access to the three components of class: wealth, power, and prestige.[29] Many entertainers and professional athletes are part of this class.

Sociologist G. William Domhoff[30] has done extensive work studying the upper class.

According to his findings, membership to this class comes from attending an exclusive prep school, belonging to exclusive social clubs, and being born into a wealthy or powerful family.

When the workday is done, many in the upper class relax in private clubs. One such club is the all-male Bohemian club. Located in northern California, the club offers luxurious retreats to its exclusive members. Members are a who's who of U.S. business tycoons and political figures, including officers or directors from 40 of the 50 largest corporations in the United States. Members come from every part of the country, and membership is highly restricted.

Domhoff suggests that such a club allows the upper class to unify.[31] At these retreats, politicians and national speakers provide information and ideas about the future. The relaxing nature of a social club such as the Bohemian also increases social integration of members because of its climate; social cohesion increases in relaxed atmospheres. The upper class's money affords them opportunities that most people only dream of having. However, members of the upper middle class come pretty close to matching the elite's status.

<<< **Paris Hilton is a celebrity primarily because she was born into extraordinary wealth,** but she has used the wealth, power, and prestige of her family name to pursue television, modeling, and musical careers.

THINK SOCIOLOGICALLY

St. Paul's Prep School

One of the luxuries that elite students enjoy is attending a high-quality college preparatory school such as St. Paul's, in Concord, New Hampshire. Founded in 1856, St. Paul's school is an Episcopal boarding school with slightly more than 500 students in grades nine through twelve. Students enjoy a variety of educational opportunities, from astronomy to Greek and can partici-

pate in 17 different sports from soccer to skiing. The student-teacher ratio is 5:1 with an average class size of 11 students. Students who wish to attend will pay more than $37,000 a year for the privilege. However, the school has one of the lowest acceptance rates of all boarding schools; it accepts approximately 19 percent of applicants.[32]

This kind of education gives the upper class the edge they need to succeed.

Graduates are most likely to attend Brown, Stanford, Harvard, Yale, and Georgetown Universities. The school has produced three presidential candidates, six U.S. senators or congressmen, 12 U.S. ambassadors, three Pulitzer Prize winners, a mayor of New York City, and many leaders of Fortune 500 corporations. The exclusive education they received ensured that they were groomed for top-paying positions that came with great power.

Upper Middle Class

As with all distinctions of class, the definition of the upper middle class is fairly subjective. For the purposes of our discussion, the **upper middle class** consists of high-income members of society who are well educated but do not belong to the elite membership of the super wealthy. These people occupy professional positions and have achieved a level of income that makes their lives comfortable. They own property, have high occupational prestige, and often hold positions of authority within their jobs.[33]

This group makes up about 15 percent of the population. Their pay tends to exceed $100,000 a year. The two primary components of this group are occupational prestige and education. Owning a small business, having a professional career, or holding a high-status job often propels a person into this group. Your dentist, your lawyer, or the owner of your local grocery store chain may belong in this group.[34]

Middle Class

Almost half of Americans claim that they are members of the middle class. This isn't exactly a new phenomenon: Studies conducted in 1957, 1979, and 1996 all show that more than 40 percent of Americans believe they are part of the middle class.[35] If you're trying to decide where you fall along the country's economic spectrum, you might think, "Well, I'm not poor, and I'm not rich, so I must be somewhere in the middle. That's middle class, right?" However, the sociological definition for middle class is a bit more complex.

In general, **middle class** people have moderate incomes. They may be lower paid white-collar workers, such as schoolteachers, or well-paid blue-collar workers, like factory foremen. Middle class workers generally aren't involved in manual labor, but they may be skilled laborers (such as electricians). The middle class makes up about 34 percent of the U.S. population, meaning that the majority of the 40 percent of people who claim to be in the middle class actually are in this class.[36]

The middle class members have at least a high school diploma and many have technical training or college credits. Such attainment affords them a moderate level of occupational prestige. When you graduate from college and get your first job, you are likely to start out in the middle class. Members own property but generally hold much less wealth than the previously discussed groups. Incomes for the middle class range a great deal, approximately anywhere from $40,000 to $80,000 a year.

Working Class

The **working class** is generally made up of people with high school diplomas and lower levels of education. This group makes up around 30 percent of the U.S. workforce,[37] and its members hold jobs that usually require manual labor or clerical skills. Blue-collar factory workers or white-collar clerical workers make up most of the working class. Unlike those in the middle- and upper middle-class, members of the working class earn an hourly wage instead of a salary. Because they work by the hour and lack formal education, the working class has very limited opportunities for job improvement. Many nontraditional college students come from the working class. They understand that "good jobs" are increasingly rare and that education opens doors. However, their ability to raise their social class is hindered by the increasing number of blue-collar and even white-collar jobs that are moving overseas. There is an increasing amount of competition for work, which is a further motivation for workers to boost their marketable skills.[38]

∧
∧ **Many nontraditional students are working-class adults who want to gain more skills**
∧ **through education.** More and more adults are going back to school for additional training and new careers.

Poverty in 2005 by Race and Age

Under 18 Years Old

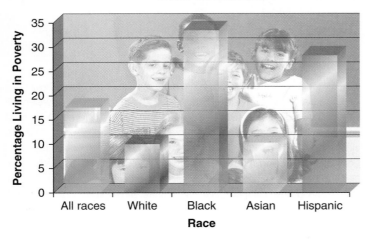

Y-axis: Percentage Living in Poverty (0 to 35)
X-axis: Race — All races, White, Black, Asian, Hispanic

18–64 Years Old

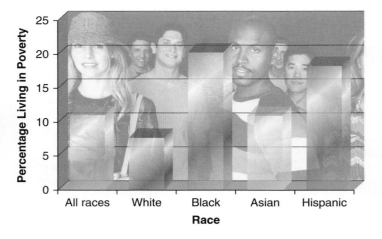

Y-axis: Percentage Living in Poverty (0 to 25)
X-axis: Race — All races, White, Black, Asian, Hispanic

65 Years and Older

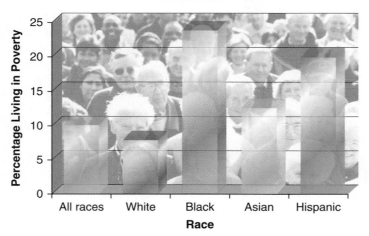

Y-axis: Percentage Living in Poverty (0 to 25)
X-axis: Race — All races, White, Black, Asian, Hispanic

Source: Carmen DeNavas-Walt, Bernadette D. Proctor, and Cheryle Hill Lee, "Income, Poverty and Heath Insurance Coverage in the United States: 2005," Current Population Reports, U.S. Census Bureau.

Lower Class

Finally, a notch below the working class are the members of society who truly feel the effects of poverty: the **lower class**. Thanks to the skyrocketing costs of tuition, food, and rent, many college students might think they understand what it means to be poor. In most cases, though, the relative poverty of their situation pales in comparison to the experiences of the working poor. After all, the privileges of attending a university and receiving a higher education are designed to lead students to employment that will land them in the middle class. When I was in college, I worked at a landscape nursery doing physical labor. Our pay was low and the hours were long. For me, a college student living at home, it was a good job. For my colleagues at the nursery who were trying to feed their families, it was not.

In the United States, a whopping 37 million people live in poverty.[39] Members of the lower class often live paycheck to paycheck, if they even have a job at all. Those people who do work are often one hospital bill or layoff away from financial ruin.

Notice, in the graphs to the left, how at all age levels **blacks have the highest rates of poverty, and the rate of poverty for whites is always lower than the national average.**

More than two-thirds of African Americans in the United States live near or below the poverty line. Hispanics follow closely behind at about 60 percent.[40] About 10 percent of senior citizens live at the poverty line, while almost half of the children in the United States are poor or near poor.[41] Why are so many children living in poverty? In *Promises I Can Keep*, Edin and Kefalas find that a poor woman is three times more likely to have a child before marriage than affluent women are. This is one reason why we have so many impoverished children in the United States, however the complete answer is more complex than this one fact.

The Urban Underclass

The homeless and chronically unemployed are also usually impoverished. Members of this group often live in substandard housing and may be receiving government assistance. They rarely have health care coverage and often lack a high school diploma. When they find a job, it's usually a minimum-wage position that propels them no higher than the working poor class. Many in this group make up what sociologists call the urban underclass.

The **urban underclass** lives in disadvantaged neighborhoods that are characterized by four components: poverty, family disruption, male unemployment, and lack of individuals in high-status occupations.[42] Many workers in disadvantaged neighborhoods are forced to take low-paying positions that go nowhere, leaving them with little hope of escaping the neighborhoods that are holding them down.

Sociologist William J. Wilson stated that these components could trigger a cycle of undermining social organization. Wilson discusses the urban underclass further in the book *The Truly Disadvantaged*, in which he notes that the U.S. urban poor are increasingly living in neighborhoods with few opportunities, poor schools, weak social structures, large amounts of crime, and rampant drug use.[43] However, what makes them truly disadvantaged is that they lack any vision and/or role models for any other way of life. These issues make life significantly more difficult for the residents and children who live in these ghettos.

NEIGHBORHOODS AND SOCIAL CLASS

Recently, sociologists have observed how neighborhoods influence behavior. Their findings have determined an increase in the geographic concentration of poverty and affluence in the United States. Over time, poor people are living in neighborhoods densely populated by other poor people. Simultaneously, the well-off members of society, particularly those who live in cities, tend to cluster in economically affluent neighborhoods such as the Gold Coast in Chicago or Manhattan's Upper East Side.[44] Looking at each end of the spectrum gives us a clear vision of the dynamics between poverty and affluence in the United States.

The concentration of poverty in a single geographic area is correlated to various issues such as high crime rates, increased drug use, and increasing numbers of single-parent homes. In *Promises I Can Keep,* Edin and Kefalas study women from the poorest areas of Philadelphia and its poorest suburb, Camden, New Jersey. The percentage of non-marital births in Philadelphia increased from 20 percent in 1950 to 30 percent in 1960 to 62 percent in 2000, which is twice the national rate. The bulk of these births were in the poor neighborhoods that they studied. Often, people who achieve any sort of economic advantage move out of these poor neighborhoods. This sort of residential segregation increases the disadvantages for those left behind.[45] Children who grow up in such neighborhoods are at increased risk for lower birth weights, poorer health, lower levels of educational attainment, and higher dropout levels.[46]

Conversely, children growing up in affluent neighborhoods do better in school, have lower rates of teen pregnancy, and have higher test scores. Interestingly, when a poor child is raised in a more affluent neighborhood, due to foster care or some type of rent control supplement, the child tends to do better than his or her peers who remain living in poor neighborhoods. In short, living in a more affluent neighborhood seems to decrease the power of the negative effect that poverty has on children. Why do you think this is the case? Apparently being "the poor kid on the block" is better for a child than being another poor kid on the block.[47] Why?

EDUCATION AND SOCIAL CLASS

We've all heard it said that the United States is the land of opportunity, and in many ways, it lives up to its name. It grants free education to every child, regardless of socioeconomic status. Unfortunately, all educational opportunities aren't exactly the same. For example, public schools frequently offer different educational opportunities. But what difference do these opportunities really make?

In a two-year study of more than 25 different communities, Jonathan Kozol observed public schools in the United States and noted that not all schools are created equal.[48] Kozol saw that urban schools frequently lacked basic supplies necessary to teach: Playgrounds often had little or no equipment, chemistry labs were missing beakers and test tubes, and students had to share textbooks. Meanwhile, suburban schools often had a surplus of supplies and staff. Kozol pointed out that while these two systems often turned out different qualities of education, the major cause for this disparity rested in the structures that supported the educational systems. Property values and taxes are higher in the suburbs, so their schools receive more funding than urban schools. This extra financial support allows suburban schools to purchase up-to-date materials and hire ample staff for the students. Unfortunately, because most urban schools are underfunded, the students who need the most help actually get the least, which adds to the endless cycle of educational inequality. Is this really "equal opportunity"?

The studies of Roscigno et al. show similar findings to Kozol's. They note that both urban and rural students frequently attend schools with fewer resources than suburban students.[49] These inequalities are directly linked to parents' socioeconomic status. Students lacking resources in school and at home are more likely to attain a lower level of educational achievement. On average, both inner-city and rural students score lower on achievement tests when compared with suburban students. These findings support the notion that college attendance is not linked to academic outcomes, but to the social class of a student's family.[50] For those in the lower classes, access to financial aid is key for students who wish to attend college.[51] Unfortunately, the availability of aid remains a serious issue for less affluent students.[52] Clearly, complete educational equality does not exist in United States. Because poor neighborhoods lack the resources necessary to succeed, many residents of these communities are denied the opportunity to overcome poverty.

> **LOWER CLASS** is a social class living in poverty.
>
> **URBAN UNDERCLASS** is a social class living in disadvantaged neighborhoods that are characterized by four components: poverty, family disruption, male unemployment, and lack of individuals in high-status occupations.

MAKE CONNECTIONS

Nickel and Dimed into Poverty

Before writing the book *Nickel and Dimed*, Barbara Ehrenreich spent a year living among the working class. Going from state to state, she worked as a waitress, a maid, a nursing home aid, and a Wal-Mart salesperson. Ehrenreich's experiences led her to dispute the idea that these jobs require low-level skills. Instead, she believes that such low-wage jobs are physically demanding and actually require a great deal of interpersonal and technical skills. These jobs don't normally provide health care or sick leave, so workers who fall ill have to choose between their health and their pay. Yet despite the hurdles society has placed in their way, these workers are actually more motivated to succeed and are not depressed by a system of low wages and long hours.

>>> **ACTIVITY** Recent college graduate Adam Shepard wrote *Scratch Beginnings: Me, $25, and the Search for the American Dream* in rebuttal to Ehrenreich's book. Read Shepard's book or search the Internet to learn his findings. Which author paints a more accurate picture of life for the working poor? Why?

SOCIAL MOBILITY is the ability to change social classes.

HORIZONTAL MOBILITY refers to moving within the same status category.

VERTICAL MOBILITY refers to moving from one social status to another.

INTRAGENERATIONAL MOBILITY occurs when an individual changes social standing, especially in the workforce.

INTERGENERATIONAL MOBILITY refers to the change that family members make from one social class to the next through generations.

STRUCTURAL MOBILITY occurs when social changes affect large numbers of people.

EXCHANGE MOBILITY is a concept suggesting that, within the United States, each social class contains a relatively fixed number of people.

MERITOCRACY ARGUMENT states that those who get ahead do so based on their own merit.

Social Mobility

Wherever we are in life, there's always the chance that something could happen to us that would change our status. Whether it's winning the lottery or investing in the right stocks, our social class could change in an instant. Likewise, the mortgage crisis and corporate downsizing have sent many middle-class families plummeting into poverty. **Social mobility** is a term that describes this ability to change social classes. If social class is a ladder, social mobility occurs when we climb either up or down it. Several patterns of social mobility are possible.

Horizontal mobility, as the name suggests, refers to moving within the same status category. For example, when a teacher leaves one school to take a position at another school, horizontal mobility has occurred. The teacher is earning the same amount of money and performs the same tasks; she just happens to be doing these things at a different location. Her movement is lateral, not vertical. **Vertical mobility** involves moving from one social status to another. This type of mobility can either be upward, in the form of a promotion at work, or downward, in the form of a demotion at work. For example, if the same teacher from our previous example got a master's degree and became a principal, then vertical mobility has occurred.

In the United States, the labor market has changed immensely. Many companies are outsourcing manual labor overseas to developing countries. **U.S. citizens who previously performed this type of work find themselves out of a job, which, in turn, slows upward mobility.**

Intragenerational mobility occurs when an individual changes social standing, especially in the workforce. Climbing the corporate ladder is a prime example of this type of mobility. For instance, if you begin your working career as an unskilled laborer doing construction work and then ten years later own a construction company, you are experiencing intragenerational mobility.

Intergenerational mobility refers to the change that family members make from one social class to the next through generations. If you hope to live a better life than your parents did, then you hope for upward intergenerational mobility. However, if you expect to do much better than your parents, the odds are probably stacked against you. A number of researchers have found that while intergenerational mobility does occur, children tend to climb only a little higher on the social class ladder when compared with their parents, if they climb at all.[53]

The effects of this kind of mobility on the poor are even greater. Edin and Kefalas describe how the young, unwed, poor men and women having children rarely have jobs and find it hard to find employment because new jobs and opportunities often require high levels of education and experience, leaving many poor struggling to survive.

Because many living in poverty are not getting the same level of education that other students receive, how can they be expected to keep up with technological advancements? Children raised in poor homes are more likely to experience poverty in adulthood. Poor black children are 2.5 times more likely to remain poor in adulthood compared with other black children who are not raised in poverty. For white children, the rates are even worse. Poor white children are 7.5 times more likely to continue being poor as adults when compared with their wealthier counterparts.[54]

Structural mobility occurs when social changes affect large numbers of people. During economic booms, some climb the ladder and benefit from changes in the economy. Think of the success that the Chrysler company experienced during the economic prosperity of the mid-1990s.

When the economy heads into a recession, workers who have lost their jobs to outsourcing experience downward structural mobility. For example, the same Chrysler company that flourished in the 1990s was forced to close many plants and lay off more than 13,000 workers a little more than a decade later.

The concept of **exchange mobility** suggests that, within the United States, each social class contains a relatively fixed number of people. If you move upward into a class above you, someone else must move down. When you consider the changes in income over time that we talked about earlier, you can see that such data generally support the idea that social stratification levels do not change much, though the people who make up each layer may be different.

think sociologically: WHAT ARE THE THEORIES BEHIND SOCIAL STRATIFICATION?

Functionalism

Functionalists believe that systems find equilibrium, or balance, so stratification must be the result of some kind of functional balance. Theorists Kingsley Davis and Wilbert Moore summarize the common argument that the U.S. stratification system is inevitable and aids in the smooth functioning of society.[55] This **meritocracy argument** states that those who get ahead do so based on their own merit.

Davis and Moore believe each society has important positions that must be filled. The more important the position, the more we reward those who choose to pursue it. Doctors in the United States generally get hefty paychecks because everyone needs a doctor to tend to their health care needs. In order to get someone to fill an important position, society offers a reward to anyone who's willing to fill it. The rarer the skill or the longer the training period, the greater the rewards can be. If you faint at the sight of blood or if you can't stand the thought of spending a good portion of your life in school, you probably shouldn't become a doctor.

On the other hand, the reason KFC is able to pay its employees minimum wage is because you can learn to fry chicken in about two hours. I should know; I once cooked chicken for the Colonel. But why would anyone become a medical doctor considering the stress and training involved? Davis and Moore say that society has to offer greater rewards to entice people to take particularly tough or stressful jobs. To sum up the functionalist view, stratification inevitably happens because people have different abilities, and those abilities are more or less important to society.

Therefore, if you get ahead, it is based on some ability or drive that you have that pushes you to get there. Delayed gratification, or the ability to wait in order to get something you want, can also determine your success. If you're willing to put in the time to go to school and work hard, you're likely to be successful.

In this sense, it means that **stratification is inevitable, since we do not all have the same intelligence, drive, and desire.** Those who get ahead in this country tend to be those who use these individual forces to reap society's rewards.

After teaching sociology for many years, I believe that most of my students are functionalists. They support the idea that people succeed or fail in the United States based on their own merit.

The graphic on the right provides information from student surveys that I have used in my classes. This nonscientific study yields the same results virtually every year. I ask students if they "agree with the following statements," and the percentages show those who agreed with the statement. What do you think? Do people in the United States determine their own success?

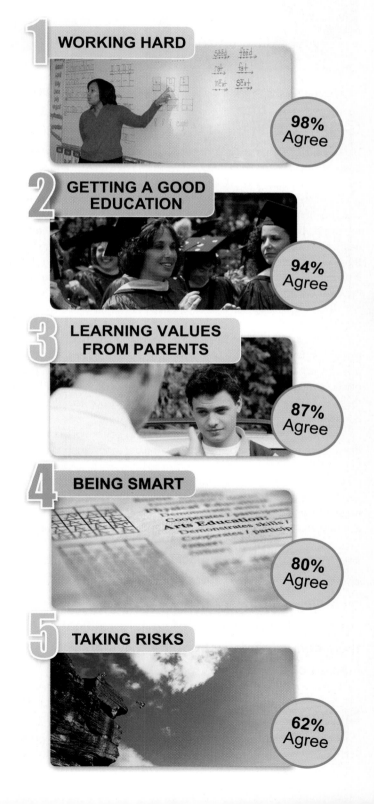

Top 5 Reasons My Students Think People Get Ahead in the United States

1. **WORKING HARD** — 98% Agree
2. **GETTING A GOOD EDUCATION** — 94% Agree
3. **LEARNING VALUES FROM PARENTS** — 87% Agree
4. **BEING SMART** — 80% Agree
5. **TAKING RISKS** — 62% Agree

<<< Teachers and police officers are essential for society, but professional athletes, like Tiger Woods, are not. **Why do you think there is such a discrepancy between salaries?**

Average Salary: $48,788[56]   Average Salary: $48,254[57]   2007 Earnings: $115 million[58]

Conflict Theory

Unlike functionalists, conflict theorists focus on the role of conflict as the basis of stratification. Every society has limited resources to go around, so groups struggle with one another for those resources. Melvin Tumin offers a critique of Davis and Moore that supports the conflict point of view. For Tumin, social inequality is rooted in a system that is more likely to reward you based on where you start—not solely based on the abilities you have.[59] There is nothing inevitable about inequality, it is merely those with wealth doing the best they can to keep that wealth and pass it on to their children. In this way, social inequality is rooted in the unjust capitalist system and not the people who live under it.

Tumin also suggests that stratification is not as simple as some might suggest. First, the societal importance of a job does not seem to be the only basis for financial rewards. Think about it: Who is arguably more important to society, a police officer or a professional athlete? Now ask yourself who makes more money? Being a soldier, firefighter, police officer, or teacher requires dedication, training, and unique skills. But these groups are actually paid very little in comparison to entertainers, corporate CEOs, and professional athletes.

Conflict theorists point out that groups with power will extract what they can from the groups beneath them. The dominant group takes control of social institutions in order to preserve the best resources for itself. By extension, conflict theorists argue, the wealthy try to maintain the status quo so that access to training will remain limited to their group, thus helping them gain even more wealth and power. Why do doctors make so much money? People need them and have very little choice about it.

Students from working-class backgrounds are far more likely to talk about social class as an issue on college campuses than upper middle-class students. **The perception of social stratification then, comes primarily from the "have-nots" instead of the "haves."**

Symbolic Interactionism

Symbolic interactionists are interested in how people perceive poverty and wealth. They seek to understand if people actually have a sense of social class. According to research by Stuber, our particular social class impacts how we talk about class in general.[60] The higher our socioeconomic status (SES), the less we believe that social class matters. For example, upper middle-class college students tend to disregard issues of class and often don't notice that others cannot do what they can do financially. They may be socialized not to care about social class, or they might not have thought much about it.

This could be because working-class students must make financial choices that upper middle-class students don't even have to consider. In addition, students from the working class have lower expectations about future earnings and successes. Basically, the disparity in these college students' social status demonstrates how ascribed positions affect expectations.

The perception of class differences is most pronounced in the dichotomous way that people look at welfare recipients. Generally, the recipient of food stamps, Section Eight housing, or cash payments incurs a serious social stigma.[61] Students in my classes frequently become angry when discussing the welfare system. As one young woman put it, "I have to work, and they get to drive around in Hummers and live off the government." Putting aside the obvious problems with this statement, this woman's words certainly illustrate the difference between what the general public perceives and the reality of welfare.

In *So You Think I Drive a Cadillac?*, Karen Seccombe investigates how female welfare recipients view the welfare system and deal with the associated stigma. Some of their coping strategies include distancing and denial: Women who avoid any discussion about their situations are distancing themselves from the fact that they receive assistance at all. Others who come up with plausible excuses—such as losing a job or fleeing an abusive marriage—are denying they are similar to other welfare recipients. But, when they viewed other women on welfare, they restated common stereotypes that echoed my student's anti-welfare tirade.

Seccombe points out that upper- and middle-class women actually have more in common with poor women than they might think. They all tend to worry about how to care for their children and homes, and they all tend to view public assistance negatively. Poor women realize society views them negatively, so they see accepting welfare as a last resort. Seccombe specifically shows that low wages and a lack of financial support from men are the driving factors behind female poverty. The reason that many of these individuals are poor is because they cannot earn enough to make ends meet or because they're not receiving court-ordered child support from their ex-husbands.

WRAP YOUR MIND AROUND THE THEORY

The average salary for a physician is over $140,000.[62] On the other hand, the average salary for a fast food cook is approximately $17,400.[63] What factors might have influenced such different outcomes for these two people?

FUNCTIONALISM

Functionalists suggest that social class is connected to a person's ability to negotiate the social world. Therefore, intelligence, drive, and personal choice influence a person's social class. All people are different, so it makes sense that differences in social class exist in the United States. Some people simply have more skills and abilities than others, and these skills naturally help them reap economic rewards. Have you ever heard the phrase "The cream rises to the top"? In many ways, this statement explains why stratification continues to occur.

CONFLICT THEORY

Conflict theorists believe that social mobility rarely occurs in a dramatic way, largely because the U.S. system doesn't allow it. Generally, one's parents and the opportunities they can provide determine social class. Parents in positions of wealth wish to make sure their children keep that advantage, so they pass wealth to their children in the form of an inheritance, they make sure their children attend the "best schools," and they use their social prestige to help their children succeed. Children who lack such things generally remain poor.

WHAT FACTORS INFLUENCE SOCIAL CLASS IN THE UNITED STATES?

SYMBOLIC INTERACTIONISM

Social class and our understanding of it are relative to our personal belief system. In *Promises I Can Keep*, Edin and Kefalas argue that middle-class citizens would not question poor people's behavior if they held similar beliefs about marriage and childbearing. According to Edin and Kefalas, "[T]he poor view childlessness as one of the greatest tragedies in life. Surveys show that the differences between the social classes are striking; female high school dropouts are more than five times as likely and male high school dropouts more than four times as likely as their college-educated counterparts to say they think childless people lead empty lives."

What future might lie in store for the children of these unwed young mothers?

Affluent parents often give their children opportunities, such as music lessons and access to organized sports, **which can influence their social class later in life.**

ENTITLEMENT PROGRAM is a program offering assistance to which a person is entitled, requiring no qualification.

Social Policy: Welfare for the Poor

When you call the fire department for help, you probably have no doubt that they will immediately respond to your call. Even if this is the tenth time your house has caught fire, firefighters will come because you are entitled to fire protection. For many years, the U.S. welfare program was a lot like the fire department because anti-poverty assistance was treated as an **entitlement program**, a program offering assistance to which a person is entitled, requiring no qualification. This all changed in 1996 when President Bill Clinton changed welfare in the United States by signing the Personal Responsibility and Work Opportunity Reconciliation Act, which created the Temporary Assistance to Needy Families (TANF) program. TANF is an ongoing government program that targets a particular section of the population to receive benefits such as cash assistance and childcare. Under the new welfare law, children in poor families are no longer entitled to poverty protection because the program is temporary.

Before the introduction of TANF, people generally believed that welfare recipients lived on the system for years. However, Edin and Kefalas found no sign that the poor women they interviewed desired to "milk the system." These women expected to have to work to make ends meet. Nevertheless, the government imposed time limits to curb abuses. The program officially allows a person to receive TANF funds for five years in their lifetime, and for only two years at a time. Thus, children cannot receive benefits throughout their childhood. But when you look at the families that participated in Aid to Families with Dependent Children (AFDC), statistics show that two-thirds of all recipients were never on the program for longer than two years. Furthermore, less than 15 percent of AFDC recipients were continuous users of the system.[64] In other words, most people were never on the system longer than the established time limits.

TANF supports the cutting of welfare benefits and argues that a job should pay more than welfare payments. Crudely put, the act established that people should not be able to stay home and live on the taxpayers' dime. However, numerous studies show that even taking food stamps and other benefits of the welfare program into account, mothers receiving TANF payments still live well below the poverty line.[65]

One of the central ideas behind welfare reform focused on job training for the poor. Conventional wisdom dictates that people need proper

> ∨
> ∨ The Temporary Assistance to Needy Families **(TANF) program left many**
> ∨ **needy people still living in poverty.**

A New Beginning
Welfare to Work

training in the requisite skills to get a good job. Unfortunately, the relatively short duration of TANF assistance prevents people from engaging in any kind of long-term training like college. Additionally, many of these programs don't accept the pursuit of higher education as an acceptable way for welfare recipients to spend their time. The system is designed in a way that effectively prevents people from improving their economic situation and ensuring they will continue to work low-wage jobs for a lifetime. Welfare reformers might argue that low-paying jobs are supposed to be a gateway to better opportunities. But do low-wage jobs really grow into more financially rewarding ones? Like many other welfare reform ideas, data do not support the answer. The transition from welfare to work usually results in a job that does not pay a living wage.[66] These low-skilled, minimum-wage jobs usually have no opportunity for growth or advancement. Although recipients technically have jobs, these jobs can't support them and their families. When jobs are not available, both individuals and communities suffer. Without sufficient jobs and training, how are people supposed to survive?

While you might categorize a minimum wage job as something limited to teenagers venturing into the workforce for the first time, **only 21.8 percent of these workers are 16–24** years old. **The greatest percentages of minimum wage workers (78.2 percent) are over 25 years old.**[67]

> **ACTIVITIES**
>
> 1. Get to know some of the homeless and poor in your community. Visit or take a tour of a shelter in your community.
> 2. Check with your state to find out the monthly welfare payments for a mother and two children. Do you think you'd be able to live on that?
> 3. Create a household budget for two parents who are both working minimum-wage jobs. Budget for rent, utilities, food, child care, and transportation for a family of four living in your local area. Don't make up expenses. Research the minimum wage and prices in your area, and provide your sources. How difficult is it to survive even with two incomes?

Social Policy: Minimum Wage

When you were in high school, your first job might have consisted of flipping burgers at McDonald's or stocking the cereal aisle at Target. Whatever the case, this job probably earned you the minimum wage. Started during the Great Depression, the minimum wage is another governmental policy designed to reduce poverty by ensuring that full-time workers could live off the income they received. Since that time, politicians have argued over the merits of raising the minimum wage to meet the demands of an evolving economy. Needless to say, there is no maximum wage in the United States.

Many of us have probably held a minimum wage job at some point in our lives, but who really are the minimum-wage workers? The demographics that make up this particular workforce might surprise you.

In their study of the impact of wages on life, Durfee et al. investigate the wages needed for a variety of family structures to be self-sufficient (or, in other words, to live without aid from the government).[68] Studying 34 states and metropolitan areas, they calculated the costs of housing, child care, food, transportation, health care, as well as tax costs and tax benefits such as the earned income tax credit. Their findings show that few low-wage workers earn enough per hour to work only 40 hours a week and be self-sufficient. Durfee found that on average both adults in a household would have to earn $10.54 an hour to be self-sufficient. Sadly, in many states this amount is well above the minimum wage.

Maybe reading about wealth and poverty has made you think about how you might use these ideas in your everyday life. One major way in which you can take action is working at a community homeless shelter. Students who lend a hand at shelters and soup kitchens get firsthand knowledge about the complexities of poverty in America.

From Classroom to Community | Helping Homeless Children

Kirk decided to seek some extra credit by volunteering to help homeless children at a school designed only for them. The program gives kids without homes a place to go to school.

"These kids are rarely anywhere for very long, and so the people at the school try really hard to make them enjoy learning and discovery while they're there," he said.

"I can remember meeting this seven-year-old girl whose only real toy was a stuffed rabbit. She told me that she'd kept it with her no matter where she went. Her mom would get jobs for a short time, and then they'd move somewhere else in search of work.

"When I met the girl's mother, she was really nice, but I could tell that she didn't have much education. She was working as a cleaning person in a hotel, but the hours were long and the work was hard. She told me that the pay barely covered the costs of her uniforms and transportation to work, so she and her daughter would be staying at the shelter for as long as they could.

"Coming from a middle-class background, I never thought about all the things I had growing up and how lucky I was to have a house with a backyard and toys. We weren't rich, but compared to this girl, I had everything. Until I volunteered at the school, I guess I really didn't understand poverty."

07

WHAT **IS SOCIAL STRATIFICATION?** 121

the ranking of people and the rewards they receive based on objective criteria, often including wealth, power, and/or prestige

WHAT **ARE THE THEORIES BEHIND SOCIAL STRATIFICATION?** 129

functionalism: stratification is the result of some kind of functional balance, is inevitable, and aids in the smooth functioning of society
conflict theory: social inequality is rooted in a system that is more likely to reward you based on where you start than based on your abilities
symbolic interactionism: a person's particular social class affects how he or she discusses class in general

WHAT **SOCIAL POLICIES HAVE BEEN CREATED TO EASE POVERTY?** 132

U.S. welfare program; Temporary Assistance to Needy Families (TANF); Aid to Families with Dependent Children (AFDC); minimum wage

get the topic: WHAT IS SOCIAL STRATIFICATION?

How Does the United States Define
Poverty? 122
Social Mobility 128

Functionalism 129
Conflict Theory 130
Symbolic Interactionism 130

Social Policy: Welfare for the Poor 132
Social Policy: Minimum Wage 133

Theory

FUNCTIONALISM 129

- social class is connected to a person's ability to negotiate the social world
- intelligence, drive, and personal choice influence a person's social class
- all people are different, so it makes sense that differences in social class exist

CONFLICT THEORY 130

- social mobility rarely occurs in a dramatic way
- generally, one's parents and the opportunities they can provide determine social class
- the higher our socioeconomic status, the less we believe social class matters

SYMBOLIC INTERACTIONISM 130

- social class and our understanding of it are relative to our personal belief system
- for example, middle-class citizens would not question poor people's behavior if they held similar beliefs about marriage and childbearing
- many poor women think childless people lead empty lives, so they place more emphasis on the maternal relationship than on marriage

Key Terms

social stratification is the ranking of people and the rewards they receive based on an objective criteria, often including wealth, power, and/or prestige. *121*

income is the money received for work or through investments. *121*

wealth is all of your material possessions, including income. *121*

transitional poverty is a temporary state of poverty that occurs when someone loses a job for a short time. *122*

marginal poverty is a state of poverty that occurs when a person lacks stable employment. *122*

residual poverty is chronic and multigenerational poverty. *122*

absolute poverty is poverty so severe that one lacks resources to survive. *122*

relative poverty is a state of poverty that occurs when we compare ourselves to those around us. *122*

power is the ability to carry out your will and impose it on others. *123*

delegated means given or assigned. *123*

power elite is a small group of people who hold immense power. *123*

prestige is the level of esteem associated with one's status and social standing. *123*

upper or **elite class** is a social class that is very small in number and holds significant wealth. *124*

upper middle class is a social class that consists of high-income members of society who are well educated but do not belong to the elite membership of the super wealthy. *125*

middle class is a social class that consists of those who have moderate incomes. *125*

working class is a social class generally made up of people with high school diplomas and lower levels of education. *125*

lower class is a social class living in poverty. *126*

urban underclass is a social class living in disadvantaged neighborhoods that are characterized by four components: poverty, family disruption, male unemployment, and lack of individuals in high-status occupations. *126*

social mobility is the ability to change social classes. *128*

horizontal mobility refers to moving within the same status category. *128*

vertical mobility refers to moving from one social status to another. *128*

intragenerational mobility occurs when an individual changes social standing, especially in the workforce. *128*

intergenerational mobility refers to the change that family members make from one social class to the next through generations. *128*

structural mobility occurs when social changes affect large numbers of people. *128*

exchange mobility is a concept suggesting that, within the United States, each social class contains a relatively fixed number of people. *128*

meritocracy argument states that those who get ahead do so based on their own merit. *129*

entitlement program is a program offering assistance to which a person is entitled, requiring no qualification. *132*

Sample Test Questions

These multiple-choice questions are similar to those found in the test bank that accompanies this textbook.

1. People with seasonal jobs most likely experience

  a. residual poverty.

  b. absolute poverty.

  c. marginal poverty.

  d. transitional poverty.

2. Which of the following is *not* a member of the power elite?

  a. The Secretary of State

  b. A military general

  c. A corporate CEO

  d. A town mayor

3. Which of the following is true of the upper, or elite, class?

  a. Most members are newly wealthy.

  b. They have higher rates of teen pregnancy.

  c. They make up one percent of the country's population.

  d. They are generally regarded highly for their specialized skills.

4. A doctor transferring from one hospital to another is an example of

  a. intergenerational mobility.

  b. horizontal mobility.

  c. vertical mobility.

  d. exchange mobility.

5. A high school graduate who works on an assembly line in a manufacturing plant is most likely a member of which social class?

  a. Urban underclass

  b. Working class

  c. Middle class

  d. Lower class

ESSAY

1. How does prestige affect one's social standing?

2. How is the mobility of the urban underclass restricted?

3. What is the relationship between social class and education?

4. In terms of marriage and family, how do the values of the low-income single mothers interviewed by Kathryn Edin and Maria Kefalas differ from the values held by most middle-class women? Why do you think this difference exists?

5. How does the concept of exchange mobility conflict with the beliefs of conflict theorists?

WHERE TO START YOUR RESEARCH PAPER

For more information on working in homeless shelters, including a complete list of shelters, go to http://www.artistshelpingchildren.org/shelters.html

http://www.hud.gov/

For more information about hunger and poverty in the world, go to http://www.poverty.com/

For more information about minimum wage laws in the United States, go to http://www.dol.gov/esa/minwage/america.htm

To view information collected from a New York Times study of social class, go to http://www.nytimes.com/pages/national/class/

ANSWERS: 1. c; **2.** d; **3.** c; **4.** b; **5.** b

Remember to check www.thethinkspot.com **for additional information, downloadable flashcards, and other helpful resources.**

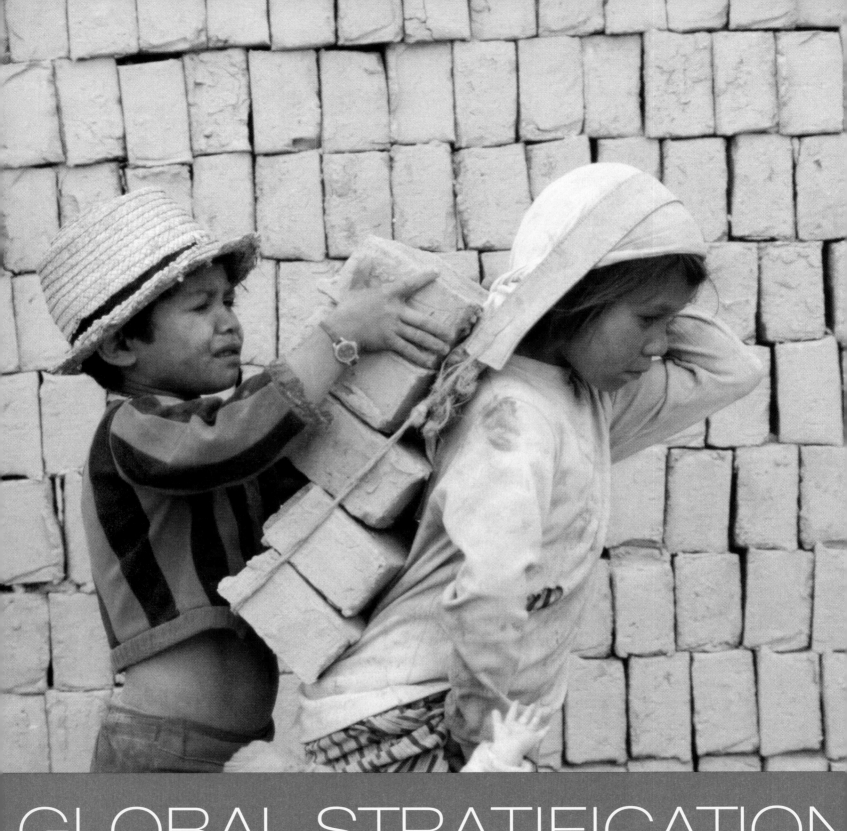

GLOBAL STRATIFICATION

"Slavery

is not a horror safely consigned to the past; it continues to exist throughout the world, even in developed countries like France and the United States. Across the world slaves work and sweat and build and suffer. Slaves in Pakistan may have made the shoes you are wearing and the carpet you stand on. Slaves in the Caribbean may have put sugar in your kitchen and toys in the hands of your children. In India they may have sewn the shirt on your back and polished the ring on your finger. They are paid nothing.

"Slaves touch your life indirectly as well. They made the bricks for the factory that made the TV you watch. In Brazil slaves made the charcoal that tempered the steel that made the springs in your car and the blade on your lawnmower. Slaves grew the rice that fed the woman that wove the lovely cloth you've put up as curtains. Your investment portfolio and your mutual fund pension own stock in companies using slave labor in the developing world. Slaves keep your costs low and returns on your investments high.

"Slavery is a booming business and the number slaves is increasing. People get rich by using slaves.

And when they've finished with their slaves, they just throw these people away. This is the new slavery, which focuses on big profits and cheap lives . . .

"Three key factors helped create the new slavery and change the old slavery. The first is the population explosion that flooded the world's labor markets with millions of poor and vulnerable people. The second is the revolution of economic globalization and modernized agriculture, which has dispossessed poor farmers and made them vulnerable to enslavement...The third factor is the chaos of greed, violence, and corruption created by this economic change in developing countries, change that is destroying the social rules and the traditional bonds of responsibility that might have protected potential slaves...

"Whether we like it or not, we are now a global people. We must ask ourselves: Are we willing to live in a world with slaves? If not we are obligated to take responsibility for things that are connected to us, even when far away."[1]

From Kevin Bales, *Disposable People: New Slavery in the Global Economy.* Copyright © 1999 by the Regents of the University of California. Reprinted by permission of the University of California Press.

137

Wealth and Poverty *in the* World

CHAPTER 08

In *Disposable People: New Slavery in the Global Economy,* sociologist **Kevin Bales estimates that 27 million people are currently enslaved around the world.**

Made in Pakistan. Made in Taiwan. In your closet, you're sure to find tags with these phrases printed on them, but you've probably never given a second thought to the laborers whose blood, sweat, and tears went into creating your designer fashions. Think about this: in these countries, children and adults alike are forced to sew and stitch for next to nothing in a form of modern-day slavery.

Today's slavery has a different look and feel than the slavery of the past. In the past, slavery was legal, and owners viewed slaves as long-term investments. Today, even though slavery is illegal, it is flourishing and new slaves are considered to be cheap, low maintenance, and disposable. Although you may think that this practice doesn't touch your life, many of the products you buy are directly or indirectly connected to slavery.

"Are we willing to live in a world with slaves?" Bales asks. Of course, most would say no, but how does one end such a widespread practice? The key is to understand the factors behind the sudden revival of slavery and why inequality exists in the world today. Clues to both can be found by studying global stratification.

get the topic: WHAT IS GLOBAL STRATIFICATION?

GLOBAL STRATIFICATION is the categorization of countries based on objective criteria, such as wealth, power, and prestige, which highlight social patterns and inequality throughout the world.

Global Stratification

Nearly three billion people, or half of the world's population, live on less than two dollars a day.[2] In the United States, that salary wouldn't be enough for someone to afford a gallon of gas. Although poverty exists in the United States and countries all around the world, the widest gap in social inequality is not within nations, but between them. Thus, when you look at the standard of living in a wealthy country, such as the United States and compare it to a poorer nation, such as Chad, you see great disparity in the way people live. **Global stratification** categorizes countries based on objective criteria, such as wealth, power, and prestige, which highlight social patterns and inequality throughout the world.

Global Stratification

an international hierarchy — *is*

key factors are — Population and geographic area — *these affect*

Measures of stratification
- Income
- Poverty/Hunger
- Literacy/Communication

for example

Rentiers – the wealthy of a society
Entrepreneurs – the business class
Petite bourgeoisie/petty bourgeoisie – small businesses owners
Bureaucrats – the managers of business and government agencies
Craftsmen – skilled laborers
Semi-skilled manual workers – workers with limited training that may work in factories
Unskilled workers – the lowest class; unorganized group who often perform manual labor jobs that are often unpleasant and sometimes dangerous

The average annual income of Luxembourg is 656 times higher than that of Burundi. This clearly illustrates one component of global stratification: **the gulf between the richest countries and the poorest countries is extremely wide.**

Gross National Income Per-Capita in 2007

Top 10 Countries

1. Luxembourg	$65,630
2. Norway	$59,590
3. Switzerland	$54,930
4. Denmark	$47,390
5. Iceland	$46,320
6. United States	$43,740
7. Sweden	$41,060
8. Ireland	$40,150
9. Japan	$38,980
10. U. K.	$37,600

Bottom 10 Countries

199. Niger	$240
200. Rwanda	$230
201. Eritrea	$220
202. Sierra Leone	$220
203. Guinea-Bissau	$180
204. Ethiopia	$160
205. Malawi	$160
206. Liberia	$130
207. Congo, D. R.	$120
208. Burundi	$100

Source: Data from The World Bank (2007).

POPULATION AND GEOGRAPHIC AREA

When comparing nations and regions, size matters. In particular, factors such as population and geographic size can determine a country's use of and access to natural resources and talented people. However, large populations and large land area do not always go hand in hand. Consider the staggering population differences between Russia and Bangladesh. Russia is the world's largest country in geographic area, but ranks 10th in population size. Bangladesh, on the other hand, is the 7th largest country in terms of population and the ranks 94th in geographic area. Why the disparity? Population is not always distributed evenly. For example, Russia includes Siberia, which is a vast desolate region with very few people. In Bangladesh, the measure of population density provides insight into life there. The cities are overcrowded with small housing units that lack the infrastructure to provide regular electricity and acceptable sanitation standards or access to clean water.[3]

INCOME

To determine a country's per-capita income, you must divide the country's total gross income by the number of people in that country and assume it is equally distributed, which, of course, it is not. However, the per-capita income can provide interesting comparisons. Look at the top and bottom income-producing countries in this graphic. Most of the top ten income-producing countries are located in Europe, while most of the bottom income-producing countries are located in Africa.

Generally speaking, the wealthiest citizens in the United States enjoy a greater share of the total income of the country than do their affluent counterparts in other rich nations. Furthermore, taxation policies allow these people to keep more of their wealth than might be the case in other places in the world. Generally, tax burdens are lowest in the United States in comparison with other developed countries.[4]

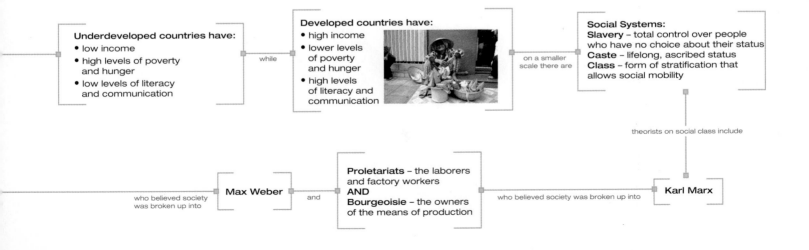

Underdeveloped countries have:
- low income
- high levels of poverty and hunger
- low levels of literacy and communication

while

Developed countries have:
- high income
- lower levels of poverty and hunger
- high levels of literacy and communication

on a smaller scale there are

Social Systems:
Slavery – total control over people who have no choice about their status
Caste – lifelong, ascribed status
Class – form of stratification that allows social mobility

theorists on social class include

who believed society was broken up into **Max Weber** *and*

Proletariats – the laborers and factory workers
AND
Bourgeoisie – the owners of the means of production

who believed society was broken up into

Karl Marx

MEASURES OF STRATIFICATION IN UNDERDEVELOPED NATIONS

Underdeveloped nations are countries that are relatively poor and may or may not be in the process of becoming industrialized. The United Nations aids the least developed countries on a basis of three criteria: a country must have a low gross national income; its population must meet health and education criteria; and factors like population size and remoteness determine need.

Developing countries are those in the process of becoming industrialized. However, issues like poverty and hunger still affect these countries as they grow.

Poverty and Hunger

According to international stratification measures, sub-Saharan Africa is the most disadvantaged region of the world. This region has the highest rates of childhood death, hunger, and people living on less than one dollar a day. Sub-Saharan Africa also has the lowest rates of sanitation, which leads to higher rates of illness and death.[5]

Disadvantaged regions illustrate disparity between wealthy countries and poor ones. For example, one in every 16 women in these poor countries dies during childbirth, whereas only one in 2,800 women dies during childbirth in rich countries.[6]

Despite the abominable living conditions poverty causes in poor countries, Kevin Bales makes a distinction in *Disposable People* that poverty is not synonymous with slavery. He says, "Slavery should not be confused with anything else: it is not prison labor, it is not all forms of child labor, it is not just being very poor and having few choices."[7] In other words, extreme poverty does not make one a slave. Although impoverished people might struggle to survive, they are not necessarily locked into a system from which there is no escape. Unlike slaves, impoverished people have more control over their own lives, although many of their destinies remain tied to the low standards of living in their countries.

MAKE CONNECTIONS

Access to Communication and Literacy

Think about different media and electronic communication forms that you use every day, such as e-mail, texting, and cell phones. You may be surprised to learn that much of the world doesn't have the same access to these communication devices as you do. These figures show selected countries' access to cell phones, personal computers, and the Internet, as well as their literacy rates.

People living in underdeveloped countries without the ability to read or write are often forced to take unskilled, labor-intensive jobs and work long hours to help support their families. As a college student in the United States, you probably can't imagine living under these conditions. But for many around the world, other options aren't available.

>>> **ACTIVITY** Spend a day without using any type of communication device. This means no cell phones, computers, books, magazines, televisions, radios, journals, etc. After spending a day without using a communication device, think about your experience. What did you spend your day doing? How did you feel? Bored? Appreciative? Peaceful? How do you think your life would be different without these items?

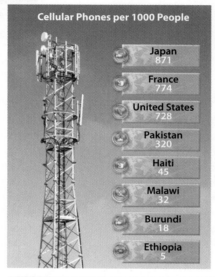

Cellular Phones per 1000 People

Japan	871
France	774
United States	728
Pakistan	320
Haiti	45
Malawi	32
Burundi	18
Ethiopia	5

Personal Computers and Internet Users per 1000 People

United States	633
Japan	502
France	413
Haiti	61
Pakistan	13.1
Malawi	3.77
Burundi	3.5
Ethiopia	1.6

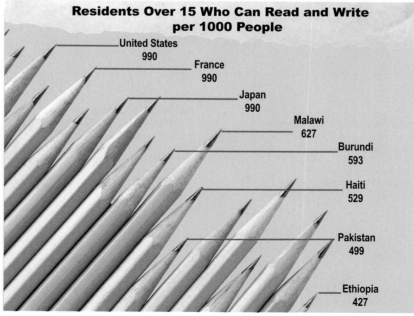

Residents Over 15 Who Can Read and Write per 1000 People

United States	990
France	990
Japan	990
Malawi	627
Burundi	593
Haiti	529
Pakistan	499
Ethiopia	427

Source: Data from World Factbook.

MEASURES OF STRATIFICATION IN DEVELOPED NATIONS

Developed countries, like the United States, have a well-educated population, regular elections, abundant industry, and free enterprise. Germany, Japan, and Great Britain are all developed nations and share many of the same characteristics, both socially and politically, with the United States.

Poverty

When studying global stratification, it's important to consider international comparisons of poverty among developed countries. Before you look at the numbers, you'll need to understand that U.S. dollars are the standard measure of income and that poverty definitions vary depending on the country. As a result, our data use half of the median income of the country as the definition for poverty, which allows for a more standardized comparison between nations. The table below shows how the poverty rates of ten developed countries stack up against one another.

Not only are you likely to find relatively high percentages of poverty in the United States, these percentages are still the highest even after welfare programs are taken into account. In part, this is because the United States has the greatest gap between the rich and poor of all high-income countries. What does that mean? Of the top 21 nations in the world by income, the distance between the top 10 percent of incomes and the bottom 10 percent is greatest in the United States. In the 1990s, for example, after taxes and other benefits, the incomes of the top 10 percent were 5.64 times higher than incomes in the bottom 10 percent in the United States. This means that if the bottom 10 percent in the United States made an average salary of $20,000, then the average salary for the top 10 percent would be 5.64 times more, which would be $112,800. This ratio represents the greatest distance between rich and poor in the industrialized world. The country with the lowest ratio was Sweden, where the wealthy earn 2.59 times more than their poor counterparts.[8] Therefore, if the bottom 10 percent of incomes in Sweden averaged $20,000, then the average for the top 10 percent would be $51,800.

Poverty Rates of 10 Developed Countries				
Country	Percentage of Total Population in Poverty (Rank)	Percentage of Children in Poverty	Percentage of Children in Poverty After Taxes and Welfare Transfers	Percentage of Elderly in Poverty
United States	17 (1)	26.6	21.9	24.7
Ireland	16.5 (2)	24.9	15.7	35.8
United Kingdom	12.4 (3)	25.4	15.4	20.5
Canada	11.4 (4)	22.8	14.9	5.9
Denmark	9.2 (5)	11.8	2.4	6.6
Germany	8.3 (6)	18.2	10.2	10.1
France	8 (7)	27.7	7.5	9.8
Belgium	8 (8)	16.7	7.7	16.4
Austria	7.7 (9)	17.7	10.2	13.7
Switzerland	7.6 (10)	7.8	6.8	18.4

Source: Data from Lawrence Mishel, Jared Bernstein, and Sylvia Allegretto, *State of Working America 2004/2005* (Ithaca, New York: Cornell University Press, 2005).

QUALITY OF LIFE

Which world city offers the best quality of life? A 2008 study shows that Zurich, Switzerland, is the best city in which to live, and Vienna, Austria, and Geneva, Switzerland, tied for a close second.[9] You might be surprised to note that a U.S. city did not make the top ten. So how might one measure the quality of life in one country or another? Many use measures of health and longevity to determine a location's quality of life. Common sense follows that the quality of life must be highest in the countries in which fewer babies die and people live longer.

The small Asian nation of Macau boasts the highest life expectancy (84.33 years), while Singapore has the lowest infant mortality rate at 2.3 deaths per 1,000 babies born. Meanwhile, Angola has 80 times the infant mortality rate of Singapore with 184.4 deaths per 1,000 births.[10] These numbers tell only part of the story about a country's quality of life.

Sociologists and economists look for variables to make international comparisons.[11] Kai Müller created a list ranking world economic and social development using a variety of measures.[12] Although income is important, it is only one of many factors to be considered. Other measures include access to telephones, televisions, and newspapers. Structural measures such as the country's debt ratio and the gross national product are also included. Finally, infant mortality, life expectancy, and literacy round out a series of items. By this method, Müller proposes that Norway is the best country in the world to live and the Congo is the worst.

Outside of Japan, New Zealand, Australia, and Canada, all of the top 20 countries are located in western Europe. Furthermore, the bottom ranked 20 countries are all in Africa. Clearly, quality of life is not equal throughout the world. My students are often surprised to see that the United States is not in the top 20. Of course, methods of weighing the factors can significantly change the ranking. For example, using older data but similar variables, Slottje found that the United States ranks 13th and Switzerland places first.[13]

Ong and Mitchell provide a slightly different list.[14] By ranking 21 different countries on four criteria—economic, social, cultural, and political—they provide another view of how to compare countries. These rankings showed that some countries might rank very high in one area, but lower in others. For example, the United States ranks first in cultural components, but 14th in social aspects and eighth over all. Ong and Mitchell combined all the tested areas to compile their quality of life list.

Efforts to compare and contrast different countries and measure quality of life often involve subjectivity. If you were to develop a schema, what variables would you use? Although the amount of air pollution is easy to measure, determining that one country has more beauty than another is very much open to debate.

Social Systems

All societies have systems by which they stratify, or rank, their members and by which those people receive the rewards of that society. Sociologists often characterize populations using wealth, power, and prestige as the basis of stratification systems. The three most common **social stratification systems** are slavery, caste, and class systems.

SLAVERY

Slavery refers to the total control over people who have no choice about their status. You may believe that slavery is a thing of the past; however, estimates suggest that there are as many as 27 million slaves worldwide.[15] That number equals the total populations of Iowa, Missouri, Illinois, and Indiana combined.[16] This staggering figure is probably difficult to believe, but the important thing to remember is that today's slavery hardly resembles the slavery of the past.

In *Disposable People,* Kevin Bales discusses "old" slavery and "new" slavery.[17] **Under old systems, slavery was legal and slaves were never paid. Today, slavery is illegal,** but today's slaves may be bound by debts, rarely earning enough to repay them.

Slaves were once expensive; in 1850, a field slave sold for approximately $1,000 to $1,800, or about $50,000 to $100,000 today. Because of their expense, slave owners viewed slaves as long-term investments. The high price and required care of slaves meant annual profits might have been only five percent of the initial investment. Today, slaves are much cheaper and virtually disposable. Once "used up" they are sent away, which increases profits. Bales estimates annual profits from modern slaves are about 50 percent of the initial investment. Owners of modern slaves are in a win-win situation; they have a continuous supply of labor and stand to make a huge profit.

Bales suggests that several new factors drive slavery today. Apart from rapid population growth and extreme poverty, weak governments, worldwide desire for cheap labor, and capital investment can support slavery. Weak governments may tolerate bribery or cannot control the behavior of local warlords and wealthy landowners. With rapid population growth, potential slaves abound. Many countries use their abundant labor supply to attract foreign investment, which can easily lead to the potential consequence of slavery.

∨
∨
∨ **Contrary to popular belief, slavery is not a thing of the past. Modern-day slaves exist in countries all around the world.** How do you think the slaves in these pictures differ?

Source: "Returning from the Cotton Fields in South Carolina," ca. 1860, stereograph by Barbard, negative number 47843. © Collection of The New-York Historical Society.

Forms of Slavery

Modern slavery takes three forms: chattel, debt bondage, and contract slavery. **Chattel slavery** is the closest to the old form of slavery because a slave is considered property. A chattel slave may work a lifetime for one family. Future generations will also become servants of the "owner."

Debt bondage occurs when a debtor is housed and fed by his or her lender. Debtors' wages are never enough to cover their expenses or debt. This form of slavery usually begins when someone borrows money in order to repay a different debt. The borrower then promises to work for the lender. Of course, the pay for the work is never high enough to decrease the debt while covering expenses for food and shelter. Thus, the person remains enslaved by his or her debt.

Contract slavery occurs when a person signs a work contract, receiving food and shelter by an employer. This is different from debt bondage because it is conducted under the façade of a legal contract. Workers sign contracts to work, often in another country, and the employer transports them to a job site. The employer also feeds and houses them. Employers deduct these costs, which often exceed the pay, and use fear and intimidation to keep workers from running away.[18]

CASTE SYSTEMS

Caste systems are similar to slave systems in that people have an ascribed status. However, unlike most slave systems, people are born into a caste system and the status is lifelong. Within **caste systems**, a person's position may be a position of power and privilege or of disadvantage, but in either case his or her place is permanently fixed. Caste systems do not allow people to move up and down the ranks, as the U.S. class system does. A person who is born to the lower class in a caste system will never have an opportunity to move vertically and join a higher class.

Perhaps the most widely known caste system is in India. Although now illegal, the caste system remains a powerful force in India today, especially in rural areas where the system decides whom you marry, what job you have, and where you live.[19] The *Go Global* box on page 144 provides a brief overview of the Indian caste system.

CLASS SYSTEMS

Unlike caste systems, class systems represent a form of stratification that allows social mobility. Sociologically speaking, there is no "official" agreement on the number and kind of social classes within the United States. In fact, the United States prides itself on being a classless society. In 2000, 20 percent of Americans thought they would make it into the top one percent of income earners during their lifetime. Another 19 percent thought they were already there, which means that a whopping 39 percent of people thought they could become rich or were already rich.[20] However, as we discussed in Chapter 7, it's unlikely for a person from the lower class to climb too high on the social class ladder. If a person does manage to climb vertically, he or she goes up only a few rungs.

THINK SOCIOLOGICALLY

Slaves in Tulsa

Could slavery still exist in the United States? According to Kevin Bales, the United States imports about 50,000 slaves every year.[21] In February 2002, the Midwestern city of Tulsa, Oklahoma, was shocked to learn that they had slaves working in their midst. Workers recruited by a Mumbai (formerly Bombay), India, company signed contracts for labor overseas. Many paid the company a fee of more than $2,000 to gain employment in the United States. Workers flew to Tulsa where they worked as welders for an industrial equipment manufacturer.

These workers left their country with a promise of long-term residency, good jobs, and high pay. What they found was signifi-

cantly different. The group lived in barracks on the factory grounds, sometimes working 12-hour days and earning as little as $2.31 an hour. The company's food was substandard, and many workers had to share beds because of a shortage of space. In the dormitory, a sign stated that workers who left the grounds could be sent back to India and that armed guards patrolled the grounds. Many also reported verbal threats and deliberate intimidation to keep the workers on the property.

After the workers were found, the U.S. firm claimed they were not involved in slavery and any fault was that of the Mumbai labor company. The corporation claimed that the workers were merely temporary trainees, so they did not deserve the mini-

mum wage or other employment benefits. The courts saw the matter differently and found the company guilty of exploiting the workers through human trafficking. A fine of 1.2 million dollars provided about $20,000 for each worker.

After the case broke, many local community members helped the Indian workers find legitimate jobs, and immigration hearings allowed them to legally stay in the country. With new jobs, the workers now seek to make their American dream come true. This case has a happy ending, largely because it occurred in a country with a free press and a strong government. Unfortunately, most contract labor occurs in countries without either of these two important components.[22]

The Indian Caste System

India is often referred to as a land of castes. India's caste system has five different levels: *Brahmin, Kshatriya, Vaishya, Shudra,* and the *Harijans (Dalit)*. Citizens are born, live, work, marry, and die within their caste. There is no room for movement up (or down) in the hierarchy of the system, and social order dictates that castes remain separate.

In India, *Brahmins* make up the priestly and scholar caste. *Kshatriyas* represent the warrior caste. These were the political leaders who protected the people and fought wars. Merchants, artists, and traders come from the *Vaishya* caste. Mohandas Gandhi,

Dalit protestors call for equal opportunities and treatment. **Although there are laws to protect *Dalits'* rights, much of Indian society still treats them poorly.**

the "father" of the Indian nation, was part of this caste. The Shudra caste represents the country's workers, such as laborers from the fields and cities. The lowest caste is "the untouchables." Gandhi referred to them as the *Harijans*, or the people of God. Today,

they are known as the *Dalit*. They were seen as unsanitary people who performed the lowest form of labor in the society. In such a system, Harijans were socially unacceptable. They lived outside the mainstream, remaining separate from the rest of society.[23]

Karl Marx on Class Systems

Remember that Karl Marx suggested that the class structure of western Europe consisted of two groups: the proletariat and the bourgeoisie.[24] The *proletariat* were the poor factory workers, while the *bourgeoisie* were the owners of the factories. They hired the workers and paid them as little as possible to help increase their own personal wealth.

Marx pointed out that **workers willingly participate in their own exploitation because they have a false consciousness,** or a false sense of their place in society.

Marx suggested that the owners foster this ideology in order to maintain their powerful position in society. Remember the 39 percent of U.S. citizens who were certain they could reach the top 1 percent? These citizens illustrate what Marx would call an ideology of false consciousness.[25] It's statistically impossible for all these people to fit into the top one percent.

Only through class consciousness, or an understanding of your position in the social system, will workers unite and eventually benefit from their labor. The bourgeoisie promote false consciousness to further exploit workers for their own benefits. The only way to break through this façade is for the exploited to unite and take power from the dominant class.[26]

According to Marx, class consciousness begins the revolution, whereby the proletariats usher in a perfect society and everyone shares resources equally.[27]

Max Weber's Class System

Max Weber expanded Marx's idea that property is the sole determinant of social class. Weber's class system included class, status, and party. When Weber discusses class, he refers to wealth, much as did Marx. However, a person's position in society is not only determined by one factor for Weber. Status or prestige includes people with fame or important positions.[28] Status matters in society. Party refers to the political dimension of power. Power elevates a person's importance, which in turn causes his or her rank to rise.

Weber's class system is more detailed than that of Marx. For Weber, **rentiers** are the wealthy of a society. They come from a privileged class who own businesses and land; they are the people with "old money." **Entrepreneurs** are the business class. They, too, may have a great deal of money, but they must work to maintain their place. They are "new money." These two groups make up social classes similar to what Marx called the bourgeoisie.

The **petite bourgeoisie** own small businesses. The people who own your local convenience store might be considered members of this group. Although they own a business and have power similar to the entrepreneurs, they do not have the same wealth, prestige, or power.

Bureaucrats make up a separate class. They are the managers of business and government agencies. They own nothing, but they have great power in the corporate structure. Corporations hire accountants and middle managers to oversee their business, often with high salaries. Weber felt this class would grow along with society's tendency to become more bureaucratic.

Next, Weber turns to laborers, which he divides into three groups. **Craftsmen** are skilled laborers such as plumbers or carpenters. They hold a special position in society because they have a needed skill that is unusual. **Semi-skilled manual workers** have some training and may work in factories. I was a semi-skilled worker when I was a bicycle mechanic. Without

RENTIERS are the wealthy members of a society, as identified by Weber.

ENTREPRENEURS are the business class, as identified by Weber.

PETITE BOURGEOISIE are small business owners in Weber's class system.

BUREAUCRATS are managers of business and government agencies.

CRAFTSMEN are the skilled laborers such as plumbers or carpenters.

SEMI-SKILLED MANUAL WORKERS are the workers who have some training and may work in factories.

UNSKILLED WORKERS are the lowest class, consisting of people who frequently perform manual labor jobs that are often unpleasant and sometimes dangerous.

∧∧∧ **Weber divides the laborer group into three classes: craftsmen, semi-skilled manual workers, and unskilled workers.** Craftsmen, like the plumber shown here, have unique skills that make them valuable members of society.

at least a little training, I would not have been able to perform well at my job. **Unskilled workers** make up the lowest class. They are an unorganized group who frequently perform manual labor jobs that are often unpleasant and sometimes dangerous. When I fried chicken at a fast-food restaurant, I was doing unskilled labor. The work was hot, dirty, and dangerous because the hot grease often burned me. However, it didn't take any specialized skills for me to fry chicken for the Colonel. Unskilled labor pays the least and frequently places the heaviest physical demands on the worker.

For Weber, people have differing levels of wealth, power, and prestige. Those with the most of all three components make up the upper class or the rentier. While Weber links social class to job type, class is also related to these other factors. Marx, on the other hand, primarily links social class to business ownership. **You are either a worker or an owner. Only through class consciousness will the poor rise up and create an egalitarian society.**[29]

Now you have a solid framework for discussing global stratification and its effect on citizens around the world. Why do you think global stratification occurs?

think sociologically: WHAT ARE THE THEORIES BEHIND GLOBAL STRATIFICATION?

Global Stratification—No Longer a Third World

When I was in college, I was told the world was divided into three parts: the first, second, and third world. The first was the United States and our allies; the second consisted of the Soviet Union and their allies; and the third world was made up of everyone else. Of course, this system bases its divisions on political and economic ideologies. Sociologists rarely use this system today. First, it's ethnocentric, inferring that the West should be first. Second, the "second world" no longer exists; the Soviet bloc has largely dissolved. Finally, lumping more than 60 percent of the world into one category hardly provides an accurate description of the included countries.

IMMANUEL WALLERSTEIN'S WORLD SYSTEMS THEORY

Immanuel Wallerstein's world systems theory presents an alternative view to the old system.[30] Wallerstein suggests that the world is divided by its connection to economic power. At the center of the system are core nations who are constantly trying to expand their capitalist markets, decrease costs, and increase profits. The economies of these nations influence the actions of others.

All core nations eventually run out of natural resources and they constantly seek expansion, so they find ways to enter *periphery* countries. Historically, core nations made colonies of periphery nations in order to expand their influence. For example, Great Britain used its Indian colony to expand its market and gain access to resources. Indians had to buy salt from British companies because it was illegal to make and use sea salt. Today, core nations do not have colonies. Instead, they use multinational corporations, trade treaties, and other techniques in order to access the periphery's resources and send the wealth home. Periphery nations hope to generate wealth through the sale of their human and natural resources. Countries like Nigeria and Iraq are periphery nations because of rich natural resources such as natural gas and petroleum.[31]

If a periphery nation can use some of its wealth to build its own economy, a small group of elites will arise who build industries of their own. In that way, the country becomes *semi-periphery*. Semi-periphery nations are developing nations who use their raw materials to manufacture goods that can be sold to the core nations while keeping more wealth in the country. Investments in future services and industries mean that the country has the chance to move closer to the core. Countries like Brazil and South Korea are semi-periphery nations.

External nations are underdeveloped nations that have little interaction with the rest of the system. They have few national resources and little ability to attract investment or interest from core nations. Burundi, Chad, and many of the nations of sub-Saharan Africa fit this category. From the perspective of the world system, they exercise little or no impact on other countries.

World Systems Theory

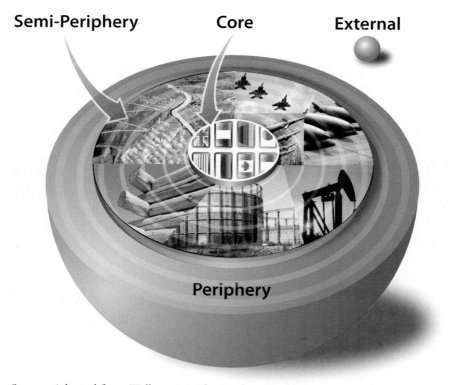

Semi-Periphery   Core   External

Periphery

<<< Wallerstein's theory suggests that **core nations are at the center of the "universe, and affect all surrounding nations.** External nations, however, are unaffected because they are seen as having little to offer to the rest of the system.

Source: Adapted from Wallerstein's The Modern World Systems, 1974.

NEOCOLONIALISM

Most of North and South America was once under colonial rule of a European power. Over time, however, it became difficult to stop rebellions, so many countries gave up their colonies.[32]

Michael Harrington says countries now use **neocolonialism**, a process in which powerful nations use loans and economic power to maintain control over poor nations.[33] Through loans for food, weapons, and development, poor nations become dependent upon rich ones. Once in debt, poor countries often cannot repay the loans and so agree to alliances, sale of natural resources, and trade agreements that primarily benefit the wealthy nation.[34]

Extending the ideas of neocolonialism, some propose that wealthy nations now use multinational corporations to control poorer nations.[35] Multinational corporations offer jobs, income, and potential riches to poor nations. The corporations benefit because they may gain tax-free status, weak environmental oversight, or some other concession that may not be in the best interest of the country. These corporations may create working conditions that lead to the enslavement of the native people. Bales points out that although company executives might not want to be involved in slave labor, they probably want to maximize their profits. Think back to the Tulsa slave case. After the slave workers were discovered, the company left Tulsa and moved to the Middle East.[36]

NEOCOLONIALISM is a process in which powerful nations use loans and economic power to maintain control over poor nations.

GLOBALIZATION is a complex process by which the world and its international economy are becoming more and more intertwined.

Through multinational corporations, wealthy countries continue to control weaker ones with corporate investment. This may, in effect, lead countries to engage in a "race to the bottom." To win the prize of foreign investment, they cut local regulations and salaries. This "race" can lead to wage and gender discrimination and less worker safety.[37] Of course, there is another side of this: they provide jobs and incomes to workers with few other opportunities.

GLOBALIZATION

Globalization involves a complex process by which the world and its international economy are becoming more and more intertwined. Globalization connects the world through business, travel, immigration, education, health issues, and production of goods.[38] Bales argues that every consumer in the world is linked to modern-day slavery in one way or another. Workers in China put together shoes made from leather tanned in Brazil, with rubber soles from Indonesia. Frequently, rich countries recruit the best and brightest from poor countries to become doctors, scientists, and other

Multinational corporations often set up factories in countries where they can **pay lower wages to the workers in order to make a heftier profit.** The Chinese women in this image are workers in the Reebok shoe factory.

vital occupations. This is **brain drain**—the best talent leaves poor countries and thereby provides an even greater advantage to wealthy countries.[39]

Some argue that an aspect of globalization is exploitation. Others suggest that it is the only hope for poor nations. As the world becomes more interconnected, are the various cultures around the world becoming more similar or less so? Those who believe cultures are becoming more similar suggest that the world's cultures are adopting more western values. On the other hand, some suggest that globalization will have the opposite effect on culture as local groups work hard to maintain their own religions, customs, and languages.[40] With this theory, globalization polarizes the world and creates gaps between groups. These theorists predict more war, terrorism, and unrest as western countries continue to expand. Do you share these views on globalization?

These countries must produce high food quantities to sustain the increasing demands of development. **Only when a country resolves its hunger issues can it begin to prosper from the benefits of global markets.[46]**

An abundance of food allowed Europeans to thrive. They created cities where they faced another hardship, which actually helped them more than hurt them. Open sewers spread disease and created high death rates for city dwellers. Consequently, their descendents developed a strong immune system and were genetically hardier than their ancestors.[47]

Those areas with great natural resources were able to acquire the power needed to function as the wealthy power brokers in the world. Remember that functionalism studies how social structures affect society. Diamond believes that Europeans and Asians advanced because they had abundant resources, strong military skills, set trade routes, and strengthened immune systems. Geographic areas with fewer advantages developed at a much slower place.[48]

Functionalism

In 1997, Jared Diamond published *Guns, Germs, and Steel,* a book explaining how the western world advanced so quickly while other regions of the world were left behind. Diamond points out that there was a time in history when all people on the earth were poor and lived in underdeveloped conditions. So why did some regions advance while other locations did not?[41]

Simply put, the fastest developing regions of the world had the climate, geography, and available natural resources that allowed them to advance. Other areas did not possess such advantages. The dawn of agrarian civilization occurred in the Fertile Crescent, an area that is present-day Iraq. The land in this region is fertile and easy to traverse. Most mountain ranges are passable, allowing for travel and trade amongst peoples. Goods and knowledge were shared throughout the region. With knowledge, civilizations became more organized, complex, and powerful because they used information to improve the quality of life. This led to greater power and wealth, which allowed for more trade.[42]

Tribal groups in Europe competed for many centuries, which built up the region's military know-how. Internal struggles led to alliances between groups, increasing trade and the transmission of information.[43]

Tribes in Europe and Asia were able to domesticate a number of animals and plants. Herders raised sheep and goats while farmers grew grains. Domesticated animals and plants allowed groups to amass more wealth and knowledge, which left people available to specialize as teachers, craftsman, artists, and warriors.[44]

Unlike Europe and Asia, native animals that live in sub-Saharan Africa defy domestication. Although native plants can be eaten, the Africans did not have the long grains that grew in the Fertile Crescent. Additionally, because the diverse African landscape ranges from desert to mountainous, regions could not share the same technologies used to grow food.[45] Jacques Diouf explains that countries cannot develop as their people starve and live in poverty.

With this theory, globalization polarizes the world and creates gaps between groups. These theorists predict more war, terrorism, and unrest as western countries continue to expand. Do you share these views on globalization?

Conflict Theory

Vilfredo Pareto provides a theory of how elite members of society reach positions of power and strive to maintain it.[49] Society seeks equilibrium, and changes in one part of society cause changes in another. This creates a circulation of the elite as the old elite members are replaced by the new.

Gaetano Mosca suggests that elites seek greater power for themselves and are unlikely to give it up.[50] Leaders use position to garnish benefits for themselves and their supporters. Consider Latin America. Cardosa and Faletto acknowledge that Latin American nations follow this pattern of leadership circulation.[51] They also discuss dependency on foreign investment and exploitation by more powerful countries. Aristocrats seek short-term rewards over long-term benefits to all. These landowners control natural resources, and they influence the government to gain more wealth. This is called the dependency theory.

It's interesting that Cardosa, one of the founding thinkers of dependency theory, led his country toward free market capitalism when he was elected President of Brazil in 1995. Cardosa, originally a financial minister, said he was an "accidental president," becoming president because he was working to quell Brazilian economic woes.[52] His two presidential terms stabilized and expanded the country's economy by increasing social programs to help the poor while opening the Brazilian economy to become a free market.[53]

Nations are dependent because they have no other choice but to borrow from wealthy places, but this often leaves them with nothing. However, the next elected president was a man who ran against Cardosa in the previous presidential elections. President Lula stood in opposition to many of Cardosa's reforms, illustrating Pareto's circulation of elites.

Pareto suggests two primary elites: lions and foxes. Lions are leaders who are patriotic, unified, and support the status quo. People choose lion leaders because they use force to create order in times of chaos. An example of this was the military dictatorship that overran Brazil prior to Cardosa's election. Cardosa was a new type of leader. Pareto refers to this type as a fox. Foxes are clever and rational with new ideas that try to change the status quo. Societies ebb and flow between leadership run by foxes or lions, balancing the desire for change with the need for stability.

Symbolic Interactionism

After World War II, European nations sought ways to prevent future wars and work together. Representatives created treaties that led to what is now called the European Union. This union grew from simple trade agreements between six countries to a group of more than 20 nations.[54]

Taken as a whole, the countries that make up the European Union have a weak central government to handle trade disputes, a common currency (the euro), and an increasingly common language (English). Although it does not have military forces, there are NATO (North Atlantic Treaty Organization) troops, which often come from a variety of European Union countries and the United States.

As a single nation, the European Union would be the richest country in the world. Business flourishes in the European Union, and many of the world's largest banks and corporations are centered here. The European Union also produces more scientific discoveries than any other country. Its inhabitants enjoy the highest standards of living, and Europeans work fewer hours, receiving more paid vacation time than U.S. workers.[55] The European Union shows how unity and cooperation can drastically benefit a region and its people. In fact, T.R. Reid suggests that the European Union residents see themselves as "Europeans," not members of a single nation. Reid suggests this collaboration could lead to a United States of Europe, becoming the world's greatest superpower.[56]

Working Hours Around the World

	Annual hours	Average per week
Mexico	1848	35.5
United States	1824	35.1
Australia	1816	34.9
Japan	1789	34.4
Canada	1751	33.7
United Kingdom	1669	32.1
Italy	1585	30.5
Sweden	1585	30.5
Germany	1443	27.8
France	1441	27.7
Norway	1363	26.2

<<< **On average, Europeans work fewer hours and have more paid vacation time than Americans.** Why do you think U.S. workers spend more hours at the office?

Source: Data from the Organization for Economic Co-operation and Development (OECD) 2005.

WRAP YOUR MIND AROUND THE THEORY

Mountains and the Sahara Desert take up almost the entire north African region. **Life exists where there are reliable water sources and vegetation**. Lush fields and plentiful resources allowed European countries to advance at a much faster rate than it did in north Africa.

FUNCTIONALISM

From a functionalist point of view, global stratification is a result of geographic conditions. Diamond states that the European countries thrived because they had natural resources that helped those societies function more efficiently. Domesticated plants and animals, trade with others, warfare, and disease all played a role in increasing the advantages for western Europe. These were the result of how societies used their resources to function more efficiently.

CONFLICT THEORY

Conflict theorists believe that an imbalance of power between the elites and the poor in a country causes stratification. Pareto argues that even among elites, power changes occur. He also believes that in times of struggle, lions will rule the day, but eventually foxes will take charge. Mosca states that leaders will do what they can to remain in power because it's in their best interests to do so. How do these power struggles between the elites affect those who are not in power?

WHAT CAUSES GLOBAL STRATIFICATION BETWEEN COUNTRIES AROUND THE WORLD?

SYMBOLIC INTERACTIONISM

Symbolic interactionists look at how language and symbolic events influence society. When the European Union was created, an entirely new notion entered the lives of Europeans. T.R. Reid suggests that Europeans increasingly identify themselves as members of Europe, not the specific country in which they were born. What impact might this have on the long-term influence of that region of the world over others?

Poor countries and their workers are exploited by richer, more powerful countries. These workers work long, hard hours for a fraction of what workers in a richer country would be paid.

Core nations have markets with local goods, but many of the cheaper items are made by slave labor in foreign countries. **Developed nations enjoy the best standards of living in the world, but at what cost to other nations?**

Social Policy: Foreign Aid

Some students in my classes are angered by the issue of foreign aid. They oppose paying huge amounts of tax dollars to help other nations when there are people in our own country in need.

"Helping the world's poor is a strategic priority and a moral imperative. Economic development, responsible governance, and individual liberty are intimately connected. **The United States must promote development programs that achieve measurable results—rewarding reforms, encouraging transparency, and improving people's lives."**[57]

The stated purpose of foreign aid by the United States is that it aids the strategic interests and safety of the nation while also promoting development and freedom in the underdeveloped parts of the world. This makes aid good for both parties involved. Many of the richest countries agree to provide 0.7 percent of their gross national product in foreign aid, so their donations depend upon a percentage of the wealth of the country. Only the top five countries meet their agreed goal. The United States ranks last on this list, giving the smallest percentage of its wealth. However, in total dollars the United States ranks first.[58]

An example may help you understand the difference. If you and I both donate $100 to charity but you only have $100 and I have $1,000, who has actually given more? We both gave the same amount, but you gave 100 percent of your wealth, while I gave only 10 percent. The United States contributes 0.14 percent of its GNP to foreign aid. In order for the United States to donate its proper percentage, 0.7 percent, it would need to contribute about six times the amount of money currently applied to foreign aid. European Union nations all give a higher percentage of their wealth, and in total, they give more than twice the total dollars of the United States in foreign aid.

ACTIVITIES

1. Check the tags of your clothes. Where were your shoes made? Do you have any assurances that slaves were used to make your apparel?
2. Discuss with a partner what can be done to combat slavery. If almost everything is connected to slavery, what can be done?
3. Take an Internet trip to www.antislavery.org. Surf the Web site. Write a paragraph explaining what you learned about modern slavery, how to stop human trafficking, and the lengths people are going to stop slavery.

From Classroom to Community | Becoming a Peace Corps Volunteer

After Caroline graduated from college, she didn't know what to do. She knew she could get a job, but somehow she wanted to see the world and use her college education to improve the lives of others. She felt her double major of sociology and Spanish could be a great asset. After joining the Peace Corps, she took a 27-month appointment in Ecuador.

"I never really thought I could live in another country, but I fell in love with Ecuador and the people there."

Caroline learned just how hospitable and welcoming the Ecuadorian people could be. "The families I encountered were so close and loving. At night, it was normal to see families crowded around a television watching soap operas with one another.

"I also learned firsthand that rules about privacy are very different in Ecuador.

"As a teenager growing up in my house, it was customary for me to hole myself up in my room surfing the Web or talking on the phone, but it's considered very rude in Ecuador! The wildlife and scenery was amazing, but my favorite experience was spending time with the kids at school."

While there, Caroline taught English in a local school and provided education to women regarding health issues. In her free time, she traveled throughout the country and taught the local children how to play soccer. "The children were so eager to learn from me. Once they got over their initial shyness, we became good friends." Once back in the United States she found a job working with abused children.

"I love my life, but a part of me will always be in Ecuador."

WHAT IS GLOBAL STRATIFICATION?   138

the categorization of countries based on objective criteria, such as wealth, power, and prestige, which highlight social patterns and inequality throughout the world

WHAT ARE THE THEORIES BEHIND GLOBAL STRATIFICATION?   146

world systems theory: the world is divided by its connection to economic power
neocolonialism: powerful nations use loans and economic power to maintain control over poor nations
globalization: a complex process by which the world and its international economy are becoming more and more intertwined; some argue that an aspect of globalization is exploitation. Others suggest that it is the only hope for poor nations.

WHAT IS BEING DONE TO ASSIST UNDERDEVELOPED COUNTRIES?   151

foreign aid, Peace Corps

get the topic: WHAT IS GLOBAL STRATIFICATION?

Global Stratification   138
Social Systems   142

Global Stratification—
    No Longer a Third World   146
Functionalism   148

Conflict Theory   148
Symbolic Interactionism   149
Social Policy: Foreign Aid   151

Theory

FUNCTIONALISM   148
- global stratification is a result of geographic conditions
- Diamond: European countries thrived because they had natural resources that helped those societies function more efficiently

- Pareto: even among elites, power changes occur; in times of struggle, lions will rule the day, but eventually foxes will take charge
- Mosca: leaders will do what they can to remain in power because it's in their best interests to do so

CONFLICT THEORY   148
- an imbalance of power between the elites and the poor in a country causes stratification

SYMBOLIC INTERACTIONISM   149
- looks at how language and symbolic events influence society
- Reid: Europeans increasingly identify themselves as members of Europe, not the specific country in which they were born

Key Terms

global stratification is the categorization of countries based on objective criteria, such as wealth, power, and prestige, which highlight social patterns and inequality throughout the world.   138

social stratification systems are slavery, caste, and class systems.   142

slavery is the total control over people who have no choice about their status.   142

chattel slavery is a form of slavery in which a slave is considered property.   143

debt bondage is a form of slavery in which someone borrows money in order to repay a different debt, and works off the new debt.   143

contract slavery is a form of slavery in which a person signs a work contract, receiving food and shelter from an employer, but is threatened when he or she tries to leave the contract.   143

caste systems are systems in which a person's position may be a position of power and privilege or of disadvantage, but in either case his or her place is permanently fixed.   143

rentiers are the wealthy members of a society, as identified by Weber.   145

entrepreneurs are the business class, as identified by Weber.   145

petite bourgeoisie are small business owners in Weber's class system.   145

bureaucrats are managers of business and government agencies.   145

craftsmen are the skilled laborers such as plumbers or carpenters.   145

semi-skilled manual workers are the workers who have some training and may work in factories.   145

unskilled workers are the lowest class, consisting of people who frequently perform manual labor jobs that are often unpleasant and sometimes dangerous.   145

neocolonialism is a process in which powerful nations use loans and economic power to maintain control over poor nations.   147

globalization is a complex process by which the world and its international economy are becoming more and more intertwined.   147

brain drain occurs when the best talent leaves poor countries and thereby provides an even greater advantage to wealthy countries.   148

Sample Test Questions

These multiple-choice questions are similar to those found in the test bank that accompanies this textbook.

1. Which of the following is characterized by the worker becoming property of an owner?
   a. False consciousness
   b. Contract slavery
   c. Chattel slavery
   d. Debt bondage

2. Which citizens illustrate what Marx would call an ideology of false consciousness?
   a. Petite bourgeoisie
   b. Bourgeoisie
   c. Proletariat
   d. Rentiers

3. Which of the following is *not* one of the three labor groups described by Weber?
   a. Craftsmen
   b. Bureaucrats
   c. Unskilled workers
   d. Semi-skilled manual workers

4. Immanuel Wallerstein's theory suggests that the world is divided by its connection to
   a. military power.
   b. economic power.
   c. political stability.
   d. technological innovation.

5. Nations that have wealth, technology, and strong military power, which they use to influence the entire global system, are called
   a. core nations.
   b. external nations.
   c. periphery nations.
   d. semi-periphery nations.

ESSAY

1. What are the positive and negative effects that globalization can have on underdeveloped nations?

2. What are the differences between a caste system and a slave system?

3. According to Marx, how does the bourgeoisie successfully promote false consciousness?

4. What characteristics does Weber use to determine social class?

5. How could wealthy nations be using multinational corporations to control poorer nations?

WHERE TO START YOUR RESEARCH PAPER

To learn more about efforts to curb slavery throughout the world, go to http://www.antislavery.org/

For more information on the Asian Development Bank, go to http://www.adb.org/

For more information about how people are ending child prostitution, child pornography, and trafficking of children for sexual purposes, go to http://www.ecpat.net/EI/index.asp

To learn more about international anti-slavery movements, go to http://www.freetheslaves.net/NETCOMMUNITY/Page.aspx?pid=183&srcid=-2

For interactive maps and data to visualize world issues, go to http://www.gapminder.org/

For more information on Guns, Germs, and Steel and a view of the ideas contained there, go to http://www.pbs.org/gunsgermssteel/

To learn more about human trafficking, go to http://www.humantrafficking.org/

To learn more about the International Monetary Fund, go to http://www.imf.org/

For information regarding health, crime, and standards of living, go to http://www.nationmaster.com/

To learn more about the OECD and read its reports on economic development throughout the world, go to http://www.oecd.org/

For more information about the Peace Corps, go to http://www.peacecorps.gov/

For information on population problems, refugees, and reports on world poverty, go to http://www.worldbank.com/

For more information regarding the use of cheap and child labor in the garment industry, go to http://www.sweatshopwatch.org/

To learn more about international aid funded by the U.S. government, go to http://www.usaid.gov/

For U.S. statistics and reports, go to the U.S. Census Bureau Web site http://www.census.gov/

For more information about the United Nations, go to http://www.un.org/english/

For more information about the World Food program, go to http://www.wfp.org/

For more information about World Health Organization and data, including issues of hunger, HIV, and other statistics from a variety of countries throughout the world, go to http://www.who.int/en/

To research how the World Trade Organization handles trade disagreements between countries, go to http://www.wto.org/

Remember to check www.thethinkspot.com for additional information, downloadable flashcards, and other helpful resources.

ANSWERS: 1. c; 2. c; 3. b; 4. b; 5. a

POPULATION AND
ENVIRONMENTAL IMPACT

"HOW

could a society that was once so mighty end up collapsing? What were the fates of its individual citizens?—did they move away, and (if so) why, or did they die there in some unpleasant way? Lurking behind this romantic mystery is the nagging thought: might such a fate eventually befall our own wealthy society? Will tourists someday stare mystified at the rusting hulks of New York's skyscrapers, much as we stare today at the jungle-overgrown ruins of Maya cities?

"It has long been suspected that many of those mysterious abandonments were at least partly triggered by ecological problems: people inadvertently destroying the environmental resources on which their societies depended.

This suspicion of unintended ecological suicide—ecocide—has been confirmed by discoveries made in recent decades by archaeologists, climatologists, historians, paleontologists, and palynologists (pollen scientists). The process by which past societies have undermined themselves by damaging their environments fall into eight categories, whose relative importance differs from case to case: deforestation and habitat destruction, soil problems (erosion, salinization, and soil fertility losses), water management problems, overhunting, overfishing, effects of introduced species on native species, human population growth, and increased per capita impact of people.[1]

How Do Societies Deal *with* Growing Numbers?

CHAPTER 09

In *Collapse*, Jared Diamond shows that even well-established, organized, and culturally stable societies can collapse under the weight of external forces like environmental or population crises.

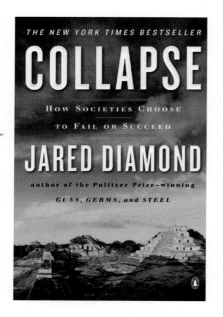

In the 2007 film adaptation of Richard Matheson's science fiction novel *I Am Legend*, Will Smith plays the last man on earth after a virus has rendered much of the world uninhabitable. The scenes featuring the movie star wandering the empty streets of an abandoned Manhattan—with man-sized weeds sprouting from the concrete streets and dilapidated skyscrapers marring the skyline—are eerie and foreboding. In a world beset by dangers, both man-made and natural, it is truly frightening to witness a once vibrant, cosmopolitan city like New York reduced to a cavernous ghost town, even if it's just a work of cinematic trickery. Seeing this, we're forced to ask ourselves, "Could this really happen to us?"

Jared Diamond discusses a number of societies and how their responses to environmental and external forces led to their eventual downfall.[2]

When these societies collapsed, it was not because of cultural or internal forces. Instead, Diamond stresses that human societies that can't adapt to changing external situations will ultimately fail. For instance, my students are very aware of the potential ecological challenges we face. Despite the "inconvenient truths" about climate change, overpopulation, and other potentially perilous circumstances, many of them still have a Darwinian belief in human societies' ability to adapt and survive. Diamond, though, knows that it takes only a small crisis to make a society fail. As frightening a notion as this is, it is vitally important to understand the influence of population and environment and the dramatic effects they have on society.

Population and Environmental Impact

includes → **Demography –** the study of population size and composition

uses key concepts → **Fertility –** number of births in a population
Mortality – number of deaths in a population

Population Control Programs – nations promote births with tax breaks and other incentives to increase population (**pronatalist**), or promote birth control to keep population down (**anti-natalist**)

get the topic: WHAT IS DEMOGRAPHY?

Population by the Numbers

Demography is the study of population size and composition. Sociologists, market researchers, and virtually all social scientists use **demographic variables**, such as population size, age, racial composition, birth rates, and death rates, to discuss populations. To better understand demography, let's get some background.

The world's population is not evenly distributed. For example, 37 percent of the world's population comes from either China or India. These two countries account for more of the world's population than the next 23 largest countries combined.[3] The United States holds only about 4.6 percent of the world's population.[4] Compared to China and India's populations, the U.S. population is about four or five times smaller, and yet the United States is the third most populated country in the world.[5]

DEMOGRAPHY is the study of population size and composition.

DEMOGRAPHIC VARIABLES are variables such as population size, age, racial composition, birth rates, and death rates used to discuss populations.

FERTILITY RATE is the number of births that occur in a population.

CRUDE BIRTH RATE is the number of births for every 1,000 people each year.

AGE-SPECIFIC BIRTH RATE is the number of births for every 1,000 women in a specific age group.

TOTAL FERTILITY RATE (TFR) is the average number of births expected from any woman in a population to bear in her lifetime.

ZERO POPULATION GROWTH is a TFR of two, meaning that each woman has two children to replace the mother and father.

TOOLS FOR STUDYING POPULATION

Somewhere in the world at this very moment, a family is celebrating the birth of a baby, while another is mourning the loss of a loved one. Every day babies are born and people die. When studying populations, sociologists frequently compare rates of fertility (birth) and rates of mortality (death). It's preferable to use rates and not total numbers when making comparisons between countries because this assures that a country's population size doesn't influence findings.

Fertility Rates

The **fertility rate** refers to the number of births that occur in a population. It is often calculated as the **crude birth rate**, which is the number of births for every 1,000 people each year. Biological and social factors both affect birth rates. The most important biological factor to consider is the **age-specific birth rate**, or the number of births for every 1,000 women in a specific age group. The greater the number of women of birthing age, the higher the number of births is. Additionally, social factors, such as health also play a part in fertility rates. For example, women who are sick or malnourished may be unable to carry a child to term. Illnesses such as AIDS lower fertility rates by reducing the number of women of birthing age or by affecting behavioral patterns. Knowledge of AIDS or other illnesses can encourage people to reduce sexual encounters, have safe sex, or practice abstinence.[6]

The **total fertility rate** (TFR) is the average number of births we might expect any woman in a population to bear in her lifetime. **Zero population growth** generally refers to a TFR of two, meaning that each woman has two children. Sometimes, demographers call this replacement level population growth because the births only replace the mother and the father. The TFR for U.S. women changes over time; in the 1950s, the TFR was 3.5 births per woman. Today, the TFR is about 2.0 to 2.1 per woman. Race and ethnicity also seem to influence fertility rates. Statistics show Hispanic women average 2.3 births per woman, while African American and non-Hispanic white women have a TFR of 1.8 to 1.9, respectively.[7]

Wealth and education also affect fertility. In general, birth rates are inversely connected to a woman's income and level of education. For example, women who are college graduates tend to have lower birth rates than women with less education. This may be due to women spending their primary reproductive years entering the workforce and continuing their education, increased availability of birth control, better understanding of reproduction, and/or different ideas about the role of women in society.

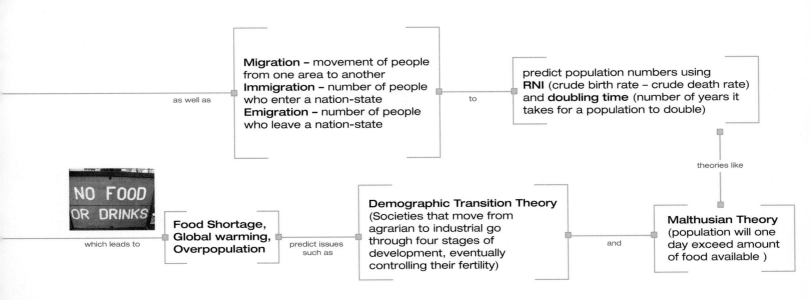

Migration – movement of people from one area to another
Immigration – number of people who enter a nation-state
Emigration – number of people who leave a nation-state

as well as

to

predict population numbers using **RNI** (crude birth rate – crude death rate) and **doubling time** (number of years it takes for a population to double)

theories like

Food Shortage, Global warming, Overpopulation

which leads to

predict issues such as

Demographic Transition Theory (Societies that move from agrarian to industrial go through four stages of development, eventually controlling their fertility)

and

Malthusian Theory (population will one day exceed amount of food available)

MORTALITY RATE is the number of deaths that occur in a population.

CRUDE DEATH RATE is the number of deaths for every 1,000 people each year.

AGE-SPECIFIC DEATH RATE is the number of deaths for every 1,000 persons of a given age group.

INFANT MORTALITY RATE is the number of children for every 1,000 born alive who die before they reach the age of one year.

LIFE EXPECTANCY is the average number of years a person is expected to live.

LIFESPAN is the maximum length of time a person can possibly live.

POPULATION PYRAMIDS are tools that visually represent data related to the age and sex of a country's population.

BABY BOOMERS are children born after WWII through the early 1960s.

POPULATION MOMENTUM is a surge in growth due to a large number of people who are of birthing age.

MIGRATION is the movement of people from one area to another.

IMMIGRATION is the movement of people into a nation-state.

EMIGRATION is the movement of people out of a nation-state.

Mortality Rates

The **mortality rate** is the number of deaths that occur in a population. It is often measured via the **crude death rate**, which is the annual number of deaths per year for every 1,000 people. Measuring the death rate in a population gives sociologists a better perspective of the society as a whole. For example, analysis of mortality rates that increase during periods of war, famine, or disease illustrates the importance of these figures. The **age-specific death rate** is the number of deaths for every 1,000 persons of a given age group. Of the age groups, particular attention is paid to the **infant**

mortality rate, which measures the number of children of every 1,000 born alive who die before they reach the age of one year. Singapore, for instance, has the world's lowest infant mortality rate with 2.3 babies dying per every 1,000 born.[8] Compare that to the African nation of Angola, which has the highest infant mortality rate at 182.3.[9] How might this affect a person's perception of life, death, and birth?

Sociologists also study **life expectancy**, the average number of years a person is expected to live. Thanks to health care improvements, trends for the last hundred years show rapid increases in life expectancy.[10] Not to be confused with life expectancy, the human **lifespan** refers to the maximum length of time a person can possibly live. Recent research indicates that a person's lifespan increased from 108 years in the 1860s to 116 years in the 1990s.[11] In short, people are living longer, but our maximum lifespan has only increased slightly, compared to our life expectancy.

One way to compare countries is to note their different life expectancies. For example, Macau, a tiny Asian nation, has the longest life expectancy (84.33 years) in the world, whereas Swaziland, a country in southern Africa, has the shortest life expectancy (31.99 years). To give you some perspective, the United States ranks 46th in the world with a life expectancy of 78.14 years.[12] Life expectancy is closely linked to health care access and environmental factors. The African HIV/AIDS epidemic, which is the leading cause of death in many African nations, contributes to that continent's low life expectancy rates.[13]

Population Pyramids

Population pyramids are tools that visually represent data related to the age and sex of a country's population. The population pyramids below show data for the United States and India. Notice how these two populations differ. The median age in India is 24.8 years, meaning that half of the population is below

Chapter 9   158

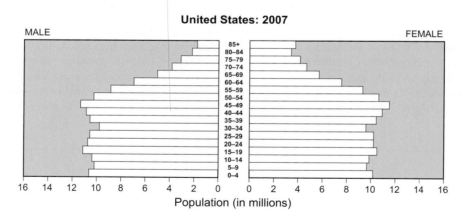

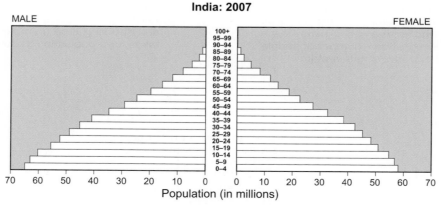

Source: Data from U.S. Census Bureau, International Data Base.

that age. Meanwhile, in the United States, the median age is significantly higher at 36.6 years.[14] What else can you see that is different about these two pyramids? Can you make predictions about each nation's future?

Population pyramids can also be used to represent population change visually. You can see the changing shape of the population pyramid for the United States from 1960 to 2050. The shape of this graph changes from a pyramid to a rectangular shape, which is known as "squaring the pyramid." This phenomenon occurs as people begin to live longer and birth rates remain stable, demonstrating the dramatic impact age can have on a society. Demographers know that the number of children or elderly people in a population will affect a society's needs. For example, children require education, so societies often provide schools for them. Children place demands on a society's resources even when they grow up: they desire jobs, homes, and other resources, but they also have the potential to create more goods for the society. Large numbers of elderly people can also put a burden on a society because their need for medical care means hospices and nursing homes need to be built and staffed.

After World War II, the United States and many other nations, experienced a rapid increase in births. We refer to this as the *baby boom*, and the children born after WWII through the early 1960s are known as **baby boomers**. Although this group has had fewer children than their parents, a quick review of the U.S. population pyramids shows that they created a **population momentum**, which is a surge in growth due to a large number of people who are of birthing age. Many college students are part of this momentum. Even if the boomers had only replacement levels of children, the population still grew because the cohort was so large. Can you see population momentum on the pyramids?

The size of a birth cohort can influence the outcomes of that group. For example, if you are born into a small cohort, you'll probably have better opportunities. This is largely because there is less competition for jobs and more individualized attention when it comes to job training and education. Better education can lead to better job opportunities.[15]

Migration

When studying population, demographers understand that issues such as life expectancy and infant mortality influence people's choices. Sometimes, those choices lead to **migration** (also discussed in Chapter 10), or the movement of people from one area to another. People from disadvantaged areas tend to move to areas where they hope to lead a more prosperous life. Migration is referenced in two ways: **Immigration** refers to the movement of people into a nation-state, and **emigration** refers to the movement of people out of a nation-state. To calculate the

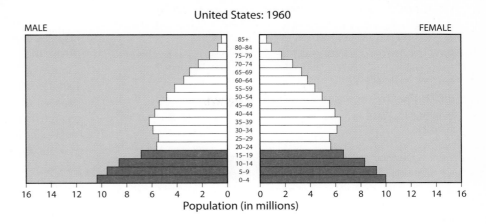

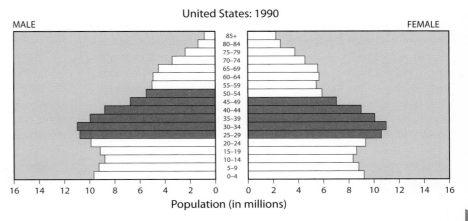

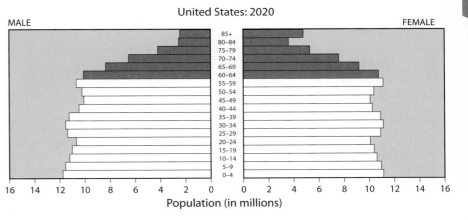

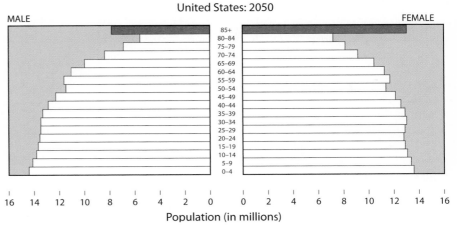

Source: Data from U.S. Census Bureau, International Data Base.

PUSH-PULL or **NEO-CLASSICAL MIGRATION THEORY** suggests that migration depends on the supply and demand for labor, both in the-sending area and the receiving one.

RATE OF NATURAL INCREASE (RNI) determines population growth and/or decline by subtracting the crude death rate from the crude birth rate and then dividing by 10.

BIRTH DEARTH is declining birth rates.

DOUBLING TIME refers to the number of years it takes for a population to double.

current population of a specific area, add births and immigrants to the base population and subtract deaths and emigrants.

Push-pull, or neo-classical migration theory, is used to explain migration, and it suggests that migration depends on the supply and demand for labor, both in the sending area as well as in the receiving one. When I was young, my family migrated from Nebraska to Oklahoma. The "push" was the closing of the meatpacking plant that employed my father. The "pull" was a pay raise and better work opportunities in Oklahoma. As a result, we migrated. Push-pull migration theory applies both to international migration, such as immigration from Mexico to the United States, and internal migration patterns, such as immigration from rural to urban areas.[16] Just like my father, my ancestors were "pushed" from Germany due to lack of work and "pulled" to the United States where there was work.

Rate of Natural Increase

When demographers calculate population growth and/or decline, they may use a simple calculation known as the **rate of natural increase (RNI)**. This is easily calculated by taking the crude birth rate and subtracting the crude death rate and then dividing by 10. Countries with a positive RNI have a growing population, and countries with a negative one have a declining population. The table below shows the crude birth rate, crude death rate, and the RNI for the world's top 10 most populated countries, and the top three fastest growing countries. As you can see from the table, the rate of increase for Uganda is six times higher than the growth rate of the United States. The table shows that the most populous countries don't necessarily have the fastest growth rates. To see this, we need to look no further than China, the world's most populous nation. Its RNI is closer to the United States, yet India is growing at a rate more than twice that of China. For this reason, many demographers predict that India will soon overtake China as the world's most-populated country.

A number of countries in the world have a declining RNI, and 25 countries actually have a negative RNI,[17] meaning that the death rate is greater than the birth rate. Most of these countries are in Europe, except for South Africa, Swaziland, and Japan. These declining birth rates, also called **birth dearth**, suggest that people in many parts of the world are opting not to have children.

Birth Rate, Death Rate, and Rate of Natural Increase for Selected Countries in 2007			
Country (Current population rank)	Crude Birth Rate	Crude Death Rate	Percentage Rate of Natural Increase (RNI)
World	20.09	8.37	1.17
1. Uganda (41)	48.12	12.64	3.55
2. Gaza Strip (151)	38.9	3.74	3.52
3. Yemen (53)	42.67	8.05	3.46
38. Nigeria (9)	40.2	16.68	2.35
53. Bangladesh (7)	29.36	8.13	2.12
66. Pakistan (6)	27.52	8.0	1.95
88. India (2)	22.69	6.58	1.61
107. Indonesia (4)	19.65	6.25	1.34
125. Brazil (5)	16.3	6.19	1.01
149. China (1)	13.45	7	0.65
153. United States (3)	14.16	8.26	0.59
203. Japan (10)	8.1	8.98	-0.88
221. Russia (8)	10.92	16.04	-0.51

Source: Data from *The World Factbook*, 2007.

Population Growth and Doubling Time

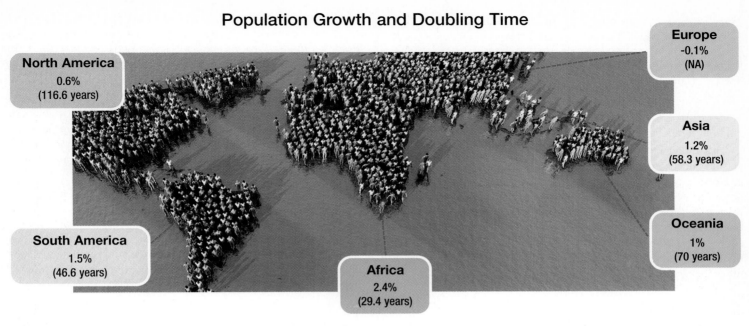

North America
0.6%
(116.6 years)

Europe
-0.1%
(NA)

Asia
1.2%
(58.3 years)

South America
1.5%
(46.6 years)

Oceania
1%
(70 years)

Africa
2.4%
(29.4 years)

Source: Data from Population Reference Bureau (PRB), 2007 World Population Data Sheet.

Doubling Time

While the people of Japan deal with decreasing numbers, other populations are experiencing rapid growth. **Doubling time** refers to the number of years it takes for a population to double. Starting at the year 10,000 BCE, when just one million people inhabited the planet, it took more than 11,000 years for the population to reach one billion. However, after 1850, it took only nine decades to double that first billion. After that, it took 42 more years to double that number. At this rate, estimates show that by 2026, the population will double once again. A country's doubling time can radically influence its future. For example, if a country's population is expected to double in 40 years, then all its resources should also double during that period.

> For each region listed, the percentage of natural increase and the doubling time is included. **Africa is predicted to double its population in 29.4 years,** while Europe's population will continue to decline.

▶▶▶ GO GL◉BAL

Birth Dearth in Japan

In the period between 1947 and 1957, Japan's total fertility rate dropped from 4.54 children per woman to about two children per woman. After this drop, fertility rates remained somewhat stable until the 1970s. From the mid-1970s to the early 1990s, fertility dropped again to a level of 1.46 children per woman, which is below replacement level.[18]

What caused this decline? Japan's defeat in World War II didn't just change the country's political culture; it also altered the economic culture. With the help of the United States, the Japanese rebuilt the national infrastructure and created efficient businesses. In a short time, Japan emerged from the ravages of war

to become a formidable economic power. Because fertility rates tend to drop as education and wealth levels increase, Japan's push toward economic success had a negative effect on births. Although measures of family values didn't seem to change, women's labor force participation increased, as did the pressure on them to get an education. This focus on career led men and women to marry and have children later in life, which made it less likely for couples to bear many children.[19]

However, the Japanese government has serious concerns over its impending demographic future. By 2050, the estimated number of children in Japan will drop by half, and the number of people of retirement age will continue to climb. This impending demographic scenario has Japanese politicians

scrambling to meet the needs of a new social reality. Schools are being closed and converted into senior citizen centers.[20] And without a replacement population, fewer people are entering the workforce. Shrinking numbers of workers could create problems for Japanese businesses. As the elderly grow in number, the pension systems for private business and the federal government are expected to have difficulty meeting their needs. These realities have resulted in an increase of government policies designed to increase births, including expanded child care assistance and more liberal child care leave laws. Lawmakers hope these policies will boost birth rates by allowing working women to keep their jobs while supporting children.[21]

MALTHUSIAN THEOREM is a population projection that suggests the population will exceed the available food supply because populations grow at geometric rates, while food supplies grow at arithmetic rates.

DEMOGRAPHIC TRANSITION THEORY is a projection that suggests people control their own fertility as they move from agrarian to industrial societies.

Thomas Malthus, an English clergyman, made one of the first and most circulated population projections in history. His essay, *An Essay on the Principle of Population*, was published in 1798. In it, Malthus theorized that populations grow at a geometric rate (2, 4, 8, 16), but food supplies increase at an arithmetic rate (1, 2, 3, 4, 5). This is often known as the **Malthusian theorem**. Increases in agricultural technology can increase the food supply, but this increase cannot keep up with the population explosion. Therefore, at some point in time the population will exceed food production. At that point, the world will experience wars over food, famine, and increases in disease.[23]

It's important to note that projections rarely occur exactly as calculated because population increases vary from year to year. In fact, previous predictions of doubling times have rarely been completely accurate.[22] Nevertheless, the use of doubling time shows some possible trends in world population growth and helps make comparisons between countries. Consider the doubling time of the world regions shown in the graphic on page 161. The population growth of Africa, South America, and Asia suggests that each continent's population will probably double within your lifetime.

During Malthus's lifetime, he saw the flowering of the Industrial Revolution. Quality of life improved, leading to increased life expectancy and rapid population growth. These events caused Malthus to consider the effects of population growth on society. He believed that a rapid rise would put a severe strain on the food supply and would eventually lead to outbreaks of famine and war. He theorized that the world's population would eventually grow itself into disaster and suggested that society would come under the influence of positive checks to curb the population. Positive population checks include war and disease. This would make worldwide health issues a positive check because they push back the day of collapse. However, you should note that during Malthus's lifetime, preventive checks such as birth control, delayed marriage, and sexual abstinence were not widely used.

Population Projections

Fertility rates, mortality rates, population pyramids, migration trends, rates of natural increase, and doubling time—all of these demographic tools help demographers make population projections that can be very useful to society. For example, if you project an increase in the elderly population, it makes sense to build retirement homes before they're needed. All population projections use estimates of birth, death, and migration rates and apply them to the future.

Malthusian Theory

In *Collapse*, Jared Diamond describes the rise of the Viking community in Greenland long ago. As their population grew, the community needed more food to sustain itself through the winters. They preferred to eat cattle over fish, even though fish were plentiful. Few fish bones were found in the archaeological digs of the ancient Viking settlements, indicating that despite the fact that their population was outgrowing the supply of beef, they did not adapt their way of life by using alternative food supplies, making it likely that they starved.

Malthus's ideas remain in the minds of many who study population. Paul Ehrlich, a famous biologist who also studied population growth, wrote an infamous book called *The Population Bomb*.[24] He suggests that there will be a point in time when the resources of the planet simply cannot keep up with the growing population. Eventually, the world's population will outgrow the world's ability to sustain it.

Malthus has greatly influenced the way people currently think about population growth. However, not everyone agrees with Malthus. Demographers who ascribe to the demographic transition theory believe that population growth will inevitably decline.

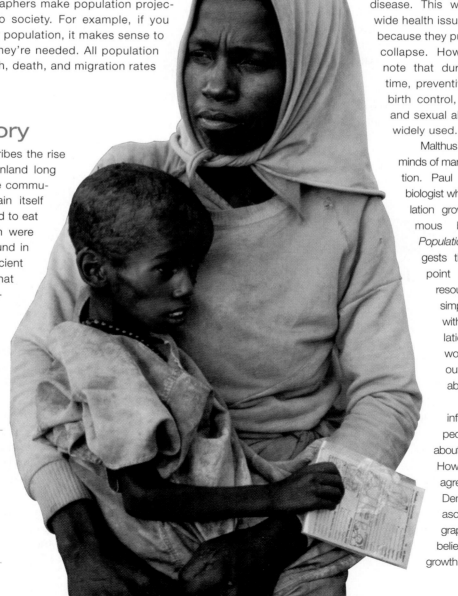

>>> **Ehrlich believes** that **unchecked population growth will lead to starvation** and death.

Demographic Transition Theory

Demographic transition theory is based on historical data of population growth in Northern Europe.[25] Demographic transition theorists suggest that people control their fertility as societies move from agrarian to industrial. This transition usually occurs in four stages.

In *stage one*, the society is not industrialized. Birth rates and death rates are high, life expectancy is short, and infant mortality is high. Economically, it's beneficial to have large numbers of children so they can assist you in day-to-day physical labor. Having a large number of children also increases the chance that some will survive into adulthood. Population grows slowly because birth rates and death rates are similar.

Things change in *stage two* when a country enters the initial phase of industrialization. New technologies mean fewer people are needed for physical labor. People migrate to urban areas seeking work in factories. Modernization brings more food, better medical care, cleaner water, and a generally higher standard of living. Birth rates remain high and infant mortality drops.[26] Life expectancy increases resulting in rapid death rate decline. Population grows fastest at this stage because of stable birth rates and rapidly declining death rates.

Birth rates decline after the country establishes itself as an industrialized nation in *stage three*. Even before artificial means of birth control were available, European nations that entered stage three had declines in birth rates. Meanwhile, life expectancy continues to improve, resulting in lower and more stable death rates. The economic and social conditions appear to influence individual choices, and people willingly control their own fertility. The rate of population growth declines although the population is still growing.[27]

World countries with constant or declining populations generally fit into *stage four* of the transition. Once a nation enters into a postindustrial economy, the population growth stabilizes and can even decline. Typically, birth and death rates are low. This theory suggests that industrialization actually improves people's quality of life. Since they are healthier and live longer, the population grows rapidly at first. However, with development, the population stabilizes. Therefore, as underdeveloped parts of the world go through this transition, the theory suggests that world population will once again stabilize and perhaps even decline.[28]

You can see the theory in action today. Agriculture-based communities, such as in the cases of families in the Midwest, tend to have more children as a means for acquiring wealth and income. However, urban areas may consider multiple children a liability. More children equal more mouths to feed, which can cause a strain on a family's finances. In the past, this notion that families in rural areas have more children has been the general rule of thumb; however, international fertility rates show that this is slowly changing.[29]

Demographic transition theory can be questioned for a number of reasons. First, although fertility did decline in Europe, this may be due to a delay in marriage and not a product of economic incentive.[30] Furthermore, fertility decline in Europe does not necessarily mean that fertility will decline in non-European countries around the world. The Eurocentric perspective of demographic transition theory is probably its greatest limitation because it ignores cultural differences around the world.

People from different cultures might behave differently. For example, the value of children and the attitude toward marriage and reproduction vary from place to place. The status of parenthood may outweigh the costs.[31]

Many demographers estimate that the entire world population growth will begin to slow by 2050 and that overpopulation will no longer be an issue by the end of the 21st century.[32] Trends show that fertility decline is already occurring worldwide, which gives credibility to the demographic transition theory.

Issues Associated with Population Growth

FOOD SHORTAGE AND HUNGER

From 1997 to 2002, thirteen million acres of cropland were no longer farmed, while acreage for grasslands increased.[33] Sounds like the world must be producing more food than it needs, right? However, food availability is associated with two important factors: wealth and geography. The poorest and most remote parts of the world, such as sub-Saharan Africa, are predicted to continue to have an inadequate food supply.[34]

Economic infrastructure, such as stable governments, doesn't exist in many parts of the developing world. Famine thrives in areas where wars and isolation exist.[35] Even though the world produces enough grain to feed everyone on the planet a sufficient diet, poor countries often lack the resources to purchase the food they need and to create the infrastructure to get that food to those who need it. These and other factors—including civil wars, weak governments, and local droughts—all result in about one in three children in the world being malnourished.[36]

ECONOMIC IMPLICATIONS

Population growth certainly can influence the country's economy. For example, assume economic growth is equally distributed in Germany, which has zero population growth. If Germany's economy grows at 2 percent in a year, then theoretically everyone in that country would have an increase in standard of living by about 2 percent. On the other hand, Uganda's population growth is 3.5 percent, so if economic growth is evenly distributed and the economy grows by 2 percent, then everyone would lose about 1.5 percent of their standard of living.

Frequently, **countries with the weakest economies have the fastest population growth,** which can cause problems in the short run. **How can a country with very little infrastructure keep up with such rapid growth? How can people who are already having problems getting their basic needs met survive with more mouths at the table?** They cannot possibly keep up with the demands of the current population, let alone a population growth.

In order to prevent the population from exceeding a country's resources, proper planning is required. Population planning is relatively easy for wealthy countries with slow growth rates. However, many of the globe's poorest nations are growing rapidly, which could result in an economic nightmare. Economist Julian Simon points out that economic forces benefit from population growth, particularly in the long run. When looking at a time period of more than 100 years, Simon finds that population growth actually improves a country's economic performance when compared with a country with stable population growth. He suggests that economies that benefit from growing populations do so because people must secure some sort of work in order to survive.[37]

Generally speaking, population growth doesn't have a major impact on developed countries' incomes and wealth. In established nations, larger populations have the freedom to encourage greater specialization of labor and increase the development of knowledge and innovation. This expands the economy by generating income and improving the quality of life for more people. The opposite is true in developing countries because rapid population increases tend to decrease incomes for most people, at least in the short run.[38]

∧∧∧∧ **As a country's population grows, the demand for public resources also grows.** New roads, schools, and hospitals must be built to accommodate the swelling population.

think sociologically: WHAT IS ENVIRONMENTAL SOCIOLOGY?

When Hurricane Katrina ravaged the Gulf Coast and submerged New Orleans under water, the public saw how intimately the environment and society are linked together. Prior to this, in the 1970s, researchers began investigating a new sociological paradigm called **environmental sociology,** which evaluates how the environment influences society, and vice versa.[39] Environmental sociologists usually concentrate on one of these areas: environmental attitudes, environmental justice, or environmental politics.[40]

Human Exemptionalism

Before we can fully comprehend environmental sociology, though, we must understand the commonly held belief in the human exemptionalism paradigm. **Human exemptionalism** considers humans as being different from other species on earth. Because we create culture and technology to expand how we fit into the environment, environmental factors don't influence humans the same way they do other living organisms. In many ways, the human exemptionalism paradigm suggests that we are

exempt from the limitations of nature.[41] For example, if we pollute the water, it has no effect on our survival because we can easily create water filters. However, the fish in the polluted streams have no such ability, and they'll die out.

Environmental Sociology

In contrast to human exemptionalism, environmental sociology considers humans to be merely one species within a global ecosystem that is interdependent upon other species.[42] While we possess greater brain capacity than other animals, we are not excluded from the forces of nature. As Jared Diamond notes in *Collapse*, several societies such as the Vikings in Greenland and inhabitants of Easter Island collapsed because their populations exceeded what the ecosystem could handle.

Humans are also limited by their biological makeup. Like other species on the planet we have a **carrying capacity,** which refers to how many members of a specific species can exist in a given environment.

When organisms live under their species' carrying capacity, resources are abundant. In such a situation, the organisms are experiencing **underpopulation**. When organisms are over carrying capacity, the organisms are experiencing **overpopulation**. In other words, the environment can no longer sustain the number of species who are trying to inhabit it.[43]

Can we sustain our standard of living in the same ecological space while consuming the resources of that space? This question is particularly relevant since we're living in an era of skyrocketing fuel costs and humans' ever-growing carbon footprints. Some argue that we're already at a breaking point because we have nearly exhausted the earth's finite carrying capacity.[44] However, it's possible that innovations and cultural changes can expand Earth's capacity. We're already seeing this as the world economies are increasingly looking at "green," renewable industries like solar and hydrogen energy. Still, many believe we will eventually reach a point at which conflict with the finite nature of resources is inevitable.[45] That means survival could ultimately depend on getting the human population below its carrying capacity. Otherwise, without population control, the demand for resources will eventually exceed an ecosystem's ability to provide it.[46]

Fortunately, our greatest asset as human beings is the ability to adapt our lifestyle to the environment. Anyone who's ever gone camping or lived where electricity is less than reliable has learned to adapt in order to survive. Unfortunately, not all wealthy nations are likely to cut their consumption of resources, even if it occurs simultaneously to their hurting the environments of other parts of the world.[47] For instance, although the United States only makes up 4.5 percent of the world's population, it consumes more than 25 percent of the world's oil.[48]

ENVIRONMENTAL JUSTICE

Julia Roberts won the 2000 Academy Award for her lead role in the film *Erin Brockovich*, the true story of a single mother who becomes a legal assistant and helps wage a successful battle against Pacific Gas & Electric. The energy giant was accused of contaminating the water supply and causing massive health problems for residents living in the vicinity of a compressor station.[49] The result of Brockovich's persistent investigations was a multi-million dollar settlement for the plaintiffs, but even an enormous sum of cash is little comfort to people who have suffered or died from the pollution.

This case illustrates an environmental truth: generally, the poor are more adversely affected by environmental damage.[50] Because the poor often don't have a way of moving away from polluted communities, they must tolerate toxic gas emissions and/or contaminated water. This is often seen as a form of environmental racism or classism.[51] Scientists explore issues like these by examining **environmental justice**, or the impact of environmental factors on social classes. This is done by looking at who uses the world's resources and in what quantities.

Even before the devastation brought on by Hurricanes Katrina and Rita in 2005, poor black residents of Norco, Louisiana, struggled against environmental hazards brought on by a Shell chemical plant. These residents suffered from health problems and even fought to be relocated from their neighborhoods.[52] In 2004, after 20 years of fighting, 300 families were relocated away from the toxic chemical plant.[53] Similarly, on a recent trip to Mexico City, the air pollution was so bad that when I awoke in my hotel, I felt as if I had a layer of soot on my skin. I was able to escape the pollution when I returned from my trip, but the residents of the city were exposed to that pollution every day. Frequently, poor states and nations have serious problems with air, land, and water pollution.

ENVIRONMENTAL SOCIOLOGY is the study of how the environment influences society, and vice versa.

HUMAN EXEMPTIONALISM is the belief that considers humans as being different from other species on earth.

CARRYING CAPACITY is the number of a specific species that can exist in a given environment.

UNDERPOPULATION occurs when a species' population lives under the carrying capacity, resulting in abundant resources.

OVERPOPULATION occurs when a species' population lives beyond the carrying capacity, resulting in too few resources.

ENVIRONMENTAL JUSTICE is the impact of environmental factors on social classes.

∨ What is the carrying capacity of this
∨ fish bowl? **What is the carrying**
∨ **capacity of the Earth?**

Alang Ship Graveyard

On a beach in the western Indian city of Alang, workers walk through the heat on their way to the graveyard. But this is not an ordinary graveyard; it is the world's largest ship graveyard. It exists in a region that was once known for its clean, sandy beaches. Now, though, it's in the business of ship breaking, which brings much needed jobs to the area, but also pollution.

India's rapidly growing population provides a plentiful supply of cheap, unskilled workers for this business. They drag former oil tankers, military ships, and cargo ships onto a stretch of beach, cut the metal from the frame, and sell it to scrap metal companies. Frequently, the workers come into contact with cancer-causing toxins that lead to a host of health issues. Due to a lack of safety regulations, some laborers are injured or killed by falling metal. Some organizations estimate that as many as 50–60 workers die per year from such accidents.[54]

With knowledge of these working conditions, why would anyone want to bring business to Alang? Because the city provides a cost-effective means for ship owners from around the world to dispose of their old vessels, despite the fact that the Alang Beach is now a polluted junkyard in which environmental toxins leach into the ocean, killing fish, and ruining the once pristine beach.[55]

Dangerous, dirty jobs continue to be outsourced to developing countries with growing populations. Generally, these countries have few pollution control regulations and rarely enforce the ones they do have. Additionally, the countries are in desperate need of an influx of wealth and will take industries from virtually anywhere for anything. This means population, globalization, and the environment interact to create wealth for some, meager wages for others, and long-term problems for subsequent generations.

>>> **ACTIVITY** Research dangerous jobs in the United States. How do they compare with the Alang ship graveyard?

∧
∧
∧ In order to work at Alang, **poorly paid workers endure numerous health dangers.**

Global Warming

These dirty jobs are not only bad for the people who work under these conditions, but these jobs also can be hazardous in the long term for the larger population. Just as investigators on the hit show *CSI: Crime Scene Investigation* analyze a crime scene for fingerprints, sociologists have developed a formula to describe a population's *environmental footprint*, or impact on the environment. The *IPAT formula* (Impacts = Population times Affluence times Technology) determines the environmental impact that population, wealth, and technology have on a society.[56] Hunter-gatherer societies generally live off the land and do not produce a footprint.[57] However, a complex postindustrial society such as the United States has a significant environmental footprint. Of course, advanced societies have a variety of technologies that can either increase or decrease their footprint. Reducing our environmental footprint by reducing what we used and recycling materials are ways to reduce global warming and battle climate change.

The issues of global warming and climate change are not just on the minds of scientists, politicians, and bloggers; it's an area that is often discussed in environmental sociology as well. **But why is the Earth warming?**

The chief suspect is increasing levels of greenhouse gases in the atmosphere. One primary greenhouse gas, carbon dioxide, is sent into the air every time you exhale. But it also occurs when fossil fuels, like the gasoline that propels the millions of cars on the road, are burned. In the atmosphere, carbon dioxide acts like a piece of glass on a greenhouse: allowing in the sun's heat and keeping its warmth from escaping.[58]

Sociologically, what is causing these warmer climates is beyond the scope of this book; however, how might these warmer climates directly change the social world? For example, one result may be dramatic changes in the world's weather patterns. Incidents of drought have increased in the Southern Hemisphere as well as in areas that previously had not experienced them. Meanwhile, rainfall totals have increased in the Northern Hemisphere. Global warming has also been blamed for raising sea levels, melting the polar ice cap, and increasing the volumes of saltwater in the oceans. As the oceans continue to rise, people who live in low-lying areas are likely to experience more and more problems with issues such as storm surges and the erosion of coastlands. One country, the small island nation of Tuvalu, located off the eastern coast of Australia, is rapidly disappearing, and its people are increasingly migrating to New Zealand and Australia. Other nations, such as Bangladesh, may experience significant loss of land and life if these trends continue as people must move to higher ground and the ocean takes over some farmland.[59]

If the globe is indeed warming due to greenhouse gases, you might wonder if this is inevitable with population growth. All you have to do is look at the increasing price of oil to know that more people are requiring more fossil fuels for their cars, homes, and workplaces. However, population increase doesn't necessarily mean that pollution and global warming are inevitable. For example, air pollution has actually declined in California, despite the state's recent population boom.[60] This environmental success story is the result of the California government's deliberate effort to address this concern. As the world becomes more aware of environmental concerns—especially in wealthy, developed nations—this example gives us hope that these trends can be reversed.[61]

WRAP YOUR MIND AROUND THE THEORY

Overpopulation can lead to a scarcity of resources. This small Indian village depends on mobile water delivery every three days.

FUNCTIONALISM

Functionalists want to know what part a growing population plays in society. Basic statistics tell us that a growing population increases opportunities and that children are absolutely essential for a society to continue. But many functionalists believe that humanity won't last long in an overpopulated state if resources become scarce and a planet's carrying capacity cannot keep up. For example, think about Easter Island. Diamond points out that natives on the island went through an ecological collapse and eventually died off due to deforestation that led to war. This example shows us that it's not a good idea to stretch resources too thin. Humans are a part of a larger integrated system, and for society to function properly, they must find their place within that larger system.

CONFLICT THEORY

Conflict theorists might view population growth using the Malthusian point of view. More people need more resources such as food, clean water, and space. Although advancements in technology can increase the food supply, at some point the population will outgrow the availability of food, causing a clear difference between the "haves" and "have-nots." The haves will obtain the necessary goods and power, while the have-nots will have fewer goods, less wealth, and therefore less power. This imbalance will lead to conflict causing war and discord. In order to prevent this and ensure survival, people must learn to adapt to changing times. For example, I recently sold my gas-guzzler for a smaller car. Oil availability and cost has been a hot topic in the news, leading many to consider hybrid vehicles and public transportation. As Diamond points out, societies must coexist within their environment. If they ignore this simple fact, even strong, thriving cultures can be destroyed.

HOW DOES POPULATION GROWTH AFFECT SOCIETY?

SYMBOLIC INTERACTIONISM

From an interactionist perspective we might want to reverse this question and ask, "How does society affect population growth?" Symbolic interactionism looks at how a society's culture influences that society. Although health and economic factors influence birth rates as well, interactionists study how society's attitude toward children influences birth rates. The changing definitions of men's and women's roles in society influence the rate of education of women, the use of birth control, and the delay of marriage. These attitudes result in fewer births and decreased population growth.

This is an image of Easter Island. **Where did all the people go?**

What **do these images tell you** about **how each family feels about children?**

discover sociology in action: HOW CAN GOVERNMENTS CONTROL POPULATIONS?

Population Control Programs

Government officials often consider population when planning for the future. Nations that promote fertility among their population are considered **pro-natalist**. The United States is a pro-natalist country because it provides tax deductions to couples who have children. The more children you have, the less income tax you pay.

On the opposite end of the spectrum are **anti-natalist** countries, or countries that do not promote fertility. This is an example of how public policy can influence population. Countries such as China have laws and tax penalties for people who have multiple births. Consider different countries and the percentages of women of birthing age in those nations who use modern means of birth control. In wealthy nations such as Canada or the United States, the rate is quite high, while poor nations have much lower rates.

In China, however, the rate of birth control being used is also quite high. Chinese fertility patterns have often differed from those in the western world. In 1979, China began what is often called

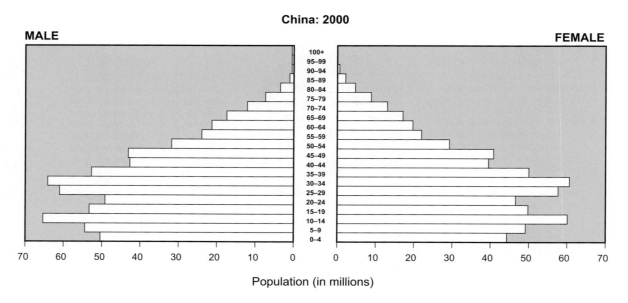

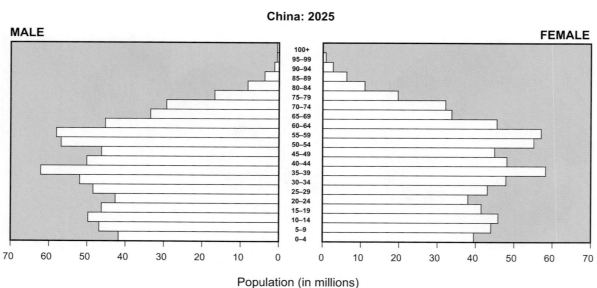

Source: Data from U.S. Census Bureau, International Data Base.

the "one-child" policy.[62] The policy was established after the Chinese government saw population projections that foreshadowed many problems such as hunger, lack of economic opportunity, and an inability to sustain the population in the future if something drastic was not done quickly.

The "one-child" policy is not as simple as it sounds, though. For example, China's family planning policy includes delaying marriage and improving access to contraception. Critics of the policy paint a darker picture of the policy by suggesting it has led to forced abortions and sterilizations.[63] Additionally, the Chinese preference for sons led some mother's to purposefully abort female fetuses, which has led to an extremely imbalanced sex ratio.[64] China's official policy also varies based on a person's geographic location. In highly concentrated urban areas, the one-child-per-couple standard is enforced, yet in more rural areas, the policy allows a couple to have a second child.[65]

China's policy basically follows the logic that bigger families use more state resources. In some areas, having only one child can give the parents bonuses in income, better health care benefits, priority for housing and school choice, and longer maternity leave. After the birth of their first child, a couple pledges to have no more children and thus can reap these benefits as long as they comply. If a couple decides to disobey the policy, the government may impose a tax penalty on their earnings.[66]

In the population pyramids on the opposite page, you can clearly see the result of the one-child policy. The policy was implemented in 1979, which can be seen on the chart for the year 2000 in the age cohort of 20-year-olds. By 2025, China's pyramid takes on an increasingly square shape, with the total number of children continuing to decline. Clearly, the policy is effective in decreasing the Chinese population.

PRO-NATALIST means concerned with promoting population growth.
ANTI-NATALIST means concerned with limiting population growth.

ACTIVITIES

1. How do you think your hometown would change if the population increased by 100,000 people? How about 1,000,000 people?
2. Contact a city official and ask them what type of data they use from the U.S. Census Bureau to help determine future needs.
3. How might population growth influence the balance of global power?
4. Go to the U.S. Census Web site and check out the international database of population pyramids for a country of interest to you. How do you think population growth will affect it in the next 50 years?

From Classroom to Community | Earth Day

First established in 1970, Earth Day was set on April 22nd as a day of environmental action and awareness. Every year, my students always participate in cleanup activities. One of those students, Janice, wrote this of her Earth Day experience.

"I decided to volunteer for Earth Day because I figured it would be a great way to get extra credit in my sociology course. Before this, I had never really thought much about the environment. I grew up in a suburban area, living close to malls and superstores that had everything I needed. I threw out bottles and cans when they were empty because I knew I could just go buy more. Spending the day cleaning up the creek near campus opened my eyes.

"Everyone met at 8:00 A.M., and we were divided into teams. Each team was given gloves and 10 trash bags. I didn't think we'd ever be able to fill all the trash bags, but after we started I began to see the problem.

"The creek runs under a road by the campus. I've driven over it many times, but I never really noticed the bridge before. Within two hours, all of our bags were filled with fast-food containers, aluminum cans, and lots and lots of paper. We divided the trash from the recyclable items, and I was amazed at how many recycling bags we were filling.

"I couldn't believe this experience. Apparently people don't think about how many reusable and recyclable items they throw away. I kept wondering, what would happen if everyone on the campus recycled? Most of the trash that ended up in the creek would have been used again, diminishing the number of resources squandered.

"All of this caused me to wonder how much wasteful dumping occurs in our country. Doing this Earth Day exercise taught me the importance of caring for the environment. **I may not be able to solve global warming, but I can do my part by picking up trash and recycling.**"

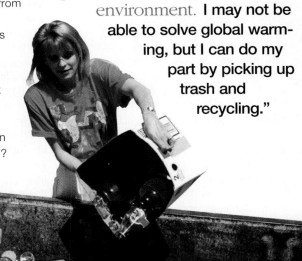

WHAT IS DEMOGRAPHY? 157

the study of population size and composition

WHAT IS ENVIRONMENTAL SOCIOLOGY? 164

a new sociological paradigm that evaluates how the environment influences society, and vice versa

HOW CAN GOVERNMENTS CONTROL POPULATIONS? 168

they can promote or discourage fertility, create fertility policies, and implement tax deductions.

get the topic: WHAT IS DEMOGRAPHY?

Population by the Numbers   157
Malthusian Theory   162
Demographic Transition Theory   163

Issues Associated with
   Population Growth   163

Human Exemptionalism   164
Environmental Sociology   164
Population Control Programs   168

Theory

FUNCTIONALISM   167

- looks at what part a growing population plays in society
- increases opportunities
- growing populations increase demand on resources
- humanity will not last if population is larger than the planet's carrying capacity

CONFLICT THEORY   167

- Malthusian point of view: population will outgrow food availability
- haves vs. have-nots will lead to war and discord
- people must learn to adapt

SYMBOLIC INTERACTIONISM   167

- looks at how society affects population growth
- culture shapes a society's population
- society's attitude toward children affect birth rates
- education of women, the use of birth control, and the delay of marriage result in fewer births and decreased population growth

Key Terms

demography is the study of population size and composition.   157

demographic variables are variables such as population size, age, racial composition, birth rates, and death rates used to discuss populations.   157

fertility rate is the number of births that occur in a population.   157

crude birth rate is the number of births for every 1,000 people each year.   157

age-specific birth rate is the number of births for every 1,000 women in a specific age group.   157

total fertility rate (TFR) is the average number of births expected from any woman in a population to bear in her lifetime.   157

zero population growth is a TFR of two, meaning that each woman has two children to replace the mother and the father.   157

mortality rate is the number of deaths that occur in a population.   158

crude death rate is the number of deaths for every 1,000 people each year.   158

age-specific death rate is the number of deaths for every 1,000 persons of a given age group.   158

infant mortality rate is the number of children for every 1,000 born alive who die before they reach the age of one year.   158

life expectancy is the average number of years a person is expected to live.   158

lifespan is the maximum length of time a person can possibly live.   158

population pyramids are tools that visually represent data related to the age and sex of a country's population.   158

baby boomers are children born after WWII through the early 1960s.   159

population momentum is a surge in growth due to a large number of people who are of birthing age.   159

migration is the movement of people from one area to another area.   159

immigration is the movement of people into a nation-state.   159

emigration is the movement of people out of a nation-state.   159

push-pull or **neo-classical migration theory** suggests that migration depends on the supply and demand for labor, both in the sending area and the receiving one.   160

rate of natural increase (RNI) determines population growth and/or decline by subtracting the crude death rate from the crude birth rate and then dividing by 10.   160

birth dearth is declining birth rates.   160

doubling time refers to the number of years it takes for a population to double. *161*

Malthusian theorem is a population projection that suggests the population will exceed the available food supply because populations grow at geometric rates, while food supplies grow at arithmetic rates. *162*

demographic transition theory is a projection that suggests people control their own fertility as they move from agrarian to industrial societies. *163*

environmental sociology is the study of how the environment influences society, and vice versa. *164*

human exemptionalism is the belief that considers humans as being different from other species on earth. *164*

carrying capacity is the number of a specific species that can exist in a given environment. *164*

underpopulation occurs when a species' population lives under the carrying capacity, resulting in abundant resources. *165*

overpopulation occurs when a species' population lives beyond the carrying capacity, resulting in too few resources. *165*

environmental justice is the impact of environmental factors on social classes. *165*

pro-natalist means concerned with promoting population growth. *168*

anti-natalist means concerned with limiting population growth. *168*

Sample Test Questions

These multiple-choice questions are similar to those found in the test bank that accompanies this textbook.

1. Which of the following is used by demographers as an indicator of the quality of a population's health care and standard of living?
   a. Age-specific death rate
   b. Age-specific birth rate
   c. Infant mortality rate
   d. Crude death rate

2. Countries entering the fourth stage of transition in the demographic transition theory are
   a. not yet industrialized.
   b. in a postindustrial economy.
   c. established as industrialized nations.
   d. entering the initial phase of industrialization.

3. Which relationship is generally true of birth rates?
   a. They are lower among women from ethnic minorities.
   b. They are lower among women with less education.
   c. They are higher among women with lower income.
   d. They are higher among women with poor health.

4. Which of the following is of major concern for Japan's demographic future?
   a. The birth rate is increasing.
   b. There will be too many workers and too few jobs.
   c. There will be significantly fewer children than there are now.
   d. The number of people of retirement age will decrease significantly.

5. Which of the following is an example of human exemptionalism in action?
   a. Wildlife conservation
   b. Mandated recycling
   c. Underpopulation
   d. Air pollution

ESSAY

1. Why doesn't population growth generally affect the income and wealth of developed countries?

2. How do sociologists describe a population's environmental footprint?

3. How can reducing one's environmental footprint help reduce climate change and global warming?

4. Describe the arguments for and against anti-natalist policies such as China's.

5. How do social factors affect birth rates?

WHERE TO START YOUR RESEARCH PAPER

To find more facts and figures for countries around the world, go to the World Factbook Web site at
https://www.cia.gov/library/publications/the-world-factbook/

For U.S. statistics and reports, go to the U.S. Census Bureau Web site at http://www.census.gov/

For more information on immigration in the United States, go to http://www.cis.org/

To learn more about the world population and issues that arise with growing numbers, go to http://www.overpopulation.org/ and www.prb.org

To find out more about what countries are doing to control their populations, go to http://www.popcouncil.org/

To see what people do to celebrate Earth Day, go to http://www.earthday.net/ and http://www.epa.gov/earthday/

Answers: 1. c; 2. b; 3. c; 4. c; 5. d

Remember to check www.thethinkspot.com for additional information, downloadable flashcards, and other helpful resources.

RACE AND ETHNIC
STRATIFICATION

WHAT IS THE DIFFERENCE BETWEEN RACE AND ETHNICITY?

WHAT CAUSES RACIST ATTITUDES, AND HOW DO THESE ATTITUDES AFFECT PEOPLE?

HOW DOES AFFIRMATIVE ACTION HELP MINORITY GROUPS IN THE UNITED STATES?

"The

traditional concept of race as a biological fact is a myth. I am going to show you that nearly everything you think you know about race is a social construct. You don't have to be a racist to be wrong about what race is. That doesn't make the effects of a belief in race any less damaging, or the situation any less perilous. Most Americans still believe in the concept of race the way they believe in the law of gravity—they believe in it without even knowing what it is they believe in.

"If you ask the average American college student if biological races exist, most will say yes. In my classes, when I asked students to identify their own race, most couldn't be any more specific than a vague catchall like "white." They couldn't say what the criteria are for membership in a racial group, and most believed that black, white, Asian, Hispanic, and American Indian are biological races. Some of them thought that every country has produced its own biological race.

"A few students responded that races had existed since the beginning of time. I asked them if they meant 1980, when the universe began for them, or 19 billion years ago, in the big bang? Several had to think about it for a while. Some thought races had existed since the break up of Pangaea, around 300 million years ago—which would have been tough, since humans didn't evolve until 299,999,999 years later! Some thought that races were formed in antiquity at about the time of the fall of the Tower of Babel, as described in the biblical book of Genesis. (Surprisingly, none related the curse of Ham as a source of modern human races.)

"Many also believed that race determined intelligence quotient (IQ) and other personality traits, as well as sexual characteristics, athletic ability, and disease predisposition, following commonly held social stereotypes. When asked about intellect, most cited the superior performance of their Asian classmates in their science courses. When asked about sex, most stated that blacks had higher sexual appetites and larger genitals. When asked about athletic ability they again cited the superior performance of black basketball and football players. Finally, almost all agreed that sickle cell anemia, Tay-Sachs, and cystic fibrosis were all proof positive of the existence of racially defined disease.

"These examples clearly show the prevailing ignorance that our society exhibits about the definitions and significance of human biological diversity, and its confusion with socially constructed races. In this book, I'm going to show you in detail how to tell the difference and why it's so important."[1]

Is It a Question *of* Color?

CHAPTER 10

In *The Race Myth: Why We Pretend Race Exists in America,* evolutionary biologist Joseph L. Graves delves into the most recent science to determine if biological differences actually exist between people.

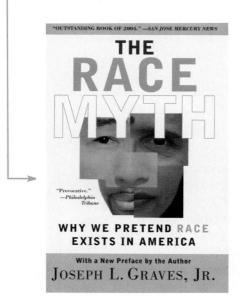

For three groundbreaking seasons, comedian Dave Chappelle used sketch comedy to satirize and lampoon the complex issue of race on *Chappelle's Show.* One skit called "Racial Draft" was set up like a mock NFL draft featuring various racial groups drafting multiracial celebrities—for instance, African Americans selected Tiger Woods while the Asian Americans drafted the Wu-Tang Clan. Through humor, this skit perfectly illustrates the arbitrary categories society uses—like skin color—to define race.

According to recent science, race is purely a social construct, not a biological one. And yet, people, especially in the United States, often seek to define race solely on biological terms. Often, this mentality is instilled at an early age because we often teach children, who don't even have a concept of race, about racial differences that do not really exist. In fact, I remember when my daughter came home from preschool and said, "Ho is different than me." Ho was a Chinese boy whose father worked with me at the university. "What makes you say that?" I asked. "The kids in the class say he's different because his skin looks different than mine," she said. "Does that make him different?" I asked. "I don't know, but I still like to play with him at recess." What is telling about this story is that it took two years of schooling and outside influence to teach a five-year-old about racial differences. This is how we learn about race: from our social experiences.

RACE **is defined as** socially-constructed divisions of people based on certain physical characteristics **differs from** Ethnicity - a shared cultural heritage

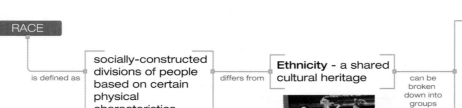

can be broken down into groups

Majority Groups - groups that have greater representation in a society and hold significant power and privilege

OR

Minority Groups - groups that hold less power than the dominant group

OR

Dominant Groups - groups who discriminate because they have greater power

Education
- schools continue to be unofficially segregated
- poorly funded schools are in poor neighborhoods where the majority of black andHispanic students live

and

Income - minorities are the most likely to live in poverty

get the topic: WHAT IS THE DIFFERENCE BETWEEN RACE AND ETHNICITY?

If you walk down any street, you'll find people with different hair-styles, fashion sense, age, body type, and, yes, skin color. Because society feels it's necessary to separate groups of people, **race**, then, refers to the divisions of people based on certain physical character-istics. The most prominent of these characteristics is skin color. Examples of racial categories include white, black, and Asian. **Ethnicity** is a little more complex than race because it usually involves grouping people who share a common cultural, linguistic, or ancestral heritage. Thus, there are many more ethnic than racial cat-egories. Examples of several ethnic groups in the United States include those from Arab, German, Italian, Jewish, Hispanic, Cuban, or Puerto Rican backgrounds.

As the population grows and intermarriage becomes more common, though, traits like skin color may no longer be such

RACE is the division of people based on certain physical characteristics.
ETHNICITY is the classification of people who share a common cultural, linguistic, or ancestral heritage.

a simple signifier of identity. However, sociological ques-tions regarding race are not fixated on the differences in looks. Instead, these questions focus on how society interprets those differences in appearance and how those interpretations affect an individual's opportunities.

CENSUS DEFINITIONS

The reality show *Survivor* has been known to engage in some interesting social experiments. One of the more controversial—and compelling—seasons of the program involved splitting each tribe by race. The tribal divisions implied that there are only four racial categories: white, black, Asian, and Latino. To highlight the fact that race is a social construct rather than a

<<< Although these women differ in physical appearance, they are the same biologically. **Why does society see fit to place them in separate racial categories?**

---

differences can sometimes lead to

Racism - discrimination based on a person's race

Genocide - the attempt to destroy or exterminate a people based on their race and/or ethnicity

Hate Groups - groups motivated by the hatred of other racial groups

Ethnic Cleansing - refers to persecution through imprisonment, expulsion, or murder of members of an ethnic minority to achieve ethnic homogeneity in a majority controlled territory.

conflicts are rooted in a number of factors, such as

Conquest - when one group uses its superior military to dominate another

Annexation - the incorporation of one territory into another

Voluntary Immigration - the willing movement of people from one society to another

Involuntary Immigration - the forced movement of people from one society to another

Migrant Superordination - occurs when a more powerful group enters an area and conquers the natives

Indigenous Superordination - occurs when immigrant groups become subordinate to the dominant group

relations are best understood by studying differences between

stratifies our society by

• our need for a scapegoat, or another group on which to blame our problems
• segregation—the separation of people on the basis of their race, gender, or ethnicity

which are caused by

Prejudice - negative attitudes about an entire category of people

AND

Discrimination - the unfair treatment of people based on a prejudice

Race by Percentage in the United States in 2006

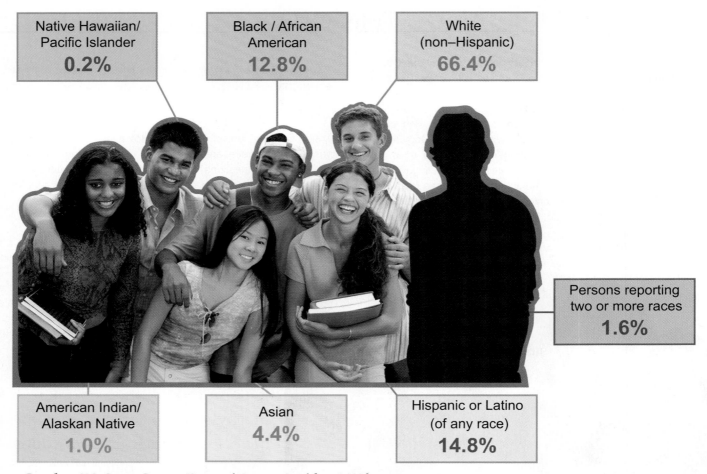

| Native Hawaiian/ Pacific Islander **0.2%** | Black / African American **12.8%** | White (non–Hispanic) **66.4%** |

Persons reporting two or more races
1.6%

| American Indian/ Alaskan Native **1.0%** | Asian **4.4%** | Hispanic or Latino (of any race) **14.8%** |

Source: Data from U.S. Census Bureau, "State and Country Quickfacts," 2006.

biological one, we can point to the U.S. Census Bureau's six definitions of race.[2] The survey choices are white, black or African American, American Indian or Alaska Native, Asian, Native Hawaiian or other Pacific Islander, or some other race. The format of this survey allows individuals to declare their own race and even provides one option for people who feel they do fit into any of the previous categories. The graphic above provides data that the U.S. Census Bureau collected in 2006 regarding race in the United States. You may be surprised to see that the Census Bureau does not classify Hispanic or Latino as a race. While Hispanics are in the photograph, they represent an ethnic group and not a race.

MAJORITY AND MINORITY GROUPS

The graphic above also provides a snapshot of race in the United States. For example, non-Hispanic whites make up more than two out of three Americans. This makes them a **majority group** that not only has a greater numerical representation in society but also holds significant power and privilege. A **minority group** refers to any group that holds less power than the majority group. Louis Wirth assigns minority group status to people who are singled out for unequal treatment. Minorities also have a collective sense of being discriminated against.[3]

In some societies, having a numeric majority isn't necessarily required to wield power or practice discrimination. Sociologists refer to those who are more powerful as the **dominant group** because even if

they may not have greater numbers, they have greater power. Apartheid, the five-decade-long system of oppression in South Africa, showed how a group's numbers don't necessarily reflect a group's political and economic power. In the era of apartheid, whites, who were the numeric minority of South Africa, passed laws that forced blacks, the native majority, into segregated housing, took away their right to vote, and generally treated them like second-class citizens.[4] The idea of a minority group ruling over a majority population, especially in periphery nations is almost always the direct result of **colonialism**, in which more powerful countries impose their will on weaker nations. More often than not, though, dominant groups tend to also be a country's numeric majority as well.

In the United States, minority populations are on the rise. By 2050, the percentage of the population that is Hispanic or Asian is expected to nearly double. Meanwhile, the percentage of whites will decline by approximately 19 percent. Migration patterns certainly influence these projections. In the future, minority group members will have greater representation in the population.[5]

RACISM

The simplest definition of **racism** is that it refers to discrimination based on a person's race. However, there is more to racism than just discrimination. To truly understand racism, you must recognize that it involves a complex calculus of intergroup privilege, power, and oppression. According to Graves, racism in the United States has relied on three assumptions that often go unchallenged: (1) Races exist; (2) Each race has distinct genetic differences; (3) Racial inequality is due to those differences. Graves provides five pillars of racist thought that run rampant in the United States.

1. Biological races exist in the human species.
2. Races have genetic differences that determine their intelligence.
3. Races have genetically determined differences that produce unique diseases and cause them to die at different rates.
4. Races have genetically determined sexual appetites and reproductive capacities.
5. Races have genetically determined differences in athletic and musical ability.

An extreme example of racism is the use of **genocide**, the attempt to destroy or exterminate a people based on their race or ethnicity. The most well-known example is the Holocaust during World War II. The Nazis slaughtered millions of Jews, Gypsies, and mentally and physically handicapped people in an attempt to cleanse Europe of people they felt were inferior. Extreme racism is not a thing of the past either. The 2004 film *Hotel Rwanda* depicted the events of 1994, when members of two Rwandan political parties began killing opposition leaders and journalists. Quickly, the violence spread to the rural areas where members of the majority Hutu tribe slaughtered members of the Tutsi tribe. In the film, Don Cheadle received an Oscar nomination for his portrayal of Paul Rusesabagina, a hotel manager who heroically saved the lives of nearly 1,300 Rwandans. Demographic data show that gender made little difference in predicting who might survive. Men, women, children, and the elderly were all killed.[6] The idea of racial purity was not just the dominion of Nazi Germany or tribal Rwanda. The history of the United States is stained by similarly horrible acts, including the Trail of Tears, Japanese

MAJORITY GROUP is the group that has the largest population in society and holds significant power and privilege.

MINORITY GROUP is a group that has a smaller population and less power than the majority group.

DOMINANT GROUP is the group that has the greatest power, but not necessarily the greatest numbers.

COLONIALISM is the imposition of control over a weak nation by a more powerful country.

RACISM is discrimination based on a person's race.

GENOCIDE is the attempt to destroy or exterminate a people based on their race and/or ethnicity.

HATE GROUPS are organizations that promote hostility or violence toward others based on race and other factors.

internment camps during World War II, slavery, lynchings, segregation, and Jim Crow laws.

Such behavior has a long history and still continues today. The Southern Poverty Law Center tracks **hate groups** in the United States. These groups are organizations that promote hostility or violence toward others based on race and other factors. They include white supremacists, neo-Nazis, and other groups that advocate hate against immigrants, gays, and other minorities. The center notes that within the United States, there were 888 organized hate groups in 2008, a 48 percent increase since the year 2000.[7]

Hate and racist groups do not always seek to exterminate those they do not like. Sometimes, they purge their society of these people by forcing the minority group to move, while abusing them in the process. Anyone who has studied the Trail of Tears knows that the U.S. government did the same thing to the Cherokee, Chickasaw, Choctaw, Creek, and Seminole tribes before the Civil War. Forcing these people to leave their homelands in the

∧
∧ **In 1994, the Hutu tribe discarded the bodies of slaughtered Tutsi tribe**
∧ **members** in mass graves.

CONQUEST is the domination over a group of people by a superior force.

ANNEXATION is the incorporation of one territory into another.

VOLUNTARY IMMIGRATION is the willing movement of people from one society to another.

INVOLUNTARY IMMIGRATION is the forced movement of people from one society to another.

ETHNIC CLEANSING refers to persecution through imprisonment, expulsion, or murder of members of an ethnic minority by a majority to achieve ethnic homogeneity in majority-controlled territory.

MIGRANT SUPERORDINATION is the conquest of a native population by a more powerful group.

INDIGENOUS SUPERORDINATION is the subordination of an immigrant group to a dominant group.

PLURALISTIC MINORITIES are groups that enter into an area voluntarily but seek to maintain their own culture while also integrating into the dominant group.

ASSIMILATIONIST MINORITIES are groups that seek to shed their old ways and integrate themselves into mainstream society.

southeastern United States, the government moved these people to modern-day Oklahoma. This forced relocation resulted in thousands of Native Americans dying on the trail.[8] Such practices are still going on around the world, from Kenya to Iraq, as armed conflicts continue to force the relocation of minority people.[9]

PATTERNS OF INTERACTION

As we've already discussed in reference to genocide and ethnic cleansing, interracial conflict is as old as history itself. But how did all this get started? To better think like sociologists, we need to understand the origins of racial and ethnic stratification.

Conquest and Annexation

Racial and ethnic tension is rooted in a number of factors. The first is **conquest**. When one group uses its superior military to dominate another, it comes in contact with people who have a different culture and often a different physical appearance. During the 16th and 17th centuries, European powers used their superior technology and military strength to colonize Africa and the Americas.[10]

Annexation is the incorporation of one territory into another. Under this system, members of ethnic and racial groups are forced to become members of a new society. For example, when James Gadsden negotiated the purchase of parts of modern-day New Mexico and Arizona from Mexico in 1853, all the people who were already living in those areas became residents of a new country in one day.[11] This annexation brought ethnic tensions as whites moved into the territories and sought ways to control land that Native American and Mexican groups had largely owned. Annexation often leads to tension between groups, as those who are annexed resist the new occupiers.

Immigration

Another pattern that can create racial and ethnic tension is immigration, whether it is voluntary or involuntary. **Voluntary immigration** refers to the willing movement of people from one society to another. Remember, people may choose to migrate for a variety of reasons as we discussed in Chapter 9. However, the countries receiving these people may not always welcome the new immigrants with open arms. The current political weather that hovers over immigration—many of whom are Mexican or Asian—is just as stormy. Some anti-immigrant activists claim "foreigners" who water down U.S. culture with bilingualism and multiculturalism are invading the country. Sometimes, politicians equate immigration with "invasion"—as the conservative pundit Pat Buchanan famously did in 2006. Does such an idea sound like it has racial overtones to you? Why or why not?[12]

Involuntary immigration refers to the forced movement of people from one society to another. Bringing millions of Africans as enslaved people against their will, forcing Native Americans onto reservations, and imprisoning hundreds of thousands of Japanese Americans in detention camps are all examples of involuntary immigration in U.S. history.[13]

Superordination

Regardless of whether the migration is voluntary or involuntary, some predictable patterns of interaction can occur when people come into

▶▶ GO GL🌐BAL

Ethnic Cleansing
Bosnia

Following the breakup of the former country of Yugoslavia in 1990, the Serbian majority seized control and forced large numbers of minority group members, particularly Bosnian Muslims, or Bosniaks, to leave their lands or face extermination. In 1992, the Serbian army launched an ethnic cleansing campaign against Bosniaks in eastern Bosnia. **Ethnic cleansing** refers to persecution through imprisonment, expulsion, or murder of members of an ethnic minority by a majority to achieve ethnic homogeneity in majority-controlled territory. Bosniak civilians were rounded up and detained in camps, Bosnian civilians, men and women, were rounded up and detained in separate camps. Many were beaten or killed during capture. The surviving men were sent to concentration camps and the women were sent to detention centers known as rape camps. In July 1995, near the end of the war, the Serbs rounded up and killed an estimated 8,000 Bosniaks in the region of Srebrenica. This act of genocide, known as the Srebrenica Massacre, is the largest mass murder in Europe since World War II.[14] The Serbian and Croatian forces carried out these tactics of torture and murder in the hope of creating ethnically pure states. During this war, armies used ethnic differences as a justification for thousands of deaths and the forced removal of millions of people from their homes.[15]

These crimes, however, have not gone unnoticed by the rest of the world. In 1995, the International Criminal Tribunal for the former Yugoslavia in the Hague indicted former Bosnian Serb leader Radovan Karadzic. Charged with multiple counts of genocide, war crimes, and crimes against humanity, Karadzic went into hiding for more than 12 years before he was eventually captured in 2008. If convicted, Karadzic could face a possible life sentence for crimes committed during the Bosnian War.[16]

contact with unfamiliar groups. Often people become involved in **migrant superordination**, which occurs when a more powerful group enters an area and conquers the native population. In the 16th century, Spain used military strength to dominate Central and South America and to elevate their own culture above the native culture. In this case, the migrants' status was elevated, or superordinated. The opposite of this is **indigenous superordination**. When arriving immigrants enter the United States today, they are expected to learn English and subordinate their old ways to their new country. In other words, they must become subordinate to the dominant group. For example, in recent years, several states have passed "English Only" laws. These laws run the gamut from nominal statutes that merely declare English to be the "official" state language to laws that limit bilingual education programs in state schools and that curb other non-English government services. The American Civil Liberties Union argues that such laws restrict or cut funding for multilingual programs that some U.S. residents can't do without such as health services, voting assistance, and driver's licensing tests.[17]

These two patterns of interaction are often justified through ethnocentric thinking. Remember, *ethnocentrism* is thinking about or defining another culture on the basis of your own. Generally, the greater the differences, the more negatively groups tend to view each other. At the same time, there is often competition between groups, which becomes more intense when resources are scarce. Consider the migrant pattern to New York City in the early 1900s. Racial and ethnic immigrants divided up the low-income jobs that were available to them. Chinese immigrants might have worked in laundries, while Jewish immigrants sewed clothing, and Italian immigrants

controlled the docks. If you were a member of one of these groups, you could find a job in those industries. But if you were a Chinese immigrant who wanted to make clothing, you were unlikely to be hired. This is because ethnic groups often had differences in power. Once a group has power, it is unlikely to let it go, unless it can somehow expand its market and wealth.[18]

Minorities

When minority groups face superordination, there are a number of ways they can choose to react. **Pluralistic minorities** are generally groups that enter into an area voluntarily. They seek to maintain their own culture, but want to integrate with the dominant group as well. Thus they hope to keep their cultural ties while participating in the political and economic system of the new society. **Assimilationist minorities**, on the other hand, seek to shed their old ways and integrate themselves into society. Groups that most closely resemble the dominant group—either racially or ethnically—are able to do this more easily.

For example, when German immigrants first came to the United States, their culture and language were generally accepted. In the original colonies, German newspapers were printed and German colonists served in the Revolutionary War. However, with the beginning of World War I in 1914 came outright hostility toward almost anything German. My grandfather was born in the United States, but is of German descent. He told me that when World War I began, his father told him to speak only English from that point on. Throughout the United States, laws were passed to forbid teaching subjects in German, and German Americans rapidly gave up their language and culture to show their loyalty to the United States.[19]

Sometimes, groups voluntarily decide to separate themselves from

∧
∧ **During WWII, nearly 120,000 Japanese**
∧ **Americans,** many of them U.S. citizens, **were forced to relocate to internment camps.**

the dominant group and become **secessionist minorities**. Such a group does not seek assimilation or cultural unification. Instead, it views the dominant group with disdain, believing that it will corrupt its belief system. The Amish of Pennsylvania can be considered an extreme example of a secessionist minority. This group has carved out a lifestyle and culture in which a Swiss German language is common and modern conveniences are rare. They emphasize the importance of family, religion, and a simple lifestyle. Their children are educated at Amish schools and a great deal of their life is exactly as it was 100 years ago. Although some Amish people are increasingly opening themselves up to other businesses besides farming, as

well as allowing in a few modern technologies, their community remains secessionist.[20]

Sometimes, minorities react to their subordination through militancy. **Militant minorities** seek to overthrow the existing system that they see as unjust. Often the militant minority is actually a numeric majority and may take the path of violence and war to fight perceived injustice, as was the case in Cuba in 1958 when Fidel Castro overthrew a government that he believed was corrupt.[21] Militants can also be peaceful, as when Mohandas Gandhi led a peaceful revolution that ended in 1947 and ultimately brought about the end of British occupation of India.[22]

Types of Minority Groups

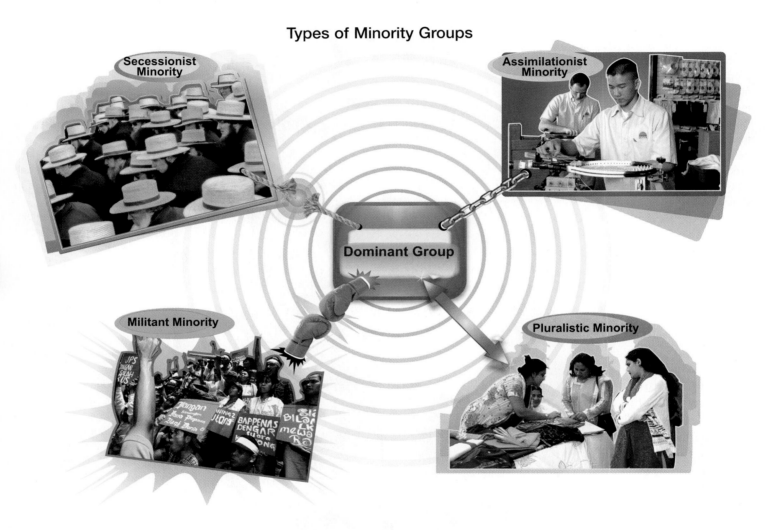

Secessionist Minority

Assimilationist Minority

Dominant Group

Militant Minority

Pluralistic Minority

Acceptance—Multiculturalism and Assimilation

Research suggests that racial and ethnic identity is related to four key factors: relative size, power, appearance, and discrimination.[23] These factors also tend to encourage a sense of solidarity among members of a single racial or ethnic group. In a sense, being different from the dominant group holds people together. The reason many minority groups tend to cluster together in neighborhoods is because their differences from the dominant group often lead to discrimination. Furthermore, the shared values of similar people make adjustment easier. Finally, their social capital increases their chances of success.

On the other hand, belonging to a group that looks like the dominant group rarely leads to discrimination. Such people often let go of their ethnic heritage because their appearance makes it easier to assimilate into the dominant culture.

This lack of privilege to belong to the dominant group is the reason many minority groups often bond together. This is especially true for new immigrants of color. It is quite common for immigrants to live in neighborhoods where people from similar cultures live together and assert cultural distinction, which are called **ethnic enclaves,** like a Chinatown or Spanish Harlem. Such enclaves assist the new immigrant in making an easier transition into the new culture.

PREJUDICE VS. DISCRIMINATION

To truly understand the complexity of race relations, it is vital to understand the differences between prejudice and discrimination. **Prejudice** usually refers to negative attitudes about an entire category of people. These prejudices are often reinforced by **stereotypes**: simplified perceptions people have of an entire group, usually based on a false assumption. Although negative stereotypes, such as believing all black people are prone to violence or that all Latinos are illegal immigrants, are absolutely wrongheaded, so-called positive stereotypes can be just as damaging. While you may think you're offering a compliment when you assume your Asian American classmate is a mathematical genius, the problem is that doing so confines that individual to a box that you have constructed in your mind. That is the danger of stereotypes. If we aren't careful, we might allow our prejudices to overtake our common sense.

These attitudes, if left unchecked, may lead to **discrimination**, or the unfair treatment of people based on a prejudice. Essentially, prejudice is an attitude, while discrimination is an action that stems from that attitude. The Jim Crow laws of the past were perpetuated by whites' attitudes toward black people. However, discrimination doesn't always have to be as blatant as the segregated water fountains of the pre–Civil Rights 1950s and 1960s to be insidious. A teacher with a prejudice against African Americans may treat black students with contempt in the classroom. Similarly, a teacher who assumes the Asian American student in class is a naturally studious person could overlook the fact that the student might actually need help.

> Essentially, prejudice is an attitude, while discrimination is an action that stems from that attitude.

Many of these prejudices and stereotypes are so prevalent, it's difficult to trace exactly where they come from. Generally, sociologists agree that while we aren't born with prejudiced attitudes, we often

SECESSIONIST MINORITIES are groups that voluntarily separate themselves from the dominant group and view the dominant group with disdain, believing that it will corrupt the group's belief system.

MILITANT MINORITIES are groups that seek to overthrow the existing system because they see it as unjust.

ETHNIC ENCLAVES are neighborhoods where people from similar cultures live together and assert cultural distinction from the dominant group.

PREJUDICE refers to negative attitudes about an entire category of people.

STEREOTYPES are simplified perceptions people have of an entire group that are usually based on false assumptions.

DISCRIMINATION is the unfair treatment of people based on a prejudice.

INSTITUTIONAL DISCRIMINATION maintains the advantage for the dominant group, while providing the appearance of fairness to all.

learn prejudice from those around us.[24] We can even learn a prejudice against a group to which we belong. This self-loathing occurs when we internalize the values of the dominant group.[25] In my classes, I often have my students take an online test designed to measure biases. Generally, minorities hold similar beliefs to their non-minority counterparts. Recently an African American student took the "Know Your Bias" test and was shocked to find that she held negative attitudes toward African Americans. This illustrates how we are all socialized to hold biases that are in accordance with the dominant society, even if we belong to a minority group.

INSTITUTIONAL DISCRIMINATION IN THE UNITED STATES

While personal biases often cause individuals to view others negatively, those attitudes can carry over into the structures of society and often go unnoticed by others who don't even hold those views. When this happens, social institutions end up supporting racial and ethnic inequality. This **institutional discrimination** maintains the advantage for

---

THINK SOCIOLOGICALLY

They're Coming to America

For centuries, immigrants have come to the United States. This trend continues to this day, constantly changing the face of the country.

Researchers are interested in what helps these immigrants not only survive but thrive in a new country. Sociologists Alejandro Portes and Alex Stepick conducted a study of Cuban immigrants in Miami, and Min Zhou studied Chinese immigration in New York City. They note that one key component of immigrant success is a successful neighborhood, or enclave, in which they can live.

A number of factors are required for a successful enclave. Location and a sense

of permanence are both very important. When Cuban immigrants first fled the regime of Fidel Castro, many of them chose to settle in Miami. After the failure of the Bay of Pigs invasion on Cuba in 1961, they decided to put down permanent roots.[26] Some suggest this will result in the Balkanization of the United States, meaning that we will have a more divided nation, much like that of the former Yugoslavia.[27] Others suggest that this is unlikely because immigrants, even in enclaves, eventually move out and assimilate into their new culture.[28]

Once the roots are in place, a stable market that small firms can control is necessary. Small businesses require very little start-up costs, and businesses related to ethnic food or culture also help. In New

York City's Chinatown, these two factors helped Chinese immigrants successfully create an economic market.[29] Once these businesses are established, the enclave provides a steady stream of cheap labor, another characteristic of a successful enclave. As immigrants continue to enter the United States, they provide a constant source of people willing to work at heavy-labor, low-wage jobs. As their children assimilate, they are less likely to take these jobs, and so a continual flow of new immigrants helps the enclave, and all who live in it, thrive.[30]

>>> **ACTIVITY** Locate the nearest ethnic enclave in your city or state. To what ethnicity does it cater? Does it appear to cater to tourists?

the dominant group, while providing the appearance of fairness to others. Such institutionalized racism is best illustrated by the Jim Crow era of U.S. history. Many of the laws that separated blacks and whites during the first half of the 20th century were based on the premise of things being "separate but equal." Unfortunately, while institutions like education and housing were separate, they were hardly equal. Jim Crow may be a relic of the past, but that doesn't mean institutional discrimination has also been erased. In fact, racism and discrimination are still institutionalized today. The U.S. education system is one area in which "separate but equal" is essentially still the norm. Jonathan Kozol's award-winning book *Savage Inequalities* supports the notion that not all education in the United States is the same. Minority children tend to be overrepresented in inner-city schools that are usually underfunded and less equipped than schools that cater to upper-middle-class, and predominantly white, children. This is largely due to the way schools are funded through property taxes. If a child lives in a poor neighborhood, his or her school is likely to struggle financially because lower property taxes mean less revenue to pay for books or teachers. Meanwhile, children from more affluent neighborhoods attend schools with state-of-the-art supplies and highly qualified educators that poorer schools can't afford. In this way, institutional discrimination works to decrease the chances of poor children using education as a vehicle to climb out of the poverty cycle and amounts to the society reinforcing the roadblocks to their success.

∧
∧   **Schools in poor neighborhoods are more likely to be**
∧   **underfunded** and unequally funded than schools in
affluent neighborhoods.

CAUSES FOR PREJUDICE AND DISCRIMINATION

So why does any kind of discrimination happen at all? John Dollard suggests that frustration leads to prejudice.[31] Often we don't have the ability to attack the real source of our irritation, and so we **scapegoat**, or unfairly accuse, another group as the cause of our problem. Usually a racial or ethnic minority becomes the target for a common societal problem like widespread poverty. If you are poor, you may not be able to increase your salary, but you can blame others for your problems. This happened in 1982 when two white unemployed autoworkers, Ronald Ebens and Michael Nitz, beat Vincent Chin, a young Chinese American man, to death. What started as a barroom brawl—Ebens and Nitz reportedly used a racial slur to refer to Chin, after which a fistfight broke out—ended in murder. The two men blamed Japanese auto companies—and by extension, all Japanese people—for the economic downturn and violently attacked Chin simply because they thought he was Japanese. To make matters worse, neither man ever spent a day in jail for Chin's murder. After they pled guilty to manslaughter, the judge sentenced Ebens and Nitz to three years' probation and fines totaling less than $4,000. The judge later defended the light sentence by claiming, "These weren't the kind of men you send to jail. We're talking here about a man [Ebens] who's held down a responsible job with the same company for seventeen or eighteen years and his son [Nitz] who is employed and is a part-time student . . . You don't make the punishment fit the crime; you make the punishment fit the criminal." In a civil trial later that year, Ebens was convicted of violating Chin's civil rights and sentenced to 25 years in jail. However, Ebens appealed the decision on the basis of a technicality and was later acquitted in a retrial, which was held in a different state.[32]

How could two men get away with committing such a hateful and racist act? Researchers often suggest the importance of education and intelligence in predicting a discriminatory type of personality. Generally, studies support the notion that people who are less educated and of lower intelligence are more likely to be prejudiced. This lends support to the idea that prejudice is learned, and can be unlearned.[33] Furthermore, structural issues such as the mix of racial and ethnic groups, as well as income inequality and differences in economic opportunities, may assist in the perpetuation of extreme forms of racism. White supremacist groups often cite these issues as evidence of minority group dominance and use these issues as a rallying cry for a white backlash against these groups.[34]

SEGREGATION

People who are discriminated against are often separated from the dominant group in terms of housing, workplace, and social settings. This enforced separation is called **segregation** when factors such as race, gender, or ethnicity are involved. Earlier, we discussed the so-called separate but equal schools, neighborhoods, restaurants, and public restrooms of the 1960s and earlier. Although these and other forms of segregation are no longer legal, issues such as unofficial segregation continue to this day.

In a study of housing segregation, Massey and Denton show that blacks of all incomes experience similar levels of segregation from whites. They note that racial segregation is linked to a number of factors, including personal choice. Sometimes, minorities prefer to live in areas that are populated by their own groups.[35] The phenomenon "white flight" refers to the housing pattern that occurs when many white people move out of a neighborhood in response to blacks or other people of color moving in.

SCAPEGOAT means making an unfair accusation against a person or group as the cause of a problem.

SEGREGATION is forced separation because of factors such as race, gender, or ethnicity.

CYCLE OF POVERTY is a generational barrier that prevents poor people from breaking into the middle and upper classes.

Racial Stratification in the United States

Now that you have a context in which to look at race and ethnicity, let's turn our attention to how race stratifies our society. Although we live in a free society that claims to be equal, there are still injustices that occur because of race. How does the well-being of different racial and ethnic groups compare? Take a look at the chart below to find out. You've seen the numbers, so now let's take a closer look at racial stratification.

INCOME

In the United States, minorities tend to be overrepresented in poverty statistics, particularly African Americans and Hispanics. This is caused in part by the **cycle of poverty**, which makes it difficult for people to break into the middle class if their parents were poor. Given that black people have been forced into poverty ever since slavery, it's easy to see how future generations could remain trapped in that cycle. Hispanic immigrants have the disadvantage of the language barrier, which makes it nearly impossible to get a high-paying job in this country. Their children will likely be born into the cycle of poverty and will have to struggle to break out of it.[36]

In 2007, the median income for Asians was $66,935 and $55,096 for whites. For people of Hispanic origin, it was $40,766, and the median income for blacks was $34,001. That same year, 9.0 percent of whites and 10.6 percent of Asians lived in poverty, whereas 20.7 percent of Hispanics and 24.7 percent of blacks did. To see how disproportionately these groups are represented, the official poverty rate for the entire U.S. population was only 12.5 percent.[37]

Racial-Ethnic Groups Compared

Racial-Ethnic Group	Median Household Income (2007)	Percentage Living at or Below Poverty Line (2007)	Percentage Without Health Insurance (2004–2007)	Home Ownership (2007)	Percentage of Children With a Computer at Home (2006)	Life Expectancy at Birth (2010 Estimate)
White	$55,096	9.0%	15.5%	74.9%	76.9%	Male: 76.5 Female: 81.3
Hispanic or Latino	$40,766	20.7%	32.7%	48.5%	40.6%	Male: 78.4 Female: 83.7
Black/ African American	$34,001	24.7%	19.4%	47.7%	41.0%	Male: 70.2 Female: 77.2
Asian	$66,935	10.6%	16.1%	58.6%*	75.7%	Male: 76.3 Female: 81.1
American Indian and/or Alaskan Native	$35,343	25.3%	31.4%	**	54.1%	Male: 76.6 Female: 81.5

*Number represents a combination number of all other racial categories.
**Data included in percentage for Asian Americans.
Source: Based on Carmen DeNavas-Walt, Bernadette D. Proctor, and Jessica Smith, U.S. Census Bureau, *Current Population Reports, P60-233, Income, Poverty, and Health Insurance Coverage in the United States: 2006; Statistical Abstract 2008:* Table 609; National Projections Program, U.S. Census Bureau.

Educational Attainment by Race/Ethnic Group

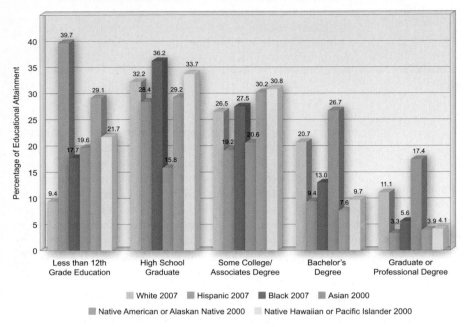

Source: U.S. Census Bureau, Current Population Survey, *2007 Annual Social and Economic Supplement and Statistical Abstract 2000.*

EDUCATION

One of the most important factors in determining income is education. Without access to quality education, it's difficult to get a well-paying job and advance in the workplace. There is a strong correlation between level of education and income, with people who have advanced degrees earning the most money. But who exactly is earning these advanced degrees? The graph on the left shows the educational attainment of the population by race. With the exception of the Asian group, minorities tend to have low educational attainment. For example, only about half of the Hispanic population over the age of 25 has graduated from college. These data help explain why such a wide gap exists between the median income of African and Americans and the median income of Asian Americans. In 1999, full-time employees with a high school diploma earned an average of $30,400 a year, while those with a bachelor's degree earned $52,200 on average. Income for those with a master's degree was $62,300 and $109,600 for those with a professional degree.[38]

As discussed earlier, schools continue to be unofficially segregated. Poorly funded schools tend to be those in which the majority of the children are black or Latino. This imbalance further adds to the income disparity between whites and other races. The lack of a proper education forces people into low-paying jobs, or worse, and the cycle of poverty continues.

MAKE CONNECTIONS

Two Towns of Jasper

In 2002, the acclaimed documentary *Two Towns of Jasper* by Whitney Dow and Marco Williams got a lot of attention for its shocking and candid portrait of race in the United States.

Two Towns of Jasper is the true story of James Byrd, Jr., a black man, who was dragged to death behind a pickup truck by three white men. The film uses two different crews, one white and one black, and each films the series with the same racial group. This provides the speakers with a level of confidence that might not have been present with a single crew.

Even before Byrd's murder, the cemetery in Jasper had a black side and a white side, with a fence running down the middle. The people of Jasper illustrate that even in death, racial segregation still occurs. The film traces the trials of the men accused and convicted of this brutal murder. It also provides reactions to the murder from both white and black townspeople. Viewers see the differences in the two racial groups' perspectives, as well as a vision of white supremacy in the United States. Despite the best efforts of city leaders in Jasper, whites and blacks tolerate each other, but continue to self-segregate.

This film leads one to question the social construction of racism, and note its proven power to injure, scapegoat, and limit human interactions.

think sociologically: WHAT CAUSES RACIST ATTITUDES, AND HOW DO THESE ATTITUDES AFFECT PEOPLE?

Symbolic Interactionism: Color-Blind Racism

Symbolic interactionists stress the importance of symbolism and language in the creation of society. In the United States, overtly racist language is socially unacceptable in most circles; however, sociologists don't believe that this means we have become a "color-blind" society. In fact, **color-blind racism**—the idea that racism still exists in more subtle ways remains a part of U.S. society to this day. For example, there is no doubt that many people of color in the United States remain in disadvantaged positions—they are poorer, achieve lower educational outcomes, live shorter lives, attend underfunded schools, experience problems with assimilation, and generally believe that the police and other social institutions work to increase their disadvantage.[39] Despite these facts, though, most whites in the United States claim these outcomes have nothing to do with racism. How can that be? Furthermore, most whites claim they are not racist.

Eduardo Bonilla-Silva suggests that this is because whites have developed a series of excuses for the status quo through four key factors: First, whites tend to hold onto ideals such as equality, individualism, and choice in an effort to explain why racial groups are disadvantaged.[40] In other words, people are only poor because they made bad choices, not because of some historical or cultural connection that supports racism. Second, white people often use cultural stereotypes to explain racial inequality. Rather than understand the source of the problem, too many people simply latch onto stereotypes to explain the issue. When radio shock jock Don Imus got into trouble for using a racially insensitive term to refer to the Rutgers University women's basketball team in 2007, the media frenzy focused more on the ills of hip-hop music rather than the racial power dynamic of Imus's words. The

third factor is the false belief that segregation is a personal choice. The suggestion is that it's natural for racial groups to prefer "their own kind." Often, this attitude prevents white people from understanding the complex role institutionalized racism has on "segregated" communities. Finally, many whites in the United States simply believe that racism is a thing of the past and deny that it has any impact on minorities' lives today. Such thinking serves to defend the way things are, and excuses the dominant group from any responsibility to make things better.

Although racism is not as overt as it once was, that doesn't mean the problem has been eradicated. Racial prejudice still exists; it's just hidden behind a series of clever language constructions. For example, white college students rarely use racist terms such as "the n-word," but they might tell racist jokes. They usually first explain that the joke doesn't really reflect their beliefs, and conclude the joke with an apologetic comment—all to eliminate the perception of racism.[41] Also, consider the recent trend of white college students attending parties in blackface, the act of whites applying makeup to mock the appearance of African Americans. The students who participate in these parties claim they're merely being "ironic," even though the act is highly offensive to most people of color.[42]

Whites may try to prove they're not racist by claiming some of their "best friends are black." This is supposed to give the speaker an air of credibility for not being racist. Unfortunately, such disclaimers are usually followed by a negative stereotype. They might try to excuse a long history of structural racism or try to take all sides when it comes to matters of race. Whites may also excuse the long history of racism and a lack of equal opportunities by denying any personal responsibility for it. Comments like "I didn't own slaves; it's not my fault" lead the conversation away from structural problems that continue to exist regarding race, while excusing the speaker from any possible advantage based on his or her race.

W.E.B. Du Bois suggested that African Americans have a sort of **double consciousness,** meaning black people have to keep a foot in two worlds, one white and one black.[43] Minority group members must learn to integrate into the dominant group in order to successfully live in the society. They must also learn to live within their own culture. Many people of color are forced to "code switch;" that is, to speak and act one way among their own group and another in white society. Du Bois considered blacks to be in a unique position because they were accountable to white culture as well as their own. This influences their sense of self and affects how they live in the world. Only through understanding this position can blacks hope to navigate the world successfully.

Du Bois's classical ideas also apply to the study of other minority groups, including Hispanics and women.[44] Generally, sociologists find that members of the dominant group do not think much about race, but as one student put it, "When you're a minority, race is always a factor."

>>> **African Americans,** and other minorities, often have to live in two worlds—one black and the other white.

WRAP YOUR MIND AROUND THE THEORY

These **protestors fight against the biases that the dominant group holds** toward them.

FUNCTIONALISM

Functionalists might view racism as having both intended and unintended consequences. For example, consider slavery in the United States. It was extremely functional to building wealth and a successful agricultural economy in the southern United States. Of course, the unintended function was to enslave fellow human beings and treat them like animals. The underlying horrors of slavery eventually became well known enough to push whites to make slavery illegal; however, it took more than 100 years for this to occur. Consider the institutional racism that occurs within the U.S. educational system today. What are the consequences of it? Are the tax savings that some receive really worth the costs of an undereducated future generation?

CONFLICT THEORY

From a conflict theorist's lens, racism is the result of one group wanting to keep its advantage over another. For example, in 1838, the U.S. government forced the relocation of Native Americans from eastern areas of the United States to western lands in a tragic episode known as the Trail of Tears. Why did this occur? It certainly was not for the good of the Native Americans; it was intended to benefit whites who wanted to expand their lands for farming. The forced relocation of native peoples resulted in more than 20 million acres of land becoming available for white settlement. This cost the government approximately three million dollars. Thus, the pursuit of even more wealth drove those with power to drive native peoples from their ancestral lands and "give" them lands that had little or no worth.[45]

HOW DO THE THREE PARADIGMS VIEW RACISM?

SYMBOLIC INTERACTIONISM

Symbolic interactionists point to the micro interactions of our daily life and how they either support or attack an issue. Had I been teaching in a college classroom 100 years ago, I may have been willing and able to utter racial slurs in class. If I were to do that today, I would be reprimanded and could even lose my job. What has changed? Certainly tolerance for negative terms of racial groups has decreased dramatically in 100 years. Interactionists would suggest that by changing the acceptable terms, we can change the reality. Perhaps we should eliminate racial slurs altogether.

Following the Indian Removal Act of 1830, **thousands of Cherokees were forced to travel from their ancestral lands** in eastern areas of the United States to designated "Indian Territory" in modern-day Oklahoma. Due to the number of Cherokees who died on the trek, **this route became known as the Trail of Tears**.

In 1957, when nine African American students attended integrated schools in Arkansas, **they were met with resistance and racial slurs from the school's white population.**

discover sociology in action: HOW DOES AFFIRMATIVE ACTION HELP MINORITY GROUPS IN THE UNITED STATES?

Affirmative Action

Affirmative action is a social policy designed to help minority groups gain opportunities through employment and education. Legal affirmative action in the United States means that if all candidates are equal, an employer or college may use minority status as a deciding factor. However, it is not acceptable to simply hire the minority member if that person is unqualified for the job. The logic behind this preference is based on hundreds of years of discrimination, as well as the obvious disadvantages that still exist for women and minorities.

A great deal of controversy surrounds affirmative action because some believe that the policy would require universities and companies to establish quotas for minority groups. The truth is that quotas are not part of acceptable affirmative action policies since that could encourage employers to hire minority members who are not qualified. While acknowledging the continuation of discrimination, sociologist William J. Wilson suggested that class-based policies should replace race-based ones.[46] He argued that financial needs and not race should determine advantage. This would allow poor whites, blacks, Hispanics, etc., to receive benefits and, since minority groups are disproportionately poor, they would still reap the lion's share of these benefits. Basing the policies on class rather than on race would eliminate the perception of racial bias. Whereas color-blind policies like this are attractive to the dominant group, they do not necessarily yield the desired results. Color-blind college entrance policies in Texas, for example, may actually lead to less qualified students entering college. Research shows that students from lower socioeconomic brackets who are admitted based on such color-blind policies have a higher likelihood of dropping out and, in the long run, may actually hurt minority educational attainment.[47]

ACTIVITIES

1. Engage someone not in this class in a conversation about race. See what you learn about his or her beliefs. Ask the following questions:
   - What are the races in the United States?
   - Are there any biological differences in races?
   - Does race play a role in opportunities?
2. Research ten ways to stop hate on a college campus. Follow this link to the list: http://www.tolerance.org/campus/index.jsp. Does your college do these things? If not, can you organize a group to address these problems?
3. Talk to your classmates about your own experiences of racial tension. Then, test your hidden biases at this Web site (http://www.tolerance.org/hidden_bias/index.html) to see what they might be.

From Classroom to Community } Teaching in a Migrant Community

A student named Maryann confronted her own notions of white privilege when she assisted at a school that was located in a poor, urban neighborhood. She was stunned to find a school filled with children who did not speak English. The experience allowed Maryann to reflect on her own upbringing.

"I never really thought that I was well-off when I was in school," she said. "What I found at this school shocked me." Some of her observations included seeing kids not allowed on the playground because of drive-by shootings in the neighborhood. She also noticed facilities that were falling apart and an environment that was not good for the students. Maryann's response to these conditions was the desire to

"get out of there as soon as possible."

She spent most of her time trying to help the students learn to read English. Though the children were smart, outside factors were affecting their schoolwork. They often lived with parents who spoke only Spanish and in enclaves where little English was spoken. Because English was not reinforced at home, these students had difficulty succeeding in class.

"One child missed school one day because he had to translate for his father at a doctor's appointment," remembered Maryann.

"I couldn't imagine being 8 years old and talking to a doctor for my dad."

The statistics show that many of these kids will never finish high school. The teachers hope to teach them enough so that they will be able to read and speak English, yet very few of them make it to college. After spending time among these students, Maryann concluded that society is not structured to help students in this situation.

"I kept wondering how this was equal education. I decided that it wasn't."

CHAPTER

10

WHAT IS THE DIFFERENCE BETWEEN RACE AND ETHNICITY?   175

race is the division of people based on certain physical characteristics, but *ethnicity* is the classification of people who share a common cultural, linguistic, or ancestral heritage

WHAT CAUSES RACIST ATTITUDES, AND HOW DO THESE ATTITUDES AFFECT PEOPLE?   184

color-blind racism, racial stereotypes, belief that segregation is a personal choice, belief that racism is a thing of the past, which denies its impact on minorities; these lead to a feeling of double consciousness for minorities

HOW DOES AFFIRMATIVE ACTION HELP MINORITY GROUPS IN THE UNITED STATES?   187

by allowing employers and educators to use minority status as a deciding factor if candidates are equal

get the topic: WHAT IS THE DIFFERENCE BETWEEN RACE AND ETHNICITY?

Racial Stratification in the United States 183   Symbolic Interactionism: Color-Blind Racism 184   Affirmative Action 187

Theory

FUNCTIONALISM   186

- racism has both intended and unintended consequences
- slavery in the South functioned to build wealth and agriculture, but it came at the expense of people being treated like animals

CONFLICT THEORY   186

- racism is a result of power conflicts among different groups
- the group with more power oppresses the weaker groups, a result of which can cause racism to occur
- 1838 relocation of Native Americans for the farmer's own personal gain

SYMBOLIC INTERACTIONISM   186

- by changing what is acceptable in society, we change reality
- racial slurs that were acceptable 100 years ago are highly discouraged today
- acceptable terms leads to what is said and thought in society

Key Terms

race is the division of people based on certain physical characteristics. *175*

ethnicity is the classification of people who share a common cultural, linguistic, or ancestral heritage. *175*

majority group is the group that has the largest population in society and holds significant power and privilege. *176*

minority group is a group that has a smaller population and less power than the majority group. *176*

dominant group is the group that has the greatest power, but not necessarily the greatest numbers. *176*

colonialism is the imposition of control over a weak nation by a more powerful country. *176*

racism is discrimination based on a person's race. *176*

genocide is the attempt to destroy or exterminate a people based on their race and/or ethnicity. *177*

hate groups are organizations that promote hostility or violence toward others based on race and other factors. *177*

conquest is the domination over a group of people by a superior force. *178*

annexation is the incorporation of one territory into another. *178*

voluntary immigration is the willing movement of people from one society to another. *178*

involuntary immigration is the forced movement of people from one society to another. *178*

ethnic cleansing refers to persecution through imprisonment, expulsion, or murder of members of an ethnic minority by a majority to achieve ethnic homogeneity in majority-controlled territory. *178*

migrant superordination is the conquest of a native population by a more powerful group. *179*

indigenous superordination is the subordination of an immigrant group to a dominant group. *179*

pluralistic minorities are groups that enter into an area voluntarily, but seek to maintain their own culture while also integrating into the dominant group. *179*

assimilationist minorities are groups that seek to shed their old ways and integrate themselves into mainstream society. *179*

secessionist minorities are groups that voluntarily separate themselves from the dominant group and view the dominant group with disdain, believing that it will corrupt the group's belief system. *180*

militant minorities are groups that seek to overthrow the existing system because they see it as unjust. *180*

ethnic enclaves are neighborhoods where people from similar cultures live together and assert cultural distinction from the dominant group. *180*

prejudice refers to negative attitudes about an entire category of people. *181*

stereotypes are simplified perceptions people have of an entire group that are usually based on false assumptions. *181*

discrimination is the unfair treatment of people based on a prejudice. *181*

institutional discrimination maintains the advantage for the dominant group, while providing the appearance of fairness to all. *181*

scapegoat means making an unfair accusation against a person or group as the cause of a problem. *182*

segregation is forced separation based on factors such as race, gender, or ethnicity. *182*

cycle of poverty is a generational barrier that prevents poor people from breaking into the middle and upper classes. *183*

color-blind racism is the idea that racism still exists in society in more subtle ways. *185*

double consciousness is the sense that a person must keep a foot in two worlds, one in the majority group's world and one in the minority group's world. *185*

Sample Test Questions

These multiple-choice questions are similar to those found in the test bank that accompanies this textbook.

1. Which of the following is *not* a racial category for the U.S. Census Bureau?
   a. White
   b. Black
   c. Latino
   d. Asian

2. Immigrants who learn their new home's language and culture while maintaining their own customs and beliefs are
   a. assimilationist minorities.
   b. secessionist minorities.
   c. pluralistic minorities.
   d. militant minorities.

3. What are the Jim Crow laws an example of?
   a. Ethnocentrism
   b. Ethnic segregation
   c. Color-blind racism
   d. Institutional discrimination

4. A dominant group
   a. always has the most in number and in power.
   b. always has the least in number and in power.
   c. usually has the most in number and in power.
   d. usually has the least in number and in power.

5. Joseph Graves states that race is a social construct, not a biological feature.
   a. True
   b. False

ESSAY

1. What are Joseph Graves' five pillars of racism?
2. Why does Wilson believe that class-based affirmative action should replace our current race-based system?
3. Why do some people have a sort of "double consciousness"?
4. What is the difference between prejudice and discrimination?
5. What are some ways that the United States is trying to break the cycle of poverty for minority groups?

WHERE TO START YOUR RESEARCH PAPER

To learn about stopping hate on campus, go to
http://www.tolerance.org/campus/index.jsp

To find more information about race and ethnicity by government standards, go to http://www.whitehouse.gov/omb/inforeg/race.pdf

To take the "Know Your Biases" test, go to
http://www.tolerance.org/hidden_bias/index.html

To learn more about multiculturalism in the United States, go to
http://www.nmci.org/

To read more about what people are doing to stop genocide in the world today, go to http://www.genocidewatch.org/

For more information about the ways the United States helps immigrants entering the country, go to
http://www.usimmigrationsupport.org/

Find out ways people are trying to stop discrimination, go to
http://www.discrimination.com/

To see what people are doing to break the cycle of poverty, go to
http://www.brakethecycle.org/

To find more information on minority groups, go to http://www.minorityrights.org/

To read about the World Conference against Racism, go to
http://www.un.org/WCAR/

ANSWERS: 1. c; 2. c; 3. d; 4. c; 5. a

Remember to check www.thethinkspot.com for additional information, downloadable flashcards, and other helpful resources.

GENDER STRATIFICATION

WHAT IS THE DIFFERENCE BETWEEN SEX
AND GENDER?
WHAT ARE THE PERSPECTIVES ON GENDER
AND GENDER INEQUALITY?
WHAT POLICIES ARE IN PLACE TO PREVENT
SEXUAL HARASSMENT AND DOMESTIC
VIOLENCE?

"She is

not the same woman in each magazine advertisement, but she is the same idea. She has that working-mother look as she strides forward, briefcase in one hand, smiling child in the other. Literally and figuratively, she is moving ahead. Her hair, if long, tosses behind her; if it is short, it sweeps back at the sides, suggesting mobility and progress. There is nothing shy or passive about her. She is confident, active, 'liberated.' She wears a dark tailored suit, but with a silk bow or colorful frill that says, 'I'm really feminine underneath.' She has made it in a man's world without sacrificing her femininity. And she has done this on her own. By some personal miracle, this image suggests, she has managed to combine what 150 years of industrialization have split wide apart—child and job, frill and suit, female culture and male.

When I showed a photograph of a supermom like this to the working mothers I talked to in the course of researching this book, many responded with an outright laugh."[1]

The Social Side *of* Sex

In their book *The Second Shift: Working Parents and the Revolution at Home*, sociologists Arlie Russell Hochschild and Anne Machung expound on the different expectations men and women have about women's roles in society.

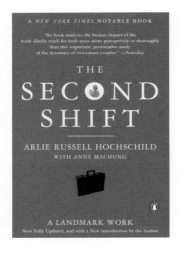

Nearly two decades after Dr. John Gray released *Men Are from Mars, Women Are from Venus*, it is still essential reading for anyone trying to figure out why his or her significant other is so annoying. The idea that the differences between men and women are so profound that we come from different planets may be a little extreme, but significant differences do exist between the sexes.

In *The Second Shift*, Hochschild and Machung contend that the women's liberation movement has actually created additional burdens for women. The movement opened up the world of work, but kept women in the world of domestic service. The image of the perfect woman involves brains, beauty, and toughness. However, as *The Second Shift* demonstrates, this image raises many problems for women. Even though women have excelled in the workforce and contributed mightily to the economy, society still expects them to fill the traditional role of mother.

In my household, we sometimes step out of our "traditional" roles. My wife and I both work, but instead of leaving all the domestic tasks to her, I pride myself on regularly doing what are typically viewed as "female" tasks. I care for our children, cook meals, and clean the house. Of course, are these really "female" tasks? Is there something biological about cleaning a toilet? Some men's attitudes have not evolved enough to share parental and domestic responsibilities. According to researchers Scott South and Glenna Spitze, men perform only 18 hours of housework per week, whereas women clock in over 32 hours.[2] Even in households in which the wife works full-time, Hochschild shows how she is often expected to be a "supermom" when she comes home. Who created these ideas of men and women?

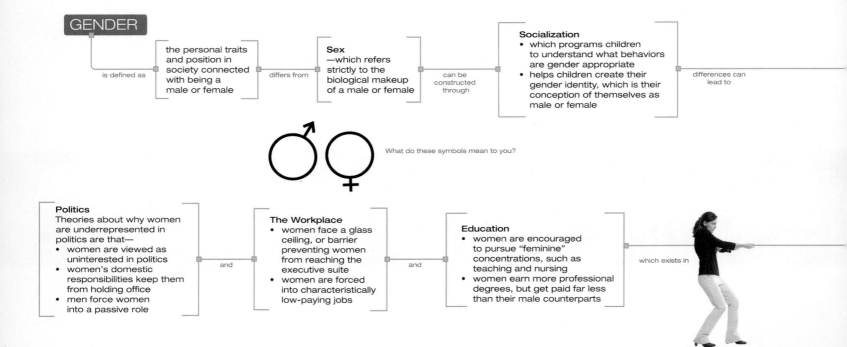

GENDER

is defined as — the personal traits and position in society connected with being a male or female

differs from

Sex —which refers strictly to the biological makeup of a male or female

can be constructed through

Socialization
• which programs children to understand what behaviors are gender appropriate
• helps children create their gender identity, which is their conception of themselves as male or female

differences can lead to

What do these symbols mean to you?

Politics
Theories about why women are underrepresented in politics are that—
• women are viewed as uninterested in politics
• women's domestic responsibilities keep them from holding office
• men force women into a passive role

and

The Workplace
• women face a glass ceiling, or barrier preventing women from reaching the executive suite
• women are forced into characteristically low-paying jobs

and

Education
• women are encouraged to pursue "feminine" concentrations, such as teaching and nursing
• women earn more professional degrees, but get paid far less than their male counterparts

which exists in

get the topic: WHAT IS THE DIFFERENCE BETWEEN SEX AND GENDER?

Gender vs. Sex

"Gender—it's bigger than sex."[3] With this phrase, many viewers were hooked to the *20/20* special called "It's More Than Just Sex: The Difference Between Men and Women" in 2006.[4] During this broadcast, anchors John Stossel and Elizabeth Vargas attempted to find out why women flock to the bathroom in groups and why men just don't listen.[5] The name of this program brings up an interesting and often overlooked point: although related, one's gender and one's sex are not necessarily the same thing.

Gender is defined as the personal traits and position in society connected with being a male or female. For instance, in traditional U.S. society, wearing a fancy dress is associated with the female gender, while wearing a tuxedo is associated with men. **Sex** refers strictly to the biological makeup of a male or female. The biological differences between men and women do correlate with some behavioral differences. For example, boys may be more aggressive, and girls more verbal. Such simple correlations support the notion that ideas about gender are based on sex.[6] However, sociologists suggest that socialization, rather than biology, determines gender.

GENDER CONSTRUCTION

In the second season of *Desperate Housewives*, Lynette Scavo's husband Tom was often seen taking care of the kids and doing housework while his wife climbed the corporate ladder. In reality, some men would scoff at Tom's actions. But why do we consider Tom's behavior atypical? Probably because we've been socially programmed with ideas of how men and women should behave. The father as the primary

> **SEX** is the biological makeup of a male or female.
> **GENDER IDENTITY** is our perception of ourselves as male or female.

> **Gender** is not a set of traits or roles; "it **is the product of social doings of some sort.**"

caregiver contradicts our traditional cultural norm. But gender is not a set of traits or roles; "it is the product of social doings of some sort."[7] Sociologists West and Zimmerman suggest that gender is developed in two ways: Not only do we "do gender" or participate in its construction, but we also have gender done to us as members of society.[8] Childhood is the prime time for development of **gender identity**, or our perception of ourselves as male or female. During our childhood, we learn what behavior is "appropriate" for each gender and how to fit in with others like us.

To find out how children display or learn their gender, sociologist Michael Messner examined the interactions between two soccer teams—the all-boy Sea Monsters and the all-girl Barbie Girls.[9] Before a season-opening ceremony began, the Barbie Girls rallied together around a miniature Barbie float decorated with their team colors. A boom box on the float played music, and the girls gathered together to sing and dance. At first the little boys watched in confused awe, but soon took up a chant of "No Barbie!" When this chant failed to get the girls' attention, the little boys invaded their space, and a game of chase ensued. The parents observed this behavior from the sidelines and remarked that little boys and little girls are like members of two different species.

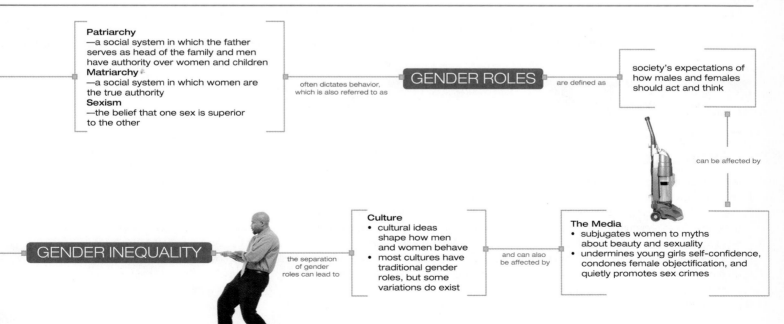

Patriarchy
—a social system in which the father serves as head of the family and men have authority over women and children
Matriarchy
—a social system in which women are the true authority
Sexism
—the belief that one sex is superior to the other

often dictates behavior, which is also referred to as

GENDER ROLES

are defined as

society's expectations of how males and females should act and think

can be affected by

GENDER INEQUALITY

the separation of gender roles can lead to

Culture
- cultural ideas shape how men and women behave
- most cultures have traditional gender roles, but some variations do exist

and can also be affected by

The Media
- subjugates women to myths about beauty and sexuality
- undermines young girls self-confidence, condones female objectification, and quietly promotes sex crimes

Messner argues that the parents easily recognized the differences, but failed to recognize the distinct similarities between the girls' and boys' teams during the rest of the season. Players on both teams regularly displayed many of the same behaviors—crying over skinned knees, racing to get snacks after the game, paying attention to birds or airplanes rather than to the coach—that would indicate a lack of major gender differences. Parents have no problem pointing out the differences between the boys and girls, but have difficulty identifying similarities due to "an institutional context that is characterized by informally structured sex segregation among the parent coaches and team managers, and by formally structured sex segregation among the children."[10] In other words, the adults couldn't see the similarities because they were socialized to see boys and girls as different.

Patriarchy and Sexism

William Wordsworth once said, "father—to God himself we cannot give a holier name." Wordsworth's sentiment was reflected in *Father Knows Best*—a definitive television program of the 1950s and 1960s. Humans have long considered the father the leader of the family unit. This role carries over into the rest of society through **patriarchy**, a social system in which men exert authority over women and children. The power position of men extends into government, business, and even religion. Few societies have been identified as a **matriarchy**, a social system in which women are the main authority and hold power over men.

The patriarchal system often results in **sexism**, or the belief that one sex is superior to the other. In many societies, attitudes often suggest

^
^ During our childhood, society shapes
^ our gender identity. **What social cues might this young girl have picked up from the world around her?**

women are the "weaker sex." This belief system may be adopted by women who seek jobs that fulfill these views. A few years ago, a very bright female student told me she wanted to be a medical doctor. I asked, "What's your major?" "Nursing" was the reply. She explained that her father, fiancé, and religious belief all dictated that women shouldn't be doctors. Clearly, these patriarchal beliefs possibly prevented a great mind from becoming a great doctor.

In *The Second Shift*, Hochschild finds that married, working women have a "second shift" when they get home from work. Although their husbands may help around the house to some extent, women come home to the tasks of cooking dinner, doing laundry, and, if there are children, helping them with homework and getting them ready for the next day of school. However, most of the women stated they were satisfied with their marriages. This shows that the patriarchal system is deeply ingrained in people's minds.

Gender Roles

Television's female characters have come a long way since Carol Brady and June Cleaver, for whom kissing their husbands good-bye and seeing the kids off to school started off a day of cleaning, baking, and homemaking. Today, we're used to seeing women portrayed as surgeons and attorneys and men actively participating in raising their children. What makes these arrangements acceptable to us now? The prevailing culture and the socialization that parents provide to their children shape ideas about gender-appropriate behaviors.

While women are succeeding in traditionally masculine fields like medicine and business, most of our children are still socialized to fit specific **gender roles**, or society's expectations of how males and females should act and think. Children's toys are an example of

▶▶▶ GO GLOBAL

The Horrors of Female Circumcision

In some of the world's most patriarchal societies, it's traditional for men to control every aspect of a woman's life, including her body. Female circumcision, also referred to as female genital mutilation (FGM), is one such tradition. The procedure consists of the alteration or removal of parts of the female genital organs for no medical purpose.[11] The intention is to keep women sexually "pure," by ensuring that they will remain virgins until marriage.[12] Women who undergo FGM may suffer from a number of long-term medical consequences, including recurrent urinary tract infections, infertility, and increased risk of childbirth complications.[13]

This practice is most common in the western, eastern, and northeastern regions of Africa, some countries in Asia and the Middle East, and certain immigrant communities in Europe and North America.[14] It's estimated that between 100 and 140 million girls and women worldwide have undergone FGM.[15] Cultural tradition and ideas about proper sexual behavior perpetuate the practice, subjecting new generations of female children to a painful and dangerous operation.

Although this practice is rooted in cultural tradition, many believe it's a violation of human rights and a sign of male domination over women. The practice represents an inequality between the sexes, and it is a major form of discrimination against women.[16]

socialization at a young age. Manhattan Toy makes a line of dolls called Groovy Girls, which allows girls to "celebrate their own unique personalities," with various fashion options for the dolls.[17] The Hasbro Company's Nerf toys—geared toward more aggressive play, like football and mock war situations—continue to be popular among young boys.[18]

However, gender roles in the United States are in a constant state of flux. This is not to say that we now encourage males to possess feminine characteristics, or vice versa, but the differences between the sexes are less pronounced than they once were. Young girls race down soccer fields or shoot hoops after school, and they're just as likely to wear jeans and T-shirts as skirts. The traditional roles of man as provider and woman as homemaker are shifting as well, since many households today have two breadwinners.

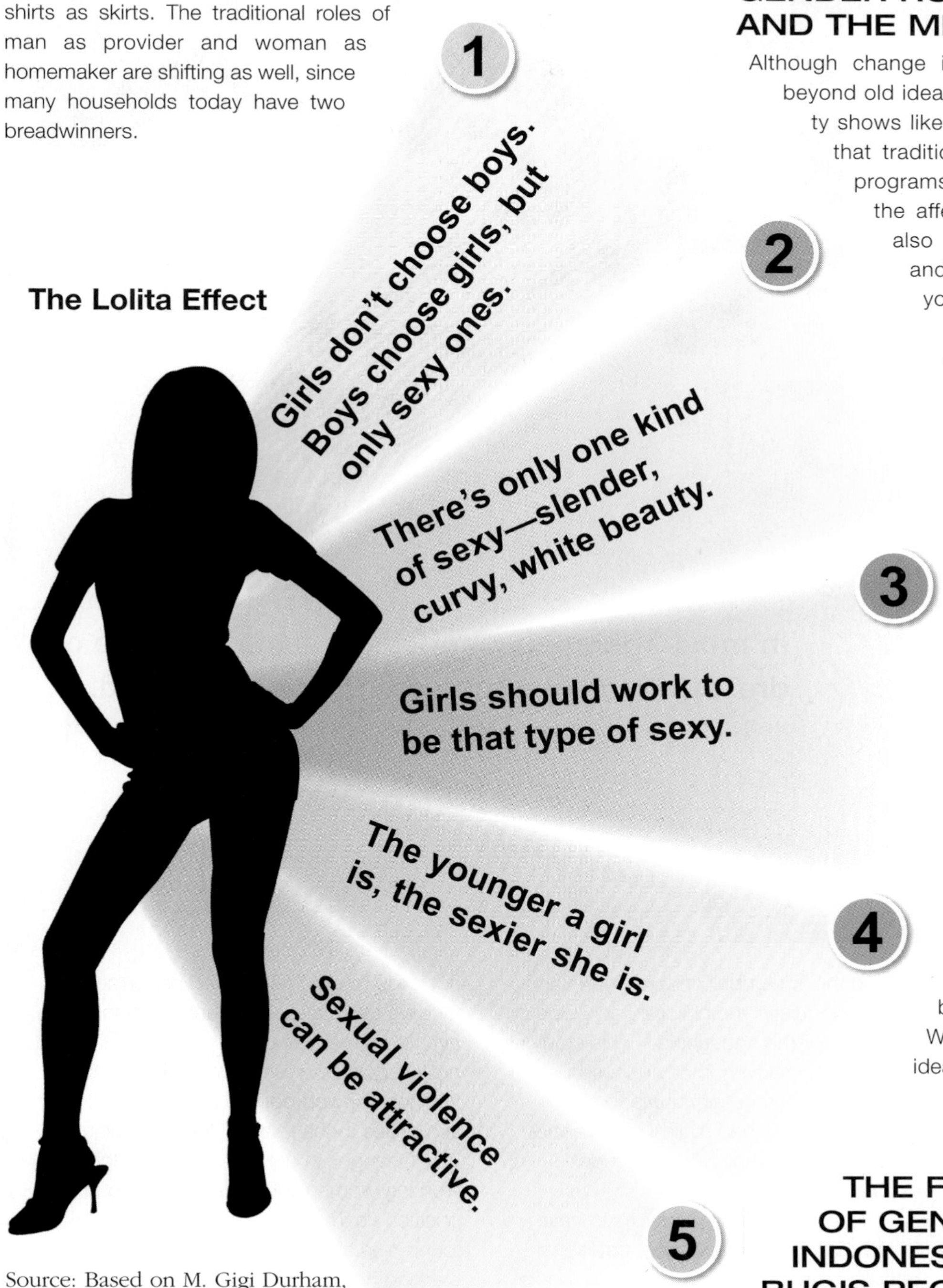

GENDER ROLES AND THE MEDIA

Although change is evident, we have not completely moved beyond old ideas about gender. Look no further than the reality shows like ABC's *The Bachelor*, and you'll see evidence that traditional gender roles are still in place. On these programs, women compete in challenges in order to win the affections of the man on the show. The shows also continue to perpetuate myths about beauty and sexuality, as the emphasis is placed on young, "sexy" girls.

In Dr. M. Gigi Durham's *The Lolita Effect: The Media Sexualization of Young Girls and What We Can Do About It*, five myths about sex and sexuality are examined. These myths, which are listed in the graphic to the left, give many impressionable young women an "if you've got it, flaunt it" attitude.

Durham has labeled these myths the "Lolita Effect," which works to undermine girls' self-confidence, condones female objectification, and quietly promotes sex crimes.[19] The goal of Durham's book is to break down these myths in order to help girls recognize ideas about healthy, progressive sexuality, and to protect themselves from media degradation and sexual vulnerability.[20] Durham hopes to empower girls to make healthy decisions about their sexuality. Although the media's portrayal of sexuality is often a skewed one, people in the real world are not forced to abide by these views. However, the media play a big role in our culture, so we cannot help but be affected by the things we see on TV and in magazines. What other effect might culture have on our ideas of gender?

The Lolita Effect

1. Girls don't choose boys. Boys choose girls, but only sexy ones.

2. There's only one kind of sexy—slender, curvy, white beauty.

3. Girls should work to be that type of sexy.

4. The younger a girl is, the sexier she is.

5. Sexual violence can be attractive.

Source: Based on M. Gigi Durham, *The Lolita Effect: The Media Sexualization of Young Girls and What We Can Do About It* (Woodstock, NY: The Overlook Press, 2008).

THE FLUIDITY OF GENDER ROLES: INDONESIA'S BUGIS PEOPLE

Some cultures, like the Bugis people living on the Indonesian island of Sulawesi, have a different view of gender and gender roles. Australian anthropologist Sharyn Davies studied the Bugis people and found that gender-specific pronouns like "he" and "she" don't exist in their language.[21] Gender stratification among the Bugis is complicated with five different gender classifications: *oroané* (masculine male), *makkunrai* (feminine female), *calalai* (masculine female), *calabai* (feminine male), and *bissu* (embodying both male and female energies, revered as a shaman).[22] Each gender has specific behaviors, articles of clothing, social and religious roles, and sexual practices. The oroané and makkunrai genders are "normal," or comparable to what we know; the calalai, calabai, and bissu are what we might call "gender benders."

The **calalai** are anatomical females who assume the characteristics of men. They hold masculine jobs and dress as men, practice homosexuality, and typically live with female partners to adopt children.

The **calabai** are anatomical males who adhere to some of the responsibilities of women. Calabai males are homosexual and dress as women, yet they don't follow all cultural suggestions for women. They do, however, take on traditionally female responsibilities, like planning weddings.

The **bissu** embody the perfect mixture of male and female. A bissu that is externally male is considered to be internally female, and vice versa if the bissu is female. The Bugis people believe that bissu embody the best characteristics of both sexes, so they are able to communicate with the spirits and therefore occupy a special place in the community.

The Bugis have ideas about gender that are different from our own, but seem to be more accepting of different kinds of people. Men and women are allowed live the gender role that suits them best in Bugis society.

> **In most societies, choosing a feminine style of dress will make a man stand out in a crowd.**
>
> Why is it less conspicuous for calabai males to dress in a feminine style?

THINK SOCIOLOGICALLY

Culture's Effect on Gender Roles

Anthropologist Margaret Mead conducted a study of gender roles among three tribes in New Guinea: the Arapesh, the Mundgumor, and the Tchambuli.[23] She concluded that gender roles are largely dependent on culture. The men and women of the Arapesh tribe would both be considered "feminine" by our standards. The Mundgumor men and women were aggressive and violent, possessing "masculine" qualities. However,

among the Tchambuli people, men stayed home and raised the children, and women provided for the household.[24] This study drew much criticism; many accused Mead of doctoring her results to show what she had hoped to find.[25] Nevertheless, this study showed that gender is culturally constructed.

Other studies of gender roles have found that, in most societies, traditional gender roles have degrees of variation for any individual task. Anthropologist George Murdock's 1937 study of more than 200

societies found that women performed farming tasks and construction of homes in almost as many societies as men. Although not every society is uniform, Murdock's findings showed definite cross-cultural similarities in the roles of men and women.[26]

Changes in gender roles have left working women with children in a tough position. In *The Second Shift*, Hochschild found that although gender roles in the working world may have changed, working women are still responsible for maintaining the home.

Gender and Inequality

In many societies, the idea of gender is not as fluid as the Bugis people suggest, and a hierarchy of sorts exists between the sexes. In the United States, for example, men and women are ranked differently in terms of power and wealth. In 2006, the Census Bureau reported that the median annual income for full-time working men was $42,261 compared to only $32,515 for full-time working women.[27] Because women are more likely to earn less than men, they're also more likely to live below the poverty line. Why is there such inequality between income levels and poverty status of men and women? We'll look into this further in the section relating to work. But first, let's look at a topic that should be relevant to everyone reading this book—gender and education.

GENDER AND EDUCATION

A few years ago, my daughter started her second grade school year very excited, but came home feeling down. When I asked why she was so upset, she said it was because she had "a boy for a teacher." I had to explain to her that "boy teachers" could be just as smart and fun as "girl teachers." Two months later, she couldn't wait to catch the bus in the morning to get to his class. Male elementary school teachers don't break any major social taboos today, but thirty years ago, when I was in school, the only men at my school were the gym teacher, the principal, and the janitor.

Historically, men and women have received vastly different educations. When Oberlin College became the first college to offer coeducational enrollment in 1837, women students were encouraged to study "feminine" concentrations, such as nursing and teaching. Men, conversely, focused on fields that either involved vocational or intellectual skills. These differences are becoming less pronounced today, but there is still a clear educational divide between men and women nationally.[28]

Even though higher education used to be a primarily masculine pursuit, women now earn the majority of associate's and bachelor's degrees. Moreover, women earn slightly more than half of all master's and professional degrees and about forty percent of doctoral degrees.[29] Although this is a major improvement for women in education, the differences in choice of major still reflect traditional gender roles. Women receive the majority of art, music, and social

The Gender Income Gap by Level of Education in 2006

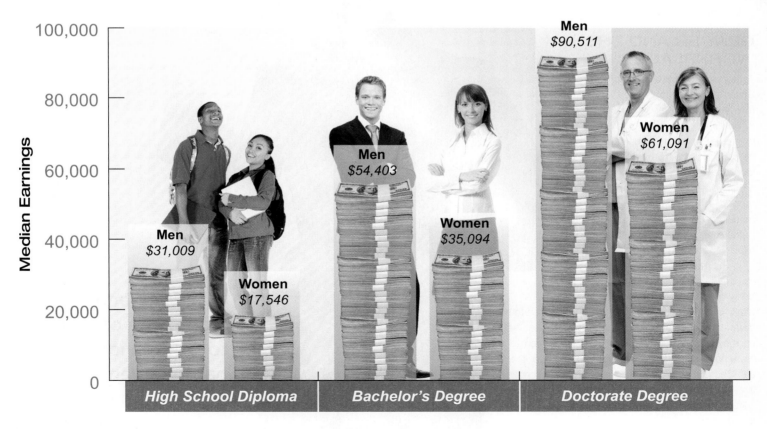

Median Earnings

100,000

80,000

60,000

40,000

20,000

0

Men $31,009

Women $17,546

Men $54,403

Women $35,094

Men $90,511

Women $61,091

High School Diploma   *Bachelor's Degree*   *Doctorate Degree*

Source: "Historical Income Tables-People," U.S. Census Bureau, 2006, http://www.census.gov/hhes/www/income/histinc/p16.html.

HUMAN CAPITAL MODEL assumes that men and women bring different natural skills to the workplace.

CHOICE MODEL explains the income gap by analyzing the kinds of jobs women choose.

PATRIARCHY MODEL assumes that we have a male-dominated society that doesn't allow women to hold upper-tier jobs.

GLASS CEILING is an invisible barrier preventing women from reaching executive-level positions in the workplace.

science degrees, while men receive the majority of engineering, chemistry, and medical degrees.[30]

If women are earning degrees in greater numbers than men, shouldn't we see the income gap between men and women decrease? Census data show that the income gap between men and women actually becomes wider with higher levels of educational background. This seems curious. To investigate this further, let's turn to women in the workplace.

GENDER AND THE WORKPLACE

Today, women make up almost half of the United States' paid labor force and more than half of all married couples depend on two incomes.[31] While it's now accepted and necessary for women to work, the types of jobs as well as the compensation for these jobs remain different for men and women. Three theoretical models—the human capital model, the choice model, and the patriarchy model—attempt to explain these discrepancies.

The **human capital model** assumes that men and women bring different natural skills to the workplace. For example, society perceives men to have more mechanical skills, thus they make better engineers. Because society considers women to be more nurturing, they are assumed to be better teachers. Such an argument suggests it is not discrimination to hire men to do jobs for which they are more suited. This explains why men seem to have advantages in higher-income professions, such as medicine, engineering, and law.[32]

The **choice model** explains the income gap by analyzing the kinds of jobs women choose. Women choose to major in social work or elementary education, therefore knowingly entering fields that pay less. This argument suggests that if you choose a career that you know pays very little, you have only yourself to blame.[33]

The **patriarchy model** assumes that we have a male-dominated society that doesn't allow women to hold upper-tier jobs or steers them away from such careers early in life. For example, when discussing majors with an enrollment counselor, students may experience stereotypical gender role expectations. Male students are asked to consider business or engineering. Female students are asked about education or communication fields as possible professions.

The patriarchy model also supports the idea of a **glass ceiling**, or the invisible barrier that prevents women from reaching the executive suite. For example, few women become the CEOs of large companies. On the 2008 Fortune 500 list, women headed only twelve companies.[34]

Cornell sociology professor Shelley J. Correll studied labor distribution by sex and found that cultural beliefs about gender shape both male and female attitudes about their abilities.[35] If this is the case, our ideas about gender may need to undergo a radical change before the income gap between men and women disappears.

<<< **Women in the workplace often have to work twice as hard as men** to break through the glass ceiling above them.

Men Are a Gender, Too

It's important to remember that men are a gender, too. As noted earlier, men have many advantages in U.S. society. Christine Williams discusses how men have a "glass elevator" when it comes to getting jobs in traditionally female-dominated occupations. Men who sought jobs in the nursing, library, and elementary education fields said they felt they had an advantage over women applying for the same job because there were fewer men in those fields.[36]

However, it's important to know that with the male gender role come gender expectations. Recently, the son of a friend was going off to college. The boy complained when his parents refused to buy him a new car. His sister got a new car when she went to college, but my friend explained, "He's a boy. It's good for him to learn how to fix a junker car."

>>> ACTIVITY Write out as many household jobs as you can think of, and place an M next to roles that are for the men and a W next to those for the women. Do you see any gender bias in your life?

GENDER AND POLITICS

Women are making huge political strides. Hillary Rodham Clinton was a widely supported female politician in her bid for the 2008 Democratic Presidential nomination, while Republican Presidential nominee John McCain tapped Alaskan governor Sarah Palin as his running mate. Clinton garnered nearly eighteen million votes and, as she famously said, caused "eighteen million cracks" in the nation's highest glass ceiling.[37]

Women regularly hold high political office in other parts of the world. England has had several women in power, beginning in 1553 with Queen Mary I. Margaret Thatcher was Prime Minister from 1979 to 1990. Golda Meir was Prime Minister of Israel from 1969 to 1973, and Benazir Bhutto was Prime Minister of Pakistan from 1988 to 1990 and 1993 to 1996.[38] Let's examine three theories that attempt to explain why women in the United States have not held similar positions.

Theory #1: Women, by nature, are uninterested in politics. This theory has been disproved time and again by data that show that women vote more regularly than men.[39] Women have also risen to political prominence, including the country's first female Speaker of the House, Nancy Pelosi.

Theory #2: The structure of women's lives does not lend itself to the rigors of political office. I like to call this theory the "baby bias." Similar to Hochschild's "supermom" responsibilities, the theory assumes a woman in office would be too overwhelmed by her mothering duties to succeed in office. During the recent election, no one questioned whether Barack Obama could be a good father and president, while many questioned how Sarah Palin could manage raising a family of five, had she been elected vice president.

Theory #3. Society forces women into a politically passive role. Traditionally, this has been the case. But women are more independent today and have an increased interest in holding political office. Furthermore, politicians tend to be lawyers and business people, traditionally "men's" worlds. Although this is changing, female representation in politics remains disproportionately low.

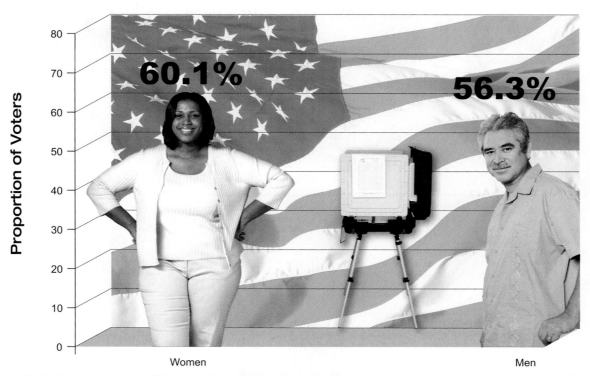

Voter Turnout by Sex in November 2004

60.1%

56.3%

Proportion of Voters

80
70
60
50
40
30
20
10
0

Women

Men

Source: Data from the U.S. Census Bureau, "Reported Voting and Registration, by Marital Status, Age, and Sex: November 2004," Table 11.

Feminism

Feminism refers to the vast collection of social movements and theories about gender differences. Feminism proposes social equality for all people. Feminist thinkers believe that women are equal to men and deserve the same opportunities as men.

The history of the feminist movement goes back to the eighteenth century. Mary Wollstonecraft's famous essay "A Vindication of the Rights of Woman" is one of the earliest examples of western feminist thought. Published in 1792, it argued for a woman's right to an education. Wollstonecraft's essay predates modern feminism, which can be divided into three "waves."

FIRST-WAVE FEMINISM

What is considered the first wave began in the late 19th and early 20th centuries and revolved around the women's suffrage movement. The fight for women's right to vote began in 1848 with activists such as Susan B. Anthony and Elizabeth Cady Stanton. Gradually, women were granted the vote at the state level, but national women's suffrage was not won until 1920. The Nineteenth Amendment, which prohibited denying the vote to anyone based on sex, was ratified after years of marches and protests in support of women's suffrage.[40]

SECOND-WAVE FEMINISM

The second wave of feminism occurred during the women's liberation movement that began in the 1960s. While first-wave feminism protested legal inequality, second-wave feminism also included equality in the workplace, equality in education, and social independence from men.

In 1963, Betty Friedan published a book called *The Feminine Mystique*, bringing attention to the idea that women should seek personal fulfillment outside her home and family. The book attacks a social system in which women are treated as nothing more than homemakers and childbearers.[41] Friedan is said to have ignited the women's lib movement with this book, although she has also been criticized for focusing exclusively on the plight of white middle- and upper-class women.[42]

In addition to equal rights in education and the workplace, second-wavers demanded reproductive rights and protection from domestic and sexual violence. These demands caused a great deal of controversy, as many conservatives felt that contraceptives and abortion go against traditional morals. Some feminists also tried to get the Equal Rights Amendment passed, which would ensure that "[e]quality of rights under the law shall not be denied or abridged by the United States or by any state on account of sex."[43] However, the bill has not been passed since its introduction to Congress in 1923. Some feminists are still trying to ratify the bill today.

One of the forces behind this proposed amendment is the National Organization for Women (NOW). NOW was founded in 1966 and remains the largest feminist organization in the United States.[44] Although the combined efforts of all those involved in the second wave of feminism did result in many successes, a new wave of feminism arose thirty years later to respond to the feelings of failure and disappointment the second wave had left behind.[45]

THIRD-WAVE FEMINISM

Beginning in the early 1990s, the third wave of feminism branched out to include multiple racial and socioeconomic groups. Gloria Anzaldua, bell hooks (née Gloria Jean Watkins), Maxine Hong Kingston, and Audre Lorde are feminist leaders associated with the third wave. Author and social activist bell hooks, for example, connected topics like race, capitalism, and gender within her works. She emphasized the fact that all three topics were interconnected and that they needed to be addressed at the same time.[46]

The History of Feminism

Second Wave Feminism

1848
Activists such as Elizabeth Cady Stanton and Susan B. Anthony fought for women's right to vote

1917
Groups such as the Silent Sentinels came together to support women's suffrage

1960s
The Women's Liberation movement began

1960s and 1970s
Women began to go to college and pursue careers

Mary Wollstonecraft Shelley's *A Vindication of the Rights of Woman* was published, which argued for a woman's right to vote
1792

Women in Wyoming were permitted to vote
1869

19th Amendment was ratified, which gave all women in the United States the right to vote
1920

Betty Friedan published *The Feminine Mystique*, which helped further ignite the Women's Lib movement
1963

First Wave Feminism

The underground feminist punk movement called "riot grrrl" is currently influencing the third wave. The subculture movement produces music, art, and magazines that address issues like rape, domestic abuse, female empowerment, and sexuality. The movement encourages the modern woman to be empowered, outspoken, and passionate.[47]

Many activist organizations resulted from the third wave. *Take Back the Night* is an organization that raises awareness and offers support to victims of rape and sexual assault. The nonprofit organization *Dress for Success* collects business suits through donations for

> **FEMINISM** is the vast collection of social movements and theories about gender differences, proposing social equality for all people.

women receiving welfare so they can interview for jobs with confidence.[48] The Third Wave Foundation and Feminist Majority Leadership Alliance are activist groups that work for gender, racial, economic, and social justice.[49]

think sociologically: WHAT ARE THE PERSPECTIVES ON GENDER AND GENDER INEQUALITY?

Feminist Theory

Feminists study how gender affects the experiences and opportunities of men and women. Although feminists may not always agree about how to achieve gender equality, they do tend to adopt four general beliefs:

1 **Increasing equality in work and education.** Year after year women are earning more professional degrees than men and entering the workforce in large numbers. However, feminists continue fighting for equality in both the workplace and schools against the gender wage gap and the glass ceiling that women commonly face in the workplace.

2 **Expanding human choice for outcomes.** In the book *Woman Hating*, feminist Andrea Dworkin comments that "Being female in this world is having been robbed of the potential for human choice by men who love to hate us."[50] Not all feminists agree with Dworkin's suggestion, but virtually all feminists work to create a society in which men

and women have equal opportunities. For example, by expanding enrollment in professional and graduate schools, women have greater opportunities to choose careers they enjoy.

3 **Eliminating gender stratification.** Feminism commits itself to assure equal rights, equal opportunity, and equal pay for women. For example, women are now successful Marines, a job that used to be an option for men only.

4 **Ending sexual violence.** Feminist theorists believe that male violence against women perpetuates gender inequality in our society.[51] For example, the "rule of thumb" refers to the alleged British common law that allowed a man to beat his wife with a stick, as long as it was not any larger than the diameter of his thumb. It's important to note that this was never an actual law; however men were allowed to punish their wives corporally.[52]

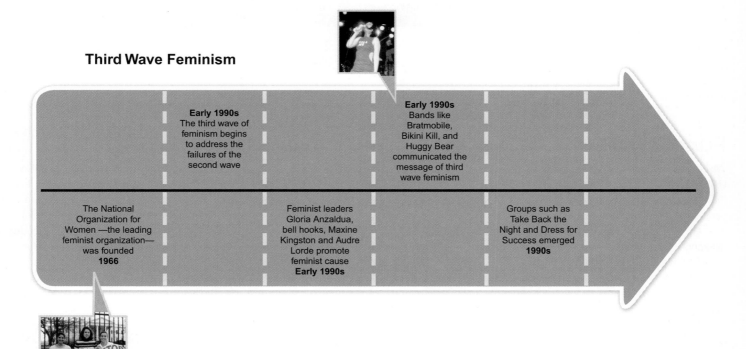

Third Wave Feminism

Early 1990s
The third wave of feminism begins to address the failures of the second wave

Early 1990s
Bands like Bratmobile, Bikini Kill, and Huggy Bear communicated the message of third wave feminism

The National Organization for Women —the leading feminist organization— was founded
1966

Feminist leaders Gloria Anzaldua, bell hooks, Maxine Kingston and Audre Lorde promote feminist cause
Early 1990s

Groups such as Take Back the Night and Dress for Success emerged
1990s

LIBERAL VS. RADICAL FEMINISM

Although there are many different kinds of feminism and there is not universal agreement about the titles of the different types, we will address two types—liberal feminism and radical feminism.

Liberal feminists tend to be in line with their historical roots, suggesting that women's equality is the primary motivation for the movement. If you believe that women should receive the same pay for the same work, have equal opportunities in the workplace, college, political office, and be free from domestic violence, then you are a liberal feminist. As you can see, this group is the larger group, because most people agree that women should not be discriminated against based on their gender. As a result, they support the idea that women should be free to pursue their own interests and achieve equality.

Radical feminists agree with the liberal agenda, but generally carry the ideas further. They might focus on capitalism and the ways that men use their historical advantage over money to maintain control over women. Radicals see that patriarchy is firmly rooted in society. Some suggest that only an overthrow of capitalism can result in equality for women. Others suggest that women should avoid "traditional activities" such as childbearing, since this often leads women to subordinate their own goals for their husbands and families.

Functionalism

While feminists fight gender inequality in the United States, functionalists examine how the separation of gender roles actually functions in a society. Society places men and women in different spheres, and these differences help maintain society. Because men and women often play different roles, competition is eliminated between the sexes, and family life runs smoothly.[53] For example, if men are expected to go out and work to provide for the family, while women are expected to perform domestic tasks and care for the children, their roles are complementary to each other. Each is doing a job that must be done. As women steadily enter the workforce, the separation of gender roles becomes less distinct. Even so, women are generally expected to maintain the home.

Talcott Parsons studied the separation of gender roles in the context of the family. Parsons noted that as children, "sex discrimination is more than anything else a reflection of the differentiation of adult sex roles."[54] Girls at a young age are socialized to display expressive qualities, such as calmness and nurturing (qualities expected of many adult women), while boys are prone to be rational and competitive, which are instrumental qualities.[55]

According to Parsons, young girls are able to step into the adult feminine role early in their development.[56] These girls see their mothers performing domestic tasks and are often expected to help out. Young boys, however, have fathers who work outside the house. As a result, boys are trained to prepare for their futures in the workforce.

Conflict Theory

Conflict theorists argue that capitalism and patriarchy are deeply intertwined. In a capitalist society, women generally are at the bottom of the system, regardless of their job. Furthermore, they often engage in unpaid, domestic tasks that serve to maintain the status quo.[57] However, men often devalue the work that women do, which reinforces the power that men have over women.[58]

Women who work tend to make less money than men in the workforce, so women are often subordinate to their better-paid husbands. Women are locked in a never-ending cycle that makes them submissive and subservient to men.

Notice the difference in dress between these male and female cheerleaders.

Conflict theorists would argue that cheerleading is just one way that men exploit women in our society.

Symbolic Interactionism

Symbolic interactionists believe that people's definition of gender develops from everyday interactions with others from the same and opposite sex.[59] Sociologists West and Zimmerman's idea of "doing gender" best illustrates the symbolic interactionists' point of view.[60] We all "do gender" every day, which means we act in a certain way that is associated with a particular gender. The way you style your hair, the mannerisms you have, and the way you talk are all part of the way you communicate your gender to others.

Sociologist Janet Chafetz argues that "doing gender" not only "(re)produces gender difference, it (re)produces gender inequality."[61] One way this happens is through conversation. Deborah Tannen's

You Just Don't Understand: Men and Women in Conversation argues that our lives are essentially a series of conversations, and we pass on "different, asymmetrical assumptions about men and women" in these conversations.[62]

Chafetz would argue that men and women communicate differently. Men often dominate conversations, and women struggle to follow the sometimes arbitrary rules that men impose on the dialogue. Women use "verbal and body language in ways that weaken their ability to assert themselves," which makes them appear less powerful than their male counterparts.[63] For example, while eating out one day, I noticed a men's softball team and a few of their wives/girlfriends at a nearby table. The guys were talking and laughing, but the women were passive. Gender socialization generally teaches boys to make their voice heard, while girls are taught to be "good," meaning quiet and docile.

Men and women often follow scripted behavior, acting in ways that are associated with their gender.[64] For example, men and women use different types of language and gesture. Men tend to be more direct in describing their wants and desires, displaying **machismo**, overt and exaggerated displays of masculinity.[65]

MACHISMO is overt and exaggerated displays of masculinity.

∨
∨
∨ Think about your conversations with people of the opposite sex. What patterns do you notice? **Do men and women really communicate differently?**

WRAP YOUR MIND AROUND THE THEORY

What functions might these boys serve in tomorrow's society? What characteristics might they have?

FUNCTIONALISM

The functionalists view society as a system of many parts, working in concert with one another to form a whole. Talcott Parsons believed that gender differences were essential in maintaining a properly functioning society. Parents socialize boys and girls for their future roles of father and mother. Boys are taught to be confident, rational, and competitive because these characteristics are instrumental qualities for men to succeed. Parents socialize girls with the primary goal of preparing to raise children. They learn nurturing qualities that Parsons refers to as expressive qualities. These complementary roles assist in the smooth functioning of society.

WHY DOES GENDER STRATIFICATION EXIST?

CONFLICT THEORY

Social conflict theorists are interested in the struggle for power between groups. In the case of gender, conflict theorists see the gender roles as beneficial to men, as their role as main breadwinner gives them power and control. Friedrich Engels, a contemporary of Karl Marx, suggested that women are the first oppressed group.[66] Although he agreed with Marx that the proletariat was oppressed, Engels points out that women, too, are exploited. This may not seem to be a major idea in today's world, but in 1884, it was staggering.

SYMBOLIC INTERACTIONISM

The symbolic interactionist perspective might focus on how people self-select by gender. For example, men may choose fields associated with "male-ness," whereas women select careers based on the types of work that are considered "normal" for them. Thus, women tend not to become engineers or work in other professions that require a mathematical background, in part, because it isn't expected of them. Gendered definitions influence career choices of men and women.[67] When I became a social worker, a job dominated by women, I had family members who actually said, "Isn't that a woman's job?" Such a definition might influence a career choice.

What are the pros and cons of selecting a career that falls **outside the traditional roles** for your gender?

Why might capitalism give men and women **reason to fight?**

discover sociology in action: WHAT POLICIES ARE IN PLACE TO PREVENT SEXUAL HARASSMENT AND DOMESTIC VIOLENCE?

Although more subtle forms of oppression can be damaging, physical, sexual, emotional, economic, and psychological abuse are all forms of oppression. The National Institute of Justice and the Centers for Disease Control and Prevention survey found that a large number of crimes go unreported. Generally, only one-fifth of rapes, one-quarter of physical assaults, and one-half of stalking committed against women by their intimate partners are reported.[68] The most common reasons for not reporting assault or rape were fear of the perpetrator, belief that police couldn't help, and worry that police wouldn't believe them.[69] Because victims begin to internalize their emotions, these women either believe they deserved the assault or that no one can help them.[70]

Resources are available to help the victims, but victims are often too scared or ashamed to come forward. However, in response to the rising concern about these crimes, such offenders are receiving longer sentences and are required to register as sex offenders in the public domain.[71]

Social Policy—Stopping Sexual Harassment and Gender Violence

Sexual harassment and gender violence are persistent issues, as stories of office harassment, domestic violence, and rape are commonplace items in the news. The National Violence Against Women survey found that approximately 25 percent of surveyed women and 7.6 percent of surveyed men claim that they were raped or physically assaulted by a spouse, cohabiting partner, or date in their lifetimes.[72] The good news is that more and more victims are reporting incidents to the police, even when the offenders are intimate partners.

Significant efforts have been made to curb sexual offenses. Law enforcement and community organizations have initiated campaigns against sexual assault and domestic violence. Shelters for battered women give victims a place to stay to recuperate from domestic violence, and counseling services help battered women with self-esteem issues, as well as other psychological trauma brought on by abuse. It is important to help men, women, and families suffering from abuse because damages extend far beyond a bruise. Abuse harms people on three levels: physical, financial, and emotional.[73]

ACTIVITIES

1. Research your state's sex offender laws. What is the suggested penalty for first-time rape offenders? Are sex offenders required to register and inform the neighborhood in which they reside of their status?
2. Locate a battered women's shelter in your area. How is the shelter funded? What services does the shelter provide?

From Classroom to Community | Visiting a Women's Shelter

Jane was in her late 40s when she decided to go back to school. As part of her class work, she volunteered some time in a local battered women's shelter, and she was surprised by how little things had changed since she was younger.

"When I was 22, I left an abusive man and lived with my son in a shelter for about six months. During that time, I learned a lot about the cycle of violence, and traced the roots of my willingness to tolerate this behavior with a counselor."

For Jane, volunteering at the shelter brought all of those memories back. "Why is it that so many men think it is their right to beat the women in their lives? Why do they need to be so controlling? If girls aren't taught to behave this way, why are men?"

Jane answered phones, filed documents, and served meals from time to time. She was so determined to help these women because of her own experience.

"I escaped this lifestyle and never wish to return. I sure hope that I helped some of those women avoid falling back into abuse. No one deserves this."

WHAT **IS THE DIFFERENCE BETWEEN SEX AND GENDER?** 193

sex: the biological makeup of a male or female
gender: the personal traits and position in society connected with being a
male or female

WHAT **ARE THE PERSPECTIVES ON GENDER AND GENDER
INEQUALITY?** 201

feminist theory: feminists share the belief that equality in work and education should increase, human choice for outcomes should be expanded,
gender stratification should be eliminated, and sexual violence should end
functionalism: the separation of gender roles eliminates competition
between the sexes and makes family life run smoothly
conflict theory: capitalism and patriarchy are intertwined; as a result,
women are locked in a never-ending cycle that makes them submissive
and subservient to men
symbolic interactionism: people's definition of gender develops from
everyday interactions with others from the same and opposite sex

WHAT **POLICIES ARE IN PLACE TO PREVENT SEXUAL
HARASSMENT AND DOMESTIC VIOLENCE?** 205

campaigns against sexual assault and domestic violence, shelters, and
counseling services

get the topic: WHAT IS THE DIFFERENCE BETWEEN SEX AND GENDER?

Gender vs. Sex   193
Patriarchy and Sexism   194
Gender Roles   194
Gender and Inequality   197
Feminism   200

Feminist Theory   201
Functionalism   202
Conflict Theory   202

Symbolic Interactionism   202
Social Policy—Stopping Sexual Harassment
    and Gender Violence   205

Theory

FUNCTIONALISM   202

- gender differences help maintain a functioning society
- parents socialize boys and girls to their future roles of fathers and mothers
- boys are taught to be competitive and confident; girls are taught to be nurturing and caring

CONFLICT THEORY   202

- gender roles are beneficial to men, as their role as main breadwinner gives them power and control
- capitalism emphasizes male domination, as women are encouraged to spend money on goods

- Engels: women are the first oppressed group

SYMBOLIC INTERACTIONISM   202

- women select careers based on the types of work that are consid-ered "normal" for women to perform
- certain careers are perceived as "masculine," which drives many capable women away from even attempting to enter these fields
- differences in the career choices of men and women begin early in life
- people "do gender" every day, which creates gender differences and inequality

Key Terms

sex is the biological makeup of a male or female. *193*

gender identity is our perception of ourselves as male or female. *193*

patriarchy is a social system in which the father serves as head of the family, and men have authority over women and children. *194*

matriarchy is a social system in which women are the main authority and hold power over men. *194*

sexism is the belief that one sex is superior to the other. *194*

gender roles are society's expectations of how males and females should act and think. *194*

calalai are anatomical females in Bugis society who assume the characteristics of men. *196*

calabai are anatomical males in Bugis society who adhere to some of the responsibilities of women. *196*

bissu are androgynous members of Bugis society who embody the perfect mixture of male and the female. *196*

human capital model assumes that men and women bring different natural skills to the workplace. *198*

choice model explains the income gap by analyzing the kinds of jobs women choose. *198*

patriarchy model assumes that we have a male-dominated society that doesn't allow women to hold upper-tier jobs. *198*

glass ceiling is an invisible barrier preventing women from reaching executive-level positions in the workplace. *198*

feminism is the vast collection of social movements and theories about gender differences, proposing social equality for all people. *200*

machismo is overt and exaggerated displays of masculinity. *203*

Sample Test Questions

These multiple-choice questions are similar to those found in the test bank that accompanies this textbook.

1. Gender identity is mostly developed at which stage in life?
- **a.** Childhood
- **b.** Middle age
- **c.** Adolescence
- **d.** Late adulthood

2. Children are socialized to fit specific
- **a.** gender roles.
- **b.** social classes.
- **c.** gender inequities.
- **d.** occupational roles.

3. Which of the following is *not* one of Dr. M. Gigi Durham's myths about sexuality?
- **a.** Girls don't choose boys. Boys choose girls, but only sexy ones.
- **b.** There's only one kind of sexy—slender, curvy, white beauty.
- **c.** Girls should be satisfied with their current body type.
- **d.** The younger a girl is, the sexier she is.

4. Which of the following is a major cause of the increase in working mothers?
- **a.** More educational opportunities for women
- **b.** Increase in homosexuality
- **c.** Rising divorce rate
- **d.** Lack of children

5. According to functionalist analysis, children are socialized in order to
- **a.** keep men in a dominant position in society.
- **b.** maintain a society that runs properly.
- **c.** establish a clear career path.
- **d.** entertain their parents.

ESSAY

1. How have gender roles in the United States changed and stayed the same since the 1950s?

2. What are the underlying causes of sexism, and will society ever be able to overcome them?

3. How might society be different if traditional gender roles were reversed?

4. Which of the three models explaining inequality in the workplace do you think is the strongest?

5. How effective do you the think the feminist movement has been in championing women's equality?

WHERE TO START YOUR RESEARCH PAPER

To learn more about the "riot grrrls" movement, go to http://eamusic.dartmouth.edu/~wowem/electronmedia/mish/riot-grrrl.html

For more information on the National Organization for Women (NOW), go to their Web site http://www.now.org/

To learn more about Take Back the Night, go to their Web site http://www.takebackthenight.org/

To learn more about Dress for Success, go to http://www.dressforsuccess.org/

ANSWERS: 1. a; 2. a; 3. c; 4. a; 5. b

Remember to check www.thethinkspot.com for additional information, downloadable flashcards, and other helpful resources.

AGING AND HEALTH

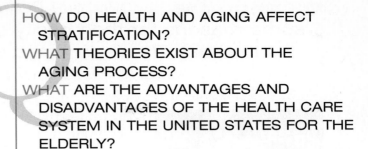

"One way

to think about America's national eating disorder is as the return, with an almost atavistic vengeance, of the omnivore's dilemma. The cornucopia of the American supermarket has thrown us back on a bewildering food landscape where we once again have to worry that some of those tasty-looking morsels might kill us. (Perhaps not as quickly as a poisonous mushroom, but just as surely.) Certainly the extraordinary abundance of food in America complicates the whole problem of choice. At the same time, many of the tools with which people historically managed the omnivore's dilemma have lost their sharpness here—or simply failed. As a relatively new nation drawn from many different immigrant populations, each with its own culture of food, Americans have never had a single, strong, stable culinary tradition to guide us.

The lack of a steadying culture of food leaves us especially vulnerable to the blandishments of the food scientists and the marketer, for whom the omnivore's dilemma is not so much a dilemma as an opportunity. It is very much in the interest of the food industry to exacerbate our anxieties about what to eat, the better to then assuage them with new products. Our bewilderment in the supermarket is no accident; the return of the omnivore's dilemma has deep roots in the modern food industry, roots that, I found, reach all the way back to the fields of corn, growing in places like Iowa."[1]

The Graying
of Society

CHAPTER 12

Journalism professor **Michael Pollan provides some reasons for the obesity epidemic in the book** *The Omnivore's Dilemma: A Natural History of Four Meals.*

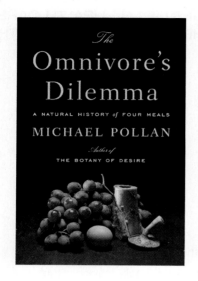

A few years ago, it dawned on me that I had gained more than 25 pounds since I got married. At the time, my weight gain equated to approximately two pounds a year. If I continued on this trend, I would weigh about 300 pounds by the time I was sixty years old. As a person who once ran 10Ks, I was shocked. How did this happen?

While many of us struggle with issues of weight and its effects on our health, **obesity**, an unhealthy accumulation of body fat, is an epidemic that threatens many people's health around the world. Michael Pollan concludes that our collective weight gain is connected to our overindulgence in certain foods, like processed corn, that are difficult for our bodies to process.

Where does most of the blame rest? According to Pollan, blame rests mainly upon the shoulders of the farm subsidies that provide the capital for growing mountains of cheap corn. This corn eventually makes its way into the chicken nuggets you had for lunch or the root beer you're drinking while reading this book. This processed corn is difficult, if not impossible, for your body to process, thereby increasing the chances that you will gain weight. Pollan adds that such a problem with corn is nothing new in the United States. In the late 1800s, Americans struggled with consumption of corn alco-

hol, drinking five times more than we do today.

Obesity is a major health concern in this country, and it's easy to frame the arguments as to why Americans are fatter today than we've ever been. Our lifestyle of watching TV and paying people to do our yard work means we are more sedentary than previous generations. We also spend more at restaurants than past generations, and when we do cook, often it includes boxed processed foods. Generally, both of these options involve lots of calories that increase the likelihood of being fat. Despite our ever-expanding waistlines and health-related problems, people in the United States are living longer.

This is not just true in the United States, but all over the world. In fact, the world's elderly population is increasing by approximately 800,000 people per month.[2] The rising number of elderly people brings a new dilemma: How do we support and take care of our aging population? What does the growing elderly population mean to society as a whole? Although health care has improved, can it overcome these mountains of fat?

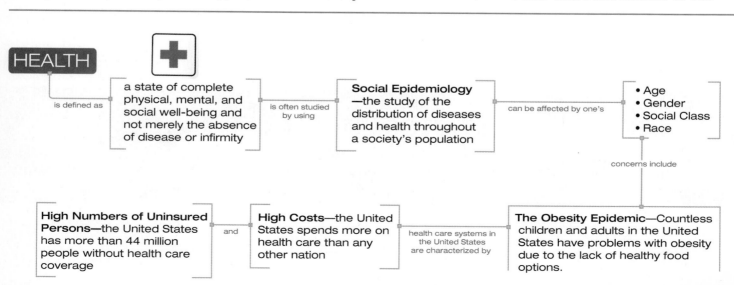

get the topic: HOW DO HEALTH AND AGING AFFECT STRATIFICATION?

Health Defined

When you are asked about your health, your response is likely to explain how you're feeling physically. However, there's more to health and being "healthy" than whether or not you're battling a cold or nursing a fever. According to the World Health Organization, **health** is "a state of complete physical, mental, and social well-being and not merely the absence of disease or infirmity."[3] In other words, several social factors determine one's health.

> **OBESITY** is an unhealthy accumulation of body fat.
>
> **HEALTH** is a state of complete physical, mental, and social well-being and not merely the absence of disease or infirmity.
>
> **SOCIAL EPIDEMIOLOGY** is the study of the distribution of diseases and health throughout a society's population.

SOCIAL EPIDEMIOLOGY

In the 2007 movie *The Bucket List*, Morgan Freeman and Jack Nicholson play two elderly, terminally ill patients who jet off to exotic places to fulfill their lifelong goals. The movie entertains while teaching about patterns of health in the United States. For example, Freeman's character is a lower-middle-class African American man, and Nicholson's character is an upper-class white owner of several hospitals. Nicholson gets the best care possible, while the doctors and nurses often ignore Freeman. Age, gender, social class, and race all have an effect on health care in the United States, and many researchers are interested in finding out why.

Social epidemiology is the study of the distribution of diseases and health throughout a society's population. Social epidemiologists want to find a link between health and the social environment. How does one's age affect his or her health? Are there health differences between the genders? Are race and social class connected to the treatment a patient receives? These are all questions that social epidemiologists seek to answer.

Age and Health

In the United States—unlike other parts of the world, particularly developing countries—death is rare among the young. The U.S. infant mortality rate is at a low point; only 6.9 infants are expected to die per 1,000 births.[4] For the most part, children and young adults are generally healthy. In 2005, only six percent of adults aged 18–44 rated their health as fair or poor, while 30 percent of adults over 75

years old believed their health to be poor.[5] With this in mind, it's no surprise that as people age, they experience more and more serious health problems. Chronic conditions such as arthritis, diabetes, heart disease, lung disease, and mental illness are major problems for older people. These conditions limit their activities, meaning that work, socializing, and exercise are often limited or become impossible to pursue.

Gender and Health

You've probably heard that older men die before older women virtually everywhere in the world.[6] In the United States, women are expected to live an average of 80.4 years, while men live only 75.2 years.[7] Sociologists attribute many factors to this trend. For example, men have higher testosterone levels than women, which may make men more likely to abuse alcohol and tobacco, drive aggressively, and engage in other life-threatening behaviors. Men also choose riskier types of work and become involved in wartime aggression, which are connected to men's decreased life expectancy. Studies also show that women are less likely to experience life-threatening illnesses and health problems than men are.[8]

Men and women differ in their desire for health care. Women are twice as likely to get preventive care and have regular checkups,[9] while men are less likely to discuss health issues with their doctors.[10]

Despite this discrepancy in doctor visits, most past research was centered on middle-class white men. However, recent studies show that some treatments are more effective for different races, like an AIDS drug that was tested in 1991. The study initially said the drug would help everyone, but the studied cohort was mostly gay white men. Further

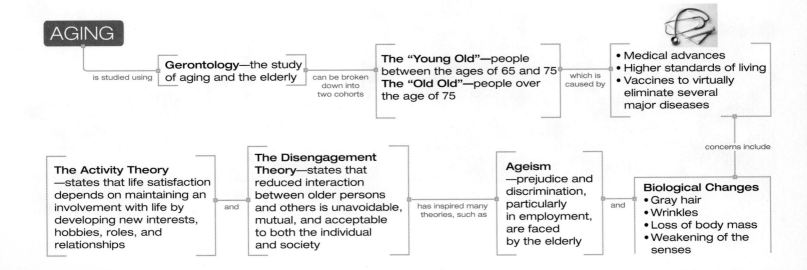

studies indicated that the drug worked better for white men than black men. Today, studies include women and minorities in testing, which could positively impact their health.[11]

Social Class and Health

In 2005, a team of *New York Times* reporters published a series of articles based on their year of exploring ways that social class influences a person's destiny.[12] The article "Life at the Top in America Isn't Just Better, It's Longer" followed three New York City residents—Mr. Miele, Mr. Wilson, and Ms. Gora—from different social classes—the upper middle class, the middle class, and the working class.[13] Although each of the three residents experienced a heart attack around the same time, each had very different outcomes. Mr. Miele, who was with friends at the time of his attack, was rushed to the hospital of his choice in an ambulance. Minutes after his arrival, a doctor assessed his condition and Mr. Miele was quickly given the treatment he needed. In another part of town, Mr. Wilson was also taken to a hospital in an ambulance, but his hospital was not able to perform the surgery he needed. After suffering through a painful night, Mr. Wilson was taken to a different facility that could treat his condition. Ms. Gora had to be persuaded to let an ambulance take her to a city-run hospital, known for its busy emergency room. She had to wait for two hours to see a doctor. In the end, Ms. Gora was finally released without ever receiving the angiogram treatment that she needed.[14] Based on these stories, can you figure out to which social classes Mr. Miele, Mr. Wilson, and Ms. Gora belong?

Sociologists believe that one's social class has a direct effect on his or her health, particularly in the United States, where health care availability is connected to your ability to pay for it. Studies show that a higher socioeconomic status leads to longer, healthier, and happier lives. When asked to rate their health, only 23.4 percent of people with an income of $20,000 or less reported excellent health compared to 46.3 percent of people making $55,000 or more.[15]

Sociologist Jason Schnittker argues that income improves health because more money means that affordable health care and basic needs are met.[16]

Neighborhoods

Neighborhoods can also have an effect on health. Neighborhoods that house poor, poorly educated, unemployed, and single mothers with little government assistance adversely affect the health of the people living there.[17] Similarly, people living in neighborhoods with high crime and drug use also report poor health.[18] These threatening environments can lead to stress, which can in turn lead to more serious health problems.

This raises the issue of environmental justice. Remember, environmental justice studies the impact of environmental factors on social classes. The poor often live in environmentally dangerous areas[19] that experience regular interaction with toxins, unclean water, and/or air.[20] For example, there is a high rate of minority children who suffer from asthma and other breathing problems as a direct result of air pollution in their Bronx and upper Manhattan neighborhoods.[21]

Race and Health

In 2005, the life expectancy of whites was 78.3 years, while African Americans were expected to live only 73.2 years.[22] Social class plays a role in explaining why whites are living longer. In the United States, 24.9 percent of African Americans and 21.8 percent of Hispanics live

---

∨
∨   Look at these two neighborhoods.
∨   **How might each one affect the health of its residents?**

Comparison: Poor Neighborhoods vs. Rich Neighborhoods

Image of Crime-infestation and Danger

Dilapidated Houses

Dirty, Littered Streets

Image of Safety and Security

Immaculate Houses

Clean Streets

below the poverty level, while only 8.3 percent of whites are impoverished.[23] Remember, people who have low incomes and live in disadvantaged neighborhoods are at an increased risk of having health problems.[24] African Americans and Hispanics are more likely to live in areas with factors that can lead to poor health.

Minorities also have higher rates of infant mortality. In a study by Thind et al., non-whites living in Newark, New Jersey, were found to have more babies with low birth weight, which increases the risk of infant mortality, than white women.[25] Possible factors contributing to this included drug and alcohol abuse, smoking, and not receiving the care they needed during pregnancy. In an effort to help the women in these poorer communities, the government created programs like Healthy Start. Infant mortality rates are down, but the mothers still live in communities that put their children at risk.[26]

The Medicalization of American Society

One way to consider the sociology of health is to look at how health and health care influence people's lives. Talcott Parsons believed that sickness can become a social role.[27] A **sick role** is the expected behaviors and responsibilities appropriate for someone who is ill. For example, part of an ill person's role is to go to the doctor in an attempt to get rid of the illness. Physicians have a primary position in society, allowing them to label sickness and health, which gives them great power over those with whom they come into contact.

This has led to what many consider the **medicalization** of American society, or the idea that the medical community is the center of many aspects of American society.[28] Americans tend to believe that we can find the right pill for anything. I attended a funeral where the widow was quite distraught, saying, "He was my whole life." Her son, a medical professional, gave her an antidepressant. Our society believes that if you take a pill, all will be okay.

One of my favorite books is *The Myth of Mental Illness* by Thomas Szasz.[29] Dr. Szasz suggests that mental illness is not really a disease at all. In fact, the diagnosis of mental illness is often used as a means of social control.[30] Paula Caplan argues that the *Diagnostic and Statistical Manual of the American Psychiatric Association*, used for the diagnosis of all mental illness, relies on personal ideology and political maneuvering.[31] In the course of ten years, the committee added

more than 70 "new" mental illnesses. In fact, according to the DSM, many women are "mentally ill" for one week a month when they menstruate.[32]

America has many issues associated with the medicalization of our society. Keeping this in mind, let's look in depth at the epidemic of obesity.

Health in the United States: Living Off the Fat of the Land

With employment, health care, and food often only a phone call or a keystroke away, the United States should be a country of healthy citizens. However, all affluent nations face a host of health concerns, including obesity. Although it's a relatively new phenomenon, the United States is in the grips of what some are calling an obesity epidemic.

Food options in the United States run the gamut from healthy (organic arugula) to unhealthy (bacon cheddar cheeseburgers). Many U.S. consumers, including myself, prefer the latter. Shopping for healthier food takes more time, effort, and money. Fast food is convenient and inexpensive, making it hugely popular, despite being unhealthy.

∧
∧ **Why is fast food so cheap,** and healthy
∧ food so expensive?

CHILDHOOD OBESITY

A 2006 study determined that the increase in childhood obesity was a direct result of the availability of energy-dense foods and drinks combined with a lack of energy expenditure.[33] That is, children are getting bigger because they are taking in more calories than they are burning. Kids today face many challenges in keeping their weight down that didn't necessarily exist before, including:

- School lunches tend to offer high-calorie foods and drinks, lacking healthier options. There are federal regulations about the nutrition content of food served in schools, but a clear standardization has not been achieved.[34]

- Dual-income and single-parent families create the need for children to eat packaged, prepared meals, which are typically unhealthy. These busy working parents are more likely to rely on carryout to feed their families. A lack of supervision also makes it difficult to monitor how much their children eat.[35]
- Television, computers, and video games are many children's primary modes of entertainment, creating sedentary behavior. This has led to a decrease in active, outdoor play.[36]

STIGMATIZATION OF THE OBESE

Another consequence of childhood obesity is that overweight children are often targets of scorn and ridicule among their peers. Numerous studies have shown that people hold prejudicial attitudes about the obese. These perceptions can cause discrimination against an obese person. This loss of status could have harmful psychological, economic, and physical consequences.[37]

Sociologists Deborah Carr and Michael Friedman performed a study to determine if obesity is in fact a stigma. The factor that separates a stigma from a prejudice is the attitude of the group in question toward their treatment. They found that obese individuals believed that other members of society treated them unfairly, which contributed to their poor self-esteem and lack of psychological well-being. Carr and Friedman found that obese professional workers were 2.5 times more likely to report work-related discrimination than their thinner counterparts.[38]

OBESITY AND RACE

Research has shown that African Americans have a substantially higher rate of obesity than whites. But does this mean certain races are more likely to be obese? We know that race is a social construct and not a biological trait. So what contributes to this statistic? One study by Boardman et al. found that socioeconomic status plays a major role in the relationship between race and obesity. According to this study, black communities are almost four times as likely as white communities to have obesity rates greater than 25 percent. However, when comparing black and white communities in more affluent areas, this relative risk drops. The comparison is even more tenuous when you compare black and white communities in poor areas.[39] So essentially, it would appear that level of affluence, not race, is a determinant of obesity.

Why are the poor more likely to be obese? Michael Pollan points to the high cost of healthier food options. Unhealthy, inexpensive foods are often necessary for those who cannot afford healthier food options. Also, a lack of education about nutrition can lead people to make uninformed choices about what they eat. Add that to a floundering health care system, and you have the recipe for an obesity problem.

MAKE CONNECTIONS

Is Keeping Kids Safe Hurting their Health?

We know that unhealthy foods, inactivity, and lack of parental control are contributing factors to childhood obesity, but location also plays a big part in packing on the pounds. In an article about contributing factors to childhood obesity, Arielle Concilio et al. assert that where a child grows up is a crucial factor in the child's health. The article explains that children growing up in poor, urban communities like the Bronx are more likely to suffer from obesity than kids in suburban areas. Their reasoning? It's too dangerous for kids to go outside and play.[40]

These kids are growing up in an area where fast food is cheaper than healthy food, and their parents might be working long hours. Add to this the facts that they live in neighborhoods where space is tight and outdoor areas available aren't safe places to play. To stay safe, kids look for indoor activities, which tend to be more sedentary. Schools may be too poor to afford physical education equipment for students, meaning that students have to find other ways to entertain themselves, and activities at home are equally limited.[41]

>>> **ACTIVITY** Do some research on youth centers where kids can go after school. What kinds of activities are available? Would these activities help or hinder a child with weight issues?

>>> **How can kids get the exercise they need** when it's too dangerous to go outside and play?

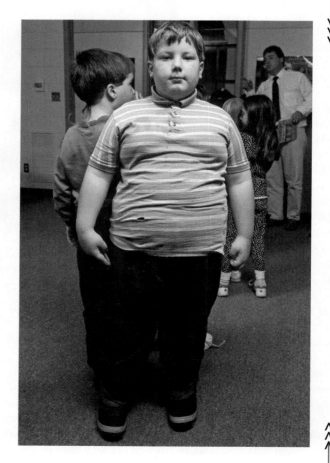

Health Care

There are many other issues in the sociology of heath other than obesity. One important issue is to consider health care. It seems that during every election cycle, **health care**—care, services, or supplies related to a person's health—is always one of the major issues. According to a recent study, only 40 percent of Americans are satisfied with their health care system.[42] A common and legitimate complaint is cost. The United States has the most expensive health care system in the world, per person, and yet not everyone has health insurance. There is no national health insurance available to cover all children and the millions of adults who can't afford to buy their own. With fewer employers offering insurance and private insurance premiums continuing to surge, over 15 percent of the U.S. population has been pushed out of health coverage.[43]

THE UNINSURED

Recently, I saw a jar with a photograph of a sick child on it. The child needed a liver transplant, but his parents had no insurance. They were trying to collect the $180,000 they needed by putting donation jars around town. An elderly local sports hero had recently just gotten a liver transplant. I couldn't help but think how strange it was: An elderly man—whose lifetime of drinking had damaged his liver—got a chance to live because he made money, while a child might die because his parents couldn't afford the surgery.

In 2005, nearly 45 million people in the United States were uninsured.[44] Of those 45 million people, more than 34 million were under the age of 44.[45] Many of these people either didn't make enough income to pay for insurance or had parents who didn't make enough. **In the United States, the uninsured "are sicker, receive inferior care, and are more likely to die prematurely."[46]**

COSTS OF SERVICES

In 1960, the United States spent $28 billion on health care. In 2007, the country spent $2.3 trillion on health care—more than any other nation in the world. By 2016, this figure is expected to double.[47] Why does the United States spend so much more than other countries? It's mainly due to the rising costs of medical technology and prescription drugs, the high numbers of people who are uninsured, and the aging of the population. The health care problem does not have an easy solution, but many people believe that universal health care could be the answer.

The U.S. government has historically rejected plans for universal health care unless they apply to senior citizens. Why the constant rejection? According to sociologist Jill Quadagno, three reasons explain this practice:

1. The Constitution states that the power of the state must be limited. Providing national health care is viewed as a form of welfare, which threatens our freedom.[48]

2. The working class and labor unions fail to support legislation that would provide universal health care.[49]

3. Private health insurance companies strongly oppose the idea of national health care.[50]

Although many of the U.S. health care companies are private firms that are provided through a person's employer or medical union, there are some public forms of health care.[51] Medicare and Medicaid, which we'll discuss later, provide the elderly, veterans, poor, and disabled with insurance.

HEALTH CARE—AN INTERNATIONAL COMPARISON

According to the American Medical Association, people without health insurance "tend to live sicker and die younger than people with health insurance."[52] With the high numbers of uninsured persons in the United States, this trend is true for a lot of the nation's population, and many question the fairness of the U.S. system.

In 2000, the World Health Organization (WHO) released a report that identified five characteristics that a good and fair health system should have. According to WHO, a good and fair health system has:

- overall good health (low infant mortality rates and high life expectancy)
- a fair distribution of good health (low infant mortality and high life expectancy across the entire population)
- a high level of overall responsiveness
- a fair distribution of responsiveness
- a fair distribution of financing health care (the health care costs are evenly distributed based on a person's ability to pay).[53]

After creating a list of criteria, **WHO compared the health systems of 191 of the world's countries. The United States was first in overall responsiveness,** meaning that our health care system does an excellent job in responding to the desires of consumers. **However, other variables present a different story.**

The world map on page 216 shows the per capita costs, life expectancy, and infant mortality of selected countries around the globe. Those selected are nations similar to the United States in that they are wealthy, industrialized, capitalist democracies.

The U.S. health care system ranks rather low compared to other wealthy democracies around the world. The United States is the only one of these countries that doesn't provide some form of universal government health care. So, it scores lower than other wealthy countries in fairness in financing and people's satisfaction with the health care system. The United States ranks 37th, leaving many policymakers wondering what can be done to improve the system.[54] One possibility could be extending the Medicare program.

A Global Look at Health Care Systems in 2005

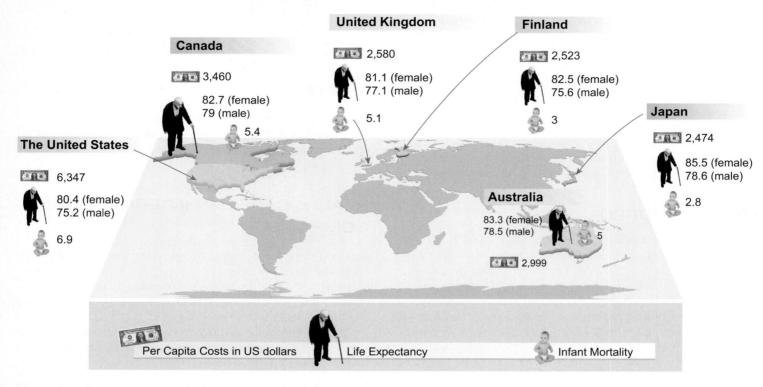

Canada
3,460
82.7 (female)
79 (male)
5.4

United Kingdom
2,580
81.1 (female)
77.1 (male)
5.1

Finland
2,523
82.5 (female)
75.6 (male)
3

Japan
2,474
85.5 (female)
78.6 (male)
2.8

The United States
6,347
80.4 (female)
75.2 (male)
6.9

Australia
83.3 (female)
78.5 (male)
5
2,999

Per Capita Costs in US dollars | Life Expectancy | Infant Mortality

Source: Data from Organization for Economic Co-operation and Development (OECD) StatExtracts, "Health Statistics."

HEALTH CARE AND THE ELDERLY— MEDICARE

Most of the U.S. elderly population has access to **Medicare**, a government-run social insurance program that provides health coverage for people 65 or older. Those who never worked and are poor are eligible for **Medicaid**, a form of government health insurance designed for the poor and disabled. People ages 65 or over qualify for coverage if they are U.S. citizens or have been legal residents for five continuous years.[55] The program covers hospital stays, skilled nursing facilities, doctor visits, and outpatient hospital services, or allows people the option of receiving their benefits through private insurance plans. There is also assistance to pay for prescription drugs, which helps seniors on tight budgets get the health care they need.

However, even with these added benefits, Medicare's cost increases as the elderly population is growing. This phenomenon is known as "the graying of the United States." The elderly now account for 13 percent of the population, and they're expected to account for 20 percent by the year 2030. With more people using Medicare, more money is required to finance the program.

The rising elderly population does not just affect health care, but also society as a whole. With people living longer than ever, we have to understand the aging process and figure out what impact aging has on the individual.

Aging: The Graying of the United States

The population of the United States has experienced a long trend of "graying" from 1900 to the present. Persons aged 65 and older

comprised about 4 percent of the population in the year 1900; in 2002, it was over 12 percent.[56] As baby boomers go into retirement, these numbers are going to skyrocket. The Census Bureau estimates that by 2050, persons over the age of 65 will comprise more than 20 percent of the total population.[57]

AGING AND DEMOGRAPHIC CHANGE IN THE UNITED STATES

Concerns about the increasing percentage of elderly people in society have drawn the attention of psychologists, medical professionals, and sociologists. The study of aging and the elderly is officially known as **gerontology**. This field of study is critically important to our future.

The elderly have been broken down into two major cohorts; the "young old" and the "old old." The **"young old"** cohort consists of people between the ages of 65 and 75, while the **"old old"** refers to those over the age of 75. The "young old" are generally in good health, live alone, and are financially independent. The "old old" tend to have failing health, live with family or in a retirement home, and rely on others for financial support. Approximately 53 percent of the elderly population fall into the "young old" category. However, living past the age of 75 is not uncommon.

Life Expectancy

Medical advances and higher standards of living dramatically increase life expectancy. At the beginning of the twentieth century, the average life expectancy was 47.3 years. In 2007, life expectancy for men reached 75.2 years while women's life expectancy was 80.4 years.[58] The development of vaccines for many infectious diseases, such as measles, diphtheria, and smallpox, virtually eliminated these diseases, allowing many more people to live longer, healthier lives.

Origins of the Baby Boomers

After WWII, social and economic restraints that were keeping couples from starting families were removed, leading to a "boom" in childbirths. Men who served in the war returned home, married, and started families. Generally, wages were high enough to support a family, so women stayed home and raised children. A period of economic prosperity also contributed to the "baby boom" that lasted from 1946 through 1964, resulting in approximately 78.2 million children born in less than twenty years.[59]

The decline in female fertility was the main factor that contributed to the end of the baby boom. Women who married after the war ended in 1945 were typically in their twenties, giving them approximately twenty more years of fertility. The introduction of the birth control pill in 1960 also

> With advances in medical technology and new vaccines popping up every day, **the life expectancy of these children could lengthen considerably in the future.**

MEDICARE is a government-run social insurance program that provides health coverage for people 65 or older.

MEDICAID is a form of government health insurance designed for the poor and disabled.

GERONTOLOGY is the study of aging and the elderly.

"YOUNG OLD" is a cohort that consists of people between the ages of 65 and 75.

"OLD OLD" is a cohort that consists of people over the age of 75.

"SANDWICHED" GENERATION is the generation that takes care of both its children and its elderly parents.

contributed to the slowing birth rate, as it became the most widely used contraceptive method.[60]

THE "SANDWICHED" GENERATION

The baby boomer generation is unique in that it is the first **"sandwiched" generation**—it takes care of its children and its elderly parents. Most future generations will probably also be sandwiched between their children and their parents because of longer lives and delays in childbearing. This can keep families closer together. The elderly can help their adult children in times of crisis by watching grandchildren, providing temporary housing, giving loans, and offering advice to their adult children.[61] This allows the elderly to stay involved in family life and increases overall life satisfaction.

Elderly in Japan

We often see the elderly as weak or bothersome if they need to rely on others for help. We live in a culture that values youth and self-sufficiency to the point that many of us fear growing old and losing our independence.

However, in countries like Japan, the elderly are revered because age is associated with wisdom. Respect for the Aged Day, celebrated on September 15th, has been an annual holiday in Japan since 1966. Three-generation homes, common in Japan, encourage respect for the elderly by making children feel more connected to their grandparents.[62]

With 21 percent of the population over the age of 65, Japan is the oldest society in the world. The elderly are expected to account for 40 percent of the population by 2050.[63] Like the population of the United States, the birth rate is going down and life expectancy is going up in Japan. But three-generation homes are less common as more elderly people live independently. At the same time, suicide rates among the elderly are soaring in Japan.[64]

Aside from depression, worries about finances and health care have been cited as the main causes of suicide among Japan's elderly. With less family support, elderly people are isolated and have to rely on their own incomes or pensions. Japan's declining economy and growing elderly population have made it difficult to supply them with affordable health care. Perhaps the Japanese elderly are having more of a difficult time adjusting to changes because they were raised in a culture that revered the elderly as beacons of wisdom.[65]

>>> **ACTIVITY** How do the changes in Japan reflect the trends in aging on an international level? Are similar trends appearing in the United States and other developed countries?

^^^ In what ways **could the decline of the three-generation home** in Japan **be detrimental to the elderly population?**

Gender and Aging: Where Are the Men?

If studies were done about the gender differences between elderly Japanese men and women, the focus would probably concentrate on Japanese women. According to sociologists John Knodel and Mary Beth Ofstedal, concerns about gender inequality have taken too much precedence, and the situation of elderly men is not being considered.[66] The Second World Assembly on Aging produced a report that is almost solely concerned with the situation of aging women called the "Madrid International Plan of Action." Knodel and Ofstedal were taken aback by the assembly's lack of "willingness to acknowledge that the relationship between gender and aging varies across settings and over time."[67] Although it is a noble goal to promote gender equality and empowerment of women, a one-sided view of the situation fails to actually promote gender equality. Knodel and Ofstedal suggest that research should also examine the "experiences of older men and women within the contexts in which they live."[68]

Data from the Philippines, Singapore, Taiwan, Thailand, and Vietnam suggest a relative equality of satisfaction with income for elderly men and women. Vietnam has the greatest disparity, with 52 percent of elderly men satisfied with their income, compared to 40 percent of elderly women. Thailand actually has a higher percentage of elderly women who are satisfied with their income than men, with 74 percent and 68 percent, respectively. Developing countries such as these are home to a large portion of the elderly population and provide useful data about the relative situation of elderly men and women.[69]

The study's authors feel that gender should not be placed above all other markers of disadvantage in old age. A more balanced approach that addresses the disadvantages of both elderly men and women would be better suited to aid current and future generations of the elderly.

CONCERNS ABOUT AGING

Biological Changes

Everyone knows that as you age, certain biological changes take place. Gray hair, wrinkles, and loss of body mass are all physical signs of aging. As you age, your senses also decline. Your senses of vision, hearing, taste, touch, and smell all become weaker. In fact, in 2006, more than 17 percent of people over the age of 65 reported that their vision was failing, while 11.4 percent reported having trouble hearing.[70] These percentages were higher than persons in any other age group.

Many people in our society associate aging with being weaker and less capable of doing normal, everyday activities. It's sentiments like these that can lead to prejudices and discrimination toward the elderly.

Ageism

Steve Richardson has worked as a contractor for Dynamic Solutions since the age of 25. Now that Steve is approaching his 65th birthday, his younger supervisor is pressuring him to retire. The company is offering him good retirement benefits, but he feels that they are attempting to gently push him out the door. However, Steve's work is an essential part of his life, and he has no desire to retire now. Dynamic Solutions views Steve as an outdated employee, who served his purpose when he was younger, but is of no use anymore. Although Steve Richardson and Dynamic Solutions don't actually exist, situations like this happen every day in the United States. With an aging population and workforce, the new concern of ageism has come into play. **Ageism** is prejudice and discrimination based solely on age.

The workplace is the main forum for ageism. Employers seek workers who are energetic and willing to work for a long duration. If an employer feels that someone is too old, the employer may be thinking that the prospective employee is going to be too slow on the job and is more likely to quit because he or she does not really need the job. It is technically illegal to discriminate in hiring on the basis of age, but many elderly people have difficulty finding new employment or find themselves being asked to leave their jobs. In the 2008 presidential election, many pundits cited Republican candidate John McCain's age as a negative factor. Others suggest his age is a plus due to his years of experience. At 72, McCain is the oldest person to run for a first presidential term in the history of the United States.[71]

Television and film are major sources of ageism, as entertainment tends to focus on the young and attractive. The elderly are typically shown as senile and frail or are just ignored. Aging movie stars, particularly females, have voiced their discontent at not getting roles. Aging female actresses must deal with what is known as "double jeopardy," or the two factors which contribute to the downfall of their career: gender and age.[72]

Generally in film and television, women have been on relatively equal footing with men, both in employment and compensation. However, the entertainment industry values physical attractiveness first and foremost, and seems to have little or no place for older, less attractive females. When a society values beauty and youth, the elderly are cast aside. This negative perception of growing old can lead to dissatisfaction in old age.

Biological Effects of Aging

A loss of body mass occurs

Hair thins and turns gray

Skin loses elasticity, which is associated with wrinkling

Chronic illnesses, such as arthritis, are prevalent

Aging brings along with it certain biological changes. **Gray hair, wrinkles, and liver spots are the inevitable physical markers of the aging process.**

think sociologically: WHAT THEORIES EXIST ABOUT THE AGING PROCESS?

Functionalism—Disengaging from Society

What happens to people's social roles as they reach old age? Many functionalists would suggest that elderly people begin to shed their old social roles and begin to take on new roles in society. Their roles as worker or spouse drop off as they retire or become widowed. Functionalists use the disengagement theory to describe the aging process. The **disengagement theory** states that reduced interaction between older persons and others is unavoidable, mutual, and acceptable to both the individual and society.[73]

Society disengages people from important positions as they get older so that the social system does not get disrupted. The disengagement theory suggests that the functions of retirement are to make older people less important in society since they are about to die, which, in turn, makes society function better. The older people move out of the way so that the younger population can take their place.

Social distance is provided between death and daily life. Death disrupts many social functions, and retirement decreases the chances that a vital person will be eliminated. Retirement allows for new generations with new ideas to move society forward. The young are promoted and expensive older workers are let go.

According to Cumming et al., the disengaging process is intrinsic and is desirable for most older people.[74] However, some sociologists would disagree. Some sociologists have found that elderly people who take part in activities such as vol-

unteering are "happiest and have the greatest expressed life satisfaction."[75] Symbolic interactionists, whom we will discuss next, often agree with this idea. Other critics of this theory suggest that elderly people don't often vacate their social roles willingly. Instead, they are often forced out of their positions through an exercise of power, because employers feel they're too old for the job or cannot afford to keep them on.

Symbolic Interactionism—Living an Active Lifestyle

Symbolic interactionists study how factors like environment and relationships with others affect how people experience aging. Sociologist Charles H. Cooley (1864–1929) suggested that people develop the "self" through their interactions with others in the social world. This development of self is a lifelong process, so social interactions continue to be important to us as we age. Symbolic interactionists believe that successful aging is a "multi-faceted phenomenon that encompasses not only health but also psychological well-being, role integration, and social engagement."[76] In other words, these theorists believe in the **activity theory**, which states that life satisfaction depends on maintaining an involvement with life by developing new interests, hobbies, roles, and relationships.

One way that the elderly population can remain active is through volunteer work. Sociologists Yunqing Li and Kenneth Ferraro suggest that volunteer work is beneficial for social life and gives people the opportunity to remain socially engaged throughout their entire lives.[77] Volunteering can reduce depression among the elderly population and improve life satisfaction. Why does volunteering have such a positive effect? Like any activity that involves helping others, volunteering provides the elderly with a sense of meaning and purpose in life. Interacting with others can also help the elderly cope with bereavement of a spouse or close friend and helps strengthen their relationships with others.

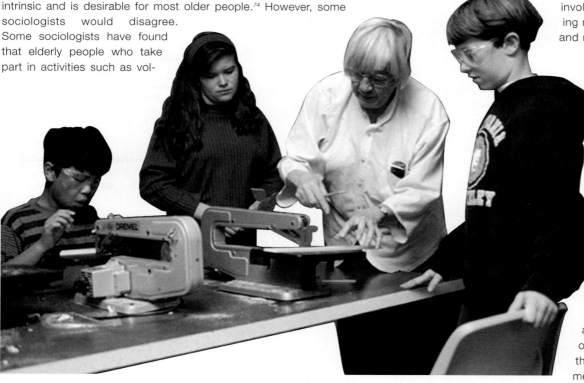

>>> **How might volunteering** at a school **help the elderly cope with the aging process?**

Conflict Theory—Aging and Inequality

Conflict theorists, unlike functionalists and symbolic interactionists, examine how power and economic forces influence aging in society. Those who accept a conflict perspective of aging might consider a number of issues. First, they note that ageism is no different than any other *ism*, like racism and sexism. By placing a negative stigma on the elderly, society segregates them from others.

If you consider retirement, for example, whose benefit does it serve? A few years ago, the college at which I teach had an early retirement buyout. Faculty members were given a bonus to retire early. Why would an organization do this? Because it was significantly cheaper to hire younger faculty at an entry-level salary than to continue to pay some who had been on campus for 25 to 30 years.

Conflict theorists might suggest age plays an important role in the formation of social policies. For example, the largest federal spending program is Social Security, accounting for 23 cents of every dollar spent

DISENGAGEMENT THEORY states that reduced interaction between older persons and others is unavoidable, mutual, and acceptable to both the individual and society.

ACTIVITY THEORY states that life satisfaction depends on maintaining an involvement with life by developing new interests, hobbies, roles, and relationships.

by the government. When you add Medicare to that number, you add 12 more cents, thus making total spending on the retired, disabled and their dependents and survivors about 35 cents of every dollar spent. Such spending has cut the poverty level for the elderly in half over the last 30 years.[78] The elderly in the United States are the only demographic group whose government benefits are tied to inflation, meaning their benefits automatically go up when the cost of living rises. They're also the only group to be guaranteed health care coverage. Now consider who votes. People over the age of 65 have the highest percentages of registered voters and the highest rate of voter turnout. Do you think these facts are related? What would a conflict theorist say?[79]

THINK SOCIOLOGICALLY

AIDS and Aging

In 2007, there were an estimated 33 million people in the world who were living with HIV/AIDS. Take a look at the graphs to the right. As you can see, a majority of these people lived in poorer regions around the world, such as sub-Saharan Africa, where an estimated 7 million people were infected, and southeast Asia, where the number was 1.7 million people.[80] Of the 33 million people, 15 million were women, and 2 million were children under the age of 15. An estimated 2 million people died from AIDS.[81]

Now look at the chart again. Interestingly, when you compare a region's number of people infected with AIDS to the region's life expectancy from birth, you can see that the data are related. Areas with high numbers of people with AIDS, such as Africa and Asia, have low life expectancies at birth. Why? As we discussed, poverty negatively affects a person's health, often because people cannot afford or do not have access to the care they require. Also recall that these regions have higher rates of infant mortality, which also contributed to low life expectancy. Also, although there is treatment available to help delay the onset of AIDS, many people in impoverished sections of Africa or Asia may not have access to this care.

Whatever the reason, the data show that areas with low life expectancies have higher numbers of people with AIDS. How would the life expectancy of an area like Africa change if information about and treatment for AIDS were more widespread?

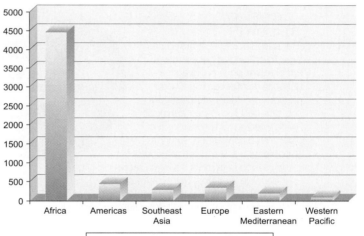

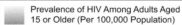

Prevalence of HIV Among Adults Aged 15 or Older (Per 100,000 Population)

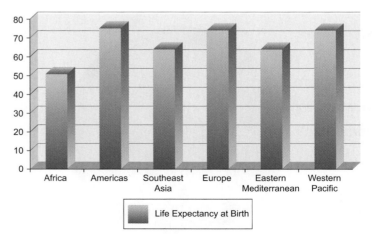

Life Expectancy at Birth

Source: World Health Organization (WHO) Statistics 2008, Part 2: Global Health Indicators.

WRAP YOUR MIND AROUND THE THEORY

Retirement is often a difficult transition for the elderly, as maintaining a sense of self-worth while not working can present a challenge.

FUNCTIONALISM

Functionalists believe that removing the elderly, whom they consider to be near death anyway, serves society well. Therefore, retirement helps both society and the elderly person disengage from jobs and other social tasks. Functionalist Elaine Cumming has written about the disengagement theory of aging. The sight of elderly people slowing down physically and approaching death disrupts the work ethic of younger people and inhibits society's ability to function. To avoid this, society gradually transfers responsibilities to younger workers, and older workers are phased out of the workplace. Society has developed Social Security and retirement programs to assist the elderly once they have left the workplace.[82]

CONFLICT THEORY

Because society is stratified by age, middle-aged people have the greatest power and access to social resources. Young people and the elderly are pushed to the side and run a greater risk of living in poverty. The elderly are perceived as washed-up, incapable workers and are removed from jobs in favor of younger, more capable workers. This type of ageism reminds one of the ideas of Karl Marx, who states that a capitalist society, with a focus on profit, has no place for less-productive workers. As the elderly become less productive, their importance to society diminishes, so they are removed from positions of importance and are largely ignored.

WHY DOES AGE STRATIFICATION EXIST?

SYMBOLIC INTERACTIONISM

The symbolic interactionist perspective on aging focuses on the life satisfaction of the elderly. The activity theory states that the elderly are more likely to have a high degree of life satisfaction if they engage in plenty of activities. When the workplace is no longer an option, it is important to replace the time and effort that was focused on work with something else. A study by Soleman Abu-Bader, Anissa Rogers, and Amanda Barusch found four core components of life satisfaction in the elderly: physical status, emotional health, social support, and locus of control. Their findings indicated that physical health was the most important indicator of overall life satisfaction in the elderly.[83]

Gray hair and wrinkles—**symbols of wisdom, or weakness?**

Maintaining a high level of activity is crucial to satisfaction at all ages, but particularly **in the elderly.**

discover sociology in action: WHAT ARE THE ADVANTAGES AND DISADVANTAGES OF THE HEALTH CARE SYSTEM IN THE UNITED STATES FOR THE ELDERLY?

Social Security and Medicare

People in the United States believe that the elderly deserve compensation for the years of hard work that they put in on the job. That's why the Social Security system is set up to take care of retired workers. The system has been a success thus far, but our population's increasing age as well as the impending retirement of the massive baby boomer generation creates concerns about our ability to assist the ones who need this help the most.

The Social Security and Medicare Board of Trustees have issued public statements about the current financial arrangement not being sufficient to sustain the Social Security and Medicare programs. Social Security estimates that by 2011, its annual surplus of tax income will begin declining. As baby boomers retire, this will rapidly grow into a deficit. Funding for Medicare is already feeling the pinch. Starting in 2008, Medicare's Hospital Insurance Fund began paying out more money than it collects in taxes and other dedicated revenues, and it expects health care costs to continue to rise faster than the income of

workers. If drastic reforms are not made, these programs may have difficulty in providing aid to the retired workers of the future.[84]

Economists Laurence J. Kotlikoff and Scott Burns warned about this generational conflict in 2003 in their book *The Coming Generational Storm: What You Need to Know About America's Economic Future*. They argued that while most U.S. citizens are unaware of how much taking care of the elderly is going to cost, the government has known all along. They accused the U.S. government of incompetence and deception when it comes to fixing these programs and informing the people of the problems.

"The American dream is becoming prohibitively expensive. And unless we act soon, the "Greatest Generation" will be the last to leave its children and grandchildren with a better country . . . The longer we delay addressing this massive red hole, the bigger it gets . . . Unfortunately, even with the best reforms, our kids are going to get clobbered. And, as a consequence, we'll never measure up to the Greatest Generation. But unless we get our act in gear, we'll end up being known as the Worst Generation."[85]

ACTIVITIES

1. Visit a nursing home or retirement center. Talk with a few residents about aging, and listen to their perceptions about how it influences them.
2. Does your college practice ageism? Do you offer discount tuition and other offers to senior citizens who want to enroll?
3. Do you think universal health care is a right or a privilege? If you think health care is a right, then what do you think must be done to provide it to those who need it? If you think it is a privilege, then rationalize why paying for it is acceptable.
4. Go to a local convenience store, watch a local news program, and read a local paper. Did you come across any articles or information about a family whose child needs some type of operation but can't afford it? Why is this occurring? Is it a lack of health insurance or health insurance coverage?

From Classroom to Community | Volunteering at a Hospital

Juan did his community learning in a hospital. He thought volunteering in a hospital would be a valuable learning experience. So, Juan welcomed people at the front desk and helped them find their way around the building.

"As I walked the hospital halls, I noticed that the rooms were primarily filled with the elderly and many of them seemed to have long-term problems related to their age.

"One day, I was asked to escort a patient's family up to his room. The patient was in his eighties and his brother, also elderly, needed my help finding his way through the maze that was the hospital. When we got to the room, we discovered that the patient was in cardiac arrest. A nurse ushered us to a waiting room to wait. Sadly, the patient died.

"A doctor walked somberly walked toward us and informed us the patient had died. Understandably,

his brother was really upset, but said something to me that I'll never forget. He said, 'When you're young, you think about dying as something far off. When you get this old, you really know that every day could be the last, and you have to learn to live with it.'"

HOW **DO HEALTH AND AGE AFFECT STRATIFICATION?**　211

race, age, social class, and gender affects health; example: people from higher social classes have better access to health care compared with members of society's lower class, so they generally have better health

WHAT **THEORIES EXIST ABOUT THE AGING PROCESS?**　220

functionalism: as people grow older, they reduce their interactions with others—a practice that is unavoidable, mutual, and acceptable to the individual and society
conflict theory: society places a negative stigma on the elderly, which segregates them from others
symbolic interactionism: successful aging encompasses health, psychological well-being, role integration, and social engagement

WHAT **ARE THE ADVANTAGES AND DISADVANTAGES OF THE HEALTH CARE SYSTEM IN THE UNITED STATES FOR THE ELDERLY?**　223

advantages: the health care system compensates the elderly for the years of hard work they put on the job; it gives retired persons access to good and reliable health care
disadvantages: the growing elderly population means that costs for health care will continue to rise, and current resources may not last long enough to provide health care for future elderly populations

get the topic: HOW DO HEALTH AND AGING AFFECT STRATIFICATION?

Health Defined　211
Health in the United States: Living Off the Fat of
　the Land　213
Health Care　215

Aging: The Graying of the United States　216
Functionalism—Disengaging from Society　220
Symbolic Interactionism—Living an Active
　Lifestyle　220

Conflict Theory—Aging and Inequality　221
Social Security and Medicare　223

Theory

FUNCTIONALISM　220

- as people age, they shed old social roles and take on new roles
- seeing the elderly slow down and approach death inhibits society's ability to function at full capacity
- retirement makes older people less important because they are close to death
- new generation moves forward

CONFLICT THEORY　221

- middle-aged people have the most power

- as the elderly become less productive, their importance in society diminishes
- the elderly are not respected and ageism occurs

SYMBOLIC INTERACTIONISM　220

- Cooley suggests that people develop the "self" through interaction
- life improves by developing new activities, hobbies, roles, and relationships
- volunteer work is socially engaging and gives a sense of purpose in life

Key Terms

obesity is an unhealthy accumulation of body fat. *210*

health is a state of complete physical, mental, and social well-being and not merely the absence of disease or infirmity. *211*

social epidemiology is the study of the distribution of diseases and health throughout a society's population. *211*

sick role is the expected behaviors and responsibilities appropriate for someone who is ill. *213*

medicalization is the idea that the medical community is the center of many aspects of American society. *213*

health care is the care, services, or supplies related to a person's health. *215*

Medicare is a government-run social insurance program that provides health coverage for people 65 or older. *216*

Medicaid is a form of government health insurance designed for the poor and disabled. *216*

gerontology is the study of aging and the elderly. *216*

"young old" is a cohort that consists of people between the ages of 65 and 75. *216*

"old old" is a cohort that consists of people over the age of 75. *216*

"sandwiched" generation is the generation that takes care of both its children and its elderly parents. *217*

ageism is prejudice and discrimination based solely on age. *219*

disengagement theory states that reduced interaction between older persons and others is unavoidable, mutual, and acceptable to both the individual and society. *220*

activity theory states that life satisfaction depends on maintaining an involvement with life by developing new interests, hobbies, roles, and relationships. *220*

Sample Test Questions

These multiple-choice questions are similar to those found in the test bank that accompanies this textbook.

1. Why do older women live longer than older men?
   a. They have more testosterone.
   b. They have less testosterone.
   c. They have more estrogen.
   d. They have less estrogen.

2. Which of the following is *not* a reason that children are struggling with obesity?
   a. Dual-income homes
   b. Nutritious school lunches
   c. The price of healthy food
   d. The popularity of sedentary activities

3. Obesity is greatly affected by
   a. race.
   b. gender.
   c. social epidemiology.
   d. socioeconomic status.

4. What was the main factor that contributed to the end of the baby boom?
   a. Women entering the workforce
   b. A period of economic decline
   c. A decline in female fertility
   d. The end of WWII

5. Which is a physical characteristic of aging?
   a. Loss of body mass
   b. Heightened senses
   c. A hunched back
   d. Senility

ANSWERS: 1. b; 2. b; 3. d; 4. c; 5. a

ESSAY

1. How does social class affect health?
2. How can television perpetuate stereotypes about people who are obese?
3. Why does the U.S. government reject universal health care plans?
4. Why has life expectancy increased?
5. How do the United States and Japan differ in their perspectives on the elderly?

WHERE TO START YOUR RESEARCH PAPER

To learn more about the elderly population around the world, go to http://www.census.gov/prod/2001pubs/p95-01-1.pdf

To learn more about health in the United States, go to http://www.cdc.gov/nchs/data/hus/hus07.pdf

To learn more about minority health concerns and disparities, go to http://www.cdc.gov/omhd/default.htm

To learn more about obesity, go to http://www.naafaonline.com/dev2/ or http://www.obesity.org/

To learn more about baby boomers and their concerns, go to http://babyboomertime.com/index.html

Remember to check www.thethinkspot.com **for additional information, downloadable flashcards, and other helpful resources.**

CRIME AND THE LEGAL SYSTEM

"A criminal

justice system is a mirror in which a whole society can see the darker outlines of its face. Our ideas of justice and evil take on visible form in it, and thus we see ourselves in deep relief. Step through this looking glass to view the American criminal justice system—and ultimately the whole society it reflects—from a radically different angle of vision.

"In particular, entertain the idea that the goal of our criminal justice system is not to eliminate crime or to achieve justice, but to project to the American public a visible image of the threat of crime as a threat from the poor.

"In the last 40 years, crime rates have gone up and down, although mostly up until the 1990s. When crime rates increase, politicians never take responsibility for it. They play to voters' fears by advocating "law and order" or the many varieties of "getting tough on crime" . . . . The plain fact is that virtually no student of the crime problem believes we can arrest and imprison our way out of the crime problem.

"So while politicians claim credit for the recent declines in crime, the real story appears to be this: The enormous growth in our prison population over the last decade, coupled with questionable police tactics, may have contributed in some measure to the decline, but most of the decline can be attributed to factors beyond the criminal justice system: the reduction in unemployment, the stabilization of the drug trade, and the decline in the popularity of crack cocaine.

"In my view, it also comes as no surprise that our prisons and jails predominantly confine the poor. This is not because these are the individuals who most threaten us. It is because the criminal justice system effectively weeds out the well-to-do, so that at the end of the road in prison, the vast majority of those we find there come from the lower classes . . . . This means that the criminal justice system functions from start to finish in a way that makes certain that "the offender at the end of the road in prison is likely to be member of the lowest social and economic groups in the country."

"For the same criminal behavior, the poor are more likely to be arrested; if arrested, they are more likely to be charged; if charged, more likely to be convicted; if convicted, more likely to be sentenced to prison; and if sentenced, more likely to be given longer prison terms than members of the middle and upper classes."[1]

How Do Societies Respond *to* Crime and Deviance?

CHAPTER 13

Jeffrey Reiman's book *The Rich Get Richer and the Poor Get Prison: Ideology, Class, and Criminal Justice* provides an excellent treatise on the criminal justice system in the United States.

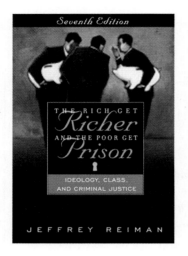

At an earlier time in my career, I had an extended practicum in a prison and noticed many of the same things Reiman mentions: most of the offenders in our overcrowded prisons were poor and did not receive enough help to change their circumstances. Where I worked, we always had three times more applicants than spaces available for treatment programs like counseling. To make matters worse, the sheer number of inmates sapped program resources. I worked in a prison designed to house one inmate per cell, yet, within five years, three or more inmates were packed into one cell. What is the reality of crime in the United States? What are the consequences of crime? What can be done about it? In this chapter, we will investigate these and other questions so we can adequately address these issues.

get the topic: WHAT IS CRIME?

Deviance vs. Crime

Most prisoners are incarcerated because they've broken a law. But how do we determine which behaviors are criminal? **Deviance** is the violation of norms that a society agrees upon. For example, teens who dye their hair in neon colors would be considered deviant in most parts of society. However, some acts that may be considered socially deviant, like refusing to bathe, for instance, aren't necessarily illegal, no matter how much you might wish they were. For something to be considered a **crime**, it has to be a violation of norms that have been written into law. Going above the speed limit is an example of a crime. Sociologists who specialize in **criminology** scientifically study crime, deviance, and social policies that the criminal justice system applies.

Everyday Crime and Deviance

Crime · Speeding · Stealing a Car · Cheating on a Test · Deviance

Crime and the Legal System

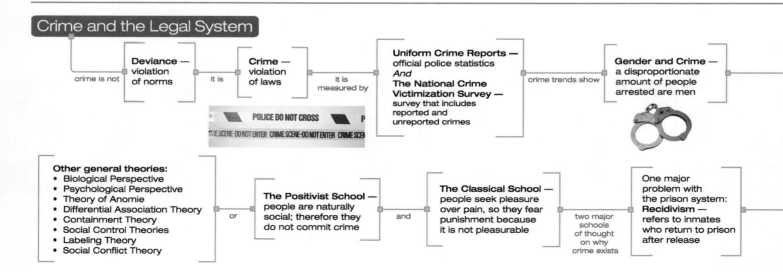

crime is not → **Deviance —** violation of norms → it is → **Crime —** violation of laws → it is measured by → **Uniform Crime Reports —** official police statistics *And* **The National Crime Victimization Survey —** survey that includes reported and unreported crimes → crime trends show → **Gender and Crime —** a disproportionate amount of people arrested are men

POLICE DO NOT CROSS — CRIME SCENE-DO NOT ENTER CRIME SCENE-DO NOT ENTER CRIME SCEN

Other general theories:
• Biological Perspective
• Psychological Perspective
• Theory of Anomie
• Differential Association Theory
• Containment Theory
• Social Control Theories
• Labeling Theory
• Social Conflict Theory

or → **The Positivist School —** people are naturally social; therefore they do not commit crime → and → **The Classical School —** people seek pleasure over pain, so they fear punishment because it is not pleasurable → two major schools of thought on why crime exists → One major problem with the prison system: **Recidivism —** refers to inmates who return to prison after release

WHAT IS DEVIANCE?

If deviance refers to violating socially agreed upon norms, then how do we determine what is and what isn't considered deviant? There are four specific characteristics that sociologists use to define deviance:

1 **Deviance is linked to time.** History changes the definition of deviance, so what is considered deviant today may not be deviant tomorrow. One hundred years ago, it was considered deviant for women to wear trousers. Today, it's normal for women to dress in trousers.

2 **Deviance is linked to cultural values.** How we label an issue determines our moral point of view. Cultural values come from religious, political, economic, or philosophical principles. For example, in Holland, active euthanasia for the terminally ill, or "mercy killing," is legal within some circumstances. In the United States, euthanasia is considered murder and is punished accordingly. Each culture defines euthanasia differently.

> **DEVIANCE** is the violation of norms that a society agrees upon.
>
> **CRIME** is the violation of norms that have been written into law.
>
> **CRIMINOLOGY** is the scientific study of crime, deviance, and social policies that the criminal justice system applies.
>
> **STREET CRIME** refers to many different types of criminal acts, such as burglary, rape, and assault.

3 **Deviance is a cultural universal.** You can find deviants in every culture on the planet. Regardless of what norms a society establishes, you can always find a small number of nonconformists who will break those rules.

4 **Deviance is a social construct.** Each society views actions differently. If society tolerates a behavior, it is no longer deviant. For example, Prohibition in the 1920s and early 30s made drinking alcohol illegal in the United States, but today it's normal.

MAKE CONNECTIONS

Crime and Media

Real-world police work is nothing like television crime. Most real-world crime involves public disturbances or missing property, but most news reports are about gang shootings or drug busts. The primetime shows don't exactly help either. Marcus Felson uses the phrase "the dramatic fallacy of crime" to describe how the media, both in news coverage and entertainment shows, paint an unreal picture of the reality of crime.[2]

Most officers never shoot their guns. They spend the majority of their time doing tedious tasks such as "driving around a lot, asking people to quiet down, hearing complaints about barking dogs, filling out paperwork, meeting with other police officers, and waiting to be called up in court."[3]

Most crime is actually rather boring and petty, like a teenager getting drunk and stealing money to buy more alcohol. Since that's not much of a story to broadcast,

the media producers prefer something more sensational.

>>> **ACTIVITY** Spend two or three nights watching different police shows and local newscasts. Record the different types of crimes being described. Then check out the police blotter in your local paper to see what type of crimes are being committed. What differences do you see?

Street Crime

Although there are many different types of crime, when most people talk about "crime," they're likely talking about **street crime**, which refers to many different types of criminal acts, such as burglary, rape, and assault. Street crime has been the focus of most criminological research, but you may wonder how much street crime actually exists. The next section will discuss street crime and how it is measured.

CRIME STATISTICS

After spending an hour watching a show like *CSI*, you'd think the police are able to solve crimes like they do on TV. Unfortunately, real life isn't as convenient as television. For example, when someone stole the tires off my car, I asked the police officer when I might get my wheels back. He said, "Probably never. These kinds of crimes are difficult to solve."

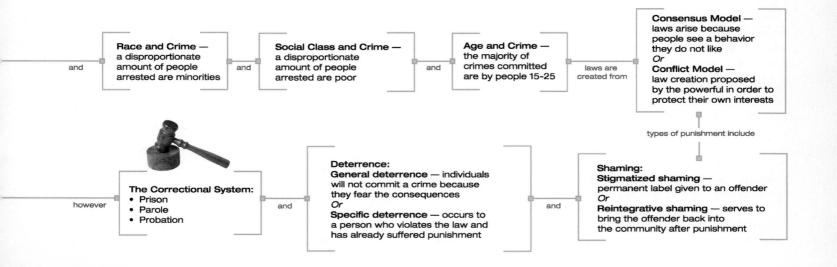

Race and Crime — a disproportionate amount of people arrested are minorities

and

Social Class and Crime — a disproportionate amount of people arrested are poor

and

Age and Crime — the majority of crimes committed are by people 15-25

laws are created from

Consensus Model — laws arise because people see a behavior they do not like
Or
Conflict Model — law creation proposed by the powerful in order to protect their own interests

types of punishment include

however

The Correctional System:
• Prison
• Parole
• Probation

and

Deterrence:
General deterrence — individuals will not commit a crime because they fear the consequences
Or
Specific deterrence — occurs to a person who violates the law and has already suffered punishment

and

Shaming:
Stigmatized shaming — permanent label given to an offender
Or
Reintegrative shaming — serves to bring the offender back into the community after punishment

UNIFORM CRIME REPORTS (UCRs) are official police statistics of reported crimes gathered from police reports and paperwork.

NATIONAL CRIME VICTIMIZATION SURVEY (NCVS) is the measurement of crime victimization based on contact with a representative sample of over 70,000 households in the United States.

CRIME INDEX is made up of eight offenses used to measure crime: homicide, rape, robbery, aggravated assault, burglary, larceny-theft, motor vehicle theft, and arson.

Uniform Crime Reports and the National Crime Victimization Survey

Another aspect of detective work often omitted from television is the paperwork that officers must file. The information in those files is vital to understand crime statistics. Criminologists use two primary sources of data to measure the amount of street crime: the UCRs and the NCVS. The Federal Bureau of Investigation (FBI) collects **Uniform Crime Reports (UCRs)**, the official police statistics of reported crimes. The **National Crime Victimization Survey (NCVS)** measures crime victimization by contacting a representative sample of over 70,000 households in the United States.

UCRs only contain data on reported crimes, so when a car is reported as stolen, it becomes a UCR statistic. This report also lists the **crime index**, which consists of eight offenses used to measure crime. These include four violent offenses: homicide, rape, robbery, and aggravated assault, as well as four property crimes: burglary, larceny-theft, motor vehicle theft, and arson.

Criminologists understand that many crimes go unreported, so they also refer to the NCVS statistics. NCVS data always account for more crime than UCR data. For example, in 2002 UCR reported fewer than 12 million offenses, whereas NCVS showed approximately 23 million crimes. This supports the criminologist's rule of thumb—about half the crimes committed go unreported.

CRIME TRENDS

UCR and NCVS data are also used to determine crime trends, and the trend that seems most constant is that the crime rates change over time. The vast majority of crime in the United States is property crime. In 2006, property crimes made up 88 percent of all reported crimes, whereas violent crimes constituted less than 12 percent.[4] These trends are in stark contrast to the media's portrayal of crime.

Gender and Crime

Throughout history, men have traditionally committed more crime than women. The demographic characteristics of street criminals in the United States have not changed much over time. In fact, 77 percent of people arrested are men.[5] This is a significant statistic because men make up less than 50 percent of the population.[6] However, several other factors also figure in crime trends.

Race and Crime

Although the gender differences in crime statistics are fairly easy to distinguish, discussing a link between race and crime is controversial. The major problem is the long history of racism in the United States. African Americans make up about 12 percent of the population, but they represent 27 percent of those arrested in the United States.[7] Does this disproportionate representation suggest African Americans commit more crimes, or does the criminal justice system unfairly pursue them?

Some argue that the police's different enforcement practices are responsible for these data. Racial profiling is a controversial police practice of targeting criminals based on their race. Cole shows that traffic police disproportionately stop people of color.[8] Jeffrey Reiman suggests that the police seek out the poor for arrest because the poor are easier to catch and easier to convict of crimes. Wealthy people can hire expensive lawyers; poor people must use the public defender system. This increases the odds that official statistics have an inherent racial bias because racial minorities disproportionately represent the poor in the United States.

Social Class and Crime

Although crime rates are higher in poorer neighborhoods, that doesn't necessarily mean people in lower classes actually commit more crime. This makes data on the link between social class and crime difficult to interpret. A number of studies have shown that poorer people are arrested at higher rates,[9] but that doesn't mean everyone who lives in poor neighborhoods breaks the law or is more likely to break the law.[10]

On the other side of the spectrum, Reiman shows that the upper classes' crimes are not prosecuted at the same rates. For example, in all 50 states, getting caught with five grams of crack cocaine can earn you up to five years in prison. However, a person would have to possess 500 grams of cocaine powder to receive the same sentence.[11] So what's the difference? People convicted of crack possession tend to be poor, while people caught with cocaine powder are usually wealthy.

Reiman believes that social class makes a huge difference in who gets caught and who goes to prison. He argues that laws are applied differently and that dangerous activities performed by the "elite" are not even considered crimes.

For example, doctors who accidentally kill a patient during an unnecessary surgery are not accused of manslaughter. Similarly, Reiman suggests that white-collar crimes are not reported because people want to avoid a scandal. Furthermore, we do not keep official records of white-collar crimes, so there is no way of knowing exactly how much of this occurs.

Age and Crime

Essentially, crime is a young person's game. This idea is supported by the relationship between age and crime. It indicates that the majority of arrests peak between the ages of 15 to 25. After that point, they follow a slow but steady decrease throughout life. Arrest data from other cultures and times in history also support this claim.[12]

The link between age and crime is very clear in criminology. According to Steffensmeier and Harer, a 60 percent decrease in crime rates in the 1980s is attributable to a decrease in the total number of 15- to 24-year-olds.[13] Clearly, age matters when discussing crime.

International Comparisons of Street Crime

In order to gain a better perspective on crime in the United States, sociologists often make international comparisons. However, making international comparisons of crime data creates certain problems for the researcher. Therefore, for this text I selected countries that are similar to the United States in a number of ways: they are all generally wealthy, and all keep good crime data. Here is a list of potentially complicating factors:

1. Crime numbers may or may not be accurate. Some countries deliberately skew their data to show lower crime rates in order to keep tourism high.
2. Legal definitions of crimes differ among nations. Some nations do not recognize marital rape as a crime; others have legalized drugs that are illegal in the United States.
3. Different methods of collecting data can result in differences in reported crimes. Some nations have extraordinarily reliable data collection systems, while others do not.
4. Cultures vary, as do programs to prevent, punish, and curb crime.

United States: Number One with a Bullet

Why does the United States have the highest murder rate in the industrialized world? Some blame easy access to guns, and others claim it's our violent history as a nation. Still others argue that it is the level of inequality in our country. Whatever the reasons, one thing is clear: U.S. citizens are three times more likely of being murdered compared to people in other developed nations.[14]

However, the graphs below present a somewhat different picture of violence with regard to international rates of rape and robbery. The countries selected are similar to the United States and give you a quick way to compare crime in the United States to that of other countries. As you can see from these data, England leads these nations in robbery, and Canada has the highest rate of rape. The United States has high rates of both crimes, but clearly is not the worst.

Property crimes present a different picture. The following graph provides data on four nonviolent crimes: theft, motor vehicle theft, drug offenses, and burglary. Generally speaking, occurrences of property crime are higher in other industrialized nations than in the United States.

These data leave a mixed picture for the international comparison of crime. Living in the United States increases the odds that one might be murdered, but it also decreases the chance of being a victim of most property crimes.[15]

Comparing international crime rates shows that crime is common to all industrial societies. Some suggest this occurs because industrial societies have more high-value, lightweight items—such as iPods or laptops—that are easily stolen and sold.[16]

International Violent Crime Rates

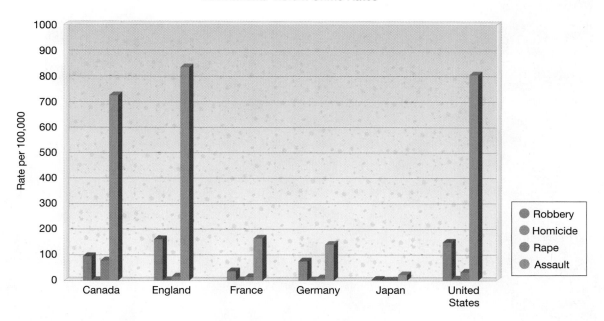

International Non-Violent Crime Rates

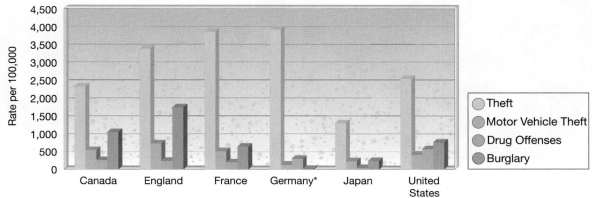

* In Germany, burglary rates are included in theft rates.

Source: *Criminal Victimization in Seventeen Industrialized Countries: Key-findings from the 2000 International Crime Victimization Survey,* Kesteren et al., 2000.

> **CONSENSUS MODEL OF LAW** suggests that laws arise because people see a behavior they do not like, and they agree to make it illegal.
>
> **CONFLICT MODEL OF LAW** proposes that powerful people write laws to protect their own interests while punishing the actions of those they wish to control.
>
> **SHAMING** is a deliberate effort to attach a negative meaning to a behavior.

SOCIETAL RESPONSES TO CRIME AND DEVIANCE

Why are certain things illegal and not others? There are two primary models as to how laws are created: the consensus and conflict models. The **consensus model of law** suggests that laws arise because people see a behavior they do not like, and they agree to make it illegal. For example, virtually everyone thinks child abuse is wrong. Laws against it arise out of a general agreement about the treatment of children.

The **conflict model of law** proposes that powerful people write laws to protect their own interests while punishing the actions of those they wish to control. Jerald Sanders, a small-time felon from Alabama, stole a $60 bicycle. Alabama has a three-strikes law, and because this was Sanders' third minor felony, he received a life sentence.[17] However, when Martha Stewart committed perjury, she received a sentence of less than two years, despite the fact that her perjury related to an amount worth several thousand dollars.[18]

Punishment

All societies must deal with rule breakers. Historically, punishments were often harsh and included physical torture, exile, forced slavery, or death. Alternative punishments included shaming an offender by placing him in the pillory and stocks in the town square.

Shaming is a deliberate effort to attach a negative meaning to a behavior. John Braithwaite suggests shame can either stigmatize or

∧
∧
∧ **Martha Stewart spent 5 months in prison.[19] With the help of an attorney, Jerald Sanders, a small-time felon from Alabama, was finally released after spending 12 years behind bars.[20]** Why is there a difference?

reintegrate.[21] **Stigmatized shame** is a permanent label given to an offender, which could actually increase the chances of reoffending because the guilty person is forever labeled. In the United States, we stigmatize former inmates when we require them to admit their prior convictions on job applications and housing forms. **Reintegrative shaming** serves to bring the offender back into the community after punishment. Justice occurs through punishments such as restitution, community service, and prison time. However, after the punishment no further stigma is placed on the offender.

The U.S. legal system relies on **deterrence**, which prevents a person from doing something because of fear of the consequences. **General deterrence** ensures individuals will not commit a crime because they see the negative consequences applied to others, and they fear experiencing these consequences. Prison is a general deterrent for many people. **Specific deterrence** occurs to individuals who have violated the law and have already been punished. When we send a criminal to prison, we hope he or she will be specifically deterred from committing future offenses because of lessons learned in prison.

STIGMATIZED SHAME is a permanent label given to an offender, which could actually increase the chances of reoffending because the guilty person is forever labeled.

REINTEGRATIVE SHAMING is an effort to bring an offender back into the community after punishment.

DETERRENCE is a measure that prevents a person from doing something because of fear of the consequences.

GENERAL DETERRENCE is a measure that ensures individuals will not commit a crime because they see the negative consequences applied to others, and they fear experiencing these consequences.

SPECIFIC DETERRENCE is a measure that changes the attitude of individuals, who have already violated the law and have been punished, by causing them never to commit crime again.

RECIDIVISM is the tendency for inmates released from prison to return to prison.

THINK SOCIOLOGICALLY

Reintegrative Justice in New Zealand

Criminal justice programs throughout the world are experimenting with the ideas of reintegrative shaming. In New Zealand, police officers use family conferencing with young offenders and their parents instead of juvenile detention. The goal is to heal the problems in the family and avoid labeling the teen. Teens return to the community as teens who have made a mistake, and not young offenders.

Although the effectiveness of this program is still being measured, a preliminary sample of police officers involved shows they strongly support the program. Using reintegrative justice philosophies in their work provides them with a sense that they are making a difference in the lives of families and youth. Furthermore, they report that this method discourages repeat offending.[22]

Corrections

The correctional system is the last leg of the criminal justice system. It supervises those who are convicted of crimes. In the last two decades, there has been a steady increase in the total number of inmates in the United States.

PRISON AND THE CHARACTERISTICS OF PRISON INMATES

Prison is a last resort in the criminal justice system. The guilty party is locked in a facility for a period of time depending on the crime. Of today's prison inmates, 64 percent belong to racial or ethnic minorities, an estimated 57 percent of inmates are under age 35, and about 21 percent are serving time for a drug offense.[23] According to the Bureau of Justice Statistics Correctional Surveys, one of every fifteen people in the United States (6.6 percent) will be incarcerated in his or her lifetime. However, the chances of going to prison are higher for certain populations.[24] As discussed earlier, 11.3 percent of men will go to prison, whereas only 1.8 percent of women will serve time, and 32 percent of black males will enter state or federal prison during their lifetime.

State and Region Incarcerations

Ever wonder why your favorite crime dramas are rarely set in Minnesota? Other than the Academy Award-winning film *Fargo*, the northern region of the United States is poorly represented in the crime genre. Meanwhile, crime films like *The Big Easy* and television shows like *The Riches, Thief*, and *K-Ville* find a southern state like Louisiana a useful backdrop for their stories.

The map on page 234 shows the incarceration rates for each state. Notice that the highest rates are in the South while the lowest rates are in the North. For example, the rate of incarceration in Minnesota is six times lower than the rate for Louisiana. Does that mean Louisiana has six times the rate of crime as Minnesota?

According to 2006 UCR data the violent crime and property crime rates for Louisiana were 698 and 3,994 per 100,000 people, respectively. Meanwhile, in Minnesota, violent crime rates were 312 and property crime rates were 3079.5 per 100,000 people. As you can see, the Minnesota rates are lower, particularly in relation to violent crimes, but not six times lower. So, why is there a discrepancy?

Some evidence shows that Southern states have higher incarceration rates because they are "tougher" on crime and assign longer sentences for offenders, whereas northern states are somewhat more lenient in sentencing. There is almost no evidence that these tougher policies actually have the desired effect.[25] Reiman suggests that as crime rates go up, politicians often use a "tough on crime" strategy to entice voters. However, this ignores the higher rates of poverty and lower educational attainment more common in the South.

Prisons in America

The Department of Corrections directs most states' prison systems. The title infers that prisons are supposed to correct the offender and assist in successful reintegration into society. Since most inmates are eventually released from prison, what will happen to them? Unfortunately, the most likely outcome for inmates released from prison is to return to prison. This is called **recidivism**. If a return to prison is a failure of the prison system,

Rate of Incarceration (per 100,000 persons)

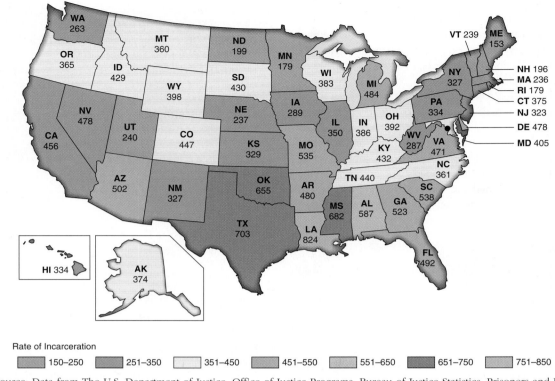

| WA 263 | | | | | | | | | VT 239 | ME 153 |
| OR 365 | ID 429 | MT 360 | ND 199 | MN 179 | WI 383 | MI 484 | NY 327 | NH 196 | MA 236 | RI 179 |

Rate of Incarceration

| 150–250 | 251–350 | 351–450 | 451–550 | 551–650 | 651–750 | 751–850 |

Map labels:
WA 263, OR 365, ID 429, MT 360, ND 199, MN 179, WI 383, MI 484, SD 430, WY 398, NV 478, UT 240, CA 456, CO 447, NE 237, IA 289, IL 350, IN 386, OH 392, PA 334, KS 329, MO 535, KY 432, WV 287, VA 471, AZ 502, NM 327, OK 655, AR 480, TN 440, NC 361, SC 538, MS 682, AL 587, GA 523, TX 703, LA 824, FL 492, HI 334, AK 374, VT 239, ME 153, NY 327, NH 196, MA 236, RI 179, CT 375, NJ 323, DE 478, MD 405

Source: Data from The U.S. Department of Justice, Office of Justice Programs, Bureau of Justice Statistics, Prisoners and Jail Inmates at Midyear 2005, Table 2: *Prisoners Under the Jurisdiction of State or Federal Correctional Authorities, June 30, 2004 to June 30, 2005.*

then clearly the system is failing. More than 50 percent of all inmates return to prison within three years of release. Over time, the recidivism rates are getting worse.[26]

What Is Prison Like?

Many of my students suggest that recidivism rates would drop if prisons were harsher. Few of these students have ever visited or been to a prison. Prisons in the United States are increasingly overcrowded and dangerous places where violence is a normal part of life. Although the homicide rate in prison is about the same as it is in free society, the frequency of rape and assault are much more common. If that weren't harsh enough, inmates have highly restricted freedoms, no privacy, and limited access to friends and family. To make matters worse, prisons in the United States continue to cut back on medical treatment and educational programs, even though the incarceration numbers continue to rise. In short, prisons are increasingly turning into human storehouses.[27]

Costs of Incarceration

The actual costs to incarcerate an individual are difficult to determine. Although all states report a dollar amount, there are "hidden" costs associated with the incarcerated—the children left behind in the foster-care system or families who must use the welfare system to survive. These social costs can't be factored in the prison budget, so the reported cost of incarceration never includes them. Nevertheless, taxpayers are left to pay for the whole broken system. Criminologists James Austin and John Irwin[28] calculated these hidden costs and determined that it actually costs $30,000 a year to incarcerate a single inmate, a number that is significantly higher than what states report. Using this estimate, Alabama taxpayers paid roughly $360,000 for the 12-year incarceration of Jerald Sanders. Remember, Mr. Sanders had no prior violent convictions, but the $60 bicycle he stole count-

<<< **Prisoners are crammed into makeshift dormitories** when overcrowding becomes an issue.

ed as his third strike.[29] Had his life sentence been enforced to the full, this amount would have been well over one million dollars.

United States Incarceration Rates vs. International Incarceration Rates

Policies like the three-strikes law have contributed to the United States' much higher incarceration rate in comparison to similar countries' rates.

In fact, the United States incarcerates at a rate six times higher than Canada and thirteen times higher than Japan. It's important to remember that, just as with crime rates, you should use caution when interpreting international data regarding prison populations. Think about what you already know about international crime and murder rates. What factors do you think contribute to the United States' role as the world's leader in crime and incarceration?

think sociologically: WHY DOES CRIME EXIST?

Historical Roots of Deviance and Crime Theories

Most crime theories arise from two philosophical schools of thought: Positivists ask why people commit crimes, and classicists ask what keeps people from committing them.

THE POSITIVIST SCHOOL

Positivists assume that people are naturally social beings and are not prone to act criminally unless some biological, psychological, or social factor is involved. To a positivist, the world is orderly and follows natural laws. And since natural law dictates that everything must have a cause, positivists are interested in what factors cause people to commit crime.

BIOLOGICAL PERSPECTIVES ON CRIME AND DEVIANCE

Physician Cesare Lombroso (1835–1905) believed that criminals could be distinguished by physical characteristics: big ears, protruding jaws, and deep-set eyes.[30] While this idea is clearly preposterous, scientists believe there might be a biological element to crime. The search for biological causes for criminality continues to this day in recent investigations, including the study of hormonal differences between men and women and how they impact criminal behavior. For example, higher testosterone levels make men more aggressive than women. Could this account for some of the difference between men and women's delinquent behaviors?[31]

Many modern-day positivists continue to seek the biological causes of crime. Some test chemical imbalances in the brain caused by genetic predisposition,[32] low blood sugar,[33] and levels of serotonin.[34] All of these factors are shown to have connections to criminal behavior, but the statistical links are often weak. The search for a biological cause for crime is far from complete and often fails to isolate social factors from genetic ones.

THE CLASSICAL SCHOOL

While positivists look for the underlying causes of criminal behavior, the classical school assumes all people are self-interested by nature. Classical thinkers also suggest that people are rational and make free will choices of how to behave. Their primary question asks what keeps us from being criminal.

The classical school emphasizes that individuals make rational choices based on pleasure/pain calculations. To a classicist, the reason most people do not commit crime is because they fear being punished. So, if the goal of the criminal justice system is to deter crime, classicists believe that the punishments must be, swift, certain, and severe enough to deter people's actions.

Cesare Beccaria's 1764 essay *On Crimes and Punishments* had a great impact on the way the western world looks at justice and crime. Beccaria argued that a legal system must treat everyone equally to protect him or her against excessive government power. In fact, many ideas contained in our Bill of Rights come from Beccaria. He believed that in order to truly deter crime, we needed a fair legal system.[35]

Another classicist, Jeremy Bentham (1748–1832), believed people were inherently *hedonistic,* seeking pleasure over pain. Being a strong supporter of the idea of deterrence, Bentham felt that people would only avoid the pleasure of crime if they feared the pain of punishment. However, the punishment must be severe enough to deter them, but not so severe as to alienate them from society. In other words, the punishment should fit the crime.[36]

Classical View

Pleasure > Pain = Crime

PSYCHOLOGICAL PERSPECTIVES ON CRIME AND DEVIANCE

The American Psychiatric Association (APA) claims that criminals suffer from an "antisocial" personality disorder that causes them to "fail to conform to social norms with respect to lawful behaviors as indicated by repeatedly performing acts that are grounds for arrest."[37] According to the APA, criminals are impulsive, aggressive, and irritable, and they tend to lie about their behaviors and feel no remorse for their actions.

Hirschi and Hindelang[38] support the idea that criminals have low IQs because the relationship between IQ and crime to official delinquency is strong. Stanton Samenow[39] proposes that criminals actually have thinking errors, including chronic lying, viewing others' property as their own, unfounded optimism, fear of injury or insult, and inflated self-image.

Psychological theories of criminality tend to be positivistic, placing the blame on something abnormal in the individual, such as a low IQ, or a thinking error. Sociological theories tend to view criminality as a social construct. Let's look at some of these theories of criminality.

Functional Explanations of Crime and Deviance

Functional theories describe crime as a response to some social factor, and theorists look for what causes crime to grow. Emile Durkheim noted that crime and deviance are needed social realities because they meet one of these three needs:

1. Crime marks the boundaries of morality. Frequently, we do not know what we like until we see something we don't like.
2. Crime promotes social solidarity because it unites people against it. People unify against a common enemy, and criminals are often a common enemy.
3. Deviance can bring about needed change in a social system.[40] Acts of civil disobedience are performed to change laws for the betterment of society.

THEORY OF ANOMIE

Robert Merton's theory of anomie—social instability caused by a wearing away of standards and ethics—questions whether social structures cause deviance. Poor individuals have limited opportunities for success. Merton suggests that Americans have common goals, including wealth, a home, career, cars, and family. Achieving these goals usually involves education, hard work, entrepreneurship, and some luck. Many in the lower classes have blocked access to these goals, so they adapt to their plight in one of five ways:

1 **Conformists** accept society's goals and use socially acceptable means to try to achieve them. They obey rules and work at low-paying jobs with little chance of advancement. One example is a janitor who works three jobs, but can't get ahead because of low pay.

2 **Innovators** accept common goals but not the means to getting them, using illegal means to achieve those goals instead. For example, a criminal might steal goods and sell them at a pawnshop instead of getting a job.

3 **Ritualists** accept the traditional means of achieving the goals, but are not as interested in the material goals. Social workers use their advanced degrees to pursue humanitarian efforts rather than monetary benefits.

4 **Retreatists** reject both the means and the goals of society. These people often live in isolation or deal with issues of drug and alcohol abuse, mental illness, or homelessness.

5 **Rebels** use their own means to create new goals, often seeking major societal changes.[41] Gandhi was a rebel who sought to change society through nonviolent methods.

Few sociologists accept Merton's theory today as it stands; however, it clearly draws a connection between social structures and crime, and it provokes more thinking about the relationships between poverty and crime. The theory is criticized for the assumption of universal goals and its inability to explain violent or white-collar crimes.

> Though the acts in which Martin Luther King, Jr., and his followers engaged were considered illegal at the time, **these "deviant" acts helped bring about much-needed change to the racist laws of the United States.**

Social Interaction Theories

Is it how we interact with people that influences our criminality? Criminals engage in social interactions that influence the likelihood of their violation of the law. Criminologists often divide such theories into social process theories and social reaction theories. Social process theories review how criminal behaviors develop, while social reaction theories examine how societal reactions affect criminal behavior.

DIFFERENTIAL ASSOCIATION THEORY

Edwin Sutherland (1883–1950) proposed the **differential association theory**, which emphasizes that criminal and deviant behavior is learned. For instance, a teen might sneak out at night to go hang out with friends. If that teen has a younger sibling, the sibling might learn that it is acceptable to sneak out and how to do so. Similarly, criminals pass on their attitudes, values, mechanisms, and beliefs about crime to others. People commit crimes because they learn that criminal activity is acceptable and/or normal. Sutherland makes this theory clear with nine propositions listed below. Clearly he is a positivist, asserting that crime must be learned from others.

Sutherland's Nine Propositions

1. Criminal behavior is learned, not inherited.
2. Criminal behavior is learned through communication.

3. The principal part of learning behavior occurs within intimate personal groups.
4. The learning includes the techniques of committing the crime and the special direction/motives, drives, rationalizations, and attitudes necessary to carry it out.
5. The specific direction of motives and drives is learned from definitions of the legal codes as favorable and unfavorable.
6. A person becomes delinquent because of an excess of definitions favorable to the violation of the law.
7. Differential associations may vary in frequency, duration, priority, and intensity.
8. The process of learning criminal behavior by association with criminal and noncriminal patterns involves all the same mechanisms that are involved in any other learning.
9. Although criminal behavior is an expression of general needs and values, it is not explained by those general needs and values.[42]

SOCIAL CONTROL THEORIES

Social control theories suggest that people are hedonistic and self-interested. Walter Reckless[43] argued that internal and external factors control behavior. His **containment theory** argues that criminals cannot resist the temptations that surround them. Everyone has different levels of internal controls, including the ability to withstand temptations, morality, integrity, self-esteem, fear of punishment, and the desire to be and do good. External forces such as the police, our family, and/or our friends also control us. However, it is the internal control that influences criminality; for example, few people speed in front of a police car.

Travis Hirschi[44] agrees that internal controls predict criminality and suggests that four social bonds—attachment, commitment, involvement, and belief—affect our inner controls. Strong bonds indicate less likelihood toward criminality.

<<< **According to Sutherland, crime must be taught.** Only then will criminal behaviors develop.

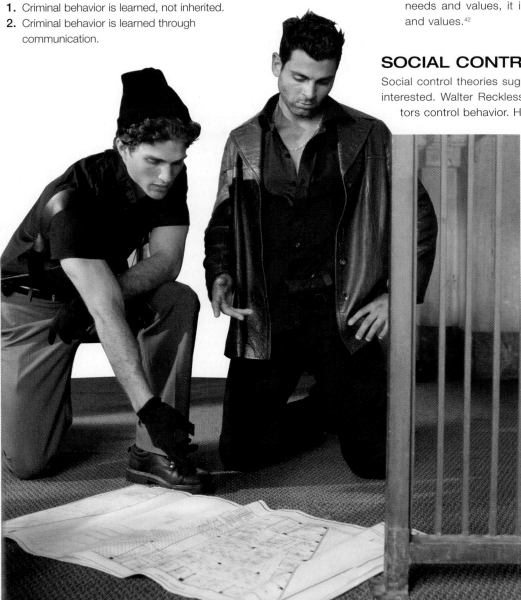

The first bond, **attachment**, refers to our relationship to others. If a teen hangs out with conformists, friends who do not drink, smoke, or use illegal drugs, they are less likely to engage in these behaviors themselves. **Commitment** refers to our dedication to live a socially acceptable life. By attending school, you are committed to a socially acceptable behavior. Thus, as we age, we are often more committed to responsible behavior. Could this explain the age-crime connection? **Involvement** refers to the level of activities in conventional things. Teens who are involved in their schools or have extracurricular activities are less likely to be delinquent. This is in part because they have less time for deviance. The final bond, **belief**, refers to a person's conviction of truth. If we believe that living a conventional life is good, then we are unlikely to deviate from that path.

Each of these bonds can act together or independently to influence a person's inner control. For example, the theory would say that cross-dressing occurs because people attach themselves to nonconformists (other cross-dressers). They involve themselves in non-normative behaviors by cross-dressing, and believe this is normal and "okay." Involvement in conforming activities may raise the level of attachment to conventional that could increase a person's belief. Likewise, low levels on these bonds might increase the likelihood that a person will engage in non-conventional activity.

Symbolic Interactionist Theory

LABELING THEORY

Some theorists believe that certain punishments can actually contribute to future deviance or crime. Edwin Lemert[45] proposes two types of deviance: primary and secondary. **Primary deviance** refers to the initial deviant act itself, such as when a group of teenagers decides to buy beer illegally. Many people can be primarily deviant, but not get caught in the act. When they get caught, they are secondarily deviant. **Secondary deviance** refers to the psychological reorientation that occurs when the system catches a person and labels him or her. The beer-buying teens become "delinquents" when they are sent to juvenile hall. Their friends' and family's perceptions of them have changed, making them secondarily deviant. According to Lemert, secondary deviance often encourages future misdeeds.

Social Conflict Theory

Reiman states that "the rich get richer and the poor get prison," meaning if you are part of the upper class, you can get away with criminal acts.[46] Social conflict theories usually focus on issues of social class, power, capitalism, and their relation to crime. For instance, Willem Bonger[47] argues that capitalism causes crime by emphasizing selfishness in individuals. Capitalism pits people against each other in a struggle for possessions. It also doesn't help that wealthy criminals often face more lenient punishment than poor criminals. Income and wealth inequality lead to abuses of the system, and this structural inequality leads to crime.

Modern conflict criminologists continue Bonger's stand that power and wealth inequality leads to crime. Reiman[48] suggests that the inequalities of the justice system are rooted in social class. Although conflict theories focus on the structural reasons for crime, they don't explain why certain individuals commit them.

General Theories of Crime Causation

Figuring out the motivation behind criminal behavior is the job of causation theorists. General theories of crime causation attempt to explain a broad range of criminal behaviors. Some integrate concepts from various theories such as Robert Agnew's[49] general strain theory or Gottfredson and Hirschi's[50] general theory of crime.

The General Strain Theory takes the basic concepts of Merton's anomie and adds a more psychological bent. According to Agnew, a person experiences strain from three sources. First, a person can suffer from a failure to achieve positively valued goals, such as proposed by Merton. Second, individuals experience strain from unpleasant life events such as losing a job or loved one. The third source of strain results from negative events such as abuse, punishment, and pain. All or any of these strains can lead a person to behave criminally. Agnew believes that everyone experiences strain, but criminality is linked to the individual's coping skills. By learning to cope with stress, people are less likely to turn to crime.[51]

Michael Gottfredson and Travis Hirschi[52] propose a general theory of crime, which states that **self-control, the ability to delay gratification, affects all criminality.** Those who trade short-term rewards for long-term consequences have low self-control. **Most crimes and other criminal-like behaviors involve spur-of-the-moment decisions; this demonstrates their lack of self-control.**

These people often engage in excessive drinking, speeding, drug use, crime, accidents, marital infidelity, and a host of other risky behaviors.[53] Thus, the solution to crime is to teach children self-control.

WRAP YOUR MIND AROUND THE THEORY

These students chose society's traditional means to reach their **goals** of success.

FUNCTIONALISM

For functionalists, crime is a part of society. Durkheim notes that crime always exists in society, and therefore must serve some function. For Merton, crime results because the pursuit of the American dream is blocked for some people. Therefore, people must adapt. Only one of these modes of adaptation leads to crime, but all occur because the system blocks some people from the goals to which they aspire.

CONFLICT THEORY

Bonger argues that capitalism causes crime in society because it teaches people to be selfish and to do what is best for themselves instead of thinking of others. The inherent competition of capitalism results in inequality of wealth and power. This leads some to strike out in criminal ways. Reiman's statement "the rich get richer, the poor get prison" points out that laws are written in the best interest of the wealthy. The wealthy often make the laws that punish poor people who might steal to survive. Meanwhile, illegal acts of the wealthy are often not considered crimes. Businessmen with power who break the law often receive little more than a slap on the wrist.

WHAT CAUSES CRIME IN OUR SOCIETY?

SYMBOLIC INTERACTIONISM

Edwin Lemert's labeling theory clearly shows the power of symbols in people's lives. Although he has no explanation for primary deviance, secondary deviance occurs as a result of the way society reacts to the first act. Thus, people learn that others see them only as criminals and so they behave in that way. Such a self-fulfilling prophecy can be enhanced by differential association theory. Sutherland suggests that we learn criminality from others, through social interactions. If for example, your friends are "gangbangers," you may believe behaving that way is acceptable. Why? Because your friends teach you that committing crimes is no big deal.

The police enforce laws written by the wealthy. These **laws often benefit the wealthy and exploit the poor.**

Society and our own social interactions influence our tendencies toward **crime.**

discover sociology in action: HOW DO WE DEAL WITH CRIME?

DISCRETION is the ability to make decisions.

PLEA BARGAIN is an out-of-court agreement between the prosecutor and the defense attorney to some concession, usually a reduced sentence.

MANDATORY MINIMUMS are fixed sentences for specific crimes.

Crime Control: The Criminal Justice System

The U.S. criminal justice system has three parts: *police, courts*, and *corrections*. Each of these parts of the system responds to violations of the law and each reflects the social policies of our country toward crime.

POLICE

Today, there are more than 18,000 law enforcement agencies in the United States.[54] Any episode of *COPS* shows that police are the ones on the front line against crime. Being on the frontlines requires police officers to have the initial **discretion**, or ability to make decisions, which often involves whether or not they will enforce the law. If you've ever received a warning instead of a speeding ticket for speeding through a school zone, you've reaped the benefit of a police officer's discretion.

COURTS

The courts are the second part of the criminal justice system. Judges and district attorneys use discretion in their work as well. District attorneys decide whether they will prosecute a crime, and under what charge they will take the case to court. For example, about 89% of cases in this country end with a guilty plea,[55] often called a **plea bargain**. This is an out-of-court agreement between the prosecutor and the defense attorney to some concession, usually a reduced sentence.

Judicial discretion exists, but state and the federal governments have limited use of judicial discretion by passing laws that mandate sentences. **Mandatory minimums** make judges give individuals fixed sentences for specific crimes. These rules eliminate discretion from judges that might impact the sentence. Mandatory sentencing laws vary by state, but they have some things in common. These rules increase the length of time people serve in prison, which creates new problems for the prison system. Since prisons have an increasingly older population, some states build nursing homes inside prison walls to care for inmates who are too weak and old to care for themselves, but cannot be released due to these laws.[56]

Studying the cost-benefit of mandatory minimum sentencing, the Rand Corporation found mandatory minimum sentences for drug offenders are not an efficient use of tax dollars when compared to drug treatment. Drug treatment actually has a stronger effect than prison, reducing drug consumption and drug-related crime while costing the taxpayers less money.[57] We have already discussed how prisons in the United States work to house criminals, but let's turn our attention to the most serious punishment meted out: the death penalty.

DEATH PENALTY

In the United States, we reserve the death penalty for offenders who commit the most serious crimes, like murder or treason. The United States is the only modern and industrialized democracy on earth that still uses the death penalty.

Supporters of the death penalty argue that it is the ultimate deterrence to crime because potential murderers would fear receiving the death penalty. However, opponents point out that states without the death penalty actually have lower rates of murder. Likewise, the costs of prosecuting and executing offenders are actually higher than lifetime incarceration. Proponents claim that these costs could be cut if appeals were shortened. However, new DNA evidence releases many from prison, and the costs of the death penalty are primarily due to the cost of trials, not the system of mandatory appeals.[58]

Finally, opponents of the death penalty point out that it is applied in a biased manner. Levine and Montgomery studied 6,000 murder cases in Maryland from 1978 through 1999. They found that **when the victim was white, blacks were twice as likely to receive a death sentence as whites.** Furthermore, blacks convicted of killing whites are four times as likely to get a death sentence than blacks whose victims were also black.[59]

ACTIVITIES

1. Read stories about prison inmates. Do you see any commonalities in their stories?
2. Research prisons in your state. What are the demographic of the inmates? How many are serving mandatory minimums?
3. What type of community service programs are available in your state for inmates to participate in?
4. Research three states that have the death penalty. How frequently are inmates executed? Do you think it acts as a deterrent for criminals?

Bill was an inmate in a local prison who took a class for college credit via a videoconferencing setup. He could listen to the class and even participate in class discussions from the prison where he was incarcerated. At about the mid-point of the semester, students were offered the chance to earn extra credit by doing community learning. Bill wanted to participate, too. The program had never had an inmate do community service, so the teacher spoke with his educational officer, who agreed that community learning could occur anywhere.

Bill wrote in his paper,

"My prison is a community of inmates, most of whom committed no violent offenses like me. I spent my time volunteering to help with the drug and alcohol group, meaning that each day I would set up the chapel for the meetings, and after the meetings I would put it back in order. Initially, I didn't stay for the meetings because it didn't seem to be important: I have no drug addiction, I haven't used since I was incarcerated. But one time the group leader invited me to stay. I was stunned to hear the stories of how alcohol and drugs caused so much damage in these men's lives. Almost all of them were under the influence when they committed their crimes.

"It made me decide that I wanted to be a drug and alcohol counselor when I got out of prison. It also made me see that a lot of inmates are just like me: normal guys trying to do their time without getting hurt, and hoping for a better life on the outside when they get released."

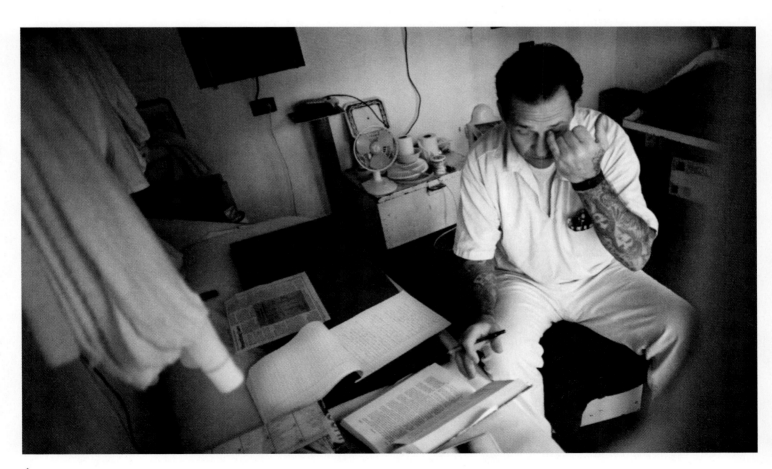

How do you think community service programs, like a support group for alcoholics, could be beneficial to inmates trying to turn their lives around?

13

WHAT IS CRIME?   228

a violation of norms that have been written into law

WHY DOES CRIME EXIST?   235

positivists: people are social and are not prone to act criminally unless some biological, psychological, or social factor is involved
classicalists: people make rational choices to commit crimes based on pleasure/pain calculations

HOW DO WE DEAL WITH CRIME?   240

through a three-part criminal justice system: police, courts, and corrections

get the topic: WHAT IS A CRIME?

Deviance vs. Crime   228
Historical Roots of Deviance and
    Crime Theories   235

Functional Explanations of Crime
    and Deviance   236
Social Interaction Theories   237
Symbolic Interactionist Theory   238

Social Conflict Theory   238
General Theories of Crime Causation   238
Crime Control: The Criminal Justice
    System   240

Theory

FUNCTIONALISM   236

- crime is a response to some social factor
- Durkheim's three functions of crime and deviance: they mark the boundaries of morality, promote social solidarity, and bring about needed change
- theory of anomie: social instability caused by a wearing away of standards and ethics
- Merton: crime results because the pursuit of the American dream is blocked for some people

CONFLICT THEORY   238

- capitalism teaches people to be selfish and competitive, resulting in inequality
- the wealthy create the laws that punish the poor, while many illegal acts committed by the wealthy are often not considered crimes
- "the rich get rich, the poor get prison"

SYMBOLIC INTERACTIONISM   238

- labeling theory
- people react to how others view them
- people learn criminality through social interactions

Key Terms

deviance is the violation of norms that a society agrees upon.   228

crime is the violation of norms that have been written into law.   228

criminology is the scientific study of crime, deviance, and social policies that the criminal justice system applies.   228

street crime refers to many different types of criminal acts, such as burglary, rape, and assault.   229

Uniform Crime Reports (UCRs) are official police statistics of reported crimes gathered from police reports and paperwork.   230

National Crime Victimization Survey (NCVS) is the measurement of crime victimization based on contact with a representative sample of over 70,000 households in the United States.   230

crime index is made up of eight offenses used to measure crime: homicide, rape, robbery, aggravated assault, burglary, larceny-theft, motor vehicle theft, and arson.   230

consensus model of law suggests that laws arise because people see a behavior they do not like, and they agree to make it illegal.   232

conflict model of law proposes that powerful people write laws to protect their own interests while punishing the actions of those they wish to control.   232

shaming is a deliberate effort to attach a negative meaning to a behavior.   232

stigmatized shame is a permanent label given to an offender, which could actually increase the chances of reoffending because the guilty person is forever labeled.   233

reintegrative shaming is an effort to bring an offender back into the community after punishment.   233

deterrence is a measure that prevents a person from doing something because of fear of the consequences.   233

general deterrence is a measure that ensures individuals will not commit a crime because they see the negative consequences applied to others, and they fear experiencing these consequences.   233

specific deterrence is a measure that changes the attitude of individuals, who have already violated the law and have been punished, by causing them never to commit crime again.   233

recidivism is the tendency for inmates released from prison to return to prison.   233

(continued)

differential association theory emphasizes that criminal and deviant behavior is learned. *237*

containment theory argues that criminals cannot resist the temptations that surround them. *237*

attachment is the social bond that refers to our relationship to others. *238*

commitment is the social bond that refers to our dedication to live a socially acceptable life. *238*

involvement is the social bond that refers to the level of activity in conventional things. *238*

belief is the social bond that refers to a person's conviction of truth. *238*

primary deviance is the initial deviant act itself. *238*

secondary deviance refers to the psychological reorientation that occurs when the system catches a person and labels him or her as a deviant. *238*

discretion is the ability to make decisions. *240*

plea bargain is an out-of-court agreement between the prosecutor and the defense attorney to some concession, usually a reduced sentence. *240*

mandatory minimums are fixed sentences for specific crimes. *240*

Sample Test Questions

These multiple-choice questions are similar to those found in the test bank that accompanies this textbook.

1. Deviance is *not* linked to
  a. time.
  b. society.
  c. legal norms.
  d. cultural values.

2. Which type of crime is most common?
  a. Violent crime
  b. Property crime
  c. White-collar crime
  d. Drug-related crime

3. Which of the following is an alternative punishment?
  a. Prison
  b. Death
  c. Torture
  d. Shaming

4. What is the last resort in the criminal justice system?
  a. Counseling
  b. Probation
  c. Parole
  d. Prison

5. According to Robert Merton, which type of lower-class person obeys social rules and works with little chance of advancement?
  a. Conformist
  b. Innovator
  c. Retreatist
  d. Ritualist

ESSAY

1. How are police shows different than real-life police work?

2. Do the poor commit more crimes than other members of society?

3. Why is it difficult to make international comparisons about crime statistics?

4. Why are only certain things illegal?

5. What is wrong with the U.S. prison system?

WHERE TO START YOUR RESEARCH PAPER

To learn more about crime in the United States, go to
http://www.fbi.gov/
http://www.usdoj.gov/

To learn more about positive deviance, go to
http://www.positivedeviance.org/

To see Uniform Crime Reports, go to
http://www.fbi.gov/ucr/ucr.htm

To see National Crime Victimization Survey information, go to
http://www.icpsr.umich.edu/NACJD/NCVS/

To learn more about international police organizations, go to
http://www.interpol.int/Default.asp

To learn more about the prison system, go to
http://www.bop.gov/

ANSWERS: 1.c; 2.b; 3.d; 4.d; 5.a

MARRIAGE AND FAMILY

"I often

ask my students to write down ideas that spring to mind when they think of the "traditional family." Their lists always include several images. One is of extended families in which all members worked together . . . Another is of nuclear families in which nurturing mothers sheltered children . . . In traditional families . . . men and women remained chaste until marriage, at which time they . . . committed themselves wholly to the marital relationship, experiencing an all encompassing intimacy.

"Such visions of past family life exert a powerful emotional pull on most Americans, and with good reason, given the fragility of many modern commitments . . . Like most visions of a "golden age," the "traditional family" my students describe evaporates on closer examination. It is an ahistorical amalgam of structures, values, and behaviors that never coexisted in the same time and place.

"The so-called "crisis of the family" is a subset of a much larger crisis of social obligation that requires us to look beyond private family relations and rebuild larger social ties.

"At first glance, it may seem depressing to think of our current family problems as part of a much larger socioeconomic crisis. But surely it is even more depressing to think that the problem is caused by people's rotten values or irredeemable selfishness . . . Maybe our personal difficulties are not all our family's fault; maybe our family's difficulties are not all our personal fault."[1]

From *The Way We Never Were* by Stephanie Coontz. Reprinted by permission of Basic Books, a member of Perseus Books Group.

How Do Societies Perpetuate Themselves?

CHAPTER 14

In her book, *The Way We Never Were: American Families and the Nostalgia Trap* historian and family studies professor Stephanie Coontz provides an overview of family life in the United States, particularly as it relates to what is often called the "crisis of the family."

Here's the story of a lovely lady, who was bringing up three very lovely girls . . . That lovely lady met a man named Brady and soon one of the most beloved sitcoms of all time—*The Brady Bunch*—was born. Families watching the show back then wanted to be just like them. In fact, the Bradys are still an ideal for many viewers. However, today's family sitcom is more likely to feature a dysfunctional family than a happy, loving family. What happened?

Stephanie Coontz suggests that most people carry with them a misconception of what the family "ought" to be, which influences their thinking.

Each semester, I ask my students to draw the "ideal family." They draw something like the image to the right. Rarely does anyone draw his or her own family. This exercise usually helps us launch into a discussion that most people never consider. What is a family? Who taught us what a family is? We will address these questions and further investigate families and marriage in this chapter.

get the topic: WHAT IS A FAMILY?

Marriage and Family

The concept of family exists in all societies and comes in all shapes and sizes. But what is a family? The term is difficult to define, but, generally, a **family** is two or more people who are related by blood,

marriage, or adoption. Often we think of marriage as the legal institution that defines family; **marriage** being the union of two people that is typically recognized by law or cultural norms. However, like family, marriage is a social construct, so the status of people who commit to each other for life is often related to social institutions and cultures.[2]

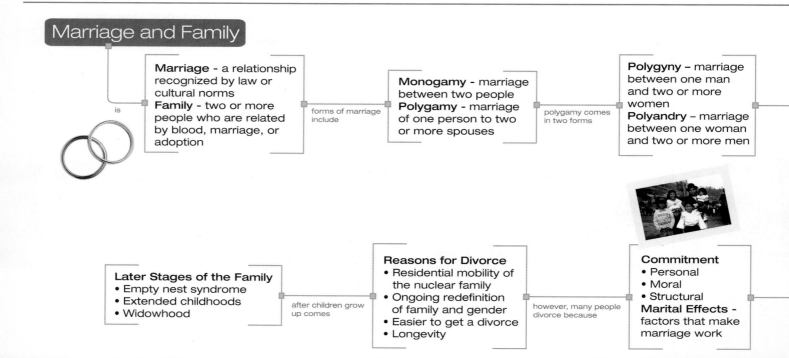

Marriage and Family

Marriage - a relationship recognized by law or cultural norms
Family - two or more people who are related by blood, marriage, or adoption

is

forms of marriage include

Monogamy - marriage between two people
Polygamy - marriage of one person to two or more spouses

polygamy comes in two forms

Polygyny – marriage between one man and two or more women
Polyandry – marriage between one woman and two or more men

Later Stages of the Family
• Empty nest syndrome
• Extended childhoods
• Widowhood

after children grow up comes

Reasons for Divorce
• Residential mobility of the nuclear family
• Ongoing redefinition of family and gender
• Easier to get a divorce
• Longevity

however, many people divorce because

Commitment
• Personal
• Moral
• Structural
Marital Effects - factors that make marriage work

My Ideal Family

>>> When I ask my students to draw their "ideal family," I get images that look like this. Neat, tidy families with a mother, father, and two and a half kids. However, **few families in our society come in such tidy packages.**

DAUGHTER DAD MOM SON BRUNO

FORMS OF MARRIAGE AND FAMILY

Take a look around and you'll notice that families come in all shapes and sizes. Some families have only one parent in the home, while others have stepparents helping to raise the children. Still others have two parents of the same sex. The drawing my students generally create consists of a husband, wife, and their children—a group that can also be referred to as a **nuclear family**. But other forms of family exist. For various reasons, another relative, like a grandparent or an uncle, may live with a nuclear family, which creates an **extended family**.

FAMILY is two or more people who are related by blood, marriage, or adoption.

MARRIAGE is the union of two people that is typically recognized by law or cultural norms.

NUCLEAR FAMILY is a household consisting of a husband, wife, and children.

EXTENDED FAMILY is a household consisting of a nuclear family plus an additional relative.

---

forms of families include

Nuclear family – family consisting of a husband, wife, and children
Extended family – family consisting of a nuclear family plus additional relatives

current marriage trends include

Increase in
- marriage age
- cohabitation
- single parent and stepfamily homes
- remarriage
- interracial marriage
- same-sex unions

many people believe

Myths about the "ideal" family
1. The Universal Nuclear Family
2. The Self-Reliant Traditional Family
3. The Naturalness of Different Responsibilities
4. The Idealized Nuclear Family of the 1950

every family goes through

once married, you need

Stimulus-Value-Role Theory
- Stimulus stage
- Value stage
- Role stage
Exchange Theory

theories of attraction include

Homogamy - marriage between people with the same characteristics
Endogamy - the practice of marrying within your group
Exogamy - the practice of marrying someone from a different group

when choosing a mate people practice

Phases of the Family
- Courtship and Mate Selection
- Marital Life
- Child Rearing
- Divorce
- Later Stages of the Family

Most of you probably grew up under a family system of **monogamy**, which is the practice of being married to one person at a time. However, some societies allow **polygamy**, the practice of having more than one spouse at a time. This practice is illegal in the United States, but in 2001, a fundamentalist Mormon named Tom Green was convicted of polygamy.[3] Green argued that his religion justified his actions, because Mormons practiced polygamy until the nineteenth century.[4] Green wondered, "How can somebody claim to be a Mormon and say that plural marriage is wicked?"[5] Nevertheless, Green was sentenced to five years in prison.[6]

Polygamy itself comes in two forms: polygyny and polyandry. **Polygyny** is more common and consists of a man marrying two or more women. This ancient practice is illegal in most developed countries, although it still exists in many developing countries around the world. **Polyandry** allows a woman to take two or more husbands. Anthropologists determined that polyandry is practiced to concentrate labor and maintain a comfortable standard of living while limiting animosity. For example, Tibetans practice fraternal polyandry, meaning a woman is married to brothers.[7] Both brothers maintain their land while limiting the number of heirs, which prevents family infighting.[8]

Most of these family types fall under the *patriarchal system*, which, if you recall from Chapter 11, means that men have power over women and children. Few would fall under a *matriarchal system*, where the woman is dominant.

>>> I live with my mom, Jeffrey, and my new baby brothers, Kevin and Scott. **On the weekends, I see my dad, his wife Anita, and my half sister Kylie.**

TRENDS OF THE AMERICAN FAMILY

Ideologies regarding the family are also changing. Years ago, female students were in a race to "get pinned," or engaged, before the end of their last semester of college. As one faculty member put it, "Springtime was for engagement parties." Today, things are different. It's no longer unusual for a woman to graduate from college without having a fiancé.

In 1900, the median age people married was 25.9 for men and 21.9 for women.[9] By the 1950s, the United States was entering an era that recognized the family as *the* social institution.[10] The median age lowered to 22.8 for men and 20.3 for women.[11] In 2007, the median ages hit an all-time high with the median age for men being 27.5 and 25.6 for women.[12] These delays in marriage may be due to a number of factors. One of these is an increase in couples who choose to live together without being legally married. Interestingly, many cohabitants begin these relationships at the same age as the people who were getting married in the 1950s.[13]

It's increasingly common for unmarried, cohabiting couples to have children. Just look at Brad Pitt and Angelina Jolie. This unmarried celebrity couple continues to add to their ever–expanding brood. It has been estimated that 40 percent of all children will spend time in a cohabiting family before their sixteenth birthdays.[14] Some researchers point out that many cohabitating couples of today resemble families of the past.[15] However, there are other forms of families that have arisen as well.

New Forms of Families

Remarriage and stepfamilies are also part of the everyday norm. Both of these trends take the traditional idea of a nuclear family and rework it to fit new forms of family. Since the 1950s, traditional roles and rules associated with families have become more varied and complex.[16] For example, I've often heard children say to an adult who is not their biological parent but is living with and providing for them, something like this; "You're not my real mom (or dad), you can't tell me what to do!" If that's true, what is that person's role in the household? Cohabitants and stepfamilies often experience such questions and stresses over these changing roles in the family.

Some children may grow up in **blended families**, which are families composed of children and some combination of biological parents. Some children grow up in a single-parent home. In fact, although the birth rate for women has decreased in the last 35 years, the birth rate for unmarried women has increased.[17] These are really two different things. First, some children live in a single-parent household because their parents are divorced. Other children live in unmarried households due to cohabitation. Either way, social norms are more accepting of unmarried women raising children today than they used to be. In fact, almost half of all children today are expected to live in a single-parent home at some time before the age of 21.[18]

Other changes in the family form include same-sex couples and interracial/ethnic marriages. Compared to the past, stigmas surrounding these unions has declined significantly, so that many people no longer keep such unions a secret.[19] What has caused such a change in family forms?

One structural event may help explain what happened. Throughout the 1950s, most children lived with their parents before getting married. During this time, the power of the parents to

help select an "acceptable mate" reigned supreme. Now there is an independent life stage as people delay marriage and often live independently from their parents prior to getting married.[20] This geographic split decreases the parent's ability to control the behavior of their grown children,[21] perhaps leading to greater diversity and partner selection. This, along with changing social norms, seems to allow people to couple with people today in a way that would not have been imaginable 40 years ago.[22]

Myths About the "Ideal" Family

In the opening excerpt, Stephanie Coontz discusses how people have idealized the traditional American family. She points out that many myths exist about family structure and family life. For example, I thought I lived in a typical home when I was growing up. My mother cooked Sunday dinners, and my father mowed the lawn. However, both of my parents worked outside the home and everyone helped with chores. In college, I visited a friend's house, and his mother waited on us hand and foot. When I got up to help with the dishes, my friend's father said, "That's women's work." That's how I learned that my family wasn't typical. Coontz discusses similar myths about families in the United States.

MONOGAMY is the practice of being married to one person at a time.

POLYGAMY is the practice of having more than one spouse at a time.

POLYGYNY is the practice of a man marrying two or more women.

POLYANDRY is the practice of a woman marrying two or more men.

BLENDED FAMILIES are families composed of children and some combination of biological parents.

The idealized 1950s family did exist, but was perpetuated by television. Shows such as *Father Knows Best* and *The Adventures of Ozzie and Harriet* depicted picture-perfect families whose problems were resolved in the span of a half-hour program.

MYTH 1 The Universal Nuclear Family
Although common belief is that all families take the form of the traditional nuclear family, the reality is that families vary in organization, membership, life cycle, social networks, and function. What many people consider the "ideal family" only came about with industrialization. When people left the farm, they often didn't take their extended family with them and created smaller family units.

MYTH 2 The Self-Reliant Traditional Family
Some people believe that family units carved out their lives on their own and that returning to a more self-reliant family structure would solve many of today's issues. The idealized image of families striking out on their own to settle the west overstates the reality of self-reliance. These families received both government support as well as support from others in the area. Early settlers relied on military protection and government programs designed to move Native Americans off the lands that they were to eventually inhabit. Slave labor also played a major role in the settlement of many states. Finally, local families often banded together for child care, construction projects, and mutual protection and support. In a complex society, no one makes it on his or her own.

MYTH 3 The Naturalness of Different Responsibilities for Wives and Husbands
We touched on this subject in the gender chapter, but many people believe that there has always been a clear division between men and women when it comes to child care and other family roles. Some suggest that if mothers stayed home and "did their jobs" (raising the children), families would function better. The truth is that prior to industrialization, men and women shared almost equally in child care tasks. Men often worked at home and their children helped them. My mother learned farming techniques from her dad. He taught her to be innovative and never afraid to try new things. So, men did take responsibility for raising their children. Women also worked hard. My grandmother worked with my grandfather and when he died, she remained on the farm, raising the children and working the fields. The notion that family roles were different is not so clear when we look at history.

MYTH 4 The Idealized Nuclear Family of the 1950s
During the 1950s, an image of the American family emerged. It was a middle-class family with a stay-at-home mom and a working dad. This image came to be idealized in television shows, and people started buying into this thinking that this is what families should look like. However, there is historical evidence to show that this "ideal" family wasn't that ideal.

Image of the Perfect Family

Stephanie Coontz argues that the image of the perfect family is just that—an image. In fact, the romanticized family portrait of the past often covered up a life of discontent and conformity. The ideal sitcom Cleaver family did exist, but only for a tiny blip in our history and only for a small portion of the population.

Looking back on it, the 1950s seemed like the golden age of happiness for all Americans. Divorce rates were down, out-of-wedlock births were low, and marriage was universally esteemed as an institution.[23] Not only was there a housing boom, but the gross national product (the estimated total value of all the goods created in the country) also rose 250 percent, and per capita income rose 35 percent.[24] This was partially because the United States was the only intact industrial nation after World War II, and so it was left to us to "rebuild the world."[25]

Even though there is a measure of truth to these points, they don't provide a clear picture of average families. Before people were ever married, they knew exactly what to expect from their lives. After a brief courtship, a couple was married, had sex, and started a family. They purchased a house, with the husband as breadwinner. His salary was high enough for the wife to stay at home as a homemaker. This routine led some women to believe life consisted of the four Bs: booze, bowling, bridge, and boredom.[26]

In fact, "[b]y 1960, almost every major news journal was using the word *trapped* to describe the feelings of the American housewife."[27] To dull the pain and tedium, some women began drinking and taking tranquilizers to make it through the day.

Men were also dissatisfied with family life and became resentful of women. Publications like *Playboy* encouraged men to take power over areas that women previously governed. Men were encouraged to have a say in the clothes they wore and the food they ate. In *Playboy*'s debut issue it published an article entitled, "Miss Gold-Digger of 1953," promoting the idea that women were interested in men for material reasons.[28] These negative stereotypes were damaging to both men and women.

Trying to gauge the frequency of events such as violence and incest is difficult because many instances were never reported. These topics were not considered appropriate for conversation. Many women suffered from physical abuse and just dealt with it, rather than face the stigma of being a member of a dysfunctional family. In the 1950s, a victim of domestic violence was often viewed "as a masochist who provoked her husband into beating her."[29] Furthermore, incest was often viewed as female "sex delinquency."[30]

>>> **ACTIVITY** What do current family sitcoms say about the role of the family in our culture? After conducting research, compare this image to reality. Do you see any discrepancies?

>>> New York bus driver Ralph Kramden wants to strike it rich, but his wife knows it's not going to happen. **Ralph threatens her by saying, "One of these days, Alice, right in the kisser . . . pow!" Incidents like this in the 1950s trivialized domestic violence in a comedic sketch.**

Networks and Family Change in Japan

Many of the family demographic changes in the United States—increased age at marriage, decreased marital stability, and lower birthrate—have been mirrored by Japan. Traditionally, Japanese family values strongly discouraged these behaviors. However, a survey conducted by Ronald R. Rindfuss et al. suggested that Japan might be on the cusp of a major demographic change.[31]

The traditional Japanese family is patriarchal; men are the authority figure, lineage is traced through the father, and fathers pass wealth on to their sons.[32] Women are left with the bulk of the housework. In 2000, Japanese women spent 29 hours per week on household labor; husbands spent just three.[33]

However, times are changing. More women are attaining higher levels of education and entering the labor force.[34] As more women enter the full-time workforce, Japan faces an increased need for day care situations. Some suggest that cohabitation may become more common.[35] In fact, recent studies indicate that 92 percent of Japanese citizens know someone who has engaged in nontraditional behaviors.[36] Japan should anticipate more changes in the future.

> ∨
> ∨ Some societies
> ∨ feel a strong need to preserve traditional culture.

What motivates societies to cling to traditional values?

PHASES OF THE FAMILY

Although every family is different and complex in its own right, there are commonalities that emerge in most unions. Traditionally speaking, people court, choose a mate, get married, have children, get divorced, and experience the later stages of family life. Let's look at these issues.

Courtship and Mate Selection

I understand that there are possibly millions of women on the planet with whom I could have a satisfying marriage. Yet, I married someone who lived in the same town I did and who happened to go to my church. Feelings of attraction and affection were part of this decision, but choosing a mate often has to do with finding people who live near you and who share similar values and social traits. Propinquity or proximity is a major factor to interpersonal attraction. It makes sense that you are attracted to people who live near you.[37]

Finding a mate comes with many unspoken or spoken rules that society, your family, or even you dictate. So, when choosing a mate, what kind of cultural questions arise?

Common Cultural Practices

Finding someone to marry can be a daunting prospect, but in the United States the options are relatively open. There are only a few rules: potential mates cannot already be married, must be of legal age, must not be closely related, and, in most states, must be of a different sex. In fact, most cultures have similar restrictions regarding age and other social issues.

David Popenoe suggests that **the traditional nuclear family is practically extinct.**

FUNCTIONALISM

The family serves as a mechanism for maintaining order. The traditional functions of the family include: (1) *Reproduction and socialization of children.* The species can't go on and the group can't exist without replacing members and training them. (2) *Affection, companionship, and recreation.* Families provide a social structure that gives us support. (3) *Sexual regulation.* A lack of sexual regulation can result in conflicts within society, both between members as well as in determining the lineage of a child. (4) *Economic cooperation.* It is cheaper to live with someone else than to live alone. (5) *Care for the sick and aged.* When you had your wisdom teeth taken out, who took care of you? Throughout history, people have had these needs and used the family to solve them.

IS THE FAMILY IN DECLINE?

CONFLICT THEORY

In *The Second Shift*, Hochschild discusses the disparity between men and women in terms of housework and how this leads to conflict between husbands and wives. This argument is about time, energy, and leisure. Wives tend to get stuck with the bulk of the work, leaving many disgruntled. This does not show a breakdown in marriage, but instead according to Coontz, is a socioeconomic problem. Both parents are forced to work outside the home to survive, unlike many families of the past, and this change creates conflict.

SYMBOLIC INTERACTIONISM

Interactionists look at the family on a micro level, by studying the relationships between individual family members. The expectation of different roles played out by men and women help determine the success of a marriage. Traditionally, men played the role of "breadwinner," while women played "homemaker." Since these roles are in a state of constant change, the way in which couples adjust to these changes defines the structure of the family. Furthermore, Coontz points out that change in ideologies show that the institution of the family is simply changing, not declining.

As **families evolve in order to keep up with social trends,** ideologies associated with the family also need to evolve.

Many **couples fight over** who gets more **free time and leisure.**

discover sociology in action: WHAT DO FUTURE FAMILIES LOOK LIKE?

Gay Marriage vs. Civil Unions vs. Nothing

A hot topic in social policies related to marriage is the current debate over same-sex unions and whether or not they should be legal. Currently, more than 20 states have constitutional amendments defining marriage as a union between a man and woman. Most of these came about after Congress passed the Defense of Marriage Act in 1996. This law states that marriage is an act between a man and a woman, but it gives individual states the power to define marriage. Furthermore, states do not have to recognize marriages from other states that do not share their definition. Thus, if you're legally married in the state of Massachusetts, it won't count in a state that does not allow same-sex marriage.[66]

Some states, like Vermont, side-stepped the word marriage, creating civil unions that allowed same-sex couples all same rights and privileges of marriage without using the word. Thus, they can enjoy the benefits of joint ownership of property and equal legal status of parenthood for any children they may have.[67]

ACTIVITIES

1. Watch a prime-time sitcom or drama and analyze the depiction of family life on that show. Are the characters married or unmarried? What roles do men and women play in the relationship? Write a paragraph analyzing the show.
2. Interview an elderly family member or acquaintance. Discuss what family life was like when he or she was your age. How did his or her experience differ from your own?
3. Research the laws in your state. Have any laws been passed in favor of or in opposition to same-sex marriage? Write a summary of those laws.

Perhaps laws banning same-sex marriage will pass away, just as laws that banned interracial marriage did. Once illegal in many places, interracial marriages now make up about seven percent of the marriages in the country.[68] Laws banning interracial marriage were deemed to be unconstitutional, because they imposed government restrictions on personal choices. Bans of same-sex marriage may eventually follow since public opinions regarding same-sex marriage seem to be headed toward greater tolerance. A poll conducted by the Pew Center shows a repeated decline in the percentage of people who oppose same-sex marriage. Even though 51% of Americans opposed gay marriage in 2006, that number was down from 63% in 2004.[69]

Even as the debate rages on, homosexual couples want the right to pass property or custody to a partner at death and social acceptance for their way of life, just like heterosexual couples. When we debate this issue in my classes, my students raise concerns over the sanctity of marriage and the welfare of children involved. However, students who raise concerns over the sanctity of marriage almost never propose eliminating divorce, which is far more common. Also, children raised in gay homes have lower rates of child abuse and neglect and better educational attainment compared to their peers in heterosexual households.[70] Regardless of whether or not a person believes homosexuality is a choice or not, the question is really, should government restrict that choice or give benefits to some but not to others?

From Classroom to Community | Adoption for Same-Sex Couples

Josephine did her community learning at a group home for orphaned children. She was assigned the task of greeting prospective foster parents and playing with the children in the home.

"The foster children are excited when prospective parents come to visit, because they all want to be part of a loving, caring home.

"Most of the foster parents were married heterosexual couples, but occasionally a homosexual couple would come in. I was upset by the attitude of some of my fellow volunteers. Several felt that gay couples should not be allowed to adopt children.

"I tried explaining that children raised by homosexuals were no more likely to be gay than those raised by heterosexuals. But willing, adoptive parents were rejected based on their sexual orientation. It's sad because many children await adoption, and a home is surely a better place than a shelter."

WHAT **IS A FAMILY?** 246

two or more people who are related
by blood, marriage, or adoption

IS **THE FAMILY IN DECLINE?** 256

functionalism: according to Popenoe, the family is declining
because the family is not cohesive, can't perform familial
functions, and has lost power
conflict theory: families are struggling to adapt to dual-career
households
symbolic interactionism: according to Coontz, the role of the
family is changing to fit the times

WHAT **DO FUTURE FAMILIES LOOK LIKE?** 259

more interracial marriages and same-sex couples
who adopt children

get the topic: WHAT IS A FAMILY?

Marriage and Family   246
Symbolic Interactionism   256

Conflict Theory   257
Functionalism   257

Gay Marriage vs. Civil Unions vs. Nothing
259

Theory

SYMBOLIC INTERACTIONISM   256

- expectations of roles help determine the success of the family
- the way couples respond to changes in their environment affect
  the structure of the family

CONFLICT THEORY   257

- Hochschild's *The Second Shift;* family is a system in which women
  are generally stuck doing the majority of the work
- husbands and wives argue over time, energy, and leisure
- both people work because of socioeconomic problems, which
  causes tension

FUNCTIONALISM   257

- family serves as a way to maintain order
- parents teach children how to behave and what is acceptable
- Popenoe: the family is no longer cohesive, functional, or powerful

Key Terms

family is two or more people who are related
by blood, marriage, or adoption.   *246*

marriage is the union of two people that is
typically recognized by law or cultural norms.
246

nuclear family is a household consisting of a
husband, wife, and children.   *247*

extended family is a household consisting of
a nuclear family plus an additional relative. *247*

monogamy is the practice of being married to

one person at a time.   *248*

polygamy is the practice of having more than
one spouse at a time.   *248*

polygyny is the practice of a man marrying
two or more women.   *248*

polyandry is the practice of a woman marrying two or more men.   *248*

blended families are families composed of
children and some combination of biological
parents.   *248*

homogamy is marriage between people with
similar backgrounds, such as religion, race,
class, or age.   *252*

endogamy is the practice of marrying within
your social group.   *252*

exogamy is the practice of marrying someone
from a different social group.   *252*

marital effects are factors that make
marriage work.   *252*

Sample Test Questions

These multiple-choice questions are similar to those found in the test bank that accompanies this textbook.

1. Which of the following is one of the four *Bs* of marriage?

   a. Billing
   b. Business
   c. Boredom
   d. Breakup

2. What is someone who marries within his or her social group practicing?

   a. Homogamy
   b. Endogamy
   c. Polyandry
   d. Exogamy

3. Women who work a "second shift"

   a. come home to hours of housework.
   b. must work two jobs to make ends meet.
   c. go back and get new jobs when they marry.
   d. equally divide responsibilities with their spouses.

4. The "appropriateness" of a spouse is dependent upon

   a. marital effects in a marriage.
   b. cultural norms and regulations.
   c. gender ideologies and gender roles.
   d. physical and mental characteristics.

5. Which of the following is *not* one of the listed reasons for the increased divorce rate in the United States?

   a. Longer life spans
   b. More mobile families
   c. Easier paperwork
   d. Lax marriage laws and tax breaks

ESSAY

1. Why do so many people consider the 1950s an ideal time for the American family?
2. What are some of the causes in the changing of the American family?
3. Why do some couples wait to have children?
4. What is the stimulus-value-role theory?
5. What are some of Coontz's myths of marriage?

WHERE TO START YOUR RESEARCH PAPER

To find information about American family values, go to the U.S. Department of State's Web site at
http://usinfo.state.gov/journals/itsv/0101/ijse/ijse0101.htm#welcome

To learn about marriage and family therapy, go to
http://www.aamft.org/

To learn about states' current stance on same-sex marriage, and to find a good definition of the Defense of Marriage Act, go to
http://www.ncsl.org/programs/cyf/samesex.htm

To find more information about the divorce rates in the United States, go to http://www.divorcerate.org/

ANSWERS: 1. c; 2. b; 3. a; 4. b; 5. d

Remember to check **www.thethinkspot.com** for additional information, downloadable flashcards, and other helpful resources.

EDUCATION AND RELIGION

"I had

begun to teach in 1964 in Boston in a segregated school so crowded and so poor that it could not provide my fourth grade children with a classroom. We shared an auditorium with another fourth grade and the choir and a group that was rehearsing, starting in October, for a Christmas play that, somehow, never was produced. In the spring I was shifted to another fourth grade that had had a string of substitutes all year. The 35 children in the class hadn't had a permanent teacher since they entered kindergarten. That year, I was their thirteenth teacher.

"After teaching for several years, I became involved with other interests . . . It wasn't until 1988, when I returned to Massachusetts after a long stay in New York City, that I realized how far I'd been drawn away from my original concerns. I found that I missed being with schoolchildren, and I felt a longing to spend time in the public schools again.

"Looking around some of these inner-city schools, where filth and disrepair were worse than anything I'd seen in 1964, I often wondered why we would agree to let our children go to school in places where no politician, school board president, or business CEO would dream of working. Children seem to wrestle with these questions too.

"According to our textbook rhetoric, Americans abhor the notion of a social order in which economic privilege and political power are determined by hereditary class. Officially, we have a more enlightened goal in sight: namely, a society in which a family's wealth has no relation to the probability of future educational attainment and the wealth and station it affords. By this standard, education offered to poor children should be at least as good as that which is provided to the children of the upper-middle class.

"If Americans had to discriminate directly against other people's children, I believe most citizens would find this morally abhorrent. Denial, in an active sense, of other people's children is, however rarely necessary in this nation. Inequality is mediated for us by a taxing system that most people do not fully understand and seldom scrutinize."[1]

How Do Societies Pass on Information?

In what has become a classic discussion of the U.S. education system, **Jonathan Kozol** describes structural differences in the public education system in his book, *Savage Inequalities: Children in America s Schools.*

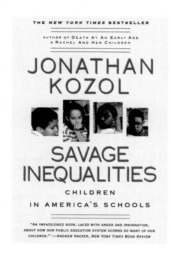

THE *NEW YORK TIMES* BESTSELLER

AUTHOR OF *DEATH AT AN EARLY AGE* & *RACHEL AND HER CHILDREN*

JONATHAN KOZOL

SAVAGE INEQUALITIES

CHILDREN IN AMERICA'S SCHOOLS

"AN IMPASSIONED BOOK, LACED WITH ANGER AND INDIGNATION, ABOUT HOW OUR PUBLIC EDUCATION SYSTEM SCORNS SO MANY OF OUR CHILDREN." —ANDREW HACKER, *NEW YORK TIMES BOOK REVIEW*

S-U-C-C-E-S-S. Success. This may not be one of Akeelah's words from 2006's *Akeelah and the Bee,* but it does sum up her journey from inner-city school spelling bee to the national competition.

Her journey isn't that simple, though. Akeelah's home life isn't easy: Her brother's in a gang, her father is dead, and her mother doesn't understand the point of wasting time on a spelling bee. With the help of a mentor, Akeelah not only overcomes the odds stacked against her, but she also gives her community something to believe in. How often do you think bright students like Akeelah, who have to deal with distractions all around them, get the attention they desperately need to succeed?

Jonathan Kozol states that poorer schools consistently received less funding compared to richer schools. Nowhere is this more obvious than in the actual school structure itself. He points out that inner-city schools in impoverished neighborhoods are often poorly maintained and lack resources that middle- and upper-class suburban neighborhood public schools take for granted.

In my own classes, many of my students choose to volunteer at a local school that could easily fit into *Savage Inequalities.* Most of its students are poor racial minorities who benefit from a "backpack program." Each weekend students are given a backpack full of food to take home so they'll have something to eat until the following Monday. These children's needs are so great that often my students cannot imagine how these kids can learn anything.

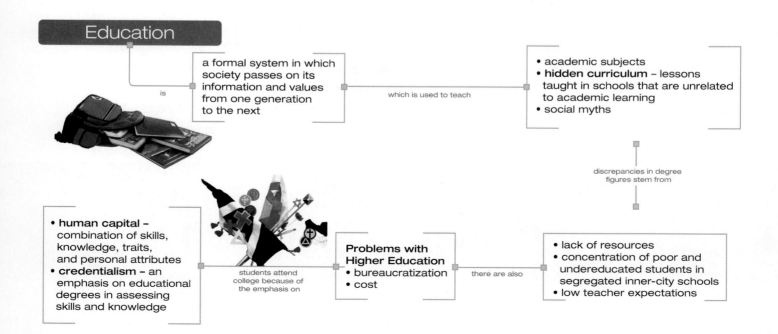

Education

is — a formal system in which society passes on its information and values from one generation to the next

which is used to teach —
- academic subjects
- **hidden curriculum** – lessons taught in schools that are unrelated to academic learning
- social myths

discrepancies in degree figures stem from

- **human capital** – combination of skills, knowledge, traits, and personal attributes
- **credentialism** – an emphasis on educational degrees in assessing skills and knowledge

students attend college because of the emphasis on

Problems with Higher Education
- bureaucratization
- cost

there are also

- lack of resources
- concentration of poor and undereducated students in segregated inner-city schools
- low teacher expectations

get the topic: HOW DO SOCIETIES PASS ON INFORMATION?

Education in Society

I often ask my students, "If I promised all of you an A, then asked those genuinely interested in learning to return, how many of you would be here tomorrow?" Rarely do I have more than five percent of my students raise their hands. Why is that? I've always found that students tend to be pragmatic about their reasons for education. They ask themselves, "What can I do with this degree?"

Since the Industrial Revolution, there has been a link between economic advancement and **education**, the formal system in which society passes on its information and values from one generation to the next.

> **EDUCATION** is the formal system in which society passes its information and values from one generation to the next.

Schools connect to the job system because they train individuals for specific types of work. For example, in order to become a surgeon, students must go through years of schooling and training. However, when they complete school, they have the benefit of a high salary, and the community benefits from their medical knowledge. In order to reach this point, students need to make an extended commitment to their education.

Educational Attainment of the Population 25 Years and Older

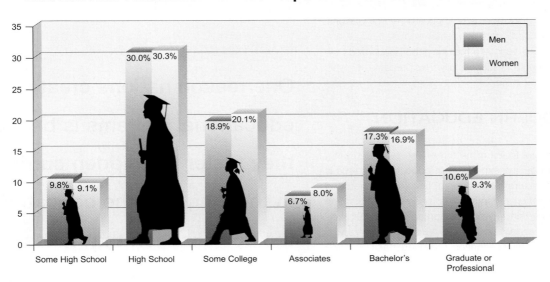

	Men	Women
Some High School	9.8%	9.1%
High School	30.0%	30.3%
Some College	18.9%	20.1%
Associates	6.7%	8.0%
Bachelor's	17.3%	16.9%
Graduate or Professional	10.6%	9.3%

Source: Data from the U.S. Census Bureau, *2006 American Community Survey*, Table S1501, Educational Attainment.

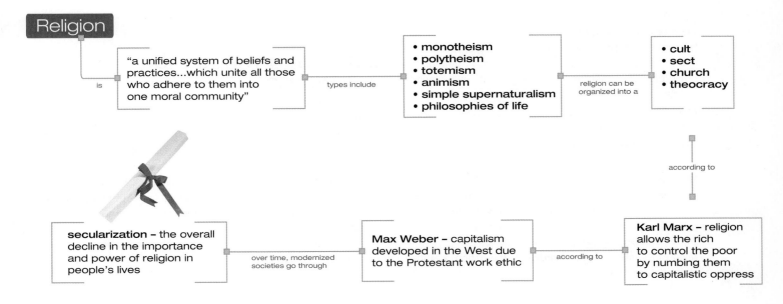

Religion

is → "a unified system of beliefs and practices...which unite all those who adhere to them into one moral community"

types include →
- monotheism
- polytheism
- totemism
- animism
- simple supernaturalism
- philosophies of life

religion can be organized into a →
- cult
- sect
- church
- theocracy

according to →

Karl Marx – religion allows the rich to control the poor by numbing them to capitalistic oppress

according to →

Max Weber – capitalism developed in the West due to the Protestant work ethic

over time, modernized societies go through →

secularization – the overall decline in the importance and power of religion in people's lives

HIDDEN CURRICULUM

When I was in elementary school, our school did not have air conditioning. With the sponsorship of a teacher, myself, and another student, we started a small school store, the proceeds of which went toward installing air conditioners throughout the school. In less than two years, we earned enough money selling school supplies to provide air-conditioners for the entire school. Through this experience, I learned about capitalism, hard work, and service.

Schools teach more than just academic subjects. If you think back to elementary school, you'll remember that you learned all kinds of things that are unrelated to academic life, like sharing and communication. Sociologists suggest that the education system plays an important role in society, because it teaches individuals the values of a community.

Certainly we want to transfer academic knowledge to the next generation, but schools also socialize students in what some call the "hidden curriculum." The term *hidden curriculum* refers to lessons taught in schools that are unrelated to academic learning. Schools teach children about citizenship when they have "mock" elections, and they teach us to follow orders, routines, and other seemingly arbitrary regulations. The hidden curriculum also applies to students' socialization of one another. Students learn how to negotiate their neighborhoods and how to deal with peers and peer conflicts successfully. This prepares students for stresses that will occur later in life.[2]

ROOTS OF MODERN EDUCATION SYSTEMS

People began going to school to learn the three R's—reading, 'riting, and 'rithmetic—right? Actually, the expansion of education systems is a social movement that stems from the ideas of building a nation and building the ideology of a nation's identity. This means that education also serves to ensure that certain "myths" are spread throughout society. These "myths" may or may not be factually true, but they are vital to the success of building a unified nation. Thinking back, do you remember any school activities that supported these myths?

Myth of the individual. The primary unit in society is the individual, not the family, clan, or ethnic group. Therefore, it is up to the individual to improve his or her place in society.

Myth of the nation as a group of individuals. The nation is no longer the property of a king or some group of elites. Individuals make up society and the nation. Therefore, by developing your skills and knowledge, you are bettering yourself and your community.

Myth of progress. Society's goal is to improve the status of both current and future residents. Thus, education for children is one way a nation can support the idea that it is working toward self-improvement.

Myth of socialization and life cycle continuity. Childhood socialization leads to adult character. Therefore, if children are socialized properly, this will lead to good character that ultimately benefits the nation in the long run. Thus, educating children plays a vital role in this endeavor.

Myth of the state as the guardian of the nation. It is the state's job to raise good, loyal, patriotic children, who will then be the next generation of good, loyal, and patriotic adults. In this way, socializing children into the nation becomes the role of the state, not the family.[3]

However, you should note that these myths are not universal. Certain groups see this forced homogenization as detrimental to their way of life. For example, the Amish refuse to participate in the state-sponsored education system out of fear of what their children might learn. Instead, they have decided to open their own schools.[4]

By looking at these five myths, you can see that **state-sponsored schools are an essential part of any strong nation.** Notice that nowhere on this list is the idea that everyone should learn to read. **One reason nations create educational systems is because they foster the hidden curriculum. In the long run, the education and the socialization that takes place in schools paves the way for a strong future.**

EDUCATION THROUGHOUT THE WORLD

Every nation has some type of educational system; however, not all educational systems are equal. The amount of resources, funding, and worth placed on education varies, which in turn creates inequalities in global education. A country's socioeconomic status has a huge effect on its education system. Systems in developing countries often fail to provide children with basic educational needs and struggle to sustain stable educational institutions. Paraguay, Sri Lanka, and the Philippines are all countries where one in five students goes to a school with no running water.[5]

Poor education systems often result in low literacy rates, or low percentages of people in the population who can read and write. In Sierra Leone, only 47 percent of men and 24 percent of women over the age of 15 are literate. This falls far below the world literacy rate of 88 percent of men and 79 percent of women.[6] Aside from showing you how poor education systems affect literacy rates, these figures also show you the imbalance of education between men and women. The number of women educated is almost half the number of men educated in Sierra Leone. Similarly, as you can see in the literacy rates map below, in every region of the world, male literacy rates are higher than female literacy rates. In Chapter 11, you learned about gender stratification and how men and women have been treated differently throughout history. Unfortunately, this is still true today.

A country's wealth plays a central role in education, so lack of funding and resources from a nation-state can weaken a system. Governments in sub-Saharan Africa spend only 2.4 percent of the world's public resources on education, yet 15 percent of the school-age population lives there. Conversely, the United States spends 28 percent of all the money spent in the world on education, yet it houses only 4 percent of the school-age population.[7]

The United States' large monetary contribution to education is in part due to the considerable number of university and college students in the nation and the high cost associated with those institutions. State colleges and universities all receive taxpayer benefits to keep their doors open. I often ask my students, "Who's on welfare in here?" Usually, no one raises his or her hand. However, if you attend a state college or university, you are on educational welfare. The taxpayers of your state are subsidizing some part of your education.

No matter what kind of college or university you attend, you'd probably agree that the main goal of attending that university is to receive a degree. Between 1997 and 2007, the number of degrees issued by higher education institutions increased from 24 percent to 29 percent.[8] But who exactly is receiving these degrees? Does one's race,

gender, or socioeconomic status affect his or her educational attainment? You bet it does.

EDUCATIONAL DISCREPANCIES IN RACE AND GENDER

Hollywood movies such as *Akeelah and the Bee, Lean on Me*, and *Freedom Writers* focus on the efforts of students who are not expected to succeed due to their environment and socioeconomic status. Unfortunately, for millions of students, these movies depict a real-life trend that exists all over the United States.

A 2007 U.S. Census survey revealed that 31.8 percent of the white population and 52.1 percent of the Asian population ages 25 and over have completed four years of college or more, while only 18.5 percent of African Americans and 12.7 percent of Hispanics showed similar attainment.[9] This discrepancy may be due to the concentration of poor and undereducated people segregated in inner-city schools. Here, African American and immigrant children are most likely to encounter teachers and administrators with very low expectations for student attainment and a lack of resources. In response to this trend, Kozol believes, society is locking them out of the competition for empowerment from the very beginning.[10]

TEACHER EXPECTANCY AND ATTAINMENT

The phenomenon known as the **teacher expectancy effect**—the impact of a teacher's expectations on a student's performance—is not just applied to poor and minority students.[11] If a teacher expects that a student will love the class and do well, the student generally does well. Of course, measuring teacher expectations is a difficult thing to do. Some studies show that expectancies influence not only individual student performance, but also the performance of the entire school.[12] Other studies suggest less obvious findings that propose that teachers may indeed influence students' self-perception, but that it is that perception that influences academic achievement.[13]

When I discuss this issue in class, I usually ask my students, "Who is afraid of math?" Many students sheepishly raise their hands. When we discuss why they fear

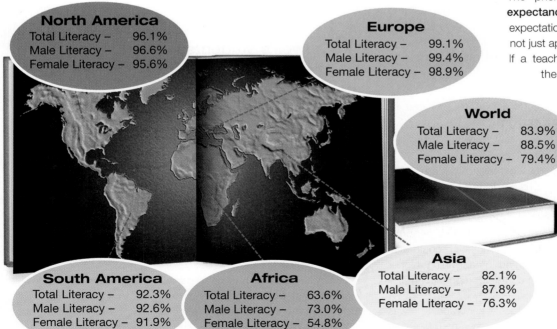

Regional Literacy Rates for Adults (15+), 2005–2007

North America
Total Literacy – 96.1%
Male Literacy – 96.6%
Female Literacy – 95.6%

Europe
Total Literacy – 99.1%
Male Literacy – 99.4%
Female Literacy – 98.9%

World
Total Literacy – 83.9%
Male Literacy – 88.5%
Female Literacy – 79.4%

South America
Total Literacy – 92.3%
Male Literacy – 92.6%
Female Literacy – 91.9%

Africa
Total Literacy – 63.6%
Male Literacy – 73.0%
Female Literacy – 54.8%

Asia
Total Literacy – 82.1%
Male Literacy – 87.8%
Female Literacy – 76.3%

Source: Data from United Nations Educational, Scientific, and Cultural Organization (UNESCO) Institute for Statistics.

mathematics, students usually say that they "don't get it," and they "hate it." When I ask the math-haters what grade they expect in their math course, the answer is usually "low." Such a self-fulfilling prophecy forms the core of most research on how educational expectations influence academic outcomes.

ACADEMIC ACHIEVEMENT

Grades

Not only is the number of college degrees increasing, but advanced placement credits for college are also rising. In fact, graduates in 2005 earned three more credits compared to graduates in 1990. Students' overall grade point averages (GPAs) also increased by roughly a third of a letter grade.[14] Improvement in student performance may have caused this increase, but grade inflation could also be the culprit. **Grade inflation** is the trend of assigning higher grades than previously assigned to students for completing the same work.

Recently, a student approached me to discuss her grade. She was very upset because she had received a B in my course. This young woman was visibly distraught, breathing hard, brow furrowed, and she rapidly began to tell me that she had "never gotten a B" in her life. She felt like a failure. Couldn't she "write an extra paper" or "do some other assignment?"

> ∧
> ∧ In the movie *Freedom Writers*, **Erin**
> ∧ **Gruwell's students were not expected to pass her class,** let alone graduate from high school. **However, all of her students graduated from high school, and many went on to college.**

"Everyone in my high school makes A's," she said. "I'm not used to failing." I pointed out that a B was not failing and thought about grade inflation. When a student views a B as failure, what do grades mean? As I said to this student, "If everyone makes an A, then an A means nothing."

Grade inflation has been perceived as something of a phenomenon at both secondary and higher education institutions. Some teachers claim it is a result of the pressure that students are under to receive high marks that is then projected onto the instructor. In 2004, Nancy W. Malkiel, dean of Princeton University's undergraduate college, imposed a plan to combat grade inflation. By the end of the 2004-2005 school year, she wanted the number of A's given to make up no more than 35 percent of the overall grades issued to students.[15] Initiatives such as this are implemented to keep the five-point grading system fair and standardized among all institutions.

Home Schooling

Some parents choose to forgo the offerings of a traditional school education. In 2005, nearly 1.1 million students were homeschooled in the United States, up from 850,000 in 1998.[16] As a professor I have taught many freshmen who were homeschooled. When I ask them why they were homeschooled, I hear a variety of reasons. Some say their parents were concerned about the quality of education at the public school they were assigned, but they couldn't afford a private school. Others cite religious reasons as the primary factor for learning at home. Still others report that a parent was an educator, and simply felt that a caring parent could do a better job of teaching his or her own children than an overworked stranger. These reports follow the general findings of researchers who study parents who homeschool. Such parents are generally motivated by a desire to be active in their children's learning, and although issues of value and quality are relevant, the strongest motivator of parents who homeschool appears to be a desire to be more deeply involved with their children.[17]

Higher Education: Bureaucratization and Cost

Traditional schools are formal organizations that have many of the aspects of any bureaucracy. Recall in Chapter 6 our discussion of Max Weber and formal organizations. The basic characteristics of bureaucracy are division of labor, rules and regulations, impersonality, hierarchy of authority, and technical qualifications. In your school, I'm sure you're aware that there is a hierarchy of authority, a division of labor between teachers, administrators, and support staff, and that most schools have student and faculty handbooks to make sure that everyone knows the rules and regulations. Schools can also take on these aspects of bureaucracy when they are impersonal to their students. For example, how many of you had to learn a unique student identification number upon entering college? Often when you enter a large population of students, you simply become a number.

Of course, by the time you reach college, you are probably used to the bureaucratic nature of education. However, I've heard some of my students say that a large part of their decision for choosing a college is based on personalization, but this is not always the case. When I was selecting a school for my undergraduate education, price was the main consideration. Although I certainly did not grow up poor, my parents were not exactly rolling in dough. Thus, my college of choice had more to do with where the scholarship money was the greatest. What made you select where you go to college?

As I'm sure you're well aware, the cost of college can have a strong influence on educational attainment. In the United States, the government only pays for primary and secondary education. Postsecondary, or higher education, is subsidized for state institutions; however, in-state tuition to a four-year university still averages about $6,185 a year.[18] Lofty tuition costs often deter low-income individuals from seeking higher education. In other industrialized countries, education at all levels is free. For example, in Sweden, government and institutionally managed schools—primary, secondary, and postsecondary—are free of tuition courtesy of the Swedish

GRADE INFLATION is the trend of assigning higher grades than previously assigned to students for completing the same work.

HUMAN CAPITAL is a person's combination of skills, knowledge, traits, and personal attributes.

CREDENTIALISM is an emphasis on educational degrees in assessing skills and knowledge.

government and taxpayers. This allows all students who meet certain academic standards to attend any school regardless of their economic status.[19]

Theories Behind Higher Education

Even though college often comes with high costs and bureaucratization, you still decided to go. Why? Sociologists propose a few theories. First, students seek an education as a way to improve their **human capital**, or their combination of skills, knowledge, traits, and personal attributes. Generally, you know that an employer will reward a worker who performs better. Education improves your attractiveness to an employer and perhaps your output for that job. Such skills are important to employers, and you understand that it improves your place in the market for jobs. Thus, through education you can improve your social status, and the education system becomes the vehicle by which you come closer to acquiring that status. What made you select where you go to college?

Similarly, I know many people who chose to go to college because of the reality of **credentialism**—an emphasis on educational degrees in assessing skills and knowledge. Many jobs

The Five Most Expensive Universities in the United States	
1. George Washington University Washington, D.C.	$39,240*
2. Kenyon College Gambier, OH	$38,140*
3. Bucknell University Lewisburg, PA	$38,134**
4. Vassar College Poughkeepsie, NY	$38,115**
5. Sarah Lawrence College Bronxville, NY	$38,090***

* Tuition and fees for 2008-09 school year.

** Tuition and fees for 2007-2008 school year.

*** Tuition for 2007-2008 school year.

Source: Data from Brian Wingfield and Louis Hau, "The World's Most Expensive Universities," *Forbes.com.*

RELIGION is a unified system of beliefs and practices, relative to sacred things, that is to say, things set apart and forbidden—beliefs and practices which unite into one single moral community called a Church, all those who adhere to them.

THEISM is the belief in a god or gods.

MONOTHEISM is the belief that there is only one god.

POLYTHEISM is the belief in multiple gods and demigods.

PHILOSOPHIES OF LIFE are ways of life that focus on a set of ethical, moral, or philosophical principles.

TOTEMISM is the practice of honoring a totem or a sacred object.

SIMPLE SUPERNATURALISM is the belief in a variety of supernatural forces that affect and influence people's lives.

ANIMISM is the belief that recognizes that animate spirits live in natural objects and operate in the world.

today require a college degree, but this was not always true. Neither of my parents had college degrees, but with hard work they held white-collar jobs in business management and accounting. Such a climb with a high school degree would be impossible in today's world. Employers use education as a type of litmus test to determine who is and who is not qualified. With the growth of public education in the United States, the status of holding a degree has become essential for success.[20]

EDUCATION AND RELIGION

It's no secret that religious instruction is not permitted in public schools in the United States. Teachers are not allowed to promote one religion over another due to the constitutional demand for a separation of church and state. Although public school students aren't getting religious instruction, sociologists have found that a student's religious affiliation and involvement play a big role in his or her educational outcome. Studies have shown that educational attainment and religious practice generally have a positive correlation.[21] In other words, religiously active students are apt to perform well in school and to graduate. In a study completed by Mark Regenerus, he found that intensely religious students scored better on standardized tests, "even after accounting for other predictors of academic success."[22] He argued that religious involvement gave students "a level of social control and motivation toward education."[23] This trend held up across all types of neighborhoods—affluent and poor—and across many different races and ethnicities. In fact, the more disadvantaged the neighborhood, the more beneficial a student's church attendance was on educational attainment.[24]

This research points to a possible connection between education and religion. Although certainly not causal, it does show that both of these social institutions perform a similar task—to socialize a person into society. Churches do this by socializing us into a value system, and schools do this through their academic mission and their pursuit of the hidden curriculum.

MAKE CONNECTIONS

Scheduling Around the Holidays

In 2007, members of the New York Muslim community called for a change in the school holiday schedule when standardized state tests were scheduled on Id al-Adha, a Muslim holy day. Although students could take excused absences, parents argued that it was unfair that children were off for Christian and Jewish holidays.

However, the New York Department of Education refused to add any additional holidays to the school schedule. Many school districts require that students be in school a certain number of days per school year, so any additional holidays would cause the school year to run even longer.[25]

>>> **ACTIVITY** Create a new school calendar for your state that includes

major religious holidays for the top five religions in the state. Remember that most school systems require that students be in school a set number of days, and that religious populations vary from state to state. Research the demographics of your state, and research the holidays of the five largest religious populations in your area. How difficult is it to create a schedule that meets everyone's religious needs?

Religion

Sociologist Emile Durkheim defined **religion** as a "unified system of beliefs and practices relative to sacred things, that is to say, things set apart and forbidden—beliefs and practices which unite into one single moral community called a Church, all those who adhere to them."[26] Although most societies have some sort of dominant religion, there are many different religions, each of which comes with its own set of beliefs and customs.

TYPES OF RELIGION

The three major religious groups of the West—Christianity, Judaism, and Islam—all practice **theism**, the belief in a god or gods. More specifically,

these religions practice **monotheism**, meaning they believe that there is only one God.[27]

Not all religions believe that there is one powerful God. Some religions believe in multiple gods or demigods; this belief is called **polytheism**. Instead of having multiple gods be all powerful, many polytheistic cultures have a single god to represent a specific power or object. For example, in ancient Nordic mythology, Odin was the god of wisdom, and Thor was the warrior god.[28] In some cases, each village in a particular area may have its own god along with a particular place or a sacred object reserved for worshipping that god.[29]

Some cultures do not have religions per se, but have philosophies that help guide people throughout life. **Philosophies of life** are ways of life that focus on a set of ethical, moral, or philosophical principles. Buddhism, Confucianism, and Taoism are all philosophies of life and are

World Religious Affiliations

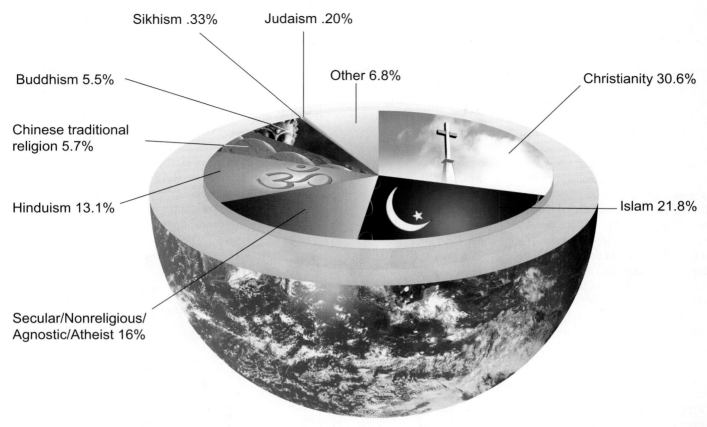

Sikhism .33%

Judaism .20%

Buddhism 5.5%

Chinese traditional religion 5.7%

Other 6.8%

Christianity 30.6%

Hinduism 13.1%

Islam 21.8%

Secular/Nonreligious/ Agnostic/Atheist 16%

Note: Total equals more than 100% due to rounding.
Source: Major Religions of the World Ranked by Number of Adherents, Adherents.com

dedicated to achieving a kind of moral enlightenment. This enlightenment is attained by following a specific set of rules, such as the teachings of Buddha or the laws of Confucius. The processes of being and becoming are key aspects of these ways of life.[30]

Preliterate societies practiced **totemism** by honoring a totem or a sacred object. These totems were symbolic objects that often depicted animals or plants that were important to the community. The totem itself was thought to have divine and mystical powers. In addition to totemism, preliterate societies also practiced simple supernaturalism. **Simple supernaturalism** is the belief in a variety of supernatural forces that affect and influence people's lives. Similarly, **animism** is the belief that recognizes that animate spirits live in natural objects and operate in the world. For example, in Shinto, which is practiced in Japan, the natural world is filled with *kami*—spirits that can bring luck or cause mischief.[31]

THINK SOCIOLOGICALLY

Hinduism in America

It should be no surprise that current immigration patterns influence religious preferences in the United States. Immigration patterns show that the majority of immigrants are coming to the United States from Mexico, China, the Philippines, and India.[32] Immigrants from Mexico and the Philippines generally follow Roman Catholic beliefs; Chinese immigrants are largely unchurched or Buddhist; and Indian immigrants are gen-

erally Hindu. These statistics are important because one of the fastest growing non-Christian religions in the United States is Hinduism. Hinduism is thought to be the oldest organized polytheistic religion, beginning more than 6000 years ago. Hinduism nearly doubled its percentage in the U.S. population over a 10-year period, from 0.13 percent to 0.23 percent in 2001.[33]

Even though Hinduism is on the rise, most Hindu temples do not qualify as "churches" from a legal point of view.

Therefore they do not enjoy the same tax benefits as their Christian counterparts. Furthermore, non-Christian doctrines are rarely acknowledged in schools and other institutions. They are tolerated, but students seldom learn about different belief patterns.[34]

National Hindu groups are growing, primarily to improve the recognition of Hinduism within this society while also supporting groups in India. These factors help unify Indian immigrants both as a religious group and as an ethnic group.[35]

ORGANIZATION IN RELIGION

Have you ever come across a religious service while flipping television channels? If so, you know that these gatherings can boast thousands of worshippers in the audience and maybe even millions at home. How do religious followings get so large?

Religions go through a series of stages before they become an integrated part of society. Sociologically, all religions begin as cults. **Cults** are new religious movements led by charismatic leaders with few followers. The teachings and practices of this religion are often at odds with the dominant culture and religion, so society is likely to reject the cult. Cults demand intense commitment and involvement of its members, and they rely on new members from outside recruitment. Most cults fail because they cannot attract enough followers to sustain themselves.

Once a cult has enough members to sustain itself, it becomes a sect. **Sects** still go against society's norms. Often, members have greater social standing and are usually better integrated into society. As a result, they are less likely to be persecuted by the dominant society. As time passes and the sect grows, the members tend to become respectable members of society.[36]

Eventually, sects can evolve into a church. The term **church** does not specifically refer to a building or a denomination of a religion; instead, it is a large, highly organized group of believers. Churches are bureaucratized institutions and may include national and international offices, and leaders must undergo special training to perform established rituals.

If a church becomes highly integrated into the dominant culture, it may join with the state. A state religion, or **theocracy**, is formed when government and religion work together to shape society. Citizenship automatically makes one a member, so most of society belongs to this religion. For example, Iran has a theocratic government, going so far as placing religious leaders at the pinnacle of executive government decisions.[37]

RELIGION IN SOCIETY

Durkheim argues that religion and society are connected so much that the elementary forms of religion are actually expressions of the importance of the social group. A united group accomplishes more than an individual, and religion became a way that primitive people sought to express and explain this mystery. Concepts of divinity or the supernatural were a means of an explanation.[38]

Religions also function to provide cultural norms like values and beliefs that societies hold important. Religions can also divide the **sacred**, things connected to God or dedicated to a religious purpose, from the **profane**, related or devoted to that which is not sacred or biblical, by labeling certain objects, events, and people as sacred. For example, few people might take offense if I burned this textbook. What if I burned a sacred book like the Bible, the Torah, or the Koran? An object's sacredness is related to the perception of the believer.

Likewise, religious rituals develop around these sacred objects further strengthening the social norm. **Rituals** are an established pattern of behavior closely associated with experience of the sacred. This allows the followers to come together and contribute to these rituals, strengthening the group's common understanding and belief. This in turn helps strengthen the group's bonds and further integrates the individuals into the group. This unity created by religion allows members to integrate by increasing cohesion and functioning as a social control mechanism.

∧∧∧ **A church choir is a ritual that strengthens bonds for the entire church.** When the choir sings, both the singers and churchgoers are participating in the activity for the same reason—to celebrate their faith together.

▶▶▶ GO GL🌐BAL

The Golden Rule Around the World

Even though many religions hold different beliefs, some ideas are practically universal. An example is the Golden Rule, which states, "Treat others as you want to be treated." As you can see, that regardless of the specific belief system, this rule manifests itself in many societies.

Buddhism (Udana-Varga 5:18): Hurt no others in ways that you yourself would find hurtful.

Christianity (Matthew 7:12): In everything do to others as you would have them do to you; this is the law and the prophets.

Confucianism (Analects 15:23): Surely it is the maxim of loving-kindness: Do not unto others what you would not have done unto you.

Hinduism (Mahabharata 5:1517): This is the sum of duty: Do naught unto others, which would cause you pain if done to you.

Islam (Fourth Hadith of an-Nawawi 13): Not one of you is a believer until you wish for others what you wish for yourself.

Judaism (Talmud Shabbat 31a): What is hateful to you, do not to your fellow man, this is the entire law: all the rest is commentary.[39]

RELIGION AND THE ECONOMY

Karl Marx

Karl Marx didn't view religion as a way to unify people and answer questions. Instead, he viewed religion as the "opium of the people." In other words, Marx believed religion was often used as a tool by the wealthy to mislead the poor about their true social class. He suggested that religion gave people an illusion of happiness but nothing of real, long-lasting value.[40]

Remember, Marx believed that the rich controlled the poor through a variety of means, one of which was ideology. If people believed that something was fair or justified, then they were unlikely to bring about change in the system. Marx thought religions did very little to change the corrupt system of capitalism; instead, they often found harmony within it.

Marx believed the wealthy used their power and influence to assure that the poor believed their plight was divinely inspired, and that some heavenly afterlife would make everything better. Marx suggested that religion helped people feel better by numbing them to their true pain. In short, religion causes people to ignore the real problem—capitalist oppression.[41]

Max Weber

Max Weber agreed with Marx's idea that there was a link between the economy and religion, but he believed the opposite was true. He pointed out a connection between Protestant and capitalist values. Weber proposed that John Calvin's teachings laid the foundation for capitalism. Therefore, Weber believed capitalism developed in the West primarily because the Calvinist Protestant belief system supported it.[42]

One of Calvin's important philosophical points was the belief in predestination. This teaching suggests that God knows in advance who will and who will not go to Heaven because God is all-knowing. Prosperity is seen as a mark of God's favor because blessings would not be given to the "damned." So hard work and the creation of wealth are positive attributes and signs that you are a "chosen one." While not explicitly stated, notice how this infers that poverty is a sign of God's disfavor. In order to avoid poverty, people have to work hard, save money, and be thrifty. Weber termed this idea the Protestant Ethic.

CULTS are new religious movements led by charismatic leaders with few followers.

SECTS are religious groups that have enough members to sustain themselves and go against society's norms.

CHURCH is a large, highly organized group of believers.

THEOCRACY is a state religion that is formed when government and religion both work together to shape society.

SACRED means connected to God or dedicated to a religious purpose.

PROFANE means related or devoted to that which is not sacred or biblical.

RITUALS are established patterns of behavior closely associated with experience of the sacred.

SECULARIZATION is the overall decline in the importance and power of religion in people's lives.

Furthermore, the Protestant work ethic emphasizes individuality. Protestantism often supports the notion of individual salvation, which lays the groundwork for individuals to focus on their own well-being first and the good of others second.[43]

Both of these components—prosperity and individuality—laid the foundation for capitalism. Notice how both Marx and Weber saw a connection between the economy and religion. However, Marx saw religion as a tool to keep the rich wealthy, while Weber saw it as a tool to make people work hard to become prosperous.

CHANGES IN RELIGION

As societies modernized, religions began going through **secularization**,[44] which is the overall decline in the importance and power of religion in people's lives. Institutional religion weakens as societies become more scientifically advanced.

Secularization theorists generally agree that as society becomes more complex people become less tied to the "old ways" and more inclined to pursue other avenues.[45] This seems to indicate that secularization is inevitable for society; however, many developing parts of the world show no obvious decline in religious influence. In fact, religion's importance in the United States and many other parts of the world seems unchanged.[46]

The Importance of Religion in People's Lives

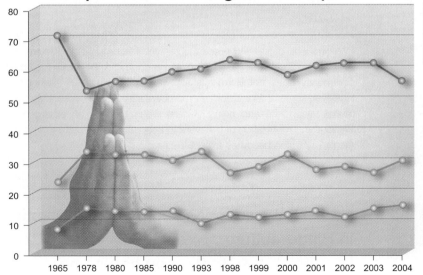

Legend:
- Very important
- Fairly important
- Not very important

Note: Data unavailable for all years.

Source: Copyright © 2006 Polling Report, Inc., and polling/sponsoring organizations POLLINGREPORT.COM

<<< **There's been a decline in the number of people in the United States who say that religion is very important in their lives, while the number of people who say it is fairly important rose.** In addition, the number of people who say that religion is not very important in their lives has doubled since the year 1965.

Religion in the United States

Robert Bellah et al. argue that there is a civil religion in the United States.[47] A **civil religion** is a binding force that holds society together through political and social issues. Civil religion elevates democracy to sacredness by giving democracy religious undertones. The flag and the cross become equally sacred.

Despite Christian influences, we have the freedom to practice whatever religion we wish. While many people in the United States are Christian, interesting trends are taking place. Since the 1900s, there has been a shift away from so-called mainstream Protestant religions, such as the Methodist, Lutheran, Presbyterian, and Episcopalian churches, and a move toward more traditionally conservative churches, like the Southern Baptist Convention, Pentecostal, Evangelical, and African Methodist Episcopal churches.

Hout et al. reviewed data in an effort to figure out why this occurred. They found that **intermarriage**, a marriage between people of different religions, is not a reason for this transition. Certainly, some mainstream members switch to a conservative religion, but conservatives also switch to mainstream religions at about the same rate. So, the rates of "switchers" balance out.[48]

Another theory proposes that mainstream churches do not organize their congregations to provide participation opportunities for members, nor do they encourage the same level of participation, which makes them less attractive.[49] However, Hout et al. show that religious participation is really an individual trait, since people who switch religions remain as active in their new church as they were in their old.

Researchers also checked to see whether U.S. churchgoers are more politically and religiously conservative. The argument suggests that values espoused by conservative churches, such as absolute standards of right and wrong and a belief in heaven and hell, appeal to more conservative people. In the political realm, conservative churches tend to oppose moral issues such as homosexuality, abortion, and cohabitation. Meanwhile, the argument goes, mainstream churches have become "too liberal" and lost their audience. Researchers actually found that conservative churches are becoming slightly more liberal, while mainstream churches are becoming more conservative.[50]

The leading cause of the conservative church growth had to do with birth rates. Most people remain in the church into which they were born. Hout et al. found that since 1900 conservatives have had larger families compared to mainstream families, and that this single factor accounts for 76 percent of the trend of conservative religious growth.[51]

However, from 1990 to 2001, the percentage of Christians in the United States has declined by approximately 10 percent. The fastest-growing category of Christians is nondenominational, while denominations such as Baptists, Roman Catholics, and Methodists decline.[52] This trend of stretching religious boundaries is called **postdenominationalism**. Churches like the Lakewood Church in Houston show the popularity of nondenominational organizations because services are housed in the former arena of the Houston Rockets basketball team and can hold over 25,000 people.[53]

think sociologically: HOW DOES RELIGION AFFECT SOCIETY?

Symbolic Interactionism

Religious believers feel that everything in the world can be interpreted or defined as either sacred or profane. Almost anything—trees, animals, even bodies of water—can be considered sacred. However, what is sacred to one group may be profane to another.

An element can be both sacred and profane by the same religious group. For example, for some Christians, red wine is profane when consumed during an ordinary meal, but the wine is sacred when consumed during the ritual of Holy Communion. The setting influences the reverence of an object.

A **system of beliefs** relates sacred objects to religious rituals and defines and protects the sacred from the profane. It labels what is a virtue and what is a sin. These labels provide meaning and morals for specific actions. For example, certain belief systems tell people that sex within marriage is acceptable, but sex outside marriage is sinful. A religion's system of beliefs is maintained by an **organization of believers**, which is a group of people who ensures the prosperity and effectiveness of the religious experience.

An organization of believers is comprised of religious leaders and followers who define and guard the sacred. The organization determines possible conflicts with the religion's moral code. For example, the Amish community does not permit its followers to use modern technology. However, some orders allow their members some leniency, such as communal telephones and riding in cars when there is an emergency.[54] Without an organization of believers to keep abreast of current developments, a religion becomes extinct.

<<< **Cows are considered sacred beasts in Hindu culture,** and as such are not to be harmed. **In India, you can sometimes see a cow sitting in the middle of traffic as cars and bikes move around it.**

Functionalism

Durkheim believed that religion binds the community together through ritual and tradition. Followers gather to celebrate the power of things that are sacred and supernatural. Rituals unite the group as they celebrate and perform the actions together. For example, Martin Luther King, Jr., was president of the Southern Christian Leadership Conference, an organization that combined religion and politics to promote the 1960s civil rights movement. Thousands of activists joined together to share their faith and beliefs while working toward equality and unity.[55]

Religion also strengthens society's norms and values by including society's values in its own lessons. Religion influences a person's actions in society, often acting as a means of social control. All religions provide rules for adherents to live by, and most suggest that disobedience of these rules leads to negative consequences.

Religion reconciles people to the hardships and inequities of society. It offers the poor and oppressed strong moral codes as a conduit to salvation after death. Religion provides both the reason and the reward to conform to social rules.

However, religion promotes stability, even if the status quo is unfair and unequal. Religion can perpetuate practices like slavery, racism, and sexism. People in power use religion to enforce social hierarchy, maintain social order, and prevent the likelihood of rebellion. Furthermore, technological advancements may go against religious beliefs. When Galileo proposed that the Earth orbited the sun, this conflicted with the geocentric views of the church. The church forced Galileo to retract his claims and then placed him under house arrest.[56]

Religion can also make it more difficult to resolve political struggles. Think about modern "religious wars." The Jewish/Muslim conflicts in the Middle East and the Protestant/Catholic tensions in Northern Ireland appear to be about religion when, in fact, they are mostly about land, who lives on it, and who controls it.

CIVIL RELIGION is a binding force that holds society together through political and social issues.

INTERMARRIAGE is marriage between people of different religions.

POSTDENOMINATIONALISM is a recent trend that stretches religious boundaries.

SYSTEM OF BELIEFS relates sacred objects to religious rituals, and defines and protects the sacred from the profane.

ORGANIZATION OF BELIEVERS is a group that ensures the prosperity and effectiveness of the religious experience.

Conflict Theory

Conflict theorists believe that religion legitimizes social inequalities. Think about slavery in the Americas. The practice of owning and abusing another human being was an accepted practice, in part, because some churches condoned it. In the hierarchy of faith, God was at the top of the list, followed by whites. Blacks and people of other races were viewed as being worth less than whites.[57]

Marx believed that religion promoted capitalism and inequality because churches often support the idea that the wealthy deserved privileges. Weber's ideology that God blesses those who will go to Heaven also indicates that religion and economics are intertwined.

Religion also promotes obedience and legitimizes governments that are not in the best interests of everyone concerned. For example, the imperial family of Japan claims lineage from Amaterasu, Shinto goddess of the sun. Therefore, to attack the emperor is to attack Amaterasu. Such a system guarantees faithful obedience to political leaders.[58]

<<< The Promise Keepers is an organization committed to helping men lead a Christian life. **When people are going through periods of uncertainty, religion can bring them together for support.**

WRAP YOUR MIND AROUND THE THEORY

One of the functions of religion is to bring people together through ritual. This family unites to celebrate a Kwanzaa tradition of lighting candles.

FUNCTIONALISM

Functionalists believe that religion binds members of the community together through participation in rituals that celebrate the supernatural. Religion also strengthens society's norms and values by teaching these beliefs in a religious context. In this way, religion also strengthens and supports the governmental authority. People tend to accept the norms of society and religion, which effectively creates social stability. This stability means that people are less likely to oppose the leadership of those in power.

CONFLICT THEORY

Conflict theorists believe that religion often serves only to further the inequalities of social classes. One aspect often discussed is the position of women ministers in churches. Conflict theorists might point out that for centuries women have been excluded from leadership in organized religions often for reasons that are more cultural than religious. Thus, why does the system perpetuate these ideas? When I discuss this with a class, I refer to God as "She" and "Her." Some students become uncomfortable, while others laugh. Eventually, someone will say, "God is a man." Feminists and conflict theorists would suggest that the reason people believe God is a man is because men run most religions, and they wish to maintain their positions.

HOW DOES RELIGION AFFECT SOCIETY?

SYMBOLIC INTERACTIONISM

Symbolic interactionists focus on labeling things as either "sacred" or "profane." Almost anything can be considered sacred, including locations, trees, caves, and animals, and these sacred objects are usually involved in rituals. The rituals themselves can also become sacred over time. Believers separate things that are sacred from things that are profane using their systems of beliefs. These systems of beliefs define meanings and morals to specific actions. In addition to this belief system, there is an organization that ensures the continuing effectiveness of the religious experience.

Religion is one way that those in power stay in control. Monarchies can use the power of the people's faith to maintain order and quell any rebellions that could threaten their thrones.

Some religions use totems to portray sacred objects and ideas. In this Native American ceremony, the totems are used as a backdrop for the ritual being performed.

Improving Education with School Vouchers

As Jonathan Kozol points out, educational outcomes are often linked to family income and structure. Generally, the poorer a child is, the lower his or her educational attainment will be. Although individual teachers can have a great impact on this situation, entire schools can also take on an active role by ensuring that their students have adequate nutrition and clothing.[59]

In an effort to give children from poorer communities an equal opportunity in education, some schools have introduced a school vouchers policy. Vouchers are essentially cash equivalents that allow parents to select a participating school—private, religious, or public—to send their child. Voucher programs further the economic model of education; performing schools will get more money and thereby thrive, leaving poor schools with fewer students.

This situation can either improve educational outcomes for poor schools or cause the school to close.

Critics of the program claim that instead of pushing students elsewhere, struggling students, teachers, and schools need assistance.[60] Kozol, a critic of the program, also claims that vouchers only works for students with involved parents. Therefore, children who need the most help and attention are stuck in a school with few resources.[61] At the other end of the spectrum, supporters of the program claim that vouchers help low-income families gain control over education.[62]

The actual research on the voucher program is rather mixed, some showing marginal effectiveness for students, while others show no effect at all. Belfield and Levin suggest that the proposed link between vouchers and improvement in schools for the poor is difficult to support, because even in areas where vouchers exist, poor children often don't have the information available to make a good school selection.[63]

ACTIVITIES

1. Research your state's position on the school voucher debate. If the voucher program is implemented, look at test scores from before and after the implementation. Do you think the program is helping struggling students? If the voucher program is not implemented in your state, look at test scores for poor and rich school districts. Do you think the voucher program would be useful? If not, what would be a good alternative?
2. Have a class debate over the pros and cons of the school voucher program.

From Classroom to Community | School Voucher Program

In high school, Sean was one of the students who benefited from the school voucher program. He left his inner-city school to attend a private Catholic school in the suburbs. When Sean was a freshman in my class, he knew he wanted to complete his community learning assignment by volunteering in an inner-city school, similar to the one from which he'd escaped.

On Sean's first day of volunteer work at the school, he immediately noticed a difference between the inner-city school and the one he had attended. "The first thing I noticed was the difference in classroom appearances. In the high school I attended, the classrooms had brightly lit rooms with large windows that looked out onto a soccer field. Every classroom had enough desks for each student, and we didn't have to share supplies. Even more impressive, every room had a computer, a television, and a working air conditioning and heating system.

"The school where I volunteer doesn't have half of the equipment my high school did.

"The next thing I noticed was how much harder the work was at my high school than it is at the inner-city school. My school had high standards of achievement, and I had to study hard and do well, or I could lose my spot in the school. Dress code and conduct requirements were also stricter. There was a list of things we could and couldn't do, and breaking these rules could get you kicked out, too.

"My classes were also different. I had a religion class in addition to my regular subjects. It was kind of strange for me, because I'm not Catholic, but the classes were required. My parents said that it was okay because I was getting a better education at a religious private school than I would in a public school.

"After completing my volunteer work, I can definitely appreciate the advantages that the school voucher program gave me."

15

HOW **DO SOCIETIES PASS ON INFORMATION?**   265

through education and religion

HOW **DOES RELIGION AFFECT SOCIETY?**   274

functionalism: religion binds people together through ritual and tradition
conflict theory: religion legitimizes social inequalities; for example,
the practice of owning slaves was accepted in part because some
churches condoned the practice
symbolic interactionism: everything in the world can be interpreted
as profane or sacred, but the setting influences the reverence
of objects or acts

WHAT **SOCIAL POLICIES HELP CHILDREN GET
A BETTER EDUCATION?** 277

school voucher policies that allow low-income parents to select a
participating school to send their child

get the topic: HOW DO SOCIETIES PASS ON INFORMATION?

Education in Society   265
Religion   270
Symbolic Interactionism   274

Functionalism   275
Conflict Theory   275
Improving Education with School Vouchers   277

Theory

FUNCTIONALISM   275

- religion strengthens norms and values
- rituals unite the group when they celebrate or perform actions
- created social stability that supports governmental authority
- acts as a means of social control by influencing a person's actions

CONFLICT THEORY   275

- religion strengthens the inequalities of social classes
- dogma created to benefit the wealthy and condemn the poor
- Marx: religion promotes capitalism because churches often support the idea that the wealthy deserve privileges that the poor do not

- religion promotes obedience and legitimizes governments that are not in the best interest of everyone

SYMBOLIC INTERACTIONISM   274

- everything is either sacred or profane
- system of beliefs define meaning and morals to specific actions
- organization that supports belief system ensures continuation and effectiveness of the religious experience

Key Terms

education is the formal system in which society passes its information and values from one generation to the next.   265

teacher expectancy effect is the impact of a teacher's expectations on a student's performance.   267

grade inflation is the trend of assigning higher grades than previously assigned to students for completing the same work.   268

human capital is a person's combination of skills, knowledge, traits, and personal attributes.   269

credentialism is an emphasis on educational degrees in assessing skills and knowledge.   269

religion is a unified system of beliefs and practices, relative to sacred things, that is to say, things set apart and forbidden—beliefs and

practices which unite into one single moral community called a Church, all those who adhere to them.   270

theism is the belief in a god or gods.   270

monotheism is the belief that there is only one god.   270

polytheism is the belief in multiple gods and demigods.   270

philosophies of life are ways of life that focus on a set of ethical, moral, or philosophical principles. *270*

totemism is the practice of honoring a totem or a sacred object. *271*

simple supernaturalism is the belief in a variety of supernatural forces that affect and influence people's lives. *271*

animism is the belief that recognizes that animate spirits live in natural objects and operate in the world. *271*

cults are new religious movements led by charismatic leaders with few followers. *272*

sects are religious groups that have enough members to sustain themselves and go against society's norm. *272*

church is a large, highly organized group of believers. *272*

theocracy is a state religion that is formed when government and religion both work together to shape society. *272*

sacred means connected to God or dedicated to a religious purpose. *272*

profane means related or devoted to that which is not sacred or biblical. *272*

rituals are established patterns of behavior closely associated with experience of the sacred. *272*

secularization is the overall decline in the importance and power of religion in people's lives. *273*

civil religion is a binding force that holds society together through political and social issues. *274*

intermarriage is marriage between people of different religions. *274*

postdenominationalism is a recent trend that stretches religious boundaries. *274*

system of beliefs relates sacred objects to religious rituals, and defines and protects the sacred from the profane. *274*

organization of believers is a group that ensures the prosperity and effectiveness of the religious experience. *274*

Sample Test Questions

These multiple-choice questions are similar to those found in the test bank that accompanies this textbook.

1. Which of the following is *not* a myth associated with education?
   a. Society is the primary unit.
   b. A nation is merely a group of individuals.
   c. Childhood socialization leads to adult character.
   d. Learning increases individual and national future progress.

2. Some parents decide to homeschool their children because they are concerned with
   a. school size.
   b. lack of resources.
   c. school segregation.
   d. academic instruction.

3. Which of the following statements is *true*?
   a. Improvements in student performance are directly related to religious practice.
   b. Religious students from all backgrounds are apt to perform well in school.
   c. Intensely religious students do not perform as well on standardized tests.
   d. Religious practice only benefits poor students.

4. A type of religious organization is a
   a. synagogue.
   b. mosque.
   c. temple.
   d. church.

5. What is Max Weber's view of religion?
   a. Scientific advancement weakens religion.
   b. Protestant teachings laid the foundation for capitalism.
   c. Religion is a way to unite people and answer questions.
   d. Elementary forms of religion express the importance of social groups.

ESSAY

1. What is the hidden curriculum?
2. How can a country's socioeconomic status affect education?
3. What factors affect educational attainment?
4. How do religions become integrated into society?
5. How can religion be related to capitalism?

WHERE TO START YOUR RESEARCH PAPER

To look at more educational statistics, go to
http://nces.ed.gov
http://www.uis.unesco.org

To learn more about grade inflation, go to
http://www.gradeinflation.com/

To learn more about homeschooling in the United States, go to
http://www.census.gov/

To learn more about college costs, go to
http://www.whitehouse.gov

To learn more about education and religion, go to
http://www.ed.gov/Speeches/04-1995/prayer.html#1

To learn more about Robert Bellah's views about the United States having a civil religion, go to
http://www.robertbellah.com/articles_5.htm

ANSWERS: 1. a; **2.** d; **3.** b; **4.** d; **5.** b

Remember to check www.thethinkspot.com **for additional information, downloadable flashcards, and other helpful resources.**

الشركة
وطني
خليج ب
تجاري
اهلي
اوسط
الدولي
برقان
بيتك
بنك بوبيان
كويتية
تسهيلات
ايفا
استثمارات
مشاريع
اهلية

40,000

31358820

أول رئيس أميركي من أصل إفريقي

0.00   0.00   0.00

ECONOMY AND POLITICS

WHAT ARE THE SYSTEMS OF ECONOMICS
AND POLITICS?
HOW DO SOCIOLOGISTS VIEW ECONOMIC
AND POLITICAL SYSTEMS?
HOW DOES THE SYSTEM WORK
FOR VETERANS?

"The world

can certainly save itself, but only if we recognize accurately the dangers that humanity confronts together. For that, we will have to pause from our relentless competition in order to survey the common challenges we face. The world's current ecological, demographic, and economic trajectory is unsustainable, meaning that if we continue with "business as usual" we will hit social and ecological crises with calamitous results. We face four causes for such potential crises:

- Human pressures on the Earth's ecosystems and climate, unless mitigated substantially, will cause dangerous climate change, massive species extinctions, and the destruction of vital life-support functions.
- The world's population continues to rise at a dangerously rapid pace, especially in the regions least able to absorb a rising population.

- One sixth of the world remains trapped in extreme poverty unrelieved by global economic growth, and the poverty trap poses tragic hardships for the poor themselves and great risks for the rest of the world.
- We are paralyzed in the very process of global problem solving, weighed down by cynicism, defeatism, and outdated institutions.

These problems will not solve themselves. A world of untrammeled market forces and competing nation-states offers no automatic solutions to the harrowing and increasing difficulties. Ecological conditions will be worsened, not improved, by the rapid economic growth that is under way in most of the world unless that growth is channeled by active public policies into resource-saving (or sustainable) technologies. The transition from high to low fertility (birth) rates, necessary for lower population growth, requires concerted public action to help guide private and voluntary fertility choices. Market forces alone will not overcome poverty traps. And the failures of global problem solving mean that we are failing to adopt even straightforward and sensible solutions lying right before our eyes."[1]

How Do Societies Support
and Govern Themselves?

In *The Common Wealth: Economics for a Crowded Planet,* economist Jeffrey Sachs explains that nations like China and India are becoming economic powerhouses.

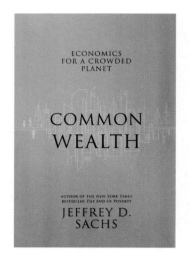

ECONOMICS FOR A CROWDED PLANET

COMMON WEALTH

AUTHOR OF THE *NEW YORK TIMES* BESTSELLER *THE END OF POVERTY*

JEFFREY D. SACHS

In 2008, the world watched as more than 2,000 Chinese performers dazzled with their precise movements and exquisite artistry in the opening ceremonies for the Beijing Olympic Games.[2] In a country long shrouded in mystery and seclusion, the Games served as a "coming-out party" for China, which is quickly becoming an economic force to be reckoned with in the global marketplace.

Jeffrey Sachs suggests to U.S. citizens that our position in the world is destined to change and that this change will not only affect our economic standing in the world, but also our political position. He identifies both the problems and solutions to many of the economic and political problems facing the world today.

Why would an economist examine political problems? Political and economic systems are tied closely to each other. For example, many laws in the United States relate to the economy. We have laws that regulate the sale of stocks and fight for truth in advertising, among others.

The world's population is growing at a rapid rate, and more and more people are falling into poverty, so how do we improve the world's economic and political systems? Sachs argues that cooperation between nations is key in making the world a safer and happier place. In a sense, cooperation and improvement of our general welfare is the focus of this chapter, which covers the social institutions of the economy and politics.

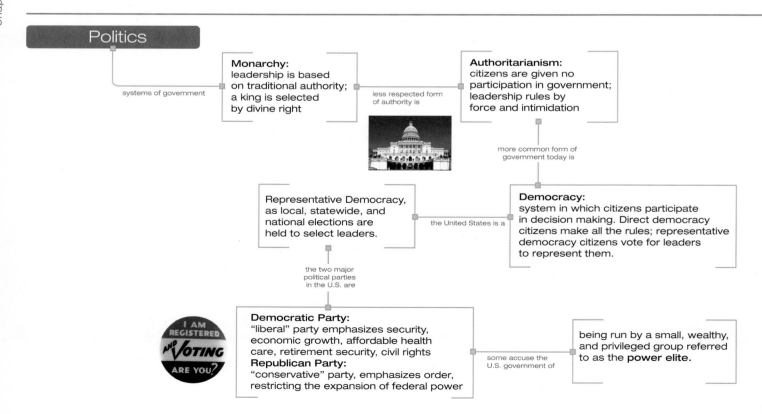

Politics

systems of government

Monarchy: leadership is based on traditional authority; a king is selected by divine right

less respected form of authority is

Authoritarianism: citizens are given no participation in government; leadership rules by force and intimidation

more common form of government today is

Representative Democracy, as local, statewide, and national elections are held to select leaders.

the United States is a

Democracy: system in which citizens participate in decision making. Direct democracy citizens make all the rules; representative democracy citizens vote for leaders to represent them.

the two major political parties in the U.S. are

I AM REGISTERED AND VOTING ARE YOU?

Democratic Party: "liberal" party emphasizes security, economic growth, affordable health care, retirement security, civil rights
Republican Party: "conservative" party, emphasizes order, restricting the expansion of federal power

some accuse the U.S. government of

being run by a small, wealthy, and privileged group referred to as the **power elite.**

People have been trading goods and services forever, and they've also attempted to establish some form of social order in every society. It is human nature to attempt to organize things that seem to be in chaos. Economic systems attempt to organize the trade of goods and services, while political systems attempt to organize the behavior of its citizens. For this reason, this chapter focuses on these systems as social institutions. *Social institutions* are organizations of society that provide a framework by which an individual can negotiate within the larger society.

Perhaps the greatest influence on these institutions was the Industrial Revolution and the changes to society associated with it. Recall our discussions in previous chapters about the importance of this economic revolution in creating new and cheaper goods, expanding the economies of the nations in which it occurred, increasing the division of labor, and changing the type of work that people do. The Industrial Revolution moved society from primarily an agrarian form of living into an urban one. People relied more on energy to power

ECONOMIC SYSTEM or **ECONOMY** is the social institution that helps a society organize what it produces, distributes, and consumes.

CAPITALISM is an economic system in which individuals can own the means of production as well as the services that others may need.

FREE MARKETS generally refer to markets that are free from government control.

machines, such as the steam engine, to reduce the amount of physical labor people had to perform. This process helped increase production. Workers became specialized, and the surplus and wealth created by industrialization changed both the economic and political structures of nations as they went through this process. In short, the Industrial Revolution influenced the form of the family, the power of the nation state, and the manner in which people traded goods and services.[3]

Economic Systems

An **economic system**, or **economy**, is the social institution that helps a society organize what it produces, distributes, and consumes, including goods and services. There are two basic types of economic systems in industrial nations—capitalism and socialism. No nation is completely capitalist or socialist in their pure forms; most countries are a mixture of both systems.

CAPITALISM

Capitalism is an economic system in which individuals can own the means of production as well as the services that others may need. The three core components of capitalism are private ownership of property, profit motivation, and competition in a "free market." **Free markets** generally refer to markets that are free from government control. Philosopher Adam Smith envisioned an economic system in which

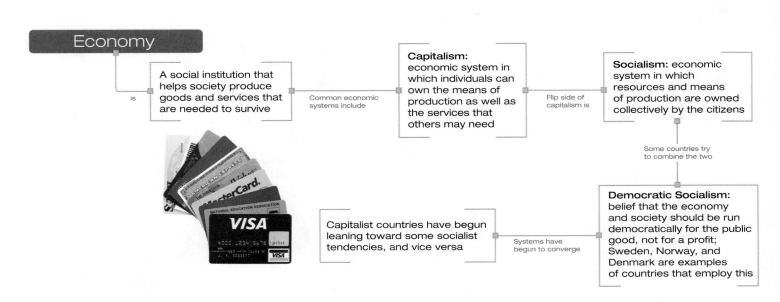

Economy

is — A social institution that helps society produce goods and services that are needed to survive

Common economic systems include — **Capitalism:** economic system in which individuals can own the means of production as well as the services that others may need

Flip side of capitalism is — **Socialism:** economic system in which resources and means of production are owned collectively by the citizens

Some countries try to combine the two

Democratic Socialism: belief that the economy and society should be run democratically for the public good, not for a profit; Sweden, Norway, and Denmark are examples of countries that employ this

Systems have begun to converge — Capitalist countries have begun leaning toward some socialist tendencies, and vice versa

DEMAND is the desire for a good or service.

SUPPLY is the amount of a good or service available.

MONOPOLY is the exclusive possession or control of the supply or trade in a service.

PRICE ELASTICITY OF DEMAND is the change in a good's demand as its price changes.

SOCIALISM is the economic system by which resources and the means of production are owned collectively by the citizens.

DEMOCRATIC SOCIALISM is the economic system that advocates running government democratically and for the good of the most people.

CONVERGENCE THEORY is the tendency for capitalism and socialism to converge.

people's own self-interest dictates what they do, not the government. In theory, the market will find a balance point on its own and meet society's needs. In free markets, the government's role is extremely limited; it is mostly involved in creating laws that govern business dealings.[4]

In such a system, market forces are supposed to meet economic needs. Economists refer to the desire for a good or service as the **demand**, while the amount of a good or service available to a customer is known as **supply**. In my day, there was a great demand for pet rocks, the fascinating toy that was essentially a rock with plastic eyes glued on. Today, I could have a great supply of pet rocks, but without demand, they only take up space, because no one wants to buy one.

The U.S. government intervenes in the marketplace when it sets a minimum wage and retirement income through Social Security. Some states regulate industries that have a **monopoly**, or the exclusive possession or control of the supply or trade in a service. For example, your state might oversee the price of electricity, because in many parts of the country, only one electricity producer controls the market. Electricity has strong **price elasticity of demand**, or the change in a

good's demand as its price changes. For example, as the price of gasoline goes up, do you stop driving? Economists find that when gas prices go up, demand declines, but only slightly, because many areas have inadequate public transportation.[5] All commodities have a different price elasticity of demand, influenced by how much people need the product as well as the number of producers of that item.

The United States has had an explosion of wealth creation over a 30-year period. In 2000, the United States had more than five million millionaires and about 267 billionaires.[6] Of course, not all capitalist countries are teeming with millionaires. Poorer countries are also capitalist, but a small group of wealthy families might control the means of production.[7] Capitalism rewards self-interest, so inequality is expected.

SOCIALISM

The polar opposite of capitalism is **socialism**, the economic system by which resources and the means of production are owned collectively by the citizens. The basic components of socialism include collective ownership of property, irrelevance of profit, and planned economy that emphasizes collective values.

Socialism's most important theorist was Karl Marx. Marx imagined socialism as a perfect or utopian society over which equality reigned. In strict socialism, the government owns all property. Workers earn a living wage, and essential goods and services are available.

Socialist governments plan the economy, meaning that governments, not people, determine what is produced. Gaining wealth is not important; meeting people's economic needs takes priority.

However, in the former Soviet Union, members of the communist party were "more equal" than non-members, and many people remained poor.[8]

Individual vs. Collective Ownership

Capitalism   Socialism

DEMOCRATIC SOCIALISM

People try to freely practice a form of socialism that takes the best from both systems. **Democratic socialism** refers to the economic system that advocates running government democratically and for the good of the most people.[9] Both individuals and government own property. The democratic socialist movement has been strongest in Europe and is often associated with the labor movements in the Eurozone.[10]

In these countries, tax rates are higher, and the government provides more services to every citizen. Governments protect worker rights, and labor unions have more power than they do in the United States. Furthermore, these nations are far more generous when we compare them to the government of the United States.[11] People view the role of government and social welfare differently, too. For example, in a study of eight industrialized nations, Stefan Svallfors found that the people in the United States have the most negative views toward the government redistributing wealth, while people in Norway are the most likely to accept such disbursement.[12] In *Common Wealth: Economics for a Crowded Planet*, Sachs examines many levels of democratic socialism and finds that democratic socialist policies benefit the poor and the economy of the countries that practice this system.

CONVERGENCE OF CAPITALISM AND SOCIALISM

The pure systems of capitalism and socialism in theory are almost exact opposites. In practice however, these two systems have shown signs of convergence. This tendency for capitalism and socialism to converge is known as the **convergence theory**.[13] For example, the capitalist U.S. government passed antitrust laws to restrict the size and scope of a corporation's reach, taking a step away from pure capitalism.

However, socialist countries are also moving away from "closed" socialism. China once practiced a brand of socialism that followed the principles espoused by Marx, Lenin, and Mao Zedong. Since the late 1970s, China has relaxed into a "purer" form of socialism. Market forces determine what goods and services are created. Individuals are allowed to own businesses, but government restrictions and taxation remain focused on improving the well-being of all Chinese people.

China's leadership remains in the hands of the Communist Party of China, and this organization controls all aspects of the government.[14] China has improved the per-capita wealth of the country as it moves toward a free market.[15] China continues to have a mixed economic system, and many state workers continue to work as government employees.[16] Although the capitalists and socialists still have their differences, the concessions made by each have led to something much closer to a middle ground.[17]

∧
∧   **When Hugo Chavez,** the elected president of Venezuela, **took over the nation's oil**
∧   **industry, he decided to practice a form of democratic socialism.** Following Mexico's lead, **he suggested that the oil and the revenues generated by the oil should belong to all the people of Venezuela.**[18]

Employment Projections by Industry: 2004 to 2014

Source: U.S. Census Bureau, "Employment Projections by Industry: 2004 to 2014," November 2005.

Trends in the U.S. Economy

As U.S. corporations find new and cheaper labor in countries overseas, the job market is shifting accordingly. According to the U.S. Census Bureau, jobs in manufacturing will continue to decline, but jobs in the medical and computer science industries will flourish. For instance, by 2014, jobs in the field of network systems are projected to increase by 54.6 percent.[19]

Workers' demographics are also changing. In 2006, whites had the highest participation rate in the labor force, followed by blacks, Asians, and Hispanics. By 2014, the participation rates for whites, blacks, and Asians are predicted to decrease, while Hispanic participation is expected to increase.[20]

These transitions in the workforce sometimes lead to unemployment. An unemployed person does not have a job, consistently seeks a new job for four weeks, and is waiting for work.[21] In August 2007, the U.S. unemployment rate was 4.6 percent, and by October 2008, it was 6.1 percent.[22]

One in four people in the United States will try to start his or her own business, which is a process known as entrepreneurship. Entrepreneurs create new organizations in response to economic and social opportunities. But, of course, you may know that many of these new ventures fail. When I was in business school, we were told that the three most important aspects of business success were "location, location, location." However, research suggests that social networks and the level of competition in the market place are crucial for a successful business. Social networks and market forces influence business success.[23]

THE U.S. ECONOMY: A SYSTEM IN CRISIS

According to the U.S. Small Business Administration, approximately 50 percent of small businesses fail in the first five years, and this is when the economy is healthy.[24] When the economy is struggling, as it has been in recent years, more and more businesses shut down, people worry about their futures, and our national leaders search for a solution. Many of us believe that the government and the economy are two distinct and separate systems, and yet there is often overlap. The 2008 economic crisis showed us all just how connected these two systems are.

In the fall of 2008, the federal government approved an approximately $700 billion "bailout" of Wall Street's mortgage industry. The economic crisis didn't happen overnight; several events contributed to the downfall. One was the rampant use of subprime mortgage lending in which banks and other credit institutions lent people money to buy houses that they wouldn't normally be able to afford. Government control of the banking and mortgage industries had also declined in the past 30 years, which led to a free market that some suggest imploded on itself. When the people who took out these loans could not pay them back, banks began to foreclose. Of course, if you take a house from someone, you assume you can sell it for more than you paid for it. But in 2008 these events came during a period when the housing market was struggling. As a result, prices for homes dropped and the country's credit system faced impending failure.[25] The government's massive purchase of bad credit followed the federal takeover of mortgage lenders Fannie Mae and Freddie Mac, leading many to question the government's role in the economy.[26]

A huge debate raged in the country about whether or not the government should even be involved in buying up parts of private companies. People often cited economist Adam Smith's philosophy that the economy was to run on an "invisible hand," meaning that the market somehow works if government stays out of the way. However, this is not a clearly accepted statement of Smith's beliefs, as he also seemed to understand that some government control is essential for an economy to survive.[27] After the Great Depression and the first stock market crash in 1929, the government imposed regulations on financial institutions in the hope of staving off a future crisis. More recently, however, the government became involved in freeing up these markets through deregulation, which may be part of the problem.[28]

During this time of economic uncertainty, some of my students wondered if their college loans would be there for them next semester. When we discussed this in class, many believed that government should not be involved in the marketplace at all. Some felt that if people made bad investments, they should lose money. Others pointed out that some of the victims of such a strategy are the elderly who live off investment income and have seen their life savings dwindle. With so many people affected by this economic situation, the financial crisis became one the most important topics in the political campaign for president between Barack Obama and John McCain, underscoring just how closely the economic and the political systems are linked.

The credit crises led to a ripple effect not just in the economy of the United States, but throughout the world. Global financial institutions had purchased some of the mortgage companies' bad loans and despite the federal government's support of companies such as Bear Stearns, this company and others still failed. **These events worked to make government a political a player in the economic markets around the world.[29]**

Global Economy

In the opening quote, Jeffrey Sachs discusses the necessity of global cooperation. As we discussed in Chapter 8, *globalization* is a worldwide trend. Businesses are spreading across the globe, seeking new markets and new areas to maximize profits.

CORPORATIONS: SPREADING ACROSS THE GLOBE

A **corporation** is viewed as a "legal person" that has some objective, usually to make a profit for its owners. It can buy property, incur debts, and become involved in legal contracts. Shareholders own the corporation, but the employees run it. In large public corporations, millions of people own pieces of the company through the purchase of stock.

Historically, individuals or a small group of people each own a part of the company, but they also work in the company to promote growth and increase the company's earnings. Today, large corporations expand across the world. The workers for these companies are often the native people from that area. Leadership is turned over to managers and executives who have increased power. This increases the importance of CEOs and others in management. This is especially true for **transnational corporations** or **multinational corporations**, corporations that operate in at least two countries and have the interests of their company at heart rather than the interests of their home country. These corporations tend to become almost like little countries in and of themselves. Multinational corporations are a dominant force in the global economy, generating huge profits and possessing major political power.

TRADE AGREEMENTS: EMBARGOES AND NAFTA

Today, the system of trade is considerably complicated. Conflicts with various nations as well as national health regulations have created the need to place certain restrictions on trade transactions. One long-standing trade restriction, or **embargo**, is between the United States and Cuba. The rivalry between the United States government and the Cuban government led the United States to impose a trade embargo on items from Cuba in 1962. This restricted trade of goods remains in effect to this day.[30] It's the longest lasting trade restriction that's currently in effect.

The United States does not have restrictions for everyone, however. **NAFTA**, or **The North American Free Trade Agreement**, was established in 1994 to allow free trade between the United States, Mexico, and Canada. All nontariff barriers to agricultural trade were removed. **Tariffs** are taxes levied on traded items, and high tariffs limit the amount of trading that occurs.[31] Canada and Mexico also reached an agreement about agricultural trade. As a result, trade has increased amongst these nations. According to the Office of the United States' Trade Representative, "From 1993 to 2007, trade among the NAFTA nations more than tripled, business investment in the United States has risen by 117 percent since 1993, compared to a 45 percent increase between 1979 and 1993."[32] Trade provides a major economic boost for these countries and the businesses within these countries.

Political Systems

NAFTA is a perfect example of how **political systems**, or social institutions that are based on an established set of practices for applying and realizing a society's goals, are linked to economic systems. All politics are about power. Max Weber defined power as the ability to achieve your own

---

CORPORATION is a business viewed as a "legal person" that has some objective, usually to make a profit for its owners.

TRANSNATIONAL CORPORATIONS or **MULTINATIONAL CORPORATIONS** are corporations that operate in at least two countries and have the interests of their company at heart rather than the interests of their home country.

EMBARGO is a long-standing trade restriction.

NAFTA (NORTH AMERICAN FREE TRADE AGREEMENT) is a policy that was established in 1994 to allow free trade between the United States, Mexico, and Canada.

TARIFFS are taxes levied on trade items.

POLITICAL SYSTEMS are social institutions that are based on an established set of practices for applying and realizing a society's goal.

---

ends despite resistance from others.[33] The distribution of power affects decision making and the course for how society will distribute resources. Authority allows decision makers to appear legitimate in an official capacity. Therefore, power does not have to be manipulative or coercive. Weber believed that political systems worked based on one of three forms of authority: traditional, charismatic, and rational legal authority.

TRADITIONAL

Social power is legitimated by respect for patterns of government. For example, European kings in the Middle Ages held power in part because it was tradition, and they supported the idea of the divine right of kings. In Iran today, theocratic principles give religious leaders great power in selecting the government leadership. Generally, in countries that follow these principles, the people share similar worldviews and come from developing nations. The traditional form of social power is definitely not as common as it once was, but it is still in place in some parts of the world.

CHARISMATIC

Power is gained because the leader has extraordinary personal attributes. Often, such leaders inspire followers and may lead "movements." In the world of politics, people like Mahatma Gandhi, John F. Kennedy, and Martin Luther King, Jr., were all influential leaders because of their charisma. Powerful public speaking skills and a charming, believable personality are essential in winning over supporters for your cause.

RATIONAL-LEGAL AUTHORITY

Rules become official when written down and codified by a bureaucracy, such as the government. When regulations are recorded, a sense of their importance is achieved. If the rules are considered to be rational by the majority of the population, the public tends to accept and follow them. For example, when the President of the United States sends troops into another country, he or she has the authority to do so, because of the authority of the commander in chief. Weber feels that this is the political system that people respect most, as it is not based on fear, but rather on an agreement as to what constitutes illegal behavior.[34]

Authority and power are important components of any government. **The amount of authority that a leader has is often dependent on the type of government that a nation operates under.**

Types of Government

Every society has some form of government. However, the types of governments in the world's societies can differ greatly. In this section, we'll review the main types of government that exist in the world today and the leaders who govern under these systems.

MONARCHY

Monarchy is a political system in which leadership is based on the idea that leaders are selected by divine right or heritage. Usually, a single family rules from generation to generation, passing power from parents to children. Many ancient societies operated under a monarchy, with royalty who had almost absolute power over society. Often the justification for this power came from "divine right," the idea that the monarch was appointed by God to be the ruler of their people. Today, most European monarchies are merely symbolic, as a parliament and prime minister make most of the important governmental decisions. However, some Middle Eastern countries, like Kuwait and Saudi Arabia, have royal families that still exercise almost complete control over society.

AUTHORITARIANISM

Citizens in authoritarian regimes are given very limited participation in the government. Unlike monarchies, **authoritarian regimes** usually involve an individual or small group taking power and using repression and other techniques to maintain it. Although some monarchs behave in a similar manner, their justification for power remains traditional. Dictators are generally authoritarians who seize power, often from elected governments. When Pervez Musharraf seized power in Pakistan in 1999, he led a military coup d'état (overthrow of the democratically elected government) and suspended the constitution of Pakistan.

Since taking power, he dismissed the national and provincial legislative assemblies, assumed the title of Chief Executive, and became Pakistan's de facto head of government. In 2001, Musharraf appointed himself to the office of President of Pakistan. He was "elected" president in 2008; however, he resigned when government officials threatened to impeach him."[35] Governing by the use of force and fear can be an effective way to control citizens, but is almost certain to create a great deal of resentment toward the government. When there is complete unrest, revolutions and political assassinations become a viable option in shifting the balance of power.

One form of authoritarianism is **totalitarianism**. Such governments attempt to control every aspect of its people's lives. They often monitor the population through a secret police designed to control and watch everything that goes on. Cuba, China, and Russia all have a history of totalitarian control. People who disagree with the government might disappear without a trace. This type of government maintains power by invoking fear and using intimidation tactics.[36]

Frequently, a dictator or an oligarchy controls an authoritarian regime. A **dictator** is a single leader with absolute power, much like a king. An **oligarchy** is a small group of very influential people who control the government. This leadership group is often unknown to many and yet wields great power behind a dictator. The players in 2008 Russian politics and finance are called oligarchs, and the entire system would classify as an oligarchy.[37]

DEMOCRACY

Unlike authoritarian regimes, a **democracy** is a political system whereby power is held by the people and exercised through participation and representation. In a pure or direct democracy, voters make all the rules. U.S. citizens are involved in a representative democracy, in which we elect leaders to make decisions for us. In fact, sociologist Robert Michels suggests that in complex societies, direct democracy is impossible, largely because there are too many people and issues to allow each person to vote on every issue. Michels warned that democracies may incur problems like corruption by giving away too much power to elites who then monopolize decisions about what should and should not happen.[38]

MAKE CONNECTIONS

Voter Apathy

In 2008, nearly 137 million people were reported to have cast their vote for either John McCain or Barack Obama. This turnout, which is the highest in more than a century, was quite surprising. Why? It turns out that since 1972, voter turnout has never been more than two of every three eligible voters. In fact, in some years it has been little more than half the eligible voters.[39] So, who hasn't been voting? People over the age of 35 have voted at rates higher than the national average, while people under the age of 35 are less likely to vote. Young adults ages 18 to 24 have the lowest voter representation. In general, women vote in a slightly higher percentage than men. Whites are most likely to vote, followed by blacks, Hispanics, and Asians. In 2004, 74 percent of people with a college degree or higher voted, while only 34 percent of high school dropouts decided to vote. Only 34 percent of the unemployed decided to vote.

Explanations for voter apathy are as ancient as Plato's *The Republic*. Plato suggests that voters are driven by their appetites and are unlikely to become involved in government as long as essential things are plentiful.[40] More recently, researchers have sought a link between alienation and voting.[41] **Alienation** refers to a person's sense of powerlessness, meaninglessness, and a general cynicism toward the political process. Findings suggest that people who feel that politics is meaningless and that their vote means nothing are less likely to vote. Cynicism can depress the likelihood of voting; however, it can also spark an increased interest in the process.[42]

Voter apathy may also be caused by structural barriers for voting. For example, some suggest that Americans cannot get off work to vote or are simply too busy to make it to the polls.[43] U.S. citizens are also required to register before they can vote, making political participation something that a person must plan ahead to do. Some states are changing their policy so that potential voters can register and vote on Election Day. However, even reducing the difficulties in registration doesn't mean that people will vote.[44] No matter what the cause for voter apathy in the past, recent elections have shown us that U.S. citizens are becoming more excited about and involved in the political process.

>>> **ACTIVITY** Create an advertising campaign, using the medium of your choice, to get young adults to vote. Share your campaign with the your class.

Politics in the United States

The United States is a representative democracy, inviting all qualified citizens to vote in governmental elections. Qualifications vary slightly from state to state, but to vote in most states you generally have to be: a citizen of the United States, at least 18 years old, mentally competent, and free of a felony conviction. Despite the wide availability of the right to vote, a growing section of the population chooses not to. However, the 2008 presidential election showed that this trend is changing.

POLITICAL PARTIES

U.S. politics has what is essentially a two-party system. The Democratic Party and the Republican Party have dominated recent politics. Smaller parties exist, but the Democrats and Republicans dominate the political landscape.

The official Web site of the Democratic Party, www.democrats.org/, gives a synopsis of the democratic vision: "The Democratic Party is committed to keeping our nation safe and expanding opportunity for every American. That commitment is reflected in an agenda that emphasizes the strong economic growth, affordable health care for all Americans, retirement security, open, honest, and accountable government, and securing our nation while protecting our civil rights and liberties."[45] The Democratic party promotes a greater involvement of government in regulating business and social programs.

MONARCHY is a political system whereby leadership is based on the idea that leaders are selected by divine right or heritage.

AUTHORITARIAN REGIMES involve an individual or small group taking power and using repression and other techniques to maintain it.

TOTALITARIANISM is a type of authoritarian government whereby the government controls everything in people's lives, and generally those who disagree are punished.

DICTATOR refers to a single leader with absolute power.

OLIGARCHY is a small group of very influential people who control the government.

DEMOCRACY is a government whereby power is held by the people and exercised through participation and representation.

ALIENATION refers to a person's sense of powerlessness, meaninglessness, and general cynicism toward the political process.

The official Web site of the Republican Party, www.rnc.org/, offers many of the same promises and hopes: "Faith in the virtues of self-reliance, civic commitment, and concern for one another. Distrust of government's interference in people's lives. Dedication to a rule of law that both protects and preserves liberty."[46] Republican politics seeks to restrict the expansion of federal power. Both Democrats and Republicans attempt to achieve the same ends, but have different ideas about how to implement the means.[47]

MAKE CONNECTIONS

The 2008 presidential election began midway through 2007 and included nearly twenty candidates. By the summer of 2008, however, U.S. voters had narrowed the list to two candidates: Republican Senator John McCain of Arizona and Democratic Senator Barack Obama from Illinois. Both men's campaigns were historic because their tickets included the first African American candidate (Obama), the oldest candidate (McCain), and the second female vice presidential candidate in history (Governor Sarah Palin). (Geraldine Ferraro, the first female vice presidential candidate, ran on the Democratic ticket in 1984.[48])

The key issues in the election were diverse in nature until the economic collapse of Wall Street and, ultimately, the United States' economy forced the candidates—and the American people—to take a look at how and why this had happened. The Democrats naturally blamed eight years of a Republican presidency, while the Republicans placed blame at the feet of a Democratically controlled

Congress. Health care reform, taxes, and the wars in Iraq and Afghanistan—while still important to voters—took a backseat to fears about the economy.

McCain and Palin's motto during the election was "Country first," a phrase that suggested that McCain, a former prisoner of war, and Palin, would place their personal and political party's interests second behind their love of the country. McCain's primary message was that he had the experience and character to lead the country during trying times. He suggested that he had the ability to work with people from all parties to do the right thing for the United States.[49]

Obama and his running mate, Joseph Biden, ran as candidates for change. They suggested that Republican policies implemented during President George W. Bush's term were responsible for the current problems in the war on terror and in the economic sector. Obama wanted to expand health care availability and funding for schools and colleges. Obama—47 at the time of the election—ushered in a new generation of U.S. politicians. His mere appearance on the Democratic ticket provided concrete evidence that the once strong racial divide in the United States was ending.[50]

Ultimately, the voters decided that change was the way to go, and Barack Obama won the election by a margin of 200 electoral votes. Voter turnout was high for a presidential election, and Obama was named the victor.

During the 2008 presidential election, **Senator John McCain and Senator Barack Obama rarely saw eye to eye on the issues.**

POLITICAL FUNDING

A great deal of funding for political parties comes from organized groups who have a vested interest in policy decisions. Traditionally, labor groups prefer the Democratic Party, while corporate groups prefer the Republican Party. A majority of the donations to political parties comes from political action committees, or PACs. PACs heavily influence the campaign for Congressional seats, as the PACs strategically allocate money to the two parties. These groups typically favor one party, but often make smaller contributions to incumbents from other parties in an attempt to gain support for the PAC's cause.[51] The world of political contributions is complex, as many groups have their personal interests at stake. For example, in the 2008 elections, leadership PACs—PACs in which lawmakers donate money in the hopes of gaining a leadership position—like AmeriPAC and Every Republican is Crucial PAC donated hundreds of thousands of dollars to the political campaigns. Leadership PACs donated over $9 million to Democrat candidates and over $11 million to Republican candidates.[52]

Special interest groups also seek to influence political candidates. Single-issue groups such as Greenpeace, PETA, and the NRA focus on one particular issue and attempt to change policy. Protection of the environment, ethical treatment for animals, and gun rights are just a few of the causes that have organized groups supporting them and attempting to influence political action.

▶▶▶ GO GL🌐BAL

Trust in Political Parties

Norway and Sweden operate under a multiple-party system, while the United States operates under what is essentially a two-party system. How does this affect the level of public trust of political parties? A study by Arthur Miller and Ola Listhaug, from the University of Iowa and University of Trondheim, Norway, respectively, examined data about the level of distrust that citizens have toward political parties.[53]

Data from this survey indicate that Norwegian citizens are more likely to trust political parties than citizens of Sweden or the United States do, and Swedish citizens are more likely to trust political parties than U.S. citizens. Swedish citizens were more likely to "say that parties were interested in their opinions as well as their votes" than U.S. citizens. Although cultural factors surely play a role, the possibility of new parties forming and providing viable candidates in Norway and Sweden may increase the voters' trust.[54]

Norway has had more success forming new political parties, due to more lax qualifications for doing so than Sweden. Sweden has typically operated under a relatively static five-party system, which still provides more variety than the two-party system of the United States. A system that allows for new parties is naturally more flexible. If a party takes on an unfavorable position, a new party can rise up in protest. These responsive parties would be a "vehicle for expressing political discontent."[55]

In a system with only two parties, people can become alienated if they are dissatisfied with both parties, which can lead to a lack of trust and a decrease in voter participation. Confidence and trust are absolutely essential in earning votes.

>>> **How important do you think trust in a political system is** to leading a satisfied life?

The Nature of Power

Regardless of our perception of the nature of power, individuals have varying amounts of it, with no one having totally unlimited power. Sociologist C. Wright Mills suggests that within the United States, a small group holds immense power. He called this group the power elite.[56] The *power elite* come from three distinct but related groups: high-ranking political officials, corporate leaders, and military leaders. They hold the power to control the knowledge that others receive and thereby direct the decisions of the country. The power elite frame every major decision of the country by using their power, position, and influence to control the direction of the country.

G. William Domhoff agrees with Mills and continues to research this overlap between economic elites and political power. Domhoff is more general in his discussion of who runs the country, but continues to suggest that the power in this country is primarily in the hands a small number of elite, white men. They form a *corporate coalition* that plays a major role in dictating who runs for office and the positions those people occupy. There also exists a *labor coalition*, which includes labor unions, and community groups who strive to exert influence as well. The interplay between these two powerful groups has great influence on the United States.[57]

MILITARY AND THE USE OF FORCE

Throughout the course of U.S. history, people have been fighting against the abuse of power. Because the United States is a democracy, no one leader or group should have absolute control over the nation. On January 17, 1961, President Eisenhower described the dangers of the **military-industrial complex**, which is a combination of the armed forces and defense industries that provide weapons and other materials to the country: "In the councils of government, we must guard against the acquisition of unwarranted influence, whether sought or unsought, by the military industrial complex. The potential for the disastrous rise of misplaced power exists and will persist. We must never let the weight of this combination endanger our liberties or democratic processes. We should take nothing for granted. Only an alert and knowledgeable citizenry can compel the proper meshing of the huge industrial and military machinery of defense with our peaceful methods and goals, so that security and liberty may prosper together."[58]

Eisenhower was the commanding general in WWII for the Allied forces and had a thorough understanding of the potential of a powerful military to dominate politics. The Cold War with the Soviet Union was a perfect example of this. Fears about Russian weaponry resulted in more tax dollars used to fund military contractors. According to Eisenhower, "The military itself, its allied contractors, and the appropriators in Congress all shared an interest in trumpeting potential perils and then building weapons to offset them." For Eisenhower, the powerful military industrial complex could hurt the essence of democracy.[59]

As a country, the United States generally views itself as a mediator in foreign disputes, and we outspend everyone else in the world to do it. Look at the table below. Although many nations in the world spend more on military by percentage, the United States spends far more than most every nation in total dollars. In fact, the United States and China combined spend more than half of the total world spending on military. Oman spends the greatest percentage in the world on military defense, but in raw dollars Oman's total is much less than other nations.

∧
∧ **Do you think it is an appropriate use of**
∧ **power to** engage the military to **change the government of a foreign country?**

The Relationship Between Military Spending and the Economy				
GDP RANK	Region	GDP (in dollars)	Military Spending as a % of GDP	Total Dollars Spent on Military
	World	$65 trillion	2%	$1.3 trillion
1	United States	13 trillion	4.06	561 billion
2	China	6 trillion	4.3	300 billion
3	Japan	4 trillion	.08	34.3 billion
4	India	2.9 trillion	2.5	74.7 billion
5	Germany	2.8 trillion	1.5	42.1 billion
6	United Kingdom	2.1 trillion	2.4	51.2 billion
7	Russia	2 trillion	3.9	81.4 billion
8	France	2 trillion	2.6	53.2 billion
9	Brazil	1.8 trillion	2.6	47.7 billion
18	Iran	753 billion	2.5	18.8 billion
22	Saudi Arabia	564 billion	10	56.4 billion
53	Israel	185 billion	7.3	13.5 billion
62	Iraq	102 billion	8.6	8.8 billion
80	Oman	61 billion	11.4	7 billion

Source: *The World Factbook*, The Central Intelligence Agency.

Guns vs. Butter: The Debate Between Military Spending and Providing for Citizens

When I was an undergraduate, we often talked about the whether the economy would benefit more from producing butter or guns. In our discussions, we used *butter* to refer to consumer goods and *guns* to refer to military spending. Does extensive military spending negatively affect the general status of the economy and the amount of funds allocated to other important areas?[60]

For example, studies show that as military spending grows, public funding of other services, such as education, declines.[61] With limited public resources, government spending in one area certainly will affect spending in others. However, the link between military spending and the economy is not complete clear. For example, studies find that when the government increases spending, it affects every other sector of the economy. Spending has been on the rise since 1940, and the request for 2009 funding is $515 billion. However, a direct link to poverty is less than clear.[62] Errol Anthony Henderson, professor at the University of Florida, determined that "peacetime military spending increases poverty, more than likely through its impact on increasing inequality and unemployment, while wartime spending has the reverse effect."[63] In other words, in times of war, military spending seems to benefit the economy, so more "guns" helps. Meanwhile, in times of peace, we're probably better off making more "butter."

Another concern is that military spending continues to rise, due to rapid increases in prices. Since the end of WWII, military hardware and technology have increased in price far greater than the price of other products.[64] At the same time, military hardware producers have generated large increases in business. From 2001 to 2006, American Body Armor Corporation increased its income from military by more than 2,000 percent.[65]

No one disputes that some level of military spending is essential. Any student who has taken a world history course knows that military conflicts are nothing new to society. From tribal wars to the Roman Empire, military conquest and defense are a part of society. We all want to be safe and secure, and providing that security is an essential function of government. Of course, we do not have unlimited resources. So, we must wrestle with how much spending is enough.

What else could the United States do with some of the money spent on national defense? Is this spending all necessary? Is it possible that a former general and president's warning about a powerful military industrial complex has come true? What do you think?

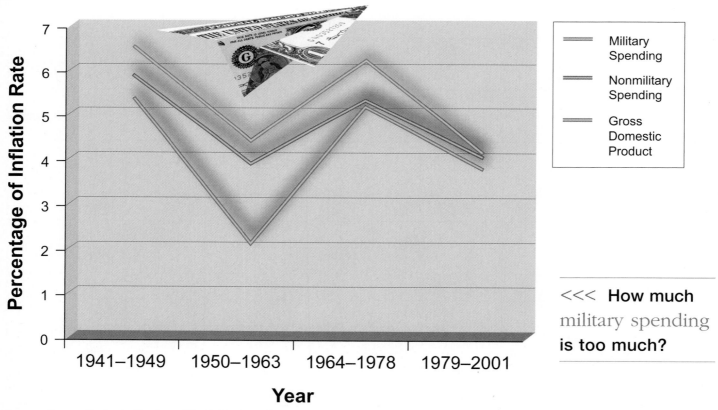

Annual Mean Inflation Rates for Selected Periods

Legend:
- Military Spending
- Nonmilitary Spending
- Gross Domestic Product

Y-axis: Percentage of Inflation Rate (0–7)
X-axis: Year — 1941–1949, 1950–1963, 1964–1978, 1979–2001

<<< **How much** military spending **is too much?**

Source: Benjamin, Fordham, "The Political and Economic Sources of Inflation in the American Military Budget," *The Journal of Conflict Resolution.* Oct 2003. Vol. 47, No. 5: 574–593.

Chapter 16 292

think sociologically: HOW DO SOCIOLOGISTS VIEW ECONOMIC AND POLITICAL SYSTEMS?

Functionalism

Politics in the United States is an ongoing series of negotiations and compromises among interested parties. No one group can assert dominance over the government, as resources are spread out among a variety of groups. This model is referred to as **pluralism**, the political system in which power is spread amongst the masses. The purpose of government is then to mediate between these various interest groups.

When you look at the system of checks and balances in the United States, you can see a functional system designed to do just this. The federal government has the executive (president), legislative (congress), and judicial (courts) branches, and each has distinct roles. This setup helps the plurality of differing voices in the country to have their needs met. For example, at the time of "separate but equal school segregation," the congress and executive branches of the government seemed unwilling to seriously look at changing a law that discriminated against blacks. However, the U.S. Supreme court, in *Brown vs. Board of Education*, struck down school segregation, thus allowing a minority voice to be heard. From watching this system for many years, it seems that Congress and the President tend to speak for the voting majority, whereas the court system is often the only recourse for minority groups. Under this system no one particular branch of government has absolute authority. Thus, government functions smoothly when each branch does its job.

Conflict Theory

According to conflict theorists, power is concentrated among a small group of individuals. The writings of both G. Williams Domhoff and C. Wright Mills discuss the dangers of a small number of the dominant elite who control the majority of society's wealth, prestige, and power. This leaves the rest of society with little power.[66] In Ben Bagdikian's book *The New Media Monopoly*, he looks at one way that elites use power to control the thinking of voters in the United States. With the exception of public radio and television, media outlets in the United States are for-profit businesses, and a very small number of corporations control most of the media outlets in this country. In 1983 there were 50 large media conglomerates in the United States; because of consolidations, today there are five.

These five giant corporations own most of the print media, as well as radio, television, and movie studios in the country and in this way, they control most of what you read and see. Who are these five corporations? They are Time Warner, Disney, Murdoch's News Corporation, Bertelsmann of Germany, and Viacom.

Conflict theorists will point out that information is power, and these five corporations hold immense power. Since funding for media comes from advertising dollars, news and information services often struggle with perceived and sometimes real conflicts of interest. For example, if a local newspaper or television station uncovers a crime committed by its largest advertiser, will it put that information in the paper or on the air? Since information is power, conflict theorists would suggest that the media become one tool by which the power elite maintain their control over the population.[67]

Symbolic Interactionism

Symbolic interactionists focus on leaders who use their charisma and personality to gain the respect and trust of citizens. Consider Weber's idea of charismatic authority and you can see that leaders arise sometimes because they have extraordinary personal magnetism. Religious figures like Jesus Christ and Muhammad used charisma to gain followers and start movements. Some politicians are able to lead people to do things they might not ordinarily do. Consider the case of Germany's Adolf Hitler. His power and skill as a charismatic public speaker convinced many Germans of the rightness of the Holocaust. Charismatic authority is an extremely powerful force over people, and it can be used for better or worse. It is important to carefully consider what a charismatic figure stands for, as his or her power can steer the public in dangerous directions.

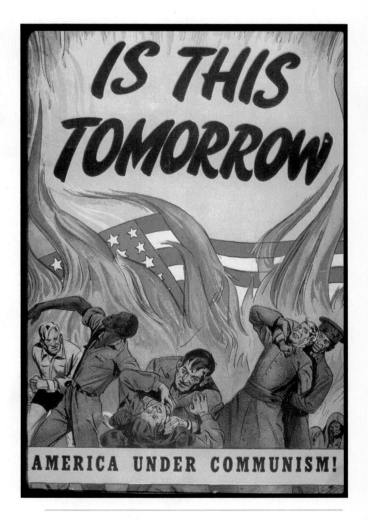

 Why do rival political **systems** often **vilify one another?**

WRAP YOUR MIND AROUND THE THEORY

Do you think that the United States cooperates well enough with its allies?

FUNCTIONALISM

Power is spread out among the masses. No one group can attain complete dominance over the rest. The functionalists believe that various power holding groups need to work together to maintain the proper functioning of society. Jeffrey Sachs advocates global cooperation in order to better the world for all people. One of the four goals that he believes to be attainable in the next couple decades is to achieve "a new approach to global problem solving based on cooperation among nations and the dynamism and creativity of the nongovernmental sector."[68]

CONFLICT THEORY

Power is concentrated among a small group of "elites." The non-elite are involved in a constant struggle to gain power, and the elite are involved a constant struggle to maintain their authority. Conflict theorists believe that the democracy of the United States is no exception to this, as a small group of rich and powerful people controls the government. Jeffrey Sachs feels that this type of power struggle is exactly what the world needs to abandon in favor of cooperation if we are to be successful in the future.

HOW IS POWER DISTRIBUTED IN ECONOMIC AND POLITICAL SYSTEMS?

SYMBOLIC INTERACTIONISM

Symbolic interactionists consider leaders' use of personality and charisma to gain power. Leaders use their oratory skills to convince followers that they are adequate for the job. The power to sway the masses can be used for both good and evil, as history has indicated. Charisma is a powerful asset, as it can be used to change people's minds and to achieve whatever ends the speaker desires. Jeffrey Sachs believes that the charismatic should use their abilities to unite people to achieve common goals.

Does a power elite dominate U.S. politics?

At a 1963 civil rights rally in Harlem, Malcolm X delivered a speech that ignited and wowed listeners. **How do speakers use facial expressions and hand gestures to emphasize their point?**

discover sociology in action: HOW DOES THE SYSTEM WORK FOR VETERANS?

Lack of Assistance for Veterans

While the military is clearly a spending machine in gearing up for war, it also creates the necessity to spend more money in aiding veterans who are damaged physically or psychologically. There are almost 24 million military veterans estimated to be living in the United States.[69] Each veteran is classified by priority to receive benefits, from priority 1 being veterans with conflict-related injuries that are 50 percent or more disabling, to priority 7, veterans with non–conflict-related injuries.[70] Many veterans do not feel that they receive the care that they need and deserve. Injured veterans have to undergo a review process, which determines the level of care that they receive. However, the process usually takes five months or more to complete.[71] The system of benefits for veterans is designed to be comprehensive, but demand for many of the services is too high to accommodate everyone in need. With so many veterans adversely affected by their experience in warfare, it is extremely difficult and expensive to care for all of them. There has been a particularly high incidence of posttraumatic stress disorder (PTSD) and other mental problems associated with veterans of the war in Iraq, with an estimated 12 to 20 percent of these soldiers suffering from PTSD.[72] Mental health has been one of the weakest areas of veteran assistance. Many veterans who seek counseling for mental problems as a result of military service are refused assistance.

ACTIVITIES

1. Research government spending on the military and veterans' affairs. What is the difference? Do you agree with these figures? Why or why not?
2. Interview a veteran about his or her experience with treatment after returning home. Have a class discussion about your findings.

SUBSTANDARD CONDITIONS AT WALTER REED

Aside from veterans not receiving care, many of those who do receive care are forced to deal with substandard conditions at veterans' facilities. Aside from bleak quarters that include roaches, mice, mold, torn walls, and stained carpets, soldiers have deal with a bureaucratic mess that is comparable to the real battlefield.[73] This is the case for many patients of Walter Reed Army Medical Center in Washington, D.C. In 2007, the *Washington Post* reported on the terrible conditions at the facility that led to the firing of the general in charge of the hospital.[74] Soldiers entering Walter Reed are being saved, but it's the administrative process afterward that is causing problems. In March 2006, seventy-five percent of soldiers polled described their hospital experience as "stressful." Problems included lost paperwork, lack of bilingual staffers, and an overall lack of organization and answers. In fact, some patients are forced to prove they fought in combat in order to get a free replacement uniform for the bloody one left behind in battle. This had led some soldiers to attend ceremonies honoring their service wearing gym clothes. Similarly, soldiers suffering from brain damage are left to figure out their own appointments, while other soldiers and their families are going hungry because they're not getting the necessary help from social workers. Prior to the *Washington Post* article, soldiers and their families complained about the conditions, but some were told, "Suck it up."[75]

From Classroom to Community | Veterans' Hospital

I had a student, Chad, who was a veteran of operation Iraqi Freedom. Injured by a roadside bomb, he was welcomed home as a hero and decided to use his military benefits to improve his life by completing his undergraduate degree. For a class project, he completed his community learning at the local veterans' hospital.

"When I returned home, I was shocked at how little medical assistance actually existed for me, so I decided to try to help other guys who were going through the same thing," Chad wrote.

"At the hospital, I mostly worked in the reception area answering questions about where certain services were available, but I got to know many of the staff. They said they had never experienced more strain on their time, budgets, and ability to help than they currently experience. The sheer numbers of veterans seeking assistance is beyond the means that they have to offer. So many vets and their families need help, and yet many go without the care they need. The mental health issues are particularly difficult to find help for. It seems the counseling centers are filled to the brim. I could understand, because when you're in Iraq, you're always on guard. You never know when a bomb may go off near you. I still have nightmares about the roadside bomb going off that nearly took my life. When you get home, it's hard to let down your guard, even though you don't need to worry like that."

WHAT ARE THE SYSTEMS OF ECONOMICS AND POLITICS? 283

economic systems: capitalism, socialism, and democratic socialism
political systems: traditional, charismatic, and rational-legal authority

HOW DO SOCIOLOGISTS VIEW ECONOMIC AND POLITICAL SYSTEMS? 293

functionalism: power is divided among groups who must work together
conflict theory: only the power elite have power
symbolic interactionism: leaders must be charismatic to gain power and prestige

HOW DOES THE SYSTEM WORK FOR VETERANS? 295

veterans do not receive all the medical care and assistance they need

get the topic: WHAT ARE THE SYSTEMS OF ECONOMICS AND POLITICS?

Economic Systems 283
Global Economy 287
Political Systems 287
Types of Government 288

Politics in the United States 289
The Nature of Power 290
Functionalism 293

Conflict Theory 293
Symbolic Interactionism 293
Lack of Assistance for Veterans 295

Theory

FUNCTIONALISM 293

- power is dispersed among different groups
- groups must work together for society to function properly
- global cooperation is beneficial for everyone
- U.S. system of checks and balances

- includes the U.S. democratic system
- consolidation of media conglomerates

SYMBOLIC INTERACTIONISM 293

- leaders must have charisma in order to gain power
- charismatic leaders can persuade people to do things they normally wouldn't do
- leader's sway can be used for good or evil

CONFLICT THEORY 293

- power is held by a small group of elites
- elites are in a struggle to keep power, and non-elite are in a struggle to gain power

Key Terms

economic system, or **economy,** is the social system that helps a society organize what it produces, distributes, and consumes. *283*

capitalism is an economic system in which individuals can own the means of production as well as the services that others may need. *283*

free markets generally refer to markets that are free from government control. *283*

demand is the desire for a good or service. *284*

supply is the amount of a good or service available. *284*

monopoly is the exclusive possession or control of the supply or trade in a service. *284*

price elasticity of demand is the change in a good's demand as its price changes. *284*

socialism is the economic system by which resources and the means of production are owned collectively by the citizens. *284*

democratic socialism is the economic system that advocates running government democratically and for the good of the most people. *285*

convergence theory is the tendency for capitalism and socialism to converge. *285*

corporation is a business viewed as a "legal person" that has some objective, usually to make a profit for its owners. *287*

transnational corporations or **multinational corporations** are corporations that operate in at least two countries and have the interests of their company at heart rather than the interests of their home country. *287*

embargo is a long-standing trade restriction. *287*

NAFTA (North American Free Trade Agreement) is a policy that was established in 1994 to allow free trade between the United States, Mexico, and Canada. *287*

(continued)

tariffs are taxes levied on trade items. *287*

political systems are social institutions that are based on an established set of practices for applying and realizing a society's goal. *287*

monarchy is a political system whereby leadership is based on the idea that leaders are selected by divine right or heritage. *288*

authoritarian regimes involve an individual or small group taking power and using repression and other techniques to maintain it. *288*

totalitarianism is a type of authoritarian government whereby the government controls everything in people's lives, and generally those who disagree are punished. *288*

dictator refers to a single leader with absolute power. *288*

oligarchy is a small group of very influential people who control the government. *288*

democracy is a government whereby power is held by the people and exercised through participation and representation. *288*

alienation refers to a person's sense of powerlessness, meaninglessness, and a general cynicism toward the political process. *288*

military-industrial complex is a combination of the armed forces and defense industries that provide weapons and other materials to the country. *290*

pluralism is a model whereby power is spread amongst the masses. *293*

Sample Test Questions

These multiple-choice questions are similar to those found in the test bank that accompanies this textbook.

1. Which is an effect of NAFTA?
   a. Canada stopped trading with Mexico altogether.
   b. The United States started trading with Mexico and Canada.
   c. No tariffs were levied between the United States, Mexico, and Canada.
   d. Heavier tariffs were levied between the United States, Mexico, and Canada.

2. Which of the following statements on rational legal authority is false?
   a. The system is based on agreement, not fear.
   b. People accept the word of those in authority.
   c. Laws are official until they are written down.
   d. The rules are accepted by a majority of the population.

3. A _____ economic system believes markets should be run by the people, but not for profit.
   a. capitalist
   b. totalitarian
   c. power elitist
   d. democratic socialist

4. Increased military spending during peacetime means that the poverty level will increase.
   a. True
   b. False

5. Which of the following is one reason why Miller and Listhaug believe Swedish citizens have more trust in their officials than U.S. citizens do?
   a. Sweden has more political parties than the United States.
   b. Swedish officials are jailed if they lie to the public.
   c. Swedish officials listen to what the citizens say.
   d. Sweden has lower taxes than the United States.

ESSAY

1. Why is it difficult for a nation to either be entirely capitalist or entirely socialist?
2. How do expanding markets affect countries' economic and political systems?
3. What are the four problems and solutions Sachs proposes?
4. Why do poorer peripheral countries usually have traditional governments?
5. Do charismatic leaders always make the best leaders? Why or why not?

WHERE TO START YOUR RESEARCH PAPER

To learn more about the Democratic Party, go to www.democrats.org/

To learn more about the Republican Party, go to http://www.rnc.org/

To find more information about other political parties in the United States, go to http://www.politics1.com/parties.htm

For more information about NAFTA, go to http://www.fas.usda.gov/itp/Policy/NAFTA/nafta.asp

For more information about the Department of Veterans Affairs, go to http://www.va.gov/

To learn more information about additional available assistance for veterans, go to http://www.veteransassistance.org/

Remember to check www.thethinkspot.com for additional information, downloadable flashcards, and other helpful resources.

ANSWERS: 1. c; 2. c; 3. d; 4. a; 5. a

SOCIAL MOVEMENTS, COLLECTIVE BEHAVIOR, AND SOCIAL CHANGE

"By any

conventional definition, this vast collection of committed individuals does not constitute a movement. Movements have leaders and ideologies. People *join* movements, study their tracts, and identify themselves with a group. They read the biography of the founder(s) or listen to them perorate on tape or in person. Movements, in short, have followers. This movement, however, doesn't fit the standard model. It is dispersed, inchoate, and fiercely independent. It has no manifesto or doctrine, no overriding authority to check with. It is taking shape in schoolrooms, farms, jungles, villages, companies, deserts, fisheries, slums—and yes, even fancy New York hotels. One of its distinctive features is that it is tentatively emerging as a global humanitarian movement arising from the bottom up.

Historically, social movements have arisen primarily in response to injustice, inequities, and corruption. Those woes still remain legion, joined by a new condition that has no precedent: the planet has a life-threatening disease, marked by massive ecological degradation and rapid climate change. As I counted the vast number of organizations it crossed my mind that perhaps I was witnessing the growth of something organic, if not biologic. Rather than a movement in the conventional sense, could it be an instinctive, collective response to threat? Is it atomized for reasons that are innate to its purpose? How does it function? How fast is it growing? How is it connected? Why is it largely ignored? Does it have a history? Can it successfully address the issues that governments are failing to: energy, jobs, conservation, poverty, and global warming? Will it become centralized, or will it continue to be dispersed and cede its power to ideologies and fundamentalism?"[1]

How Do Societies Change?

In *Blessed Unrest: How the Largest Social Movement in History is Restoring Grace, Justice, and Beauty to the World,* author, journalist, and environmentalist Paul Hawken gives readers a reason to hope while facing the vast, potentially disastrous environmental and social problems that loom on our horizon.

A NEW YORK TIMES BESTSELLER

Blessed Unrest

When it rains, it pours. However, sometimes the downpours signal the beginning of a new Ice Age. At least, in the 2004 movie *The Day After Tomorrow* they do. Big-budget disaster movies give viewers a visual to associate with the discussion of climate change. However, do movies like these actually do anything to help awareness? Some may say that spreading the word that there is a problem to the masses is not enough.

Blessed Unrest is the result of years of collecting information on groups working to make the world a better place. Author Paul Hawken notes that this is not a groundswell of people who want to make the world a better place. He argues that it's easy to be terrified of the problems we have from explosive global population growth and oppression to pollution and global warming. However, thinking about the millions of organizations dedicated to making tomorrow a little brighter should put those fears to rest.

What drives changes, and how do we react to those changes? In this chapter, we review these and others questions as we study social change, collective behavior, and social movements.

Social Movements and Cultural Change

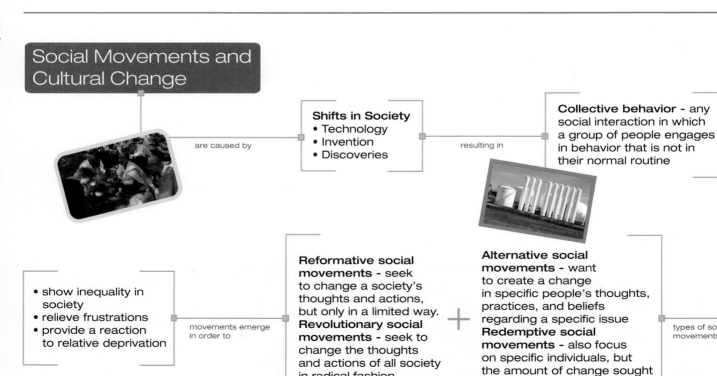

are caused by

Shifts in Society
• Technology
• Invention
• Discoveries

resulting in

Collective behavior - any social interaction in which a group of people engages in behavior that is not in their normal routine

• show inequality in society
• relieve frustrations
• provide a reaction to relative deprivation

movements emerge in order to

Reformative social movements - seek to change a society's thoughts and actions, but only in a limited way.
Revolutionary social movements - seek to change the thoughts and actions of all society in radical fashion.

+

Alternative social movements - want to create a change in specific people's thoughts, practices, and beliefs regarding a specific issue
Redemptive social movements - also focus on specific individuals, but the amount of change sought is radical, rather than limited

types of social movements include

get the topic: WHAT DRIVES SOCIAL CHANGE?

Shifts in Society

Changes in society are often caused by reactions to events and new opportunities, like the Industrial Revolution. This event brought about great **social change**, the way in which culture, interaction, and innovation change social institutions over time. Recall how the Industrial Revolution brought about changes in social classes. Capitalists became more powerful and wealthy than the old landed aristocracy, while workers struggled to make ends meet.[2]

Around the same time, new ways to think about the world arose, including the science of sociology. Some of these ideas helped form the intellectual basis for creating a new nation, based on common ideals. One merely needs to look at the Preamble of the Declaration of Independence to read some of these ideas. Ideas often drive social change. For example, no one recycled in my neighborhood when I was growing up. Someone realized that people were wasting too many natural resources and came up with the idea to reuse these materials. Today, recycling is a common practice.

Populations also grew, bringing about demographic changes such as immigration. Immigration and internal migration have changed the United States. Over time, the U.S. population grew and shifted westward. For example, in 1800, the population center (the imaginary point where half the population lives both east and west) of the United States was Baltimore, MD. By 1880 it was Covington, KY. According to the 2000 Census, the population center of the Unites States is now Edgar Springs, MO.[3]

Currently, we are experiencing globalization, a new trend in the world in which we are more interconnected to other nations than ever before. We've discussed this issue at length in previous chapters, but recall that the world is becoming smaller through technology and globalization. **For example, the Disney Channel is available all over the world, including Japan, Australia, France, southeast Asia, India, Germany, the United Kingdom, and Mexico. What's the significance of this?**

Well, the Disney Channel's television programs pass along American information, ideals, and beliefs to children all over the world. Kids around the globe learn about U.S. culture from the teen crews on *Hannah Montana* and *Wizards of Waverly Place*. How could this affect foreign cultures and bring about social change?

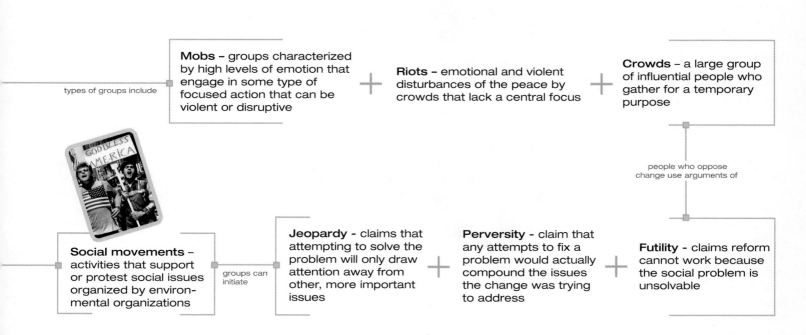

types of groups include

Mobs – groups characterized by high levels of emotion that engage in some type of focused action that can be violent or disruptive

Riots – emotional and violent disturbances of the peace by crowds that lack a central focus

Crowds – a large group of influential people who gather for a temporary purpose

people who oppose change use arguments of

Social movements – activities that support or protest social issues organized by environmental organizations

groups can initiate

Jeopardy - claims that attempting to solve the problem will only draw attention away from other, more important issues

Perversity - claim that any attempts to fix a problem would actually compound the issues the change was trying to address

Futility - claims reform cannot work because the social problem is unsolvable

TECHNOLOGY

One specific vehicle to social change is technology. **Technology** deals with the creation, use, and application of knowledge and its interrelation with life, society, and the environment. Technology often inspires change because it offers new possibilities for people to improve their environment and their lifestyles. Sociologist William Ogburn suggests that all social change is a result of technology.[4] Technology is usually the product of invention. An **invention** is the creation of a new device or way of thinking. Look at the graphic to the right to see how a simple invention can change society.

The term "technology" is not simply restricted to objects and things. Systems are also considered technologies, and new systems offer similar opportunities and changes that new objects might bring. The capitalist system offers the opportunity to rise in society's ranks by gathering material wealth and power. Similarly, the democratic system changes society by providing everyone a chance to be involved in the political process.

Technology also leads to new discoveries, which mean new opportunities. A discovery does not just have to be a place or object. A discovery can be a new way to see the world. However, discoveries cannot have a big impact on society unless they are made known. This is done by **diffusion**. It's by this process that new technologies, discoveries, and ideas are shared and spread from one person to another, extending the knowledge far beyond its point of origin. This in turn creates opportunities for someone to improve upon these ideas, further advancing and improving the original technologies while creating new technologies and discoveries.

Take, for instance, the automobile. Karl Benz created the first gasoline-fueled automobile in 1885 in Germany. Ten years later, U.S. inventor

Effects of Invention on Society: Tractors

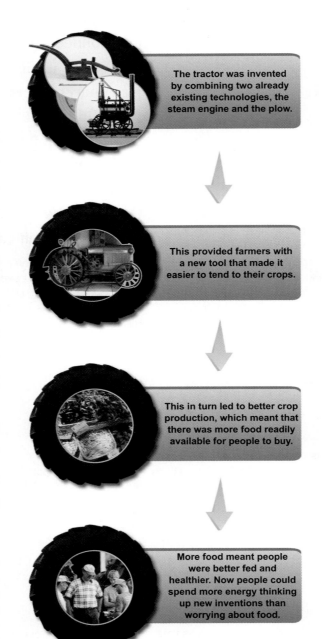

The tractor was invented by combining two already existing technologies, the steam engine and the plow.

This provided farmers with a new tool that made it easier to tend to their crops.

This in turn led to better crop production, which meant that there was more food readily available for people to buy.

More food meant people were better fed and healthier. Now people could spend more energy thinking up new inventions than worrying about food.

George Selden improved on this design by combining an internal combustion engine with a carriage. In 1893, brothers Charles and Frank Duryea created the first successful gas-powered car, and the two set up the first American automobile-manufacturing company.[5] Fast-forward to today's automotive industries. Automobiles continue to change as rising gas prices spur interest in new fuels and alternative energy. Technology changes and improves as new ideas and inventions from around the world are put into practice.

The rapid pace at which technology spreads and changes can leave some cultures lagging behind. *Cultural lag,* as we discussed in Chapter 3, occurs when some parts of a culture cannot keep up with the inventions, discoveries, and diffusion of ideas. Technology changes first, leaving other parts of the culture scrambling to keep up. For example, India's rapid industrialization has created a new affluence for some members of society, but other parts of the culture suffer from cultural lag. Trash piles up behind buildings because of the pressure on the area's resources and inability to keep up with industrial progress. People are fighting to keep up with the technological and societal changes that industrialization brings.[6]

Resistance to Change

Change happens in a culture, whether it is directly related to technology or not. However, although many people might be pushing for this change to occur, there may be some people who wish to resist it. They are happy with the way things are, and they strive to maintain the status quo. Sociologist Albert Hirschman noted that every new idea for constructive change is met with three types of attack by people who want things to stay the way they are.

First, Hirschman says that these protesters will argue **futility**, which claims that the reform cannot work because the social problem is unsolvable. One example of this type of arguing can be heard from people who criticize efforts to find cleaner, more efficient alternative energy sources for our motor vehicles. They claim that we're stuck with oil because it's the only thing that really works and that changing to alternative fuels would make transportation unreliable and more costly. People using this and the other forms of attack are often those who benefit from the use of oil and other fossil fuels and desire to maintain the status quo to protect their profits.

Another form of attack that protesters might choose as their argument is **perversity**, which claims that any attempt to fix a problem would actually compound the issues the change was trying to address. This argument is often used in the debate for electric cars. Although plugging in your car might sound like a cleaner solution for the environment, these protesters point out that this electricity must come from somewhere. Most electricity comes from power plants that burn coal, the process of which releases harmful gases and fumes into the air. More electric cars mean that there will be a greater demand for electricity, and more demand for electricity means more coal burning. Their argument is that the additional burning of more coal would be worse than the damage we are already doing with oil.

Yet another way to attack change is the argument of jeopardy. **Jeopardy** claims that attempting to solve the problem will only draw attention away from other, more important issues. People who support the use of oil might say that researching alternative fuels is not only costly, but it's also a waste of time. They say that there is plenty of oil and that

we do not need to worry about shortages; instead, we need to drill more. Spending money to find new energy sources then draws our attention away from other more important issues such as national security, education, or some other social problem.[7]

TECHNOLOGY deals with the creation, use, and application of knowledge and its interrelation with life, society, and the environment.

INVENTION is the creation of a new device or way of thinking.

DIFFUSION is the spreading of something more widely.

FUTILITY is the claim that a reform cannot work because the social problem is unsolvable.

PERVERSITY claims that any attempts to fix a problem would actually compound the issues the change was trying to address.

JEOPARDY is the claim that attempting to solve a problem will only draw attention away from other, more important issues.

Attack Strategies

Futility

Alternative Energy

Perversity

Electric Vehicle Fueling Station

Jeopardy

CALIFORNIA NEEDS ZERO-EMISSION CARS!

=

Leads To More

Draws Attention From

Internet Petitions

Many people who want society to change will sign a petition. Traditionally, this entails someone going around with a piece of paper for others to sign or mark up as a way to show their views on the subject. In recent years, petitions and polls have switched from paper to online. In *Blessed Unrest*, Hawken says, "The Internet and other communication technologies have revolutionized what is possible for small groups to accomplish."[8] The Internet is beneficial because it allows for thousands of replies, as well as links to further information about the topics being addressed.

However, these Internet petitions are not as effective as people would think. For instance, the distinct handwriting of many participants you find on paper petitions proves that many people signed the petition. However, once a petition is moved to an online format, the individual writing styles become typed text, indistinguishable from one person to the next. Another issue is that the intended audience is often not explicitly mentioned, or the topic itself is too vaguely outlined for readers to understand everything that is being proposed in the petition. There is no guarantee that the petition will reach its intended audience or that the specified recipient actually has the credentials or ability to act upon the petition's results. There's also the fact that signing a petition doesn't actually get anything accomplished. People can sign a petition stating that they want something to be done about global warming, but they themselves do not take the initiative to go out and do something about it with this petition.[9]

A California task force looked into the matter of making official petitions that voters could use in an effort to make online petitions more effective and trustworthy. However, they decided that there were too many issues to deal with. An official government petition program would require voters to sign in each time to verify their identification. Hacking and identity theft could result in a user's being unable to sign a petition, or the user might sign multiple petitions that he or she did not choose to sign. In addition, petitions can be signed at any time of the year, making it a costly program to update and maintain.[10]

Despite these issues, the Internet is still a potential way to reach a broader voting population and audience. Online petition companies like http://www.ipetitions.com/, http://www.thepetitionsite.com/, and http://www.gopetition.com/ have sprung up around the Web, allowing anyone to create a petition. These companies may offer to "make sure" that the petition gets to the person it needs to get to. However, even if the petition doesn't get signed, it may still influence people's opinions. Online petitions can expose people to opinions and causes that they had never thought about before. Even if people don't end up signing the petition, they might be interested in the cause. This may encourage them to go out and do something about the issue themselves, which, in effect, accomplishes what the petition set out to do in the first place.[11]

>>> **ACTIVITY** Find and read through an online petition. What is the issue the petition is trying to address? Is this an effective petition? Why or why not?

COLLECTIVE BEHAVIOR

People who gather in groups often react and think in the same way when they gather together. **Collective behavior** is any social interaction in which a group of people engages in behavior that is not in their normal routine. Depending on the type of collective behavior, this can be harmful and dangerous.

Violence

When discontent and tempers run high, violence often follows. Riots and mobs are likely to break out when people assemble in anger, and chaos ensues. **Mobs** are groups characterized by high levels of emotion that engage in some type of focused action that can be violent or disruptive. In 1999, peaceful protests against the World Trade Organization turned violent as 30,000 protesters surrounded the Seattle Convention Center to give voice against WTO policies. There were over 500 arrests, and emotions were high on both sides.[12] Mobs can lead to **hysteria**, a heightened emotional state that can lead a group to violence.

Riots are emotional and violent disturbances of the peace by a crowd. Riots involve high levels of emotion and violence, but unlike mobs, the people taking part in riots have no centralized focus and lash out at any and everything. Rioters express rage and anger and often spontaneously attack property and people. For example, the Watts Riots of 1965 in Los Angeles ignited after the arrest of Marquette Frye and his family. Witnesses to the arrest were enraged and released their anger on the city of Los Angeles. For six days, property was destroyed, people fought in the streets, and the town was in complete mayhem. The police were forced to retaliate. When the dust settled, 42 people were dead, more than 1,000 were injured, 4,000 had been arrested, and property damage was estimated at $40 million. Another part of the outrage that continued to simmer was that the parts that were destroyed were never rebuilt.[13]

Consumerism

Consumerism, rather than hate, often causes people to go out in droves, but to buy things en masse, instead of protesting social injustice. For instance, people might buy into the newest fad, like iPhones or the latest Sony PlayStation. A **fad** is a temporary fashion, notion, or action that the public embraces. Fads can take many forms. Last year, my daughter wanted a Wii gaming system for Christmas, and I was thrown into the midst of an object fad. Finding a Wii was nearly impossible. Fortunately, Santa was able to get one.

Fads may also include popular ideas, such as using feng shui to increase the chi, or energy, in one's home. They can also include activities, like rollerblading. Finally, fads can be people. The latest teen sensation, Miley Cyrus, is a human fad that's taking the nation, or at least tween girls, by storm.

Sociologist Joel Best suggests that fads such as the hula hoop are one thing, but fads in institutions are another.[14] Institutional fads follow a predetermined cycle: *emerging, surging,* and *purging*. At the emerging and surging stages, we embrace institutional change because we are optimistic and believe in progress. Thus, the latest trends take over the way we do business, regardless of their effectiveness.[15] Look at the DARE—Drug Abuse Resistance Education—program. Police officers teach children about the dangers of drugs, but the results are dubious at best, and some studies actually show that the program makes drug use worse, not better.[16]

The problem with institutional fads is that at the time they are surging, no one really knows if they will work. Usually, the media publicize someone or something as the latest trend in business, education, or medicine. This fad promises to solve a problem or change society. Americans tend to jump on the bandwagon of the latest institutional fad, so it's only after the fad has proved itself to be a total failure that this changes.

But some fads can actually leave lasting effects on a society. When this occurs, we call it a **craze**. When I was in college, you had to go to video arcades to play games. They were so new, that people actually took dates to the arcade. Such a craze has largely ended, but the lasting effect of this craze is that most homes have some type of gaming system.

Fear also instigates consumerism. A **panic** is an extreme fear based on something that might happen. I'm sure you remember the Y2K panic, when many people were convinced that modern life would stop because computers would fail to recognize "00" as 2000. However, when January 1, 2000, passed, people realized that they'd panicked for nothing.[17] The panic caused by the 9/11 terrorist attacks led the government to encourage the public to buy duct tape and plastic to seal doors and windows against a chemical attack. This panic caused a large increase in purchases of these items.[18]

Crowds

You might not join in the latest fad, craze, or panic, but at some point everyone is part of a large group of influential people, called a crowd. A **crowd** is a large group of people who gather for a temporary purpose. When you attend a football game, you're in a crowd. Members can easily influence each other. For example, when you cheer, others will often join in with you. Other crowds may focus on a cause, like those protesting a death penalty execution. Protest crowds can be large or small. For instance, the March on Selma in 1965 included 600 civil rights marchers, whereas the Million Man March in 1995 had more than 400,000 people.[19]

Rumors

People connect in other ways, too. Sociologists suggest that passing on **rumors**, stories or statements that lack confirmation or certainty, is part of American culture. A common type of rumor is an urban legend. **Urban legends** are rumors that are presented as true stories and act as cautionary tales. These are stories that circulate that claim to have happened to other people, but are actually false. We spread them as if we really saw or heard the event personally to entertain our listeners.[20] One of my favorite rumors is one I call "How long must I wait?"

This legend deals with the supposed rules pertaining to how long students must wait for a tardy professor. When a professor is late, students worry that they might miss something if they leave too soon. The rumor suggests that there's a tardiness policy that dictates how long students must wait before they can assume they will not be penalized for leaving class. Wait times vary depending on the rank of the professor: graduate assistants get the shortest leeway, while full doctoral professors receive the most patience. Truthfully, few colleges have an official faculty tardiness policy. Of those that do, academic rank doesn't affect how long you must wait. To be safe, check your student handbook or ask your professor what policy he or she has about this matter.[21]

The Million Man March was a social movement in which African American men gathered to call for social reform, including an end to violence and getting jobs to support their families.

Rescuing Rainforests

As sociologists, it's important to study and understand the effects that humans have on the environment. Deforestation, pollution, and poaching are just three ways that humans have negatively impacted their environment.[22] It's no surprise, then, that conservation movements are gaining popularity in the United States and other parts of the world.

One conservation movement is rainforest conservation. Rainforests clean the air, provide food and raw materials, and are home to half of the world's population of plants and animals.[23] To maintain and protect these vital areas, organizations like the World Wildlife Foundation and the Rainforest Alliance work alongside individuals, governments, and other organizations. Members can help by donating money to the conservation projects or by volunteering in local and national conservation efforts.[24] The WWF also focuses on helping the people who live in the area surrounding the rainforests. These people rely on the forest for their livelihood, so they work with organizations to safely harvest items from the forest while protecting its valuable natural resources.[25]

Activist groups like the Rainforest Action Network (RAN) employ different methods to get their point across. In 1987, RAN's successful boycott against Burger King stopped the fast-food chain's practice of buying cheap beef from areas that were once rainforests.[26] The group calls for nonviolent protests to make the public aware of important issues.

The modern environmental movement is spreading; in fact, this book you bought is totally recyclable. I'm happy to say that this book is made with post-consumer fiber, and it should leave no footprint. How would our world be different if we printed every book, newspaper, and magazine this way?

NATURE OF SOCIAL MOVEMENTS

Social movements are activities that support or protest social issues organized by nongovernmental organizations. In other words, social movements allow regular folks to participate in the political process, diffusing ideas and beliefs. Many social movements want to bring about social change, while others seek to maintain the status quo. According to sociologist Charles Tilly, there are three elements that exist in all social movements.[27]

The first element in a social movement is the promotional campaign. **Campaigns** are organized and ongoing efforts of claims making that target a specific authority in the society. For instance, when it's time for elections, politicians have campaigns geared to the voters. They make claims of what they will do if they are elected to office and try to convince the voter that they would be the best candidates for the position.

Another element used is repertoire. **Repertoires** are actions used to promote interest and involvement within the movement. For example, protesters who oppose the death penalty might lobby in Congress, protest at executions, and complete research into that social policy.

Finally, you have the members of a movement who want to show the public the worthiness, unity, numbers, and commitments of their movement (**WUNC**). They're the people who organize the events, participate in the activities, and do what they can to get the word out about their organization. Remember, people committed to a cause do not constitute a movement. Movements need WUNC members to help lead and keep it focused.

Tilly suggests that before the eighteenth century, there was no such thing as a true "social movement." It's true that there were violent revolutions and rebellions demanding changes in society before this period; however, these movements were not social movements because they didn't bring about organizations. It was not until the 1800s that movements arose over issues such as unionism in response to capitalism, women's suffrage, abolition of slavery, and many other issues.

<<< **Protesters demonstrated outside the White House in the months leading to the 2008 Olympics and in front of the Chinese Embassy in Berlin, Germany, the day before the Games began.** They wanted freedom for Tibet, which has been under China's rule since 1959.

Stages of Social Movements

All social movements go through a set of predictable stages of development. In the first stage, **emergence**, people become aware of a problem and begin to notice that others feel the same way. Forty years ago, few were aware of the pitfalls of pollution. A few people took notice, though, and began the first step for any social movement—making people aware of a problem.

In the next stage, social movements seek to define their goals and design a plan to get their goals met. This state is known as **coalescence**. In this stage, groups reach out to other groups and individuals to gain membership. The movement then grows and increases the public awareness of the problem. In 1980, independent John Andersen ran for President. He took note of the pollution problems associated with burning fossil fuels. He ran on a 50 cents a gallon gasoline tax, which would all go into the research and development of clean energy. With gasoline prices on the rise and global warming a reality, it seems he was ahead of his time.

The environmental movement became a political force, moving it into **bureaucratization**. The myriad of social movements dedicated to the environment shows that this concern will not go away. Organizations like the Northeast Sustainable Energy Association strive to achieve what John Andersen dreamed possible in 1980.

SOCIAL MOVEMENTS are activities that support or protest social issues organized by nongovernmental organizations.

CAMPAIGNS are organized and ongoing efforts of claims making that target a specific authority in society.

REPERTOIRES are actions used to promote interest and involvement within the movement.

WUNC refers to the members of a movement who want to show the public the worthiness, unity, numbers, and commitments of their movement.

EMERGENCE is the first stage of a movement when people become aware of a problem and begin to notice that others feel the same way.

COALESCENCE is the second stage of a movement when groups reach out to other groups and individuals to gain membership.

BUREAUCRATIZATION is the third stage of a movement when it becomes a political force.

DECLINE is the final stage of a movement when an organization completes its goal or is seen as irrelevant.

When an organization completes its goal or is seen as irrelevant, it falls into the final stage, **decline**. If and when the day comes that we have clean energy and recycling becomes the norm, the environmental movement should simply go into decline, because it will have achieved its goals.[28]

THINK SOCIOLOGICALLY

Funeral Protests

Soldiers who die in action serving their country are usually treated with the utmost respect, and their funerals are quiet, somber events. However, over the past few years, a group of religious protestors has been causing a stir at services by holding up signs and shouting at the mourners in the funeral procession.

The Westboro Baptist Church, led by Pastor Fred Phelps, has been protesting funerals for American soldiers, carrying signs that say, "Thank God for dead soldiers" and "God hates you." The group claims that God has killed the soldiers because they fought for a country that accepts homosexuality. Phelps's congregation of more than 70 people is mostly made up of his family members and has protested at over 100 military funerals, as well as the funeral of Matthew Shepard, a college student who was beaten to death because he was gay. They travel around the country exercising their rights to protest and free speech by claiming the soldiers' deaths were the result of God's wrath and displeasure with America.

Although they are within their rights to protest, laws have been passed to protect the rights of the mourners and show respect for the dead. Now, protesters must be at least 500 feet away from the procession, and some states are passing laws that only allow protesting an hour before and an hour after the funeral. Lawmakers believe that these

laws will allow the family some respite while maintaining the protestors' rights.

In addition to legal backing, American citizens have come forth to show their support for the soldiers and their families as well. In opposition to the Westboro Baptist Church, a group of more than 400 bikers around the country have formed the "Patriot Guard Riders." Their goal is to drown out the sounds of the protestors by escorting the soldiers to their resting places while shielding the mourners from the protesters. The Phelps family says they will continue to exercise their right to protest, and the Patriot Guard Riders say they will continue to protect the soldiers' families.

The U.S. Bill of Rights gives us the freedom to assemble and the freedom of speech. But are there situations when it's not appropriate to exercise this right? Should there be laws that curb these rights under certain circumstances? Where do we draw the line between what is constitutionally right and what is socially wrong?[29]

∧∧∧ While **members of the Westboro Baptist Church protest at a funeral,** a Patriot Guard Rider holds up a U.S. flag across the street. **Is a soldier's funeral the right forum for these actions?**

TYPES OF SOCIAL MOVEMENTS

Although all social movements are essentially sustained campaigns that support a goal, there is no standard type of social movement. They have different methods of approaching their goals and identifying potential followers. David F. Aberle developed an early typology of social movements in 1966.[30] He categorized movements based on two dimensions: the orientation of change (society as a whole or individuals) and the amount of change sought (limited or radical). This classification created four categories of social movement: alternative, redemptive, reformative, and revolutionary.[31] Each category seeks a different combination of target audience and level of change.

The Four Categories of Social Movements

How much change is sought?

Who is changed?

	Limited	Radical
Society	 Alternative Social Movement	 Redemptive Social Movement
Specific Individuals	 Reformative Social Movement	 Revolutionary Social Movement

Alternative Social Movements

Alternative social movements want to create a change in specific people's thoughts, practices, and beliefs regarding a specific issue. Their goal is to encourage a small, defined change in the way a particular group of people think and act in order to solve a problem. La Leche League (LLL) is an alternative social movement organization that encourages mothers to breastfeed their babies. In 1959, seven women, who were alarmed by the fact that the breastfeeding rate in the United

States had dropped to nearly 20 percent, organized the group. Shortly after its incorporation, the group published and distributed the first edition of *The Womanly Art of Breastfeeding* in an effort to promote LLL's purpose. The publication expressed the organization's philosophy that breastfeeding is the most natural and effective way to satisfy a baby's needs, and it also gave helpful advice to new and expecting mothers on how to perform the practice.[32]

LLL also protects a nursing mother's rights. In 2006, a woman was escorted off an airplane because she began breastfeeding her daughter. Angered by the airline's actions, mothers from the LLL organized a "nurse-in" protest in front of the airline's counter. The women argued that it was a mother's right to feed her child in public.[33]

Over the last 50 years, the group established a presence in 68 countries and helped the breastfeeding rate in the United States reach nearly 77 percent.[34] The organization has grown dramatically, but its purpose remains the same. The organization does not ally itself with any other movement and continues to focus solely on its single goal.

Redemptive Social Movements

Redemptive social movements also focus on specific individuals, but the amount of change sought is radical, rather than limited. Religious movements, such as those involving evangelical Christians, are typically categorized as redemptive because they encourage a specific group of nonbelievers to make a dramatic lifestyle change by converting to or adopting a new religion. Christian missionaries have held a quiet presence in traditionally Islamic states in the Middle East for centuries. However, this missionary movement has surged in recent years. According to the Center for the Study of Global Christianity at Gordon-Conwell Theological Seminary in South Hamilton, Massachusetts, the number of missionaries to Islamic countries has increased from about 15,000 in 1982 to more than 27,000 in 2001.[35] The 9/11 attacks pushed the movement even farther. Some Christian missionaries enter Islamic countries with the sole intention of providing aid to the region's struggling communities; however, evangelical missionaries proceed with the primary goal of converting Muslims to Christianity. This practice is controversial in both Muslim and Christian communities.

Reformative Social Movements

Not all social movements are targeted to specific individuals or groups. Some social movements attempt to tether all of society to their mission. **Reformative social movements** seek to change a society's thoughts and actions, but only in a limited way. This type of movement can be **progressive**, favoring or promoting change, or **regressive**, seeking to stop change. Progressive reformative social movements ask society to accept something new into the social order. For example, environmental groups ask society to participate in or support conservation efforts like recycling programs, clean air legislation, or alternative fuel funding. This movement has grown by leaps and bounds, as conservation has become a growing global concern. Journalist Paul Hawken reveals in *Blessed Unrest*, "The modern environmental movement is spreading" and individuals, communities, and corporations are making an effort to take part in this movement.

> **ALTERNATIVE SOCIAL MOVEMENTS** want to create a change in specific people's thoughts, practices, and beliefs regarding a particular issue.
>
> **REDEMPTIVE SOCIAL MOVEMENTS** focus on specific individuals, but the amount of change sought is radical, rather than limited.
>
> **REFORMATIVE SOCIAL MOVEMENTS** seek to change a society's thoughts and actions, but only in a limited way.
>
> **PROGRESSIVE** means favoring or promoting change.
>
> **REGRESSIVE** means seeking to stop change.
>
> **REVOLUTIONARY SOCIAL MOVEMENT,** or sometimes called the transformative social movement, seeks to change the thoughts and actions of all society in radical fashion.

REVOLUTIONARY SOCIAL MOVEMENTS

The most ambitious type of social movement is the **revolutionary social movement**, or sometimes called the transformative social movement. This type of movement seeks to change the thoughts and actions of all society in radical fashion. Social movement groups that are considered revolutionary aim to completely restructure society. When a revolutionary social movement organization attempts to fulfill its missions, it is called a revolution.

On July 26, 1953, Fidel Castro organized rebel forces and launched an attack on the Moncada military barracks in Santiago de Cuba. The revolution was an attempt to spark an uprising against Fulgencio Batista's regime. After the attack failed to dismantle the existing government, Castro moved his efforts to Mexico, where he organized Cuban exiles into a revolutionary group called the 26th of July Movement. After gaining the support of numerous Cuban citizens through the distribution of political propaganda, the movement's guerilla forces defeated the existing Cuban government and enlisted Castro as president in 1960. The movement asked all citizens on the island of Cuba to change their ideology and support a government that would reinstate full civil and political liberties and assume moderate reforms. Unfortunately, the initial goals of the movement were never realized as Castro changed his policies once he was in power.[36]

<<< Groups protest the presence of Christian missionaries in many countries. **New Delhi inhabitants protest against Christian missionary conversions, which increase violence and tension between India's Christians and Hindus.**

think sociologically: WHAT ARE THE THEORIES BEHIND SOCIAL MOVEMENTS?

Conflict Theory

Conflict theorists believe that social movements are normative events in a social world that has inequality. This can be because of social inequalities or because of a perceived inequality. As Marx suggested, inequality makes social change not only necessary, but likely. Why? Because people eventually notice their plight and decide to do something about this. Sociologists such as Charles Tilly suggest that discontent is always present because there will always be haves and have-nots in every society.[37] This applies to social movements.

Social movements are in competition with each other for resources. Resource mobilization theory suggests that those organizations that are best able to gain access to money, media, and larger audiences are more likely to succeed. The nature of the scarcity of resources causes movements to compete for those resources. The ones that compete most effectively are the ones that are going to survive.[38]

Functionalism

Functionalists do not believe that social movements are actually activities per se. Instead, they are a way for participants to relieve the frustrations and emotions they have about a particular subject. In this way, social movements challenge the equilibrium of society, and change is likely to occur.

Sociologists Park and Burgess discuss how successful social movements become more organized and eventually institutionalized.[39] First, crowds gather together to protest something they object to or something that is stressful or uncertain. Within this crowd, leaders eventually emerge to take on the responsibility of guiding the crowds toward their purpose. In this way, the crowd begins to organize under the leadership, and an organization will begin to form. This organization is based on ideology, and more people may join the organization's ranks. Eventually, the mainstream accepts this ideology, and the organization becomes institutionalized.

For example, a diverse group of people went to our town's city council meetings to complain about the lack of bike lanes on the roads. At the meetings, we met others who had similar feelings, and, over time, leaders began to emerge from our group. We formed an organization to promote bicycling as an alternative mode of transportation. The group now meets regularly with the park's board and the city council to discuss progress on new bike lanes.

William Kornhauser supports Park and Burgess's idea. He went on to say that not only do social movements bring together people who are like-minded, these movements also allow people who feel less important or isolated in society to come together with others. These people relish the idea of being a part of something bigger, and they feel fulfilled because they take part. Therefore, social movements take on a personal, individualistic component to them, filling the need of those who feel separate from the rest of society.[40]

Symbolic Interactionism

Symbolic interactionists believe that social movements are less of a unifying force of individuals and more of a reaction to relative deprivation. **Relative deprivation** points to the gaps between what people have and what they expect. For example, you may have a cheap car, but you believe that you should have an expensive car. This makes you feel deprived when you see cars that you think are better than your own. You forget to consider the people who drive cars that are not as nice as your car or the people who don't have cars at all. You focus on the envy you feel when you see people with things that are "better" than yours.[41]

Davies applies this theory to social movements by explaining that when people's expectations are met, they are unlikely to organize and work to make changes.[42] They are satisfied with what they have and are unlikely to complain. So, it's only natural to assume that people will be unhappy and more willing to rebel when their expectations are not being met. Collective violence will most likely occur after a period of rising expectations, and a steep decline and reversal of the people's fortunes follows increased gratification.

Ted Gurr suggests that deprivation creates discontent, which leads to civil strife. If social institutions can absorb some of the stress or channel it into something other than violence, revolution is unlikely. Nonviolent strife consists of turmoil such as riots and demonstrations. Violent strife consists of revolution and terrorism.[43]

FRAMING PROCESSES

In social movement studies, the idea of frames in social movements has its root in the work of Erving Goffman.[44] Frames provide the individual the opportunity to identify, understand, and label events as they occur in the social world. Frames are templates that organize how we behave publicly. They do not completely limit our understanding of social events, like

<<< People like author Paul Hawken have spoken about the state of the environment for years, but **it wasn't until 2006 that environmental awareness got a huge boost from Al Gore's** *An Inconvenient Truth.*

Overview of Politicized Communal Groups by Region and Type of Group in 1990

WORLD REGIONS	Number of countries with politicized groups	Number of politicized groups	Ethno-classes	Types of Groups			
				Ethno-nationalists	Militant sects*	Indigenes	Communal contenders
Advanced industrial democracies (21)	12	23	8	10	3 (1)	4	0
Eastern Europe and the USSR (9)	5	32	4	17	14 (1)	11	0
East, Southeast, and South Asia (21)	15	42	7	19	8 (2)	25	3
North Africa and the Middle East (19)	11	29	5	13	9 (5)	11	8
Africa South of the Sahara (36)	29	72	10	21	5	12	51
Latin America and the Caribbean (21)	17	29	9	1	0 (1)	19	0
Totals (127)	89	227	43	81	39 (10)	82	62

*Listed first are numbers of Muslim minorities; numbers in parentheses are non-Muslim religious minorities: Northern Irish Catholics, Jews (in the ex-USSR and Argentina), Copts in Egypt, Maronites in Lebanon, Hindus (in Pakistan and Bangladesh), Sikhs in India, Baha'is in Iran, and Ahmadis in Pakistan. The latter two have been condemned as non-Muslin heresies in Iran and Pakistan, respectively, which is a warrant for discrimination against their followers. The total number of sects is 49.
Source: Ted Robert Gurr, "Why Minorities Rebel: A Global Analysis of Communal Mobilization and Conflict Since 1945," *International Political Science Review*, 1993. 14 (2): 161-201.

∧
∧ This table shows the number of political groups in different countries around the world. Notice how
∧ more industrialized areas have fewer politicized groups and no contenders for resources, **but in poorer regions like southern Africa, there are as many as 72 political groups and 51 contending groups. Do you think the number and types of groups have anything to do with social stratification and strife?**

a picture frame limits the end of a photo; instead, they provide the building blocks by which we understand the world. Frames exist before us, and we become part of them through social processes that teach us how to dress, communicate, and interact within them.[45] For example, if you're on an elevator, you probably do not speak to strangers. At a sporting event, you might hug a stranger if you're caught up in the moment. The frames of the events provide the parameters for understanding that interaction.

Successful social movements use frames to further their cause. If a movement hopes to bring about a change, it must frame its argument successfully. There are three core tasks in framing:

1 **Diagnostic framing:** Creates a frame that states the problem clearly. Is this really a problem? Why? For example, the movement to move the U.S. economy away from petroleum relies on accurately and effectively pointing to the problems associated with continued dependence on oil from other nations.[46]

2 **Prognostic framing:** Provides the solution to this problem. Currently, there are a host of social movements competing to be the solution to the problem. Is natural gas the best alternative, or are solar, wind, nuclear energy, and biofuels the better choice? Each group competes against the other and provides a prognosis of how its solution will be the best one.[47]

3 **Motivational framing:** This calls people to take action. It makes an argument that people need to do more than merely talk about a problem—they must also take action. When groups urge you to buy a hybrid car or put up a windmill, they are using the motivational frame.[48]

Of course, in an environment such as this, where energy concerns continue to take center stage in the national debate, it is not surprising that some groups are coming together to provide answers. This **frame alignment process** occurs when social movement organizations link their goals to the goals of other organizations. Four processes occur when organiza-

tions are involved in the frame alignment process: Bridging, Amplification, Extension, and Transformation.[49]

Frame bridging occurs when two or more groups that may be somewhat opposed to each other join forces. Within the public debate over the oil-based economy, solar and natural gas power proponents have bridged, suggesting that both sources of energy are renewable and clean and they should work together to change the country's collective understanding about how to power their homes and cars.[50]

Amplification occurs when ideas become elaborated and sometimes exaggerated. Groups seek to engage people by illuminating the social issue. The closer this issue is to an already existing value or cultural belief, the more likely amplification can work.[51] For example, in the 1980s, I was a member of a group that proposed using wind power for electricity generation. However, we had little success because the price of oil was still cheap, and energy seemed plentiful. As times change, Americans are warming up to the idea of wind power if that means they can continue to have air conditioning they can afford.

Extension of the frame alignment refers to the way in which social movement organizations seek to align their interests with those of other groups that are related, sometimes furthering ideas that were not originally in their frame. For example, the solar movement is often connected in the public discourse to the use of biological fuels. Finally, frames can experience transformation when they become aligned.[52]

Transformation changes the old meanings and understandings of the problem and creates new and innovative ones. To push our example further, the energy independence frame is transforming into an organization that once sought to foster only renewable and clean energy, but now often includes a discussion of coal and nuclear power as well.[53]

WRAP YOUR MIND AROUND THE THEORY

These South Koreans are protesting the import of U.S. beef after a mad cow disease scare. **Emotions often run high when people gather to dissent from something.**

FUNCTIONALISM

Functionalists tend to focus on how systems find balance. In general, they would suggest that social movements cause imbalance, but that they will be short term. For example, Talcott Parsons suggested that social movements follow a predictable pattern that eventually leads the movement into harmony and balance with the rest of society.[54] If you consider the environmental movement, it has become a much more accepted part of society today compared to its status 25 years ago. According to Hawken, over two million organizations worldwide are organizing and uniting because of people's concerns for the environment. These groups are not a part of the status quo.

CONFLICT THEORY

Conflict theorists believe that social structures are the cause of social movements. Inequality causes discontent. This discontent causes people to seek out change, either from within the system or with outside forces. Opposing parties fight for resources, so social movements are a way for groups to mobilize and seize power and resources. Whichever group is most effective at mobilizing "wins" the conflict. An exception to this rule would be with regard to climate concerns. The origin of environmental organizations is a much more organic creation marked by concern for ecological degradation.

WHAT ARE THE RESULTS OF SOCIAL MOVEMENTS **?**

SYMBOLIC INTERACTIONISM

Some believe that social movements are caused by the perception of relative deprivation. When a person's expectations are not met, they are discontent. If their expectations are continually not met, they are likely to resort to social movements. For example, environmental hazards seen in countries with few safety regulations can spur people to make a change. Perception is the big key: What do people perceive as unfair? In addition, people react differently because of different framing situations. Bridging, amplification, extension, and transformation are all ways in which organizations react to a framing situation and problem.

Conflict theorists believe that **social movements are a result of people wanting what others have.**

Workers will often strike if their expectations are not met. Verizon workers went on strike when their contracts expired without a plan in place for new contracts.

discover sociology in action: HOW DO SOCIAL MOVEMENTS INFLUENCE SOCIOLOGICAL THEORY AND STUDY?

Social Policy: Corporate Average Fuel Economy

The movements that Hawken discusses are people and organizations working without a formal system of leadership to oversee their actions. They make up groups that focus on human rights, the environment, and a plurality of other issues dedicated to improving the people's lives. They make up a loose configuration of groups dedicated to change. These independent movements have a strong force behind them, despite their unconventional structure. So, what will happen if the government decides to take part, too?

One way the government is joining in is by changing Corporate Average Fuel Economy (CAFÉ) automotive standards. These are the average miles per gallon an automobile maker should attain in its entire selection of vehicles. The increase in the CAFÉ standards is part of an effort to get cleaner, more efficient vehicles on the road. The government will help do this by increasing the required miles per gallon levels for automobiles that are sold in the United States. The new laws will force manufacturers to produce more efficient cars to meet the new requirements. Currently, cars need to average (between highway and city mileage) 27.5 miles per gallon, and trucks need to average 22.5. By 2011, CAFÉ standards increase the average to 31.6 miles per gallon, and by 2020 vehicles must average 35 miles per gallon. In order to conform to these standards, car companies have two options: make vehicles lighter or make them more fuel efficient. However, fuel efficiency changes can add up, leading car companies to increase their price by $4,000 to $6,000.

More fuel-efficient cars are already in production, and companies like Ford, Dodge, and General Motors hope to have more environmentally friendly vehicles ready for the U.S. market by 2010. It's predicted that in the future, people will drive smaller, more efficient vehicles and use less gas.[55]

As you fill your car with expensive gas, think how glad you would be to have increased fuel efficiency. Of course, what will happen to those large SUVs and gas-guzzling pickups? Who will be able to afford these new, more efficient cars? Are there other sources of energy that we could use, other than gasoline? These and other questions remain to be answered, but the policy of setting standards is one way the government is trying to control the marketplace and force cultural change by making demands on industry to use technology to create more efficient cars.

ACTIVITIES

1. Think about some of the social policies in our nation. Choose three and look for information about when these policies came into effect, and what spurred the movement.
2. Use the Internet to find out the popular fads in the United States beginning with the 1900s and continuing today. Create a timeline or graphic showing what the latest fads were from each decade.
3. Research an environmental group that is located in your community or state. Find out what the group's mission statement is and what steps they've taken to improve the environment. Design an advertisement for the group that might inspire others to join.

From Classroom to Community ⟩ Carpooling

With gas prices increasing all the time, many of my students were complaining about their decreasing funds. Some students decided that biking to school would be their best money-saving option. Devante, who drove twenty minutes to get to class, suggested a campus-wide carpool. Using the school's online community board, he set up a page where commuters could find other students in their area.

"I wanted one or two other people to share the cost of travel. I didn't expect to hear back from more than twenty people. The online community board made it easy for us to get in touch and figure out scheduling details. It also helped us form a commuter community on campus. We ended up creating a commuter's lounge where students could relax between classes and wait for their rides.

"Then, the campus' conservation club wrote an article for the school newspaper about how carpooling helps the environment by decreasing pollution. Even more students joined our online group. It was great to see so many people in one group for so many different reasons. I got to meet a lot of really interesting people, and I felt closer to our school community. By the end of the semester, the money I saved on gas was just one of the many perks I received by starting this group."

WHAT **DRIVES SOCIAL CHANGE?** 301

reactions to events and new opportunities

WHAT **ARE THE THEORIES BEHIND SOCIAL MOVEMENTS?** 309

functionalism: social movements challenge the equilibrium of society and give people a way to relieve their frustrations and emotions about a particular subject

conflict theory: social inequality creates discontent among some, which can lead to social movements

symbolic interactionism: people protest in reaction to a need that is not being met

HOW **DO SOCIAL MOVEMENTS INFLUENCE SOCIOLOGICAL THEORY AND STUDY?** 313

social movements: provide an ever-changing sociological landscape; encourage the development of new theory and the application of existing theory

get the topic: WHAT DRIVES SOCIAL CHANGE

Shifts in Society 301
Resistance to Change 302
Conflict Theory 309
Functionalism 310
Symbolic Interactionism 310
Social Policy: Corporate Average Fuel Economy 313

Theory

FUNCTIONALISM 310
- social movements are not the actual activities, but are ways for people to vent their frustrations and emotions
- venting upsets the balance of society
- movements also bring individuals together, allowing those who feel isolated and alone to feel as though they are part of something bigger

CONFLICT THEORY 309
- social structures are the cause of social movements
- people concentrate on the things that they do not have, and inequality causes discontent

- discontent causes people to seek out change, either from within the system or with outside forces
- opposing parties fight for resources, so social movements are a way for groups to mobilize and seize power and resources

SYMBOLIC INTERACTIONISM 310
- social movements are caused by relative deprivation
- when a person's expectations are not met, he or she are discontent
- if their expectations are continually not met, they are likely to resort to social movements
- perception is key

Key Terms

social change is the way in which culture, interaction, and innovation change social institutions over time. 301

technology deals with the creation, use, and application of knowledge and its interrelation with life, society, and the environment. 302

invention is the creation of a new device or way of thinking. 302

diffusion is the spreading of something more widely. 302

futility is the claim that a reform cannot work because the social problem is unsolvable. 302

perversity claims that any attempts to fix a problem would actually compound the issues the change was trying to address. 303

jeopardy is the claim that attempting to solve a problem will only draw attention away from other, more important issues. 303

collective behavior is any social interaction in which a group of people engages in behavior that is not in their normal routine. 304

mobs are groups characterized by high levels of emotion that engage in some type of focused action that can be violent or disruptive. 304

hysteria is a heightened emotional state that can lead a group to violence. 304

riots are emotional and violent disturbances of the peace by a crowd that lacks a central focus. 304

fad is a temporary fashion, notion, or action the public embraces. 304

craze occurs when a fad leaves a lasting effect on society. 305

panic is an extreme fear based on something that might happen. 305

crowd is a large group of influential people who gather for a temporary purpose. 305

rumors are stories or statements that lack confirmation or certainty. 305

urban legends are rumors that are presented as true stories that act as cautionary tales. 305

social movements are activities that support or protest social issues organized by nongovernmental organizations. 306

campaigns are organized and ongoing efforts of claims making that target a specific authority in society. 306

repertoires are actions used to promote interest and involvement within the movement. 306

WUNC refers to the members of a movement who want to show the public the worthiness, unity, numbers, and commitments of their movement. 306

(continued)

emergence is the first stage of a movement when people become aware of a problem and begin to notice that others feel the same way. *307*

coalescence is the second stage of a movement when groups reach out to other groups and individuals to gain membership. *307*

bureaucratization is the third stage of a movement when it becomes a political force. *307*

decline is the final stage of a movement when an organization completes its goal or is seen as irrelevant. *307*

alternative social movements want to create a change in specific people's thoughts, practices, and beliefs regarding a particular issue. *308*

redemptive social movements focus on specific individuals, but the amount of change sought is radical, rather than limited. *308*

reformative social movements seek to change a society's thoughts and actions, but only in a limited way. *309*

progressive means favoring or promoting change. *309*

regressive means seeking to stop change. *309*

revolutionary social movement, or sometimes called the transformative social movement, seeks to change the thoughts and actions of all society in radical fashion. *309*

relative deprivation points to the gaps between what people have and what they expect. *310*

frame alignment process occurs when social movement organizations link their goals to the goals of other organizations. *311*

frame bridging occurs when two or more groups that may be somewhat opposed to each other join forces. *311*

amplification occurs when ideas become elaborated and sometimes exaggerated. *311*

extension refers to the way social movement organizations seek to align their interests with those of other groups that are related, sometimes furthering ideas that were not originally in their frame. *311*

transformation changes the old meanings and understandings of the problem and creates new and innovative ones. *311*

Sample Test Questions

These multiple-choice questions are similar to those found in the test bank that accompanies this textbook.

1. Which of the following statements about mobs is *false*?
   a. They are violent and disruptive.
   b. They have high levels of emotions.
   c. They have no central focus or intent.
   d. They are one form of collective behavior.

2. Social protesters who argue perversity claim that
   a. there is no solution to the problem.
   b. any change will only make the problem worse.
   c. the "so-called problem" is not really a problem at all.
   d. focusing on the problem means ignoring more important things.

3. Which of the following statements about technology is *false*?
   a. Technology encompasses more than objects and things.
   b. As technology changes, culture remains the same.
   c. Technology is the product of invention.
   d. Technology leads to new discoveries.

4. Which of the following is an example of a craze?
   a. People redecorating their home using feng shui techniques
   b. People going on a date at a video arcade
   c. People attending a DARE presentation
   d. People waiting in line to buy a Wii

5. Which type of social movement seeks to create limited change for the entire society?
   a. An alternative social movement
   b. A redemptive social movement
   c. A reform social movement
   d. A revolutionary social movement

ANSWERS: 1. c; 2. b; 3. b; 4. b; 5. d

4. How do sociologists from the three sociological paradigms view social movements?
5. How does the environmental movement Hawken discusses differ from other social movements?

WHERE TO START YOUR RESEARCH PAPER

For more information on all countries, including maps and profiles, go to http://www.cia.gov/cia/publications/factbook/index.html http://www.unesco.org/women/sta/index.htm

To find United Nations data on children, go to http://www.unicef.org/statistics/index.html

To find more information on national and international population projections and reports as well as inequality and poverty numbers, go to http://www.census.gov

To learn more about the World Values Survey (which includes data from surveys of 66 countries), go to http://wvs.isr.umich.edu/

To find religious data on the Web, go to http://www.adherents.com/

For comparison data on education, go to http://nces.ed.gov/

For more information on the world population report, data, and trends, go to http://www.un.org/esa/population/unpop.htm

To find summary data on topics related to population growth, go to http://www.prb.org/

To learn more about the United Nations environmental report, including data on environmental trends, go to http://www.unep.org/Evaluation/default.htm

For international earth science information, including numerous reports and various data sources, go to http://www.ciesin.org/

To find information on health indicators, international comparisons or health care systems, and health-related data, go to http://www3.who.int/whosis/menu.cfm

For data on income and inequality throughout the world, go to http://www.wider.unu.edu/wiid/wiid.htm

To find international data and analysis of poverty and wealth throughout the world, go to http://www.worldbank.org/

Remember to check www.thethinkspot.com **for additional information, downloadable flashcards, and other helpful resources.**

ESSAY

1. Discuss the four types of social movements and the features of each one.
2. How does new technology affect society?
3. What is relative deprivation?

GLOSSARY

Parenthetical numbers refer to the pages on which the term is introduced.

absolute poverty   is poverty so severe that one lacks resources to survive. (122)

achieved status   is a type of position that you earn or do something to attain. (68)

activity theory   states that life satisfaction depends on maintaining an involvement with life by developing new interests, hobbies, roles, and relationships. (220)

ageism   is prejudice and discrimination based solely on age. (219)

agents of socialization   are the people and groups who shape our self-concept, beliefs, and behavior. (92)

age-specific birth rate   is the number of births for every 1,000 women in a specific age group. (157)

age-specific death rate   is the number of deaths for every 1,000 persons of a given age group. (158)

alienation   refers to a person's sense of powerlessness, meaninglessness, and general cynicism toward the political process. (288)

alternative social movements   want to create a change in specific people's thoughts, practices, and beliefs regarding a specific issue. (308)

altruistic suicides   are suicides that occur when the level of solidarity is exceptionally high and when the individual views the group's interest as superior to all other interests. (7)

amplification   occurs when ideas become elaborated and sometimes exaggerated. (311)

animism   is the belief that recognizes that animate spirits live in natural objects and operate in the world. (271)

annexation   is the incorporation of one territory into another. (178)

anomic suicides   are suicides that occur as a result of social unrest. (8)

anti-natalist   means concerned with limiting population growth. (168)

ascribed status   is a position in society that is given or assigned. (68)

assimilation   is the process by which minority groups adopt the patterns of the dominant culture. (56)

assimilationist minorities   are groups that seek to shed their old ways and integrate themselves into mainstream society. (179)

attachment   is the social bond that refers to our relationship to others. (238)

authoritarian regimes   involve an individual or small group taking power and using repression and other techniques to maintain it. (288)

authoritarian style   is a parenting style with which children experience high levels of social control but low levels of emotional support. (92)

authoritative style   is a parenting style in which parents listen to their children's input while consistently enforcing the preset rules. (92)

autocratic leaders   are leaders who determine the group policies and assign tasks. (106)

baby boomers   are children born after WWII through the early 1960s. (159)

backstage   is the demeanor that incorporates our true feelings and beliefs. (75)

belief   is the social bond that refers to a person's conviction of truth. (238)

birth dearth   is declining birth rates. (160)

bissu   are androgynous members of Bugis society who embody the perfect mixture of male and female. (196)

blended families   are families composed of children and some combination of biological parents. (248)

bounded relationships   are relationships that exist only under specific conditions. (103)

bourgeoisie   refers to members of the capitalist class. (14)

brain drain   occurs when the best talent leaves poor countries and thereby provides an even greater advantage to wealthy countries. (147)

bureaucracies   are formal organizations that are organized into a hierarchy of smaller departments. (111)

bureaucratization   is the third stage of a movement when it becomes a political force. (307)

bureaucrats   are managers of business and government agencies. (145)

calabai   are anatomical males in Bugis society who adhere to some of the responsibilities of women. (196)

calalai   are anatomical females in Bugis society who assume the characteristics of men. (196)

campaigns   are organized and ongoing efforts of claims making that target a specific authority in the society. (306)

capitalism   is an economic system in which individuals can own the means of production as well as the services that others may need. (283)

carrying capacity   is the number of a specific species that can exist in a given environment. (164)

case studies   are investigations of one person or event in detail. (37)

caste systems   are systems in which a person's position may be a position of power and privilege or of disadvantage, but in either case his or her place is permanently fixed. (143)

causal relationship   is a relationship in which one condition leads to a certain consequence. (32)

causation   is the relationship between cause and effect. (32)

central tendency   is the numbers in the middle of an array of numbers. (38)

chattel slavery   is a form of slavery in which a slave is considered property. (143)

choice model   explains the income gap by analyzing the kinds of jobs women choose. (198)

church   is a large, highly organized group of believers. (272)

civil religion   is a binding force that holds society together through political and social issues. (274)

class consciousness   is an understanding of one's position in the class system. (15)

coalescence   is the second stage of a movement when groups reach out to other groups and individuals to gain membership. (307)

coercive organizations   are organizations that people are forced to join. (110)

cognitive development   is a person's ability to think and reason. (88)

cohort   is a specific group of people used in a study. (33)

collective behavior   is any social interaction in which a group of people engages in behavior that is not in their normal routine. (304)

colonialism   is the imposition of control over a weak nation by a more powerful country. (176)

color-blind racism   is the idea that racism still exists in society in more subtle ways. (184)

commitment   is the social bond that refers to our dedication to live a socially acceptable life. (238)

community learning   occurs when individuals and groups work to identify and address issues of public concern. (25)

comparative studies   use data from different sources in order to evaluate them against each other. (33)

concepts   are abstract ideas that are impossible to measure. (32)

concrete operational stage is the stage (ages 7 through 12 years) at which children can think about objects in the world in more than one way and start to understand causal connections in their surroundings. (88)

conflict model of law proposes that powerful people write laws to protect their own interests while punishing the actions of those they wish to control. (232)

conflict theory is a theoretical framework that views society as an unequal system that brings about conflict and change. (9)

conformity is the degree to which we will alter our behavior, attitudes, and points of view to fit into our perceived expectation of what is appropriate. (107)

conquest is the domination over a group of people by a superior force. (178)

consensus model of law suggests that laws arise because people see a behavior they do not like, and they agree to make it illegal. (232)

contagion is a rapid, irrational mode in which people do not think rationally or clearly. (20)

containment theory argues that criminals cannot resist the temptations that surround them. (237)

content analysis is a type of research in which the sociologist looks for common words or themes in newspapers, books, or structured interviews. (41)

contract slavery is a form of slavery in which a person signs a work contract, receiving food and shelter by an employer, but is threatened when they try to leave the contract. (143)

control variables are variables that are kept constant to accurately test the impact of an independent variable. (31)

conventional level is the second stage of moral development that arises before puberty and uses the lens of norms and rules to determine what is right and wrong. (90)

convergence theory is the tendency for capitalism and socialism to converge. (285)

corporation is a business viewed as a "legal person" that has some objective, usually to make a profit for its owners. (287)

correlation is an indication that one factor might be a cause for another factor. (32)

countercultures are groups with value systems that are in opposition to the dominant group's values. (56)

craftsmen are the skilled laborers such as plumbers or carpenters. (145)

craze occurs when a fad leaves a lasting effect on society. (305)

credentialism is an emphasis on educational degrees in assessing skills and knowledge. (270)

crime is the violation of norms that have been written into law. (228)

crime index is made up of eight offenses used to measure crime: homicide, rape, robbery, aggravated assault, burglary, larceny-theft, motor vehicle theft, and arson. (230)

criminology is the scientific study of crime, deviance, and social policies that the criminal justice system applies. (228)

cross-sectional studies look at one event at a single point in time. (33)

crowd is a large group of influential people who gather for a temporary purpose. (305)

crude birth rate is the number of births for every 1,000 people each year. (157)

crude death rate is the number of deaths for every 1,000 people each year. (158)

cults are new religious movements led by charismatic leaders with few followers. (272)

cultural lag happens when social and cultural changes occur at a slower pace than technological changes. (55)

cultural relativism means making a deliberate effort to appreciate a group's ways of life without prejudice. (55)

cultural transmission is culture passing from one generation to the next through language. (50)

culture is the language, beliefs, values, norms, behaviors, and material objects that are important enough to pass on to future generations of a society. (48)

culture shock occurs when a person encounters a culture foreign to his or her own and has an emotional response to the differences between the cultures. (56)

cycle of poverty is a generational barrier that prevents poor people from breaking into the middle and upper classes. (183)

debt bondage is a form of slavery in which someone borrows money in order to repay a different debt, and works off the new debt. (143)

decline is the final stage of a movement when an organization completes is goal, or is seen as irrelevant. (307)

delegated means given or assigned. (123)

demand is the desire for a good or service. (284)

democracy is a government whereby power is held by the people and exercised through participation and representation. (288)

democratic leaders are leaders who strive to set group policy by discussion and agreement. (106)

democratic socialism is the economic system that advocates running government democratically and for the good of the most people. (285)

demographic similarity refers to shared characteristics such as race, gender, or age. (76)

demographic transition theory is a projection that suggests people control their own fertility as they move from agrarian to industrial societies. (163)

demographic variables are variables such as population size, age, racial composition, birth rates, and death rates used to discuss populations. (157)

demography is the study of population size and composition. (157)

dependent variables are the response to the manipulated variable. (31)

deterrence is a measure that prevents a person from doing something because of fear of the consequences. (233)

deviance is the violation of norms that a society agrees upon. (228)

dictator refers to a single leader with absolute power. (288)

differential association theory emphasizes that criminal and deviant behavior is learned. (237)

diffusion is the spreading of something more widely. (303)

discreditable stigma is a stigma that can be concealed from others. (69)

discredited stigma is a stigma that cannot be hidden from others or is no longer hidden from others. (69)

discretion is the ability to make decisions. (240)

discrimination is the unfair treatment of people based on a prejudice. (181)

disengagement theory states that reduced interaction between older persons and others is unavoidable, mutual, and acceptable to both the individual and society. (220)

dominant group is the group that has the greatest power, but not necessarily the greatest numbers. (176)

double consciousness is the sense that a person must keep a foot in two worlds, one in the majority group's world and one in the minority group's world. (185)

doubling time refers to the number of years it takes for a population to double. (161)

dramaturgy is a theory of interaction in which all life is like acting. (20)

dyad is a group consisting of only two people. (106)

economic system or economy, is the social institution that helps a society organize what it produces, distributes, and consumes. (283)

education is the formal system in which society passes on its information and values from one generation to the next. (265)

egoistic suicides are suicides that result from a lack of solidarity, occurring among those who have few social connections, feel isolated and alone, and are more likely to fall into despair. (7)

elite class is a social class that is very small in number and holds significant wealth. (124)

embargo is a long-standing trade restriction. (287)

embarrassment is a state that occurs when we realize our act has failed. (75)

emergence   is the first stage of a movement when people become aware of a problem and begin to notice that others feel the same way. (307)

emigration   is the movement of people out of a nation-state. (159)

endogamy   is the practice of marrying within your social group. (252)

entitlement program   is a program offering assistance to which a person is entitled, requiring no qualification. (132)

entrepreneurs   are the business class, as identified by Weber. (145)

environmental justice   is the impact of environmental factors on social classes. (165)

environmental sociology   is the study of how the environment influences society, and vice versa. (164)

ethics   is a system of values or principles that guide one's behavior. (40)

ethnic cleansing   refers to persecution through imprisonment, expulsion, or murder of members of an ethnic minority by a majority to achieve ethnic homogeneity in a majority-controlled territory. (178)

ethnic enclaves   are neighborhoods where people from similar cultures live together and assert cultural distinction from the dominant group. (180)

ethnicity   is the classification of people who share a common cultural, linguistic, or ancestral heritage. (175)

ethnocentrism   occurs when a person uses his or her own culture to judge another culture. (55)

ethnography   is a research method that aims to understand the social perspective and cultural values of a particular group by participating with or getting to know their activities in detail. (37)

exchange mobility   is a concept suggesting that, within the United States, each social class contains a relatively fixed number of people. (128)

exogamy   is the practice of marrying someone from a different social group. (252)

extended family   is a household consisting of a nuclear family plus an additional relative. (247)

extension   refers to the way social movement organizations seek to align their interests with those of other groups that are related, sometimes furthering ideas that were not originally in their frame. (311)

face-saving work   is a reaction to embarrassment; either humor, anger, or retreat. (75)

fad   is a temporary fashion, notion, or action the public embraces. (304)

false consciousness   is a person's lack of understanding of his or her position in society. (15)

family   is two or more people who are related by blood, marriage, or adoption. (246)

fatalistic suicides   are suicides that result from a lack of social control. (8)

feminism   is a vast collection of social movements and theories about gender differences, proposing social equality for all people. (200)

feral   means wild. (86)

fertility rate   is the number of births that occur in a population. (157)

field research   is research conducted in a natural setting. (36)

folkways   are informal types of norms. (54)

formal operational stage   is the stage (ages 12 years and above) at which people become able to comprehend abstract thought. (88)

formal organizations   are groups created for a certain purpose and built for maximum efficiency. (110)

formal rationality   is the reasonable actions that organizations and bureaucracies take to achieve goals in the most effective way. (111)

formal structures   are the explicit rules, goals, and guidelines of an organization. (110)

frame alignment process   occurs when social movement organizations link their goals to the goals of other organizations. (311)

frame bridging   occurs when two or more groups that may be somewhat opposed to each other join forces. (311)

free markets   generally refer to markets that are free from government control. (283)

front stage   is what the audience sees, or the part of ourselves that we present to others. (75)

functionalism   is a theoretical framework that defines society as a system of interrelated parts. (9)

functions   are social factors that affect people in society. (13)

futility   is the claim that a reform cannot work because the social problem is unsolvable. (303)

game stage   is Mead's third stage of development that never truly ends, and is the stage in which we begin to understand that others have expectations and demands placed upon them. (87)

Gemeinschaft   refers to community connections involving personal relationships based on friendship and kinship ties, such as family. (73)

gender   is the expectations of behavior and attitude that a society considers proper for males and females. (95)

gender identity   is our perception of ourselves as male or female. (193)

gender roles   are society's expectations of how males and females should act and think. (194)

gender socialization   teaches members of society how to express their masculinity or femininity. (95)

general deterrence   is a measure that ensures individuals will not commit a crime because they see the negative consequences applied to others, and they fear experiencing these consequences. (233)

generalization   is the extent that what is learned from a sample can be applied to the population from which the sample is taken. (35)

generalized other, the   is our sense of others. (87)

genocide   is the attempt to destroy or exterminate a people based on their race and/or ethnicity. (177)

gerontology   is the study of aging and the elderly. (216)

Gesellschaft   refers to societal connections that are more formal and impersonal. (73)

gestures   are symbols that we make using our bodies, such as facial expressions, hand movements, eye contact, and other types of body language. (51)

glass ceiling   is an invisible barrier preventing women from reaching executive-level positions in the workplace. (198)

global stratification   is the categorization of countries based on objective criteria, such as wealth, power, and prestige, which highlight social patterns and inequality throughout the world. (138)

global village   refers to the "shrinking" of the world through immediate electronic communications. (57)

globalization   is a complex process by which the world and its international economy are becoming more and more intertwined. (147)

grade inflation   is the trend of assigning higher grades than previously assigned to students for completing the same work. (268)

groups   are any number of people with similar norms, values, and behaviors who frequently interact with one another. (67)

groupthink   is the term for group decisions that are made without objective thought. (107)

hate groups   are organizations that promote hostility or violence toward others based on race and other factors. (177)

Hawthorne effect   occurs when people behave differently because they know they are part of an experiment. (36)

health   is a state of complete physical, mental, and social well-being and not merely the absence of disease or infirmity. (211)

health care   is the care, services, or supplies related to a person's health. (215)

hedonism   is seeking pleasure over pain. (90)

hidden curriculum   refers to the lessons taught in schools that are unrelated to academic learning. (94)

homogamy   is marriage between people with similar backgrounds, such as religion, race, class, or age. (252)

horizontal mobility   refers to moving within the same status category. (128)

human capital   is a person's combination of skills, knowledge, traits, and personal attributes. (269)

human capital model   assumes that men and women bring different natural skills to the workplace. (198)

human exemptionalism   is the belief that considers humans as being different from other species on earth. (164)

hypothesis   involves a suggestion about how variables relate. (32)

hysteria   is a heightened emotional state that can lead a group to violence. (304)

"I" self   is the subjective part of the self. (87)

imitation stage   is Mead's first stage of development, which is the period from birth to about age 2, and is the stage at which children merely copy the behaviors of those around them. (87)

immigration   is the movement of people into a nation-state. (159)

impression management   is management of the impression that the performer makes on others. (75)

income   is the money received for work or through investments. (121)

independent variables   are variables that are deliberately manipulated in an experiment. (31)

indigenous superordination   is the subordination of an immigrant group to a dominant group. (179)

infant mortality rate   is the number of children for every 1,000 born alive who die before they reach the age of one year. (158)

informal structures   are friendships, allegiances, and loyalties among members of an organization. (110)

in-group   is a group to which we feel an affinity or closeness. (104)

in-group bias   is the feeling that a person's in-group is superior to others. (104)

institutional discrimination   maintains the advantage for the dominant group, while providing the appearance of fairness to all. (181)

intergenerational mobility   refers to the change that family members make from one social class to the next through generations. (128)

intermarriage   is marriage between people of different religions. (274)

intimate distance   is distance reserved for those with whom we are very close. (74)

intragenerational mobility   occurs when an individual changes social standing, especially in the workforce. (128)

invention   is the creation of a new device or way of thinking. (302)

involuntary immigration   is the forced movement of people from one society to another. (179)

involvement   is the social bond that refers to the level of activity in conventional things. (238)

iron cage   is a concept introduced by Max Weber that refers to the way in which bureaucracies make workers feel trapped and turn them into little more than robots accomplishing tasks. (111)

jeopardy   is the claim that attempting to solve a problem will only draw attention away from other, more important issues. (303)

laissez-faire leaders   are leaders who lead by absence and may in fact not want to be leaders at all. (106)

language   is a system of speech and/or written symbols used to convey meaning and communicate. (49)

latent functions   are functions that lead to unforeseen or unexpected consequences. (13)

leadership style   is a behavioral mode that leaders use to influence group members. (106)

life expectancy   is the average number of years a person is expected to live. (158)

lifespan   is the maximum length of time a person can possibly live. (158)

literature review   is a study of relevant academic articles and information. (32)

longitudinal studies   include data from observations over time using a cohort. (33)

looking-glass self theory   is the theory that the self develops through a process of reflection, like a mirror. (87)

lower class   is a social class living in poverty. (126)

machismo   is overt and exaggerated displays of masculinity. (203)

macro   means large-scale. (6)

macrosociology   is the study of large-scale society, focusing on the social structures that exist within a society and examining how those structures create the social world. (67)

majority group   is the group that has the largest population in society and holds significant power and privilege. (176)

Malthusian theorem   is a population projection that suggests the population will exceed the available food supply because populations grow at geometric rates, while food supplies grow at arithmetic rates. (162)

mandatory minimums   are fixed sentences for specific crimes. (240)

manifest functions   are functions that lead to an expected consequence or outcome. (13)

marginal poverty   is a state of poverty that occurs when a person lacks stable employment. (122)

marital effects   are factors that make marriage work. (253)

marriage   is the union of two people that is typically recognized by law or cultural norms. (246)

mass media   are any print or electronic resource that is used to communicate to a wide audience. (95)

master status   is the status toward which we gravitate. (68)

material culture   consists of the items within a culture that you can taste, touch, and feel. (49)

matriarchy   is a social system in which women are the main authority and hold power over men. (194)

"Me" self   is the objective part of the self. (87)

mean   is an average. (38)

mechanical solidarity   refers to the state of community bonding in traditional societies in which people share beliefs and values and perform common activities. (12)

median   refers to the midpoint in a distribution of numbers. (38)

Medicaid   is a form of government health insurance designed for the poor and disabled. (216)

medicalization   is the idea that the medical community is the center of many aspects of American society. (213)

Medicare   is a government-run social insurance program that provides health coverage for people 65 or older. (216)

meritocracy argument   states that those who get ahead do so based on their own merit. (129)

micro   means small-scale. (6)

microsociology   is the study of the small interactions of daily life. (67)

middle class   is a social class that consists of those that have moderate incomes. (125)

migrant superordination   is the conquest of a native population by a more powerful group. (179)

migration   is the movement of people from one area to another. (159)

militant minorities   are groups that seek to overthrow the existing system because they see it as unjust. (180)

military-industrial complex   is a combination of the armed forces and defense industries that provide weapons and other materials to the country. (290)

minority group   is a group that has a smaller population and less power than the majority group. (176)

mobs   are groups characterized by high levels of emotion that engage in some type of focused action that can be violent or disruptive. (304)

mode   refers to the most common value in a distribution of numbers. (38)

monarchy   is a political system whereby leadership is based on the idea that leaders are selected by divine right or heritage. (288)

monogamy   is the practice of being married to one person at a time. (248)

monopoly   is the exclusive possession or control of the supply or trade in a service. (284)

monotheism   is the belief that there is only one god. (270)

morality of care   is morality decided by a standard of how best to help those who are in need. (91)

morality of justice   is morality based on the rule of law. (91)

mores are norms that represent a community's most important values. (54)

mortality rate is the number of deaths that occur in a population. (158)

multiculturalism is a concept that supports the inherent value of different cultures within society. (56)

multinational corporations are corporations that operate in at least two countries and have the interests of their company at heart rather than the interests of their home country. (287)

NAFTA (North American Free Trade Agreement) is a policy that was established in 1994 to allow free trade between the United States, Mexico, and Canada. (287)

National Crime Victimization Survey (NCVS) is the measurement of crime victimization based on contact with a representative sample of over 70,000 households in the United States. (230)

nature theory states that the genes we get from our parents at conception are the primary causes of human behaviors. (85)

needs assessment is an analysis that studies the needs of a specific group and presents the results in a written statement. (43)

negative correlation occurs when variables move in opposite directions. (32)

neocolonialism is a process in which powerful nations use loans and economic power to maintain control over poor nations. (147)

neo-classical migration theory suggests that migration depends on the supply and demand for labor, both in the sending area as well as in the receiving one. (160)

nonmaterial culture consists of the nonphysical products of society, including our symbols, values, rules, and sanctions. (49)

normative organizations are organizations that exist to achieve a worthwhile goal. (110)

normative relativism is the evaluation of a society based on that society's norms. (55)

norms are rules developed for appropriate behavior based on specific values that are conditional; they can vary from place to place. (54)

nuclear family is a household consisting of a husband, wife, and children. (247)

nurture theory states that our environment influences the way we think, feel, and behave. (85)

obesity is an unhealthy accumulation of body fat. (210)

objectivity is the ability to conduct research without allowing personal biases or prejudices to influence you. (31)

"old old" is a cohort that consists of people over the age of 75. (216)

oligarchy is a small group of very influential people who control government. (288)

operationalizing is turning abstract ideas into something measurable. (32)

organic solidarity occurs when people live in a society with a diverse division of labor. (12)

organization of believers is a group of people who ensures the prosperity and effectiveness of the religious experience. (274)

organizations are formal groups that exist to achieve a desired goal. (110)

out-group is a group from which we are disconnected. (104)

overpopulation occurs when a species' population lives beyond the carrying capacity, resulting in too few resources. (165)

oversampling is the process of taking a bigger sample if the group you wish to study makes up a small percentage of the whole population. (35)

panic is an extreme fear based on something that might happen. (305)

paradigm refers to a theoretical framework through which scientists study the world. (9)

parsimony is extreme unwillingness to use resources. (35)

participant observation is a type of field research in which the researcher poses as a person who is normally in the environment. (37)

patriarchy is a social system in which the father serves as head of the family, and men have authority over women and children. (194)

patriarchy model assumes that we have a male-dominated society that doesn't allow women to hold upper-tier jobs. (198)

permissive style is a parenting style in which parents provide high levels of support but an inconsistent enforcement of rules. (92)

personal distance is distance that ranges from 18 inches to 4 feet; this distance is for normal conversations. (74)

personal space is the invisible bubble that each of us has around us that insulates us from others. (74)

perversity claims that any attempt to fix a problem would actually compound the issues the change was trying to address. (303)

petite bourgeoisie are small business owners in Weber's class system. (145)

philosophies of life are ways of life that focus on a set of ethical, moral, or philosophical principles. (270)

play stage is Mead's second stage of development, which occurs around the ages of 2–4 years, during which children play roles and begin to take on the characteristics of important people in their world. (87)

plea bargain is an out-of-court agreement between the prosecutor and the defense attorney to some concession, usually a reduced sentence. (240)

pluralism is a model whereby power is spread amongst the masses. (293)

pluralistic minorities are groups that enter into an area voluntarily, but seek to maintain their own culture while also integrating into the dominant group. (179)

political systems are social institutions that are based on an established set of practices for applying and realizing a society's goal. (287)

polyandry is the practice of a woman marrying two or more men. (248)

polygamy is the practice of having more than one spouse at a time. (248)

polygyny is the practice of a man marrying two or more women. (248)

polytheism is the belief in multiple gods and demigods. (270)

population momentum is a surge in growth due to a large number of people who are of birthing age. (159)

population pyramids are tools that visually represent data related to the age and sex of a country's population. (158)

populations are target groups from which researchers want to get information. (35)

positive correlation includes two variables that move in a parallel direction. (32)

postconventional level is the third stage of moral development that refers to a morality based on abstract principles. (90)

postdenominationalism is a recent trend that stretches religious boundaries. (274)

power is the ability to carry out your will and impose it on others. (123)

power elite is a small group of people who hold immense power. (123)

preconventional level is the first stage of moral development that lasts through the elementary school years; at this level, children make their moral judgments within a framework of hedonistic principles. (90)

prejudice refers to negative attitudes about an entire category of people. (181)

preoperational stage is the stage (ages 2 through 7 years) at which the ability to speak grows rapidly. (88)

prestige is the level of esteem associated with one's status and social standing. (123)

price elasticity of demand is the change in a good's demand as its price changes. (284)

primary deviance is the initial deviant act itself. (238)

primary groups are groups that are small, intimate, and enduring. (67)

primary socialization   is socialization that occurs during childhood. (85)

profane   means related or devoted to that which is not sacred or biblical. (272)

progressive   means favoring or promoting change. (309)

proletariat   refers to members of the poor working class. (15)

pro-natalist   means concerned with promoting population growth. (168)

psychosocial crisis   is a crisis occurring during each of Erikson's stages that will be resolved either positively or negatively, and each outcome will have an effect on our ability to deal with the next one. (88)

public distance   is the zone of interaction that is used in highly formal settings; this distance includes everything greater than 12 feet. (75)

push-pull   suggests that migration depends on the supply and demand for labor, both in the sending area and in the receiving one. (160)

qualitative data   include words, pictures, photos, or any other type of information that comes to the researcher in a non-numeric form. (41)

quantitative data   refer to data based on numbers. (41)

race   is the division of people based on certain physical characteristics. (175)

racism   is discrimination based on a person's race. (176)

random sample   is a group of subjects arbitrarily chosen from a defined population. (35)

rate of natural increase (RNI)   determines population growth and/or decline by subtracting the crude death rate from the crude birth rate and then dividing by 10. (160)

recidivism   is the tendency for inmates released from prison to return to prison. (234)

redemptive social movements   focus on specific individuals, but the amount of change sought is radical, rather than limited. (308)

reference group   is the group that you use to evaluate yourself. (105)

reformative social movements   seek to change a society's thoughts and actions, but only in a limited way. (309)

regressive   means seeking to stop change. (309)

reintegrative shaming   is an effort to bring an offender back into the community after punishment. (233)

relative deprivation   points to the gaps between what people have and what they expect. (310)

relative poverty   is a state of poverty that occurs when we compare ourselves to those around us. (122)

reliable   means able to be trusted. (33)

religion   is a unified system of beliefs and practices, relative to sacred things, that is to say, things set apart and forbidden—beliefs and practices which unite into one single moral community called a Church, all those who adhere to them. (270)

rentiers   are the wealthy members of a society, as identified by Weber. (145)

repertoires   are actions used to promote interest and involvement within the movement. (306)

research design   refers to the process used to find information. (33)

research methods   are the scientific procedures that sociologists use to conduct research and develop knowledge about a particular topic. (30)

residual poverty   is chronic and multigenerational poverty. (122)

resocialization   is the process of learning new norms, values, attitudes, and behaviors and abandoning old ones. (93)

revolutionary social movement,   or sometimes called the transformative social movement, seeks to change the thoughts and actions of all society in radical fashion. (309)

riots   are emotional and violent disturbances of the peace by crowds that lack a central focus. (304)

rituals   are established patterns of behavior closely associated with experience of the sacred. (272)

role   is the behavior of a specific status. (68)

role conflict   is a phenomenon occurring when one is forced to choose between the competing demands of multiple roles. (68)

role expectations   are the anticipated behaviors for a particular role. (68)

role performance   is the degree to which a person plays the role in a manner we expect. (68)

role strain   occurs when the demands and expectations of one role are impossible for us to satisfy. (69)

rumors   are stories or statements that lack confirmation or certainty. (305)

sacred   means connected to God or dedicated to a religious purpose. (272)

sample   is a subset of the population. (35)

sample of convenience   is a nonrandom sample available to the researcher. (35)

sanction   is a prize or punishment you receive when you either abide by a norm or violate it. (54)

"sandwiched generation"   is a generation that takes care of both its children and its elderly parents. (217)

Sapir-Whorf Hypothesis   is a hypothesis, first advanced by Edward Sapir in 1929 and subsequently developed by Benjamin Whorf, that the structure of a language determines a native speaker's perception and categorization of experience. (50)

scapegoat   means making an unfair accusation against a person or group as the cause of a problem. (182)

secessionist minorities   are groups that voluntarily separate themselves from the dominant group and view the dominant group with disdain, believing that it will corrupt the group's belief system. (180)

secondary data   are data that others have already collected and published. (37)

secondary data analysis   is the process of using and analyzing data that others have collected. (37)

secondary deviance   refers to the psychological reorientation that occurs when the system catches a person and labels him or her as a deviant. (238)

secondary groups   are groups that are formal, superficial, and temporary. (67)

secondary socialization   is the dynamic whereby socialization continues throughout our lives. (85)

sects   are religious groups that have enough members to sustain themselves and go against society's norms. (272)

secularization   is the overall decline in the importance and power of religion in people's lives. (273)

segregation   is forced separation because of factors such as race, gender, or ethnicity. (182)

selection effects   are the likelihood that a nonrepresentative sample of the population may lead to inaccurate results. (35)

self   refers to a person's identity and what makes that person different from others. (19)

self-focused impression management   refers to techniques that include acting modest about your accomplishments (even if that modesty is false), boasting occasionally about your successes, and showing your friendliness and self-assuredness through smiles and eye contact. (76)

semi-skilled manual workers   are the workers who have some training and may work in factories. (145)

sensorimotor stage   is the stage (birth to age 2 years) at which infants learn to experience and think about the world through their senses and motor skills. (88)

sex   is the biological makeup of a male or female. (193)

sexism   is the belief that one sex is superior to the other. (194)

shaming   is a deliberate effort to attach a negative meaning to a behavior. (232)

sick role   is the expected behaviors and responsibilities appropriate for someone who is ill. (213)

simple supernaturalism   is the belief in a variety of supernatural forces that affect and influence people's lives. (271)

slavery   is the total control over people who have no choice about their state. (142)

social capital is a sociological concept that refers to the individual and collective resources available to a person. (109)

social change is the way in which culture, interaction, and innovation change social institutions over time. (301)

social class is a group with similar access to power, wealth, and prestige. (67)

social control refers to the social mechanisms that regulate a person's actions. (7)

social Darwinism is a notion that suggests strong societies survive and weak ones become extinct. (11)

social distance is distance that ranges from about 4 feet to 12 feet and is usually reserved for formal settings. (75)

social dynamics are the change in the structural elements of society. (10)

social epidemiology is the study of the distribution of diseases and health throughout a society's population. (211)

social groups are groups that consist of two or more people who interact with one another and share a common identity. (102)

social institutions are structures that provide for patterned relationships. (71)

social laws are statements of fact that are unchanging under given conditions and can be used as ground rules for any kind of society. (10)

social mobility is the ability to change social classes. (128)

social movements are activities that support or protest social issues organized by nongovernmental organizations. (306)

social network is the web of ties you have with others. (109)

social policies are deliberate strategies designed to correct recognized social problems. (97)

social research is investigation conducted by social scientists. (32)

social statics are the existing structural elements of society. (10)

social stratification is the ranking of people and the rewards they receive based on an objective criteria, often including wealth, power, and/or prestige. (121)

social stratification systems are slavery, caste, and class systems. (142)

social structures are patterns of relationships that endure from one generation to the next. (67)

socialism is the economic system by which resources and the means of production are owned collectively by the citizens. (284)

socialization is the process that teaches the norms, values, and other aspects of a culture to new group members. (84)

sociological imagination is the ability to look beyond the individual as the cause for success and failure and see how one's society influences the outcome. (6)

sociology is a science guided by the basic understanding that "the social matters: our lives are affected, not only by our individual characteristics but by our place in the social world." (5)

solidarity refers to the level of connectedness and integration a person feels to others in the environment. (7)

specific deterrence is a measure that changes the attitude of individuals, who have already violated the law and been punished, by causing them never to commit crime again. (233)

spurious correlation occurs when two variables appear to be related, but actually have a different cause. (32)

status is the position that you occupy within the social structure, which is often closely linked to social class. (68)

stereotypes are simplified perceptions people have of an entire group that are usually based on false assumptions. (181)

stigma is a mark of disgrace associated with a particular status, quality, or person. (69)

stigmatized shame is a permanent label given to an offender, which could actually increase the chances of reoffending because the guilty person is forever labeled. (233)

street crime refers to many different types of criminal acts, such as burglary, rape, and assault. (229)

structural mobility occurs when social changes affect large numbers of people. (128)

subculture is a subset of the dominant culture that has distinct values, beliefs, and norms. (56)

supervisor-focused impression management refers to techniques that involve flattering your boss and agreeing with your boss's opinions (or at least avoiding disagreements whenever possible). (76)

supply is the amount of a good or service available. (284)

survey is an investigation of the opinions or experience of a group of people by asking them questions. (35)

symbols represent, suggest, or stand for something else. (49)

symbolic interactionism is a theoretical framework that focuses on how people interact with others in their everyday lives. (9)

system of beliefs relates sacred objects to religious rituals, and defines and protects the sacred from the profane. (274)

taboo is an act that is socially unacceptable. (54)

tariffs are taxes levied on trade items. (287)

teacher expectancy effect is the impact of a teacher's expectations on a student's performance. (268)

technology deals with the creation, use, and application of knowledge and its interrelation with life, society, and the environment. (302)

theism is the belief in a god or gods. (270)

theocracy is a state religion that is formed when government and religion both work together to shape society. (272)

theory is a comprehensive and systematic explanation of events that lead to testable predictions. (32)

Title IX is a 1972 educational amendment that prohibits the exclusion of any person from participation in an education program on the basis of gender. (97)

total fertility rate (TFR) is the average number of births expected from any woman in a population to bear in her lifetime. (157)

total institutions are places in which the most effective forms of resocialization can occur because they isolate people from outside influences so they can be reformed and controlled. (93)

totalitarianism is a type of authoritarian government whereby the government controls everything in people's lives, and generally those who disagree are punished. (288)

totemism is the practice of honoring a totem or a sacred object. (271)

transformation changes the old meanings and understandings of the problem, and creates new and innovative ones. (311)

transitional poverty is a temporary state of poverty that occurs when someone loses a job for a short time. (122)

transnational corporations are corporations that operate in at least two countries and have the interests of their company at heart rather than the interests of their home country. (287)

triad is a group consisting of three people. (106)

triangulation is the process of using multiple approaches to study a phenomenon. (42)

underpopulation occurs when a species' population lives under the carrying capacity, resulting in abundant resources. (165)

Uniform Crime Reports (UCRs) are official police statistics of reported crimes gathered from police reports and paperwork. (230)

unskilled workers are the lowest class, consisting of people who frequently perform manual labor jobs that are often unpleasant and sometimes dangerous. (145)

upper class is a social class that is very small in number and holds significant wealth. (124)

upper middle class is a social class that consists of high-income members of society who are well educated but do not belong to the elite membership of the super wealthy. (125)

urban legends are rumors that are presented as true stories that act as cautionary tales. (305)

urban underclass is a social class living in disadvantaged neighborhoods that are characterized by four components: poverty, family disruption, male unemployment, and lack of individuals in high-status occupations. (126)

utilitarian organization is an organization in which people receive wages in exchange for work. (110)

validity assures that you're actually measuring the thing you set out to measure in the first place. (33)

value clusters are two or more values that support each other. (51)

value conflict occurs when two or more values are at odds. (51)

value pairs help us define values, usually in terms of opposites. (51)

values are a part of a society's nonmaterial culture that represent cultural standards by which we determine what is good, bad, right, or wrong. (51)

vertical mobility refers to moving from one social status to another. (128)

voluntary association is the act of joining an organization that offers no pay and that expands social networks through interaction. (110)

voluntary immigration is the willing movement of people from one society to another. (178)

wealth is all of your material possessions, including income. (121)

working class is a social class generally made up of people with high school diplomas and lower levels of education. (125)

WUNC refers to the members of a movement who want to show the public the worthiness, unity, numbers, and commitments of the movement. (306)

xenocentrism is perceiving other groups or societies as superior to your own. (55)

xenophobia refers to fear and hostility toward people who are from other countries or cultures. (55)

"young old" is a cohort that consists of people between the ages of 65 and 75. (216)

zero population growth is a TFR of two, meaning that each woman has two children to replace the mother and the father. (157)

ENDNOTES

CHAPTER 1

1. Reprinted with the permission of The Free Press, a Division of Simon & Schuster, Inc., *Tell Them Who I Am: The Lives of Homeless Women* by Elliot Liebow. Copyright © 1992 by Elliot Liebow. All rights reserved.

2. "Health of Sociology," *American Sociological Association*, 2007, http://www.asanet.org/galleries/Research/SocHealthsheet_Intro.pdf, Accessed August 25, 2008.

3. C. Wright Mills, *The Sociological Imagination* (New York: Oxford, 1959).

4. Ibid.

5. Ibid.

6. Emile Durkheim, *Suicide*, edited by George Simpson, translated by John A. Spaulding and George Simpson (New York: The Free Press, 1897/1966).

7. Ibid.

8. Ibid.

9. Emile Durkheim, *Suicide*, edited by George Simpson, translated by John A. Spaulding and George Simpson (New York: The Free Press, 1897/1966); Robert Travis, "Halbwachs and Durkheim: A Test of Two Theories of Suicide," *British Journal of Sociology*, 1990. 41: 225–243.

10. Jean Stockard and Robert M. O'Brien, "Cohort Effects on Suicide Rates: International Variations," American Sociological Association, *American Sociological Review*, 2002. 67(6): 854–872.

11. Centers for Disease Control and Prevention, "Suicide: Fact Sheet" Atlanta, GA: Centers for Disease Control and Prevention, 2005, http://www.cdc.gov/ncipc/ factsheets/suifacts.htm, Accessed August 19, 2008.

12. Elliot Liebow, *Tell Them Who I Am: The Lives of Homeless Women* (New York: Penguin Books, 1995).

13. Kenneth Thompson, *Auguste Comte: The Foundation of Sociology* (New York: Halsted Press, 1975).

14. Jonathan Turner, Leonard Beeghily, and Charles H. Powers, *The Emergence of Sociological Theory* (Albany, NY: Wadsworth Publishing Company, 1998).

15. Emile Durkheim, *The Division of Labor in Society*, with introduction by Lewis A. Coser, translated by W.D. Halls (New York: Free Press, 1893/1997).

16. Ibid.

17. Ibid.

18. Vernon K. Dibble, *The Legacy of Albion Small* (Chicago: University of Chicago Press, 1975).

19. Talcott Parsons, *The Social System* (Glencoe, IL: The Free Press, 1951).

20. Ibid.

21. Robert K. Merton, *Social Theory and Social Structure* (Glencoe, IL: Free Press, 1957).

22. Ibid.

23. David A. Cotter, Joan M. Hermsen, Seth Ovadia, and Reeve Vanneman, "The Glass Ceiling Effect," *Social Forces*, Dec 2001. 80(2): 655–681.

24. Ieva M. Augstums, "Wachovia Board Forces Out CEO Ken Thompson," *ABC News*, June 2, 2008, http://abcnews.go.com/Business/IndustryInfo/wireStory?id5497 7739, Accessed November 12, 2008.

25. Karl Marx, *Selected Writings in Sociology & Social Philosophy*, edited by, T. B Bottomore and Maximilien Rubel, translated by T. B. Bottomore (New York: McGraw-Hill, 1964); Karl Marx, "Economic and Philosophic Manuscripts of 1844," pp. 37–42 in *Readings in Social Theory: The Classical Tradition to Post-Modernism*, 4th edition, edited by James Farganis (New York: McGraw-Hill, 1844/2004); Karl Marx, *Capital: A Critique of Political Economy, Vol. 1* (New York: International Publishers, 1867/1967); Karl Marx and Friedrich Engels, "Manifesto of this Communist Party" pp. 26–36 in *Readings in Social Theory: The Classical Tradition to Post-Modernism*, 4th edition, edited by James Farganis (New York: McGraw-Hill, 1845/2004); Karl Marx and Friedrich Engels, "The German Ideology," pp. 43–46 in *Readings in Social Theory: The Classical Tradition to Post-Modernism*, 4th edition, edited by James Farganis (New York: McGraw-Hill, 1974/2004).

26. Susan Hoecker-Drysdale, *Harriet Martineau: First Woman Sociologist* (New York: St. Martin's Press, 1992).

27. Ibid.

28. "W.E.B. Du Bois," NAACP, http://www.naacp.org/about/history/dubois/, Accessed October 21, 2008.

29. W.E.B. Du Bois (William Edward Burghardt), "The Philadelphia Negro: A Social Study," pp.167–170 in *Readings in Social Theory: The Classical Tradition to Post-Modernism,* 4th edition, edited by James Farganis (New York: McGraw-Hill, 1899/2004).

30. Tukufu Zuberi, "Being Here and Being There: Fieldwork Encounters and Ethnographic Discoveries: W.E.B. Du Bois's Sociology: The Philadelphia Negro and Social Science," *The Annals of the American Academy of Political and Social Science,* 2004. 595: 146–156.

31. Joseph P. DeMarco, *The Social Thought of W.E.B. Du Bois* (Lanham, MD: University Press of American Inc., 1983).

32. Allen F. Davis, *American Heroine: The Life and Legend of Jane Addams* (New York: Oxford University Press, 1973).

33. Mary Jo Deegan, *Jane Addams and the Men of the Chicago School, 1892–1918* (New Brunswick, NJ: Transaction Books, 1988).

34. John Bellamy Foster, "The End of Rational Capitalism," *Monthly Review*, March 2005, http://findarticles.com/p/articles/mi_m1132/is_10_56/ai_n16126168/pg_1? tag5artBody;col1, Accessed September 11, 2008.

35. George H. Mead, *Mind, Self, and Society: From the Standpoint of a Social Behaviorist* (Chicago: University of Chicago Press, 1934/1962).

36. Suzanne Speak and Dr. Graham Tipple, "Perceptions, Persecution, and Pity: The Limitations of Interventions for Homelessness," *International Journal of Urban and Regional Research*, 2006. 30(1): 172–188.

37. Herbert Blumer, "Society as Symbolic Interaction," in Arnold M. Rose, *Human Behavior and Social Process: An Interactionist Approach* (Boston: Houghton-Mifflin, Reprinted in 1969).

38. Erving Goffman, *The Presentation of Self in Everyday Life* (Edinburgh: University of Edinburgh, Social Sciences Research Centre, 1958).

39. Jonathan Turner, Leonard Beeghily, and Charles H. Powers, *The Emergence of Sociological Theory* (Albany, NY: Wadsworth Publishing Company, 1998).

40. Elliot Liebow, *Tell Them Who I Am: The Lives of Homeless Women* (New York: Penguin Books, 1995).

CHAPTER 2

1. From Laud Humphreys, *Tearoom Trade: Impersonal Sex in Public Places*. Copyright © 1970. Reprinted by permission of Transaction Publishers.

2. Carl Hulse and David Stout, "Guilty Plea Stands, but Craig Won't Quit Senate," *New York Times*, sec. A, October 5, 2007.

3. Laud Humphreys, *Tearoom Trade: Impersonal Sex in Public Places* (Chicago: Transaction Publishing Co., 1970).

4. Max Weber, "Class, Status, Party," in *Readings in Social Theory: The Classical Tradition to Post-Modernism* 4th edition, ed. James Farganis (New York: McGraw-Hill, 1978/2004).

5. Elizabeth Lanthier, Ph.D., "Correlation," Elizabeth Lanthier, http://www.nvcc.edu/ home/elanthier/methods/correlation.htm, Accessed August 26, 2008.

6. Earl Babbie, *The Practice of Social Research 8th edition* (Belmont, CA: Wadsworth Publishing Company, 1998).

7. Steven Stack and Jim Gundlach, "The Effect of Country Music on Suicide," *Social Forces* 1992. 72: 211–218.

8. Jeffery B. Snipes and Edward R. Maguire, "Reassessing the Link Between Country Music and Suicide," *Social Forces* 1994. 72: 1239–1243.

9. Jeffery B. Snipes and Edward R. Maguire, "Reassessing the Link Between Country Music and Suicide," *Social Forces* 1994. 72: 1239–1243; Jeffery B. Snipes and Edward R. Maguire, "Country Music, Suicide, and Spuriousness," *Social Forces* 1995. 74: 327–330; Steven Stack and Jim Gundlach, "The Effect of Country Music on Suicide," *Social Forces* 1992. 72: 211–218; Steven Stack and Jim Gundlach, "Country Music and Suicide, A Reply to Maguire and Snipes," *Social Forces* 1994. 72: 1245–1248; Steven Stack and Jim Gundlach, "Country Music, Suicide—Individual, Indirect, and Interaction Effects: A Reply to Snipes and Maguire," *Social Forces* 1995. 74: 331–336.

10. United States Department of State, "Global Issues," http://usinfo.state.gov/gi/ Archive/2005/Jul/18-258720.html, Accessed May 21, 2008.

11. Drug Policy Alliance, "Drug Policy Around the World," http://www.drugpolicy.org/global/drugpolicyby/westerneurop/thenetherlan/, Accessed May 21, 2008.

12. Ibid.

13. Office/ of/ National/ Drug/ Control/ Policy,/ "Arrests/ and/ Sentencing," http://www.whitehousedrugpolicy.gov/drugfact/marijuana/index.html#arrests, Accessed May 21, 2008.

14. Stanley Milgram, *Obedience to Authority: An Experimental View* (New York: Harper and Row, 1974).

15. Fritz J. Roethlisberger and William J. Dickson, *Management and the Worker* (Cambridge, MA: Harvard University Press, 1939).

16. Anthony R. Ward, "Isabelle," Feral Children, http://www.feralchildren.com/en/ showchild.php?ch5isabelle, Accessed August 26, 2008.

17. Robert Yin, *Applications of Case Study Research, 2nd edition* (Thousand Oaks, CA: Sage Publishing, 2003).

18. Ralph A. Weisheit, "The Intangible Rewards from Crime: The Case of Domestic Marijuana Cultivation," *Crime and Delinquency* 1991. 37: 506-527; Ralph A. Weisheit, "Marijuana Subcultures: Studying Crime in Rural America," in *Ethnography at the Edge: Crime, Deviance, and Field Research,* ed. Jeff Ferrell and Mark S. Hamm (Boston: Northeastern University Press, 1998).

19. Joint United Nations Programme on HIV/AIDS (UNAIDS) and World Health Organization (WHO), "2007 AIDS Epidemic Update," http://www.unaids.org/en/KnowledgeCentre/HIVData/EpiUpdate/EpiUpdArchive/2007/, Accessed May 21, 2007.

20. American Sociological Association, "Code of Ethics," Washington D.C.: American Sociological Association, http://www.asanet.org/page.ww?section5Ethics&name5 Ethics, Accessed August 26, 2008.

21. Norman K. Denzin, *The Research Act in Sociology* (Chicago: Aldine Publishing Company, 1970).

22. Barry Glassner, *The Culture of Fear: Why Americans are Afraid of the Wrong Things: Crime, Drugs, Minorities, Teen Moms, Killer Kids, Mutant Microbes, Plane Crashes, Road Rage, and So Much More* (New York: Basic Books, 1999).

23. Factcheck.org, "Misstatement of the Union: The President Burnishes the State of the Union through Selective Facts and Strategic Omissions," http://factcheck. org/article376.html#, Accessed August 26, 2008.

CHAPTER 3

1. "The Medium is the Metaphor", from *Amusing Ourselves to Death* by Neil Postman, copyright © 1985 by Neil Postman. Used by permission of Viking Penguin, a division of Penguin Group (USA) Inc.

2. The World Factbook, "Rank Order—Electricity—Consumption," Central Intelligence Agency, https://www.cia.gov/library/publications/the-world-factbook/ rankorder/2042rank.html, Accessed March 30, 2006; The World Factbook, "Rank Order—Oil—Consumption," Central Intelligence Agency, https://www. cia.gov/library/publications/the-world-factbook/rankorder/2174rank.html, Accessed March 30, 2006; The World Factbook, "Rank Order—Population," Central Intelligence Agency, https://www.cia.gov/library/publications/the-world-factbook/rankorder/2174rank.html, Accessed March 30, 2006.

3. Jan Kavan, "International Mother Language Day: Address to the Fifty-seventh Session of the United Nations General Assembly," Office of the President of the General Assembly, http://www.un.org/ga/president/57/pages/speeches/statement 210203-MotherTongue.htm, Accessed September 18, 2008.

4. Noam Chomsky, *Reflections on Language* (New York: Pantheon Books, 1975).

5. Marie Coppola and Elissa L. Newport, "Grammatical Subjects in Home Sign: Abstract Linguistic Structure in Adult Primary Gesture Systems without Linguistic Input," *Proceedings of the National Academy of Sciences of the United States,* 2005. 103(52): 19249–19253.

6. Peter Gordon, "Numerical Cognition without Words: Evidence from Amazonia," *Science,* 2004. 306(5695): 496–499.

7. Benjamin L. Whorf, *Language, Thought, and Reality* (New York: Wiley, 1956)

8. Richard Monastersky, "Speak Before You Think," *Chronicle of Higher Education,* 00095982, 2002. 48(29): p. A17–A19.

9. Robin M. Williams, Jr., *American Society: A Sociological Interpretation,* 3rd ed., (New York: Alfred A. Knopf, 1970).

10. Organization for Economic Cooperation and Development, "Employment Outlook Statistical Annex—2008," OECD, http://www.oecd.org/searchResult/0,3400,en_2649_201185_1_1_1_1_1,00.html, Accessed September 18, 2008.

11. Jacqueline L. Salmon and Leef Smith, "Two-Thirds of Katrina Donations Exhausted," The *Washington Post,* 27 February 2006,http://www.washington-post.com/wp-dyn/content/article/2006/02/26/AR2006022601383_pf.html, Accessed September 18, 2008.

12. One Laptop Per Child Foundation, http://laptopfoundation.org/en/program/, Accessed September 5, 2008.

13. Robert N. Bellah, Richard Madsen, William M. Sullivan, Ann Swidler, and Steven M. Tipton, *Habits of the Heart, Individualism and Commitment in American Life* (Berkley, CA: University of California Press, 1996).

14. Freedom House, *Freedom in the World; Selected Data from Freedom House's Annual Global Survey of Political Rights and Civil Liberties* (Washington D.C: Freedom House, 2006) http://www.freedomhouse.org/uploads/pdf/Charts 2006.pdf, Accessed September 18, 2008.

15. Harry C. Triandis, *Individualism and Collectivism* (Boulder, CO: Westview, 1995).

16. Darryl Fears, "La. Town Fells 'White Tree,' but Tension Runs Deep," *The Washington Post,* 4 August 2007, http://www.washingtonpost.com/wp-dyn/content/ article/2007/08/03/AR2007080302098.html, Accessed September 5, 2008.

17. Peijia Zha, Jeffrey J. Walczyk, Diana A. Griffith-Ross, Jerome J. Tobacyk, Daniel F. Walczyk, "The Impact of Culture and Individualism-Collectivism on the Creative Potential and Achievement of American and Chinese Adults," *Creativity Research Journal,* 2006. 18(3): 355–366.

18. B. Quiroz, P. M. Greenfield, and M. Altchech, "Bridging Cultures with a Parent-Teacher Conference," *Educational Leadership,* 1999. 56 (7): 68–70.

19. Chuansheng Chen, Shin-ying Lee, and Harold W. Stevenson, "Response Style and Cross-cultural Comparisons of Rating Scales Among East Asian and North American Students," *Psychological Science,* 1995. 6(3): 170–175.

20. Richard Ball, "Individualism, Collectivism, and Economic Development," *Annals of the American Academy of Political and Social Science,* 2001. 573: 57–84.

21. CDC, "Overweight and Obesity: Obesity Trends: U.S. Obesity Trends 1985–2004," Centers for Disease Control and Prevention, http://www.cdc.gov/nccdphp/dnpa/obesity/trend/maps/index.htm, Accessed September 18, 2008.

22. John D'Emilio and Estelle B. Freedman, *Intimate Matters: A History of Sexuality in America* 2nd ed. (Chicago: University of Chicago Press, 1997).

23. NRF, "Cupid Strikes Again as Valentine's Day Spending Set to Top $13 Billion: More Than Half of Consumers to Celebrate on Feb. 14," National Retail Federation, http://www.nrf.com/content/default.asp?folder5press/release2005&file5valentines0105.htm, Accessed September 18, 2008.

24. William Sumner, *Folkways and Mores* (New York: Schocken Books, 1911/1979).

25. Bronislaw Malinowski, *Magic, Science, and Religion and Other Essays* (Garden City, NY: Doubleday, 1954).

26. Elizabeth Cashdan, "Ethnocentrism and Xenophobia: A Cross-cultural Study," *Current Anthropology,* 2001. 42(5): 760–765.

27. Robert B. Edgerton, *Sick Societies: Challenging the Myth of Primitive Harmony* (New York: Free Press, 1992).

28. Daniel M. Kammen, "Cookstoves for the Developing World," *Scientific American,* 1995. 273(1): 72–76.

29. David Wallace Adams, *Education for Extinction: American Indians and the Boarding School Experience* (Lawrence, KS: University of KS Press, 1995).

30. Marshall McLuhan, *The Gutenberg Galaxy: The Making of Typographic Man* (Toronto: University of Toronto Press, 1962).

31. Stanley Milgram, "The Small-World Problem," *Psychology Today,* 1967. 1: 61–67.

32. Peter Sheridan Dodds, Roby Muhamad, and Duncan J. Watts, "An Experimental Study of Search in Global Social Networks," *Science,* 2003. 301(5634): 827–829.

33. Marshall Fishwick, *Probing Popular Culture: On and Off the Internet* (Binghamton, NY: The Haworth Press, Inc, 2004).

34. Andrew Murphie and John Potts, *Culture and Technology* (New York: Palgrave McMillian. 2003).

35. Wayne Baker, *America's Crisis of Values: Reality and Perception* (Princeton, NJ: Princeton University Press, 2005).

36. Amitai Etzioni, *The Spirit of Community: The Reinvention of American Society* (New York, Simon & Schuster, 1994).

37. George Ritzer, *The McDonaldization of Society: Revised New Century Edition* (Thousand Oaks, CA: Pine Forge Press, 2004).

38. Wayne A. Santoro, "Conventional Politics Takes Center Stage: The Latino Struggle against English-Only Laws," *Social Forces,* 1999. 77(3): 887–909

39. Rubén G. Rumbaut, "Assimilation and its Discontents: Between Rhetoric and Reality," *International Migration Review,* 1997. 31: 923–968.

40. Alejandro Portes and Rubén G. Rumbaut, *Immigrant America: A Portrait* (Berkeley: University of California Press, 1996).

41. Valerie/ Barker/ and/ Howard/ Giles,/ "Who/ Supports/ the/ English-Only Movement? Evidence for Misconceptions about Latino Group Vitality," *Journal of Multilingual and Multicultural Development,* 2002. 23(5): 353–370.

CHAPTER 4

1. Reprinted by permission of the publisher from *The Dignity Of Working Men: Morality and the Boundaries of Race, Class, and Immigration* by Michèle Lamont, p. 234, Cambridge, Mass.: Harvard University Press, Copyright © 2000 by the Russell Sage Foundation.

2. Charles H Cooley, *Human Nature and Social Order,* Revised ed. (New York: Scribner and Sons, 1922).

3. Dennis Gilbert, *The American Class Structure in an Age of Growing Inequality,* 6th ed. (Belmont CA: Wadsworth, 2003).

4. Yanjie Bian, "Chinese Social Stratification and Social Mobility." *Annual Review of Sociology,* 2002. 28: 91–116.

5. Julian A. Oldmeadow, Michael J. Platow, Margaret Foddy, and Donna Anderson, "Self-categorization, Status, and Social Influence," *Social Psychology Quarterly,* 2003. 66(2): 138–152.

6. Ibid.

7. Ibid.

8. Robert K. Merton, "The Role-Set: Problems in Sociological Theory," *British Journal of Sociology,* 1957. 8: 106–120; Robert K. Merton, *Social Theory and Social Structure,* Revised and Enlarged ed. (New York: Free Press, 1968).

9. Erving Goffman, *Stigma: Notes on the Management of Spoiled Identity* (Englewood Cliffs, NJ: Prentice-Hall, 1963).

10. Gerhard Lenski, Jean Lenski, and Patrick Nolan, *Human Societies* (New York: McGraw-Hill, 1990).

11. Douglas S. Massey, "A Brief History of Human Society: The Origin and Role of Emotion in Social Life: 2001 Presidential Address," *American Sociological Review,* 2002. 67(1): 1–29.

12. Gerhard Lenski, *Power and Privilege: A Theory of Social Stratification* (Chapel Hill, NC: University of North Carolina Press, 1966).

13. Jared Diamond, *Collapse: How Societies Choose to Fail or Succeed* (New York: Viking Penguin Press, 2005).

14. Douglas S. Massey, "A Brief History of Human Society: The Origin and Role of Emotion in Social Life: 2001 Presidential Address," *American Sociological Review,* 2002. 67(1): 1–29.

15. Gerhard Lenski, Jean Lenski, and Patrick Nolan, *Human Societies* (New York: McGraw-Hill, 1990).

16. Ibid.

17. Ibid.

18. Douglas S. Massey, "A Brief History of Human Society: The Origin and Role of Emotion in Social Life: 2001 Presidential Address," *American Sociological Review*, 2002. 67(1): 1–29.

19. Gerhard Lenski, Jean Lenski, and Patrick Nolan, *Human Societies* (New York: McGraw-Hill, 1990).

20. Ibid.

21. Douglas S. Massey, "A Brief History of Human Society: The Origin and Role of Emotion in Social Life: 2001 Presidential Address," *American Sociological Review*, 2002. 67(1): 1–29.

22. Daniel Bell, *The Coming of Post Industrial Society: A Venture in Social Forecasting* (New York: Basic Books, 1973, 1999).

23. Stephanie Coontz, *Marriage, A History: How Love Conquered Marriage* (New York: Penguin Publishing, 2005).

24. Ferdinand Tonnies, *Community and Society (Gemeinschaft und Gesellschaft)*. Translated and edited by Charles P. Loomis, (East Lansing, Michigan: Michigan State University Press, 1887).

25. Steven Brint, "Gemeinschaft Revisited: A Critique and Reconstruction of the Community Concept," *Sociological Theory*, 2001. 19(1): 1–23.

26. Michèle Lamont, *The Dignity Of Working Men: Morality and the Boundaries of Race, Class, and Immigration* (Cambridge, Massachusetts: Harvard University Press, 2000).

27. Ibid.

28. Edward T. Hall, *The Hidden Dimension* (New York: Anchor Books, 1966, 1982).

29. Ibid.

30. Erving Goffman, *The Presentation of Self in Everyday Life* (Edinburgh: University of Edinburgh, Social Sciences Research Centre, 1958).

31. Sandy J. Wayne and Robert C. Liden, "Effects of Impression Management on Performance Ratings: A Longitudinal Study," *The Academy of Management Journal*, 1995. 38(1): 232–260.

32. Mario Bruno-Britz, "Spitzer Exposed by Bank's Anti-Money Laundering Technology," March 27, 2008, at http://www.banktech.com/showArticle.jhtml?articleID=206904957, Accessed November 12, 2008.

33. Sandy J. Wayne and Robert C. Liden, "Effects of Impression Management on Performance Ratings: A Longitudinal Study," *The Academy of Management Journal*, 1995. 38(1): 232–260.

34. W. I. Thomas and Dorothy Swaine Thomas, *The Child in America: Behavior Problems and Programs* (New York: Alfred A. Knopf, 1928).

35. Emile Durkheim, *Rules of Sociological Method*, Edited by George E. G. Catlin, Translated by Sarah A. Solovay & John H. Mueller, (New York: The Free Press of Glenco, 1895).

36. Jared Diamond, *Collapse: How Societies Choose to Fail or Succeed* (New York: Viking Penguin Press, 2005).

37. Jared Diamond, *Guns, Germs, and Steel: The Fates of Human Societies* (New York: W.W. Norton and Company, 1999).

38. Emile Durkheim, *Rules of Sociological Method*, Edited by George E. G. Catlin, Translated by Sarah A. Solovay & John H. Mueller. (New York: The Free Press of Glenco, 1895); D. F. Aberle, A. K. Cohen, A. K. Davis, M. J. Levy Jr., and F. X. Sutton, "The Functional Prerequisites of a Society," *Ethics*, 1950, 60(2): 100–111; Raymond W. Mack and Calvin P. Bradford, *Transforming America: Patterns of Social Change*, 2nd ed. (New York: Random House, 1979); Jared Diamond, *Guns, Germs, and Steel: The Fates of Human Societies* (New York: W.W. Norton and Company, 1999); Jared Diamond, *Collapse: How Societies Choose to Fail or Succeed* (New York: Viking Penguin Press, 2005).

39. Evon Z. Vogt, "Acculturation of American Indians." *Annals of the American Academy of Political Science*, 1957. 311: 137–146.

40. Colin G. Calloway, *First Peoples: A Documentary Survey of American Indian History*, 2nd ed. (Boston: Bedford/St. Martin's, 2004).

41. Ibid.

42. David P. Weikart, "An Early Education Project that Changed Students' Lives: The Perry School Program, 20 Years Later," *Education Digest*, 1985. 51: 32–35.

43. Lawrence J. Schweinhart, The High/Scope Perry Preschool Study through Age 40: Summary, Conclusions and Frequently Asked Questions, *High/Score Educational Research Foundation*, http://www.highscope.org/productDetail.asp?intproductID=52164, Accessed October 11, 2006.

CHAPTER 5

1. Brief excerpts as submitted (six paragraphs in total) from *Genie* by Russ Rymer. Copyright © 1993 by Russ Rymer. A portion of this book appeared in somewhat different form in The New Yorker magazine. Reprinted by permission of HarperCollins Publishers.

2. Talcott Parsons, *The Social System* (New York: Free Press, 1951).

3. Talcott Parsons and Robert Bales, *Socialization and the Interaction Process* (New York: Free Press, 1955).

4. Orville G. Brim, Jr., "Socialization Through the Life Cycle," In: Orville Brim and Stanton Wheeler (eds.), *Socialization after Childhood: Two Essays* (New York: Wiley, 1966).

5. Theodore E. Long and Jeffrey K. Hadden, "Reconception of Socialization," *Sociological Theory*. 1985. 3(1): 39–49.

6. Orville G. Brim, Jr., "Socialization Through the Life Cycle," In: Orville Brim and Stanton Wheeler (eds), *Socialization after Childhood: Two Essays*. (New York: Wiley, 1966).

7. Richard Dawkins, *The Selfish Gene* (Oxford: Oxford University Press, 1989).

8. W. L. Reese, *Dictionary of Philosophy and Religion: Eastern and Western Thought* (Atlantic Highlands, NJ: Humanities Press Inc., 1987).

9. Paul R. Ehrlich, *Human Natures: Genes, Cultures, and the Human Prospect* (Island Press. Washington, D.C., 2000), p. 6, at http://books.google.com/books?id=5mHFsScY8ewMC&dq=5Human1Natures1Paul1Ehrlich&pg=5PP1&ots=5XW4w7TDMLU&sig=5MjKy9QADe0TPCKe0fZZ8h_ahKLM&hl=5en&sa.5X&oi.5book_result&resnum=51&ct.5result.

10. Harry F. Harlow and Margaret Harlow, "Social Deprivation in Monkeys," *Scientific America*, 1962. November: 137–146.

11. Susan Donaldson James, "Wild Child Speechless After Tortured Life," *ABC News*, May 7, 2008, at http://abcnews.go.com/Health/story?id=54804490; "What Drove Father Who Built House of Horror?" *CNN News*, April 29, 2008, at http://www.cnn.com/2008/WORLD/europe/04/29/austria.cellar.profile/, Accessed November 12, 2008.

12. Russ Rymer, *Genie: An Abused Child's Flight from Silence* (New York, NY: Harper-Collins Publishers, 1993).

13. Ibid.

14. Ibid.

15. Louis De Maio, "Stages of Language Development," at www.mnstate.edu/pccp/ stages%20of%20language%20development.pdf, Accessed June 5, 2008; "Isabelle," http://www.feralchildren.com/en/showchild.php?ch=5isabelle, Accessed June 26, 2008.

16. Charles H. Cooley, *Human Nature and the Social Order* (New York: Schocken Books, 1902, 1964).

17. King-To Yeung and John L. Martin, "The Looking Glass Self: An Empirical Test and Elaboration," *Social Forces*, 2003. 81(3): 843–879.

18. Ibid.

19. George Herbert Mead, *Mind, Self, and Society*, Charles W. Morris, ed. (Chicago: University of Chicago Press, 1934, 1962).

20. Ibid.

21. Ibid.

22. Erik Erikson, *Childhood and Society* (New York: Norton Press, 1963).

23. "Secret of the Wild Child," *Nova*, March 4, 1997, http://www.pbs.org/wgbh/nova/transcripts/2112gchild.html, Accessed November 12, 2008.

24. Jean Piaget and Barbel Inhelder, *The Psychology of the Child* (New York: Basic Books, 1969, 2000).

25. Ibid.

26. Ibid.

27. Ibid.

28. Ibid.

29. Lawrence Kohlberg, *The Psychology of Moral Development: The Nature and Validity of Moral Stages* (New York: Harper & Row, 1981).

30. Ibid.

31. Ibid.

32. Ibid.

33. Charles Helwig and Urszula Jasiobedzka, "The Relation Between Law and Morality: Children's Reasoning about Socially Beneficial and Unjust Laws," *Child Development*, 2001. 72: 1382–1394.

34. Anne Colby and William Damon, *Some Do Care: Contemporary Lives of Moral Commitment* (New York: Free Press, 1992).

35. Carol Gilligan, *In a Different Voice: Psychological Theory and Women's Development* (Cambridge, MA: Harvard University Press, 1982).

36. Ibid.

37. Elliott Turiel, "The Development of Morality," In: W. Damon (ed.), *Handbook of Child Psychology*, 5th ed., Vol. 3, 863–932 (New York: Wiley, 1998).

38. Eva A. Skoe and Alethia Gooden, "Ethics of Care and Real-Life Moral Dilemma Content in Male and Female Early Adolescents," *Journal of Early Adolescence*, 1993. 13(2): 154–167.

39. Eva A. Skoe and Rhett Diessner, "Ethics of Care, Justice, Identity and Gender: An Extension and Replication," *Merrill–Palmer Quarterly*, 1994. 40: 102–119. Eva A. Skoe and Anna L. von der Lippe, "Ego Development and the Ethics of Care and Justice: The Relations Among Them Revisited," *Journal of Personality*, 2002. 70(4): 485–508.

40. Andrew J. Cherlin, *Public and Private Families: An Introduction*, 2nd ed. (Boston: McGraw–Hill College, 1999).

41. Diana Baumrind, "Current Patterns of Parental Authority," *Developmental Psychology Monographs*, 1971. 4(1, pt. 2):103; Diana Baumrind, "Parental Disciplinary Patterns and Social Competence in Children," *Youth and Society*, 1978. 9: 239–276. Diana Baumrind, "The Discipline Controversy Revisited," *Family Relations*, 1996. 5(4): 405–415.

42. Ibid.

43. Ruth K. Chao, "Beyond Parental Control and Authoritarian Parenting Style: Understanding Chinese Parenting Through the Cultural Notion of Training," *Child Development*, 1994. 65(4): 1111–1119.

44. Ibid.

45. Min Zhou, *Chinatown: The Socioeconomic Potential of an Urban Enclave* (Philadelphia, PA: Temple University Press, 1992).

46. Min Zhou and Carl L. Bankston, III, "Social Capital and the Adaptation of the Second Generation: The Case of Vietnamese Youth in New Orleans," *The New Second Generation*, Alejandro Portes (ed.), (New York: Russell Sage Foundation, 1996), 197–220.

47. Melvin L Kohn, "Social Class and Parent-Child Relationships: An Interpretation," *American Journal of Sociology*, 1963. 571–580.

48. William J. Wilson, *The Truly Disadvantaged: The Inner City, The Underclass, and Public Policy* (Chicago: University of Chicago Press, 1987).

49. Jeanne Brooks–Gunn, Greg Duncan, Pamela Klebanove, and Naomi Sealand, "Do Neighborhoods Influence Child and Adolescent Development?" *American Journal of Sociology*, 1993. 99(2): 353–395.

50. Ibid.

51. Gary Solon, Marianne Page, and Greg J. Duncan, "Correlations Between Neighboring Children and Their Subsequent Educational Attainment," *Review of Economics and Statistics*, 2000. 82(3): 383–393.

52. John D. Carl, "Social Capital and Sport Participation," Ph.D. dissertation, Department of Sociology, University of Oklahoma, Norman, OK, 2002.

53. Erving Goffman, *Asylums: Essays on the Social Situation of Mental Patients and Other Inmates* (Chicago: Aldine, 1961).

54. Harold Garfinkel, "Conditions of Successful Degradation Ceremonies," *American Journal of Sociology*, 1956. 61(2): 420–424.

55. Howard S. Becker, "The Politics of Presentation: Goffman and Total Institutions," *Symbolic Interaction*, 2003. 26(4): 659–669.

56. Charles Tittle and Michael Welch, "Religiosity and Deviance: Toward a Contingency Theory of Constraining Effects," *Social Forces*, 1983. 61(3): 653–682.

57. Harold Grasmick, Karyl Kinsey, and Kent Smith, "Framing Justice: Taxpayer Evaluations of Personal Tax Burdens, *Law and Society Review*. 1991. 25: 845–873.

58. "Prisoners of Time," Education Commission of the States, April 1994, www.eric.ed.gov/ERICDocs/data/ericdocs2sql/content_storage_01/0000-019b/80/1b/b9/60.pdf, Accessed November 12, 2008..

59. Annette Hemmings, "The 'Hidden' Corridor Curriculum," *High School Journal*, 2000. 83(2): 1–10.

60. Philip Jackson, *Life in Classrooms* (New York, NY: Holt, Rinehart, and Winston, 1968).

61. Kirstie Farrar, Dale Kunkel, Erica Biely, Keren Eyal, Rena Fandrich, and Edward Donnerstein, "Sexual Messages During Primetime Programming," *Sexuality & Culture*, 2003. 7(3): 7–38.

62. "Patsy T. Mink Equal Opportunity in Education Act," *K12 Academics*, http://www.k12academics.com/patsy_t_mink_equal_opportunity_education_act.htm, Accessed June 27, 2008.

63. NWLC: National Women's Law Center, "Quick facts on women and girls in athletics," June 2002, www.nwlc.org/pdf/quickfacts_June2002.pdf; NWLC: National Women's Law Center, "The Battle for Gender Equity in Athletics: Title IX at Thirty," 2002, http://www.nwlc.org/pdf/Battle%20for%20Gender%20Equity%20in%20Athletics%20Report.pdf.

CHAPTER 6

1. From *Extraordinary Groups: An Examination of Unconventional Lifestyles, 8th Edition* by Richard T. Schaefer and William W. Zellner. © 2007 by Worth Publishers. Used with permission.

2. "Super Bowl FAQs," http://azsuperbowl.com/super_bowl_faqs.aspx, Accessed July 2, 2008.

3. Charles H. Cooley, *Human Nature and the Social Order* (New York: Schocken Books, 1902/1964).

4. Ibid.

5. Henry Tajfel, "Social Categorization, Social Identity, and Social Comparison," in *Differentiation between Social Groups: Studies in Social Psychology of Intergroup Relations*, ed. Henry Tajfel (London: Academic Press, 1978), 61–76; Robert K. Merton, *Social Theory and Social Structure* (New York: Free Press, 1968).

6. Robert K. Merton, *Social Theory and Social Structure* (New York: Free Press, 1968).

7. Daan Scheeners, Russell Spears, Bertjan Doosje, and Antony S.R. Manstead, "Diversity in In-group Bias: Structural Factors, Situational Features, and Social Functions," *Journal of Personality and Social Psychology*, 2006. 90(6): 944:960.

8. B. Ann Bettencourt, Kelly Charlton, and Nancy Dorr, "Status Differences and InGroup Bias: A Meta-analytic Examination of the Effects of Status Stability, Status Legitimacy, and Group Permeability," *Psychological Bulletin*, 2001. 127(4): 520–542.

9. Henry Tajfel and John Turner, "The Social Identity Theory of Intergroup Behavior," In: S. Worschel and W.G. Austin, eds, *Psychology and Intergroup Relations*, (Chicago: Nelson-Hall, 1986), pp. 7–24.

10. Courtney D. Von Hippel, "When People Would Rather Switch Than Fight: Out-group Favoritism Among Temporary Employees." *Group Processes and Intergroup Relations*, 2006. 9(4): 533–546.

11. Ibid.

12. Ibid.

13. Charles H. Cooley, *Human Nature and the Social Order* (New York: Schocken Books, 1902/1964).

14. Ron Adams, "Hikikomori/Otaku Japan's Latest Out-Group," eclip5e.visual-assault. org/assets/Hikikomori_Japans_Latest_Outcasts.pdf, Accessed June 11, 2008.

15. Ibid.

16. Ibid.

17. Ibid.

18. Richard T. Schaefer and William W. Zellner, *Extraordinary Groups: An Examination of Unconventional Lifestyles, 8th ed.* (New York: Worth Publishers, 2007).

19. Georg Simmel, *The Sociology of Georg Simmel*. Kurt Wolfe ed. (New York: Free Press, 1902/1950).

20. Ibid.

21. James Tucker and S. Thomas Friedman, "Population Density and Group Size," *American Journal of Sociology*, 1972. 77(4): 742–749.

22. Henry Hamburger, Melvin Guyer, and John Fox, "Group Size and Composition," *The Journal of Conflict Resolution*, 1975. 19(3): 503–531.

23. Kurt Lewin, Ronald Lippit, and Ralph K. White, "Patterns of Aggressive Behavior in Experimentally Created Social Climates," *Journal of Social Psychology*, 1939. 10: 271–299.

24. Ibid.

25. Ibid.

26. Ibid.

27. Litsa Nicolaou-Smokovita, "Business Leaders, Work Environment, and Leadership Styles. *Current Sociology*, 2004. 52(3): 404–427.

28. Solomon Asch, *Social Psychology* (Englewood Cliffs, NJ: Prentice-Hall, 1952).

29. Irving L. Janis, *Victims of Groupthink: A Psychological Study of Foreign-Policy Decisions and Fiascoes* (Boston: Houghton Mifflin, 1972); Irving L. Janis, *Groupthink: Psychological Studies of Policy Decisions and Fiascoes* (Boston: Houghton Mifflin, 1983).

30. Irving L. Janis, *Groupthink: Psychological Studies of Policy Decisions and Fiascoes* (Boston: Houghton Mifflin, 1983).

31. Irving L. Janis, *Victims of Groupthink: A Psychological Study of Foreign-Policy Decisions and Fiascoes* (Boston: Houghton Mifflin, 1972).

32. Ibid.

33. "Shock and Awe Campaign Launched in Iraq," *CNN.com*, March 22, 2003, http:// www.cnn.com/2003/fyi/news/03/22/iraq.war/, Accessed November 12, 2008.

34. Dan Glasiter, "Bush Voices Regret for Macho Rhetoric in Run-up to Iraq War," *Guardian.co.uk*, June 11, 2008, http://www.guardian.co.uk/world/2008/jun/11/georgebush.usforeignpolicy.

35. George W. Bush, "Address to a Joint Session of Congress and the American People," September 20, 2001, http://www.whitehouse.gov/news/releases/2001/09/20010920-8.html, Accessed November 12, 2008.

36. Bob Woodward, *Plan of Attack* (London: Simon and Schuster, 2004).

37. Mike Celizic, "Network Anchors Differ on Iraq War Coverage," *msnbc.com*, May 28, 2008, http://www.msnbc.msn.com/id/24855902/, Accessed November 12, 2008.

38. "Colin Powell on Iraq, Race, and Hurricane Relief," *ABC News*, September 8, 2005, http://abcnews.go.com/2020/Politics/story?id51105979&page51, Accessed November 12, 2008.

39. James S. Coleman, "Social Capital in the Creation of Human Capital," *American Journal of Sociology*, 1988. 94(S): 95–120.

40. James S. Coleman, "Social Capital in the Creation of Human Capital," *American Journal of Sociology*, 1988. 94(S): 95–120; Pierre Bourdieu, "The Forms of Capital," *Handbook of Theory and Research for the Sociology of Education*, John G. Richardson ed., (New York: Greenwood, 1986), pp. 241–258.

41. Carlos Garcia, "Buscando Trabajo: Social Networking Among Immigrants from Mexico to the United States," *Hispanic Journal of Behavioral Sciences*, 2005. 27(1): 3–22.

42. Ibid.

43. Ibid.

44. Ibid.

45. Ibid.

46. Mark S. Granovetter, "The Strength of Weak Ties," *American Journal of Sociology*, 1973, 78(6): 1360–1380.

47. Robert D. Putnam, "Bowling Alone: America's Declining Social Capital," *Journal of Democracy*, 1995. 6(1): 65–78.

48. Jennifer Barber, Lisa D. Pearce, Indra Chaudhury, and Susan Gurung, "Voluntary Associations and Fertility Limitation," *Social Forces*, 2002. 80(4): 1369–1401.

49. Amitai Etzioni, *A Comparative Analysis of Complex Organizations: On Power, Involvement, and Their Correlates* (New York: Free Press, 1975).

50. Ibid.

51. Ibid.

52. Ibid.

53. Amitai Etzioni and Edward W. Lehman, *A Sociological Reader on Complex Organizations. 3rd ed.* (New York: Holt, Rinehart and Winston, 1980).

54. Max Weber, "Max Weber Bureaucracy," in *Readings in Social Theory: The Classical Tradition to Post-modernism, 4th edition*, James Farganis ed. (New York: McGraw-Hill, 1978/2004), pp. 99–108; Max Weber, *Max Weber: Essays in Sociology*.

Translated and edited by Hans H. Gerth and C. Wright Mills. (New York: Oxford University Press, 1946).

55. Ibid.

56. George Ritzer, *The McDonaldization of Society: Revised New Century Edition* (Thousand Oaks, CA: Pine Forge Press, 2004).

57. John C. Maxwell, *Leadership 101: What Every Leader Needs to Know* (Nashville, TN: Thomas Nelson Publishers, 2002).

58. Ibid.

59. George Wallingford Noyes, *Free Love in Utopia: John Humphrey Noyes and the Origin of the Oneida Community*, (Chicago, The University of Illinois, 2001), p. xvii.

60. Critique of Hegel's Philosophy of Right Karl Marx, 1843, http://www.marxists.org/archive/marx/works/1843/critique-hpr/ch03.htm#027, Accessed August 28, 2008.

61. Richard D. Rosenberg and Eliezer Rosenstein, "Participation and Productivity: An Empirical Study," *Industrial and Labor Relations Review*, 1980, 33(3): 355–367; Henry Levin, "Worker Democracy and Worker Productivity," *Social Justice Research*, 2006. 19(1): 109–121.

62. Tove H. Hammer, Steven C. Curral, and Robert N. Stern, "Worker Representation on Boards of Directors: A Study of Competing Roles," *Industrial and Labor Relations Review*, 1991. 44(4): 661–680.

63. "Most U.S. Workers Not Living the Dream," *msnbc.com*, January 25, 2007. http://www.msnbc.msn.com/id/16795881/, Accessed November 12, 2008.

64. Randy Hodson, *Working With Dignity* (Cambridge: Cambridge University Press, 2000).

65. Joyce Rothschild-Whitt and J. Allen Whitt, *Cooperative Workplace: Potentials and Dilemmas of Organizational Democracy and Participation* (New York: Cambridge University Press, 1986).

66. Ibid.

67. Ibid.

68. Joyce Rothschild, "Utopian Visions: Engaged Sociologies for the 21st Century: Creating a Just and Democratic Workplace: More Engagement and Less Hierarchy," *Contemporary Sociology*, 2000. 29(1): 195–213.

69. Oprah Fansite, http://www.oprah-fansite.com/, Accessed August 29, 2008.

70. "Oneida Community," Encyclopedia Britannica Online, 2008, http://search.eb. com/eb/article-9057124, Accessed August 29, 2008.

71. Ibid.

72. Robert D. Putnam, "Bowling Alone: America's Declining Social Capital," *Journal of Democracy*, 1995. 6(1): 65–78.

73. Daniel A. McFarland and Reuben J. Thomas, "Bowling Young: How Youth Voluntary Associations Influence Adult Political Participation," *American Sociological Review*, 2006. 71: 401–425.

74. Ibid.

75. Ibid.

CHAPTER 7

1. From Kathryn Edin and Maria Kefalas, *Promises I Can Keep: Why Poor Women Put Motherhood Before Marriage.* Copyright © 2007 by the Regents of the University of California. Reprinted by permission of the University of California Press.

2. Jane Lawler Dye, "Fertility of American Women: June 2004," U.S. Census Bureau, http://www.census.gov/prod/2005pubs/p20–555.pdf, Accessed July 21, 2008.

3. Philip Carl Salzman, "Is Inequality Universal?" *Current Anthropology*, 1999. 40: 31–61.

4. Carmen DeNavas-Walt, Bernadette D. Proctor, and Cheryle Hill Lee, "Income, Poverty and Heath Insurance Coverage in the United States: 2006," *Current Population Reports,* U.S. Census Bureau, http://www.census.gov/prod/2007pubs/ p60-233.pdf, Accessed February 9, 2007.

5. David Cay Johnson, *Perfectly Legal: The Covert Campaign to Rig our Tax System to Benefit the Super Rich and Cheat Everybody Else* (New York: Penguin Group Inc., 2003).

6. Lawrence Mishel, Jared Bernstein, and Sylvia Allegretto, *State of Working America 2006/2007* (Ithaca, New York: Cornell University Press, 2007).

7. Ibid.

8. Barry W. Johnson and Brian G. Raub, "Personal Wealth, 2001," *Statistics of Income Bulletin, 2005*, Internal Revenue Service, http://www.irs.ustreas.gov/pub/irs-soi/98perwel.pdf, Accessed August 29, 2008.

9. Lisa A. Keister and Stephanie Moller, "Wealth Inequality in the United States," *Annual Review of Sociology*, 2000. 26: 63–81.

10. U.S. Department of Health & Human Services, "Frequently Asked Questions Related to the Poverty Guidelines and Poverty," http://aspe.hhs.gov/poverty/faq. shtml, Accessed July 15, 2008.

11. Ibid.

12. Carmen DeNavas-Walt, Bernadette D. Proctor, and Cheryle Hill Lee, "Income, Poverty and Heath Insurance Coverage in the United States: 2005," *Current Population Reports, 2006,* U.S. Census Bureau, www.census.gov/prod/2004pubs/ p60-226.pdf, Accessed February 9, 2007.

13. Robert Rosenheck, Ellen Bassuk, and Amy Saloman, "Special Populations of American Homeless," United States Department of Health and Human Services, http://aspe.hhs.gov/progsys/homeless/symposium/2-Spclpop.htm, Accessed July 15, 2008.

14. Mark Haugaard, "Reflections on Seven Ways of Creating Power," *European Journal of Social Theory*, 2003. 6: 87–113.

15. C. Wright Mills, *The Power Elite* (New York: Oxford University Press, 1956).

16. Ben Bagdikian, *The New Media Monopoly* (Boston: Beacon Press, 2004).

17. Disney, "The Walt Disney Company and Affiliated Companies—Investor Relations," http://corporate.disney.go.com/investors/index.html, Accessed July 16, 2008.

18. Kelly Holder, "Voting and Registration in the Election of November 2004," *Population Characteristics,* 2006, U.S. Census Bureau, http://www.census.gov/prod/ 2006pubs/p20-556.pdf, Accessed August 29, 2008.

19. Keiko Nakao, and Judith Treas, "Updating Occupational Prestige and Socioeconomic Scales: How the New Measures Measure Up." *Sociological Methodology*, 1994. 24: 1–72.

20. Lee Rainwater and William Yancey, *The Moynihan Report and the Politics of Controversy* (Cambridge, MA: The MIT Press, 1968).

21. U.S. Census Bureau, "U.S. Census Bureau Press Releases," http://www.census.gov/Press-Release/www/releases/archives/income_wealth/010583.html, Accessed June 18, 2008.

22. U.S. Census Bureau, *Federal Interagency Forum on Child and Family Statistics,* http://www.childstats.gov/americaschildren/tables/econ3a.asp, Accessed August 29, 2008.

23. Catherine E. Ross, John Reynolds, and Karlyn Geis, "The Contingent Meaning of Neighborhood Stability for Residents Psychological Well-being," *American Sociological Review*, 2000. 65: 581–597.

24. *ChildStats.gov*, "America's Children in Brief: Key National Indicators of Well-Being, 2008," http://www.childstats.gov/americaschildren/econ_fig.asp, Accessed July 21, 2008.

25. Robert Frank, "US Led a Resurgence Last Year Among Millionaires Worldwide," *Wall Street Journal*, June 15, 2004, A1–A8.

26. Ralph Dannheisser, "Rich Candidates Abound as Presidential Campaign Costs Rise," *America.gov*, http://www.america.gov/st/washfile-english/2007/October/ 20071016174359ndyblehs0.8567926.html, Accessed July 21, 2008.

27. Elia Kacapyr, "Are You Middle Class? Definitions and Trends of the U.S. Middle-class Households," *American Demographics*, 1996. 18: 30–36.

28. Harold R. Kerbo, *Social Stratification and Inequality: Class Conflict in Historical, Comparative and Global Perspective, 6th edition* (New York: McGraw-Hill, 2006).

29. Austin Scaggs, "Paris Hilton," *Rolling Stone*, 2004. 964: 92–94.

30. G. William Domhoff, *Who Rules America?: Power and Politics* (New York: McGraw-Hill, 2002); G. William Domhoff, *The Higher Circles* (New York: Random House, 1970).

31. *Boarding School Review*, "St. Paul's," http://www.sps.edu/Default.asp?bhcp51/, Accessed February 19, 2007.

32. G. William Domhoff, *Bohemian Grove and Other Retreats: A Study in Ruling Class Cohesiveness* (New York: Harper Books, 1975); G. William Domhoff, "Social Clubs, Policy-Planning Groups, and Corporations: A Network Study of Ruling-class Cohesiveness," *The Insurgent Sociologists*, 1975. 5:173–184; G. William Domhoff, "Social Cohesion & the Bohemian Grove: The Power Elite at Summer Camp," *Who Rules America,* http://plebe.ucsc.edu/sociologynew/whorule-samerica/power/bohemian_grove.html, Accessed February 19, 2007.

33. Harold R. Kerbo, *Social Stratification and Inequality: Class Conflict in Historical, Comparative and Global Perspective, 6th edition* (New York: McGraw-Hill, 2006).

34. Dennis Gilbert, *The American Class Structure in an Age of Growing Inequality, 6th edition* (Belmont CA: Wadsworth, 2003).

35. Elia Kacapyr, "Are You Middle Class? Definitions and Trends of the U.S. Middle-class Households," *American Demographics*, 1996. 18: 30–36.

36. Dennis Gilbert, *The American Class Structure in an Age of Growing Inequality, 6th edition* (Belmont CA: Wadsworth, 2003).

37. Ibid.

38. Bettina Lankard Brown, "Effects of Globalization on Careers: Myths and Realities No. 29," http://eric.ed.gov/ERICDocs/data/ericdocs2sql/content_storage_01/ 0000019b/80/1b/8b/1c.pdf, Accessed July 15, 2008.

39. Paul Harris, "37 Million Poor Hidden in the Land of Plenty," *The Observer*, February 19, 2006, http://www.guardian.co.uk/world/2006/feb/19/usa.paulharris, Accessed August 29, 2008.

40. Carmen DeNavas-Walt, Bernadette D. Proctor, and Cheryle Hill Lee, "Income, Poverty and Heath Insurance Coverage in the United States: 2005," *Current Population Reports,* U.S. Census Bureau, www.census.gov/prod/2004pubs/p60–226.pdf, Accessed February 9, 2007.

41. Ibid.

42. Lauren J. Krivo and Ruth D. Peterson, "Extremely Disadvantaged Neighborhoods and Urban Crime," *Social Forces*, 1996. 75: 619–648.

43. William J. Wilson, *The Truly Disadvantaged: The Inner City, The Underclass, and Public Policy* (Chicago: University of Chicago Press, 1987).

44. Paul A. Jargowsky, "Take the Money and Run: Economic Segregation in U.S. Metropolitan Areas," *American Sociological Review*, 1996. 61: 984–998; Martha A. Gephart, "Neighborhoods and Communities as Contexts for Development," in *Neighborhood Poverty: Context and Consequences for Children. Vol. 1,* ed. Martha A. Gephart and Jeanne Brooks-Gunn, (New York: Russell Sage Foundation,

1997); Craig St. John, "Interclass Segregation, Poverty, and Poverty Concentration: Comment on Massey and Eggers," *The American Journal of Sociology,* 1995. 100 (1995):1325–1333; Craig St. John, "The Concentration of Affluence in the United States," *Urban Affairs Review,* 2002. 37: 500–520.

45. Catherine E. Ross, John Reynolds, and Karlyn Geis, "The Contingent Meaning of Neighborhood Stability for Residents Psychological Well-being," *American Sociological Review,* 2000. 65: 581–597.

46. Jeanne Brooks-Gunn, Greg Duncan, Pamela Klebanove, and Naomi Sealand, "Do Neighborhoods Influence Child and Adolescent Development?" *American Journal of Sociology,* 1993. 99; 353–395; Catherine L. Garner and Stephen W. Raudenbush, "Neighborhood Effects on Educational Attainment: A Multilevel Analysis," *Sociology of Education,* 1991. 64: 251–262; Gary Solon, Marianne Page, and Greg J. Duncan, "Correlations Between Neighboring Children and Their Subsequent Educational Attainment," *Review of Economics and Statistics,* 2000. 82: 383–393.

47. Jeanne Brooks-Gunn, Greg Duncan, Pamela Klebanove, and Naomi Sealand, "Do Neighborhoods Influence Child and Adolescent Development?" *American Journal of Sociology,* 1993. 99: 353–395.

48. Jonathan Kozol, *Savage Inequalities: Children in America's Schools* (New York: Crown Publishers Inc., 1991).

49. Vincent Roscigno, Donald Tomaskovic-Devey, and Martha Crowley, "Education and the Inequalities of Place," *Social Forces,* 2006. 84: 2121–2145.

50. Karl L. Alexander, Scott Holupka, and Aaron M. Pallas, "Social Background and Academic Determinates of Two-year Versus Four-year College Attendance: Evidence from Two Cohorts a Decade Apart," *American Journal of Education,* 1987. 96: 56–80; Robert Haveman and Timothy Smeeding, "The Role of Higher Education in Social Mobility," *Opportunity in America,* 16 (2):125–150, http://www.futureofchildren.org, Accessed February 9, 2007.

51. Susan M. Dynarski, "Does Aid Matter? Measuring the Effect of Student Aid on College Attendance and Completion," *The American Economic Review,* 2003. 93: 279–288.

52. Ilana Fried, "Governor Preys on Weak Student Clout," *The Daily Bruin,* February 6, 2004, www.dailybruin.ucla.edu; "Editorial: Accountability, Reason Needed in Funding Debate," *Kansas State Collegian,* October 28, 2004, http://collegian. ksu.edu, Accessed November 12, 2008.

53. Gary Solon, "Intergenerational Income Mobility in the United States," *The American Economic Review,* 1992. 82: 393–408; David J. Zimmerman, "Regression Toward Mediocrity in Economic Stature," *American Economic Review,* 1992. 82: 409–429.

54. Mary Corcoran, "Rags to Rags: Poverty and Mobility in the United States," *Annual Review of Sociology,* 1995. 1995. 21: 237–267.

55. Kingsley Davis and Wilbert E. Moore, "Some Principles of Stratification," *American Sociological Review,* 1944. 10: 242–249.

56. Salary.com, "Salary Wizard," http://swz.salary.com/salarywizard/layouthtmls/swzl_compresult_national_ED03000010.html, Accessed June 18, 2008.

57. Salary.com, "Salary Wizard," http://swz.salary.com/salarywizard/layouthtmls/swzl_compresult_national_LG12000003.html, Accessed June 18, 2008.

58. "The Celebrity 100," *Forbes,* http://www.forbes.com/lists/2008/53/celebrities08_The-Celebrity-100_Rank.html, Accessed June 18, 2008.

59. Melvin Tumin, "On Inequality," *American Sociological Review,* 1963. 28: 19–26.

60. Jenny M. Stuber, "Talk Of Class: The Discursive Repertoires of White Working and Upper Middle Class College Students," *Journal of Contemporary Ethnography,* 2006. 35: 285–318.

61. Kathryn Edin and Laura Lein, "Stratification Processes: Women, Work, and Wages: Work, Welfare, and Single Mothers' Economic Survival Strategies," *American Sociological Review,* 1997. 62: 253–266.

62. Salary.com, "Salary Wizard," http://swz.salary.com/salarywizard/layouthtmls/ swzl_compresult_national_HC07000025.html, Accessed June 17, 2008.

63. Salary.com, "Salary Wizard," http://www.cbsalary.com/national-salary-chart.aspx? speciality5Food/Fast/Food/Cook&cty5&sid5 &kw5Food&jn5jn035&edu5&tid563803, Accessed June 17, 2008.

64. Harvard Law Review, "Dethroning the Welfare Queen: The Rhetoric of Reform," *Harvard Law Review,* 1994. 107: 2013–2030.

65. Ibid.

66. Kathryn Edin and Laura Lein, "Stratification Processes: Women, Work, and Wages: Work, Welfare, and Single Mothers' Economic Survival Strategies," *American Sociological Review,* 1997. 62: 253–266.

67. U.S. Department of Labor, Bureau of Labor Statistics 2006, "Current Population Survey (CPS)," http://www.bls.gov/cps/minwage2006.htm, Accessed March 25, 2007.

68. Aimee Durfee, Meryl Haydock, and Noelle Simmons, *Setting the Standard for American Working Families: A Report on the Impact of the Family Economic Self-Sufficiency Project Nationwide,* ed. Joan Kuriansky and Jennifer Brooks (Wider Opportunities for Women, 2003).

CHAPTER 8

1. From Kevin Bales, *Disposable People: New Slavery in the Global Economy.* Copyright © 1999 by the Regents of the University of California. Reprinted by permission of the University of California Press.

2. "The Millennium Development Goals Report: Statistical Annex 2006," *United Nations,* http://unstats.un.org/unsd/mdg/Default.aspx, Accessed April 23, 2007.

3. "UNFPA Annual Report 2007," United Nations Population Fund, at http://www. unfpa.org/, Accessed July 8, 2007.

4. "OECD Country Taxes as Share of GDP 2000," *Tax Policy Center,* Washington D.C., 2003, http://www.taxpolicycenter.org/TaxFacts/tfdb/TFTemplate.cfm?topic2id5 95, Accessed April 21, 2006.

5. "The Millennium Development Goals Report: Statistical Annex 2006," *United Nations,* at http://unstats.un.org/unsd/mdg/Default.aspx, Accessed April 23, 2007.

6. "Mortality," World Health Organization, http://www.who.int/en/, Accessed May 10, 2007.

7. Kevin Bales, *Disposable People: New Slavery in the Global Economy* (Berkeley, CA: University of California Press, 1999).

8. Timothy M. Smeeding and Lee Rainwater, *Comparing Living Standards Across Nations: Real Incomes at the Top, the Bottom, and the Middle,* Social Policy Research Centre, December 2002, http://www.sprc.unsw.edu.au/dp/DP120.pdf.

9. "Swiss and German Cities Dominate Ranking of Best Cities in the World," *Mercer Consulting,* June 10, 2008, http://www.citymayors.com/features/quality_ survey.html.

10. Eric Neumayer, "HIV/AIDS and Cross-National Convergence in Life Expectancy," *Population and Development Review,* 2004. 30(4): 727–742. Central Intelligence Agency, "Life Expectancy at Birth 2008," *The World Factbook,* https://www.cia.gov/library/publications/the-world-factbook/rankorder/2102rank.html, Accessed October 24, 2008.

11. Daniel J. Slottje, "Measuring the Quality of Life Across Countries," *Review of Economics and Statistics,* 1991. 73(4): 684–693.

12. Kai Müller, "The World Economic and Social Development Ranking List," *Global Policy Forum,* March 18, 2000, http://www.globalpolicy.org/nations/kaiswork.htm.

13. Daniel J. Slottje, "Measuring the Quality of Life Across Countries," *Review of Economics and Statistics,* 1991. 73(4): 684–693.

14. Li Lian Ong and Jason D. Mitchell, "Professors and Hamburgers: An International Comparison of Real Academic Salaries," *Applied Economics,* 2000. 32: 869–876.

15. Kevin Bales, *Disposable People: New Slavery in the Global Economy* (Berkeley, CA: University of California Press, 1999).

16. "American Fact Finder: Population," *Census.gov,* http://www.census.gov, Accessed April 15, 2007.

17. Kevin Bales, *Disposable People: New Slavery in the Global Economy* (Berkeley, CA: University of California Press, 1999).

18. Ibid.

19. John Henry Hutton, *Caste in India, its Nature, Function and Origin,* 4th ed (Oxford: Oxford University Press, 1963).

20. David K. Shipler, *The Working Poor: Invisible in America* (New York: Vintage Books, 2005).

21. Kevin Bales, *Disposable People: New Slavery in the Global Economy* (Berkeley, CA: University of California Press, 1999).

22. Michael Overall, "Workers Allege Abuses," *Tulsa World,* February 1, 2002, p. 1; Michael Overall, "Workers Free to Leave, Pickle Testifies," *Tulsa World,* September 11, 2003, p. A1; Michael Overall, "Verdict: Guilty: Judgment Exceeds $1 Million," *Tulsa World,* May 25, 2006, p. A1.

23. John Henry Hutton, *Caste in India: Its Nature, Function, and Origins* (Bombay: Oxford University Press, 1963); Narendra Jadhav, *Untouchables: My Family's Triumphant Journey Out of the Caste System in Modern India* (New York: Scribner, 2007).

24. Karl Marx, "Economic and Philosophic Manuscripts of 1844," *Readings in Social Theory: The Classical Tradition to Post-Modernism,* 4th edition, edited by James Farganis (New York: McGraw-Hill, 1844/2004), 37–42; Karl Marx, *Capital: A Critique of Political Economy,* Vol. 1. (New York: International Publishers, 1867/1967); Karl Marx and Friedrich Engels, "Manifesto of this Communist Party," *Readings in Social Theory: The Classical Tradition to Post-Modernism,* 4th edition, edited by James Farganis (New York: McGraw-Hill, 1845/2004), 26–36.

25. David K. Shipler, *The Working Poor: Invisible in America* (New York: Vintage Books, 2005).

26. Karl Marx, "Economic and Philosophic Manuscripts of 1844," *Readings in Social Theory: The Classical Tradition to Post-Modernism,* 4th edition, edited by James Farganis (New York: McGraw-Hill, 1844/2004), 37–42; Karl Marx, *Capital: A Critique of Political Economy,* Vol. 1. (New York: International Publishers, 1867/1967); Karl Marx and Friedrich Engels, "Manifesto of this Communist Party," *Readings in Social Theory: The Classical Tradition to Post-Modernism,* 4th edition, edited by James Farganis (New York: McGraw-Hill, 1845/2004), 26–36.

27. Ibid.

28. Max Weber, *Economy and Society: An Outline of Interpretive Sociology, 2 Volumes,* edited by Guether Rothe and Claus Wittich (Berkeley: University of California Press, 1978); Max Weber, "Class, Status, Party," *Readings in Social Theory: The Classical Tradition to Post-Modernism,* 4th edition, edited by James Farganis (New York: McGraw-Hill, 1978/2004), 116–126.

29. Karl Marx, "Economic and Philosophic Manuscripts of 1844," *Readings in Social Theory: The Classical Tradition to Post-Modernism,* 4th edition, edited by James Farganis (New York: McGraw-Hill, 1844/2004), 37–42; Karl Marx, *Capital: A Critique of Political Economy,* Vol. 1. (New York: International Publishers, 1867/1967); Karl Marx and Friedrich Engels, "Manifesto of this Communist

Party," *Readings in Social Theory: The Classical Tradition to Post-Modernism*, 4th edition, edited by James Farganis (New York: McGraw-Hill, 1845/2004), 26–36.

30. Immanuel Wallerstein, *The Modern World System: Capitalist Agriculture and the Origins of the European World-Economy in the Sixteenth Century* (New York: Academic Press, 1974); Immanuel Wallerstein, *The Capitalist World- Economy* (New York: Cambridge University Press, 1979).

31. "Nigeria," The World Factbook, https://www.cia.gov/library/publications/the-world-factbook/print/ni.html, Accessed July 24, 2008; "Iraq," The World Factbook, at https://www.cia.gov/library/publications/the-world-fact-book/print/iz.html, Accessed July 24, 2008.

32. Richard H. Robbins, *Talking Points on Global Issues: A Reader* (Boston: Allyn and Bacon, 2004); Richard H. Robbins, *Global Problems and the Culture of Capitalism* (Boston: Allyn and Bacon, 1999).

33. Michael Harrington, *The Vast Majority: The Journey to the World's Poor* (New York: Simon and Schuster, 1977).

34. Margaret Hanson and James J. Hentz, "Neocolonialism and Neoliberalism in South Africa and Zambia," *Political Science Quarterly*, 1999. 114(3): 479–502.

35. Leslie Sklair, "The Transnational Capitalist Class and Global Politics: Deconstructing the Corporate State Connection," *International Political Science Review*, 2002. 23(2): 159–174.

36. Michael Overall, "Workers Allege Abuses," *Tulsa World*, February 1, 2002, p. 1; Michael Overall, "Workers Free to Leave, Pickle Testifies," *Tulsa World*, September 11, 2003, p. A1; Michael Overall, "Verdict: Guilty: Judgment Exceeds $1 Million," *Tulsa World*, May 25, 2006, p. A1.

37. Günseli Berik, Yan van der Meulen Rodgers, and Joseph E. Zveglich, "International Trade and Gender Wage Discrimination, Evidence from East Asia," *Review of Development Economics*, 2004. 8(2): 237–254.

38. A. Aboubakr Badawi, "The Social Dimension of Globalization and Health," *Perspectives on Global Development and Technology*, 2004. 3(1–2): 73–90.

39. Jonathan Crush, "The Global Raiders: Nationalism, Globalization and the South African Brain Drain," *Journal of International Affairs*, 2002. 56(1): 147–173.

40. Ibid.

41. Jared Diamond, *Guns, Germs, and Steel: The Fates of Human Societies* (New York, NY: W.W. Norton & Company, 1997).

42. Ibid.

43. Ibid.

44. Ibid.

45. Ibid.

46. Jacques Diouf, "Food Security and the Challenge of the MDGs," *UN Chronicle*, No. 4, 2007.

47. Ibid.

48. Jared Diamond, *Guns, Germs, and Steel: The Fates of Human Societies* (New York, NY: W. W. Norton & Company, 1997).

49. Vilfredo Pareto, *The Rise and Fall of Elites: An Application of Social Theory.* (New Brunswick, NJ: Transaction Publishers, 1901/2000).

50. Gaetano Mosca, *The Ruling Class.* (New York: McGraw-Hill, 1895/1965).

51. Fernando Cardosa and Enzo Faletto, *Dependency and Development in Latin America*, Translated by Marjory Mattingly Urquidi (Berkeley, CA: University of California Press, 1979).

52. Fernando Enrique Cardosa, *The Accidental President of Brazil: A Memoir* (New York: Public Affairs, 2006).

53. Caspar W. Weinberger, "Brazil in 1997," *Forbes*, July 28, 1997. 160(2): 37.

54. T.R. Reid, *The United States of Europe: The New Superpower and the End of American Supremacy* (New York: Penguin, 2004).

55. Jeremy Rifkin, *The European Dream* (New York: Jeremy P. Tarcher/Penguin, 2005).

56. T.R. Reid, *The United States of Europe: The New Superpower and the End of American Supremacy* (New York: Penguin, 2004).

57. USAID, "New Frontiers in U.S. Foreign Aid," http://www.usaid.gov/policy/, Accessed July, 9, 2007.

58. Organization for Economic Co-operation and Development, "Official Development Assistance," OECD, http://www.oecd.org/, Accessed November 12, 2008.

CHAPTER 9

1. From *Collapse: How Societies Choose to Fail or Succeed* by Jared Diamond, copyright © 2005 by Jared Diamond. Used by permission of Viking Penguin, a division of Penguin Group (USA) Inc.

2. Ibid.

3. Central Intelligence Agency, "Population 2007," *The World Factbook*, https://www.cia.gov/cia/publications/factbook/rankorder/2119rank.html, Accessed April 20, 2007.

4. Ibid.

5. Ibid.

6. U.S. AID, "Fertility Differences and Decline," *The INFO Project*, http://www.infoforhealth.org/pr/m17/m17chap1_1.shtml, Accessed July 16, 2008.

7. Jane Lawler Dye, "Fertility of American Women: June 2004," *Current Population Reports*, http://www.census.gov, Accessed September 24, 2007.

8. Central Intelligence Agency, "Infant Mortality Rate," *The World Factbook*, https://www.cia.gov/library/publications/the-world-factbook/rankorder/2091rank.html, Accessed September 19, 2008.

9. Ibid.

10. Eric Neumayer, "HIV/AIDS and Cross-National Convergence in Life Expectancy," *Population and Development Review*, 2004. 30(4): 727–742.

11. John R. Wilmoth and Jean-Marie Robine, "The World Trend in Maximum Life Span," *Population and Development Review*, 2003. 29: 239–257.

12. Central Intelligence Agency, "Life Expectancy at Birth 2008," *The World Factbook*, https://www.cia.gov/library/publications/the-world-factbook/rankorder/2102rank.html, Accessed October 24, 2008.

13. Eric Neumayer, "HIV/AIDS and Cross-National Convergence in Life Expectancy," *Population and Development Review*, 2004. 30(4): 727–742.

14. U.S. Census Bureau, "Midyear Population, by Age and Sex," International Data Base, http://www.census.gov/cgi-bin/ipc/idbpyry.pl?cty5US&maxp514348291&maxa585&ymax5250&yr52007&.submit5Submit1Query, Accessed July 22, 2008.

15. Richard Easterlin, *Birth and Fortune*, 2nd edition (Chicago: University of Chicago Press, 1987).

16. Douglas Massey, Rafael Alarecon, Jorege Durand, and Humberto Gonzalez, *Return to Aztlan: The Social Process of International Migration from Western Mexico* (Berkeley, CA: University of California Press, 1987); Alejandro Portes and Ruben G. Rumbaut, *Immigrant American: A Portrait* (Berkeley, CA: University of California Press, 1996).

17. Central Intelligence Agency, "Population 2007," *The World Factbook*, https://www.cia.gov/cia/publications/factbook/rankorder/2119rank.html, Accessed April 20, 2007.

18. Naohiro Ogawa and Robert D. Retherford, "The Resumption of Fertility Decline in Japan: 1973–92," *Population and Development Review*, 1993. 19(4): 703–741.

19. Robert D. Retherford, Naohiro Ogawa, and Satomi Sakamoto, "Values and Fertility Change in Japan," *Population Studies*, 1996. 50(1): 5–25.

20. Cynthia G. Wagner, "Promoting Parenthood in Japan," *Futurist*, 2007. 41(3): 9–13.

21. Hayashi Yuka and Sebastian Moffett, "Cautiously, and Aging Japan Warms to Foreign Workers," *Wall Street Journal*, May 25, 2007, Vol. 249, Issue 122, p. A1–A12.

22. John R. Bermingham, "Exponential Population Growth and Doubling Times: Are They Dead or Merely Quiescent?," *Population and Environment*, 2003. 24(4): 313–327.

23. Kingsley Davis, "The World Demographic Transition," *The Annals of the American Academy of Political and Social Science*, 1945. 237: 1–11; Edward M. Crenshaw, Matthew Christenson, and Doyle Ray Oakey, "Demographic Transition in Ecological Focus," *American Sociological Review*, 2000. 65(3): 371–391.

24. Paul Ehrlich, *The Population Bomb* (Cutchogue, NY: Buccaneer Books, 1968).

25. Kingsley Davis, "The World Demographic Transition," *The Annals of the American Academy of Political and Social Science*, 1945. 237: 1–11; Sarah F. Harbison and Warren C. Robinson, "Policy Implications of the Next World Demographic Transition," *Studies in Family Planning*, 2002. 33(1): 37–48.

26. Dudley Kirk, "Demographic Transition Theory," *Population Studies*, 1996. 50(3): 361–387.

27. Kingsley Davis, "The World Demographic Transition," *The Annals of the American Academy of Political and Social Science*, 1945. 237: 1–11.

28. Edward M. Crenshaw, Matthew Christenson, and Doyle Ray Oakey, "Demographic Transition in Ecological Focus," *American Sociological Review*, 2000. 65(3): 371–391; Richard A. Easterlin, "The Worldwide Standard of Living Since 1800," *The Journal of Economic Perspectives*, 2000. 14(1): 7–26; Julian L. Simon, *Population Matters: People, Resources, Environment, and Immigration* (New Brunswick, NJ: Transactions Press, 1990); Julian L. Simon, *Theory of Population and Economic Growth* (New York: Basil Blackwell, 1986); Julian L. Simon, "One Aggregate Empirical Studies Relating to Population Variables to Economic Development," *Population and Development Review*, 1989. 15(2): 323–332.

29. Robert Woods, "Urban-Rural Mortality Differentials: An Unresolved Debate," *Population and Development Review*, 2003, Vol. 29, No. 1: 29–46.

30. Dudley Kirk, "Demographic Transition Theory," *Population Studies*, 1996. 50(3): 361–387.

31. Ibid.

32. "International Data Base," U.S. Census Bureau, http://www.census.gov/ipc/www/idb/, Accessed September 19, 2008.

33. "Briefing Room: Land Use, Value and Management," *United States Department of Agriculture Economic Research Service*, www.ers.usda.gov/Briefing/LandUse, Accessed January 29, 2008.

34. Mark W. Rosegrant and Mercedita A Sombilla, "Critical Issues Suggested by Trends in Food, Population, and the Environment to the Year 2020," *American Journal of Agricultural Economics*, 1997. 79(5): 1467–1470.

35. Mark W. Rosegrant and Mercedita A Sombilla, "Critical Issues Suggested by Trends in Food, Population, and the Environment to the Year 2020," *American Journal of Agricultural Economics*, 1997. 79(5): 1467–1470; Gretchen Daily, Partha Dasgupta, Bert Bolin, Pierre Crosson, Jacques du Guerny, Paul Ehrlich, Carl Folke, Ann Mari Jansson, Bengt-Owe Jansson, Nils Kautsk, Ann Kinzig,

Simon Levin, Karl-Göran Mäler, Per Pinstrup-Andersen, Demenico Siniscalco, and Brian Walker, "Food Production, Population Growth, and the Environment," *Science*, 1998. 281(5381): 1291–1292.

36. Gerald C. Nelson, "Drivers of Ecosystem Change: Summary Chapter," *Ecosystems and Human Well-being: Current State and Trends, volume 1,* edited by Rashid Hassan, Robert Scholes, and Neville Ash (Washington: Island Press, 2005), 73–77; Carl Jordon, "Genetic Engineering, the Farm Crisis, and World Hunger," *Bioscience,* 2002. 52(6): 523–529; Vaclav Smil, "Eating Meat: Evolution, Patterns, and Consequences," *Population and Development Review,* 2002. 28(4): 599–639; Kenneth G. Cassman, Stanley Wood, Poh Sze Choo, H. David Cooper, C. Devendra, John Dixon, Joanna Gaskell, Shabaz Khan, Rattan Lal, Leslie Lipper, Jules Pretty, Jurhenna Primavery, Navin Ramankutty, Ernesto Viglizzo, and Kieth Wiebe, "Cultivated Systems," *Ecosystems and Human Well-Being: Current State and Trends, volume 1,* edited by Rashid Hassan, Robert Scholes, and Neville Ash (Washington: Island Press, 2005), 747–787; Gerhard K. Helig, "Neglected Dimensions of Global Land-use Change: Reflections and Data," *Population and Development Review,* 1994. 20(4): 831–859.

37. Julian L. Simon, *Theory of Population and Economic Growth* (New York: Basil Blackwell, 1986); Julian L. Simon, "One Aggregate Empirical Studies Relating to Population Variables to Economic Development," *Population and Development Review,* 1989. 15(2): 323–332.

38. Gary S. Becker, Edward L. Glaeser, and Kevin M. Murphy, "Population and Economic Growth," *The American Economic Review,* 1999. 89(2): 145–149.

39. William R. Catton and Riley Dunlap, "Environmental Sociology: A New Paradigm," *The American Sociologist,* 1978, 13: 41–49; Frederich H. Buttel, "New Directions in Environmental Sociology," *Annual Review of Sociology,* 1987. 13: 465–488.

40. Thomas K. Rudel, "Sociologists in Service of Sustainable Development: NGO's and the Environment – Case Studies in the Development World," *Society and Natural Resources,* 2002. 15: 263–268.

41. William R. Catton and Riley Dunlap, "Environmental Sociology: A New Paradigm," *The American Sociologist,* 1978, 13: 41–49; Riley E. Dunlap, "Environmental Sociology: A Personal Perspective on its First Quarter Century," *Organization and Environment,* 2002. 15: 10–29.

42. Riley E. Dunlap, "Environmental Sociology: A Personal Perspective on its First Quarter Century," *Organization and Environment,* 2002. 15: 10–29.

43. William R. Catton, *Overshoot: The Ecological Basis of Revolutionary Change* (Chicago: University of Illinois Press, 1980).

44. Maurie Cohen, "Sustainable Development and Ecological Modernization: National Capacity for Rigorous Environmental Reform," *Environmental Policy and Societal Aims,* edited by D. Requier-Desjardins, C. Spash, and J. va der Straaten (Dordrecht, Netherlands: Kluwer, 1999), 103–128.

45. William R. Catton and Riley Dunlap, "Environmental Sociology: A New Paradigm," *The American Sociologist,* 1978. 13: 41–49.

46. Riley E. Dunlap, "Environmental Sociology: A Personal Perspective on its First Quarter Century," *Organization and Environment,* 2002. 15: 10–29; Riley E. Dunlap and William R. Catton, Jr., "Which Function(s) of the Environment do We Study? A Comparison of Environmental and Natural Resource Sociology," *Society and Natural Resources,* 2002. 15: 239–249.

47. Paul Hawken, *The Ecology of Commerce* (New York: Harper-Collins, 1994).

48. "Energy Statistics," Nation Master, http://www.nationmaster.com/red/pie/ene_ oil_con-energy-oil-consumption, Accessed July 17, 2008.

49. Duncan Campbell, "What Erin Brockovich Did Next," *Guardian.co.uk,* December 10, 2001, http://www.guardian.co.uk/world/2001/dec/10/gender.uk.

50. Robert E. Bullard, *Confronting Environmental Racism: Voices from the Grassroots* (Boston: South End Press, 1993); Robert E. Bullard, "Anatomy of Environmental Racism and the Environmental Justice Movement," *The Environment and Society Reader,* edited by R. Scott Free (Needham Heights, MA: Allyn and Bacon, 2001), 97–105.

51. Natgan Keyfitz, "Population Growth, Development, and the Environment," *Population Studies,* 1996. 50(3): 335–359; Beverly H. Wright, "Endangered Communities: The Struggle for Environmental Justice in Louisiana's Chemical Corridor," *Journal of Public Management and Social Policy,* 1998. 4: 181–191.

52. "About the Film: Fenceline," *Public Broadcasting Service,* July 23, 2002, http://www.pbs.org/pov/pov2002/fenceline/.

53. "Margie Eugene Richard of Norco, Louisiana Campaigned For Justice Against Oil Giant Shell and Won Relocation for 300 Families from Toxic Releases," *Global Community Monitor* press release, April 19, 2004, http://gcm.live.radicaldesigns. org/article.php?id5195.

54. "Ship-breakers in India Disabled by Asbestos, Report Says," *International Herald Tribune,* September 6, 2006, http://www.iht.com/articles/ap/2006/09/06/asia/ AS_GEN_India_Ship_Graveyard.php.

55. Anand Krishnamoorthy, "Behind the Hype, the Real India: Unskilled Workers Stoke Economy as Tech Sector Takes Glory," *The International Herald Tribune,* July 12, 2006, p 17; Ken Moritsugu, "Many Environmental Fears: Ship Breaking, Big Industry in India Falters," *The Philadelphia Inquirer,* November 12, 2006, p E02.

56. Richard York, Eugene A. Rosa, and Thomas Deitz, "Bridging Environmental Science with Environmental Policy: Plasticity of Population, Affluence, and Technology," *Social Science Quarterly,* 2002. 83(1): 18–34; Richard York, Eugene

A. Rosa, and Thomas Deitz. "Footprints on the Earth: The Environmental Consequences of Modernity," *American Sociological Review,* 2003. 68(2): 279–300.

57. Andrew K. Jorgenson and Thomas J. Burns, "The Political-Economic Causes of Change in the Ecological Footprints of Nations, 1991–2001: A Quantitative Investigation," *Social Science Research,* 2007. 36: 834–853.

58. "Climate change 2007: Synthesis Report," *Intergovernmental Panel on Climate Change: Fourth Assessment,* November 17, 2007, http://www.ipcc.ch/.

59. Ibid.

60. James Cramer, "Population Growth and Air Quality in California," *Demography,* 1998. 35(1): 45–56.

61. Paul Hawken, *The Ecology of Commerce* (New York: Harper-Collins, 1994).

62. James Lee and Feng Wang. *One Quarter of Humanity: Malthusian Mythology and Chinese Realities, 1700–2000* (Cambridge, MA: Harvard University Press, 1999); Rachel Murphy, "Fertility and Distorted Sex Ratios in a Rural Chinese County: Culture, State, and Policy," *Population and Development Review,* 2003, 29(4): 595–626; Nancy E. Riley, "China's Population: New Trends and Challenges," *Population Bulletin,* 2004. 59(2): 3–36.

63. "Report: China's One-Child Policy has Prevented 400 Million Births." *The International Herald Tribune,* November 9, 2006, http://www.iht.com/articles/ap/2006/11/09/asia/AS_GEN_China_One_Child_Policy.php.

64. Ibid.

65. Rachel Murphy, "Fertility and Distorted Sex Ratios in a Rural Chinese County: Culture, State, and Policy," *Population and Development Review,* 2003. 29(4): 595–626; Nancy E. Riley, "China's Population: New Trends and Challenges," *Population Bulletin,* 2004. 59(2): 3–36.

66. James Lee and Feng Wang, *One Quarter of Humanity: Malthusian Mythology and Chinese Realities, 1700–2000* (Cambridge, MA: Harvard University Press, 1999).

CHAPTER 10

1. "Introduction: The Problem Simply Stated", from *The Race Myth* by Joseph L. Graves, Jr., copyright © 2004 by Joseph L. Graves, Jr. Used by permission of Dutton, a division of Penguin Group (USA) Inc.

2. U.S. Census Bureau, "Race," American FactFinder, http://factfinder.census.gov/home/en/epss/glossary_r.html, Accessed August 14, 2008.

3. Louis Wirth, 1945, "The Problem of Minority Groups," In *The Science of Man in the World Crisis,* Ralph Linton, ed. (New York: Columbia University Press, 1945).

4. Apartheid, *Africana: The Encyclopedia of the African and African American Experience,* ed. Kwame Anthony Appiah and Henry Louis Gates, Jr., in Featured Selections, http://www.africanaencyclopedia.com/apartheid/apartheid.html, Accessed August 12, 2008.

5. U.S. Census Bureau, "Population Projections," www.census.gov/ipc/www/usinterimproj, Accessed August 12, 2008.

6. "Children Targeted in the Genocide," Human Rights Watch, http://hrw.org/reports/2003/rwanda0403/rwanda0403–03.htm, Accessed September 10, 2008.

7. SPLC, "Stand Strong Against Hate," Southern Poverty Law Center, Montgomery, Alabama. http://www.splcenter.org/center/petitions/standstrong/, Accessed August 14, 2008.

8. Gloria Jahoda, *Trail of Tears: The Story of American Indian Removals 1813– 1855* (New York: Wings Books, 1995).

9. Jeffrey Gettleman and Kennedy Abwao, "U.S. Envoy Calls Some Kenya Violence Ethnic Cleansing," *New York Times,* January 31, 2008;-- James Hider, "Ethnic Cleansing Claim as Iraqi Hostages Found Dead," *The Times,* April 21, 2005.

10. Jared Diamond, *Guns, Germs, and Steel: The Fates of Human Societies* (New York: W.W. Norton and Company, 1999).

11. Benjamin Banneker Center for Economic Justice and Progress, "The Gadsden Purchase: Odd Land Deal," The Progress Report, http://www.progress.org/gads.htm, Accessed August 12, 2008.

12. Media Matters for America, "Buchanan said Immigration will Cause the 'Complete Balkanization of America' Create 'a Giant Kosovo in the Southwest," June 6, 2006, http://mediamatters.org/items/200606060011, Accessed August 12, 2008.

13. Martin N. Marger, *Race and Ethnic Relations: American and Global Perspectives,* 4th edition (Belmont, CA: Wadsworth Publishing, 1997).

14. Public Broadcasting Service, "Srebrenica: A Cry from the Grave," http://www.pbs.org/wnet/cryfromthegrave/massacre/massacre.html, Accessed August 12, 2008.

15. Marcus Cox, "The Right to Return Home: International Intervention and Ethnic Cleansing in Bosnia and Herzegovina," *The International and Comparative Law Quarterly,* 1998. 47(3): 599–631.

16. Chris Stephen, "Court Wants Exemplary Karadzic Trial," *BBC News,* July 24, 2008, http://news.bbc.co.uk/2/hi/europe/7522908.stm, Accessed August 12, 2008.

17. The 'Lectric Law Library, "ACLU Briefing Paper Number 6: 'English Only,'" http://www.lectlaw.com/files/con09.htm, Accessed August 12, 2008.

18. Roger Waldinger, *Still the Promised City?: African-Americans and New Immigrants in Postindustrial New York* (Cambridge, Mass: Harvard University Press, 1996).

19. William L. Reinshagen, "German Immigrants" in *Immigration in U.S. History*, ed. Carl L. Bankston III, Danielle Hidalgo, and R. Kent Rasmussen (Pasadena, CA: Salem Press Inc., 2006).

20. Donald Kraybill, *The Riddle of Anabaptist Culture*, 2nd edition (Baltimore: Johns Hopkins University Press, 2001).

21. "Castro, Fidel," Encyclopædia Britannica, 2008, Encyclopædia Britannica Online, http://search.eb.com/eb/article-9020736, Accessed September 30, 2008.

22. "Gandhi, Mohandas Karamchand," Encyclopædia Britannica, 2008, Encyclopædia Britannica Online, http://search.eb.com/eb/article-22639, September 30, 2008.

23. Ashley W. Doane, Jr., "Dominant Group Ethnic Identity in the United States: The Role of "Hidden" Ethnicity in Intergroup Relations," *The Sociological Quarterly*, 1997. 38(3): 375–397.

24. Kathryn Blee, *Inside Organized Racism: Women in the Hate Movement* (Berkley, CA: University of California Press, 2002).

25. Mark E. Hill, "Skin Color and Perception of Attractiveness Among African Americans: Does Gender Make a Difference?" *Social Science Quarterly*, 2002. 65(1): 77–91.

26. Alejandro Portes and Alex Stepick, *City on the Edge: The Transformation of Miami* (Berkeley, CA: University of California Press, 1993).

27. William Frey, "Immigration, Domestic Migration and Demographic Balkanization in America: New Evidence for the 1990's," *Population and Development Review*, 1996. 22: 741–763.

28. Mark Ellis and Richard Wright, "The Balanization Metaphor in the Analysis of U.S. Immigration," *The Annals of the Association of American Geographers*, 1998. 88: 686–708.

29. Min Zhou, *Chinatown: The Socioeconomic Potential of an Urban Enclave* (Philadelphia: Temple University Press, 1992).

30. Alejandro Portes and Rueben G. Rumbaut, *Immigrant America* (Berkeley, CA: University of California Press, 1996).

31. John Dollard, *Frustration and Aggression,* (New Haven, Connecticut: Yale University Press, 1939).

32. "Vincent Chin," Vincent Who?, posted June 14, 2007, http://vincentchin.net/vincent/, Accessed August 12, 2008.

33. M. Brewster Smith, "The Authoritarian Personality: A Re-review 46 Years Later," *Political Psychology* 1997. 18(1): 159–163; John Levi Martin, "The Authoritarian Personality, 50 Years Later: What Lessons Are There for Political Psychology?" *Political Psychology* 2001. 22(1) : 1–26.

34. Rory McVeigh, "Structured Ignorance and Organized Racism in the United States," *Social Forces*, 2004. 82(3): 895–936.

35. Douglas Massey and Nancy Denton, *American Apartheid: Segregation and the Making of the Underclass,* (Cambridge MA: Harvard University Press, 1993).

36. Mary Corcoran, "Rags to Rags: Poverty and Mobility in the United States," *Annual Review of Sociology*, 1995. 21: 237–267.

37. Carmen DeNavas-Walt, Bernadette D. Proctor, and Jessica Smith, "Income, Poverty, and Health Insurance Coverage in the United States: 2006; Statistical Abstract 2008: Table 609," Current Populations Report, P6—233, National Projections Program, U.S. Census Bureau; "Number in Poverty and Poverty Rate: 1959 to 2007," Current Population Survey, U.S Census Bureau, http://www.census.gov/ hhes/www/poverty/povertyrate.html, Accessed October 17, 2008.

38. "The Big Payoff: Educational Attainment and Synthetic Estimates of Work-Life Earnings," U.S. Census Bureau, http://www.census.gov/prod/2002pubs/p23-210.pdf, Accessed September 9, 2008.

39. Jonathan Kozol, *Savage Inequalities: Children in America's Schools* (New York: Crown Publishers 1991); Mary C. Waters and Karl Eschbach, "Immigration and Ethnic and Racial Inequality in the United States," *Annual Review of Sociology*, 1995. 21: 419–446; Grace Kao and Jennifer S. Thompson, "Racial and Ethnic Stratification in Educational Achievement and Attainment," *Annual Review of Sociology*, 2003. 29: 417–443; Rory McVeigh, "Structured Ignorance and Organized Racism in the United States," *Social Forces* 2004. 82(3): 895–936.

40. Eduardo Bonilla-Silva, "The Linguistics of Color Blind Racism: How to Talk Nasty about Blacks Without Sounding 'Racist,'" *Critical Sociology*, 2002. 28(1–2): 41–64.

41. Ibid.

42. Adam Peck, "Blackface: Racism Across College Campuses," *The Statesman*, February 22, 2007, http://media.www.sbstatesman.com/media/storage/paper955/news/2007/02/22/News/Blackface.Racism.Across.College.Campuses-2734300.shtml, Accessed August 12, 2008.

43. W.E.B. Du Bois, *The Souls of Black Folk* (New York: Penguin, 1903/1996).

44. Patricia Hill Collins, *Black Feminist Thought* (New York: Routledge, 1990); Darlene Clark Hine, "In the Kingdom of Culture: Black Women and the Intersection of Race, Gender, and Class," in *Lure and Loathing: Essays on Race, Identity and the Ambivalence of Assimilation,* ed. Gerald Early (New York: Penguin Press, 1993).

45. Gloria Jahoda, *Trail of Tears: The Story of American Indian Removals 1813–1855* (New York: Wings Books, 1995).

46. William J. Wilson, *The Declining Significance of Race: Blacks and Changing American Institutions, 2nd ed.* (Chicago: University of Chicago Press, 1980).

47. Roland G. Fryer and Glenn C. Loury, "Affirmative Action and Its Mythology," *The Journal of Economic Perspectives,* 2005. 19(3): 147–162.

CHAPTER 11

1. "A Speed-up in the Family", from *The Second Shift* by Arlie Hochschild and Ann Machung, copyright © 1989, 2003 by Arlie Hochschild. Used by permission of Viking Penguin, a division of Penguin Group (USA) Inc.

2. Scott J. South and Glenna Spitze, "Housework in Marital and Nonmarital Households," *American Sociological Review*, 1994. 59(3): 327–347.

3. "20/20: The Difference Between Men and Women: 9/29/06," *ABC News*, at http://abcnewsstore.go.com/webapp/wcs/stores/servlet/DSIProductDisplay?catalogId511002&storeId520051&productId52003060&langId5-1&categoryId5100032.

4. Ibid.

5. Ibid.

6. Ivy Kennelly, Sabine N. Merz, and Judith Lorber, "What is Gender?" *American Sociological Review,* 2001. 66(4): 598–605.

7. Candace West and Don H. Zimmerman, "Doing Gender," *Gender and Society,* 1987. 1(2): 125–151.

8. Ibid.

9. Michael A. Messner, "Barbie Girls versus Sea Monsters: Children Constructing Gender," *Gender and Society,* 2000. 14(6): 765–784.

10. Ibid.

11. "Female Genital Mutilation," World Health Organization, http://www.who.int/mediacentre/factsheets/fs241/en/, Accessed July 28, 2008.

12. Ibid.

13. Ibid.

14. Ibid.

15. Ibid.

16. Ibid.

17. Manhattan Toy Online Store, http://store.manhattantoy.com, Accessed July 28, 2008.

18. Nerf, http://www.hasbro.com/nerf, Accessed July 28, 2008.

19. M. Gigi Durham, *The Lolita Effect: The Media Sexualization of Young Girls and What We Can Do About It* (Woodstock, NY: The Overlook Press, 2008).

20. Ibid.

21. Sharyn Graham Davis, *Challenging Gender Norms: Five Genders Among the Bugis in Indonesia* (Belmont, CA: Thomson Wadsworth, 2007).

22. Ibid.

23. Margaret Mead, *Sex and Temperament* (New York, Harper Perennial, 1935).

24. Ibid.

25. Derek Freeman, *Margaret Mead and Samoa: The Making and Unmaking of an Anthropological Myth* (Cambridge, MA: Harvard University Press, 1983).

26. G. P. Murdock, "Comparative Data on the Division of Labor by Sex." *Social Forces*, 1937. 15: 551–553.

27. Carmen DeNavas-Walt, Bernadette D. Proctor, and Jessica Smith, *Income, Poverty, and Health Insurance Coverage in the United States: 2006,* U.S. Census Bureau, Current Population Reports, P60-233, U.S. Government Printing Office, Washington, DC, 2007.

28. "Colleges for Women," National Women's History Museum, http://www.nmwh.org/exhibits/education/1800s_6.htm, Accessed August 18, 2008.

29. Jerry A. Jacobs, "Gender and the Stratification of Colleges." *The Journal of Higher Education,* 1999. 70(2): 161–187.

30. Ibid.

31. Carmen DeNavas-Walt, Bernadette D. Proctor, and Jessica Smith, *Income, Poverty, and Health Insurance Coverage in the United States: 2006,* U.S. Census Bureau, Current Population Reports, P60-233, U.S. Government Printing Office, Washington, DC, 2007.

32. Brian L. Rich, "On Inequality," *Sociological Perspectives*: Papers from the 56th Annual Meeting, Autumn, 1995. 38(3): 357–380.

33. Miriam David, "Choice, Diversity and Equity in Secondary Schooling," *Oxford Review of Education*, 1997. 23(1): 77–87.

34. David A. Cotter, Joan M. Hermsen, Seth Ovadia, and Reeve Vanneman, "The Glass Ceiling Effect," *Social Forces*, 2001. 80(2): 655–682; CNN.com, "Fortune 500 Women CEOs," http://money.cnn.com/galleries/2008/fortune/0804/gallery500_women_ceos.fortune/index.html, Accessed August 15, 2008.

35. Shelley J. Correll, "Gender and the Career Choice Process: The Role of Biased Self-Assessments." *The American Journal of Sociology,* 2001. 106(6): 1691–1730.

36. Christine Williams, "The Glass Escalator: Hidden Advantages for Men in the "Female" Professions." *Men's Lives,* 2007, http://jan.ucc.nau.edu/hdh9/e-reserves/ Williams_-_The_glass_escalator_PDF-1.pdf, Accessed August 15, 2008.

37. Hendrik Hertzberg, "Exhillaration," *The New Yorker*, June 23, 2008, http://www.newyorker.com/talk/comment/2008/06/23/080623taco_talk_hertzberg, Accessed August 26, 2008.

38. "Prime Minister Golda Meir," The President and Prime Minister Memorial Council, http://www.pmo.gov.il/PMOEng/Government/Memorial/PrimeMinisters/ Golda.htm, Accessed August 15, 2008; "Benazir Bhutto," *Benazirbhutto.org,* http://www.benazirbhutto.org/mbb-profile.html, Accessed August 15, 2008; "Benazir Bhutto," Encyclopædia Britannica Online, 2008, http://search.eb.com/eb/ article-9079076, Accessed August, 27, 2008.

39. Susan Carroll, "Women Voters and the Gender Gap," http://www.apsanet.org/ content_5270.cfm, Accessed August 18, 2008.

40. "Topics in Feminism," *Standford Encyclopedia of Philosophy*, March 15, 2004, http://plato.stanford.edu/entries/feminism-topics/#Oth.

41. Betty Friedan, *The Feminine Mystique* (New York: W.W. Norton and Company, 1963).

42. Barbara Epstein, "Feminist Consciousness After the Women's Movement," *Monthly Review*, 2002, Vol. 54, No. 4, http://www.monthlyreview.org/0902epstein.htm.

43. "The Equal Rights Amendment," *EqualRightsAmendment.org*, http://www.equalrightsamendment.org/era.htm, Accessed August 15, 2008.

44. "About NOW," National Organization for Women, http://www.now.org/about.html, Accessed August 15, 2008.

45. Mountain Writer, "Feminism in Waves: A Brief Overview of the First, Second and Third Wave." *Associated Content*, October 1, 2007, at http://www.associatedcontent.com/article/392800/feminism_in_waves_a_brief_overwiew. html?page5&cat575.

46. "Bell hooks," *Contemporary Educational Thought,* University of Miami, http://www.education.miami.edu/ep/contemporaryed/Bell_Hooks/bell_hooks.html, Accessed August 15, 2008.

47. Sofia Klatzker, "Riot Grrls," 1998, http://eamusic.dartmouth.edu/;wowem/electronmedia/mish/riot-grrrl.html, http://www.riotgrrrlink.com/.

48. "Take Back the Night," http://www.takebackthenight.org/, Accessed August 26, 2008; "Dressed for Success," http://www.dressforsuccess.org/, Accessed August 26, 2008.

49. Third Wave Foundation, http://www.thirdwavefoundation.org/, Accessed August 26, 2008; Feminist Majority Leadership Alliance, http://www.feministcampus.org/, Accessed August 26, 2008.

50. Mary F. Brewer, *Race, Sex, and Gender in Contemporary Women's Theatre: The Construction of "Woman,"* (Sussex, UK: Sussex Academic Press, 1999), p. 106.

51. Janet Saltzman Chafetz, "Feminist Theory and Sociology: Underutilized Contributions for Mainstream Theory," *Annual Review of Sociology,* 1997. 23: 97–120.

52. "Rule of Thumb," The Phrase Finder, http://www.phrases.org.uk/meanings/rule-of-thumb.html, Accessed August 28, 2008.

53. Talcott Parsons, "Age and Sex in the Social Structure of the United States," *American Sociological Review,* 1942. 7(5): 604–616,

54. Ibid.

55. Ibid.

56. Ibid.

57. Janet Saltzman Chafetz, "Feminist Theory and Sociology: Underutilized Contributions for Mainstream Theory," *Annual Review of Sociology,* 1997. 23: 97–120.

58. Ibid.

59. Ibid.

60. Candace West and Don H. Zimmerman, "Doing Gender," *Gender and Society,* 1987. 1(2): 125–151.

61. Janet Saltzman Chafetz, "Feminist Theory and Sociology: Underutilized Contributions for Mainstream Theory," *Annual Review of Sociology,* 1997. 23: 97–120.

62. Deborah Tannen, *You Just Don't Understand: Women and Men in Conversation* (New York: HarperCollins Publishers, 2007).

63. Janet Saltzman Chafetz, "Feminist Theory and Sociology: Underutilized Contributions for Mainstream Theory," *Annual Review of Sociology,* 1997. 23: 97–120.

64. Ibid.

65. Gloria Gonzalez-Lopez, "Beyond Machos and Machoism: Mexican Immigrant Men, Sexuality, and Intimacy," *Men's Lives,* July 11, 2003, http://www. allacademic.com/meta/p_mla_apa_research_citation/1/0/9/1/5/pages109159/p109159-1.php.

66. Friedrich Engels, *The Origin of the Family, Private Property and the State* (Resistance Books, 1884).

67. Shelley J. Correll, "Gender and the Career Choice Process: The Role of Biased Self-Assessments." *The American Journal of Sociology,* 2001. 106(6): 1691–1730.

68. Patricia Tjaden and Nancy Thoennes, "Extent, Nature, and Consequences of Intimate Partner Violence," Findings From the National Violence Against Women Survey, Washington, DC: National Institute of Justice and Centers for Disease Control, July 2000, http://www.ncjrs.gov/pdffiles1/nij/181867.pdf

69. Patricia Tjaden and Nancy Thoennes, "Extent, Nature, and Consequences of Intimate Partner Violence," Findings From the National Violence Against Women Survey, Washington, DC: National Institute of Justice and Centers for Disease Control, July 2000, http://www.ncjrs.gov/pdffiles1/nij/181867.pdf; "Sexual Violence Prevention," Centers for Disease Control and Prevention, http:// www.cdc.gov/ncipc/dvp/SV/svp-consequences.htm, Accessed August 18, 2008.

70. United States Department of Justice. "About Domestic Violence," http://www. ovw.usdoj.gov/domviolence.htm, Accessed August 15, 2008.

71. Ibid.

72. Patricia Tjaden and Nancy Thoennes, "Extent, Nature, and Consequences of Intimate Partner Violence," Findings From the National Violence Against Women Survey, Washington, DC: National Institute of Justice and Centers for Disease Control, July 2000, http://www.ncjrs.gov/pdffiles1/nij/181867.pdf.

73. "Cost of Intimate Partner Violence Against Women in the United States," Centers for Disease Control and Prevention, http://www.cdc.gov/ncipc/pub-res/ipv_ cost/01_executive.htm, Accessed September 17, 2008.

CHAPTER 12

1. "Introduction: Our National Eating Disorder", from *The Omnivore's Dilemma* by Michael Pollan, copyright © 2006 by Michael Pollan. Used by permission of The Penguin Press, a division of Penguin Group (USA) Inc.

2. Kevin Kinsella and Victoria A. Velkoff, U.S. Census Bureau, Series P95/01-1, *An Aging World: 2001* (Washington, D.C.: U.S. Government Printing Office, 2001).

3. Preamble to the Constitution of the World Health Organization as adopted by the International Health Conference, New York, 19–22 June, 1946; signed on 22 July 1946 by the representatives of 61 States (Official Records of the World Health Organization, no. 2, p. 100) and entered into force on 7 April 1948.

4. National Center for Health Statistics, *Health, United States, 2007 With Chartbook on Trends in the Health of Americans* (Hyattsville, MD: 2007).

5. Ibid.

6. John Knodel and Mary Beth Ofstedal, "Gender and Aging in the Developing World: Where Are the Men?" *Population and Development Review,* 2003. 29: 677–698.

7. National Center for Health Statistics, *Health, United States, 2007 With Chartbook on Trends in the Health of Americans* (Hyattsville, MD: 2007).

8. John Knodel and Mary Beth Ofstedal, "Gender and Aging in the Developing World: Where Are the Men?" *Population and Development Review,* 2003. 29: 677–698.

9. "Women Visit Doctors More Than Men," *CNN.com,* http://transcripts.cnn.com/TRANSCRIPTS/0606/17/hcsg.01.html, Accessed August 28, 2008.

10. Clarian Health "Healthy Living for Men," *The Commonwealth Fund News Release,* http://www.clarian.org/portal/patients/healthyliving?paf_gear_id5200001&paf_dm5full&paf_gm5content&task_name5articleDetail&articleId59764&sectionId59, Accessed August 28, 2008.

11. Gina Kolata, "Ideas & Trends: In Medical Research Equal Opportunity Doesn't Always Apply," *New York Times,* March 14, 1991.

12. Janny Scott, "Class Matters: Life at the Top in America Isn't Just Better, It's Longer," *New York Times,* May 16, 2005, http://www.nytimes.com/2005/05/16/national/ class/HEALTH-FINAL.html.

13. Ibid.

14. Ibid.

15. "Social Class and Health: A Data-Driven Learning Guide," Inter-University Consortium for Political and Social Research, http://icpsrdirect.com/cocoon/OLC/PRINT/classhealth.xml, Accessed August 28, 2008.

16. Jason Schnittker, "Education and the Changing Shape of the Income Gradient in Health," *Journal of Health and Social Behavior,* 2004. 45: 286–305.

17. Terrence D. Hill, Catherine E. Ross, and Ronald J. Angel, "Neighborhood Disorder, Psychophysiological Distress, and Health," *Journal of Health and Social Behavior,* 2005. 46: 170–186.

18. Ibid.

19. Robert E. Bullard, *Confronting Environmental Racism: Voices from the Grass Roots* (Boston: MA: South End Press, 1993); Robert E. Bullard, "Anatomy of Environmental Racism and the Environmental Justice Movement," in *The Environment and Society Reader,* ed. R. Scott Free (Needham Heights, MA: Allyn and Bacon, 2001).

20. Natan Keyfitz, "Population Growth, Development, and the Environment," *Population Studies,* 1996. 50: 335–359; Beverly H. Wright, "Endangered Communities: The Struggle for Environmental Justice in Louisiana's Chemical Corridor," *Journal of Public Management and Social Policy,* 1998. 4: 181–191.

21. R. Charon Gwynn and George D. Thurston, "The Burden of Air Pollution: Impacts Among Racial Minorities," *Environmental Health Perspectives,* 2001, http://www.ehponline.org/members/2001/suppl-4/501-506gwynn/EHP109s4p501PDF.pdf.

22. National Center for Health Statistics, *Health, United States, 2007 With Chartbook on Trends in the Health of Americans* (Hyattsville, MD: 2007).

23. Ibid.

24. Terrence D. Hill, Catherine E. Ross, and Ronald J. Angel, "Neighborhood Disorder, Psychophysiological Distress, and Health," *Journal of Health and Social Behavior,* 2005. 46: 170–186.

25. Inderjit S. Thind, Donald B. Louria, Rosemary Richter, Elizabeth Simoneau, and Martin Feurman, "Infant Mortality in Newark, New Jersey," *Public Health Reports*, 1979. 94:349–356, at http://www.pubmedcentral.nih.gov/picrender.fcgi? artid51431779&blobtype5pdf.

26. U.S. Department of Human and Health Resources, "Preventing Infant Mortality," http://www.hhs.gov/news/factsheet/infant.html, Accessed August 28, 2008.

27. Talcott Parsons, "The Sick Role and the Role of Physicians Reconsidered," *Milbank Medical Fund Quarterly Health and Society*, 1975. 53: 257–278.

28. Ivan Ilich, *Medical Nemesis* (New York: Pantheon Books, 1975); Peter Conrad and Joseph Schneider, *Deviance and Medicalization: From Badness to Sickness* (Philadelphia: Temple University Press, 1992).

29. Thomas Szasz, *The Myth of Mental Illness: Foundations of a Theory of Personal Conduct* (New York: Harper and Row, 1974).

30. Ibid.

31. Paula Caplan, *They Say You're Crazy: How the World's Most Powerful Psychiatrists Decide Who is Normal* (New York: Perseus Books Group, 1995).

32. Ibid.

33. Pamela M. Anderson and Kristin F. Butcher, "Childhood Obesity: Trends and Potential Causes," *The Future of Children*, 2006. 16: 19–45.

34. Ibid.

35. Ibid.

36. Ibid.

37. Deborah Carr and Michael A. Friedman, "Is Obesity Stigmatizing? Body Weight, Perceived Discrimination, and Psychological Well-Being in the United States," *Journal of Health and Social Behavior*, 2005. 46: 244–259.

38. Ibid.

39. Jason D. Boardman, Jarron M. Saint Onge, Richard G. Rogers, and Justin T. Denney, "Differentials in Obesity: The Impact of Place," *Journal of Health and Social Behavior*, 2005. 46: 229–243.

40. Arielle Concilio, Sydney Lake, and Gabrielle Milner, "Lack of Resources and Outdoor Space Lead to High Rate of Obesity in Bronx," *New York Daily News*, August 19, 2008.

41. Ibid.

42. James W. Russell, *Double Standard: Social Policy in Europe and the United States* (Lanham, MD: Rowman & Littlefield Publishers, Inc., 2006).

43. Leighton Ku, "Census Revises Estimates of the Number of Uninsured People," *Center on Budget and Policy Priorities*, http://www.cbpp.org/4-5-07health.htm, Accessed August 28, 2008.

44. Ibid.

45. Ibid.

46. Jill Quadagno, "Why the United States Has No National Health Insurance: Stakeholder Mobilization against the Welfare State, 1945–1996," *Journal of Health and Social Behavior*, 2004. 45: 25–44.

47. National Coalition on Health Care, "Facts About Health Care: Health Insurance Costs," http://www.nchc.org/facts/cost.shtml, Accessed August 28, 2008.

48. Jill Quadagno, "Why the United States Has No National Health Insurance: Stakeholder Mobilization Against the Welfare State, 1945–1996," *Journal of Health and Social Behavior*, 2004. 45: 25–44.

49. Ibid.

50. Ibid.

51. Ibid.

52. Dr. Ronald M. Davis, "Resolutions for a Healthy New Year," *American Medical Association*, January 3, 2008, http://www.ama-assn.org/ama/pub/category/18240. html.

53. World Health Organization, *The World Health Report 2000—Health Systems: Improving Performance* (Geneva: WHO, 2000).

54. World Health Organization "World Health Organization Assesses the World's Health Systems," http://www.who.int/whr/2000/media_centre/press_release/en/, Accessed August 28, 2008.

55. Medicaid, "Are You Eligible?" http://www.cms.hhs.gov/MedicaidEligibility/02_ AreYouEligible_.asp≠TopOfPage, Accessed August 28, 2008.

56. "No. HS-3. Population by Age: 1900 to 2002," *U.S. Census Bureau*, Statistical Abstract of the United States: 2003, http://www.census.gov/statab/hist/ HS-03.pdf, Accessed August 28, 2008.

57. "Population: Estimates and Projection by Age, Sex, Race/Ethnicity," U.S. Census Bureau, http://www.census.gov/compendia/statab/cats/population/estimates_and_projections_by_age_sex_raceethnicity.html, Accessed August 28, 2008.

58. "Life Expectancy," National Center for Health Statistics, http://www.cdc.gov/nchs/fastats/lifexpec.htm, Accessed August 28, 2008.

59. U.S. Census Bureau, "Facts for Features," http://www.census.gov/Press-Release/www/releases/archives/facts_for_features_special_editions/006105.html Accessed August 28, 2008.

60. Charles F. Westoff and Elise F. Jones, "The End of 'Catholic Fertility,'" *Demography*, Vol. 16, No. 2, (May 1979), pp. 209–217.

61. Berit Ingersoll-Dayton, Margaret B. Neal, and Leslie B. Hammer, "Aging Parents Helping Adult Children: The Experience of the Sandwiched Generation," *Family Relations*, 2001. 50: 262–271.

62. Global Action on Aging, "Moving Beyond Respect for Age," *The Yomiuri Shimbun Daily*, September 15, 2000, http://www.globalaging.org/elderrights/world/ respect.htm.

63. Mari Yamaguchi, "Number of Elderly in Japan Hits High Record," *USA Today.com*, May 20, 2008, http://www.usatoday.com/news/world/2008-05-20-1807510551_ x.htm; BBC News, "Elderly Suicides Surge in Japan," June 19, 2008. http://news. bbc.co.uk/2/hi/asia-pacific/7463139.stm.

64. U.S. Library of Congress, "Japan: The Elderly," http://countrystudies.us/japan/74.htm, Accessed August 28, 2008.

65. Ibid.

66. John Knodel and Mary Beth Ofstedal, "Gender and Aging in the Developing World: Where Are the Men?" *Population and Development Review*, 2003. 29:677–698.

67. Ibid.

68. Ibid.

69. John Knodel and Mary Beth Ofstedal, "Gender and Aging in the Developing World: Where Are the Men?" *Population and Development Review*, 2003. 29: 693.

70. National Center for Health Statistics, *Health, United States, 2007 With Chartbook on Trends in the Health of Americans* (Hyattsville, MD: 2007).

71. Dana Bash, "With McCain, 72 is the new . . . 69?" International CNN.com, September 4, 2006, http://edition.cnn.com/2006/POLITICS/08/29/mccain.birthday/index.html.

72. Anne E. Lincoln and Michael Patrick Allen, "Double Jeopardy in Hollywood: Age and Gender in the Careers of Film Actors, 1926–1999," *Sociological Forum*, 2004. 19: 611–631.

73. Elaine Cumming, Lois R. Dean, David S. Newell, and Isabel McCaffrey, "Disengagement—A Tentative Theory of Aging," *Sociometry*, 1960. 23: 23–35.

74. Ibid.

75. *Aging and Everyday Life*, eds. Jaber F. Gubrium and James A. Holstein (Malden, Massachusetts: Blackwell Publishers Ltd, 2000).

76. Robert Crosnoe and Glen H. Elder, Jr., "Successful Adaptation in the Later Years: A Life Course Approach to Aging," *Social Psychology Quarterly*, 2002. 65: 309–328.

77. Yunqing Li and Kenneth F. Ferraro, "Volunteering and Depression in Later Life: Social Benefit or Selection Processes?" *Journal of Health and Social Behavior*, 2005. 46: 68–84.

78. United States Census Bureau, "Table 3" http://www.census.gov/hhes/www/poverty/histpov/hstpov3.html, Accessed August 28, 2008.

79. "Voting and Registration of the Voting-Age Citizen Population," United States Census Bureau, http://www.census.gov/prod/2002pubs/p20-542.pdf, Accessed October 2, 2008.

80. World Health Organization,"World Health Statistics 2008: Part 2, Global Health Indicators," http://www.who.int/whosis/whostat/EN_WHS08_Table1_Mort.pdf, Accessed August 28, 2008.

81. UNAIDS, "Global Summary of the AIDS Epidemic, December 2007," http://www.who.int/hiv/data/2008_global_summary_AIDS_ep.png, Accessed August 28, 2008.

82. Elaine Cumming, Lois R. Dean, David S. Newell, and Isabel McCaffrey, "Disengagement—A Tentative Theory of Aging," *Sociometry*, 1960. 23: 23–35.

83. Soleman H. Abu-Bader, Anissa Rogers, and Amanda S. Barusch, "Predictors of Life Satisfaction in Frail Elderly," *Journal of Gerontological Social Work*, 2002. 38: 3–17.

84. Social Security Online, "Status of the Social Security and Medicare Programs," http://www.socialsecurity.gov/OACT/TRSUM/trsummary.html, Accessed August 28, 2008.

85. Laurence J. Kotlikoff and Scott Burns, *The Coming Generational Storm: What You Need to Know about America's Economic Future* (Cambridge, MA: MIT Press, 2003).

CHAPTER 13

1. Reiman, Jeffrey, *The Rich Get Richer and the Poor Get Prison* © 2007. Reproduced by permission of Pearson Education, Inc.

2. Marcus Felson, *Crime & Everyday Life* (Thousand Oaks, CA: Pine Forge Press, 1998).

3. Ibid.

4. "2006 Crime in the United States," *Federal Bureau of Investigation*, at http://www.fbi.gov/ucr/cius2006/offenses/property_crime/index.html, Accessed July 30, 2008.

5. "*Crime in the United States: Uniform Crime Reports*," *Federal Bureau of Investigation, Department of Justice* (Washington, D.C.: Government Printing Office, 2002).

6. "U.S. Summary 2000," *U.S. Census Bureau*, April 2000, http://www.census.gov/prod/2002pubs/c2kprof00-us.pdf.

7. Ibid.

8. David Cole, *No Equal Justice: Race and Class in the American Criminal Justice System* (New York: New Press, 1999).

9. John Braithwaite, "The Myth of Social Class and Criminality Reconsidered," *American Sociological Review*, 1981. 46: 36–57; Margaret Farnsworth, *Social Background and the Early Onset of Delinquency: Exploring the Utility of Various Indicators of Social Class Background* (Albany: Hindelang Criminal Justice Research Center, 1990).

10. Elijah Anderson, "Ideologically Driven Critique," *American Journal of Sociology*, 2002. 197(6):1533–1550.

11. Alexandra Marks, "More Equity in Cocaine Sentencing," *The Christian Science Monitor*, November 2, 2007, http://www.csmonitor.com/2007/1102/p01s02-usju.html.

12. Michael Gottfredson and Travis Hirschi, *A General Theory of Crime* (Stanford, CA: Stanford University Press, 1990).

13. Darrell Steffensmeier and Miles Harer, "Did Crime Rise or Fall During the Reagan Presidency?" *Journal of Research in Crime and Delinquency*, 1991. 28: 330–359.

14. J. N. van Kesteren, P. Mayhew, and P. Nieuwbeerta, *Criminal Victimization in Seventeen Industrialized Countries: Key-findings from the 2000 International Crime Victimization Survey* (The Hague, Ministry of Justice, WODC, 2000).

15. Ibid.

16. Marcus Felson, *Crime & Everyday Life* (Thousand Oaks, CA: Pine Forge Press, 1998).

17. Adam Liptake, "Sentences are Too Long or Too Short. Rarely, Just Right," *The New York Times*, August 24, 2003, http://www.nytimes.com/2003/08/24/weekinreview/24LIPT.html.

18. Susan Saulny, "Martha Stewart is Denied New Trial by U.S. Judge," *The New York Times*, May 6, 2004, http://www.nytimes.com/2004/03/06/business/06martha.html.

19. Kate DuBose Tomassi, "Martha Stewart Closes the Book," *Forbes*, August, 7, 2006, http://www.forbes.com/business/2006/08/07/martha-stewart-settle-cx_kt_0807martha.html.

20. "EJI Wins Relief for Persons Sentences to Die In Prison for Nonviolent Crimes." *Equal Justice Initiative*, September 13, 2007, http://eji.org/eji/node/48.

21. John Braithwaite, *Crime, Shame, and Reintegration* (New York: Cambridge University Press, 1989).

22. L. Thomas Winfree, Jr., "New Zealand Police and Restorative Justice Philosophy," *Crime and Delinquency*, 2004. 50: 189–213.

23. "Criminal Victimization in the United States," *Bureau of Justice Statistics* (Washington, D.C.: Government Printing Office, 2002).

24. Ibid.

25. James Austin and John Irwin, *It's About Time: America's Imprisonment Binge*, 3rd ed. (Belmont, CA: Wadsworth Publishing Company, 2001).

26. "Criminal Victimization in the United States," *Bureau of Justice Statistics* (Washington, D.C.: Government Printing Office, 2002).

27. James Austin and John Irwin, *It's About Time: America's Imprisonment Binge*, 3rd ed. (Belmont, CA: Wadsworth Publishing Company, 2001).

28. Ibid.

29. Adam Liptake, "Sentences Are Too Long or Too Short. Rarely, Just Right," *The New York Times*, August 24, 2003, http://www.nytimes.com/2003/08/24/weekinreview/ 24LIPT.html.

30. Cesare Lombroso, "Introduction," in Gena Lombroso-Ferrero, *Criminal Man According to the Classification of Cesare Lombroso* (Montclair NJ: Patterson Smith, [1911] 1972).

31. Alan Booth and D. Wayne Osgood, "The Influence of Testosterone on Deviance in Adulthood: Assessing and Explaining the Relationship," *Criminology*, 1993. 31: 93–117; J.R. Sanchez-Martin, E. Fano, L. Ahedo, J. Cardas, P.F. Brain, and A. Azpiroz, "Relating Testosterone Levels and Free Play Social Behavior in Male and Female Preschool Children," *Psychoneuroendocrinology*, November 25, 2000, 773–783.

32. James J. Hudziak and Lawrence P. Rudiger, "A Twin Study of In-attentive Aggressive and Anxious/Depressed Behaviors," *Journal of American Academy of Child and Adolescent Psychiatry*, 2000. 39: 469–476.

33. William Duffy, *Sugar Blues* (Pandor, PA: Childton Book Co., 1975).

34. Abdulla Badawy, "Alcohol and Violence and the other Possible Role of Serotonin," *Criminal Behaviour and Mental Health*, 2003. 12: 31–45.

35. Cessare Beccaria, *Essays on Crimes and Punishments*, translated by Henry Paolucci (Indianapolis: Bobbs-Merrill, [1764] 1963).

36. Jeremy Bentham, *An Introduction to the Principles of Morals and Legislation*, edited by J.H. Burns and H.L.A. Hart (London: Athlone Publishing, [1789] 1970).

37. DSM, *Diagnostic and Statistical Manual of Mental Disorders, 4th edition*. (Washington, D.C.: American Psychiatric Association, 1994).

38. Travis Hirschi and Michael J Hindelang, "Intelligence and Delinquency: A Revisionist Review," *American Sociological Review*, 1977. 42: 57–87.

39. Stanton E. Samenow, *Inside the Criminal Mind: Revised and Updated Edition* (New York: Crown Publishers, 2004).

40. Emile Durkheim, *The Rules of Sociological Method*, 8th ed, Translated by Sarah A. Solovay and John H. Mueller, and edited by George E. G. Catlin (New York: Free Press, [1895] 1964).

41. Robert K. Merton, "Social Structure and Anomie," *American Sociological Review*, 1938. 3: 672–682.

42. Edwin Sutherland and Donald Cressey, *Principles of Criminology*, 10th edition. (Philadelphia: Lippincott, 1978).

43. Walter C. Reckless, *The Crime Problem* (New York: Appleton-Century-Crofts, 1955).

44. Travis Hirschi, *Causes of Delinquency* (Berkeley, CA: University of California Press, 1969).

45. Edwin M. Lemert, *Social Pathology* (New York: McGraw-Hill, 1951); Edwin M. Lemert, *Human Deviance, Social Problems and Social Control* (Englewood Cliffs, NJ: Prentice-Hall, 1967).

46. Jeffrey Reiman, *The Rich Get Richer and the Poor Get Prison: Ideology, Class and Criminal Justice* (Needham Heights, MA: Pearson Education, 1998).

47. Willem A. Bonger, *Criminality and Economic Conditions* (Bloomington, IN: Indiana University Press, 1969).

48. Jeffrey Reiman, *The Rich Get Richer and the Poor Get Prison: Ideology, Class and Criminal Justice* (Needham Heights, MA: Pearson Education, 1998).

49. Robert Agnew, "Foundation for a General Strain Theory of Crime and Delinquency," *Criminology*, 1992. 30: 47–66.

50. Michael Gottfredson and Travis Hirschi, *A General Theory of Crime* (Stanford, CA: Stanford University Press, 1990).

51. Robert Agnew, "Foundation for a General Strain Theory of Crime and Delinquency," *Criminology*, 1992. 30: 47–66.

52. Michael Gottfredson and Travis Hirschi, *A General Theory of Crime* (Stanford, CA: Stanford University Press, 1990).

53. H. Grasmick, C. R. Tittle, R. Bursik, and B. Arnkelev, "Testing the Core Empirical Implications of Gottfredson and Hirschi's General Theory of Crime," *Journal of Research in Crime and Delinquency*, 1993. 30: 5–29; Marianne Junger and Richard E. Tremblay, "Self-Control, Accidents, and Crime," *Criminal Justice and Behavior*, 1999. 26: 485–502; Carter Hay, "Parenting Self-Control, and Delinquency: A Test of Self-Control Theory," *Criminology*, 2001. 39: 707–736; Richard Tremblay, Frank Vitaro, Lucie Bertrand, Marc Leblanc, Helene Beauchesne, Helene Boileau, and Lucille David, "Parent and Child Training to Prevent Early Onset Delinquency: The Montreal Longitudinal Experimental Study," *Life-Course Criminology: Contemporary and Classic Readings*, edited by Alex Piquero and Paul Mazerolle (Belmont, CA: Wadsworth Publishing Co., 2001); Charles R. Tittle, David Ward, and Harold Grasmick, "Gender, Age, and Crime/Deviance: A Challenge to Self Control Theory," *Journal of Research in Crime and Delinquency*, 2003. 40: 426–454.

54. Joseph J. Senna and Larry J. Siegel, *Introduction to Criminal Justice*, 8th ed. (Belmont, CA: West/Wadsworth Publishing Co., 1999).

55. Jodi M. Brown and Patrick A. Langan, *State Court Sentencing of Convicted Felons, 1994* (Washington, D.C.: Government Printing Office, 1998).

56. Ronald H. Aday, *Aging Prisoners: Crisis in American Corrections* (Westport, CN: Praeger Press, 2003).

57. "Are Mandatory Minimum Drug Sentences Cost-Effective?" *Rand Corporation: Drug Policy Research Center*, RB-6003, 1997, http://www.rand.org/publications/RB/RB6003/.

58. Richard Dieter, "Costs of the Death Penalty," March 27, 2003, Testimony before Joint Committee on Criminal Justice of the Legislature of Massachusetts, http://www.deathpenaltyinfo.org/MassCostTestimony.pdf.

59. Susan Levine and Lori Montgomery, "Large Racial Disparity Found in Study of Maryland Death Penalty," *Washington Post*, January 8, 2003.

CHAPTER 14

1. From *The Way We Never Were* by STEPHANIE COONTZ. Reprinted by permission of BASIC BOOKS, a member of Perseus Books Group.

2. Ted L. Huston, "Social Ecology of Marriage and Other Unions," *Journal of Marriage and Family*, 2000. 62: 298–320.

3. Cable News Network, "Utah Polygamist Found Guilty," http://archives.cnn.com/ 2001/LAW/05/19/utah.polygamy/index.html, Accessed August 11, 2008.

4. Ibid.

5. Ibid.

6. CBS News, "Polygamist Will Appeal," http://www.cbsnews.com/stories/2002/08/28/national/main520012.shtml, Accessed August 11, 2008.

7. Melvyn C. Goldstein, "Pahair and Tibetan Polyandry Revisited," The Center for Research on Tibet, http://www.case.edu/affil/tibet/tibetanSociety/marriage.htm, Accessed July 28, 2008.

8. Ibid.

9. U.S. Census Bureau, "Estimated Median Age at First Marriage, by Sex: 1890 to the Present," http://www.census.gov/population/www/socdemo/hh-fam.html#ht, Accessed August 1, 2008.

10. Steven L. Nock, "Marriage as a Public Issue, The Future of Children," *Marriage and Child Wellbeing*, 2005. 15, 2: 13–32.

11. U.S. Census Bureau, "Estimated Median Age at First Marriage, by Sex: 1890 to the Present," http://www.census.gov/population/www/socdemo/hh-fam.html#ht, Accessed August 1, 2008.

12. Ibid.

13. Larry L. Bumpass, James A. Sweet, and Andrew Cherlin, "The Role of Cohabitation in Declining Rates of Marriage," *Journal of Marriage and the Family*, 1991. 53: 913–927.

14. Urban Institute, "Introduction," http://www.urban.org/publications/310962.html, Accessed July 20, 2008.

15. Larry L. Bumpass, James A. Sweet, and Andrew Cherlin, "The Role of Cohabitation in Declining Rates of Marriage," *Journal of Marriage and the Family*, 1991. 53: 913–927.

16. Andrew J. Cherlin and Frank F. Furstenberg, Jr., "Stepfamilies in the United States: A Reconsideration," *Annual Review of Sociology*, 1994. 20: 359–381.

17. Herbert L. Smith, S. Philip Morgan, and Tanya Koropeckyj-Cox, "A Decomposition of Trends in the Nonmarital Fertility Ratios of Blacks and Whites in the United States, 1960–1992." *Demography*, 1996. 33: 141–151.

18. Sara McLanahan and Christine Percheski, "Family Structure and the Reproduction of Inequalities," *The Annual Review of Sociology*, April 14, 2008. 34: 12.1–12.19.

19. Michael J. Rosenfeld and Byung-Soo Kim, "The Independence of Young Adult and the Rise of Interracial and Same-Sex Unions," *American Sociological Review*, 2005. 70: 541–562.

20. Ibid.

21. David Popenoe, "American Family Decline, 1960–1990: A Review and Appraisal," *Journal of Marriage and the Family*, 1993. 55: 527–542.

22. Michael J. Rosenfeld and Byung-Soo Kim, "The Independence of Young Adult and the Rise of Interracial and Same-Sex Unions," *American Sociological Review*, 2005. 70: 541–562.

23. Stephanie Coontz, *The Way We Never Were: American Families and the Nostalgia Trap* (New York: Basic Books, 2000), 24.

24. Ibid.

25. Mitchell, Graham. "The Global Context for U.S. Technology Policy." U.S. Department of Commerce, Accessed September 4, 2008. http://64.233.167.104/search?q5cache:vwk_7M-5KoJ:www.technology.gov/Reports/globalcontext/nas.pdf/WWII/US/government/industrial/gov/site:.gov&hl5en&ct5clnk&cd519&gl5us

26. Stephanie Coontz, *The Way We Never Were: American Families and the Nostalgia Trap* (New York: Basic Books, 2000), 37.

27. Ibid.

28. Stephanie Coontz, *The Way We Never Were: American Families and the Nostalgia Trap* (New York: Basic Books, 2000), 172.

29. Stephanie Coontz, *The Way We Never Were: American Families and the Nostalgia* (New York: Basic Books, 2000), 35.

30. Ibid.

31. Ronald R. Rindfuss, Minja Kim-Choe, and Larry L. Bumpass, "Social Networks and Family Change in Japan," *American Sociological Review*, Dec, 2004. 69: 838–861.

32. Ibid.

33. Noriko O. Tsuya, "Gender, Employment, and Housework in Japan," Paper presented at the annual meeting of the Population Association of America, Boston, MA, April 1–3, 2004.

34. Minja Kim-Choe, Larry L. Bumpass, and Noriko O. Tsuya, "Employment," from *Marriage, Work, and Family Life in Comparative Perspective: Japan, South Korea, and the United States*, ed. Noriko O. Tsuya and Larry L. Bumpass (Honolulu, HI: University of Hawaii Press, 2004), 95–113.

35. Ronald R. Rindfuss, Minja Kim-Choe, and Larry L. Bumpass, "Social Networks and Family Change in Japan," *American Sociological Review*, Dec, 2004. 69: 838–861.

36. Ibid.

37. Maurice R. Davie and Ruby Jo Reeves, "Propinquity of Residence Before Marriage," *The American Journal of Sociology*, 1939. 44: 510–517; Joseph R. Marches and Gus Turbeville, "The Effect of Residential Propinquity on Marriage Selection," *The American Journal of Sociology*, May, 1953. 58: 592–595; James H. S. Bossard, "Residential Propinquity as a Factor in Marriage Selection," *The American Journal of Sociology*, 1932. 38: 219–224.

38. Michael P. Johnson, John P. Caughlin, and Ted L. Huston, "The Tripartite Nature of Marital Commitment: Personal, Moral, and Structural Reasons to Stay Married," *Journal of Marriage and the Family*, 1999. 61, 1: 160–177.

39. Duane W. Crawford, Renate M. Houts, Ted L. Huston, and Laura J. George, "Compatibility, Leisure, and Satisfaction in Marital Relationships," *Journal of Marriage and the Family* 2002. 64, 2: 433–449.

40. Ibid.

41. Daphne Stevens, Gary Kiger, and Pamela Riley, "Working Hard and Hardly Working: Domestic Labor and Marital Satisfaction Among Dual-Earner Couples," *Journal of Marriage and Family*, 2002. 63: 514–526.

42. Ibid.

43. Ibid.

44. Center for Nutrition Policy and Promotion, United States Department of Agriculture, "Expenditures on Children by Families, 2006," Pub. No. 1528–2006 http://www.cnpp.usda.gov/Publications/CRC/crc2006.pdf.

45. Sara McLanahan and Christine Percheski, "Family Structure and the Reproduction of Inequalities," *The Annual Review of Sociology*, 2008. 34: 12.1–12.19.

46. Lisa Strohschein, "Household Income Histories and Child Mental Health Trajectories," *Journal of Health and Social Behavior*, 2005. 46: 359–375.

47. Robert Schoen, Young J. Kim, Constance A. Nathanson, Jason Fields, and Nan Marie Astone, "Why Do Americans Want Children?" *Population and Development Review*, June 1997. 23: 333–358.

48. S. H. Preston and J. McDonald, "The Incidence of Divorce Within Cohorts of American Marriage Contracted Since the Civil War," *Demography* 1979. 16:1–26.

49. U.S. Census Bureau, http://www.census.gov/population/socdemo/marital-hist/ 2004/Table3.2004.xls, Accessed July 2008.

50. "Live Births, Deaths, Marriages, and Divorces: 1950 to 2001," 2003 Abstract of the United States, U.S. Census Bureau, http://www.census.gov/prod/2004pubs/03statab/vitstat.pdf, Accessed October 8, 2008.

51. Stephanie Coontz, *Marriage, A History: How Love Conquered Marriage* (New York, Penguin: 2006).

52. Lillian B. Rubin, "Women of a Certain Age: The Midlife Search for Self," *Contemporary Sociology*, May, 1981. 10: 460–462.

53. Arlene Saluter and Terry Lugaila, "Marital Status and Living Arrangements: March 1996," *Current Population Reports: Population Characteristics*, http://www.census.gov/prod/3/98pubs/p20-496.pdf, Accessed August 21, 2008.

54. Michael J. Rosenfeld, *The Age of Independence: Interracial Unions, Same Sex Unions and the Changing American Family* (Cambridge, MA: Harvard University Press, 2007).

55. Michael J. Brien, Stacy Dickert-Conlin, and David A. Weaver, "Widows Waiting to Wed? (Re)Marriage and Economic Incentives in Social Security Widow Benefits," *The Journal of Human Resources*, Summer, 2004. 39: 585–623.

56. Stephanie Coontz, *Marriage, A History: How Love Conquered Marriage* (New York, Penguin: 2006); Divorce Reform, "No Fault Divorce Laws and Divorce Rates in the United States and Europe," http://www.divorcereform.org/DivorceLawAbstract.html, Accessed August 7, 2008; Divorce Reform, "European Divorce Rates, Waiting Periods, and Reconciliation Counseling Laws," http://www.divorcereform.org/EuropeanRatesChart.html, Accessed August 7, 2008.

57. A. Kroska, "The Division of Labor at Home: A Review and Reconceptualization," *Social Psychology Quarterly*, 1997. 60: 304–322.

58. Stephanie Coontz, *Marriage, A History: From Obedience to Intimacy, or How Love Conquered Marriage* (New York: Viking Adult, 2005), Stephanie Coontz, *The Way We Never Were: American Families and the Nostalgia Trap* (New York: Basic Books, 2000), 18.

59. Steven L. Nock, *Marriage in Men's Lives* (New York: Oxford University Press, 1998).

60. Daphne Stevens, Gary Kiger, and Pamela Rilely, "Working Hard and Hardly Working: Domestic Labor and Marital Satisfaction Among Dual-Earner Couples," *Journal of Marriage and Family*, 2002. 1963: 514–526.

61. Arlie Russell Hochschild with Anne Machung, *The Second Shift: Working Parents and the Revolution at Home* (New York: Penguin Books, 1989/2003).

62. Herbert Bynder, "Émile Durkheim and the Sociology of the Family," *Journal of Marriage and Family*, 1969. 31: 527–533.

63. David Popenoe, "American Family Decline, 1960–1990: A Review and Appraisal," *Journal of Marriage and the Family*, Aug, 1993. 55: 527–542.

64. Ibid.

65. Ibid.

66. "States Issues," DOMA Watch: Your Legal Source for Defense of Marriage Acts Information, http://www.domawatch.org/index.php, Accessed October 8, 2008.

67. "The Vermont Guide to Civil Unions," Civil Unions/Marriage, http://www.sec. state.vt.us/municipal/civil_mar.htm, Accessed October 8, 2008.

68. Michael J. Rosenfeld, *The Age of Independence: Interracial Unions, Same Sex Unions and the Changing American Family* (Cambridge, MA: Harvard University Press, 2007).

69. "Less Opposition to Gay Marriage, Adoption, and Military Service," The Pew Research Center for the People and the Press, http://people-press.org/report/273/less-opposition-to-gay-marriage-adoption-and-military-service, Accessed October 8, 2008.

70. William Meezan and Jonathan Rauch, "The Future of Children," *Marriage and Child Wellbeing*, 2005. 15: 97–115.

CHAPTER 15

1. From *Savage Inequalities* by Jonathan Kozol, copyright © 1991 by Jonathan Kozol. Used by permission of Crown Publishers, a division of Random House, Inc.

2. Annette Hemmings, "The 'Hidden' Corridor Curriculum," *High School Journal*, 2000. 83(2): 1–10.

3. Francisco O. Ramirez and John Boli, "The Political Construction of Mass Schooling: European Origins and Worldwide Institutionalization," *Sociology of Education*, 1987. 60:2–17.

4. John Andrew Hostetler, *Amish Society* (Baltimore: The Johns Hopkins University Press, 1993).

5. "Under-privileged Children Also Disadvantaged in the Classroom," *UNESCO Institute for Statistics*, May 29, 2005, http://www.uis.unesco.org/ev.php?ID5 7200_ 201&ID25DO_TOPIC.

6. "Literacy Rates," *UNESCO Institute for Statistics*, http://stats.uis.unesco.org/ unesco/TableViewer/document.aspx?ReportId5121&IF_Language5eng&BR_Co untry56940, Accessed August 12, 2008; "Sierra Leone," The Central Intelligence Agency's *World Fact Book*, https://www.cia.gov/library/publications/the-world-factbook/print/sl.html, Accessed July 17, 2008.

7. "Global Education Spending Concentrated in a Handful of Countries," *UIS Global Education Digest 2007*, October 2007, www.uis.unesco.org/GED2007.

8. "Digest of Education Statistics: 2007," *Institute of Educational Sciences*, http://nces.ed.gov/programs/digest/d07/, Accessed July 17, 2007.

9. "Percent of People 25 Years and Over Who Have Completed High School or College, by Race, Hispanic Origin and Sex: Selected Years 1940 to 2007," *U.S. Census Bureau*, http://www.census.gov/population/socdemo/education/ cps2007/tabA-2.xls, Accessed September 2, 2008.

10. Jonathan Kozol, *Savage Inequalities: Children in America's Schools* (New York: Crown Publishers, 1992).

11. Robert Rosenthal and Lenore Jacobson, *Pygmalion in the Classroom* (New York: Holt, 1968).

12. Hussain Al-Fadhili and Madhu Singh, "Teachers' Expectancy and Efficacy as Correlates of School Achievement in Delta, Mississippi," *Journal of Personnel Evaluation in Education*, 2006. 19(1–2): 51–67.

13. Margaret R. Kuklinksy and Rhona S. Weinstein, "Classroom and Developmental Differences in a Path Model of Teacher Expectancy Effects," *Child Development*, 2001. 72(5): 1554–1579.

14. "America's High School Graduates: Results from the 2005 NAEP High School Transcript Study," *The National Center for Educational Statistic*, http://nces.ed. gov/nationsreportcard/pdf/studies/2007467.pdf, Accessed September 4, 2008.

15. Rebecca Aronauer, "Princeton's War on Grade Inflation Drops the Number of A's," *Chronicle of Higher Education*, 2005. 52(6): A41.

16. "Homeschooling in the United States: 2003," *U.S. Department of Education*, http://nces.ed.gov/pubs2006/2006042.pdf, Accessed July 17, 2008.

17. Crista L. Green and Kathleen Hoover-Dempsey, "Why do Parents Homeschool?" *Education & Urban Society*, 2007. 39(2): 264–285.

18. "2007–2008 College Cost," College Board, http://www.collegeboard.com/ student/pay/add-it-up/4494.html, Accessed July 14, 2008.

19. "Higher Education," Estia in Sweden, http://www.estia.educ.goteborg.se/sv-estia/edu/edu_sys5.html, Accessed September 2, 2008.

20. Randall Collins, *The Credential Society* (New York: Academic Press, 1979); Randall Collins, "Functional and Conflict Theories of Educational Stratification," *American Sociological Review*, 1971. 36: 1002–1019.

21. Mark D. Regenerus, "Religion and Positive Adolescent Outcomes: A Review of Research and Theory," *Review of Religious Research*, 2003. 44(4): 394–413.

22. Ibid.

23. Ibid.

24. Min Zhou and Carl L. Bankston, III, "Social Capital and the Adaptation of the Second Generation: The Case of Vietnamese Youth in New Orleans," in *The New Second Generation*, Alejandro Portes (ed.) (New York: Russell Sage Foundation, 1996), 197–220.

25. "Selected Characteristics of Public School Teachers: Selected Years, Spring 1961 Through Spring 2001," *Digest of Educational Statistics*, http://nces.ed.gov/ programs/digest/d05/tables/dt05_068.asp, Accessed July 9, 2008; "Secondary Education: Teacher's Characteristics," *Institute of Educational Sciences*, http://nces.ed.gov/surveys/international/intlindicators/ index.asp?SectionNumber53&SubSectionNumber56&IndicatorNumber584, Accessed July 9, 2008; "2008 Federal Holidays," *National Archives News*, http://www.archives.gov/news/federal-holidays.html, Accessed July 9, 2008; Emily Brady, "For Muslim Students, A Drive to Deem Holy Days as Holidays," *The New York Times*, April 29, 2007, http://www.nytimes. com/2007/04/29/nyregion/thecity/29holi.html.

26. Emile Durkheim, *Elementary Forms of the Religious Life*, translated by Karen Fields (New York: Free Press, 1912/1995).

27. Ibid.

28. Huston Smith, *The World's Religions: Our Great Wisdom Traditions* (New York: Harper-Collins, 1958/1991).

29. Ibid.

30. Emile Durkheim, *Elementary Forms of the Religious Life*, translated by Karen Fields (New York: Free Press. 1912/1995); Huston Smith, *The World's Religions: Our Great Wisdom Traditions* (New York: Harper-Collins, 1991/1958).

31. Emile Durkheim, *Elementary Forms of the Religious Life*, translated by Karen Fields (New York: Free Press. 1912/1995); Huston Smith, *The World's Religions: Our Great Wisdom Traditions* (NY: Harper-Collins, 1958/1991); Mark Schumaker, "Shintoism-The Way of the Gods," *Gods of Japan: A-to-Z Photo Dictionary*, February 26, 2008, http://www.onmarkproductions.com/html/ shinto.shtml.

32. "Yearbook of Immigration Statistics, 2007, Table 3," *Department of Homeland Security*, April 2, 2008, http://www.dhs.gov/ximgtn/statistics/publications/ LPR07.shtm.

33. Ariela Keysar and Barry A. Kosmin, "International Survey: Worldviews and Opinions of Scientists: India 2007–2008 Summary Report," *Institute for the Study of Secularism in Society and Culture*, Trinity College, http://www.trincoll.edu/ secularisminstitute/, Accessed September 2, 2008.

34. Prema A. Kurien, "Multiculturalism and 'American' Religion: The Case of Hindu Indian Americans," *Social Forces*, 2006. 85(2): 723–741.

35. Prema Kurien, "Multiculturalism, Immigrant Religion, and Diasporic Nationalism: The Development of an American Hinduism," *Social Problems*, 2004. 51(3): 362–385.

36. Benton Johnson, "On Church and Sect," *American Sociological Review*, 1963. 28: 539–549.

37. Hoa Omid, "Theocracy or Democracy? The Critics of 'Westoxification' and the Politics of Fundamentalism in Iran," *Third World Quarterly*, 1992. 13(4): 675–690.

38. Emile Durkheim, *Elementary Forms of the Religious Life* (London: George Allen and Unwin, 1976).

39. "A Humanist discussion of . . . The Golden Rule," *British Humanist Association*, February 2006, http://www.humanism.org.uk/site/cms/contentViewArticle. asp? article51222.

40. Karl Marx, *Karl Marx: Selected Writings*, 2nd edition, David McLellan ed (Oxford: Oxford University Press, 1844/2000).

41. Ibid.

42. Max Weber, *The Protestant Ethic and a Spirit of Capitalism: and Other Writings*, Translated by Peter Caehr and Gordon C. Wells (New York: Penguin Books, 2002).

43. Ibid.

44. Peter Berger, *The Sacred Canopy: Elements of the Sociology of Religion* (Garden City, NY: Doubleday, 1969).

45. Ibid.

46. Peter Berger, "The Desecularization of the World, a Global Overview. In: *The Desecularization of the World: Resurgent Religion and World Politics*, Peter Berger ed. (Grand Rapids, MI: Eerdmans, 1999) 1–18.

47. Robert Bellah, Richard Madsen, William M. Sullivan, Ann Swidler, and Steve Tipton, "Habits of the Heart: Individualism and Commitment in American Life," (University of California Press, 1996).

48. Michael Hout, Andrew Greeley, and Melissa Wilde, "The Demographic Imperative in Religious Change in the United States," *The American Journal of Sociology*, 2001. 107(2): 468–500

49. James Henslin, *Sociology: A Down to Earth Approach*, 6th edition (Boston: Pearson Custom, 2005).

50. Michael Hout, Andrew Greeley, and Melissa Wilde, "The Demographic Imperative in Religious Change in the United States," *The American Journal of Sociology*, 2001. 107(2): 468–500.

51. Ibid.

52. "Self-Described Religious Identification of Adult Population: 1990 and 2001," The American Religious Identification Survey 2001, *Statistical Abstract of the United States*, http://www.census.gov/compendia/statab/tables/08s0074.pdf, Accessed August 29, 2008.

53. Luisa Kroll, "Megachurches, Megabusinesses," *Forbes.com*, September 17, 2003, http://www.forbes.com/2003/09/17/cz_lk_0917megachurch.html.

54. "The Amish," Encyclopedia Britannica, http://search.eb.com/eb/article-233461, Accessed July 11, 2008.

55. "Martin Luther King, Jr.: Biography," The Nobel Foundation, http://nobelprize. org/nobel_prizes/peace/laureates/1964/king-bio.html, Accessed September 3, 2008.

56. Megan Wilde, "Galileo and the Inquisition," *The Galileo Project*, http://galileo. rice.edu/bio/narrative_7.html, Accessed September 2, 2008.

57. Shirley Ann Rainey, "Great Chain of Being," *Encyclopedia of Race and Racism*, (New York: MacMillan, 2007), at http://personal.uncc.edu/jmarks/pubs/ Enc percent20race percent20GCOB.pdf.

58. "Amaterasu," Encyclopedia Britannica. http://search.eb.com/eb/article-9006019, Accessed September 2, 2008; "Religion & Ethics: Shinto—The Imperial Family," *BBC.com*, http://www.bbc.co.uk/religion/religions/ shinto/texts/stories_5.shtml, Accessed September 2, 2008.

59. Barbara L. Schneider and Venesa Keester, "School Reform 2007: Transforming Education into a Scientific Enterprise," *Annual Review of Sociology*, 2007. 33: 197–217.

60. "Vouchers," National Education Association, http://www.nea.org/vouchers/index.html, Accessed September 24, 2008.

61. "Kozol Sees Hypocrisy with Testing Craze," Wisconsin Education Association Council, October 27, 2000, http://www.weac.org/News/2000-01/oct00/kozol.htm.

62. Terry M. Moe, *Private Vouchers* (Stanford: Hoover Institute Press, 1995).

63. Clive Belfield and Henry M. Levin, "Vouchers and Public Policy: When Ideology Trumps Evidence," *American Journal of Education*, 2005. 111(4): 548–568.

CHAPTER 16

1. "Common Challenges, Common Wealth", from *Common Wealth: Economics for a Crowded Planet* by Jeffrey Sachs, copyright © 2008 by Jeffrey Sachs. Used by permission of The Penguin Press, a division of Penguin Group (USA) Inc.

2. "Beijing Lights Up Olympic Dream," http://beijingolympic2008.wordpress.com/category/ opening-ceremony/, Accessed September 16, 2008.

3. Pat Hudson, *The Industrial Revolution: Reading History* (New York: Hodder Arnold, 1992).

4. Jerry Evensky, "Adam Smith's 'Theory of Moral Sentiments' On Morals and Why They Matter to a Liberal Society of Free People and Free Markets," *The Journal of Economic Perspectives*, 2005. 19(3): 109–130.

5. Molly Espey, "Explaining the Variation in Elasticity Estimates of Gasoline Demand in the United States: A Meta-analysis," *Energy Journal*, 1996. 17(3): 49–60.

6. James M. Poterba, "Stock Market Wealth and Consumption," *The Journal of Economic Perspectives*, 2000. 14(2): 99–118.

7. Leslie Sklair and Peter Robbins, "Global Capitalism and Major Corporations from the Third World," *Third World Quarterly*, 2002. 23(1): 81–100.

8. Tamas Krausz, "Stalin's Socialism-Today's Debates on Socialism: Theory, History and Politics," *Contemporary Politics*, 2005. 11(4): 235–257.

9. Democratic Socialists of America, http://www.dsausa.org/dsa.html, Accessed July 16, 2008.

10. Noel Thompson, *Political Economy and the Labour Party: The Economics of Democratic Socialism 1884–1995* (London: UCL Press, 1996).

11. T.R. Reid, *The United States of Europe: The New Superpower and the End of American Supremacy* (New York: Penguin, 2004).

12. Stefan Svallfors, "Worlds of Welfare and Attitudes to Redistribution: A Comparison of Eight Western Nations," *European Sociological Review*, 1997. 13(3): 283–304.

13. Jan Tinbergen, "Do Communist and Free Economies Show A Converging Pattern?" *Soviet Studies*, 1961. 12(4): 333–341.

14. Lev Deliusin, "Chinese Capitalism or Socialism with Specific Chinese Features?" *Problems of Economic Transition*, 1994. 37(3): 24–45.

15. Dwight Perkins, "Completing China's Move to the Market," *The Journal of Economic Perspectives*, 1994. 8(2): 23–46.

16. Xiaogang Wu and Yu Xie, "Does the Market Pay Off? Earnings Returns to Education in Urban China," *American Sociological Review*, 2003. 68(3): 425–442.

17. Jan Tinbergen, "Do Communist and Free Economies Show A Converging Pattern?" *Soviet Studies*, 1961. 12(4): 333–341.

18. BBC News. "Profile: Hugo Chavez," December 5, 2002, http://news.bbc.co.uk/1/ hi/world/americas/1925236.stm.

19. U.S. Census Bureau, "Employment Projections by Occupation: 2004 to 2014," http://www.census.gov/compendia/statab/tables/08s0600.pdf, Accessed September 9, 2008.

20. U.S. Census Bureau, "Civilian Labor Force and Participation Rates With Projections: 1980 to 2014," http://www.census.gov/compendia/statab/tables/08s0570.pdf, Accessed September 9, 2008.

21. Bureau of Labor Statistics, "Labor Force Statistics From the Current Population Survey: Frequently Asked Questions," http://www.bls.gov/cps/faq.htm#Ques5, Accessed September 9, 2008.

22. Bureau of Labor Statistics, "Employment Status of the Civilian Population by Gender and Age," http://www.bls.gov/news.release/empsit.t01.htm, Accessed September 9, 2008.

23. Patricia Thornton, "The Sociology of Entrepreneurship," *Annual Review of Sociology*, 1999. 25: 19–46.

24. "Get Ready," U.S. Small Business Administration, http://www.sba.gov/smallbusinessplanner/plan/getready/SERV_SBPLANNER_ISENTFORU.html, Accessed October 10, 2008.

25. Eddie Evans and Keven Krolicki, "Congress Passes Bailout, Focus Shifts to Fallout," October 3, 2008, Reuters.com, www.reuters.com/article/topnews/idUSTRE42967J20081003, Accessed October 10, 2008.

26. Paul Krugman, "The Power of DE," *New York Times,* 8 September 2008, Section A, Column O, p. 23.

27. Emma Rothschild, "Adam Smith and the Invisible Hand," *The American Economic Review*, 1994. 84(2): 319–322.

28. Vernon Hill, "Financial Crisis—How'd We Get Here, and What's Next?" *U.S. News and World Report,* 1 October 2008, http://www.usnews.com/articles/opinion/2008/10/01/the-financial-crisis—howd-we-get-here-and-whats-next.html, Accessed October 10, 2008.

29. Edmund L. Andrews and Mark Landler, "Treasury and Fed Looking at Options," *New York Times,* 30 September 2008, nytimes.com, www.nytimes.com/2008/09/30/business/30plan.html, Accessed October 10, 2008.

30. Rémy Herrera, "The Effects of the US 'Embargo' Against Cuba," *Alternatives.ca,* October 7, 2003, http://www.alternatives.ca/article876.html.

31. North American Free Trade Agreement, *usda.com*, http://www.fas.usda.gov/itp/Policy/NAFTA/nafta.asp, Accessed August 5, 2008.

32. "NAFTA Facts," *Office of the United States Trade Representative*, March 2008, http://www.ustr.gov/assets/Document_Library/Fact_Sheets/2008/asset_upload_file855_14540.pdf.

33. Max Weber, *Economy and Society: An Outline of Interpretive Sociology* (New York: Bedminster Press, 1968).

34. Max Weber, *Economy and Society: An Outline of Interpretive Sociology*, ed. Guether Roth and Clause Wittich (Berkeley: University of California Press, 1925/1978).

35. Jane Perlez, "In Musharraf's Wake, U.S. Faces Political Disarry," *The New York Times,* August 18, 2008, http://www.nytimes.com/2008/08/19/world/asia/19pstan.html?hp; "Profile: Pervez Musharraf," *BBC Online*, August 18, 2008, http://news.bbc.co.uk/2/hi/south_asia/4797762.stm.

36. Norman Naimark, "Totalitarian States and the History of Genocide," *Telos,* 2006. 136:10–25; Marie O'Brien, "Dissent and the Emergence of Civil Society in Post-totalitarian China," *Journal of Contemporary China*, 1998. 7(17): 153–167.

37. Norman Naimark, "Totalitarian States and the History of Genocide" *Telos,* 2006. 136: 10–25.

38. Robert Michels, *Political Parties: A Sociological Study of the Oligarchical Tendencies of Modern Democracy,* translated by Eden and Cedar Paul (New York: Free Press, 1911/1962).

39. "Voting Age Population, Percent Reporting Registered, and Voted: 1972 to 2006," *U.S. Census,* http://www.census.gov/compendia/statab/tables/08s0404.xls, Accessed September 15, 2008.

40. Plato, *The Republic*, translated by Desmond Lee (New York: Penguin Classics, 2007.)

41. Dwight G. Dean, "Alienation and Political Apathy," *Social Forces*, 1960. 38(3): 185–189.

42. Priscilla L. Southwell, "The Effect of Political Alienation on Voter Turnout 1964–2000," *Journal of Political and Military Sociology,* 2008. 36(1): 131–145.

43. "Busier Lifestyles, Increased Apathy Mean Fewer Voters," *Population Today,* 1998. 26(10): 8–14.

44. Seymour Lipset, *American Exceptionalism* (New York: Norton, 1997).

45. "What We Stand For," www.democrats.org/, Accessed September 15, 2008.

46. "2008 Republican Platform," http://www.gop.com/pdf/PlatformFINAL_With Cover.pdf, Accessed September 8, 2008.

47. Carl Grafton and Anne Permaloff, "Liberal and Conservative Dissensus in Areas of Domestic Public Policy Other than Business and Economics," *Policy Sciences,* 2005. 38(1): 45–67.

48. "Geraldine A. Ferraro," Encyclopædia Britannica, 2008, Encyclopædia Britannica Online, http://search.eb.com/eb/article-9034089, Accessed October 14, 2008.

49. McCain-Palin 2008, http://www.johnmccain.com/, Accessed October 14, 2008.

50. Obama for America, http://www.barackobama.com/index.php/, Accessed October 14, 2008.

51. Thomas L. Brunell, "The Relationship between Political Parties and Interest Groups: Explaining Patterns of PAC Contributions to Candidates for Congress, *Political Research Quarterly,* 2005. 58(4): 681–688.

52. The Center for Responsive Politics, "Leadership PACS," http://www.opensecrets. org/pacs/industry.php?txt5Q03&cycle52008, Accessed September 11, 2008.

53. Arthur H. Miller and Ola Listhaug, "Political Parties and Confidence in Government: A Comparison of Norway, Sweden and the United States," *British Journal of Political Science,* 1990. 20(3): 357–386.

54. Ibid.

55. Ibid.

56. C. Wright Mills, *The Power Elite. A New Edition* (New York: Oxford University Press, 1956/2000).

57. C. Wright Mills, *The Power Elite. A New Edition* (New York: Oxford University Press, 1956/2000); G. Williams Domhoff, *Who Rules America? Power, Politics, and Social Change,* 5th edition (New York: McGraw-Hill, 2006).

58. Dwight D. Eisenhower, "Military-Industrial Complex Speech," 1961, http://www.yale.edu/lawweb/avalon/presiden/speeches/eisenhower001.htm, Accessed August 5, 2008.

59. James Fallows, "The Military-Industrial Complex," *Foreign Policy,* 2002. 133: 46–48.

60. Stacy May, "Butter, Guns or Both," *Proceedings of the Academy of Political Science,* Jan. 1942. 19(4), American Industry in a War of Machines: 7–13.

61. Alex Mintz and Chi Huang, "Guns versus Butter: The Indirect Link," *American Journal of Political Science,* 1991. 35(3): 738–757.

62. Jim Garamone, "Defense Officials Discuss Budget Assumptions," *American Forces Press Service*, February 6, 2008, http://www.defenselink.mil/news/newsarticle. aspx?id548881.

63. Errol A. Henderson, "Military Spending and Poverty," *The Journal of Politics,* May 1998. 60(2): 503–520.

64. Benjamin Fordham, "The Political and Economic Sources of Inflation in the American Military Budget," *The Journal of Conflict Resolution*, 2003. 47(5): 574–593.

65. William Hartung and Frida Berrigan, "Top Pentagon Contractors, FY 2006: Major Beneficiaries of the Bush Administration's Military Buildup," *A World Policy Institute Special Report,* March 2007.

66. C. Wright Mills, *The Power Elite. A New Edition* (New York: Oxford University Press, 1956/2000); G. Williams Domhoff, *Who Rules America? Power, Politics, and Social Change,* 5th edition (New York: McGraw-Hill, 2006).

67. Ben Bagdikian, *The New Media Monopoly* (Boston: Beacon Press, 2004).

68. Jeffrey D. Sachs, *Common Wealth: Economics for a Crowded Planet* (New York: Penguin Press, 2008).

69. U.S. Department of Veterans Affairs, "VA Benefits & Health Care Utilization," http://www1.va.gov/vetdata/docs/436_summer08_sharepoint.pdf, Accessed September 12, 2008.

70. Department of Veterans Affairs, "Health Status," http://www1.va.gov/vetdata/docs/HEALTH_STATUS.doc, Accessed September 12, 2008.

71. Hal Bernton, "Returning Veterans Say Benefits Aren't Keeping up with Needs," *The Seattle Times*, August 4, 2005, http://seattletimes.nwsource.com/html/localnews/2002419658_murrayhearing4m.html.

72. U.S Department of Veterans Affairs: National Center for PTSD, "How Common is PTSD?" http://www.ncptsd.va.gov/ncmain/ncdocs/fact_shts/fs_how_common_is_ptsd.html?opm51&rr5rr1363&srt5d&echorr5true, Accessed September 12, 2008.

73. Dana Priest and Anne Hull, "Soldiers Face Neglect, Frustration At Army's Top Medical Facility," *Washington Post*, February 18, 2007, http://www.washingtonpost.com/wp-dyn/content/article/2007/02/17/AR2007021701172.html.

74. Guy Raz, "Walter Reed Scandal Unfolds with General's Firing," *NPR*, March 2, 2007, http://www.npr.org/templates/story/story.php?storyId57681867.

75. Dana Priest and Anne Hull, "Soldiers Face Neglect, Frustration At Army's Top Medical Facility," *Washington Post*, February 18, 2007, http://www.washingtonpost.com/wp-dyn/content/article/2007/02/17/AR2007021701172.html.

CHAPTER 17

1. "The Beginning", from *Blessed Unrest* by Paul Hawken, copyright © 2007 by Paul Hawken. Used by permission of Viking Penguin, a division of Penguin Group (USA) Inc.

2. Pat Hudson, *The Industrial Revolution: Reading History* (New York: Hodder Arnold, 1992).

3. U.S. Department of Commerce News, April 2, 2001, http://www.census.gov/Press-Release/www/2001/cb01cn66.html.

4. William Fielding Ogburn, *Social Change with Respect to Cultural and Original Nature* (New York: Dell Publishing Co., 1923/1966).

5. Library of Congress, "Everyday Mysteries: Who Invented the Automobile?" March 1, 2007, http://www.loc.gov/rr/scitech/mysteries/auto.html.

6. "India: Environmental Issues," Energy Information Administration, February 2004, www.earthscape.org/p1/ES2_6242/6242.pdf, Accessed November 6, 2008.

7. Albert Hirschman, *The Rhetoric of Reaction: Perversity, Futility, Jeopardy* (Cambridge, MA: Harvard University Press, 1991).

8. Paul Hawken, *Blessed Unrest: How the Largest Social Movement in History is Restoring Grace, Justice, and Beauty to the World* (New York: Viking Penguin, 2007), 6.

9. "Internet Petitions," *Snopes.com*, http://www.snopes.com/inboxer/petition/internet.asp, Accessed September 11, 2008.

10. Ibid.

11. Ibid.

12. Chris Plante and Rusty Dornin, "Troops sent to Seattle as Part of Terrorism Contingent Plan," *CNN.com*, December 2, 1999; Don Knapp, "Activists to WTO: Put People over Profits," *CNN.com*, November 29, 1999, http://www.cnn.com/US/ 9911/29/wto.seattle.02/; John Vidal, "The Real Battle for Seattle," *Guardian.co.uk*, December 5, 1999, http://www.guardian.co.uk/world/1999/dec/05/wto.globalisation.

13. "Watts Rebellion," King Encyclopedia, http://www.stanford.edu/group/King/about_king/encyclopedia/watts_rebellion.html, Accessed September 11, 2008.

14. Joel Best, *Flavor of the Month: Why Smart People Fall for Fads* (Berkeley, CA: University of California Press, 2006).

15. Ibid.

16. Ibid.

17. "FEMA for Kids: Y2K for Kids," *Federal Emergency Management Agency*, http://www.fema.gov/kids/y2k.htm, Accessed September 11, 2008; "Are You Ready?" *The White House*, February 3, 2003, http://www.whitehouse.gov/news/releases/2003/02/20030207-10.html; Jeanne Meserve, "Duct Tape Sales Rise Amid Terror Fears," *CNN.com*, February 11, 2003, http://www.cnn.com/2003/US/02/11/emergency.supplies/.

18. Jeanne Meserve, "Duct Tape Sales Rise Amid Terror Fears," *CNN.com*, February 11, 2003, http://www.cnn.com/2003/US/02/11/emergency.supplies/.

19. "Selma-to-Montgomery March," National Park Service, http://www.nps.gov/nr/ travel/civilrights/al4.htm, Accessed September 11, 2008; Cindy Hall, "Washington's Great Gatherings," *USA Today*, http://www.usatoday.com/news/index/ nman006.htm, Accessed September 11, 2008.

20. Bernard Guerin and Yoshihiko Miyazaki, "Analyzing Rumors, Gossip, and Urban Legends through Their Conversational Properties," *Psychological Record*, Winter 2006. 56(1): 23.

21. "The Obligatory Wait," *Snopes.com*, http://www.snopes.com/college/admin/wait.asp, Accessed August 5, 2008.

22. Rhett Butler, "Rainforests Face Array of Emerging Threats," *mongabay.com*, June 15, 2008, http://news.mongabay.com/2008/0614-laurance.html.

23. Rainforest Alliance, "Research & Resources: Tropical Forests in Our Daily Lives," http://www.rainforest-alliance.org/resources.cfm?id5daily_lives, Accessed September 11, 2008; J. Louise Mastrantonio and John K. Francis, "A Student Guide to Tropical Forest Conservation," October 1997, http://www.fs.fed.us/global/lzone/student/tropical.htm.

24. World Wildlife Fund, http://wwf.worldwildlife.org/site/PageServer?pagename5can_home&JServSessionIdr01256kimssfum2.app13a, Accessed September 11. 2008; The Nature Conservancy 2008, http://www.nature.org/?src5logo, Accessed September 11, 2008.

25. WWF Amazon Project 2008, http://www.worldwildlife.org/what/wherewework/amazon/item1376.html, Accessed September 11, 2008.

26. Rainforest Action Network: Our Mission and History, http://ran.org/who_we_ are/our_mission_history/, Accessed September 11, 2008.

27. Charles Tilly, *Social Movements, 1768–2004* (Boulder, CO: Paradigm Publishers, 2004).

28. Charles Tilly, *From Mobilization to Revolution* (Reading MA: Addison-Wesley, 1978).

29. Ed Lavendara, "Dodge City Showdown at Funeral," *CNN.com*, March 7, 2006, http://www.cnn.com/2006/US/03/06/btsc.lavandrera.funerals/index.html; Adrienne Mand Lewin, "Military Funeral Protests Outrage Families, Lawmakers," *ABC News*, March 15, 2006, http://abcnews.go.com/US/Politics/Story?id51728788& page 51; Will Rothschild, "Anti-Gay Group to Protest at Soldier's Funeral," *Herald Tribune.com*, January 21, 2006, http://www.heraldtribune.com/apps/pbcs.dll/ article?AID5/20060121/NEWS/601210405.

30. David F. Aberle, *The Peyote Religion Among the Navaho* (University of Oklahoma Press: OK, 1966).

31. Frances A. DellaCava, Norma Kolko Phillips, and Madeline H. Engel, "Adoption in the U.S.: The Emergence of a Social Movement," *Journal of Sociology and Social Welfare*, Dec. 2004, http://findarticles.com/p/articles/mi_m0CYZ/is_4_31/ai_n8681413.

32. "About Us," La Leche League International, http://www.llli.org/ab.html?m51, Accessed September 11, 2008.

33. Emily Bazar and Sam Hemingway, "Nursing Mom Files Complaint Against Airlines," *USA Today*, October 11, 2006, http://www.usatoday.com/travel/news/2006-11-16-breastfeeding_x.htm; Associated Press, "Breast-feeding mothers stage nurse-in" *MSNBC.com*, November 16, 2006, http://www.msnbc.msn. com/id/15755898/.

34. Mike Stobbe, "CDC says Breast-feeding Rates Hit New High of 77 Percent in US," *The Seattle Times*, May 1, 2008, http://seattletimes.nwsource.com/html/health/2004382901_webbreastfeeding30.html.

35. Danuta Otfinowski, "Should Christians Convert Muslims?" *Time*, June 22, 2003, http://www.time.com/time/magazine/article/0,9171,1101030630-460157,00. html?CNN5yes.

36. "Fidel Castro," Encyclopedia Britannica Online, http://www.britannica.com/EBchecked/topic/98822/Fidel-Castro, Accessed September 11, 2008.

37. Charles Tilly, *From Mobilization to Revolution* (Reading, MA: Addison-Wesley Publishing Co., 1978).

38. David A. Locher, *Collective Behavior* (Upper Saddle River: NJ Prentice-Hall, 2002).

39. Robert E. Park and Ernest W. Burgess, *Introduction to the Science of Society, 3rd edition* (Chicago: University of Chicago Press, 1921/1969).

40. William Kornhauser, *The Politics of Mass Society* (New York: Free Press, 1959).

41. Denton E. Morrison, "Some Notes Toward Theory on Relative Deprivation, Social Movements and Social Change," *American Behavioral Scientists*, 1971, 14(5): 675–690; David A. Locher, *Collective Behavior* (Upper Saddle River, NJ: Prentice-Hall, 2002).

42. James Chowning Davies, "The J-Curve and Power Struggle Theories of Collective Violence," *American Sociological Review*, 1974, 39(4): 607–610; James Chownng Davies, *When Men Revolt and Why: A Reader in Political Violence and Revolution* (New York: Free Press, 1970).

43. Ted Robert Gurr, *Why Men Rebel* (Princeton, NJ: Princeton University Press, 1970).

44. Erving Goffman, *Frame Analysis: An Essay on the Organization of Experience* (Cambridge, MA: Harvard University Press, 1974).

45. David A. Snow, E. Burke Rochford, Jr., Steven K. Worden, and Robert D. Benford, "Frame Alignment Processes, Micromobilization, and Movement Participation," *American Sociological Review*, 1986. 51: 464–481.

46. Robert D. Benford and David A. Snow, "Framing Processes and Social Movements: An Overview and Assessment," *Annual Review of Sociology*, 2000. 26: 611–639.

47. Ibid.

48. Ibid.

49. David A. Snow, E. Burke Rochford, Jr., Steven K. Worden, and Robert D. Benford, "Frame Alignment Processes, Micromobilization, and Movement Participation," *American Sociological Review*, 1986. 51: 464–481.

50. Ibid.

51. Ibid.

PHOTO CREDITS

Front Cover Inside Art: Corbis/Jupiter Images, Inc.

CHAPTER 1 PAGE 2: ©BananaStock, Ltd. **4 (from top):** Penguin Group USA, Inc.; Prentice Hall School Division; David Mager/Pearson Learning Photo Studio; **5:** Laima Druskis/Pearson Education/PH College; **6:** ©Louis DeLuca/Dallas Morning News/CORBIS All Rights Reserved; **7 (from top):** Shutterstock; Shutterstock; Shutterstock; Shutterstock; **9:** AP Wide World Photos; **11:** Harry Taylor ©Dorling Kindersley, Courtesy of the Natural History Museum, London; **12:** StockTrek/Getty Images, Inc. Photodisc; **13 (from top):** Courtesy of the Library of Congress; Library of Congress; Corbis/Bettmann; ©American Sociological Association; Harvard University News Office; ©Pictorial Parade/Getty Images **15 (from top):** Shutterstock; Shutterstock; Shutterstock; **16:** Corbis—Brand X Pictures; **17:** Courtesy of the Library of Congress; The Granger Collection, New York; MPI/Getty Images Inc.—Hulton Archive Photos; The Granger Collection; Jack Liu/Jack Liu; **18:** Reza Estakhrian/Getty Images Inc.—Stone Allstock; **21 (from top):** University of Chicago Archive; Courtesy of P.K. Wright, Lyrl Ahern/Lyrl Ahern; Sophie Bassouls/Corbis/Sygma; **23:** Library of Congress; **24 (from top):** Michelle D. Bridwell/PhotoEdit, Inc.; Susanna Price ©Dorling Kindersley; Jose Azel/Aurora Photos, Inc.; SuperStock, Inc.; Spike Mafford/Photodisc/Getty Images; **26 (from top):** Laima Druskis/Pearson Education/PH College; CORBIS All Rights Reserved; Michelle D. Bridwell/PhotoEdit, Inc.

CHAPTER 2 PAGE 28: Tyler Olsen/Shutterstock; **30 (from top):** Transaction Publishers; ©Dorling Kindersley; **31 (from top):** Thomas Kruesselman/Corbis Zefa Collection; Tim Ridley ©Dorling Kindersley; **33:** Angelo Cavelli/Corbis Zefa Collection; **34 (from top):** Shutterstock; Shutterstock; Stephen Aaron Rees/Shutterstock; Bolt/Shutterstock; **36:** Vincent Bensnault/Jupiter Images-Stock Image; **40:** Getty Images; **41 (from top):** Fotocrisis/Shutterstock; Shutterstock; Dreamstime LLC-Royalty Free; **42 (from top):** Zsolt Nyulaszi/Shutterstock; Vospales/Shutterstock; ©Graham Bell/CORBIS All Rights Reserved; ©Graham Bell/CORBIS All Rights Reserved; ©Cultura/CORBIS All Rights Reserved; **44 (from top):** Thomas Kruesselman/Corbis Zefa Collection; Vincent Bensnault/Jupiter Images-Stock Image; Getty Images.

CHAPTER 3 PAGE 46: Mitchell Funk/Getty Images; **48 (from top):** Penguin Group USA, Inc.; ANCIENT ART & ARCHITECTURE/DanitaDelmont.com; ©Perter Harholdt/CORBIS All Rights Reserved; Guy Ryecart ©Dorling Kindersley; **49 (from top):** William Thomas Cain/Stringer/Getty Images; National Archives and Records Administration/THE NATIONAL ARCHIVES STILL PICTURE BRANCH image #179-W-256; **50 (from top):** Iker Caniklgil/Shutterstock; Thomas Sztanek/Shutterstock; Thomas Sztanek/Shutterstock; Lucian Coman/Shutterstock; Frank Micelotta/Getty Images; **51 (from top):** Eduardo Miller/Shutterstock; Andy Z./Shutterstock; **52:** Peter Menzel Photography; **53:** ©Larry W. Smith/CORBIS All Rights Reserved; **54:** Tanushree Punwani/Landov Media; **55 (from top):** National Archives and Records Administration/THE NATIONAL ARCHIVES STILL PICTURE BRANCH image #179-W-256; Dmitriy Aseev/Shutterstock; **57:** Public Citizen; **58 (from top):** Tomislav Forgo/Shutterstock; Jonas Staub/Shutterstock; Oddphoto/Shutterstock; T-Design/Shutterstock; Shutterstock; Junial Enterprises/Shutterstock; James Steidl/Shutterstock; **59:** AP Wide World Photos; **60 (from top):** BRECELJ & HODALIC/Peter Arnold, Inc.; Reuters/Landov; Chad Ehlers/Stock Connection; **62 (from top):** Mitchell Funk/Getty Images; AP Wide World Photos; Tanushree Punwani/Landov Media.

CHAPTER 4 PAGE 64: Hemera Technologies/AbleStock; **66 (from top):** Book cover from THE DIGNITY OF WORKING MEN: MORALITY AND THE BOUNDARIES OR RACE, CLASS, AND IMMIGRATION by Michele Lamont, Cambridge, Mass.: Harvard University Press, Copyright ©2000 by the Russell Sage Foundation.; Cecile Treal and Jean-Michel Ruiz ©Dorling Kindersley **67 (from top):** Shutterstock; Getty Images; Valerie Schultz/Merrill Education; EMG Education Management Group; **69:** Corbis Digital Stock; **70 (from top):** Jupiter Images—Comstock Images; Levgeniia Tikhonova/Shutterstock; ©Alexander Chelmodeev/www.shutterstock.com; **71 (from top):** ©Stephanie Maze/CORBIS All Rights Reserved; Dave Wetzel/Shutterstock; ©Jim Sugar/CORBIS All Rights Reserved; **73 (from top):** Corbis Digital Stock; Natalia Lukiyanova/Shutterstock; Gautier Wilaume/Shutterstock; Getty Images; Inta Eihmane/Shutterstock; Lisa F. Young/Shutterstock; Shutterstock; Yuri Arcurs/Shutterstock; Getty Images, Inc—Stockbyte Royalty Free; Knud Nielsen/Shutterstock; Clara Natoli/Shutterstock; Shutterstock; Fred Goldstein/Shutterstock; ©C. LYTTLE / CORBIS All Rights Reserved; **74 (from top):** Andresr/Shutterstock; Phil Date/Shutterstock; Getty Images; Andresr/Shutterstock; istockphoto.com; istockphoto.com; **75:** ©Ramin Talaie/CORBIS All Rights Reserved; **77:** ©Corbis/SuperStock; **78 (from top):** Picture Desk, Inc./Kobal Collection; Lions Gate/Picture Desk, Inc./Kobal Collection; Peter Anderson ©The British Museum; Angelo Cavalli/Corbis Zefa Collection; **80 (from top):** Corbis Digital Stock; ©Corbis/SuperStock; Angelo Cavalli/Corbis Zefa Collection.

CHAPTER 5 PAGE 82: Ken Karp/Pearson Education/PH College; **84 (from top):** Harper Collins Publishers, Inc.; Dorling Kindersley ©Bethany Dawn; Laura Bolesta/Merrill Education; **85 (from top):** ©Tarhill Photos/CORBIS All Rights Reserved; Trish Gant ©Dorling Kindersley; **86:** Shutterstock; **89 (from top):** Getty Images; Dave King ©Dorling Kindersley; Vanessa Davies ©Dorling Kindersley; Andy Sacks/Getty Images Inc.—Stone Allstock; David Young-Wollf/PhotoEdit; Stephen Derr/Getty Images Inc.—Image Bank; ©Ken Seet/CORBIS All Rights Reserved; Getty Images; **90:** Corbis/Bettmann; **91 (from top):** Shutterstock; Getty Images; Photo by Jerry Bauer. Courtesy of Harvard Graduate School of Education; **92 (from top):** Shutterstock; Shutterstock; **94:** Getty Images; **96 (from top):** Gunter Marx ©Dorling Kindersley; Frank Siteman/Creative Eye/MIRA.com; Pierre Tremblay/Masterfile Corporation; **98 (from top):** ©Tarhill Photos/CORBIS All Rights Reserved; Gunter Marx ©Dorling Kindersley; Frank Siteman/Creative Eye/MIRA.com.

CHAPTER 6 PAGE 100: Dennis MacDonald/PhotoEdit Inc.; **102 (from top):** W.H. FREEMAN AND COMPANY/WORTH PUBLISHERS/ Extraordinary Groups: An Examination of Unconventional Lifestyles by Richard T. Schaefer and William W. Zellner; Keith Brofsky/Getty Images, Inc.—Photodisc; **103 (from top):** ©Rick Gomez/CORBIS All Rights Reserved; ©Jim Craigmyle/CORBIS All Rights Reserved; Shutterstock; istockphoto.com; **104:** Getty Images; **105 (from top):** Kiselev Anddrew Valerevich/Shutterstock; Jochen Sands/Getty Images—Digital Vision; **107:** John Noltner/Aurora Photos, Inc.; **108:** Photofest; **109 (from top):** Monkey Business Images/Shutterstock; Monkey Business Images/Shutterstock; Brian Chase/Shutterstock; Brian Chase/Shutterstock; Dmitriy Shironosov/Shutterstock; Yuri Arcurs/Shutterstock; Andresr/Shutterstock; **110:** A. Ramey/PhotoEdit Inc.; **111:** ©Owen Franken/CORBIS All Rights Reserved; **113 (from top):** argus/Thomas Raupach/Peter Arnold, Inc.; Getty Images; **114 (from top):** Newscom; ©Tom Wagner/Corbis; Getty Images; **116 (from top):** Keith Brofsky/Getty Images, Inc.—Photodisc.; Photofest; istockphoto.com.

CHAPTER 7 PAGE 118: AP Wide World Photos; **120 (from top):** "Promises I Can Keep: Why Poor Women Put Motherhood Before Marriage" by Kathryn Edin and Maria Kefalas; University of California Press, Copyright March 2005; Shutterstock; **121 (from top):** AP Wide World Photos; Shutterstock; **122 (from top):** Valentin Mosichev/Shutterstock; Shutterstock; **123:** ©Nathan Benn/CORBIS All Rights Reserved; **124:** ©Kurt Krieger/CORBIS All Rights Reserved; **125:** Geri Engberg/Geri Engberg Photography; **126 (from top):** Richard Hutchings/Photo Researchers, Inc.; Ryan McVay/Getty Images, Inc.—Photodisc.; Bob Thomas/Getty Images Inc.—Stone Allstock; **129 (from top):** Laura Bolesta/Merrill Education; Laima Druskis/Pearson Education/PH College; Carolyn A. Mckeone/Photo Researchers, Inc.; PhotoDisc/Getty Images, Inc.-Photodisc; Ken Fisher/Getty Images Inc.—Stone Allstock; **130 (from top):** Frank Siteman/Omni-Photo Communications, Inc.; Michal Heron/Pearson Education/PH College; Getty Images; **131 (from top):** Will & Deni McIntyre/Photo Researchers, Inc.; ©Kurt Krieger/CORBIS All Rights Reserved; KEVIN LAUBACHER/Getty Images, Inc.—Taxi; ©Shepard Sherbell/CORBIS All Rights Reserved; **132:** Stephen Jaffe/Getty Images, Inc—Liaison; **134 (from top):** Wally Santana, Stringer/AP Wide World Photos; ©Nathan Benn/CORBIS All Rights Reserved; Stephen Jaffe/Getty Images, Inc—Liaison.

CHAPTER 8 PAGE 136: J.P. Laffont/ZUMA Press—Gamma; **138 (from top):** "Disposable People New Slavery in Global Economy" by Kevin Bales, University of California Press, Copyright November 2004; Dorling Kindersley ©Bethany Dawn; **139 (from top):** Tim Ridley ©Dorling Kindersley; ©John Wilkes/CORBIS All Rights Reserved; EMG Education Management Group; Barnabas Kindersley ©Dorling Kindersley; **140 (from top):** Shutterstock; Shutterstock; Shutterstock; Christopher Conrad/Getty Images, Inc.—Photodisc; **142 (from top):** "Returning from the Cotton Fields in South Carolina", ca. 1860, stereograph by Barbard, negative number 47843. ©Collection of The New-York Historical Society; Malcolm Linton/Getty Images, Inc—Liaison; **144:** Getty Images; **146 (from top):** istockphoto.com; istockphoto.com; istockphoto.com; Shutterstock; Shutterstock; Shutterstock; Shutterstock; **147:** ©Michael S. Yamashita/CORBIS All Rights Reserved; **149:** Shutterstock; **150 (from top):** Victor Englebert/Photo Researchers, Inc.; Dorling Kindersley ©Jamie Marshall; Eric Lansner/Black Star; ©Jon Hicks/CORBIS All Rights Reserved; **152 (from top):** Malcolm Linton/Getty Images, Inc—Liaison; ©Michael S. Yamashita/CORBIS All Rights Reserved; Victor Englebert/Photo Researchers, Inc.

CHAPTER 9 PAGE 154: Uli Wiesmeier/Getty Images Inc.—Stone Allstock; **156 (from top):** Penguin Group USA, Inc.; Shutterstock; **157:** Shutterstock; **161:** Shutterstock; **162:** Photo Researchers, Inc.; **164:** Dr. Jeremy Burgess/Photo Researchers, Inc.; **165 (from top):** ©David Aubrey/CORBIS All Rights Reserved; NASA/Dorling Kindersley Media Library; **166:** Getty Images; **167 (from top):** Argus Fotoarchiv/Peter Arnold, Inc.; Dorling Kindersley ©Rowan Greenwood; ©Spencer Tirey/CORBIS All Rights Reserved; Tony Freeman/PhotoEdit Inc.; **169:** Tomi/Getty Images, Inc.—Pho-

INDEX

Page numbers followed by *f* refer to figures. Page numbers followed by *t* refer to tables.

Absolute poverty, definition, 122, 134

Achieved status, in social structure, 68-69, 80

Achievement and success, dominant value in the U. S., Williams, 52

Activity and work, dominant value in the U. S., Williams, 52

Activity theory
aging process, 220-221
definition, 211, 220-221, 225

Addams, Jane, 16-17

Adoption, same-sex couples, 259

Affirmative action, 187-188

Age, crime and, 229-230

Ageism, definition, 211, 219, 225

Agendas, of research studies, 43

Age-specific birth rate, definition, 157, 170

Age-specific death rate, definition, 158, 170

Aging
biological effects, 211, 219*f*
conflict theory, 221
demographic changes in the U. S., 216-217
functionalism, 220
gender and, 219
health stratification and, 208-225
symbolic interactionism, 220

Agnew, Robert, 238

Agricultural societies, 67, 70-71

Aid to Families with Dependent Children (AFDC), 132

Akeelah and the Bee (film), 264

Akihito, Emperor, 121

Alang ship graveyard, 166

Alienation, definition, 288-289, 297

Allegretto, Sylvia, 141

Alternative social movements, definition, 300, 308*f*-309, 315

Altruistic suicide, 7, 26

Americanization, under the Dawes Act, 77

American Sociological Association
code of ethics, 43
sociology defined, 5

Amplification, definition, 310-311, 315

Amusing Ourselves To Death (Postman), 48, 57

Andersen, John, 307

Animism, definition, 265, 270-271, 279

Annexation, definition, 175, 178, 188

Annual mean inflation rates, U. S., 292*f*

Anomic suicide, 7-8, 26

Anti-natalist, definition, 156, 168-169, 171

Asch, Solomon, cards, 107

Ascribed status, in social structure, 67-69, 80

Assimilation
definition, 49, 56, 63
multiculturalism and, 56, 180
social policy, 61

Assimilationist minorities, definition, 178-179, 188

Attachment, definition, 238, 243

Attack strategies, 303*f*

Authoritarianism, definition, 282

Authoritarian parenting style, 92*f*-93, 98

Authoritarian regimes, definition, 288-289, 297

Authoritative parenting style, 92*f*-93, 98

Autocratic leader, definition, 106, 116

Autonomy *vs.* shame and doubt, Erikson's stages of development, 89*f*

Baby boomers
definition, 158-159, 170
origins, 217

The Bachelor (TV show), 195

Backstage, definition, 66, 75, 80

Bagdikian, Ben, 293

Bales, Kevin, 137-138, 140-143, 147

Batista, Fulgencio, 309

Beccaria, Cesare, 235

Becker, Howard, 20-22

Belief, definition, 238, 243

Belief in inherent morality, in groupthink, 108

Bentham, Jeremy, 235

Bernstein, Jared, 141

Biological changes, aging, 211, 219

Biological perspective, crime, 228, 235

Birth dearth
definition, 160, 170
in Japan, 161

Birth rate, selected countries, 2007, 160

Bissu, definition, 196-197, 206

Blended families, definition, 248-249, 260

Blessed Unrest: How the Largest Social Movement in History is Restoring Grace, Justice, and Beauty to the World (Hawken), 300, 304

Blumer, Herbert, 20-22

Bonilla-Silva, Eduardo, 184

Bosnia, ethnic cleansing, 178

Bounded relationships, definition, 103, 116

Bourdieu, 109

Bourgeoisie
definition, 14, 27, 139
Karl Marx, 14-15, 145

Brahman, Indian priestly and scholar caste, 144

Brain drain, definition, 148, 152

Brazil, toward free market capitalism, 148

Brien, Michael J., 255

Brokovich, Erin, 165

Bugis people, gender roles, 195-196

Bureaucracies
conflict theory and, 113
definition, 103, 110-111, 117

Bureaucratization, definition, 306-307, 315

Bureaucrats, definition, 145, 152

Burns, Scott, 223

Bush, George W., 108

Byrd, James, Jr., 185

Calabai, definition, 196-197, 206

Calalai, definition, 196-197, 206

Calvin, John, 273

Campaigns, definition, 306-307, 315

Capitalism
convergence with socialism, 285-286
definition, 283-284*f*, 296

Capitalist system
cycle of wealth, 15
Karl Marx, 14-15

Caplan, Paula, 213

Cardosa and Faletto, 148

Carr, Deborah, 214

Carrying capacity, definition, 164-165, 170

Case studies, definition, 37, 44

Caste systems
as a social system, 143
definition, 143, 152

Castro, Fidel, 309

Caughlin, John P., 252-253

Causal relationship, definition, 32, 44

Causation, definition, 32, 44

Causes, definition, 30, 32

Cellular phones, access in selected countries, 140*f*

Center for Nutrition Policy and Promotion, USDA, cost of raising a child, 254

Central tendency, measures of, 38-39, 45

Chafetz, Janet, 203

Chappelle's Show (TV show), race issue, 174

Charismatic authority, 101-102

Chattel slavery, definition, 143, 152

Chavez, Hugo, Venezuela and democratic socialism, 285

Cheney, Dick, 108

Childhood obesity, 213-214

Child rearing, 254-255

Chin, Vincent, 182

China
mixed economic system, 285
population control program, 168-169
social systems, 68

Choice model, definition, 198, 206

Church, definition, 272-273, 279

Church networks, 109

Civil religion, definition, 274-275, 279

Class consciousness
definition, 14, 27
Karl Marx, 15

Classical school, crime, 228, 235*f*, 242

Class structure, 121
in the U. S., 124-126

Class systems
Karl Marx, 145
Max Weber, 145
as a social system, 142-143

Clinton, Hillary, 60, 199

Coalescence, definition, 306-307, 315

Coercive organization, definition, 110-111, 117

Cognitive development
definition, 88, 98
stages (Piaget), 85, 88

Cohesiveness, groupthink and, 107

Cohort, definition, 33, 44

Coleman, 109

Collapse (Diamond), 155-156, 162, 164

Collective behavior, 304-305, 314

Collective rationalization, in groupthink, 108

Collectivist views, 53

Colonialism, 16, 176, 188

Color-blind racism, definition, 184–185, 189

The Coming Generational Storm: What You Need to Know About America's Economic Future (Kotlikoff and Burns), 223

Commitment, 246
definition, 238, 243
three types, 253t

The Common Wealth: Economics for a Crowded Planet (Sachs), 282, 285

Communication, access to, 140f

Communitarianism, 26, 59

Community learning. *see* Volunteering

Comparative hypothesis, 58

Comparative studies, definition, 33, 44

Computers and Internet, access in selected countries, 140f

Comte, Auguste, 4

Concentration of power, in an organization, 110

Concepts, definition, 32, 44

Concilio, Arielle, 214

Concrete operational stage, cognitive development, 85, 88, 98

Conflict model of law, definition, 229, 232, 242

Conflict theory, 4–5, 9, 60
aging process, 221–222, 224
bureaucracy, 113
characteristics, 26
comparison of paradigms, 10t, 76–78
culture differentiation, 62
crime, 239
criticism, 18
definition, 8, 26
economic and political systems, 293–294, 296
family, 258, 260
feminism, 202, 204, 206
global stratification, 148, 150, 152
leadership, 116
marriage and family, 256
McDonaldization of the U.S., 59
Native American culture, 77
overlapping theories, 22t
population growth, 170
racism, 186, 188
religion and, 275–276, 278
resocialization and, 94
socialization and, 96, 98
social movements, 309, 313–314
social stratification, 130, 134
social structures, 80
worldview, 14–18

Conformists, definition, 236

Conformity, definition, 103, 106–107, 116

Conquest, definition, 175, 178, 188

Consensus model of law, definition, 229, 232, 242

Consumerism, collective behavior, 304–305

Contagion, definition, 20–21, 27

Containment theory, crime, 228, 243

Content analysis, definition, 41, 45

Contract networks, 109

Contract slavery, definition, 143, 152

Control variables, definition, 31, 44

Conventional level, moral reasoning, 84, 90, 98

Convergence theory, definition, 284–285, 296

Cooley, Charles H., 85
looking-glass self, 87
primary and secondary groups, 103f

Coontz, Stephanie, 245–246, 256

Core nations, world systems theory, 146

Corporate average fuel economy (CAFE), 313

Corporate coalition, power and, 290

Corporation, definition, 286–287, 296

Correctional system, 229

Correlation, definition, 30, 32, 44

Countercultures, definition, 49, 56, 63

Courts, 240

Courtship and mate selection, 251–252
stages, 252

Craftsmen, definition, 138, 145, 152

Craig, Larry, 30

Crash (motion picture), 78

Craze, definition, 304–305, 314

Credentialism, definition, 264, 269, 278

Crime, 227–243. *see also* Street crime
age and, 229–230
biological perspectives, 228, 235
definition, 228–229, 242
everyday deviance and, 228f
gender and, 228, 230
general theories of causation, 238
international comparison, 230–231f
media and, 229
psychological perspectives, 236
race and, 229–230
social class and, 229–230
societal response, 232–233
structural-functional explanations, 236
Sutherland's nine propositions, 237

Crime index, definition, 230, 242

Criminal justice system, 240

Criminology, definition, 228–229, 242

Cross-sectional study, definition, 33, 44

Crowds, definition, 301, 304–305, 314

Crude birth rate, definition, 157, 170

Crude death rate, definition, 158, 170

Cults, definition, 272–273, 279

Cultural lag, 26
definition, 54–56, 63

Cultural relativism, 49
definition, 54–55, 63

Cultural shock, 52, 63

Cultural transmission, 26, 48, 50
definition, 50, 62

Culture, 26, 47–61
changes, 299–315
courtship and mate selection, 251–252
definition, 48, 62
differentiation, 58–59, 62
influence on sociology theory, 61–62
in social structure, 67
study of, 48–49, 54–57

Culture and Technology (Murphie and Potts), 57

Culture shock, definition, 56

Cycle of poverty, definition, 182–183, 189

Dalit, lowest Indian caste, 144

Darwin, Charles, natural selection, 11

Data evaluation, 39

Davies, 310

Davis, Kingsley, 129

Dawes Act, 77

Death penalty, 240

Death rate, selected countries, 2007, 160

Debt bondage, definition, 143, 152

Decline, definition, 306–307, 315

Delegated, definition, 123, 134

De Maio, Louis, 86
"Stages of Language Development," 86f

Demand, definition, 284, 296

D'Emilio, John, 54

Democracy
definition, 282, 288–289, 296
dominant value in the U.S., Williams, 53

Democratic leader, definition, 106, 116

Democratic socialism, definition, 283–285, 296

Demographic similarity, definition, 76–77, 80

Demographic transition theory, 157
definition, 162–163, 170

Demographic variables, definition, 157, 170

Demography, definition, 157, 170

Dependency theory, Cardosa, 148

Dependent variable, definition, 31, 44

Desperate Housewives (TV show), 193

Deterrence, definition, 229, 233, 242

Developed countries, 139–141

Deviance
definition, 228–229, 242
everyday deviance and, 228f
societal response, 232–233

Deviance and crime theories, historical roots, 235

Diagnostic and Statistical Manual of the American Psychiatric Association, 213

Diagnostic framing, definition, 310–311, 315

Diamond, Jared, 148, 155–156, 162, 164

Differential association theory, crime, 228, 237, 243

Diffusion, definition, 303, 314

The Dignity of Working Men: Morality and the Boundaries of Race, Class, and Immigration (Lamont), 66, 69, 73

Diouf, Jacques, 148

Direct pressure on dissenters, in groupthink, 108

Discreditable stigma, definition, 67, 69, 80

Discredited stigma, definition, 67, 69, 80

Discretion, definition, 240, 243

Discrimination, definition, 175, 180–181, 189

Disengagement theory
aging process, 220–221
definition, 211, 220–221, 224

Disposable People: New Slavery in the Global Economy (Bales), 137–138, 141–142

Distribution hypothesis, 58

Division of labor, in an organization, 110–111

Divorce
ease of obtaining, 255
rates by country, 254
reasons for, 246
sociological reasons, 255

Domestic violence, 250

Domhoff, G. William, 124, 290, 293

Dominant groups, definition, 174, 177, 188

Double consciousness, definition, 184–185, 189

Doubling time, prediction of population numbers, 157, 161–162, 170
Dow, Whitney, 184
Dramaturgy
definition, 20–21, 27, 66, 74–75, 80
social structures, 66, 74–75
Drug problems, U. S. *vs.* the Netherlands, 34*f*
Du Bois, W. E. B., 4, 16–18, 185
Durfee, 133
Durham, M. Gigi, 195
Durkheim, Emile, 4
families, 257
four types of suicide, 7*f*
functional requisites, 76–77
religion, 275
solidarity theory, 12–13
theory of suicide, 7
Dworkin, Andrea, 201
Dyads, definition, 103, 106, 116

Earth Day, 169
Ebens, Ronald, 182
Economics
politics and, 281–297
population growth and, 163–164
Economic systems, 72
China, 285
definition, 283–286, 296
global, 286–287
military spending and, 291
power distribution in, 294
U. S., 286
Venezuela, 285
Edin, Kathryn, 119–120, 126–128, 131–132
Education. *see also* Higher education
academic achievement, 268–270
attainment by race, 184*f*
attainment in the U.S., 265
definition, 264–265, 278
discrepancies in race and gender, 267–268
effect on participation in organized sports, 93*f*
effects of social policies, 277
effects on socialization, 93
equality, 201
functionalism and, 94
gender and, 197
gender *vs.* sex, 192
grades, 268–269
home schooling, 269
income and, 184
institutional discrimination, 182
myths, 266
race and ethnicity in, 174
religion and, 263–279
roots of modern systems, 266
scheduling around the holidays, 270

school voucher programs, 277
social class and, 127
teacher expectancy effect, 268
throughout the world, 266–267
Educational systems, 72
Efficiency and practicality, dominant value in the U. S., Williams, 52
Egoistic suicide, 7, 26
Ehrenreich, Barbara, 127
Ehrlich, Paul, 85, 162
Eighth United Nations Survey on Crime Trends and the Operations of Criminal Justice Systems, 34
Eisenhower, Dwight D., 290–291
Eisner, Michael, 123
Elite. *see* Upper (elite) class
Embargo, definition, 287, 296
Embarrassment, definition, 75, 80
Emergence, definition, 306–307, 315
Emigration, definition, 157–160, 170
Empty nest syndrome, 255
Endogamy, definition, 247, 252, 260
Entitlement program, definition, 132, 134
Entrepreneurs, definition, 138, 145, 152
Environmental justice, 165, 170
Environmental Sociology, definition, 164–165, 170
Equality, dominant value in the U. S., Williams, 52
Erikson, Erik, 85
eight stages of development, 88–89*f*
An Essay on the Principle of Population (Malthus), 162
Ethics, definition, 40, 45
Ethnic cleansing, 177–178
Ethnic enclaves, definition, 180–181, 188
Ethnicity, 40
definition, 175, 188
general comparison of racial–ethnic groups, 183*t*
race and, 173–189
Ethnocentrism, 49
definition, 54–55, 62
Ethnography, definition, 37, 44
Etzioni, Amitai, 59, 110
European Union, 149
Exchange mobility, definition, 128, 134
Exchange theory, 252
Exogamy, definition, 247, 252, 260
Experiments, definition, 35–36
Extended childhood, 255
Extended family, definition, 247–248, 260

Extension, definition, 310–311, 315
External conformity, dominant value in the U. S., Williams, 52
External nations, world systems theory, 146
Extraordinary Groups: An Examination of Unconventional Lifestyles (Schaefer and Zellner), 102

Façade, for study of sociology, 5
Facebook, subcultures of, 56
Face-saving work, definition, 75, 80
Fads, definition, 304–305, 314
False consciousness
definition, 14, 27
Karl Marx, 15, 145
Family
American trends, 248–249
child rearing, 254
definition, 245–247, 260
divorce, 254–255
erosion of the TV family, 256*f*–257*f*
future, 259
ideal image, 247*f*
ideal, myths, 249
later stages, 246, 255
perfect, image of, 250
phases of, 247, 251–253
Fatalistic suicide, 7–8, 26
Female circumcision (female genital mutilation, FGM), 194
Feminism
definition, 200–201, 206
first-wave, 200
history of, 200*f*–201*f*
liberal *vs.* radical, 202
second-wave, 200
third-wave, 200–201
Feral, definition, 86–87, 98
Fertility rate
definition, 157, 170
Japan, 161
Field research, definition, 36, 44
Fishwick, Marshall, 57
Folkways, 26, 48
definition, 54, 62
Food shortage
population control and, 156–157
population growth and, 163
Fordham, Benjamin, 292
Foreign aid, underdeveloped countries, 151
Formal operational stage, cognitive development, 85, 88, 98
Formal organization, definition, 110–111, 117
Formal rationality, definition, 110–111, 117
Formal structures, definition, 110–111, 117
Foster, John Bellamy, 17–18

Frame alignment process, definition, 310–311, 315
Frame bridging, definition, 310–311, 315
Freedman, Estelle B., 54
Freedom, dominant value in the U. S., Williams, 52
Freedom Writers (film), 264–265
Free markets, definition, 283, 296
Friedman, Michael, 214
Fritzl, Josef, 86
Front stage, definition, 66, 75, 80
Functionalism, 4–5, 9, 24, 60
adaptation and replacement, 76
aging process, 220, 222, 224
characteristics, 26
communitarianism, 59
comparison of paradigms, 10, 78
crime, 239, 242
criticisms, 13–14
culture differentiation, 62
definition, 8, 26
economic and political systems, 293–294, 296
family, 258, 260
feminism, 204, 206
global stratification, 148, 150, 152
leadership and, 112, 116
marriage and family, 256
overlapping theories, 22
population growth, 170
production and economy production, 77
racism, 186, 188
religion and, 275–276, 278
resocialization and, 94
Robert Merton, 12–13
socialization and orientation, 76–77, 96, 98
social movements, 310, 312, 314
social order, 77
social stratification, 129, 134
social structures, 80
Talcott Parsons, 4, 12–13
unity and purpose, 77
Functions, definition, 13, 27
Funding, research studies, 43
Futility, definition, 301–303*f*, 314

Game stage, 85
definition, 87, 98
Garcia, Carlos, 109
Gay marriage, 259
Gemeinschaft
definition, 72–73*f*, 80
in personal space, 66
Gender
aging and: where are the men?, 219
bias in the media, 95
in conflict theory, 95
crime and, 228, 230

definition, 95, 99, 193, 206
education and, 197
education discrepancies,
267–268
health and, 211–212
income gap, 197*f*
inequality and, 193, 196–197
male, 199
politics and, 199
vs. sex, 190–205
workplace and, 198
Gender identity, definition, 193,
206
Gender roles
definition, 194–195, 206
fluidity of, 195–196
media and, 195
Gender (sexual) violence, 201,
205–206
domestic violence in families, 250
social policies, 205
Gender stratification, elimina-
tion of, 201
General deterrence, definition,
233, 242
Generalization, definition, 35,
44
Generalized other, definition,
87, 98
General strain theory, crime,
238
Generativity *vs.* stagnation, Erikson's stages of development,
89*f*
Genie: A Scientific Tragedy
(Rymer), 83–84, 86
Genocide, definition, 175, 177,
188
Gere, Richard, 54
German immigrants in America,
178
Gerontology, definition, 211,
216–217, 225
Gesellschaft
definition, 72–73*f*, 80
in personal space, 66
Gestures, definition, 48, 51, 62
International Gestures Quiz,
51
Gilligan, Carol, morality of care,
84, 90–91
Glass ceiling, definition, 198,
206
Global economy, 287
Globalization, definition, 147,
152, 301
Global stratification
definition, 138–139, 152
theories behind, 146–150
Global village, 26
definition, 56–57, 63
Global warming
population control and,
156–157
sociology and, 166
Goffman, Erving, 20–22, 75
Golden Rule, around the world,
272

Gottfredson and Hirschi's gen-
eral theory of crime, 238
Government types, 288
Grades, 268–269
Grade inflation, definition,
268–269, 278
Granovetter, 108
Grasmick, Harold, 94
Graves, Joseph L., 175
Gray, John, 192
Gross national income per-
capita, 2007, highest and
lowest countries, 139*f*
Groups
definition, 67, 80
leading of, 115
size, structure, and interac-
tion, 106
in social structure, 67
Groups and societies, 100–115
Groupthink
definition, 103, 106–108, 116
history of, 108
Gruwell, Erin, 268
Gundlach, Jim, 33
Guns, Germs, and Steel (Dia-
mond), 148
Gurr, Ted, 310

Harijans (now *Dalit*), lowest
Indian caste, 144
Harlow, Harry and Margaret, 86
Harrington, Michael, 147
Hate groups, definition, 175,
177, 188
Hau, Louis, 269
Hawken, Paul, 300, 304, 310,
313
Hawthorne effect, 36, 44
Headlines, *vs.* statistics, 43
Health
age and, 211
definition, 210–211, 225
race and, 212–213
social class and, 212, 224
in the U. S., 213–214
Health care
costs of services, 215
definition, 215, 225
disadvantages for the elderly,
U. S., 223–224
global look, 216*f*
international comparison,
215
Hedonistic, definition, 235
Hidden curriculum, definition,
264, 266
Hierarchy of authority, in an
organization, 111
Hierarchy of knowledge, Marx's
interpretation of bureau-
cracy, 113
Higher education, 264. *see also*
Education
most expensive universities
in the U. S., 269*t*
problems with, 269
theories behind, 269–270

Hilton, Paris, celebrity, 124
Hinduism, in America, 270–271
Hirschman, Albert, 303
HIV/AIDS
aging and, 221
life expectancy, 221*f*
statistics, 2007, 39*t*
Hochschild, Arlie Russell,
190–192, 257
Homelessness, 4
individual choice *vs.* social
forces, 8
labels around the world, 19
Home schooling, 269
Homogamy, definition, 247, 252,
260
Horizontal mobility, definition,
128, 134
Hotel Rwanda (film), 177
Hukou system, China, 68
Human capital, definition, 264,
269, 278
Human capital model, defini-
tion, 198, 206
Human exemptionalism, defini-
tion, 164–165, 170
Human interaction, deprivation
of, 86–87
Humanitarianism, dominant
value in the U. S., Williams,
52
Humphreys, Laud, 30, 37, 42
Hunger
most disadvantaged world
region, 140
population growth and, 163
Hunting and gathering society,
67, 70
Huston, Ted L., 252–253
Hutu tribe, genocide, 177
Hypothesis, definition, 32, 44
Hysteria, definition, 304–305,
314

Ideal culture
definition, 49
vs. real culture, 56
Identity *vs.* role confusion, Erikson's stages of development,
89*f*
Iger, Robert, 123
Illusion of invulnerability, in
groupthink, 108
Illusion of unanimity, in groupthink, 108
Imitation stage, 85
definition, 87, 98
Immigration
coming to America, 181
definition, 157–160, 170
Impersonality, in an organization, 111
Impression management, 66,
75, 80
getting ahead in the workplace, 76
Inactivity, childhood obesity
and, 214

Incarceration rates and costs,
234*f*
Income
cycle of poverty, 183–184
definition, 120–121, 134
distribution, 121–122
educational attainment and,
184
effects on socialization, 93
per-capita, rich and poor
countries, 139
Independent variable, definition, 31, 44
India
Alang ship graveyard, 166
caste system, 143–144
Indian Removal Act of 1830,
186
Indigenous superordination,
definition, 175, 178–179, 188
Individual choice, *vs.* social
forces, 8
Individualism, 53
Individual personality, dominant
value in the U. S., Williams,
53
Individuals, a framework for,
47–61
Industrial societies, 67, 71
Industry *vs.* inferiority, Erikson's
stages of development, 89*f*
Infant mortality rate, definition,
158, 170
Informal structures, definition,
110–111, 117
In-groups
bias, 104, 116
definition, 103–104, 116
Initiative *vs.* guilt, Erikson's
stages of development, 89*f*
Innovators, definition, 236
Institutional discrimination
definition, 180–182, 189
education systems, 182
Integrity, definition, 40
Integrity *vs.* despair, Erikson's
stages of development, 89*f*
Intergenerational mobility, defi-
nition, 128, 134
Intermarriage, definition,
274–275, 279
*International Crime Victimiza-
tion Survey, 2000,* 231
Internet petitions, societal
change and, 304
Intimacy *vs.* isolation, Erikson's
stages of development, 89*f*
Intimate distance, in personal
space, 66, 74*f*, 80
Intragenerational mobility, definition, 128, 134
Invention, definition, 302–303,
314
Involuntary immigration, defini-
tion, 175, 178, 188
Involvement, definition, 238,
243
IPAT formula, 166

Iron cage, definition, 110-111
I self, definition, 87, 98

Janis, Irving, 108
Japanese immigrants in America, 178
Japanese society
    birth in social stratification, 121
    elderly population, 218
    networks and family change, 251
    xenophobia, 105
Jeopardy, definition, 301-303f, 314
Johnson, Michael P., 252-253
Journal of Marriage and the Family, types of commitment, 253

Kefalas, Maria, 119-120, 126-128, 131-132
Keister, 122
King, Martin Luther, Jr., 236
Klum, Heidi, 104
Kohlberg, Lawrence, 84
    theory of moral development, 90
Kornhauser, William, on social movements, 310
Kotlikoff, Laurence J., 223
Kozol, Jonathan, 127, 182, 264, 277
Kshatriya, Indian warrior caste, 144

Labeling theory, crime, 228, 238
Labor coalition, power and, 290
Lamont, Michéle, 66, 69, 73, 78
Language, 48-50f, 62
Laissez-faire leader, definition, 106, 116
Latent functions, definition, 13, 27
Leadership styles, definition, 103, 106, 116
Lean on Me (film), 264
Legal systems, 72, 227-243
Leibow, Elliot, 3, 4-5, 8, 10, 14, 19, 25
Lemert, Edwin, 238
Lenin, socialism and, 285
Liden, R. C., 75-76
Life expectancy
    AIDS, 221f
    definition, 158, 170
    medical advances, 216-217
Lifespan, definition, 158, 170
Listhaug, Ola, 290, 297
Literacy
    access to, 140f
    throughout the world, 267f
Literature review, definition, 32, 44
Locke, John, 85

The Lolita Effect: the Media Sexualization of Young Girls and What We Can Do About it (Durham), 195
Lombroso, Cesare, 235
Longitudinal studies, definition, 33, 44
Looking-glass self theory (Cooley), 85
    definition, 87, 98
Lower class, definition, 126-127, 134

Machismo, definition, 203, 206
Machung, Anne, 190-192
Macro (large-scale reference), 6, 26
Macrosociology, definition, 66-67, 80
Maguire, 33
Majority groups, definition, 174-175, 188
Malthus, Thomas, 162
Malthusian theory, 157
    definition, 162, 170
Mandatory minimums, definition, 240, 243
Manifest functions, definition, 13, 27
Marginal poverty, definition, 122, 134
Marital effects, definition, 252-253, 260
Marriage
    definition, 245-247, 260
    effects, 246
    men's lives and, 256
    types of commitment, 253
Marriage, a History: From Obedience to Intimacy, or How Love Conquered Marriage (Coontz), 256
Marriage and family, 245-261
Marriage in Men's Lives (Nock), 256
Martineau, Harriet, 4, 15-18
Marx, Karl, 4, 14-18
    bureaucracy, 113
    on class systems, 145
    on productivity, 222
    religion, 265, 275
    religion and the economy, 273
    social class, 139
    socialism and, 284-285
Mass media
    in conflict theory, 95
    crime and, 229
    definition, 95, 99
    gender bias in, 95
    gender roles in, 195
Master status, in social structure, 67-69, 80
Material comfort, dominant value in the U. S., Williams, 52
Material culture
    definition, 48, 62
    rap music and, 50

Matheson, Richard, 156
Matriarchies, definition, 194-195, 206
Maxwell, John C., leadership model, 112
McCain, John, 199, 286, 289
    ageism, and, 211, 219
McDonaldization, 59
Mead, George Herbert, 4, 19-21, 85
    three stages of the "I-Me" self, 87
Mean, definition, 38-39, 45
Mechanical solidarity, 12-13, 27
    in social structure, 66, 72-73
Median, definition, 38-39, 45
Medicaid, definition, 216-217, 225
Medicalization, definition, 213, 225
Medicare
    definition, 216-217, 225
    disadvantages, 223
Men are from Mars, Women are from Venus (Gray), 192
Meritocracy argument, definition, 128-129, 134
Merton, Robert, 4, 104, 236
    functionalism, 12-13
Me self, definition, 87, 98
Methods of succession, in an organization, 110
Michiko, Empress, 121
Micro (small-scale reference), 6, 26
Microsociology, definition, 66-67, 80
Middle class, definition, 125, 134
Migrant superordination, definition, 175, 178, 179, 188
Migration, definition, 157-160, 170
Milgram, Stanley, 36
Milgram Obedience Study, 36
Militant minorities, definition, 180-181, 188
Military-industrial complex, definition, 290-291, 296
Military spending
    debate, 292
    economy and, 291t
Miller, Arthur, 290, 297
Million Man March, 305
Mills, C. Wright, 5-6, 123, 290, 293
Mind, Self, and Society (Mead), 19, 87
Minimum wage
    definition, 120
    social policy, 133
Minority groups
    definition, 174-175, 188
    patterns of interaction, 179-180
    types of, 180f
Miscegenation, definition, 259
Mishel, Lawrence, 142

Mobs, definition, 301, 304-305, 314
Mode, definition, 38-39, 45
Moller, 122
Monarchy, definition, 282, 288-289, 296
Monogamy, definition, 246, 248-249, 260
Monopoly, definition, 284, 296
Monotheism, 265
    definition, 270, 278
Moore, Wilbert, 129
Moral development theories, 90
Morality of care (Gilligan), 84, 90-91, 98
Morality of justice (Gilligan), 84, 90-91, 98
Moral orientation, dominant value in the U. S., Williams, 52
Moral reasoning (Kohlberg), 84
Mores, 26, 48
    definition, 54, 62
Mortality rate, definition, 156, 158, 170
Mosca, Gaetano, 148
Motivational framing, definition, 310-311, 315
Müller, Kai, 142
Multiculturalism, 26
    assimilation and, 180
    definition, 49, 56, 63
    social policy, 61
Multinational corporation
    definition, 287, 296
    neo-colonialism and, 147
Murphie, Andrew, 57
The Myth of Mental Illness (Szasz), 213

NAFTA (North American Free Trade Agreement), definition, 287, 297
National Crime Victimization Survey (NCVS), 228, 230, 242
Nationalism and patriotism, dominant value in the U. S., Williams, 53
Native American culture, example of conflict theory, 77
Natural selection, Charles Darwin, 11
Nature theory, definition, 85, 98
Nature *vs.* nurture debate, 85
Needs assessment
    community learning and, 43
    definition, 42-43, 45
Negative correlation, definition, 32, 44
Neighborhoods
    health and, 212f
    impact of wealth and poverty, 121, 127
    social class and, 93, 127
Neo-classical (push-pull) migration theory, definition, 160, 170

INDEX

Neo-colonialism, definition, 147, 152

The New Media Monopoly (Bagdikian), 293

Nickel and Dimed (Ehrenreich), 127

Nitz, Michael, 182

Nock, Steven L., 256

Nonmaterial culture, definition, 48–49, 62

Normative organization, definition, 110–111, 117

Normative relativism, definition, 54–55, 63

Norms, definition, 54, 62

Noyes, John Humphrey, 101–102, 112–113

Nuclear family, definition, 247, 260

Nurture theory, definition, 85, 98

Obama, Barack, 60, 199, 286, 289

Oberlin College, first coeducational enrollment, 197

Obesity
childhood, 213–214
definition, 210–211, 225
race and, 214
stigmatization of, 214

Objectivity, definition, 30–31, 44

"Old old cohort," definition, 211, 216–217, 225

The Omnivore's Dilemma: A Natural History of Four Meals (Pollan), 210

Oneida community, 101–104, 106
leadership in, 112, 114

Ong and Mitchell, quality of life rankings, 142

Operationalizing, definition, 32, 44

Organic solidarity, 12–13, 27
in personal space, 66, 72–73

Organization for Economic Cooperation and Development (OECD), health statistics 216f working hours around the world, 149t

Organization of believers, definition, 274–275, 279

Organizations, definition, 103, 110–111, 117

Out-groups, definition, 103–105, 116

Outsiders: Studies in the Sociology of Deviance (Becker), 20–21

Overpopulation, 156–157
definition, 165, 171

Oversampling, definition, 35, 45

Palin, Sarah, 199, 289

Panic, definition, 305, 314

Paradigm, definition, 8–9, 27

Parenting styles, 92f
Asian cultures, 92
civic engagement, 115
keeping kids safe, 214

Pareto, Vilfredo, 148–150, 152

Park and Burgess, on social movements, 310

Parsimony, definition, 35, 44

Parsons, Talcott, 4
functionalism, 12–13

Participant observation, definition, 37, 45

Pastoral and horticultural societies, 70

Patriarchy, definition, 193–195, 206

Patriarchy model, definition, 198, 207

Peace Corps, 151–152

People development leaders, 112

Perfectionists, 101

Periphery nations, world systems theory, 146

Permission leaders, 112

Permissive parenting style, 92f–93, 99

Perry Preschool Project, social policy, 79

Personal distance,
definition, 66, 74, 81
in personal space, 66, 74f, 80

Personal Responsibility and Work Opportunity Reconciliation Act, 132

Personal space, definition, 66, 74, 81

Personhood leaders, 112

Perversity, definition, 301, 303f, 314

Petite bourgeoisie/petty bourgeoisie, definition, 138, 145, 152

Phelps, Fred, 307

The Philadelphia Negro (Du Bois), 16

Philosophies of life, 265, 270, 279

Physical fitness and youthfulness, new value in the U. S., 54

Piaget, Jean, theory of cognitive development, 85, 88

Plan of Attack (Woodward), 108

Play stage, 85
definition, 87, 98

Plea bargain, definition, 240, 243

Pluralism, definition, 293, 297

Pluralistic minorities, definition, 178–179, 188

Police, 240

Political action committees (PACs), 290

Political groups, 311t

Political parties, 289
trust in, 290

Political systems
definition, 287, 297
parties in the U. S., 289
power distribution in, 294
rival, 293
trust in parties, 290
types of, 289, 296

Politics
economy and, 281–297
gender and, 199

Pollan, Michael, 210, 214

Polyandry, definition, 246, 248–249, 260

Polygamy, definition, 246, 248–249, 260

Polygymy, definition, 246, 248–249, 260

Polytheism
definition, 270, 278

Popenoe, David, erosion of the family, 257–258, 260

Population
definition, 35, 44
geographic area and, 139
growth, issues associated with, 163–164
growth, PRB 2007 World Population Data Sheet, 161f
projections, 162
tools for study, 157–162

Population control programs
definition, 156
government, 168–169

Population momentum, definition, 158–159, 170

Population pyramids, definition, 158, 170

Portes, Alejandro, 181

Positional leaders, 112

Positive correlation, definition, 32, 44

Positivist school, crime, 228, 235, 242

Postconventional level,
definition, 90, 99
moral reasoning, 84, 90, 98

Postdenominationalism, definition, 274–275, 279

Postindustrial societies, 67, 71

Postman, Neil, 48, 57

Posttraumatic stress disorder (PTSD), veterans in the U. S., 295

Potts, John, 57

Poverty
by race and age in 2005, 126f
children in the U. S., 123
developed nations, 141–142
in the world, 137–151
social policies, 132–134
underdeveloped nations, 140–141
U. S. definition, 122

Poverty line, U. S., 122

Powell, Colin, 108

Power
definition, 123, 134
nature of, 290–291

Power elite, definition, 123, 135

Preconventional level,
definition, 90, 99
moral reasoning, 84

Prejudice
causes for, 182
definition, 175, 181, 189
vs. discrimination, 181

Preoperational stage, 85
cognitive development, 88, 98

Preschool, in social policies, 79–80

Prestige, definition, 121, 123, 135

Price elasticity of demand, definition, 284, 296

Primary deviance, definition, 238, 243

Primary groups
definition, 67, 80, 103–104
vs. secondary groups, 103f

Primary socialization, definition, 84–85, 98

Prison
as an organization, 110
characteristics of inmates, 233–235

Production leaders, 112

Profane, definition, 272–273, 279

Professional and scientific responsibility, 40

Professional competence, definition, 40

Prognostic framing, definition, 311

Progress, dominant value in the U. S., Williams, 52

Progressive, definition, 309, 315

Project Runway (reality show), 104

Proletariat
definition, 14–15, 27, 139, 144
Karl Marx, 14–15

The Promise Keepers, 275

Promises I Can Keep: Why Poor Women Put Motherhood Before Marriage (Edin and Kefalas), 119–120, 126–127, 131

Pro-natalist, definition, 156, 168–169, 171

The Protestant Ethic and the Spirit of Capitalism (Weber), 23

Psychological perspectives, crime and deviance, 236

Psychosocial crisis, definition, 88, 98

Psychosocial stages (Erikson), 85, 89

Public distance, in personal space, 66, 74f–75, 81

Public resources, population growth and, 164
Punishment, crime and, 232–233
Push-pull (neo-classical) migration theory, definition, 160, 170
Putnam, Robert, 110

Qualitative data, definition, 30, 40–41, 45
Qualitative research methods, 41f
Quality of life, in world cities, 141–142
Quantitative data, definition, 30, 40–41, 45
Quantitative research methods, 41f

Race
    crime and, 229–230
    definition, 174–175, 188
    education discrepancies, 267
    educational attainment, 184f
    ethnicity and, 173–189
    general comparison of racial–ethnic groups, 183t
    health and, 212–213
    obesity and, 214
The Race Myth (Graves), 174
Racial stratification, in the U.S., 183–184
Racism
    color-blind, 184–185, 189
    definition, 175–177, 188
    related group superiority, dominant value in the U.S., Williams, 53
Random sample, definition, 35, 45
Rate of natural increase (RNI), prediction of population numbers, 157, 160, 170
Real culture, definition, 49
Rebels, definition, 236
Recidivism, definition, 228, 233, 242
Reckless, Walter, 237
Redemptive social movements, definition, 300, 308f–309, 315
Reference groups, definition, 105, 116
Reformative social movements definition, 300, 308–309, 315
    progressive or regressive, 309
Regressive, definition, 309, 315
Reiman, Jeffrey, 228, 230, 233, 238–239
Reintegrative shaming, definition, 229, 233, 242
Relative deprivation, 310, 315
Relative poverty, definition, 122, 134
Reliable, definition, 33, 44

Religion
    changes in, 273–274
    church networks, 109
    conflict theory, 275
    definition, 265, 270, 278
    education and, 263–279
    functionalism and, 94, 275
    importance in people's lives, 273f
    major religions of the world ranked, 271f
    Marx, 265, 273, 278
    organization in, 272
    scheduling around the holidays, 270
    society and, 272
    symbolic interactionism, 274
    types, 270–271
    Weber, 265, 273
Religious holidays, 270
Remarriage, 248
Rentiers, definition, 138, 145, 152
Repertoires, definition, 306–307, 315
Research design, definition, 33, 44
Research methods
    see also Social research
    comparison, 37t
    definition, 30, 44
    sociologist use of, 41, 44
    three paradigms and, 42
Research studies
    agendas, 43
    funding groups, 43
    headlines, 43
    spuriousness and selection effects, 43
Residual poverty, definition, 122, 134
Resistance to change, 302–309
Resocialization, definition, 93, 99
Respect for rights, dignity, and diversity, 40
Respect for the Aged Day, Japan, 218
Restorative justice, New Zealand, 233
Retreatists, definition, 236
Revolutionary social movements, definition, 300, 308f–309, 315
Rhesus monkey study, nature vs. nurture, 86
The Rich Get Richer and the Poor Get Prison: Ideology, Class, and Criminal Justice (Reiman), 228
Rindfuss, Ronald R., 251
Riots, definition, 301, 304–305, 314
Ritualists, definition, 236
Rituals, definition, 272–273, 279
Ritzer, George, 59
Role, definition, 67, 69, 80

Role conflict, definition, 67, 69, 80
Role expectation, definition, 67, 69, 80
Role performance, definition, 67, 69, 80
Role set, definition, 67, 69
Role stage, courtship, 252f
Role strain, definition, 67, 69, 80
Rothschild, Joyce, 113–114
Rules and regulations, in an organization, 111
Rumbaut, Ruben, 61
Rumors, definition, 305, 314
Rymer, Russ, 84

Sachs, Jeffrey, 282, 285, 287, 294, 297
Sacred, definition, 272–273, 279
Saddam Hussein, 108
Same-sex couples, adoption for, 259
Sample of convenience, definition, 35, 44
Samples, definition, 35, 44
Sanction, definition, 54, 62
"Sandwiched generation," definition, 217, 224
Sapir, Edward, 50
Sapir-Whorf hypothesis, 50, 62
Savage Inequalities: Children in American Schools (Kozol), 182, 264
Scapegoat, definition, 175, 182–183, 189
Schaefer, Richard, 102
School voucher programs, 277–278
Science and secular rationality, dominant value in the U.S., Williams, 53
Seccombe, Karen, 130
Secessionist minorities, definition, 180–181, 189
Secondary data, definition, 37, 45
Secondary data analysis, definition, 37, 45
Secondary deviance, definition, 238, 243
Secondary groups
    definition, 67, 80, 103
    vs. primary groups, 103f
Secondary school net enrollment, world regions, 72t
Secondary socialization, definition, 84–85, 98
The Second Shift: Working Parents and the Revolution at Home, 190–192, 257–258
Sects, definition, 272–273, 279
Secularization, definition, 265, 273, 279
Secular values, vs. traditional values, 58
Segregation, definition, 182–183, 189
Selection effects, definition, 35, 44

Self, definition, 19, 27
Self-appointed mind guards, in groupthink, 108
Self-censorship, in groupthink, 108
Self-focused impression management, definition, 76–77, 81
Self stages of development (Mead), 85, 87
Semi-periphery nations, world systems theory, 146
Semi-skilled manual workers, definition, 138, 145, 152
Sensorimotor stage, cognitive development, 85, 88, 98
Sex. see also gender
    definition, 192–193, 206
    vs. gender, 193–194
Sexism, definition, 193–195, 206
Sexual harassment, social policies, 205–206
Sexuality and romance, new value in the U.S., 54
Shaming, crime, 229, 232, 242
Sheerman, Jill, 67
Shetty, Shilpa, 54
Shudra, India's worker caste, 144
Sick role, definition, 213, 225
Simmel, Georg, 106, 117
Simple supernaturalism, 265, 270–271, 279
The Sims, for study of sociology, 5
Sitcoms, role of the family in culture, 250, 256f–257f
Slavery
    definition, 142–143, 152
    forms of, 143
    as a social system, 142–143
    Tulsa, Oklahoma, 143
Slottje, quality of life rankings, 142
Snipes, 33
Social capital, definition, 102, 109f, 116
Social change, definition, 301, 314
Social class
    character traits and, 73
    crime and, 229–230
    definition, 67, 80
    education and, 127
    health and, 212
    neighborhoods and, 93, 127
    opportunities for socialization, 93
Social conflict theory, crime, 228, 238
Social construction of reality, 76, 80
Social control, definition, 5, 7, 26
Social control theories, crime, 228, 237–238
Social Darwinism, definition, 10–12, 27

INDEX

Social distance, in personal space, 66, 74f-75, 81
Social dynamics
  change, 299-315
  definition, 10, 27
Social epidemiology, definition, 210-211, 225
Social forces, *vs.* individual choice, 8
Social groups
  characteristics, 102, 111
  definition, 102, 116
Social institutions
  definition, 71-72, 80, 283
  in social structure, 67
Social interaction, 65-81
  theories, crime, 237-238
Socialism
  convergence with capitalism, 285-286
  definition, 283-284f, 296
Socialization, 83-99
  agents of, 84, 92-93
  definition, 84, 98
  media role in, 95
  opportunities for, 93
  parenting styles, 92
  theorists on, 87-91
Social laws, definition, 10, 26
Social mobility, definition, 128, 134
Social movements
  cultural change and, 299-315
  four categories of, 308f
  influence on sociological theory and study, 313-314
  nature of, 306-307, 315
  stages of, 307
Social network, definition, 102, 109, 117
Social policy
  applying sociological thinking, 97
  definition, 97, 99
  education and, 277, 278
  foreign aid, 151
  improvement in society and, 79-80
  minimum wage, 133
  statistics and, 43
  stopping sexual harassment and gender violence, 205-206
  welfare for the poor, 132-133
Social research. *see also* Research methods
  definition, 32, 40-44
  six steps, 30-39
Social responsibility, 40
Social roles, 68-69
Social statics, definition, 10, 27
Social stratification, 118-135
  conflict theory, 130, 134
  definition, 120-121, 134
  developed nations, 141
  functionalist beliefs, 129, 134
  reasons for getting ahead, 129f

symbolic interactionism, 130, 134
  three most common systems, 142-143
  underdeveloped countries, 140
Social structure, 65-81
  definition, 67, 80
  elements, 66-76
Social systems, 139, 142-145
Societal change
  invention effects, 302
  resistance to, 303
  shifts, 300-302
  stages, 70f-71f
  technology and, 302
Society
  holding together, 72-74
  religion and, 274-275
Society in America (Martineau), 15
Sociological imagination, definition, 4, 6-7, 26
  developing a, 5-6
Sociological paradigm
  characteristics of, 4-9, 23
  comparison, 10
  overlapping theories, 22t
Sociology, definition, 4-26
Solidarity
  definition, 5, 7, 26
  Emile Durkheim, 12
So You Think I Drive a Cadillac? (Seccombe), 130
Special interest groups, politics and, 290
Specific deterrence, definition, 229, 233, 242
Spencer, Herbert, 4, 11-12
Spitzer, Eliot, 75
Spurious correlation, definition, 32, 44
Spuriousness, in research studies, 43
Spurlock, Morgan, 59
St. Paul's Prep School, elite college preparatory school, 124
Stack, Steven, 33
Stages of Language Development (De Maio), 86f
State of Working America 2004/2005 (Mishel, Bernstein and Allegretto), 141t
Statistics, effects on social policy, 43
Status
  definition, 67-69, 80
  in social structure, 68-69
Stepfamilies, 248
Stepick, Alex, 181
Stereotyped view of out-groups, in groupthink, 108
Stereotypes, definition, 181, 189
Stewart, Martha, 232
Stigma, definition, 67, 69, 80
Stigmatized shaming, definition, 229, 233, 242
Stimulus stage, courtship, 252f

Stimulus-value-role theory, 247, 252f
Street crime. *see also* Crime
  definition, 229, 242
  international comparison, 230-231f
Strong leadership, groupthink and, 107
Structural mobility, definition, 120, 128, 135
Subcultures
  definition, 49, 56, 63
  Facebook, 56
Suicide
  country music and, 33
  Emile Durkheim's theory on, 7f-8
Super Size Me (Spurlock), 59
Supervisor-focused impression management, definition, 76-77, 81
Supply, definition, 284, 296
Survey, definition, 35, 44
Survivor (TV show), 175
Sutherland, Edwin, 237, 239
Symbolic interactionism
  aging process, 220, 222, 224
  characteristics, 26
  color-blind racism, 184-185
  comparison of paradigms, 10t
  crime, 238-239, 242
  criticism, 22
  culture differentiation, 4, 62
  definition, 4, 8-9, 26
  economic and political systems, 293-294, 296
  family, 256, 258, 260
  feminism, 202, 204, 206
  global stratification, 149-150, 152
  just and democratic workplace, 113
  leadership, 114, 116
  overlapping theories, 22t
  population growth, 167, 170
  racism, 186, 188
  religion, 274, 276, 278
  resocialization and, 94
  social class differences, 78
  socialization and, 96, 98
  social movements, 310, 312, 314
  social stratification, 130-131, 134
  social structures, 80
  Thomas Theorem, 76
  values, 58, 60
  worldview, 18-22
Symbols, 48-49, 62
System of beliefs, definition, 274-275, 279
Szasz, Thomas, 213

Taboos, definition, 54, 62
Tajfel, 105
Tannen, Deborah, 202-203
Tariffs, definition, 287, 297
Teacher expectancy effect

and attainment, 267-268
  definition, 267, 278
Tearoom Trade: Impersonal Sex in Public Places (Humphreys), 30, 37-48
Technology, definition, 302-303, 314
Tell Them Who I Am: The Lives of Homeless Women (Liebow), 3-4, 8, 25
Temporary Assistance to Needy Families (TANF) program, 132-133
Term definitions, in research studies, 43
Theism, definition, 270, 278
Theocracy, definition, 272-273, 279
Theory, definition, 32, 44
Theory of Anomie, crime, 228, 236
Thomas Theorem, 76
Threats, groupthink and, 107
Tilly, Charles, 306
Title IX, 97, 99
Tittle, Charles, 94
Total fertility rate (TFR), definition, 157, 170
Total institutions, definition, 93, 99
Totalitarianism, definition, 288-289, 297
Totemism, definition, 270-271, 279
Traditional networks, 109
Traditional values, *vs.* secular values, 58
Transformation, definition, 310-311, 315
Transitional poverty, definition, 122, 134
Transnational corporation, definition, 287, 296
Trend hypothesis, 58
Triads, definition, 103, 106, 116
Triangulation
  definition, 42, 45
  Tearoom Trade, 42f
The Truly Disadvantaged (Wilson), 126
Trust *vs.* mistrust, Erikson's stages of development, 89f
Tumin, Melvin, 130
Turner, 105
Twitter, 57
Two Towns of Jasper (Dow and Williams), 185

U. S. Bureau of Labor Statistics, marriage and divorce rates by country, 254
U. S. Census Bureau
  college attendance, 268
  educational attainment, 265f
  educational attainment by race, 184f
  employment projections by industry, 286f

gender income gap, 197*f*
geography of American poverty, 122*f*
income by educational attainment, 185*f*
population data, 158
profile of general demographic characteristics, 176*f*
racial-ethnic groups compared, 183*t*
voter turnout by sex, 2005, 199*f*
U. S. Department of Justice, incarceration rates, 234
Ugly Betty (TV show), 120
Underdeveloped countries, 139
social policy: foreign aid, 151
Underpopulation, definition, 165, 171
UNESCO Institute for Statistics, adult literacy throughout the world, 267*f*
Unhealthy foods, childhood obesity and, 214
Uniform Crime Reports (UCRs), 228, 230, 242
Uninsured, in the U. S., 215
Universal grammar, 48, 50
Unskilled workers, definition, 138, 145, 152
Upper (elite) class, definition, 124, 135
Upper middle class, definition, 125, 135
Urban legend, definition, 305, 314
Urban underclass, definition, 126–127, 135
Utilitarian organization, definition, 110–111, 117

Vaishya, Indian merchants, traders caste, 144
Validity, definition, 33, 44
Value clusters, definition, 51, 62
Value conflict, definition, 51*f*, 62
Value pairs, definition, 51, 62
Values, 48
definition, 51, 62
three hypotheses, 58
U. S., 52–53
Value stage, courtship, 252*f*
Variables, definition, 30–31
Vertical mobility, definition, 128, 135
Veterans, assistance in the U. S., 295
Video games, 5
Violence
collective behavior, 304
domestic, 250
gender, 201
social policies, 205
Voluntary association, definition, 102, 110–111, 117
Voluntary immigration, definition, 175, 178, 188
Volunteering (community learning), 25–27, 43, 61, 79, 97, 115, 133, 151, 169, 187, 205, 220, 223, 241, 259
Von Hippel, Courtney, 105
Voter apathy, 288–289
Voter turnout, by sex, 199*f*
Voting, adult civic engagement effects, 115

Wallerstein, Immanuel, 146
Wayne, S. J., 75–76

The Way We Never Were: American Families and the Nostalgia Trap, 245–246
Wealth
definition, 120, 134
distribution, 122
in the world, 137–151
Wealthy, Healthy, and Aged 85: The Women Living Even Longer (Sheerman), 67
Weber, Max, 4
characteristics of bureaucracy, 111*f*
classification, 23
on class systems, 145
idea of bureaucracy, 111
political systems, 287
religion, 265
religion and the economy, 273
social class, 139
verstehen, 31
Welch, Michael, 94
Welfare
definition, 120
social policy, 132
Westboro Baptist Church, protests, 307
Whorf, Benjamin, 50
Why people get ahead, functionalism, 129
Williams, Christine, 199
Williams, Marco, 184
Williams, Robin, U. S. values, 52–53
Wilson, William J., 93, 126
Wingfield, Brian, 269
Woman Hating (Dworkin), 201
Woodward, Bob, 108
Working class, definition, 125, 135

Working hours around the world, 149*f*
Workplace
equality, 201
gender and, 198
gender *vs.* sex, 192
World Factbook, 2007,
birth rate, death rate, and rate of natural increase, 160*t*
income per capita in 2007, 139*f*
World Health Organization (WHO)
comparison of health systems, 215
life expectancy and AIDS, 221*f*
World systems theory, Wallerstein, 146*f*, 152
Worldview, conflict theorists, 14–18
WUNC, definition, 307, 314

Xenocentrism, 26, 49
definition, 54–55, 63
Xenophobia, 26, 49
definition, 54–55, 62
in and out in Japan, 105

You Just Don't Understand: Men and Women in Conversation (Chafetz), 203
"Young old cohort," definition, 211, 216–217, 225

Zedong, Mao, socialism and, 285
Zellner, William, 102
Zero population growth, definition, 157, 170